NEWS

REPORTING AND WRITING

Alfred Lawrence Lorenz
LOYOLA UNIVERSITY, NEW ORLEANS

John Vivian
WINONA STATE UNIVERSITY

ALLYN AND BACON
Boston   London   Toronto   Sydney   Tokyo   Singapore

Vice President, Editor in Chief, Humanities: Joseph Opiela
Editorial Assistant: Susannah Davidson
Cover Administrator: Linda Knowles
Prepress and Manufacturing Buyer: Aloka Rathnam
Editorial-Production Service: Electronic Publishing Services Inc.
Cover Designer: Susan Paradise

Copyright © 1996 by Allyn & Bacon
Simon & Schuster/A Viacom Company
Needham Heights, Massachusetts 02194

Library of Congress Cataloging-in-Publication Data
Lorenz, Alfred Lawrence.
  News: reporting and writing / Alfred Lawrence Lorenz,
John Vivian.
     p.   cm.
  Includes bibliographical references and index.
  ISBN 0-205-13975-2
  1. Journalism—Handbooks, manuals, etc. 2. Reporters and
reporting—Handbooks, manuals, etc. 3. Mass media—Handbooks,
manuals, etc. 4. Public relations—Handbooks, manuals, etc.
I. Lorenz, Alfred Lawrence.   II. Title.
PN4781.V58   1995
070.4—dc20   95-14806
                                                  CIP

Printed in the United States of America

10 9 8 7 6 5 4 3 2 1   99 98 97 96 95

CONTENTS

PREFACE

The day 17-year-old Robert Musel went to work for the United Press news service, the New York bureau manager handed him a press card.

"This is what you make of it," the editor told Musel, who would have a half-century career as an outstanding news correspondent. "It can be so much cardboard or a ringside seat to history. One thing it's not is a license to bore people."

Like that press card, this book is what you make of it.

AN INTEGRATED APPROACH

Many college news writing and news reporting textbooks have been written over the years. So why this one? Times are changing. In our journalism classrooms, we are finding dramatic shifts in students' career plans. It's happening everywhere. The number of students intent on broadcast careers is growing. We have more public relations students. Too often, it seems, these students ask us: "What am I doing here? Is this course for me?" In part, the traditional textbooks fuel those questions. Some books have a chapter on broadcast news or public relations tacked on, but those chapters come across to students as afterthoughts. Some journalism books focus myopically on newspapers.

We are also aware that news people are making more numerous career shifts among media. Prominent examples are Tom Johnson's move from the Los Angeles Times to CNN, Michael Gartner's switch from the Des Moines Register to NBC and then back to newspapers, and Peter Arnett's move from the AP to CNN. Increasingly common are early career shifts back and forth from news and public relations. No longer is it enough to learn skills unique to newspapers.

This book, "News," is a significant departure. We have written it as a "news book," not a "newspaper book." We want every student to be comfortable with it, regardless of whether they are in news-ed, broadcast or public relations curriculum tracks. We have also tried to show photography and broadcast production students why news skills are vital to them.

Broadcast

In every chapter broadcast students will find information and examples drawn from radio and television journalism. This is a text that reminds broadcast students why their curriculum includes a news course. By integrating broadcast news, we are serving not only broadcast students but also others who don't know it but who may very well end up in a radio or television newsroom.

Public Relations

A significant part of public relations involves the news media, a fact lost in many traditional textbooks and also on many public relations students. We remind public relations students in every chapter why news skills are relevant to them. We have examples of news releases, tips on arranging news conferences, and suggestions on media relations in a broad sense.

To be sure, this is not a comprehensive book on public relations writing. We don't try to teach speechwriting, nor fund-raising appeals, nor non-news aspects of public relations. That's for another course. But we have given the news aspects of public relations a strong presence throughout.

Print News

By many measures, newspapers still are the dominant news medium in the country, and students planning on newspaper careers will find "News" is for them. Many examples are from people who once worked for newspapers but who now report for broadcast stations or work in public relations—and the other way around too. We also talk about journalists who have spent their entire careers productive and satisfied in newspapers.

In short, "News" is designed for all the students who fill today's news writing and news reporting courses. The book can be used profitably in either course or both.

HOW THIS BOOK IS ORGANIZED

The text is organized to first introduce students to news writing. So important do we believe the writing to be that we have devoted more than one-third of the text to it.

Next, students will learn the basics of reporting, moving from various aspects of general assignment reporting to the specific demands of beat reporting. We give special attention to the techniques of interviewing, observation and research.

The text ends with a detailed discussion of law and ethics as they apply to the mass media. We highlight the opportunities young reporters will find provided to them by the First Amendment and the American legal system and some of the legal pitfalls that await them. We look at ethical thickets they might encounter and offer a road map for getting through them.

The structure allows instructors to use the text advantageously in a stand-alone news writing and reporting course or in writing and reporting courses spread over two or even, in some cases, three terms.

SPECIAL FEATURES

News is exciting, and we believe students will find this book, "News," captures that excitement. We have tried for a writing style that's as lively and substantive as a well-crafted newscast. We have used up-to-date examples, including the horrific terrorist bombing of the Oklahoma City Federal Building—a story that will still be unfolding when students first use this book.

Cyberjournalism

You will find a whole chapter on how reporters are using the Internet and commercial on-line services as reporting tools. Students will find tips they can use right away for everyday tasks like verifying information and making routine checks. But we also have combed newsrooms around the country for the best examples of enterprise stories that come from new computer tools. We hope to excite students about the potential that computer access to databases and sources holds for them in their careers over the next few decades.

Introductory Vignettes

Every chapter begins with a story about a journalist at work, such as Molly Moore covering the Persian Gulf war for the Washington Post, Howard Weaver's leadership at the Anchorage Daily News uncovering rural despair as a social issue, and the Fargo Forum's Jim Corcoran following up on a North Dakota shootout for a revealing portrait of the rural Radical Right in America. These introductory vignettes are meant to excite students and hook them on the lessons ahead in the chapter.

Reporting Experiences

We have leaned on dozens of journalists, some of them recognized globally, some only to their local audiences, for experiences to share with students. What better way to learn the rules of direct quotation than by reading about Janet Malcolm's trials for playing loose, or how Truman Capote trained himself to remember detail without taking notes.

Historical Context

We have drawn on historical experiences for many lessons so that the next generation might learn from successful journalists of the past. Consider the enterprise exhibited by St. Louis Post-Dispatch reporter Frank Woodward, who joined the Army for an inside story on life in uniform but found himself court-martialed when he left the post to write his story. Woodward's lesson is as riveting today as in 1889 when he joined up. Students learn accuracy when they read about the garbled accounts of Abraham Lincoln's Gettysburg Address. No stronger lesson about the importance of securing communication back to the newsroom exists than that of UPI's Merriman Smith covering the assassination of President Kennedy.

Ethics and Issues

"News" not only has an entire chapter on ethics, but discussions on ethics issues appear throughout at appropriate points. In the section on video news releases, for example, students will learn the problems of public relations people who do stand-ups in which they come across as news reporters. What about reporters who conceal their identities and purposes in going after stories? Can such misrepresentation be justified? That discussion comes in the observation chapter's discussion on participatory and immersion projects.

PEDAGOGICAL FEATURES

We believe "News" breaks new ground in its array of features to help students master the material in each chapter.

Learning Goals

Students get a road map at the start of every chapter in bulleted learning goals. These coincide with headings that break the chapters into manageable learning units.

Study Previews

Every learning unit within a chapter has a brief summary of the main points in the paragraphs that follow. These study previews orient students to what's ahead.

Review Questions

Every chapter ends with questions that students should be able to handle after reading the chapter. These flow sequentially from the chapter and coincide with study previews to facilitate checking back on any weak areas.

Bulleted Lists

To help students grasp material quickly, we use many bulleted lists. Students can zip through these lists for an instant sense of how to go about certain tasks. For example, one bulleted list tells student what things to consider when putting together an analytical piece.

Annotated Bibliography

Students interested in further learning will find suggested reading at the end of every chapter. The bibliography ranges from seminal works to the latest thinking.

Reinforcing Photographs

We have used photographs and captions to reinforce primary points in the chapters.

Exercises

We invite students to put their learning to work with exercises at the end of every chapter. Some of these are thought-provoking exercises. Others ask students to create stories from information that is provided.

SUPPLEMENTARY MATERIALS

Workbook

You will find more than 200 writing exercises in a workbook that is available to accompany "News." The workbook is structured so exercises coincide with the chapters in the textbook. Many of these exercises are adapted from real events.

CNN Videos

Professors who adopt "News" can receive a video with selected features from the CNN series "Reliable Sources." The series, hosted by veteran journalist Bernard Kalb, examines journalistic issues with rotating panelists who bring expertise to the discussion. These make an excellent springboard for class discussions.

Instructor's Resource Guide

Instructors have a comprehensive manual available with chapter synopses, outlines, terms and definitions, lecture and exam questions, and discussion on the "Putting Your Learning to Work"exercises in the text and on the exercises in the workbook. The manual also includes additional reading suggestions.

For further information on these supplementary materials, contact your local publisher's representative.

IMITATION AS A LEARNING TOOL

Benjamin Franklin tells us in his autobiography that as an apprentice in his brother's print shop he would rewrite essays that he read in the Spectator, an English publication whose writing he admired, and then compare his efforts with the originals. In that way, he said, "I discovered many faults and corrected them." From time to time he found he had improved on the original, and that, he said, "encouraged me to think that I might in time come to be a tolerable English writer, of which I was extremely ambitious."

Believing with Franklin that imitation is a useful tool for learning, we have included examples in each chapter so that students can see how professionals have succeeded in putting into practice the principles we discuss. We also have examples that show how pros sometimes fall short.

With the diverse interests of our audience in mind, we have public relations releases, both print and broadcast, and house publications. We have also included examples from student-produced college media. We hope they will give the text special relevance to students who are or will be involved with campus newspapers, newscasts and magazines.

When students are done with the text, we hope they will be well prepared to go forth and, like the UP's Robert Musel, take their seats at the ringside of history—and never bore their audiences.

ACKNOWLEDGMENTS

We appreciate the thoughtful suggestions of the following colleagues who reviewed the manuscript in whole or in part, at various stages of its development: Jean Chance, University of Florida; Jim Highland, Western Kentucky University; Harry Marsh, Kansas State University; James Hoyt, University of Wisconsin; and David C. Nelson, Southwest Texas State University.

We also wish to thank the many people who gave help and advice to us during the making of this book: Mike Adams, ChicagoLand Television News; Ed Anderson, New Orleans Times-Picayune; Betty Bertrang, Winona State University; Rev. David Boileau, Loyola University; Sharon Donovan, freelance writer, New Orleans; Sandra Driggin, Extra Extra; Joe Duke, television station KHOU, Houston; Cathy Rogers Franklin, Loyola University; Bill Holden, University of North Dakota; Hoda Kotb, television station WWL, New Orleans, John Lorenz, MVP Training, Inc., Newport Beach, Calif.; Bruce Nolan, New Orleans Times-Picayune; Charles Pizzo, PR PR Inc., New Orleans; Steve Schild, St. Mary's University of Minnesota; Mark Schleifstein, New Orleans Times-Picayune; Liz Scott, Loyola University; Scott Shaw, radio station WIZM, La Crosse, Wis.; Jim Smorada, South Dakota State University; Alexandra Walsh, Recording Industry Association of America; Bill Withers, Winona State University; and Linda Yasnyi, You Ain't Seen Nothing Yet Ink.

We also appreciate the efforts of Paula Wiczek, the Mass Communication Department secretary at Winona State University. She never failed in helping us while simultaneously meeting the needs of a busy academic department. At Loyola University, we likewise are indebted to Department of Communications secretaries Lynda Favret and Diane Howard.

A debt also is owed to the hundreds of news people whose work we cite as examples. In some cases, we have made slight adjustments in the original work to underscore a pedagogical point or to conform with Associated Press style.

We owe special thanks to those from whom we have learned along the way, for their influence is surely present in this book. Warren Bovee, Albion Ross and Louis Belden were our colleagues when we served together on the faculty of the College of Journalism at Marquette University. We each turned to them as mentors, and we were rewarded beyond measure by their friendship and their example. Their love of teaching and their goodness have inspired our lives and our careers.

The professionals with whom we have worked taught us too, and we are grateful to them as well. Patrick J. Craig, William G. Ferguson, Thomas L. McGann and John I. Pelletreau were senior editors on United Press International's National Broadcast News desk in Chicago when Professor Lorenz was a young newsman. Bobbie Ulrich was Professor Vivian's bureau manager when he joined UPI in Spokane, and Paul Lloyd, Bill Mertena and Burl Osborn were in charge of the Associated Press bureau there when he crossed the street to work for that news agency. These all were excellent writers and patient editors, and from them we learned that writing should be spare and clear, even when crafted under deadline pressure, and that editing should always encourage a writer to improve—lessons we hope have benefited our students through the years.

Although they didn't realize it at the time, hundreds of students in our journalism classes over the years, first at Marquette, New Mexico State and the University of North Dakota, and now at Loyola and Winona State, are our most important contibutors. Just as we taught them, they taught us by pressing our assumptions and seeking new and better explanations. To them we cannot overstate our appreciation.

Sharing Your Experiences

We hope to improve this text in future editions in order to increase its value as a teaching tool, so we ask that you give us your suggestions.

You may write to Larry Lorenz at the Department of Communications, Loyola University, New Orleans, LA 70118; by e-mail, lorenz@beta.loyno.edu.

John Vivian can be reached at the Mass Communication Department, Winona State University, Winona, MN 55987; or you can contact him by e-mail, jvivian@vax2.winona.msus.edu.

Alfred Lawrence Lorenz
New Orleans, Louisiana

John Vivian
Fountain City, Wisconsin

Grateful acknowledgment is extended to the following for permission to reprint excerpts from news materials:

ABC News, Radio, broadcast excerpts. Reprinted by permission.

Associated Press, articles by Stephanie McGehee and others. Reprinted by permission of the Associated Press.

Atlanta Constitution, Atlanta, Ga., articles by Bill Husted and John Blake, 3/4/91 p. A-1 and 11/9/92 p. B-1. The Atlanta Journal/The Atlanta Constitution/AJC Newsearch, Atlanta, Ga. Reprinted by permission.

Boca Raton News, Boca Raton, Fla., articles by Anthony Marx and others. Reprinted with permission of The News.

Chicago Tribune, Chicago, Ill., articles by Peter Kendall and Susan Kuczka. Copyright © 1991 Chicago Tribune Company. All rights reserved. Used with permission.

Daily Northwestern, Northwestern University, Evanston, Ill., article by Mark Mensheha. Reprinted by permission.

Dallas Morning News, Dallas, Texas, articles by Dan Shine, George Kuempel, and others. Reprinted by permission.

Dow Jones & Company, Inc., articles in the Wall Street Journal by Tony Horwitz and Geraldine Brooks, Bruce Ingersoll, Robert Greenberger, and William Carley. Reprinted by permission of the Wall Street Journal. Copyright © 1991, 1994 Dow Jones & Company, Inc. All Rights Reserved Worldwide.

Gannetteer, Gannett Co. house organ, article by Mary Hardie, February 1993. Reprinted with permission of the Gannetteer, Gannett Co., Inc.

Houston Chronicle, Houston, Texas, articles by Geoff Davidian and Patti Muck. Copyright © Houston Chronicle. Reprinted by permission.

L'Observateur, New Orleans, La., article by Amy Miller. Reprinted by permission.

Martin/Williams Advertising, Minneapolis, Minn., public service announcement for the American Humane Association. Lyle Wedemeyer, creative director; Sally Wagner, art director; Christopher Wilson, copywriter; Anne Swarts, producer; Janet Jones, account supervisor.

Miami Herald, Miami, Fla., articles by Ana Santiago, Mimi Whitefield, and Michael Browning. Reprinted by permission.

Milwaukee Journal, Milwaukee, Wis., articles by Dave Hendrickson, Richard Jones, Manuel Mendoza. Reprinted by permission.

Munster, Ind., Times, Carol Napolitano, CAR Coordinator.

New Orleans Times-Picayune, New Orleans, La., a selection of articles. Reprinted by permission.

Newsweek Magazine, article by Tom Post from Newsweek February 14, 1994. Copyright © 1994 Newsweek, Inc. All rights reserved. Reprinted by permission.

New York Times, New York, N.Y., "Explosion at the Twin Towers; The Investigation; Bomb Is Definite Answer, But All Else is Mystery," by Ralph Blumenthal, February 28, 1993. "War in the Gulf," by James Barron, January 17, 1991. "Bernard Malamud Dies at 71," March 19, 1986. "Tender Trap," by Bill Carter, August 23, 1992. "NBC, Hiding Behind the Lawyers," February 17, 1993. "The Fall of the House of Bingham, " by Alex S. Jones, January 19, 1986. Reprinted by permission.

Continued on the folowing page

NEWS

REPORTING AND WRITING

CHAPTER 1

Applying News Skills in Mass Media Careers

In this chapter you will learn:

+ News reporting and writing skills are important in all fields of mass communication.

+ Journalism is a field that includes all media of mass communication, not only newspapers.

+ Public relations people need to understand how journalists go about their work.

+ The tight, sharp writing that is stressed in journalism is essential in creating effective advertising messages.

+ Photojournalists often are eyewitnesses to events that no one else sees, which means their writing skills are as important as their photographic skills.

+ Most television station jobs involve news, which is the bulk of most stations' production.

+ People with news skills are sought after in many fields outside the mass media, including law.

THE EXCITEMENT OF NEWS

High in the press box at Fenway Park, Larry Whiteside of the Boston Globe taps out a story on a Red Sox victory on a portable computer as soon as the game ends, transmits it to his editors across town, and rushes down to the locker room for color and comment for a revision he will write for the final edition 30 minutes away.

John Holliman of CNN adjusts his microphone seconds before he begins a live report from Baghdad on an Iraqi government announcement.

At the Barcelona Olympics, Mary Lou Retton, who herself was the first U.S. gymnast to win a gold medal, at the 1984 Los Angeles games, keeps track of U.S. medals for USA Today. She punches stories into a laptop computer, plugs the machine into a telephone line, and transmits her copy instantly to USA Today's sports editors on the Potomac outside Washington.

In Iowa, photographer David Peterson of the Des Moines Register spends most of his day in rural towns interviewing people as part of his scouting for photogenic material. Later, after processing his film, Peterson sits down to write the captions.

Lauri Fitz-Pegado, a public relations executive, coaches a client on how to answer Washington reporters at a news conference scheduled on the Capitol steps.

In Aspen, Colorado, Hunter Thompson, who has procrastinated on a magazine piece, faxes one paragraph at a time, as he pulls them from his typewriter, to his editors in New York, who are biting their nails as the clock ticks toward their deadline.

These writers—at Fenway Park, in Baghdad, at the Barcelona Olympics, in rural Iowa, in a District of Columbia office, and in the Colorado Rockies— work for different media organizations, but they have much in common. Whatever their medium, they are all journalists. They have the same goals: to seek and tell truth about the day's public events accurately and fairly.

Another similarity among good reporters is that they make their work seem easy—at least that is how the audience sees their polished final products. This fluency is a developed skill. Nobody is born knowing how to tell news.

This chapter is intended to help you realize that the skills you develop in a news course are important not only if your career intention is journalism but also if you plan to go into other fields, including public relations. The ability to ask probing questions, to absorb and understand complicated background information, and to explain it in simple, lucid, compelling terms to a busy audience is much in demand, not only in the mass media but also in law, banking, politics and many other fields.

NO STOPPING THE NEWS. When Communism toppled through most of central and eastern Europe in 1989, people were eager for information. Even in less tumultuous times, people have an insatiable appetite for news on what is happening around them and far away.   (Charles Platiau/Reuters/The Bettmann Archive)

JOURNALISTS AND THEIR WORK

STUDY PREVIEW   Journalists work in many media, and some of their tools are unique to a particular medium—such as microphones for radio and television, and cameras for photojournalism—but there is incredible similarity in how they go about their work and overcome obstacles. All face deadlines. All communicate with mass audiences. All use the written language, whether they are writing newspaper articles or scripting newscasts or composing captions.

Meeting Deadlines

Journalists all face deadlines. While not every news story is written against severe deadlines, every journalist must write quickly when the pressure is on. With breaking news, like the 1994 California earthquake, a fumble at a television network can mean surrendering an advantage to competitors. Viewers tune to the affiliate that is on top of the story. At the global news agencies, writers know that a one-minute delay will mean that some publication or broadcast station somewhere in the world will miss receiving a story in time for an edition or a newscast. Its business, UPI used to say, was meeting "a deadline every minute."

Thinking Clearly

Whatever their medium, journalists all need highly developed analytical abilities to sort through what's going on around them. The challenge is to be accurate, quick and interesting, and also to explain why the information they are conveying is important. The editors and producers who make final decisions on using a reporter's story need the same kind of analytical abilities to make good decisions on deadline. It is no wonder that most editors and producers and many public relations executives are veteran reporters.

Serving Mass Audiences

All news people also have mass audiences in common—huge masses of people of diverse backgrounds and interests. Many of the techniques developed over time for serving these heterogeneous audiences apply to all media, not just news.

Because readers, viewers and listeners cannot give immediate feedback to the reporter, the story must be clear the first time. This requires good writing skills. The challenge of communicating news successfully is heightened by the fact that people in the mass audience have varying degrees of attentiveness and are distracted easily.

Using the Language

Like other mass communicators, journalists are adept with the language. They have mastered the tedious mechanical details like comma placement and the rules of spelling. In addition, they have cultivated a feel for language that gives their reports clarity and flourish. Even when they are doing unscripted, unrehearsed live television standups from the scene of an unfolding event, reporters are employing the same rules of effective communication that they use in writing news.

MASS MEDIA CAREERS

STUDY PREVIEW   News work requires finding truth and then telling it accurately, fairly and compellingly. These abilities are also at the heart of mass media fields outside of journalism.

Public Relations

When several people died in Chicago after taking Tylenol capsules, the manufacturer Johnson & Johnson had a major public relations problem on its hands. Somebody had laced the capsules with cyanide. Johnson & Johnson, which had built Tylenol into the leading headache remedy, was suddenly faced with the reality that its product had become a vehicle of death. There was also the possibility that public loss of confidence in the product could ruin the company.

Hundreds of reporters deluged Johnson & Johnson with questions. The company response, which has become a classic case study in effective public relations, was to communicate to the public as much information as could be learned about the situation. The company's willingness to communicate through the mass media stemmed a loss of confidence and laid the groundwork for the restoration of Tylenol's market dominance. Johnson & Johnson's success was due in no small part to the journalistic savvy of its public relations staff.

In less dramatic situations too, the news media are important in public relations. There is no more effective, efficient way to reach great numbers of people. Media relations, an essential element of public relations, involves:

✦ Issuing news releases that communicate an institution's message through newspapers, television, magazines and radio.

✦ Arranging news conferences.

✦ Answering reporter inquiries.

✦ Arranging news interviews.

It is no wonder that the model curriculum endorsed by the Public Relations Society of America and the Public Relations Division of the Association for Education in Journalism and Mass Communication includes journalism courses. News skills have wide applications in public relations, not just for news releases but for in-house magazines and newsletters, corporate reports and internal documents.

Journalism courses also introduce public relations students to the ways in which news people go about their work and how they think. To not know what makes journalists tick is to go about media relations blindly.

PUBLIC RELATIONS WRITING. The importance of writing in public relations work can be measured by the ratio of employees to keyboards at a PR agency. In their widely used public relations textbook, Doug Newsom and Bob Carrell say: "Public relations professionals are expected to be effective writers—real wordsmiths—whose fact-finding and analytical skills are exceeded only by their ability to mold information into any format needed for presentation in any medium."   (Courtesy of The Pepsi-Cola Company)

Advertising

Advertising people have a rule of thumb for billboards: Keep the message to seven words maximum. At 60 miles an hour, anything longer will be missed. Even a 15-second radio commercial can accommodate only 35 or 40 words.

Effective advertising messages require disciplined thinking and writing, just as news does, which is why many college advertising curricula include courses in news writing. Just as in news work, the challenge in advertising is to pack as much connotative value as possible into a message for an audience which, like the news audience, cannot be assumed to be looking between the lines for nuance and subtlety. Although advertising draws more on the techniques of persuasion than on those of news, both rely on the same techniques to reach mass audiences through a mass medium with convincing, credible nonfiction messages.

Advertising genius Bill Bernbach gave testimony to the importance of writing as part of the disciplined creative process when he said: "Merely to let your imagination run riot, to dream unrelated dreams, to indulge in graphic aerobatics and verbal gymnastics, is not being creative. The creative person has

THE VALUE OF NEWS SKILLS. An assumption about educated people is that they know how to write. When she was an Olympic gymnast, Mary Lou Retton probably wasn't thinking she would someday be covering the Olympics. But that was exactly what she found herself doing at the Barcelona summer games, on assignment for the newspaper USA Today.   (Erica Lanser/Black Star)

harnessed his imagination. He has disciplined it so that every thought, every idea, every word he puts down, every line he draws, every light and shadow in every photograph he takes, make more vivid, more believable, more persuasive the original theme or product advantage he has decided he must convey."

Techniques that make for effective news writing also make for effective advertising writing. Mastery of the language is essential in both, as is a sense of the opportunities and limitations of different media. Writing against a deadline is a fact of life in both news and advertising. Practitioners in both fields face the problems of delayed feedback and of inattentive, even uninterested audiences.

Learning how to write news for a mass audience can help an advertising student develop methods for crafting effective pitches. The fact is that the news audience and the advertising audience are the same.

Photography and Videography

At age 24 Stephanie McGehee took up residence in Kuwait and over the next 13 years worked as an Associated Press photographer. In 1990, when the Iraqi blitzkrieg began, McGehee found that the AP needed more than her skills as a photojournalist. She was the only AP staffer in the country, and the news service's only journalistic witness to what was happening.

Nineteen days after the invasion, after a daring convoy escape across the desert to Saudi Arabia, McGehee put her writing skills to work in a first-person account. An excerpt:

> The bomb blasts shook me out of bed.
>
> It was actually happening. The Iraqis were invading and their tanks were rumbling brazenly into Kuwait City.
>
> I told my Canadian flatmate, Kathy McGregor, that the Iraqis were there and ran to the roof.
>
> There was gunfire. The TR-72s were rolling through the streets. The Iraqi soldiers stopped all motorcyclists and pedestrians at gunpoint. They yanked the mobile phones out of cars and threw them away. They shot at motorists who did not stop.
>
> I called the Associated Press with the news, then rushed back to the roof.
>
> Iraqi army vehicles were heading to the oil area of al-Ahmadi. Helicopter gunships swooped low over the city. There was no sign of Kuwaiti troops.
>
> The Iraqis were shooting indiscriminately. It was frightening.

Not infrequently, photographers like McGehee, and videographers too, find themselves exclusive witnesses to major events, and they need to record the story both pictorially and in words.

Most college photojournalism programs require news-writing courses so that their graduates will be ready when they find themselves in the middle of an earth-jarring event, like the Iraqi invasion. Also, many entry-level photojournalism positions are with rural weekly newspapers, which for financial reasons often need staff members who are as handy with a keyboard as with a shutter. At small-market television stations, videographers sometimes are sent alone to get a story, which means both shooting and writing.

Broadcast Production

Many students intent on careers in broadcast production will find themselves working in news. At almost every network-affiliated television station, news involves more staff and resources than any other station activity. Even small-market stations produce at least 1½ hours of news a day—far more than any dramatic or entertainment programming or other kinds of local shows. As part of the team that brings news to the air, broadcast production people need an intimate understanding of how journalists decide what to report and the techniques they use to do it.

In radio not only the people with "news" in their job titles but almost every on-air person has something to do with news. At most stations even the most junior announcer delivers the news, and news provides the basis for the patter of many entertainment programs.

Beyond the Mass Media

At many law schools, admissions committees attach special value to applicants who majored in journalism as undergraduates. Law professors have learned from experience that good J-grads, as well as students with other majors but with substantial experience in news courses, have the sharp writing and thinking skills that make them good prospects for graduate work in law.

News courses require students to develop analytical skills that are valuable not only in law but in other fields as well. When students go through the exercise of deciding which stories are most worth reporting, they are putting their intellectual abilities to a test. The cerebral stretching continues when students are required to articulate rationales to support their choices.

News courses also emphasize the analytical process of encoding data, emotions and reactions about changing situations into messages that will reach and affect mass audiences. These are skills valued in every professional field.

CHAPTER WRAP-UP

News people and other mass communicators have a lot in common, but the heart of their work is that they craft messages for mass audiences. The techniques for reaching these audiences are similar whether the object is informing, entertaining or persuading. For this reason, mastering these techniques is invaluable not only in news- and journalism-related fields like public relations and broadcast production but also in other media fields including advertising.

STUDY QUESTIONS

1.   What value is there for public relations students in studying news? For photography students? For broadcast production students?

2.   Advertising people seldom write news, yet developing news-writing skills can help them in their work. How so?

3.   How does the development of journalistic skills help hone a student's analytical abilities?

PUTTING YOUR LEARNING TO WORK

EXERCISE 1   **Writing and Media Careers**

Talk with a leading mass media person in your community about how much of a typical day's work involves writing. Ask to see a typical day's output. Then write a brief report on the role of writing in that media person's work.

Most media people are flattered when a student asks about their work. In most communities, arranging time to meet a person should be no problem. Follow these steps:

+   Call the media person when he or she is at work.

✦ Introduce yourself as a student in an introductory news course.

✦ Explain that you would like to visit the media person at work and discuss the role of writing in the job. You could elaborate that you are interested in how much of a typical day is spent at the keyboard, what form the finished written product takes, and how the writing fits into the total product that the person's media organization produces.

✦ Explain that you will be writing a report for class on what you learn.

✦ Say you would be interested in seeing what the person writes in the course of a typical day.

✦ Be clear that your visit will require no more than 15 minutes.

✦ If the person is agreeable, set a time to get together.

Be sure to coordinate with classmates so two students don't call the same media person.

How do you choose a media person? Your instructor may be able to help, but you also can proceed on your own:

✦ If advertising especially interests you, check with the advertising manager at a local television or radio station or newspaper. Also, check the Yellow Pages for advertising agencies.

✦ For news, check newspaper and magazine bylines for people who write about subjects that particularly interest you. Do the same watching television news or listening to radio news.

✦ If you like photojournalism, look for credit lines on published photographs, and also check the staff credits at the end of television newscasts.

✦ If you are interested in public relations, inquire at large companies, hospitals, colleges or large government agencies for the name of a person in public relations.

EXERCISE 2   Writing in Your Future

Writing is an essential skill for an educated person. Write a few paragraphs on the role you see writing taking in your career. Even if your career plans don't include writing news, explain how the skills you expect to polish in this course will help your writing in general.

FOR FURTHER LEARNING

Debra Gersh. "Into Iraq, Out of Kuwait," Editor & Publisher 123, No. 35 (Sept. 1, 1990): 7–9, 34–35. Accompanying Gersh's account of early coverage of the Iraq-Kuwait war is AP photographer Stephanie McGehee's diary, which AP newspapers published after she escaped from occupied Kuwait.

Jane T. Harrigan. "Read All About It! A Day in the Life of a Metropolitan Newspaper." The Globe Pequot Press, 1987. Harrigan, a journalist, captures the excitement of producing a newspaper, tracking hundreds of Boston Globe people from 6 a.m. through midnight as they produce the issue of June 5, 1986. Along the way, she explains how journalists decide which events to report.

CHAPTER 2

Deciding What Makes News

In this chapter you will learn:

+ Journalism has the potential to inspire people to improve public policy to meet both community and individual needs.

+ Hard news deals with significant events and issues.

+ Soft news deals with matters that tend to be more interesting than significant.

+ Common elements in news stories are timeliness, proximity, prominence, currency, drama and consequence.

+ Journalists have to understand their audiences in order to reach them.

AN ALASKA TRAGEDY

Howard Weaver, managing editor of the Anchorage Daily News, looked over a state agency report on suicides. The Alaska state epidemiologist had found that local officials, especially in rural areas, often failed to report suicides to the state agency although the law required it. The underreporting had been massive, which meant that Alaska's suicide data had been misrepresented for years. The report, with its serious charge, made headlines throughout Alaska. At the Anchorage Daily News, however, it did more. Weaver sensed a bigger story. Most suicides, he knew, were more than individual acts of self-destruction. They originated in personal problems, usually rooted in family, community or the larger society. Weaver had a feeling that the statistical underreporting, although an important news story in itself, was only the tip of the iceberg. He wanted to know more.

Weaver asked his reporters to check newspaper obituaries on rural Alaskans for the past several months and then conduct interviews to find out whether the deaths were from natural causes. In one village, population 550, reporters discovered that there had been eight suicides in 16 months—a shocking number. Weaver and his reporters pushed on with more questions. In that same village in those same 16 months, there were also dozens of suicide attempts, four drownings and two homicides.

Over the next few months, 30 Daily News reporters and photographers—almost the whole news staff—worked on the story. In a package of 44 stories over 10 days, the newspaper began telling what it had learned. Readers were told about the extent of despair in rural Alaska and how it had led to the state's alarming suicide rate. Among native men 20 to 24, suicide was 10 times the national frequency. Not surprisingly, two often-related problems, alcoholism and child abuse, were rampant.

In this chapter, you will learn how stories like the Anchorage series on rural despair can help a democratic society work better, and can also help to improve the lives of individual members of the society. You also will learn about different kinds of news. And how do you reach a mass audience effectively? You'll learn that too.

THE IMPORTANCE OF NEWS

STUDY PREVIEW   Journalists can play an important role in democracy by providing information that helps people become involved in the political and social processes that determine the kind of society we have. Information that journalists offer can also help individuals lead better lives.

Journalism and Democracy

Asked what journalism does in a democracy, most people will answer: "It informs." That's only part of the answer. A follow-up question is needed: What is accomplished by doing the informing?

Journalism succeeds to the extent that it helps individuals participate in creating public policy—by buttonholing a county commissioner, calling a radio talk show, discussing public issues with neighbors, firing off a letter to a legislator, voting, supporting a lobby, writing a letter to the editor. This concept is well summed up in the mission statement in the masthead of the Marquette University campus newspaper, the Tribune: "To promote intelligent citizen involvement."

This goal, promoting intelligent citizen involvement, was accomplished by the Anchorage Daily News revelations about rural despair. Alaskans had a vague sense of the problem, but not until the Daily News portrayed the devastation to families and individuals in wrenching detail did everyone know enough to conclude for certain that something had to be done.

On the second day of the series, the governor called for programs aimed at preventing rural suicide and stemming alcohol and drug abuse. Legislators drafted bills to create alcoholism programs and proposed banning mail-order liquor sales and stiffening punishments for bootlegging.

Alaskans acquired information that helped them create public policies to correct serious social problems. It was no surprise that the series won the 1989 Pulitzer Prize for community service.

Journalism and Individuals

Public dialogue spurred by journalistic enterprise works at a personal level too. Doug Modig, an alcohol-abuse counselor in Anchorage, told a magazine reporter: "Instead of holding the shame inside, people are beginning to talk. When you don't talk about living in terror in your own villages, you cannot heal."

HARD NEWS

STUDY PREVIEW   The term "hard news" applies to event-based stories, like a city council meeting or an airplane crash, and to depth coverage, which involves stories that explore issues.

Spot Coverage

When the Alaska state epidemiologist first released his study on suicides, which led eventually to the Anchorage Daily News series on rural despair, reporters extracted numbers from the study, interviewed the epidemiologist, and wrote stories for their next edition and for the evening newscasts. These first stories were spot news based on an event—the release of a significant study. No reporter could miss the story. In the unlikely event that a reporter did not sense the inherent newsworthiness of the epidemiologist's report, the flurry of interest by competing reporters would be a tip-off that it was worth writing about.

Besides important public announcements, examples of spot news stories include plane crashes, assassinations, fires, elections and trial verdicts. Spot news is also called "breaking news," especially when events unfold over a period of time. A story on a disaster, for example, is spot news, but so are follow-up stories on the causes of the disaster and on the casualties as they become known.

Here are characteristics of spot news stories:

✦ Lead-off sentences are event based, telling the most significant or interesting development. Lesser aspects follow.

✦ With fast-breaking stories, in which news elements of great significance are occurring over time, the latest development is placed at the top.

✦ Witnesses and expert sources are cited.

✦ Coverage reacts to events, whether a natural phenomenon, like a storm, or something that is scheduled, like a news conference.

✦ Almost always, information for spot news stories is gathered and written against a deadline.

✦ Coverage is competitive. Reporters from numerous news organizations simultaneously cover the same event.

These characteristics are present in the following stories adapted from the Daily Northwestern, the campus newspaper at Northwestern University:

A Northwestern student monitoring the door at the kick-off dance for Bisexual, Gay and Lesbian Culture Month was hit on the arm by an unidentified man late Friday night, university police said.

The candidate list for Associated Student Government elections just got shorter. Tim Bhattacharyya announced yesterday he was dropping out of the race for academic vice president, trimming the number of candidates to two.

A 13-year-old girl was fatally shot in the forehead Saturday night as she and her friends stood in the front yard of a house in south Evanston.

An Evanston man was arrested Saturday in a Florida drug-smuggling investigation that ended in seven arrests and the seizure of 2½ tons of Jamaican marijuana.

Depth Coverage

While spot news focuses on events, depth coverage is concerned with providing detail and explanation of broad phenomena. Depth coverage is also hard news, but it goes beyond spot developments. In part it is a response to the call of the landmark Hutchins Commission on a Free and Responsible Press in 1947 for journalists to go beyond simply reporting events to put those events "in a context which gives them meaning." The difference between spot and depth coverage is obvious in comparing the brief, event-based stories on an evening television newscast with the treatments done on ABC's "Nightline" and PBS's "Washington Week in Review," which try to provide background, explication and analysis.

When Howard Weaver of the Anchorage Daily News sensed that there was a bigger story behind the epidemiologist's report, he wasn't focusing on an event. Rather, he wanted to see whether there was an issue worth exploring. The resulting series was depth reporting. As with a lot of depth coverage, Howard Weaver's enterprise created news. Had he not pursued the truths underlying the shocking data in the epidemiologist's study, those stories would never have been written. In depth news, the coverage is initiated by the news organization itself, often with daring and resourcefulness.

Here are the characteristics of the best depth coverage:

+ Journalists rely on their curiosity and enterprise to decide what to cover, rather than letting sources or events set their agendas.
+ Information gathering is extensive, sometimes taking months.
+ Because depth coverage is proactive, with journalists deciding what to pursue, stories are scoops that competitors don't have.
+ Written without pressing deadlines, depth news stories are fine-tuned and show advanced writing skills.

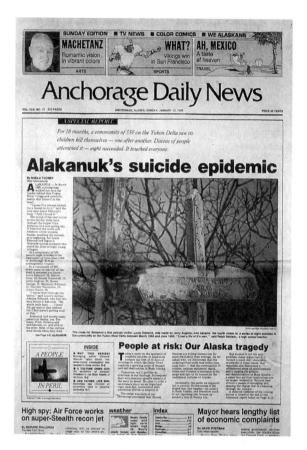

ENTERPRISE REPORTING. The Anchorage Daily News's managing editor, Howard Weaver, mobilized almost all his reporters and photographers to follow up on a report that the state's published suicide statistics were erroneously low because of false reports from local officials. The resulting series alerted Alaskans to serious problems of rural despair and prompted dialogue that led to new public policies to address the problems. The series, which won a Pulitzer Prize, demonstrated the role of journalists in a democratic society to focus public concern on issues.   (Courtesy of Alaska Daily News)

Enterprise Coverage

Taking the initiative, called "enterprise" in the news business, can be important in both spot and depth coverage.

Reuters, the British news service, exhibited enterprise in setting up satellite transmission facilities that gave it an edge in covering the dramatic ousting of Communist regimes in central and eastern Europe in 1990. CNN led early coverage of the coalition war against Iraq in 1991 because, months earlier, it arranged for backup communication systems in case regular lines went down.

When ABC's Barbara Walters sought an exclusive White House interview with Barbara Bush, it was enterprise reporting. The story would not have come into existence if Walters had not asked for the interview.

Public Relations and Hard News

Public relations practitioners and journalists are close allies, at least most of the time, as journalists go about gathering spot information and digging into situations for depth stories. Public relations people frequently answer journalists' questions as their organization's spokespersons—the people who are quoted in print or whose voices you hear on the radio. When a hurricane hit New Orleans, knocking out electrical power, it was public relations person Mike Sanders, a former television reporter, who was seen and heard describing the extent of power losses and advising his company's customers when they could expect to have their lights back on.

Public relations people also act as brokers between the individuals in their organizations who have information and the journalists who want that information. And when individuals in their organizations do not want to give up information, the public relations people often are in a position to persuade them to cooperate with journalists.

SOFT NEWS

STUDY PREVIEW   The widely used term "soft news" is difficult to define. One useful attempt at a definition is that soft news is about things that people instinctively want to know, as opposed to things they feel duty-bound to know.

Defining Soft News

Stories whose purpose is more to entertain than to inform are called "soft news." Sometimes the terms "feature" and "human interest" are used to describe soft news, although a neat definition is elusive. People use the term "soft news" loosely.

In general, though, soft news has a discretionary quality. Imagine that a Chicago subway accident has paralyzed the city's mass transit system. A Chicago radio station would be remiss not to cover the accident, which clearly would be hard news. The same station could hardly be faulted, however, for not reporting the retirement of a school janitor that a competing station included in its newscast. The competing station talked about the changes the janitor had seen over 40 years at an urban grade school—information that was interesting and worthwhile to an audience but was not hard news. The mass audience would not be seriously misserved if the story never aired.

Soft news can have a news peg. A story based on an interview with the spouse of someone who died in our hypothetical subway accident, discussing the psychological, social and economic impact on the family, would be an excellent follow-up to the accident. It would be a story worth telling, full of emotion and insight, even though it didn't demand the priority placement of a major breaking story, like the accident itself.

One definition of soft news is that it is less important than hard news—less important, but not necessarily unimportant. Compare the first few paragraphs of the following event-based hard news story from the Winona, Minn., Daily News with the soft news story that follows:

By Tim Schultz

Fire destroyed the abandoned Mapleleaf Lanes, one of Winona's oldest bowling alleys, Wednesday night, sending smoke over much of the city.

The fire blew out the back wall shortly after firefighters arrived.

"We're lucky no one got hurt," said Fire Chief Ed Kohner.

Three firefighters got out of the building just before the explosion, and another firefighter narrowly missed being hit by debris.

It was too early to speculate about the cause or whether foul play was involved, Kohner said.

Here is a soft news story that accompanied the preceding main story:

By Tim Schultz

When it was built, Mapleleaf Lanes was "the Cadillac of bowling alleys," says Josephine Biltgen, widow of one of the men who started the bowling alley.

When the smoke cleared Wednesday night, Mapleleaf Lanes was totaled. Fire had gutted it.

"I feel really bad," Biltgen said. "The boys are gone, but it's still kind of a legend, still a part of the family."

The "boys" were brothers Roger and Harold Biltgen, and the legend was the bowling alley they built in 1947 after returning from the Army in World War II.

Soft news stories that focus on a single event, person or issue may not seem of great importance at first glance, but some soft news offers significant insights into important matters. Here is an example from the Sagamore, the campus newspaper at Indiana University–Purdue University at Indianapolis:

By Stacey McArthur

When senior Beth Terrell found out she was in the same oceanography class as her 62-year-old father, she tried to be discreet.

She had just moved into her own apartment and was struggling to maintain independence.

"He sat in the front of the class as close as he could to the teacher, and I always sat as far away from the teacher as possible," said Terrell, a 24-year-old French and supervision major.

But Terrell discovered that little girls almost always need their daddies sooner or later.

McArthur went on to discuss the dynamics of parent-adult child relationships when both are in college.

Some soft news is frivolous. Celebrity gossip stories can be tantalizing, but rarely are they important. Some people in the mass audience might "want to know" such news, but it is not news they "need to know." It hardly affects the future of the republic or even how individuals will go about their daily affairs. Supermarket tabloids like the National Enquirer specialize in this kind of frivolous soft news: bizarre, odd, novel, offbeat, crazy, wacky stuff—interesting but of only transitory value.

Soft news stories that focus on personalities are not necessarily frivolous. The kind of personality profile that the New Yorker magazine pioneered in the 1920s and that Playboy magazine developed in the 1960s with the modern question and answer format can be significant pieces of journalism. Consider this news release from Playboy, issued to news organizations on the eve of publication of the January 1991 issue:

Japan's refusal to open its markets is responsible for America's $50 billion trade imbalance, says Lee Iacocca, embattled chairman of the Chrysler Corp.

In the January issue of Playboy magazine, Iacocca, a cultural icon known as much for his intense patriotism as his business acumen, talks about the Persian Gulf crisis, running for president and his reputation as a Japan basher.

"I am not a Japan basher," Iacocca says in the Playboy interview. "Newsweek once put out a list of the Top 10 Japan bashers and I didn't even make the list.

"Every time you turn up the volume in any way, the Japanese yell racist and everybody backs off. Why? Because we've got a guilty conscience in this country, and they know that over in Japan."

Because they come out infrequently and therefore do not deal with spot news, company publications more often than not contain soft news stories. Personality profiles of company officers or stories about an organization's activities or products are the stuff of such newsletters, so the stories are, by their very nature, soft rather than hard.

Mass media scholar Wilbur Schramm struggled to come up with distinctions among various kinds of news in the 1940s, finally concluding that many stories of the soft news type give the audience an immediate reward. The satisfaction of knowing the story is immediate: "Gee, that was interesting!" The reward with hard news comes later, said Schramm. A story on congressional debate over the national debt, for example, helps thoughtful readers keep on top of an ongoing issue, providing a small piece of information that fits into their larger and developing mosaic of information and ideas on the issue.

While it is helpful, Schramm's delayed-immediate reward continuum lacks universal applicability, as do all attempts to categorize news. The fact is that journalistic work is an art, not a science. Neat, clean definitions are elusive. Even so, the terms "soft news" and "hard news" are widely used among journalists to try to describe the approach they take with particular stories.

A problem with this looseness in the definition of soft news is that young writers sometimes assume they have a license to be self-indulgent, choosing subjects to write about simply because the topics interest them, regardless of whether a mass audience would be interested. That approach to choosing subjects contradicts the whole premise that news reporting should be audience oriented. It is not enough that the writer like the subject. A key to newsworthiness, for hard or soft news, is whether the audience is interested too.

Balancing Hard and Soft News

Most newsrooms seek a balance of hard and soft news. This balance is based on how they see their role in the community and how they perceive their audience's needs and interests.

Broadcasters are heaviest with hard news programs in the morning and evening, when people look for wrap-ups on what has happened overnight or during the day. The Phil Donahue, Oprah Winfrey and Geraldo Rivera programs, which generally feature soft news, run at other times of the day.

Practical considerations also affect the hard-soft mix. Morning newspapers, with their deadlines the night before, have the whole previous day's events to report, and thus they emphasize hard news.

Evening papers, on the other hand, with deadlines about noon or earlier, go to press before much news has happened since readers saw the morning paper. Evening newspapers generally tend to a softer mix.

Radio news, which emphasizes immediacy, lends itself to hard news.

Lacking the edge of timeliness, many weekly newspapers and magazines opt for softer approaches. So do many house organs and other news vehicles produced by public relations people.

LOOKING FOR NEWS

S T U D Y   P R E V I E W   No easy formula can determine whether something is newsworthy, but most events reported in the media have at least one of the common elements of news: timeliness, proximity, prominence, currency, drama and, the most important, consequence. Novelty also can be an element in news.

Elements of News

Some journalists know intuitively what will interest an audience. Their "nose for news" gets them to the right place at the right time, they ask the right questions, and they spin great tales. Those who weren't born with a mystical feel for news can use a more methodological approach, looking for qualities in events around them that should interest a mass audience.

Timeliness. Because people look to the news media to keep them up to date, they are more interested in today's vote by the city council than in one a week or a year ago. In most stories about events you will find the "when" element in the lead sentence, as in these stories adapted from the Milwaukee Journal:

> **By Richard Jones**
> MADISON, Wis.—The session that Wisconsin legislators begin Monday could become a budget brawl by spring.

> **By Manuel Mendoza**
> One of four people trying to win a boat by sitting outside in the cold weather during a Milwaukee endurance contest was hospitalized Saturday night after his body temperature dropped to 95.7 degrees.

Proximity. A Boston television news producer knows her audience will be more interested in an airliner crash at Logan International Airport, right in Boston, than in a crash half a world away in Timbuktu. This Milwaukee Journal story about astronaut Dan Brandenstein would interest more readers in Watertown, Wis., than in Watertown, N.Y.:

> Capt. Dan Brandenstein, a Watertown, Wis., native, will be heading into the heavens again in 1992 as he commands the new space shuttle Endeavor.

GETTING TO THE STORY FIRST. Life magazine reporter Lee Hall leans precariously from a tugbot rail for porthole interviews with survivors from the ocean liner Andrea Doria. The luxury ship sank after being struck by the liner Stockholm off New York, and the Stockholm, its bow smashed flat, as you can see, brought survivors to port. Hall and Life photographer George Silk wangled their way onto the tug for the first interviews on a story whose news elements included timeliness, drama and consequence.   (George Silk/Time-Life Pictures)

Proximity is the "where" element of news. The "where" almost always shows up in the lead sentence of an event-based story so the audience knows whether the event was local. For out-of-town stories, most newspapers use a device called the "dateline" to immediately orient readers to where the event occurred:

> WASHINGTON (AP)—The worst three-month stretch of job losses since the depths of the 1981–82 recession pushed the nation's unemployment rate to 6.1 percent in December, the government reported Friday.

At some newspapers, including the New York Times, the dateline includes the date on which the dispatch was written, but this 19th-century practice has been largely abandoned because, in this age of instantaneous global transmission of stories, almost every story has been written within 24 hours of its publication.

Many news service broadcast stories carry a dateline in parentheses to help the newsroom people quickly identify stories from places of special interest to their listeners and viewers. The dateline is in parentheses to alert announcers that it is there for reference and is not meant to be aired:

> (WASHINGTON)—The government has gloomy economic news. The unemployment rate nationwide reached six and two-tenths percent in December. That means that the last three months of the year was the worst stretch of job losses since the depths of the 1981 to 1982 recession.

Prominence. Journalists know that there is more interest in some people than in others. When the president of the United States comes down with the sniffles, there is global concern. The president's well-being has far greater implications than yours or mine. This is the "who" element of news.

Some media critics complain that journalistic coverage of celebrities goes too far. The fact is that there is a double standard. The American news media, for example, cover the extramarital dallying of a celebrity with a degree of detail that would repulse readers and listeners if attempted for nonpublic persons.

From the St. Paul, Minn., Pioneer Press, here are two stories whose newsworthiness is rooted in the prominence of the people involved:

> MADISON, Wis. (AP)—A former policeman has been charged with having sexual contact with two boys while he was Florence County sheriff.

> SANTA MONICA, Calif. (AP)—Actor Marlon Brando's son, Christian, pleaded guilty Friday to voluntary manslaughter in the shooting death of his sister's Tahitian lover.

Currency. Some topics are on people's minds more at some times than at others. A hot topic in the early 1980s was herpes, but as people tired of it, it lost currency, and then AIDS took its place as the dominant health issue. Glasnost and the dramatic events in central and eastern Europe in 1989 prompted Western news organizations to cover Russia more closely. In 1990 and again in 1994, when U.S. troops were deployed in Saudi Arabia, CNN added Middle East weather reports to its programming, for all the viewers who had developed a sudden interest in Persian Gulf military developments and for friends and families of the troops.

Drama. Some events, like an unfolding murder trial, have inherent suspense. There is also suspense when individuals or institutions are in conflict. Which will prevail? Is a resolution possible? What are the issues? When conflict involves an issue on which society is split, like abortion, news coverage helps people define the issue and come to individual conclusions, but also contributes to working out public policy for dealing with the issue.

Consequence. The greater an event's effect on people, the more likely it will be reported. Wake-up radio programs emphasize weather information because it affects every listener. Here are stories built around consequence:

MADISON, Wis. (AP)—Law enforcement and medical services may suffer throughout Wisconsin if the number of military reservists called for active duty increases, officials say.	LOS ANGELES (AP)—The first few storms of the rainy season have arrived in California, bringing a little moisture and a torrent of hope that the state will dodge a disastrous fifth year of drought.

Consequence can be dramatic. At the height of the Cold War, a wag joked that the most important news he could conceive of would be either "The Russians are coming" or "A tornado is coming." Both events would affect people's lives in major ways. As high-impact events, they would stand a better chance of being reported than less consequential events. Of consequence too is coverage of ongoing debates on public policy, whether they concern war and peace, taxes, or a rabid dog on the loose in a community.

To the original list of basic news elements, the Five Ws–Who, What, When, Where and Why—some journalists add the Sixth W, "So what?" Many editors insist that the "So what?" factor be prominent in a story, to let the audience know right away why a story is worth paying attention to. Look at the following treatments, one of which fails to explain the significance of the event:

A bankruptcy judge Tuesday approved the sale of Behrens Manufacturing Co., a Winona sheet metal company founded in 1911, to a Wisconsin businessman for $450,000.	A bankruptcy judge Tuesday approved the sale of Behrens Manufacturing Co., a Winona sheet metal company, raising hopes that the company's remaining 60 employees would keep their jobs.

Consequence can be measured in many ways. In a society based on traditions that cherish human life, an airplane crash that kills 100 people is more consequential than a crash in which no one dies. A volcanic explosion that is witnessed by thousands of people or that threatens a community is more newsworthy than an undersea eruption that is of consequence mainly to scientists. A fire in a theater from which 1,200 people flee has more inherent interest than a similar fire at 4 a.m. when no one is in the building.

Novelty. The unusual can be newsworthy, sometimes because it is significant and sometimes just because it will interest people. The election of a black person to a position formerly held only by whites is news because it is a first.

It also says something significant about race relations. Journalists know too that people are interested in oddball items, like a man biting a dog. These are sometimes called "human interest stories," sometimes "soft news."

News by Formula

When some people see a list of the elements of news—timeliness, proximity and the others—they conclude that journalism can be reduced to a formula. To them, it seems that all a journalist has to do is identify events with intrinsic qualities like proximity, timeliness and prominence, and write them up. But news judgment—the process of deciding what events to report—is too complicated to be reduced to a formula. Although there are similarities in coverage among competing media, journalists don't all see eye to eye on what events are most worth their audience's attention.

Nowhere is this better illustrated than at Southwest Texas State University, where the campus newspaper, the Star, gave nearly one-third of its news space to covering a $20 check bounced by the student body president. Critics, including some journalism students, argued that a $20 bounced check was hardly worth such treatment, even if it involved an elected leader. Others defended the coverage, noting among other things that elected leaders have special responsibilities and should be subject to special scrutiny.

THE NEWS AUDIENCE

STUDY PREVIEW   News lacks purpose unless it touches people and affects their lives. Numerous methods are available to journalists to help them keep their fingers on the audience's pulse. Because the public's interests change over time, sometimes quickly, formulas for deciding what stories are worth telling and how to tell them cannot be inscribed in granite.

Reaching the Audience

When people look to the weather forecast to help them decide how to dress for the day, news is put to a practical use. At a more sweeping level, a level that puts journalism at the heart of democratic ideals, news can fuel public dialogue on the great social issues of the day, expanding the number of people who participate in public policy.

In one sense, the journalist's work is only beginning when news is aired or printed. News accomplishes a purpose only when it is received and has an effect. Police reporter Edna Buchanan of the Miami Herald puts it this way: "The best day is one when I can write a lead that will cause a reader at the breakfast table the next morning to spit up his coffee, clutch at his heart, and shout, 'My God! Martha, did you read this?' "

News succeeds also when it prompts a reader to chuckle or sigh or groan, or a viewer to recount a story to a neighbor across the backyard fence, or a listener to get on the phone to the mayor to applaud or condemn a new initiative before the city council.

How does a journalist develop the ability to reach the audience in meaningful ways? The key is knowing the audience. This can be done by:

- ✦ Paying attention to ongoing social and language changes among all segments of the audience.
- ✦ Studying surveys of the audience to determine its demographic characteristics.
- ✦ Devising a composite picture of the audience.
- ✦ Knowing about audience preferences.
- ✦ Participating in focus groups, in which experts tap selected individuals for their values, opinions and reactions.

Talking with People

Reporters have to live among the people in their audience and develop local wisdom about why they think and feel the way they do. Media scholar Linda Steiner says this immersion in their communities is also necessary if reporters are to know how their messages are perceived. An obvious but often overlooked fact is that communication occurs only when people pick up a message and incorporate it into their lives.

Joseph Pulitzer, the influential 19th-century newspaper publisher, knew that learning writing techniques from a textbook was an incomplete approach to reaching the news audience successfully. Pulitzer roamed the streets when new editions came off his press so he could look over people's shoulders to see which stories they were reading. Today, a television news anchor, new in a city, would be well advised to avoid the $50 styling salon and hit Ernie's $7-haircut barbershop or Erma's bargain beauty shop to see what interests ordinary people.

Another way to develop a sense for the local grass roots is to become a regular at working-class cafes, campus hangouts, church clubs, political caucuses, health clubs and shopping malls, and other places where people of diverse backgrounds congregate. Neighborhood newsletters and church bulletins are revealing too.

Public relations people, similarly, should interact regularly with their company's other employees to learn what they are thinking about and talking about. Their interests should be addressed in company publications. And because PR practitioners give personality to their company or organization in all that they write, the better that PR persons understand that personality, the better they can communicate to other groups of people what the company is all about.

Some journalists, especially those with major media in urban areas, run the risk of gradually losing touch with their audiences. After they advance beyond entry-level jobs, they are earning enough to afford "the good life"—nice vacations, a house in the suburbs, an American Express card. The downside is that their lives become shaped by values and forces in a relatively narrow segment of the whole society, and they lose the deft touch necessary for their communication to be received and internalized effectively by people at other strata in the mass audience. It requires conscious, continuing effort to be in tune with issues among the diverse components of the mass audience. Bernard Shaw, the CNN anchor who has maintained a common touch, made the point this way: "Be wary of anchors who arrive in limousines."

Writing to Be Understood

Journalists can lose touch with their audiences by immersing themselves in their subjects to the point that the arcane language and jargon of their sources show up in their stories. In their book "Coaching Writers," Roy Peter Clark and Don Fry observe: "It may take a new city hall reporter a month to learn the acronymic alphabet soup of municipal government. Suddenly, she feels comfortable sneaking things like 'UDAG' in her stories."

Acronyms and specialized language work against effective communication with the mass audience. At the Wall Street Journal, whose staff works hard to be clear for a mass audience, the term "gross national product" is defined whenever it is introduced in a story: "the total market value of the output of goods and services in the nation."

No enduring, cookie-cutter formula keeps journalists in tune with the language of their audiences. Linda Steiner, the media scholar, makes the point that language is always changing and, further, that it is going in different directions simultaneously. Even within the range of a single radio station, different people will interpret the same message differently.

The solution, Steiner says, is for writers to think not only in their own terms about the story they are telling but also in terms of the diverse social and language contexts of the people receiving the message. This point was made in a classic Gimbels department store advertisement:

> When a teenager asks, "How's the apple pie?" and she's told it's gone— does she order peach?
>
> "No!" She shrieks, "Give me a double hunk of that gone apple pie."
>
> "Gone" to her means good—tops— out of this world.
>
> "Real gone" means absolute tops.
>
> That's how Gimbels feels about Russel Wright dinnerware, Winter pianos,

| Bigelow broadlooms, antique paper- | They're tops, the best—they're real |
| weights. | gone. |

For a mass audience, which includes more than teenagers, "gone" won't work—at least not without the kind of context that the Gimbels copywriter so skillfully employed. Even for a teenage audience, a reporter must be sure that "gone" hasn't been replaced by "awesome," "bad" or "wow" in teen lingo.

Another kind of specialized language, corporate gibberish, also can contaminate stories for a mass audience. This is a special problem for public relations people, who themselves are immersed in a corporate culture.

Demographic Profiles

Most news organizations generate data about their audiences, which give reporters a statistical feel for the people who will receive their stories. New York Times reporters, for example, know that their readers, on average, have more schooling and greater incomes than do readers of screaming tabloids like the New York Post and the Daily News.

Statistical profiles, which come from surveys, can be illuminating on all kinds of demographic details, including career patterns, age ranges, and political, religious and sexual preferences.

Knowing audience demographics helps journalists choose what to report. In Chicago, which has more Polish people than many cities in Poland, news people are especially alert to stories from the Old Country. People in Ames, Iowa, a college town with few Poles, would be much less interested in stories from Poland than in stories from Washington on federal education policies. Editors of Business Week magazine know that the median income of their readers is close to $80,000 and that many of them are corporate executives. This knowledge guides the editors in producing a magazine whose business coverage is very different from the business section of Newsweek, whose readership, in general, is much less involved in business. Network broadcasters have daily information on audiences from the Nielsen overnights, which provide data every morning on viewership the night before.

Composites

While demographics help journalists know their audiences statistically, many reporters—especially beginning reporters—have a difficult time relating to impersonal statistics. Some newsroom veterans suggest writing stories in ways that would be understood by somebody the writer knows—a favorite aunt or brother or sister. The reporter asks: "How can I write this so it would be clear to Aunt Tillie?"

These composite personifications about the mass audience can be useful, but they can go too far. One television news director told reporters to write their stories so that a derelict at the downtown bus depot would be interested and would understand. That advice underscores the weakness of writing to just one person. The mass audience includes a broad range of people, most of whom would find a newscaster condescending if all the stories were geared to a bus depot wino.

Content Surveys

News organizations that commission audience surveys sometimes ask questions about audience interests to get clues on coverage that will be popular. Their surveys yield useful information, but as with demographic data, the findings are broad sweeps and the lessons are no better than the questions that went into them.

By their nature, surveys are one-dimensional with no opportunity for the kind of conversation about issues and preferences that can help writers touch readers, viewers and listeners.

Focus Groups

Some news organizations arrange focus groups in which writers sit down with community people to talk. A focus group leader, trained in encouraging lively, productive discussions, draws out the reactions of readers, viewers and listeners to coverage and tries to identify directions that they would like to see coverage go. Focus groups typically range from 12 to 20 people, and reporters often sit in on them.

When well done, focus group discussions can help put news reporters in touch with their mass audiences. Focus groups, however, are seldom a cross-section of the whole audience.

A variation for encouraging writer-audience contact has been town hall meetings sponsored by news organizations. Hundreds of people, sometimes the whole community, are invited to come and talk.

Changing Audience Values

In competing for audience, the news media are always looking for new ways to attract people. This was demonstrated dramatically when Generoso Pope Jr., publisher of the National Enquirer, concluded in 1966 that his paper, which featured police news and reveled in gore and blood, had reached its circulation plateau at one million. Pope dropped the emphasis on decapitations and mutilations and switched to stories designed to attract housewives at the supermarket checkout. The only crime stories in the new Enquirer were offbeat, and most of them were lost amid celebrity gossip news and hyped stories on the occult, parapsychology and medical research. With its new emphasis on "happy news," as it's been derisively called, the Enquirer's circulation quintupled.

Mainstream news media also adapt to the reality that audience values are in continuing flux. In 1978 researcher Ruth Clark's study for the American Society of Newspaper Editors and UPI found that people were hungry for news they could use. Many newspapers heeded Clark's report, "Changing Needs of Changing Readers." The most notable change was in business sections, which traditionally had been edited for investors and for people in finance and business. These sections added articles on such topics as where to get the best deal on a checking account, how to find the lowest airfare to Las Vegas, and where to invest if you have only $1,000 to spare. Other sections of newspapers added how-to and advice articles on health, hobbies, fitness and interpersonal relations.

Clark also recommended that news be presented in quickly digestible forms. Celebrity news became a staple. The Gannett chain's USA Today, which was introduced in 1982, embodied much of Clark's consumer-oriented, news-you-can-use advice.

In 1984, only six years after her influential study, Clark issued a follow-up report concluding that newspaper readers now wanted more serious treatment of traditional news subjects—public policy, international news and economics. Changing needs were indeed changing. This time Clark said: "During the last six years, the United States has undergone inflation, recession, unemployment, international crises and developing concern about its prestige abroad and ability to compete in world markets. Underlying all of this is a deep-seated anxiety about the danger of nuclear war, not in the distant future but in our own lifetime."

Asked whether the job of a newspaper was to help them keep up with the issues of the day or to help them with their daily lives, Clark's respondents, 1,200 individuals by telephone plus people in focus groups, favored hard news over soft news by a 60:40 ratio. There was a demand for both, but there had been a dramatic shift in only six years.

Pandering to changing audience preferences can go too far. Few journalists, for example, would go as far as Generoso Pope Jr., who virtually banned the Vietnam war from his National Enquirer after focus group studies in the 1970s discovered people were sick of hearing about the war. Some subjects, like war and peace, are too important not to cover, no matter how distasteful.

CHAPTER WRAP-UP

Journalists make decisions on things around them that are worth telling to other people. Many criteria can be used in making these decisions, but the most important news is that which helps society develop better public policies and helps individuals improve their lives. To identify stories that accomplish these goals, and to communicate those stories effectively, journalists need a good sense of their audiences.

Stories on events, significant phenomena and issues are called "hard news." Hard news that focuses on events is called "spot coverage," and that which focuses on phenomena and issues is called "depth coverage." Spot news reacts to events. Depth coverage is characterized by journalistic initiative.

Both spot and depth news are important. Providing information and being a forum for ideas, the news contributes to an informed populace. Without high-quality reporting, intelligent citizen involvement in discussion that leads to good public policy is impossible.

"Soft news" is a term for stories that generally lack the importance of hard news. It is a slippery concept with lots of exceptions, but generally, soft news attracts people for the immediate kick they get out of it.

Hard news, in contrast, is more what people "need" to know than what they "want" to know. Elements of hard-news stories include timeliness, proximity, prominence, currency, drama and, most important, consequence. Novelty is a strong element in most soft news.

Journalism is an art, not a science. Judgment rather than formulas determines which events and issues are reported and how—and no two journalists would do any story exactly the same. This leaves the whole process of gathering and telling news subject to second-guessing and criticism. Journalists themselves ask all the time if there are ways to do a better job. All that journalists can do is honestly seek to find and to relate truth accurately.

STUDY QUESTIONS

1. What events are most worth reporting? How do journalists make the decision to cover one event rather than another?

2. The masthead motto of the Marquette University Tribune says that the newspaper's purpose is "to promote intelligent citizen involvement." Is this a desirable goal? If so, how can it be achieved?

3. Why is it essential for journalists to keep in touch with how their audiences live their daily lives? What are the risks of losing touch?

4. What is the problem with using formulas for choosing which events and issues to cover and for trying to reach the mass audience?

5. Can you describe the difference between the National Enquirer's concept of mission and audience and that of any other newspaper? Between that of tabloid television programs like "A Current Affair" and any other television news program?

6. What are the common characteristics of hard news and soft news?

7. Is all soft news frivolous?

8. Take any story from your morning newspaper or a morning newscast, and look for the presence of timeliness, proximity, prominence, currency, drama, consequence or novelty. Perform this exercise on a second story, then a third.

9. As you identified elements of news in the preceding exercise, were you able to come to any conclusions about how the newspaper or station conceives of its audience and of its audience's interests?

PUTTING YOUR LEARNING TO WORK

EXERCISE 1   The Wide Range of News

Consider the introductory sentences of the following sampler of stories from college newspapers and assign each to one of these categories:

✦ Hard spot news.

✦ Hard depth news.

✦ Soft news.

By Catherine Sabatos

Three female Fordham University students were robbed and abused at a student deli party in the Pugsley Pizza basement Saturday night.

—The Ram, Fordham University

By William Rubenstein

Memorial services will be held Friday for Ray Hampton Park, the head of a media empire and long-time Ithaca College board of trustees member who died Monday in New York City.

He was 83.

—Ithacan, Ithaca College

By Jenni Hohnke

For seven months, a former Winona State University student lived in an igloo in the mountains of Crested Butte, Colo.

It took Dave Zimbric, 23, a week and a half to build his home out of snow and ice.

When completed, the igloo was 15½ feet in circumference and seven feet high. Visitors crawled in through a 20-foot tunnel.

—Winona Campus Life, Winona State University

By Raymond Lombardo

For a majority of Fordham students, Ben Soper is not a household name.

Yet he, along with many Fordham students, are getting professional on-air and technical training at one of New York's most powerful radio stations.

That's right: It's WFUV, and the signal that most students would identify with hearing over their phone lines has developed into a 50,000-watt radio station pumping music out to people far beyond the gates of Rose Hill.

It's not just polka any more.

—The Ram, Fordham University

By John Burstein

TUCSON, Ariz.—Indecent exposure is a touchy subject at the University of Arizona main library.

In a recent two-week period, six offenses were reported in the library, leaving police baffled, psychologists trying to provide explanations, and library officials saying they were unaware of the incidents.

—Arizona Daily Wildcat

| EXERCISE 2 | **Identifying Elements of News** |

Among elements that make a news story interesting to a mass audience are:

- ✦ Timeliness
- ✦ Proximity
- ✦ Prominence
- ✦ Currency

- ✦ Drama
- ✦ Consequence
- ✦ Novelty

Which of these elements appear in this news release from the public relations staff at Amsterdam-based KLM Royal Dutch Airlines for a company magazine edited for international travelers?

KLM's first direct service between Amsterdam and Detroit, which took off Jan. 7, has proved so popular that it will soon be a daily operation.

Since January there have been flights three times a week, on Tuesdays, Fridays and Saturdays.

With the introduction of the airline's summer schedule on March 29 a fourth flight, on Saturdays, will be added. By June 1 there will be daily flights.

Detroit was recently placed third on the list of U.S. cities best situated for industrial growth.

Also, Detroit is the busiest hub of KLM's U.S. partner, Northwest Airlines. From Detroit, Northwest operates 340 daily flights to 80 destinations both in and outside the United States.

Which elements of news appear in these stories?

By Kathleen Ragan

Andrew Brown can't believe anyone would shoot his best friend.

His 5-year-old half-Labrador, half-chow dog was shot once, the bullet entering through his back, a quarter inch from his spine, and exiting through his skin.

Brown, a University of Georgia graduate student, was at a parking meter outside.

Squire didn't need surgery or even stitches, but he's on antibiotics.

Robert Lee Cox, 34, of Athens, was arrested and charged with aggravated assault, discharging a firearm in the city, reckless conduct and cruelty to animals, police said.

Police quoted Cox as saying that the dog barked and came after him and that he pulled his gun out of its holster and shot at the dog.

—Red & Black, University of Georgia

By Jacinthia Jones

Whoopi Goldberg and Ted Danson ruffled a lot of feathers Friday.

At a Friars Club roast honoring Goldberg, her "best friend," Danson, appeared in blackface makeup with large white lips and told racial jokes.

Some people weren't laughing.

Talk show host Montel Williams walked out seven minutes into Danson's monologue and terminated his Friars Club membership.

"I was confused as to whether or not I was at a Friars event or a rally for the KKK and Aryan Nation," Williams told reporters.

Williams, who is black, was especially upset at jokes Danson told about racially mixed children. William's wife, who is white, recently gave birth to their first child.

New York City Mayor David Dinkins also criticized Danson's actions.

—Daily Helmsman,
Memphis State University

By Richard Turner

BURBANK, Calif.—Walt Disney Co. outlined plans for its third U.S. theme park complex, a historically themed "Disney's America," about 30 miles outside the nation's capital in Prince County, Va.

—Wall Street Journal

FOR FURTHER LEARNING

William R. Amlong. "The High Priest of Low Brow," Tropic (Miami Herald magazine) (Jan. 14, 1973). Amlong describes how the National Enquirer built its massive readership by adjusting its news values. This transition also is covered in George Bernard's "Inside the National Enquirer: Confessions of an Undercover Reporter" (Port Washington, N.Y., 1977). Other insights into the popularity of the newspaper are in S. Elizabeth Bird's "For Inquiring Minds: A Cultural Study of Supermarket Tabloids" (University of Tennessee Press, 1992).

Andrew Radolf. "A Return to Hard News," Editor & Publisher, 117, No. 20 (May 19, 1984): 10–11, 19. Radolf summarizes the 1978 and 1984 studies of changing newspaper readership by Ruth Clark.

Wilbur Schramm. "The Nature of News," Journalism Quarterly, 26, No. 3 (Autumn 1949): 259–69. Schramm develops his idea that news can be divided into two categories: stories that offer an immediate reward to the audience and stories that offer delayed reward.

Michael Schudson. "Discovering the News: A Social History of American Newspapers." Basic Books, 1978. Schudson, a scholar, traces the development of journalists and their self-perceptions through U.S. history, with continuing attention to the evolving concept of news.

Linda Steiner. "The Role of Readers in Reporting Texts." Journalism Quarterly, 65, No. 3 (Autumn 1988): 642–47. Steiner calls on her fellow journalism professors to emphasize an audience orientation in teaching news skills, rather than passing on dubious formulas that ignore the heterogeneous nature of the mass audience.

CHAPTER 3

Starting the Spot News Story

In this chapter you will learn:

+ To relate the elements of news to types of leads for news stories.

+ Circumstances determine which news element to highlight in the lead.

+ Following a clean and thoughtful process will result in well-constructed and compelling leads. The lead plays a key role in every story.

+ Leads can be either simple or complex.

+ Newspaper leads differ in construction from broadcast leads because of the forms of the media.

+ Broadcast writing makes special demands on the writer.

+ Question and quotation leads are used only in special circumstances.

THE LEAD

The Bible's Book of Genesis begins with a clear, declarative sentence: "In the beginning, God created heaven and earth." Charles Dickens began "A Tale of Two Cities" with the line: "It was the best of times, it was the worst of times." More recently, Janet Malcolm began her magazine profile of psychoanalyst Jeffrey Masson with: "Every journalist who is not too stupid or too full of himself to notice what is going on knows that what he does is morally indefensible." In each of these instances, as in many other literary works, a strong first line rivets the audience's attention and draws readers into the story. The first lines are compact and potent, and they capture the gist of what the author has to say.

News writers working for newspapers or broadcasting stations or in public relations capacities have much more competition for their readers' or listeners' attention. It's all the more important, then, that they "top" their stories with clear, concise leads, or "ledes," as journalists sometimes spell the word. They try to encapsulate the main element or elements of the story in such a way as to grab the attention of busy readers and entice them to read further. They try to make every word count. And they try to achieve a tone that fits the story's tone—one that is appropriate to the event or situation they are recounting.

News writers take great pride in their leads and admire the well-written leads of others. When journalists get together it is not uncommon to hear them talk about the excellent leads they have written or read.

Some leads have become a part of the literature of journalism. Civil War correspondent Whitelaw Reid of the Cincinnati Gazette provided readers with a glimpse of the chaos of warfare in the lead to his story of what became known as the Battle of Shiloh:

Fresh from the field of the great battle, with its pounding and roaring of artillery, and its keener-voiced rattle of musketry sounding in my ears; with all its visions of horror still seeming seared upon my eye-balls, while scenes of panic-stricken rout and brilliant charges, and obstinate defences, and succor, and intoxicating success are burned alike confusedly and indelibly upon my brain, I essay to write what I know of the battle of Pittsburg Landing.

Reid's lead may be too flowery and long for the modern newspaper. Nevertheless, it stands out as an attention-getter that gives the reader a clear and colorful glimpse of what's ahead in the story. More in keeping with today's style and taste was Andrew Rosenthal's spare but fact-filled lead to his New York Times report on the start of the war against Iraq on Jan. 16, 1991:

> The United States and allied forces
> tonight opened the long-threatened war
> to drive President Saddam Hussein's
> army from Kuwait, striking Baghdad
> and other targets in Iraq and Kuwait
> with waves of bombers and cruise mis-
> siles launched from naval vessels.

LEADS FOR SPOT NEWS STORIES

STUDY PREVIEW   Like the stories that follow them, leads are of two types, hard leads and soft leads. The most common is the hard lead, which states in a direct way what happened. In so doing it tells the audience what is coming in the story. It is used most often for hard news stories. The second type, the soft lead, delays the main news. It is most frequently used on depth stories, feature stories and broadcast copy, though some news writers top hard news stories with an indirect lead as a way to tickle the reader's or listener's interest.

Hard Leads for Print Media

The hard news lead provides a readable, straightforward statement of the information that the writer has decided is most important. After telling what is most important, the writer moves to secondary items, then to even less important points. That means the writer must decide what basic information readers need and want to know very early, or high, in the story. Normally this lead-worthy information answers the questions posed by "the Five Ws and H": Who? What? When? Where? Why? and How?

+ Who is involved or affected?
+ What happened?
+ When did it happen?
+ Where did it take place?
+ Why did the event occur as it did?
+ How did it happen?

Each of these questions reflects one of the essential elements that make an event or situation news. By summarizing the answers in the lead, the writer tells the reader what the story is about and why it is being singled out for news

CATCHY INTRODUCTIONS. Whitelaw Reid covered the Civil War for the Cincinnati Gazette. His writing style is considered florid by today's standards, but his reporting attracted readers. Modern newswriters attract readers with leads that are more tightly written yet give a glimpse of what follows.   (Culver Pictures, Inc.)

coverage. Just how that is done is shown in this lead adapted from a story that appeared in The Daily Iberian of New Iberia, La.

Nine representatives of the U.S. Environmental Protection Agency and its subcontractor, ICF Kaiser Engineers, were out in the damp cold **this morning** to begin a week-long **soil and water sample collection** of the closed **New Iberia landfill**.	*who* *when* *what* *where*

There was a time when news writers tried to pack all the Five Ws and H into the first sentence of the story. That has changed, in part because we know now that shorter sentences make for easier reading. News writers now try to limit their leads to fewer than 40 words. Some editors, in fact, prefer even shorter leads. As a result, a writer may have to use two or three sentences to cover all of the Five Ws and the H.

Writers of newsletters and news releases also know that the lead is a critical element. For one example, consider this lead on a Loyola University news release:

> At the Loyola Death Penalty Resource Center, 31 dates are marked in red on the calendar. They aren't holidays or birthdays or anniversaries, but the dates Louisiana death row inmates are scheduled to be executed.

The writer, Christine Guillory, then an intern with the university's news bureau, chose one aspect of the center's work to focus on in her lead. That aspect was a dramatic one, and made more so by her graphic description. What could have been a plain vanilla recitation of detail about the center became, instead, a lively "grabber" that made readers want to continue.

Writing spot news leads does not require literary genius, just the ability and the practiced skill to decide which facts are most important and start with them.

Soft Broadcast Leads

One difference between spot news stories for newspapers and for radio and television is that newspaper leads start with the main news. Broadcast stories, in contrast, delay the main news until the listener is primed to the subject and really listening.

Look at these two treatments. The first is a newspaper hard lead:

> Seven members of country-western singer Reba McEntire's band and her road manager were among 10 people killed Saturday when a private jet crashed just north of the Mexican border.

In contrast, the lead below is a radio soft lead. The news nut is in the second sentence:

> Country-western singer Reba McEntire is in grief today. Her road manager and seven members of her band are dead in a plane crash just north of the Mexican border near San Diego.

The soft lead for broadcast news dates from the late 1920s, when radio writers followed the dictum: "Tell 'em what you're gonna tell 'em, then tell 'em, and then tell 'em what you told 'em." In part, that is done because people ordinarily listen much less attentively than they read. Broadcast writers have to go to special lengths to catch their attention. The soft lead tells listeners what you are going to tell 'em. Consider, for example, the United Press International sports desk lead reporting that Notre Dame's football team had snapped Oklahoma's 48-game winning streak:

> The inevitable finally has caught up with the invincible.

On the day of the Notre Dame victory, when sports fans were eager for the game's outcome, UPI's reference to "the invincible" caught immediate attention. Fans knew this was the story they were waiting for, and they were set up to listen to the real news, the score, which came in the follow-up sentence.

The first sentence is critical. The Associated Press Broadcast Stylebook says it is, "in many respects, the equivalent of a newspaper headline." It should, first, catch the listeners' attention. Second, it should orient them for what is to follow. United Press International told broadcast news writers that their "first sentence should be a snappy attention-getter, similar to the banner line in a newspaper. It alerts and 'warms up' the listener." Both AP and UPI, keen news service rivals, agree that the first line of a broadcast story says to the listener, in effect, "Hey, listen up! This story will interest you!" Then, like a one-two punch, comes the main news in the next sentence:

> The police chief in Los Angeles is sticking to his guns. Chief Daryl Gates says he will not resign. Calls for Gates to resign have been mounting since a black motorist was beaten savagely by police two weeks ago. Gates reaffirmed today that he will not, using his words, "slink away" under pressure from community and civil rights groups. The chief, who is white, denied that he is insensitive to minority concerns about police brutality.

In giving examples of extraordinary soft leads, the UPI stylebook gives this example for a story on the anniversary of the liberation of Paris from the Nazis:

> France is celebrating the memory of a day grown men cried for joy in the streets of Paris.

A news writer for the CBS Evening News chose a soft lead for the obituary of actor-director-producer Orson Welles. It was particularly appropriate for Welles, and all the more effective, because it mimicked the newsreel obituary of Charles Foster Kane at the beginning of Welles' best-known film, "Citizen Kane":

> As it must to all men, death came today to Orson Welles.

An NBC radio news writer picked another familiar and appropriate theme to lead the report that Johnny Carson had signed a contract to emcee "The Tonight Show" for his 30th, and final, year:

> It will be "Here's Johnny" for another year.

Other examples are only as far away as the next news broadcast on your radio or your television set. If you listen carefully, and with discrimination, you will hear them.

One variation of the broadcast soft lead is the incomplete sentence, which has become a convention among some radio and television news people as an attention getter and as a way to flag stories and alert listeners to what is to come. Here are two examples, both of which were written by NBC radio news writers:

> A few more orbits on tap for shuttlenauts aboard Atlantis. Their landing today was postponed.

> A new clue in the mysterious memory disease Alzheimer's.

The incomplete sentence introduction to a broadcast story saves words, and for broadcasters, words eat up precious time. A disadvantage is that the incomplete sentence, like any convention, can be annoying if it is overused. And a sentence fragment can throw off an announcer who is reading copy cold. Unless you are writing copy that you will read yourself, or unless the announcers for whom you write always take the time to rehearse, it is best to go sparingly with this technique.

Soft broadcast leads sometimes work well for the print media, too. When Horizon Airlines scrapped its widely recognized corporate symbol, a stylized sun intersected by numerous horizon lines, editors in the Seattle bureau of the Associated Press dispatched this catchy soft lead to both broadcast stations and newspapers, and it was used word for word on the air and in print:

> The sun is setting on Horizon Air's familiar logo. The Seattle-based airline Monday revealed a new logo that will more clearly associate the carrier with its sister company, Alaska Airlines.

Effective though that lead is, it is best to go with hard leads for newspaper spot-news stories.

Further Tips for the Ear

Broadcast news is written for the ear, not the eye. It must be written so that it sounds like ordinary speech, not text on a page. It has to be conversational. Many broadcast writers literally write conversationally. That is, they speak their copy aloud as they punch it into a typewriter or key it into a word processor, as if they were talking to someone. That also helps them catch any words or phrasing that might prove to be a problem when their copy is read on the air, including alliterations and sibilants.

Broadcast writers also seek to make their writing clear and easy for the ear to grasp. Listeners may have their minds on their driving or their ironing or some workbench task. Even for the attentive audience, broadcast news is fleeting, on the air for just moments, so listeners cannot go back over the material again if they do not understand something. For that reason, broadcast writers, for the most part, normally write short, simple sentences. No dependent clauses at the start of sentences to befuddle listeners. No modifying clauses in the middle to lead them astray.

Consider the difficulty a listener might have with a lead like this one:

> Following an automobile chase that occasionally reached 100 miles an hour, police early this morning captured two suspects in a convenience store holdup. The suspects, both identified as escaped convicts, gave up only after their car crashed into a barricade.

The problem is that most people do not ordinarily talk that way, beginning sentences with subordinate clauses or inserting them in the middle of a sentence. Far better for the listener's understanding to put the story in simple, active sentences. This is one way to handle the problem:

> Two men led police on a chase at speeds up to 100 miles an hour early this morning after a holdup. The two were wanted in the armed robbery of a convenience store. Police nabbed them when they crashed their car into a barricade. Police say both are escaped convicts.

As we have done here, you can usually break a sentence containing more than one clause into two sentences rather easily, and the result is greater clarity. At the same time, however, you should avoid making all sentences extremely short. You do not want them coming out in machine gun bursts.

Similarly, avoid polysyllabic words. You can count on your audience understanding most one-syllable words, but some might not understand those with more than one syllable. In reading, too, you will be less likely to stumble over words of just one syllable.

Newspaper writers most often put the attribution, the phrase that tells the reader who made the statement, at the end of a direct or indirect quotation. Broadcast writers put the speaker first so that listeners will have no doubt who made the statement. For a newspaper story, you might write:

> "There is no such thing as a false idea," said Lewis F. Powell Jr., associate justice of the U.S. Supreme Court.

If you used the same form in a newscast, you might puzzle your listeners. They might think you are making the statement. Or, they might be left at the end of the sentence wondering "Who said what?" For the broadcast writer, the proper form is

> Supreme Court Justice Lewis Powell says he believes "there is no such thing as a false idea."

Note the tense of the word "says." Broadcast writers try to exploit fully the competitive advantage that their immediacy gives them over the print media, and one way they do that is by using the present tense or present perfect whenever possible. It is true that it was in the past that Justice Powell made the statement quoted in the previous paragraph, but "says" gives the statement a fresh ring. To use another example, by the time a newspaper comes out, "President Clinton **flew** to Little Rock Wednesday," will be correct. For the broadcast writer reporting the story on Wednesday, it should be "President Clinton **is flying** to Little Rock at this hour," or "President Clinton **has arrived** in Little Rock," or "President Clinton **is in** Little Rock."

The following soft leads from Wisconsin Public Radio newscasts also were written in present and present perfect verb tenses. Each takes advantage of broadcasting's immediacy.

> The Wisconsin Supreme Court has decided that merchants who sell second-hand goods may be liable for defects in the goods.

> A Wisconsin Democratic state lawmaker says Republican

Governor Tommy Thompson's ambitious prison-building plans translate into an effort to imprison more black men.

An outside study of the Wisconsin state bureaucracy is being proposed by some lawmakers who want to hire a consulting firm to evaluate the efficiency of state agencies.

Wisconsin Governor Tommy Thompson is taking a second look at his proposal to decriminalize the penalties for minor crimes.

LEADS AND THE ELEMENTS OF NEWS

STUDY PREVIEW   While leads summarize the Five Ws and H, news writers select one to emphasize. The one they choose depends on their analysis of the news they are writing about and the impact they wish to make with their stories. We classify leads according to the primary questions they seek to answer: Who? What? When? Where? Why? or How? Below are examples of leads written for newspapers or newsletters.

"Who" Leads

The "who" lead focuses on a person or a group of persons. Most personality profiles, of course, have "who" leads, as did this story by Cheryl Miller of the staff of Santa Clara University's newspaper:

> **As a freshman in 1979, Dee Dee Myers** had no idea what she could do with a political science major. Now, as President Clinton's press secretary, she's finding out.

Stories that have the individual as the main element also employ a "who" lead, as in this story by Peter Kendall of the Chicago Tribune:

> **A Western Illinois University professor** of tourism and leisure, and perhaps the nation's foremost academic authority on nude beaches, was sent on a permanent vacation Thursday.

In a "who" story—and thus in "who" leads—the individuals involved are given a more prominent place than the events in which they are the actors. If they are well known, they are featured prominently. If not, they may be referred to by their profession or by a label that lets the reader know why they are in the news. Such was the case of the individual featured in another Associated Press story:

> **A woman** believed to be one of the first patients to be infected with AIDS by **a health-care worker** has reached a $1 million settlement with her dentist's insurance company.
>
> The agreement, reached Tuesday with the CNA Insurance Company, followed a report by the Federal Centers for Disease Control last week confirming that the 23-year-old woman, **Kimberly Bergalis**, as well as two other patients, had probably contracted the AIDS virus while being treated by **Dr. David Acer** of Stuart, Fla.

The two individuals are not well known, so their names are not immediately important in the story. But both names are needed in the second sentence to particularize the persons.

"What" Leads

A "what" lead focuses on the event or situation being reported, as in this story by Aline McKenzie of the Dallas Morning News:

> **The Texas Department of Transportation will hold two meetings this week to gauge public opinion** of the controversial eastern route proposed for State Highway 190.

Ana E. Santiago of the Miami Herald watched the unexpected happen at a Miami ceremony, then went back to the newsroom and wrote a "what" lead for her story:

> **The traditionally solemn commemoration of the Bay of Pigs invasion ended Wednesday with a fight** between two politically differing groups of veterans of the failed mission.

"When" Leads

"What" and "who" leads are the most frequently used approaches for spot-news stories. But the other "Ws" and the "H" can be used with care for definite purposes. As you analyze news stories, you will soon become aware that the time element ordinarily is subordinate to other elements. The day an event occurred or will occur is usually put at some point inside the lead, or at the end—most often following the verb or the object of the verb. Here are two examples adapted from the Associated Press:

> Actor Marlon Brando's son Christian was sentenced **Thursday** to 10 years in prison for voluntary manslaughter in the shooting death of his half-sister's lover.

> The Record Plant, one of the music industry's leading recording studios and rock hangouts for more than two decades, closed its doors **Thursday**.

While the "when" usually is subordinate to other elements, it can provide a current angle on a story that doesn't have any other strong news peg. In the following lead Amy Henderson, writing in the Clemson University Tiger, employed the "when" to give a newsy angle to a story that otherwise lacked a recent event to justify it as a news story.

> **Monday** marked the fifth anniversary since the explosion of the space shuttle Challenger, which has special meaning for Clemson University mechanical engineering professor Norman Knight, who was instrumental in getting the space program back on its feet.

James Barron of the New York Times used a "when" lead to construct a story that captured the mood of America at the start of the war in the Persian Gulf. His use of the time element served to freeze the moment when Americans heard the news.

> **In one long moment yesterday**, word that the United States had attacked Baghdad swept the country. In split level suburban homes on the East Coast where dinner was in the oven, in big-city restaurants in the Midwest where bars were jammed with the happy-hour crowd and in skyscraper offices on the West Coast where people were still at work, there was an odd mixture of apprehension, sadness and relief.

In "when" leads, writers often link the time to another element. William M. Carley of the Wall Street Journal found that a "when" lead, written in conspiratorial generalities, fit well with the facts he uncovered about the mysterious circumstances surrounding an attempted political assassination:

> **Early last year**, an Iraqi diplomat in New York telephoned a man living in Modesto, Calif. He was trying to recruit an assassin.

Edward R. Murrow used time to good effect in this lead to one of his celebrated CBS broadcasts from London during the Battle of Britain in World War II.

> **Christmas Day** began in London nearly an hour ago. The church bells did not ring at midnight. When they ring again it will be to announce invasion. And if they ring, the British are ready.

"Where" Leads

"Where" leads direct the reader's attention to the location of an event, and as with "when" leads, they usually do so for effect. Also like "when" leads, "where" leads are seldom used for spot news stories. The "where" is seldom the most important element. Starting with the "where," however, can help establish a mood or an atmosphere, as Richard Dodds of the New Orleans Times-Picayune did in beginning a story on the city's annual Tennessee Williams Festival. Dodds' "where" lead concretized the planning for the event for his readers:

> **Down in the French Quarter in 1986**, the crazies were doing Halloween. But **out at Mandina's Restaurant**, a table of four worked over some fried oysters while cooking up what has become a New Orleans spring tradition.

While Dodds used the "where" to help set a festive tone, Michael A. Hiltzik of the Los Angeles Times used it to create a somber mood for a story he filed from El Obeid, Sudan:

> This is the graveyard of good intentions.

> On the outskirts of this town, the capital of Kordofan province and the

epicenter of one of the worst famines to strike this region in many years, about 40,000 destitute Sudanese have camped, awaiting shipments of relief food.

John Flinn employed the "where" for a different purpose in a San Francisco Examiner story on the violence in national parks:

Up in the Yosemite high country near Tioga Pass, the newly born Dana Fork of the Tuolumne River rushes and tumbles through wildflower-dotted meadows, and snowfields glisten on the bulky pyramid of Mount Gibbs.

It is a scene French mountaineer Gaston Rebuffat might have had in mind when he described the alpine world as "a place between heaven and Earth." In such a setting, it might seem odd that a Yosemite Park ranger would feel the need to patrol this paradise while wearing a bulletproof vest.

"Why" and "How" Leads

"Why" and "how" leads provide explanations for actions or events. They are appropriate when the writer believes the reason something happened is as important to know as the fact that it happened at all. Such was the case in the example below, adapted from a story by Doug Myers, capitol reporter for the Advocate of Baton Rouge, La.:

A state education board Thursday reinstated the teaching certificate of convicted felon and former Pardon Board Chairman Howard Marsellus **so he can seek a teaching job in Texas.**

Interpretive stories, editorials and op-ed-page columns also frequently begin with "why" leads as their writers attempt to explain the reasons something occurred or the consequences of an action. Los Angeles Times business writer Tom Petruno used a "why" lead to explain a Federal Reserve Bank report that the amount of currency in circulation had dropped dramatically:

If you have any doubt that **people are deeply troubled over the economy and the war**, consider this: The public has suddenly begun stashing cash, literally hoarding hard currency.

THINKING YOUR WAY TO A LEAD

STUDY PREVIEW   Choosing the elements for a hard news story's lead sentence is not as daunting as it may seem. The challenge is to choose the most important information and then build it into a single, simple, direct sentence.

Sorting Through Information

For months a criminal case against an Adams State College student had been moving through the Alamosa County judicial system. Tom Brightman, editor of the Southern Coloradan, a campus newspaper, looked at the information he had amassed on the case as the first step in putting the story together:

> Unauthorized use of a credit card is a Class 5 felony in Colorado. The maximum sentence is four years in prison and $1,000 fine. Eleven months ago, Melanie Patten, an Adams State student, realized that her father's Visa Gold card had disappeared, and she reported the card as lost to Visa authorities. The next month, Patten's father received a Visa bill with charges exceeding $600. Patten had never made the charges. About the same time, the supervisor of Patten's dorm, Ron Holman, somehow received the card and returned it to Patten. A later Visa bill to Patten's father had more unauthorized charges, bringing the total to $752.46. Police investigator Jim Lanier decided to arrest Patten's roommate, Cristal Seefluth. San Luis Valley District Attorney Doug Primavera filed charges of unauthorized use of a credit card and eight charges of second-degree forgery against Seefluth. Seefluth, an Adams State cheerleader, was a prominent campus person. Records showed that Seefluth had been convicted in Arapahoe County, 300 miles away, of Class 4 theft two years ago, and issued a two-year sentence, but jail time was deferred in favor of probation. Class 4 theft in Colorado law exceeds $200. It is a felony. Latest development: Seefluth pleaded guilty in Alamosa County District Court in Alamosa to charge of unauthorized credit card use. That was Friday. There was plea bargaining, and the eight second-degree forgery charges were dropped. The judge scheduled sentencing for next month. Primavera, the prosecutor, said he will recommend probation and restitution of the $752.46 unauthorized charges. Side note: This conviction constitutes a violation of the Arapahoe County probation, which means Seefluth faces a maximum of eight years for violating terms of probation. Seefluth's future as a cheerleader is in doubt. Anne Greenwood, cheerleading adviser, said she will wait until sentencing to decide what to do. Greenwood quote: "I have to be fair and support her until I have all the facts."

How does a reporter sort through so much information to come up with a neat, clean and direct sentence to start the story? Because of his experience writing leads for hard news stories, Brightman reflexively put the Five Ws and H to work. Subconsciously, he asked these questions:

Who? Who is the most important or interesting "who" in the information?

What? What is the most important or interesting thing that happened?

When? What is the most important or interesting "when"?

Where? What is the most important or interesting "where"?

Why and how? Of the explanations for the most important or interesting thing that happened, which is the likeliest?

Novice news reporters, not as experienced as Brightman, should go through these questions step by step for their first few sorties, even diagramming the information to sort it through. The diagramming takes the form of lists. The first can be a list of all the "whos":

Melanie Patten

Melanie Patten's father

Ron Holman

Jim Lanier

Cristal Seefluth

Doug Primavera

Judge

Anne Greenwood

This categorizing process continues by listing all the "whats," all the "wheres," all the "whens," all the "whys" and all the "hows." This may seem a time-consuming process, but it will pay off in a good lead. With practice, the process becomes almost automatic. Don't be concerned if you categorize information differently from other classmates. Inconsistencies from person to person won't affect the lead sentence that emerges from the process. Inconsistencies that do affect the lead are simply differences that reflect the idiosyncrasies of individuals. There is no one, single, perfect lead sentence for any story.

Once the six lists are complete, one for each of the Five Ws and H, you then move to a second step in the process: identifying the most important who, what, where, when, why and how. This step, organizing the information according to importance, involves judgment calls. Not every writer will choose the same items, but that doesn't matter as long as you apply your intellect in both the categorizing and organizing steps in the process. Brightman's analysis resulted in this refined list of the most important Ws and H:

Who: Cristal Seefluth

What: Sentencing

Where: Alamosa County District Court

When: Friday

Why: Unauthorized use of a credit card

How: No "hows" emerged in the categorizing process

Creating a Core Sentence

After boiling down a mass of information to the most important or interesting components, the writer then creates a core sentence. This is done by plugging the remaining components into what is the core structure of most sentences in the English language—a subject, followed by a predicate, followed by a sentence complement like a direct object. Another label for this structure is "SVO"—which stands for Subject, Verb, Object.

Here is the model:

Subject | Predicate | Complement

In the Adams State story, Brightman did this:

Seefluth | pleaded | guilty

Writers who followed different courses during the categorizing and arranging steps might have different cores. This core takes a future angle:

Seefluth | will be sentenced | next month

This lead capitalizes on an angle of special interest to a campus audience:

Cheerleader status | to be decided | by Greene

Once a grammatical core has been created, the writer fleshes it out—in effect packing meat onto the skeletal bare-bones core. That was Brightman's next step:

> Cristal Seefluth pleaded guilty in district court Friday to unauthorized use of a credit card.

Although he had a solid core sentence, Brightman wasn't satisfied. He wanted to point out Seefluth's campus prominence, so he built that into the sentence:

> Cristal Seefluth, **an Adams State College cheerleader**, pleaded guilty in district court Friday to unauthorized use of a credit card.

Still Brightman wasn't satisfied. He wanted to include some background, so he expanded the sentence:

> Cristal Seefluth, an Adams State College cheerleader **who is already on probation for a felony conviction**, pleaded guilty in district court Friday to unauthorized use of a credit card.

Brightman realized that the lead had become unwieldy, so he decided to drop Seefluth's name, reasoning that it would be less recognized among readers than her status as a cheerleader, and he did some other trimming:

> An Adams State College cheerleader, already on probation for a felony conviction, pleaded guilty in district court Friday to unauthorized use of a credit card.

Brightman was satisfied, and the lead ended up atop a story on Page 1 of the Southern Coloradan.

In summary, the steps in this process for writing lead sentences for spot news stories are:

+ Assemble all the information available.
+ Use the Five Ws and H to categorize the information.
+ Narrow the information in each category to the one most interesting or significant item.
+ Create a core sentence from the items that emerged in the categorizing process.
+ Flesh out the core sentence so it reads well.
+ Incorporate additional information to embellish the sentence, taking care that the sentence doesn't become unwieldy or cumbersome.

Applying the Five Ws and H to a mass of information is time well spent. Rushing to the keyboard without first sorting through the information results inevitably in false starts. Starting over, perhaps over and over and over, takes more time than using the Five Ws and H to organize the material before hitting the keyboard. And although the process may seem laborious at first, it becomes automatic with practice.

WRITING ABOUT THE SIMPLE AND THE COMPLEX

STUDY PREVIEW   Long ago we all learned how to distinguish among simple sentences, compound sentences, and complex sentences. In a nutshell, simple sentences deal with one thing while compound and complex sentences are constructed to deal with several. Like sentences, news stories can be categorized according to their complexity, and that is based on the number of elements with which they must deal.

Single-Incident Leads

Open any section of any newspaper any day of the week, or thumb through a stack of news releases, and you will find many good examples of single-incident leads. A single-incident story may recount a relatively simple event. Accidents of one kind or another would fall in the simple category. So would many of the sorts of things that show up on police blotters. So would many of the situations that are reported in news releases or employee newsletters.

The person assigned to write such a story has a relatively simple task: analyze the situation, decide which news element to highlight, thus which type of lead to begin with, and then recount the event that occurred.

Single-incident leads on a series of local briefs from the Boca Raton News illustrate the construction well:

A 21-year-old Boca Raton woman was killed Wednesday afternoon when she was struck by a car while crossing Glades Road near Powerline Road in Boca Raton.

Boca Raton police arrested three teen-age boys Wednesday in connection with 31 area business, auto and home burglaries in late February.

The School Board is going to consider installing a $35,000 traffic signal at the entrance of Olympic Heights High School on Lyons Road in West Boca Raton.

In each instance, the lead focuses on one event, one situation, that will be developed in the story that follows. It is important to note that the event or situation in the lead is the story's climax, the most important element.

Not that all single-incident leads are so lean. Consider the lead that Houston Chronicle reporter Geoff Davidian put on his story about a police sting operation. Though somewhat more complicated because of the detail included, it is still a single-incident lead.

> Houston police used a mannequin, an ambulance, a U-Haul trailer and a Channel 26 TV news crew Thursday in a phony murder staged to bring drug suspects into the open.

Multi-Incident Leads

Other stories are more complex. The situations they recount may require that they give equal weight to a variety of elements. Leads for such stories must summarize what is of equal import. An Associated Press writer, for example, gave equal weight to the latest military and diplomatic developments in filing a story during the war with Iraq, so the lead combined both:

> The U.S. military said Sunday no date has been set for an allied ground offensive in the Persian Gulf war, **and** Washington said it would reject any Soviet peace plan calling for a cease-fire.

A writer assigned to do a story on two studies of nuclear radiation effects published in the Journal of the American Medical Association believed the studies were of equal importance, and the lead showed that:

> Workers in nuclear weapons plants who were exposed to levels of radiation previously thought safe had higher rates of fatal cancer, **but** persons living near nuclear plants showed no more susceptibility to the disease than persons living at a distance.

Governmental activities frequently involve a number of aspects that writers seek to put together in the lead. Jack Wardlaw of the New Orleans Times-Picayune capital bureau packed three elements into his page one story on a Louisiana governor's budget proposal:

> Gov. Roemer handed the Legislature a **proposed $8.57 billion state budget** Tuesday, one that **he hopes will grow by $310 million** if he can **persuade lawmakers to renew temporary sales taxes** on groceries and utility bills.

The lead pointed out what the governor did, reported that he wanted the budget to be higher, and told what he planned to do to bring in more revenue. The story that followed the lead amplified all three points.

Obviously, multi-incident leads can become unwieldy if writers try to put too much into them. Just think of the problem a reporter covering an appeals court has on a day when the court hands down a variety of decisions. Or of the problem of a legislative reporter when a large number of bills are filed at one time. Does the person cram all of the decisions or all of the bills into the lead, select only a few to highlight, or focus on just one? In this day of simplified writing, the decision more often than not is to choose one item. That puts a burden on the writer, who must decide which point is most important. But it simplifies the reader's job.

Consider the lead on this story filed by one of Wardlaw's capital bureau associates, Ed Anderson. Anderson's job was to summarize the bills filed in advance of an upcoming legislative session. To Anderson only one of those in the hopper stood out, so he focused on that one in the lead, developed it briefly, then listed some of the others.

> A state lawmaker from New Orleans wants to limit the number of terms a governor can serve from two in a row to one four-year stint.

Why did Anderson choose to highlight what he did? Think back to the criteria for news. The governor is the most important political figure in the state, and the legislator represents a district in which the New Orleans newspaper is circulated. Because he had two of the criteria in one story, Anderson's decision was relatively easy. On the other hand, a reporter for the Advertiser of Lafayette might have weighed the news criteria differently and chosen to point up a bill that had been introduced by one of Lafayette's legislators to forbid legislators to do business with the state. A reporter for the Ville Platte, La., Gazette might have centered on two bills filed by that town's house member.

On another day, assigned to go through another batch of bills filed in advance, Anderson found two that he thought would be of particular interest to his readers, based on reaction to similar legislation in the past. His lead reflected his judgment:

> Two bills sure to be controversial at the Legislature's April 15 regular session—one outlawing most abortions, the other establishing a superboard of higher education—have been filed in the Senate.

Umbrella Leads

In a story that detailed an even longer list of bills that Louisiana lawmakers had prepared for consideration, no one or two of them stood out enough to single out in the lead. Anderson and Wardlaw responded with what is called an umbrella lead. Avoiding particulars, the umbrella lead makes a general statement about the elements that will follow, or a statement that broadly covers what is to come. It is a handy device for dealing with multi-incident stories and can be an effective tool in the hands of a clever writer.

> Like robins heralding spring, the first batch of bills was filed Tuesday for the regular legislative session, which starts April 15.

In neighboring Texas, John Gonzalez of the Fort Worth Star-Telegram's Austin bureau used an umbrella lead to attract readers to an otherwise routine government dollars-and-cents story:

> They must be doing something right in the Tarrant County public schools.
> As part of the Texas Successful Schools Award System, the Texas Education Agency awarded 80 area campuses a total of $1.1 million in cash prizes yesterday for raising test scores and curbing dropout rates in 1992-93.

The umbrella lead is especially useful to broadcast writers, who seldom use multi-incident leads on their stories. Detailing many incidents in the lead would become clumsy, and the complexity would be difficult for listeners to follow. When riots swept Rochester, N.Y., in the 1960s, a UPI news writer led one story for morning drivetime newscasts with an umbrella lead:

> The night was long in Rochester and full of violence.

An umbrella lead for a national weather story:

> The nation is covered with a crazy quilt of weather this morning.

In broadcasting, an umbrella lead can be as brief as a sentence fragment. A White House reporter's umbrella covered a variety of stories from his beat:

> A busy morning for President Clinton.

A similar lead came from a Capitol Hill broadcast correspondent:

> A stern reprimand today for nations that haven't paid what they pledged to the war effort in the Persian Gulf.

Writers of such leads follow the advice laid out in a UPI broadcast stylebook: "Often it's best to use a soft lead . . . a lead with little or none of the story's essentials. A soft lead can hit on the feel of a story . . . or the humor of an event . . . or simply set the stage for telling the story."

Hooking the Audience

Reporters and editors for the Wall Street Journal, published by Dow Jones & Company, Inc., perfected story introductions in which complex issues are explained in terms of the people involved and affected. The technique, which some call "Dow-Jonesing," works well for depth stories. In the following Associated Press piece, note how Dow-Jonesing hooks the reader. Everybody can relate to the problem of Roy Gafvert. Either we have a Roy or two in the family or we've honked at them on the road. Contrast this straight lead with the Dow Jones approach of the lead that follows:

> Older drivers are more likely to fail to yield right of way, turn improperly and run stop lights, a study says.

The Dow Jones approach, as an Associated Press writer applied it in the following passage, gives life to the situation by showing how an individual is affected:

Four years ago, Roy Gafvert of Green Bay faced an unpleasant choice: either give up his driver's license or risk becoming dangerous.

He gave up his license.

At age 85, after being the cause of two minor traffic accidents, he sensed his judgment was deteriorating, so he voluntarily quit driving.

Now almost 90, Gafvert said that although his choice has condemned him to "watching the boob tube," he is sure he made the right decision.

"Often when you get older, you get a little stubborn, where you say, 'I'm just as good as ever.' But you're really not," said Gafvert.

"Our faculties are not the same. Our sight is not the same," he said. "My mind is active enough as far as some things go but on others, well, I probably should have quit sooner than I did."

Driving skills decay with age. A 1987 study by the Insurance Institute for Highway Safety found that older drivers are more likely than younger ones to fail to yield the right of way, to turn improperly, and to run stop lights.

"Older drivers don't deal as well as younger ones with complex traffic situations," the study says. "Multiple-vehicle crashes at intersections increase markedly with age."

This depth story reflects the reporter's initiative. It's not an account of an event, although two events triggered the story: proposed legislation to require more frequent tests for older drivers, and new statistics on accidents involving older drivers.

But the reporter went further. He interviewed the legislator proposing that drivers 75 and older take vision tests every two years. He also interviewed a social worker on the trauma for an older driver and quoted the people involved with the insurance study. Numerous older people discussed how their deteriorating driving skills were affecting their lives. All of that took the facts of the study off the flat page and made them three-dimensional.

When reporter Joan Rigdon sat down to write a story on where companies get cheap labor during tough economic times, she also chose a Dow Jones lead:

Christine Sparta works full time as an assistant editor at Meredith Corp.'s Ladies' Home Journal.

She sits in on story meetings, covers news conferences and researches articles. Her first byline will appear in the July issue.

But Ms. Sparta, who graduated from New York University in December with a bachelor's degree in journalism, is no ordinary junior executive: She is a $6-an-hour intern.

Without her, the magazine's health department would have to hire a

Rights Fight

'Militant Integrationist' Rethinks a Coalition By Ditching Liberals

For Michael Meyers, Strict Adherence to Philosophy Required Radical Moves

Anger Over the 'Pod People'

By DOROTHY J. GAITER
Staff Reporter of THE WALL STREET JOURNAL

NEW YORK — There was a time when Michael Meyers fit snugly in the bosom of American liberalism. A child of the 1960s who helped integrate his high school in the Bronx, he has followed an activist creed ever since. Friends respectfully refer to him as "a militant integrationist."

Thus, after whites chased a black youth to his death in the Howard Beach section of New York in 1986, Mr. Meyers was in the forefront of faulting the New York Civil Rights Coalition to rally this city's racially fractured communities. His model: the teachings of Martin Luther King Jr. — nonviolence, understanding through education and an integrated society where people are judged by the content of their character, not the color of their skin.

Please Turn to Page A4, Column 2

What's News—

Business and Finance

THE DOW JONES industrials closed at a record 3986.17 on growing confidence that the economy is slowing down, easing interest-rate fears. The average at one point was within 2.05 points of 4000, and the S&P 500 set a second consecutive record, edging up to 484.54. Stocks were helped by a report that industrial output rose in January at about half the pace of the prior two months. But there were signs that inflation may be picking up.
(Articles on Pages A2 and C1)

The Justice Department is leaning strongly toward appealing a rejection of its Microsoft antitrust settlement, and people close to the software maker say it would likely join in an appeal.
(Article on Page A3)

Mexico's markets were thrown into turmoil as interest rates on Mexican treasury bills soared to 40% and a major conglomerate defaulted on some short-term debt. The stock market's IPC index fell 6.41%. The peso lost 2.7% of its value against the dollar.
(Article on Page A10)

Kohlberg Kravis Roberts will sell more of RJR Nabisco than expected as part of its planned Borden acquisition, reducing its stake to 8% from 18%.
(Article on Page A3)

Many Blue Cross plans are looking at ways to take part of their companies public as one such partial spinoff, WellPoint, attracts takeover interest.
(Article on Page A3)

Piper Jaffray settled the largest lawsuit arising from its derivatives-investment strategy, agreeing to pay $70 million to investors in one of its funds.
(Article on Page A3)

Dow Chemical was found liable for 20% of a $5.2 million verdict in a breast-implant case in a Texas court, the first such finding against the company in silicone-device litigation.
(Article on Page B7)

Morrison Knudsen will report a fourth-quarter loss more than twice as wide as analysts' expectations.

Democrats unleashed a plan for telecommunications reform that resists GOP deregulation efforts and sticks close to a bill considered last year.

Conseco reported a fourth-quarter loss of 17 cents a share and said it spent $23.3 million on its failed Kemper bid. Its share price fell 9.1%.

Figgie plans to sell 12 of 16 remaining businesses in a bid to reduce debt. Separately, the conglomerate reported a narrowed fourth-quarter loss.

Bell Atlantic plans to drop AT&T as overseer of the Baby Bell's multibillion-dollar effort to build an interactive network, taking on the role itself.

AT&T and LIN Broadcasting differed widely on a market valuation for LIN under which AT&T could purchase the 48% of the cellular-phone company it doesn't already own.
(Articles on Page B5)

German shipbuilder Jos. L. Meyer is negotiating to build large vessels at the Philadelphia Naval Shipyard.
(Article on Page A4)

Markets—

Stocks: Volume 377,942,530 shares. Dow Jones industrials 3986.17, up 37.92; transportation 1575.66, up 16.07; utilities 193.94, up 0.92.

Bonds: Lehman Brothers Treasury index 5345.53, up 30.62.

Commodities: Oil $18.42 a barrel, up 19 cents. Dow Jones futures index 133.46, up 0.04; spot index 147.99, up 0.33.

Dollar: 98.35 yen, off 0.15; 1.5098 marks, up 0.003.

World-Wide

A WELFARE BILL CLEARED a House panel amid rising anger from Democrats.
All eight GOP members of the Ways and Means human-resources panel voted for the bill, which would save $23 billion in federal welfare spending during the next five years. All five Democrats voted against it. The bill would bar unwed mothers under the age of 18 and their children, as well as legal aliens, from receiving some benefits. While the panel's approval is the first step in a long legislative process, it foreshadows a bitter debate.
(Article on Page A2)

Senate Majority Leader Dole said projected spending for Medicare and Medicaid would have to be cut by unprecedented amounts to balance the budget, as Republican leaders considered putting first-ever limits on how much the health programs can grow.
(Article on Page A16)

Mexico called off a manhunt for Chiapas rebel leader Marcos and officials said they were ready to offer him an amnesty. President Zedillo has ordered the army to halt its advance against the guerrillas.

North Korea warned it might scrap a nuclear agreement if it means accepting South Korean-made reactors, but the U.S. said Pyongyang's statement may just be a bargaining position for new talks.

China and the U.S. resumed full-scale talks aimed at averting a trade war, with both sides adopting a more conciliatory tone ahead of a Feb. 26 deadline. The negotiators in Beijing will try to hammer out an accord on protection of intellectual property, including copyrights, patents and trademarks.
(Article on Page A11)

The Justice Department reached an agreement with the Lawyers' International Union of North America that it intended to rid the union of what the government says is organized-crime influence.

Confirmation hearings will provide a chance to rebut "a lot of the" sergeant general nominee Foster said as he began making courtesy calls on senators. The celebrity has been under fire from anti-abortion groups and conservatives.

U.N. peacekeeping efforts would face new constraints under a GOP bill expected to be approved by the House today. Democrats, meanwhile, last night managed in an initial vote to defeat another provision of the bill: the deployment of an antimissile defense system.

The Israeli army sealed off the West Bank area of Hebron ahead of memorial ceremonies planned by some right-wing Jewish settlers for a gunman who killed 29 Muslims at a mosque one year ago.

A fugitive computer hacker was arrested in Raleigh, N.C., the Justice Department announced. Kevin Mitnick, 31, allegedly has broken into corporate and communications networks in several states. He was convicted in 1988 on related charges in California.

A 10-truck U.N. food convoy briefly came under fire but managed to safely reach Bosnia's northwest Bihac region, where thousands of civilians are reported to be threatened with starvation.

Club-wielding white protesters shouted racial insults and attacked black students bused to a high school near Cape Town, but the demonstrators were pushed back by South African riot police. The incident was the first major confrontation over the country's post-apartheid integration policy.

Russian and Chechen troops reinforced their cease-fire and extended it by 48 hours as Yeltsin prepared to defend Moscow's assault in Chechnya. The Russian leader, in an advance text of an address to be delivered today, said force was used after authorities "exhausted all other forms of action."

Peru's president said a day-old law, in holding in a disputed border zone where Ecuadoran and Peruvian forces had clashed. But Ecuador accused Peru of mobilizing two armored divisions along the border.

A nightclub fire killed at least 67 people and injured 11 in the Taiwanese port city of Taichung. The cause of the blaze, which destroyed a karaoke bar and restaurant, wasn't immediately known.

Consumer Prices
Year-to-year percent change

CONSUMER PRICES rose 2.8% in the 12 months ended in January. Excluding the food and energy sectors, the change was 2.9%.
(Article on page A2.)

Business Bulletin

A Special Background Report On Trends in Industry And Finance

TIMBERRRR! Volatile wood prices keep lumber dealers on their toes.

Lumberyards, home centers and builders deal with today's erratic wood prices by substituting varieties, stocking up on staple items when prices allow and leaving room in client price quotes. Requarth Lumber Co. in Dayton, Ohio, regularly sends faxes to builders to warn them of potential price rises. While still historically high, many lumber prices are lower than a year ago, says Random Lengths newsletter, based in Eugene, Ore.

On the West Coast, a still weak construction market hurts demand, says Rod Jones, head of Jones Lumber Co., Los Angeles. He says a standard 2-by-4 stud sells for 33 cents per board foot, down from 40 cents last year. But imports help keep supply ample. "You can buy today all the lumber you want — if you have the money," says Michael Modansky of Home Depot in Atlanta. Still, he warns of shortages down the road. So, Home Depot and others offer lessons in using wood alternatives for building.

Redwood is scarce, say Dykes Lumber in Weehawken, N.J., and Beronio Lumber in San Francisco.

MANAGING UNRULY DESKTOP computers costs businesses dearly.

Big companies spend $3,830 annually to maintain each personal computer in their realm, says Forrester Research Inc., Cambridge, Mass. That's the bad news. The good news is the cost of managing those PCs is expected to drop by 30% during the next three years as standards and technologies improve, says Waverly Deutsch, a computing strategy analyst at the market-research outfit.

In the meantime, costs associated with the PC remain "subtle, hidden and excessive," she says. Today's biggest expense: providing one support person for every 10 PC users. This "friend of the desktop" costs $1,435 per user, including salary, benefits, tools and overhead, Forrester says. Downtime is a close second, costing users about six days per year of productive time, or $1,350 per PC a year.

PAIN-RELIEF PROGRAMS grow, but insurance coverage is, well, a pain.

An aging population and repetitive-stress injuries bolster demand for treating such chronic pain as migraines and back aches, says Marianicola Enterprises Inc. The Valley Stream, N.Y., research firm says the pain-management market at $4 billion a year and sees growth of 16.3% for 1995. While early clinics in the 1970s were tied to hospitals, now the growth area is solo practice by anesthesiologists and other practitioners.

Marketdata says the rate of gain will slow to 5.3% a year by 1996-98, partly due to insurers' efforts to curb medical costs. Average treatment cost already has dropped 25% from 1992 to $8,366. At the Mayo Clinic Pain Management Program in Rochester, Minn., the cost of services hasn't fallen, says Jeffrey D. Rome, medical director, but patients may be adopting some of the available treatments because of curbs on medical benefits, like higher co-payment provisions.

The American Society of Anesthesiologists says that 34% of its 35,000 members practice pain management.

SAILING FOR SALES. Chevrolet sponsors "stadium sailing," a sport in which two specially designed, one-person boats propelled by giant fans compete in Olympic-sized pools. The events, taking place on college campuses and such, tie in with the America's Cup race.

A GUTTER BALL goes to Mother Nature. Bowl America Inc. in Alexandria, Va., says profits fell 14% to 37 cents a share in its second quarter ended Jan. 1, mainly due to unusually mild weather which diverted people from bowling. Colder weather since then will help offset the drop, it says.

CUTTING WITHOUT A NET? Independent Sector, the Washington umbrella group for nonprofits, says 116 organizations ranging from the American Cancer Society to Dance/USA signed and sent to Congress a statement saying charities cannot fill the gap envisioned by substantial cuts in federal funding of social services.

WINNER-TAKE-ALL salaries gain ground in the business world.

The astronomical earnings of top sports and entertainment figures have marked a clear difference for some ties between the stars and the lesser lights in glamorous fields. Now, the business community, too, is showing a bothersome gap between top executives and the rest of the staff, say economists Robert Frank and Philip Cook in their book due out this fall: "The Winner-Take-All Society." The gap reaps losers in a purgatory-like land of vice presidents.

"The downside is, you get too many people competing for these prizes," Mr. Frank says. Since only a few can rise to the top, "there's a lot of waste," he adds. The simplest solution is to make the "prizes" less attractive, the authors say. Raising the tax rate on the top performers would divert marginal contestants who would then find other, more fruitful professions. In such a setup, higher taxes actually could spur growth rather than deter it.

"One of the goals is to steer the 'scamblers' into other areas by making the top payoff smaller," Mr. Frank says.

BRIEFS: Furniture giant Ikea says that Americans — unlike Europeans — use the television set as focal point when decorating a room. . . . A Morton International billboard alongside Chicago's Kennedy Expressway provokes a hot line on how to use table salt as a home cleaning aid, and the hot line is peppered with calls from car phones.

—PAMELL SEBASTIAN

Grim Reapers

Farm Subsidies Face Almost Certain Cuts In the GOP Congress

Deficit Hawks Will Question Rationale of Programs Dating From the 1930s

Sen. Lugar: Chop Billions

By SCOTT KILMAN AND BRUCE INGERSOLL
Staff Reporters of THE WALL STREET JOURNAL

WELLINGTON, Kan. — As a new Congress focused on deficits scours the budget for programs to rewrite, one big target keeps popping up: farm subsidies, $10 billion a year.

Robert White knows the farm program is in the gun sights, and it worries him. Mr. White is a Kansas wheat farmer, and an annual check from Washington is a critical part of the middle-class living he manages to earn on 1,400 owned and rented acres. Last year, Mr. White got $14,000 from the government.

Although Mr. White is a frugal operator and reaped a good crop last year, wheat-farming margins are so thin that he also sells crop insurance to help make ends meet. "If you take away the subsidies," he says, sitting in his 1964 Ford pickup, "I made zip last year."

Such grim economics are part of the mix Congress will be struggling with as it takes up farm legislation with a fresh and very skeptical eye. By chance, the five-year farm bill has come up for renewal just as balanced-budget forces are storming Capitol Hill. The Republican chairman of the Senate Agriculture Committee is Richard Lugar of Indiana, the owner of a farm himself, who says that farm-state lawmakers must help devise a plan to "budget sanity."

Proposing to Cut

Today, in an appearance before the Senate Budget Committee, Mr. Lugar will propose two simple but drastic steps to cut farm spending by almost $5 billion over five years. At the risk of alienating wheat growers like Mr. White, he would scuttle export subsidies—saving $3.4 billion—and lop off $11.5 billion with a phase-down of crop subsidies.

This spring, Mr. Lugar plans to hold hearings challenging nearly all the many tools the U.S. Department of Agriculture uses to steer the farm economy, from price supports to land-idling requirements to the Farmers Home Administration, which has written off billions of dollars in loans.

Congress isn't expected to abolish subsidies outright. But although farm-program spending has already fallen steeply from its peak in 1986, more spending cuts seem inevitable now. And a growing number of U.S. officials, industry executives and farm leaders say that virtually the whole complex system—which aims not only to support farm incomes but also to guarantee America's food security—could be gone in a decade.

"I've never been this worried before," says Democratic Sen. Kent Conrad of wheat-growing North Dakota. "We're having to fight over why we even have a farm bill."

Without any commodity programs at all, say economists, tens of thousands of

Farm-Program Spending

Net outlays to the USDA's Commodity Credit Corp., in billions; fiscal years shown

Source: U.S. Department of Agriculture

farm families would probably quit as the incomes fell and as slipping land values shrank their borrowing power. The borders of the Farm Belt might contract as wheat growing became uneconomic in the Great Plains region. But fertile corn states in the Midwest could see a planting boom as the government no longer restricted acreage, with business strength gaining for everything from fertilizer to tractors. Big supplies of cheap grain might make U.S. exports more competitive and lower the cost of feeding livestock.

Kansas has three favorite sons who stand in the way of any radical assault on farm programs: Senate Majority Leader Bob Dole, Agriculture Secretary-nominee Dan Glickman and the head of the House Agriculture Committee, Pat Roberts. Still, Congress may be less beholden to farmers than ever before. The November election riddled agriculture's Old Guard, as 33 House members from farm districts were replaced by newly elected Republicans.

"This is an acid test for them," says Rep. Charles Schumer, a New York Democrat. "Welfare reform is fine for poor people; will it be fine for farmers?"

Skeptical Farmers

Interestingly, large numbers of farmers themselves seem to be fed up with the government's involvement in farming. Cutbacks, red tape and tillage restrictions to protect the environment have so eroded the appeal of federal farm programs that surveys find only one-third of farmers wish

Please Turn to Page A6, Column 1

Today's Contents

Please Turn to Page A4, Column 2

DOW-JONESING THE NEWS. While the Wall Street Journal's focus is on financial news, it is anything but stodgy. In fact, the newspaper's writing style is widely emulated as a method for telling how individuals are affected by world and national situations.

salaried assistant editor, says her boss, health editor Nelly Edmondson Gupta.

But that's "not in the budget," Ms. Gupta explains, adding: "We're getting the best and brightest for a very low rate."

Tough economic times are changing corporate attitudes about college interns. Only a few years ago, companies could afford to design internships around the interns, investing time and money to squire them through the business, hoping to woo the most promising to full-time employment after graduation. Now, as more companies cut their salaried staffs, they are increasingly tapping interns as a source of inexpensive labor.

Bill Wells, a reporter for the Nicholls Worth of Nicholls State University, turned an ordinary announcement of a university service organization's sponsorship of Handicap Awareness Week into a compelling feature by Dow-Jonesing it:

Stacey Zeringue looked at her watch. It was 8:50 a.m., leaving her five minutes to get to her class. As she rounded the corner near Talbot Hall, a university maintenance truck was parked, blocking the sidewalk.

To most students, the truck was merely a nuisance, and they could simply walk around it. To Stacey, who is a paraplegic and confined to a wheelchair, it meant finding another route to class or waiting until the truck moved. It also meant she would probably be late for class.

The rest of the story deals with the problems of other handicapped students and what the university was doing to make all facilities accessible to them.

Dow Jones leads aren't limited to newspaper stories. They can be used effectively in a variety of publications. Steve Schild, a public relations writer in La Crosse, Wis., Dow-Jonesed this article in the Lutheran Health System annual report.:

Ruth Moore is hired to clean house and care for 64-year-old Gordy Knudson of La Crosse.

But the two have a deeper relationship than just employer and employee.

"If Gordy is down in the dumps and I'm washing windows, I won't wash them. We'll visit," says Ruth.

And every now and then, she'll coax a smile from Gordy through good-natured teasing.

Her responsibilities with Gordy are part of her job as a Supportive Home Care provider. Supportive Home Care is a Lutheran Health System subsidiary that provides care and service—in their homes—for the elderly, disabled and those recuperating from an illness.

To tell the story of what the Gannett Co. was doing to increase understanding among the diverse elements in American society, Mary Hardie, a writer for the Gannetteer, the company's house organ, also used a Dow Jones approach:

Six months ago, a light went on in Judy Diebolt's head. The managing editor at the Burlington, Vt., Free Press and chair of the paper's diversity committee was reading through surveys from employees about their jobs and life in their workplace. One thing kept turning up, she says.

"People had a lot of misconceptions about each other." But the misconceptions weren't about how employees thought of their co-workers, as she'd expected. "Many were about how employees felt co-workers perceived them."

For instance, those with large families thought others considered them "irre-sponsible for having so many kids," Diebolt explains. Many older employees also felt tension. Some Catholics did too. "In Vermont, there's some anti-Catholic sentiment because the state has a lot of French Canadians who are discriminated against and most are Catholic."

As more women, minorities, immigrants, older and disabled workers than ever before fill the labor pool in the United States—by the year 2000, they'll surpass white males, according to Workforce 2000, a report prepared by the Hudson Institute for the U.S. Labor Department—companies face complex issues of race, sex, age, religion and ethnicity in the workplace.

Hardie's story went on to tell what Gannett's newspapers and broadcasting stations were doing to break down barriers among its employees. With its focus on an individual, the lead was effective at interesting readers in the story. What if the fourth paragraph had been the lead? Would it have stirred the same interest?

To write Dow Jones leads, writers must be sensitive to the human impact of issues and situations. If a government or a company sets a policy, if the courts hand down a decision, if a new product goes into production, if a television program is taken off the air, individuals are affected. By focusing on those individuals and the ways in which they are affected, writers can make their stories more pertinent and more interesting to the reader. The result is that the stories have more impact on the reader.

CHAPTER WRAP-UP

One thing news writers should keep in mind is that there is no formula lead for any one story. And there is no formula that will tell them which type of lead to employ. What is needed is clear, hard thinking about the story at hand. The question that you or any other writer should ask in sitting down at the word processor is, "What is it about this event or this situation that makes it news? Is it the 'who,' the 'what,' the 'when,' the 'where,' the 'why' or the 'how'?" You also should ask yourself whether the subject matter allows the Dow Jones approach, in which the effect of a situation on an individual is examined. Coming to a carefully thought-out answer will put you well on your way to constructing the lead_and the story below the lead.

STUDY QUESTIONS

1. What is the purpose of the lead?
2. What does the news writer want the lead to do for the reader?
3. Explain the differences between hard leads and soft leads?
4. How do broadcast leads normally differ from newspaper leads, and why?
5. How does the writer determine when to use a "who" lead? A "what" lead? A "when" lead? A "where" lead? A "why" or "how" lead?
6. How do single-incident leads differ from multi-incident leads?
7. Under what circumstances would a writer use a multi-incident lead rather than a single-incident lead?
8. What is an umbrella lead, and when would a writer use it?
9. How is attribution handled in broadcast stories and in newspaper stories? Why is it handled differently?

PUTTING YOUR LEARNING TO WORK

EXERCISE 1   **Writing Basic Leads**

Write a "who" lead based on these facts for the Middle State Mercury:

A local woman, Anna Johns, recently received her Ph.D. from Middle State University. She graduated from Middleton High School in 1984, received her B.S. in history from Ivy College in 1988, and a master of arts degree in history from Middle State in 1990. She wrote her dissertation on the history of farming in Apple County. It's entitled "A Century of Farming in Apple County: A Social and Economic History, 1875-1975."

In an interview she said, "When I was a child, I rode with father on his tractor while he worked the fields. He told me stories about his father and grandfather. That sparked my interest in the area's history. My great-great-grandfather settled in Apple County in 1900, when he was 25. He came over from Belgium, and built the farmhouse I grew up in. When he first came here, the whole county was farmland, and Middleton was just a crossroads with a general store."

Write a "what" lead based on these facts:

Police arrested three suspects in a rash of burglaries in the Rapid River and Middleton areas: Edward Anthony, 20, 888 Atlantic Ave., Middleton; Polly Henry, 30, 225 Park Place, Middleton; and John Terry, 18, 313 Marvin Gardens Drive, Rapid River.

Anthony and Henry were arrested yesterday after they were pulled over for failure to stop at a red light. They were booked on charges of six counts of simple burglary and one count of possession of stolen goods. Terry was arrested on the 16th of last month. He was charged with seven counts of simple burglary and two counts of felony theft. He has been held on $100,000 bond.

The announcement was made by Chief Detective Louise Palmer. Police are looking for a fourth suspect, Palmer said.

Write a "when" lead based on these facts:

The board of supervisors of Apple County have designated the week of July 15 as "Farmer Recognition Week." The resolution passed on a vote of 6-0 at the supervisors meeting last night. Supervisor E. W. "Bare" Bones introduced the resolution, as he has every year for the past 25. He told the supervisors this would be the 25th anniversary of the celebration, which includes awards to area farmers, the annual Apple County Tri-county League championship baseball game and the traditional ox roast.

"This is the most outstanding festival in the state and we all need to work to make this year's the best ever," Bones said. Bones estimated the cost of the event at $10,000. The board allocated $5,000. Bones said the rest would come from donations from area merchants.

Write a "where" lead based on these facts:

Gov. Myrna Williams will cut the ribbon Monday at ceremonies marking the opening of the newly completed San Luis Bridge that will carry State Highway 22 traffic over the Style River one mile east of Middleton. The bridge is named in honor of Anthony San Luis, Middleton mayor from 1950 to 1980. It was built at a cost of $25 million to replace the old bridge that had been condemned as unsafe by state engineers. Construction began 16 months ago.

Write a "why" lead based on these facts:

The Apple County School Board adopted a revised version of its policy on drugs and alcohol possession and consumption in the schools. The new policy does away with automatic expulsion for possession of drugs or alcohol on school grounds. However, any students caught with drugs or alcohol will be ineligible to participate in extracurricular or cocurricular activities, Superintendent Selwyn Arbogast said. Arbogast said he proposed the change in order to give students a second chance. In his presentation to the board, Arbogast said: "We need to let the students know we won't tolerate drug use, but we need to let them know we have compassion and concern for them too."

EXERCISE 2   **Writing Broadcast Leads**

Write broadcast leads based on the facts given in Exercise 1.

EXERCISE 3   **Writing Complex Leads**

Using the following facts, write a multiple-incident lead and an umbrella lead:

At its meeting last night, the Student Government Association, accomplished the following:

Voted 20–4 to approve publication of a book of syllabuses for all of the courses in the university. The vote followed two years of negotiations that involved a student referendum and negotiations between the SGA and the Faculty Senate. The SGA established a Syllabus Handbook Office to publish the book.

Voted 16-8 to provide funding of up to $2,500 for a forum on the First Amendment and political correctness. The forum was proposed by Philomena Freneau, representative from the Department of Journalism and Mass Communications.

Voted 22-2 to establish an SGA information booth in Greeley Memorial Union. The proposal was made by Herbert Bush, representative from the Department of Political Science. Bush argued: "The students have little idea what SGA does for them and this information booth will help inform them."

Voted 23-1 against recommending to the athletic board that the university's team nickname be changed from the Chipmunks to the Pythons. The proposal had been made in an editorial in the University Bugle and submitted to SGA by Rhonda Town, representative from the College of Business.

Tabled a motion by Willy Painter, representative from the Department of Visual Arts, to establish an annual Erase the Graffiti Week.

FOR FURTHER LEARNING

"Best Newspaper Writing." The Poynter Institute. Excellent newspaper stories begin with excellent leads, as shown by the examples in this annual series.

The Wall Street Journal. Every day, this national newspaper has a column-one story that builds from an individual to a general situation. Those stories well illustrate the technique we call Dow-Jonesing.

Fixing Weak and Troubled Leads

In this chapter you will learn:

+ Significant differences exist between strong leads and weak leads.

+ A weak lead often contains no news, in contrast to a strong lead that holds the nut of the news.

+ Quotation leads are seldom appropriate, but they can be used on occasion.

+ One common pitfall in writing leads is to formularize them.

+ Sometimes it is possible to break the rules of writing leads.

WEAK AND TROUBLED LEADS

Edgar Allan Poe crafted tales that still hold readers in suspense from the first paragraph to the last. In "The Pit and the Pendulum," for example, we suffer the doomed prisoner's terror until, in the final paragraph, he is saved by the French general, Lasalle. But while readers go to Poe and other mystery writers for suspense, in their news reports they want the what-was-done and the who-dunit near the beginning. And they would like it told with both grace and economy. We can disappoint those readers unless we take care to avoid some construction problems that might not be apparent immediately.

PROBLEM LEADS

STUDY PREVIEW   The art of news writing cannot be reduced to a series of inviolable rules, but journalists recognize that some approaches to lead sentences do not work. Among them are leads that ignore the story completely or back into it, leads that consist primarily of direct quotations, and leads that ask questions.

Non-News Leads

When readers or listeners turn to an item in a newsletter or newspaper or tune in to a news broadcast, they unconsciously say to the writer, "Get to the point. Don't beat around the bush." They want the news kernel, or "nut," and they want it first. They are impatient with leads that give them no news. The following is an example of a non-news lead adapted from the daily newspaper of a university:

> Middle State students had the opportunity to present questions and comments about the university to MSU administrators at a student forum Thursday.

This lead provides no news. Meetings of all sorts are held regularly. The forum probably had been announced in a calendar of events or in a previous story. The lead doesn't even say whether the students presented their "questions and comments." They only had the opportunity to do so, according to the lead.

The news should center on the action that occurred or any major announcement that was made. Buried in the forum story was this item that could have been turned into a lead:

> One business major said that much of the advising for undergraduates in the business and economic department is done by graduate students instead of faculty. Provost Arms responded that he was exploring adding advising as a part of the faculty performance evaluation.

That the administration is considering taking a step to change the advising process is one substantive matter that came out of the meeting, a change that could affect students and faculty alike. It could be turned into a lead that contains news:

> The Middle State University administration is considering giving all faculty members responsibility for academic advising.
>
> University Provost Ivan Arms told students at a forum Thursday that he is considering making advising a part of the faculty performance evaluation.
>
> Arms' comment came in response to a business major's complaint that graduate students are doing most of the advising for undergraduates in the business and economics department.

The new lead contains news, something that could have an impact on nearly everyone who reads the Middle State newspaper. It will also spark people to wonder what else happened at the meeting and to read more of the story to find out.

Backing into the Story

What some call "backing into the lead" is a related fault common among young journalists. An example adapted from a university newspaper illustrates what the term means:

> Liberal Arts faculty members voted at a meeting Thursday whether or not to give Alexander Bartleby, senior vice president and dean of faculty, a vote of confidence regarding his position as chief academic officer.

Rather than getting to the heart of the matter immediately and giving the result of the vote, the reporter chose to tell readers, first, only that the faculty voted. This bit of information is hardly as important to the reader as how the vote came out. Notice how the following variations on the lead both emphasize the meeting's outcome, which is what made the event newsworthy:

Liberal Arts faculty members gave a vote of confidence to Alexander Bartleby, senior vice president and dean of faculty, Thursday.	Alexander Bartleby, senior vice president and dean of faculty, won a vote of confidence from the College Assembly of the College of Arts and Sciences Thursday.

The writer of the following story also was slow in getting to the point. Readers had an idea of what was to come after reading the headline "Polluter gets break on taxes," but they had to plod through four long paragraphs before getting the details.

PPG Industries, a major industrial polluter with a history of environmental problems, recently applied for $393,000 in industrial tax exemptions for an expansion of its Lake Charles Plant.

The application was one of the first to be evaluated under a new Roemer administration policy that links tax breaks to a company's record of compliance with environmental laws.

Environmentalists hoped that PPG would be harshly penalized under the new policy. The PPG plant has spilled toxic chemicals into the Calcasieu River for years, and poisonous organic chemicals that leaked from a PPG tank farm for several years have seeped into the Chicot Aquifer, the underground drinking water source for Lake Charles. The company also has a huge groundwater cont-amination problem from an old toxic waste dump that officials do not expect to be cleaned up in their lifetimes.

But when the Department of Environmental Quality evaluated PPG's record under the new policy, the company scored quite high. The policy's formula, devised by the executive branch, recommended that PPG get 91.5 percent of its $393,000 request. **So the Board of Commerce and Industry approved a $360,000 property-tax exemption in December.**

That PPG should get so generous an exemption, critics say, **underscores sizable loopholes** in a formula that the Roemer administration has touted as the state's first serious attempt to encourage environmental responsibility through tax incentives.

The question to ask is what good purpose the writer served by taking the reader on that convoluted route to the main point. Was it to make the story more readable? Or was the aim to entertain the reader? In either case, did the topic lend itself to such treatment?

A more readable way to handle it would be to give the reader the startling fact, the newsworthy element, immediately, then get into the details. The fact that a heavy polluter "received" a substantial tax break under a formula designed to reward companies that did not pollute is more newsworthy than the fact that the company "applied for" the tax break. One way to shift the emphasis to reflect the news element would be simply to change one word in the lead paragraph:

> PPG Industries, a major industrial polluter with a history of environmental problems, recently **won** $360,000 in industrial tax exemptions for an expansion of its Lake Charles Plant.

The lead could be rewritten to emphasize that the exemption is evidence of loopholes in the law:

> A new Roemer administration policy that links tax breaks to a company's record of compliance with environmental laws has major loopholes, according to critics.

When covering a speech, some novice writers back into the news, telling only the speaker's subject in the lead sentence rather than telling what the speaker said. Consider this variation on a story reported by Ulrike Dauer of the Kansas State University Collegian:

> A criminology professor opened Native American Heritage Month with a lecture **about** American Indians and the prison system Friday at K-State Union.
> Karen Baird-Olson said the United States has one of the harshest criminal and justice systems in the world.

That lead says nothing more than that something that was expected to occur did so. Undoubtedly there had been a story in an earlier edition that said the speaker was scheduled to discuss the subject. It hardly is news that a scheduled event occurred. In contrast, a more appropriate lead immediately identifies a point that the speaker made:

> A criminology professor, opening Native American Heritage month at K-State Friday, charged that the United States has one of the harshest criminal and justice systems in the world.

Some beginning news writers back into their stories by piling up relatively unimportant information at the front of their lead sentences. That sometimes reflects young writers' lack of confidence, which is overcome with experience and time. They hesitate to charge into the main event. A frequent signal of timidity is a "when" lead:

> **On Nov. 14** a surprise health inspection of the McNeil Room kitchen at Rensselaer Polytechnic Institute yielded no citations and B-plus rating from a public health inspector.

Contrast that with the lead as it actually appeared in the Rensselaer Polytechnic campus newspaper:

> **A surprise health inspection** of the McNeil Room kitchen at Rensselaer Polytechnic Institute **on Nov. 14** yielded no citations and a B-plus rating from a health inspector.

Stephen Chan, the reporter, says he wrote the lead to alert readers to the "surprise right away, in the first few words." As you can see, that was more interesting and significant than the particular day on which it occurred.

Many "where" leads also are symptoms of writer timidity:

> **At a posh Manhattan penthouse**, the 4-year-old son of rock legend Eric Clapton plunged 49 stories to his death yesterday.

Even worse would be burying the news behind both the "where" and the "when":

> **At a posh Manhattan penthouse yesterday,** the 4-year-old son of rock legend Eric Clapton plunged 49 stories to his death.

Here is how New York Post editors organized the information for a March 21, 1991, story to emphasize the strongest material:

> **The 4-year-old son of rock legend Eric Clapton plunged 49 stories to his death** from a posh Manhattan penthouse yesterday.

WRITING THE DAY'S NEWS. Experienced writers like these CNN staff members know that busy readers and viewers want them to get to the point and tell the story. They avoid problem leads like the non-news lead, the quotation lead, and the question lead.

Unwieldy Leads

A reality in all writing is that everything worth telling cannot be told at once. Information has to be paced, which means that news writers must overcome a temptation to load the lead sentence with too much information. They can do that by avoiding obscure names and cluttering detail and by narrowing the focus.

Avoid obscure names. Naming people can bog down a lead sentence if their names aren't widely recognized. In lead sentences, where every word is so important, giving a title or credential or reason for being in the news usually is better than identifying a person who is not well known by name. In these leads from the Associated Press, the names would only clutter:

> A **spelunker** whose broken leg has kept her in the nation's deepest cave four days said Wednesday that the ordeal would not deter her from exploring caverns.

> An anti-treaty rights **activist** predicts a dangerous, violent Chippewa spearfishing season on northern Wisconsin lakes.

There are exceptions. You can be confident identifying well-known entertainers and celebrities and major political figures in leads. President Clinton would qualify, but probably not a state legislator from the next county. Even with well-known people, a supportive adjective is usually advisable: comedian Whoopi Goldberg, inventor Thomas Edison, talk-show host Larry King, First Lady Hillary Rodham Clinton, actress Elizabeth Taylor.

The justification for using names, even obscure ones, is strongest when the focus is on an individual, as in obituaries and stories about appointments, promotions and resignations. Even so, leads will be easier for the audience if the obscure name is delayed.

Avoid cluttering detail. Becoming overly specific in a lead sentence can overwhelm the audience with detail. Leads can be cluttered by official titles, addresses and jargon. For example, when police conduct a raid, the address should be prominent and fairly high in the story but not in the lead sentence:

> Police raided a Pulliam College fraternity party at **127 Wallace Drive** Saturday night, arresting 42 people on a variety of charges which included drunkenness and disorderliness.

The college's name is a sufficient localizing reference to a neighborhood in the lead sentence. The address in the lead only clutters. It is best held for a second or third sentence.

> Police raided a Pulliam College fraternity house party Saturday night, arresting 42 people on a variety of charges which included drunkenness and disorderliness.

Organizations develop all kinds of high-sounding labels, titles and abbreviations. Public relations becomes "information management," the personnel department takes on the name "human relations," and work permits are designated "occupational licenses." Titles abound: chairman and chief executive officer; vice president for finance and investor relations; senior vice president and president, publishing group; Legendre-Soule professor of business ethics and professor of management. Government agencies on all levels have become known as alphabet agencies because of their abbreviations: CIA, FCC, TVA, UNESCO, CINCPAC. All of these have the potential for creating alphabet soup or turning a meat and potatoes lead into goulash. Don't let your leads become mired in the officialese of the institutions you cover.

> A worker at the Smith Hardware **Retail Support Center** at Blue Isle was crushed to death Tuesday when she was caught behind a truck that was backing up to a loading dock.

Just call it a warehouse.

> A Department of Communication–Theatre Arts associate professor has been named director of the new Western State University residential college.

By finding out the professor's teaching specialty, you can avoid the drawn-out departmental name and offbeat spellings like "theatre." Also, specific academic ranks like "associate professor" clutter and can be avoided unless the rank is germane. Even if rank is an issue, it seldom will merit a place in a lead sentence:

> A theater professor has been named director of the new Western State University residential college.

Leaving officialese out of the lead gives a writer room in the sentence for additional detail that contributes to telling the story:

> A theater professor, new to the Western State University faculty last year, has been named director of the university's residential college.

As for abbreviations, follow the Associated Press rule. In general, avoid them. And while an abbreviation like FBI may be easily recognizable, be especially wary of using abbreviations that are not commonly before the public. DAC may be acceptable in a Pentagon newsletter and TA recognizable on a campus, but for general publication, put them in words. DAC stands for Department of the Army civilian. In a news story, translate that to "a civilian employee of the Army." TA, of course, should be "teaching assistant."

Public relations writers have a special problem with official titles and labels and oddball spellings. Their corporate or institutional superiors may insist on them, although PR people should persevere in making the case that news releases should follow journalistic style and preferences. It's a strong case: A news release has a greater chance of making it to print and on the air if it's ready to go without editing. While many news organizations will not use a news release without editing it, many will, especially those with small staffs.

If newsroom people decide to convert a release to journalistic style, the release will be subject to a process that can result in significant rewriting. That can lead to additional information-gathering and questions, and when that happens the organization that issued the release loses control over the message that ends up going to the public. These arguments will be persuasive with bosses who put function ahead of their idiosyncratic corporate or institutional cultures.

Narrow the focus. A single lead sentence that covers too many points is like a lone cop on a very long waterfront. It's overextended. Although multi-point leads are warranted at times, the trend in this fast-paced age is narrowly focused leads that don't require readers and listeners to work at sorting it all out. Work your way through this lead:

Co-anchor Deborah Norville of the NBC morning program "Today," who was widely believed to have pushed Jane Pauley, a 13-year veteran of the show, out of a job 14 months ago, and who most recently was the subject of criticism for posing for People magazine breast-feeding her newborn son, probably will not return to the show, with her substitute during a recent maternity leave, Katie Couric, 34, who joined the show last May as national correspondent, taking over the co-anchoring responsibilities, according to sources close to Michael Gartner, president of NBC News, who has been pleased with "Today's" improved ratings, which have been approaching those of the show's No. 1 rival, ABC's "Good Morning America," in recent weeks.

A skilled grammarian might be able to diagram that lead sentence and pronounce it properly constructed, but that hardly matters to the news audience. Possibilities abound for reducing such a lead to a palatable sentence:

> A substitute co-anchor on the NBC "Today" program, Katie Couric, whose presence has been tied to improved ratings, has been tabbed to replace the controversial Deborah Norville, insiders say.

> Co-anchor Deborah Norville of the NBC "Today" show, under fire for posing breast-feeding her newborn son, will not return to the program, according to network sources.

> Buoyed by recent ratings for the morning program "Today," NBC reportedly will stick with substitute co-anchor Katie Couric and dump Deborah Norville.

A danger in boiling down a multi-point lead is to become so general that the lead lacks anything substantive. In this lead from a college newspaper, for example, there is nothing for readers to dig their teeth into:

> Monday night's Student Association senate meeting ran smoothly despite the diverse topics that needed to be addressed by the senators.

The writer could have made that a news lead rather than a non-news lead by highlighting one or more of those "diverse topics" and telling readers what the senators accomplished—or failed to accomplish.

Here is another umbrella summary lead, also from a college newspaper, that fails to tell much of anything about what happened:

> The results of the student government survey conducted in the last election are in.

"So what?" the reader could ask. It would have been better to identify the survey's most significant or interesting finding and focus on it for the lead sentence.

Quotation Leads

If you want to see an editor frown, perhaps growl, write a direct quotation lead for a spot news story. On rare occasions a master writer can handle a quote lead, but editors have seen so many bad ones that some even ban them entirely.

The worst direct quote leads come from writers who either have not mastered the mental process for crafting good leads or who are too hurried or lazy to go through the process. They scan their notes in the hope that something will pop up as leadworthy. In effect, they sidestep the process of thinking through their material. They are counting on the source to have said something that will do their job for them, even down to the exact wording. Some direct quote leads are splendid, but so many bad ones have been written that the good ones, sadly, get a bad rap.

One problem with direct quotes for spot news leads is rooted in the fact that quotations originated as oral utterances, with all the wonderful reinforcing elements that speakers have at their command: inflection, paced delivery, gestures, facial expressions. Those reinforcing elements are not available to a writer trying to put together a lead sentence.

In the relatively barren environment of the written word, quoted words have to stand on their own merits. To be effective in the written media, however, most quotes require explanation, and it is rare that a lead sentence can accommodate both a quotation and the additional information that will make it as effective as it was when it came from the speaker's mouth.

Packing so much into a single sentence will almost always result in something unwieldy and cumbersome, as was this lead adapted from a university newspaper.

> "Reporting on the environment does not mean Geraldo showing up at a plant gate with the manager diving under the desk," William Smith, city editor of the Merrimac Tribune, said as part of a panel on environmental reporting held Saturday in Jones Hall of the journalism building.

Also illustrative of the problem is this lead adapted from a university film reviewer's story about a film and a symposium on the film:

> "Russia is perishing and you are dancing in its ruins," exclaims the young, pompous leader of a revolutionary organization in the new Russian film "Whiskers," directed by Soviet filmmaker Yuri Mamin, which had its premiere last Friday in Bartleby Hall as part of a two-day "Conference on Satire and Soviet Cinema," coordinated by Dr. William James, professor of cinema studies.

The difficulty with direct quote leads is that they are given to the reader without context. The reader has no feel for the situation in which the statement was made. The quote stands alone, naked and without explanation. Not many quotable sentences are that good.

Another problem is that the lead quote seldom is neatly tied to the paragraph that follows, so coherence in the story is absent from the start. To get the point, readers have to work hard, and readers going through a newspaper at the breakfast table or on a bus or subway don't have the time or energy to do that.

In the following lead, note how the reader has to wait halfway through the lead sentence to find out who "I" is:

> "I'm bullish on the cattle industry in the state of Kansas over the coming years," said Don Smith, president of the National Cattlemen's Association, at a cattleranchers' convention Friday at Kansas State University.

In the following variation on the same story, which was reported by Jodell Lamer of the Kansas State Collegian, the speaker's credential comes before the assertion. The reader doesn't have to guess for half a sentence whether "I" is credible or a crackpot:

> The president of the National Cattlemen's Association told Kansas cattle ranchers Friday that he is "bullish" about the state's cattle industry over the coming years.

Another seldom effective approach to spot news leads is quoting a famous person:

> "One should be either sad or joyful. Contentment is a warm sty for eaters and sleepers." — Eugene O'Neill.

The quote is provocative, but as a lead it is obscure. Is the story that follows about moods? Dieting? Sleeping? At best, the words-of-wisdom approach to journalism does no more than introduce the subject of a story. Such introductions fail to tell what the story has to say, which is the purpose of a lead.

Even with depth stories, words of wisdom rarely are as effective as other approaches to compelling the reader into the story. Many readers perceive such quotes as pedantic, and nobody likes being lectured at. Other readers find them dowdy, like plastic "words to live by" plaques.

As for quotation leads in broadcast stories, the word is: "Verboten!" Listeners cannot see the quotation marks, so they have no idea who may be making the statement. In fact, broadcast stylebooks caution against use of quotes at all because they slow the pace of a broadcast. To set off quotes, broadcast writers have to use phrases like "in these words," "as the President put it," "what she calls," and the like, and those eat up broadcasters' precious time.

Despite problems with direct quote leads, a reporter occasionally will hear a source utter something that cries out as leadworthy. Such moments will be rare. When they occur, it normally will be for a depth story, not a spot story. It happened to Ted Landphair, a reporter for the now-defunct National Observer. When Landphair sat down to write his interview with baseball star Henry Aaron, he picked a striking quote out of his notes that embodied the sheer joy Aaron got out of playing the game:

> "Baseball is a simple game," to hear Henry Aaron tell it. It's all instinct.
>
> Grinning and *degage*, the 36-year-old Atlanta Braves slugger romps after a butterfly. For him spring training is a lark. He guffaws at the barroom-brawl yarns of scrappy coach Clint Courtney. He whiffs at an imaginary ball. He beams, arm around an old man seeking sun and a souvenir picture. "I gotta look busy," he laughs, trotting off to dabble at playing shortstop.

Direct quote leads as good as Landphair's have a common characteristic: The quotation is simple and brief, and it is tied to the paragraph that follows. Note, too, that Landphair does not just hang the quote out by itself, as an inexperienced writer might do: "Baseball is a simple game," said Henry Aaron. Rather, using the conversational attributive "to hear Henry Aaron tell it" ties the quotation to the story, and in such a way that the quotation sets the mood for the story.

Alex Jones of the New York Times used an apt quote in much the same way in a story about the Bingham family's sale of its Louisville newspapers to the Gannett Co. It was a story that would win him a Pulitzer Prize:

> "It's a sad day for all of us," said Paul Janensch, executive editor of the Courier-Journal and the Louisville Times, hoarsely addressing several hundred somber co-workers who had jammed the company cafeteria to consider their uncertain future.

The story was a Sunday edition depth wrap-up, and Jones used the simple and brief direct quote to help recreate the seriousness of the meeting to discuss the sale. His purpose was to establish a mood at the outset, not to relate a spot news event. The spot stories had been written earlier in the week as the drama of the sale unfolded.

While effective direct quote leads are a rarity in spot news stories, a fragment from a quotation can work well, as shown in Lynn Bostian's lead adapted here from the Milwaukee Sentinel:

> The county solid waste manager called on the Walworth County Board Tuesday to take immediate action to curb the flow of out-of-area wastes entering the county "before it is too late."

Normally, writers avoid partial quote leads. Partial quotes can break up the writing. But Bostian composed a solid spot news story lead, using her words to tell what most warranted being told at the outset. Then she strengthened her lead by replacing a few of her own words with carefully selected words from the source. The result was added credibility that comes with verbatim words from the county waste manager.

At the same time, Bostian retained control of the sentence instead of surrendering control to the source, as happens with problematic full-sentence direct quote leads. Later in the story, she provided the full quote to give readers the context.

Even so, writers sometimes will find an occasion to incorporate a full-sentence direct quote into a lead sentence, as long as it is simple and brief, and as long as a context is established ahead of the quote. Here, Associated Press writer Vera Haller built a full-sentence quote into a lead to capitalize on the terror of a New York subway mishap:

> Panicked subway passengers screamed "We're going to die!" when waves of smoke filled a subway tunnel Friday, killing one person and injuring more than 150 others.

Question Leads

Is there a school newspaper in the country that has not run a story that begins something like this?

> Have you ever walked down the hall to the door just past the principal's office and wondered what's behind it?

A WRITER'S WRITER. Syndicated columnist George Will is considered a fine stylist, whether he is writing about politics or baseball, and whether he is writing for print or television. Will, shown here on the set of ABC's This Week With David Brinkley, knows the rules of good writing, and if he breaks one, he has a reason for doing so. (A/P/Wide World Photos)

Besides being trite, it is not even interesting. Those are two reasons why the best news writers avoid question leads. Such leads also read like advertisements — or, in broadcast copy, sound like commercials. Only on rare occasions does a question lead work, as this one did for syndicated columnist George F. Will.

What person was most directly responsible for the broadest improvement of life in this century? Douglas MacArthur, whose contribution to the liberalization of Japan should be remembered as America approaches the problems and possibilities of victory in another war.

Bill Husted, a staff writer for the Atlanta Constitution, also turned to a question lead as a reader-grabbing device in a story on information about telephone callers that companies have at their disposal:

> So you think your privacy is invaded each time Caller ID shows your telephone number to someone you call?
>
> Stop worrying. You haven't had any real privacy in years.

In those rare instances when a question lead seems right, be sure to answer the question immediately. The purpose of news writing, after all, is to report and explain, not tease.

Note how reporter Mark Tosczak of the North Carolina State University Technician skillfully began an interview story with a question and then answered it right away:

> In the year 2010, will there be fraternities on American college campuses?
>
> According to Al Calarco, a local Greek expert, if they don't clean up their act, there won't be.
>
> "We haven't been a good role model," he said.

Another question lead that worked topped a story by Katy Robinson and Anna Gilson of Santa Clara University's newspaper, the Santa Clara:

> Is there room for controversial or offensive material in the classroom?
>
> Yes, say many professors. Without it learning becomes a process of memorization, and students are not challenged to defend their convictions.

In this case, the question lead was an excellent choice. But even when question leads work, some editors have such disdain for them that they will never get into print.

FORMULA LEADS

STUDY PREVIEW   Imitation, it is said, is the sincerest form of flattery. But in writing, imitation that leads to triteness can be a crutch for the writer and a bore for the reader, and that is certainly true of leads that are written almost by formula.

"His or Her Way" Leads

Two formulas that lazy writers have come to use over the years are the "his or her way" construction and its "at least" corollary. They work this way:

> Middle State University students will pay more tuition next year, **if university president Arnold Jones has his way.**
> He plans to ask for the tuition hike at the meeting of the board of trustees next week.

It's an all-season, all-purpose formula that is as shopworn on Page 1 of the local newspaper as it is in the sports segment of the nightly news.

The "at least" lead is just as tired, and found in all media, as these broadcast leads attest:

> The legislature is likely to win its latest showdown with the governor. **At least**, that's what legislative leaders are saying.

It is also possible to combine the two formulas in one:

> The Chicago Bulls will hang another championship banner in the stadium this year, **at least if Scotty Pippen has his way**.

"Good News, Bad News" Leads

Another trite usage is the "good news, bad news" lead. Too many writers, apparently inspired by the slew of jokes that rely on the "good news, bad news" routine, believe it is clever to use the formula in their news stories, and over and over again. It looks like this:

> For Frank Fleer, the **good news** was that he had won Tuesday's lottery. The **bad news** was that officials learned he was wanted in Nebraska on armed robbery charges.

Such leads are bad news.

"Wrong Place, Wrong Time" Leads

The "wrong place, wrong time" lead is used less frequently, but enough so that it is overused anytime it appears:

> Sandra Saver was in the **wrong place** at the **wrong time** yesterday. She parked her car in front of the Gaiety Building and a piano fell on it.
>
> A cable on a crane hoisting the piano to the third floor gave way and the piano plummeted onto the hood of Saver's car, police said.

Suspense Leads

It's used so often, in so many newspapers and on so many broadcasts, that writers have to be careful not to overdo it. But when well done, it's a useful tool to draw readers into a story.

It's called a suspense lead. It delays providing the subject of a story while it builds suspense and, thus, interest in the subject. Such leads are used on soft news stories or provide a soft news tone to the start of a hard news story. Note, however, that the suspense is not drawn out. Even in a suspense lead, the nut of the story must be given in the first paragraph or two.

Dan Shine of the Dallas Morning News could have put a hard news lead on a story of a city council member's complaint of racial discrimination:

> Carrollton City Council member Shirley Demus Tarpley charged Tuesday that she and another African-American council member were denied the chance to be named mayors pro tem because they are black.

Instead, Shine chose a delayed lead that created more interest:

> The way City Council member Shirley Demus Tarpley sees it, there's only one reason she and Bernie Francis weren't elected by their colleagues as mayor pro tems. It wasn't their qualifications or their tenure on the council. It was the color of their skin.

The following suspense lead was written by Cecil Scaglione for the Los Angeles Times:

> We smelled **it** as soon as we left the oppressive Pennsylvania humidity outside and swooshed through the cool glass doors into the revitalizing air-conditioned low brick building.
>
> "Crayons," my wife said. She always says things like that before I do.

Dan Froomkin and Marc S. Posner put a delayed lead on a hard news police story for the Orange County Register:

> **It** had "student prank" written all over it, but the booby-trapping of toilet seats that disrupted finals for 4,000 California State University, Fullerton, students was the work of a chemistry professor.
>
> Campus police said Tuesday that Professor Wayne Taylor, 44, was responsible for the May 28 prank, which led to small explosions in two campus rest rooms.

A depth story in the Houston Chronicle by Patti Muck also carried a delayed lead:

> To investigators who spent more than a year examining Prairie View A&M University, **it** was an aberration.
>
> About $15.1 million in university funds unaccounted for—records so poorly kept that investigators say no one will ever know exactly where all that money went.
>
> They placed much of the blame on Prairie View A&M president from 1983 to 1989, Percy Pierre. In fact, Pierre, his controller Charles White and vice president of fiscal affairs Herbert Watkins would face charges of misapplication of fiduciary funds had the statute of limitations not expired, according to a final report to the Texas A&M University System.

As the examples show, the suspense lead can be effective. If overused, however, it will become ineffective.

CHAPTER WRAP-UP

The lead should draw the reader into the story by letting the reader know in an interesting way what is in the story. Some leads repel rather than attract, including leads that contain no news or highlight subordinate elements at the expense of the main news, leads that are difficult to decipher and quotation and question leads. Leads written by formula repel because they are trite. However, practically all the rules of good writing can be broken now and then, but only if writers know what they are doing—why they are breaking the rules. That is true of leads also. The rules can be broken to achieve particular effects, but they should be broken only sparingly.

STUDY QUESTIONS

1. What is meant by "backing into a story"?
2. What types of leads most often provide the occasion for backing into a story?
3. How would you remedy the situation?
4. Why are quotation leads frowned upon by editors?
5. When can quotation leads be used safely?
6. Why are question leads a problem?
7. Why are question leads a special problem for broadcasters?
8. How can question leads be used effectively?
9. How do news writers normally deal with the names of people who are not prominent?
10. What is a "his or her way" lead?
11. What is a "good news, bad news" lead?
12. What is a "wrong place, wrong time" lead?
13. What is a suspense lead?

PUTTING YOUR LEARNING TO WORK

EXERCISE 1   **Finding Faults**

Describe the faults, if any, in each of the following leads. How could each be corrected?

Four water-loving Middle State University students may have thought they were at the right place last summer when they moved into a boathouse on

Sleepy Island, but it was the wrong time because it was the summer of the big flood.

The Student Government Association met Tuesday to consider impeachment proceedings against President Catherine Barkley on charges she misappropriated funds to pay her boyfriend's rent and voted 35-0 in favor of impeaching her.

At Wednesday's Faculty Senate meeting, President Richard Diver said Middle State and all state universities are facing the uncertainty of such things as "closure of the 1993 Summer school session, a cap on freshman enrollment, increased tuition, reduction of scholarships and elimination of evening and off-campus classes," regarding the state's budget problems.

Understanding how and why the choices made by societies make their cultures different helps people understand their own cultures, said a Harvard anthropologist.

Anthropologist David Maybury-Lewis shared anecdotes Tuesday in the Greeley Memorial Union Ballroom from the time he spent gathering information about Brazilian tribal societies for his documentary series.

EXERCISE 2   Strengthening Leads

Rewrite each lead below to strengthen it.

"The Chamber wants to help you," so eloquently stated Middleton Chamber of Commerce Member Sandy Reed at the regular meeting of the Sons of Confederate Veterans on Monday, August 30, 1993.

Assembling at the Camp Lee Museum, Rapid River, the Middleton Chamber of Commerce hosted the dinner meeting and presented the program. Reed, the featured speaker, told that "the Chamber was ready and willing" to do all it can to promote Camp Lee as a tourist attraction.

Tommy Ensenar, president of the Apple County Association of Educators, asked to speak at last week's bi-monthly meeting of the Apple County School Board.

The approval of the 1993-94 school board budget was on the agenda for later that evening and Ensenar asked the board to consider a two percent permanent pay raise for all school board employees.

"We are losing good teachers to the schools in Bartlett, Concord and Sweet Counties because of low pay," Ensenar told the board.

He also said, "If you can't include a two percent raise in the budget, I'd like to know why."

This week's list for Grand Jury duty included the name of Betsy Andrews of Middleton. There's nothing strange about that: after all Grand Jury selection is made up of names of registered voters in the county. And Mrs. Andrews is definitely that, having voted in every election since she first registered as a young woman. However, while Mrs. Andrews was delighted to have made the list, and would be honored to serve, she gracefully declined. After all, at 101 years of age, she has plenty of other things to keep her busy—like enjoying the company of her children, grandchildren, great-grandchildren and a multitude of friends and other family members who consider a visit to Grammaw, as she is fondly known, as part of their weekly routine.

Have you ever been stuck behind the traffic light on Oak Street around 2 p.m on a week day? Traffic flows through that light like blood flows through the arteries of a guy who exists on nothing but fried mozzarella sticks for 30 years. It seems as if you are going nowhere.

Sometimes a car will sit through that light two or three times before it can pass under it. The red light stays on for about two and a half minutes at a time. That is quite a long wait when you are sitting in traffic under the sweltering April sun.

Middle State University is mainly a commuter college and it does not even have enough parking spaces to conveniently handle the massive influx of cars that come here every day. Naturally, there are going to be many traffic jams with commuters coming in from Rapid River, Swirl City and Poinsett and other surrounding areas.

The Middle State University men's golf team wrapped up yet another season over the weekend.

The Pythons finished the spring season on a positive note with a good showing at the Rivington College Invitational in Pressville.

"I was pleased with the showing," head coach Walter Burns said. "We gave a couple of underclassmen a shot, and we did well."

The Pythons finished second out of ten in the am competition, paced by seniors Bill Bogie and Charles Niblick.

FOR FURTHER LEARNING

Rene J. Cappon. "The Word: An Associated Press Guide to News Writing." The Associated Press, 1982. This is a fine brief discussion of news writing. Cappon, an AP editor, subtitled his chapter on leads "The Agony of Square One."

CHAPTER 5

Organizing the News Story

In this chapter you will learn:

✦ The inverted pyramid has special characteristics for a special purpose.

✦ The writer plays a far more important role in a depth story than in a spot news story.

✦ A single-incident story can be constructed using the inverted pyramid.

✦ The inverted pyramid lends itself to construction of the multiple-incident story.

✦ Two types of stories that support main stories are the sidebar and the point of entry story.

✦ A brief tells the central point of a story concisely.

✦ Stories must be organized differently for print and for broadcast.

TECHNOLOGY AND NEWS STORY FORM

Every schoolchild learns the first sentence that Samuel F. B. Morse clicked out on his newly invented telegraph key on May 24, 1844: "What hath God wrought?" The dots and dashes that made up the message were sent electronically from Washington to Baltimore where they were decoded by an assistant. Less well-known is another message Morse sent across the wire that day. It became the lead for a news story later printed by the Baltimore Patriot:

> One o'clock — There has just been made a motion in the House to go into committee of the whole on the Oregon question. Rejected — ayes, 79; nays, 86.

Looking back through the prism of daily satellite transmissions of words and pictures from whatever place news events are occurring, those simple messages and the device that carried them were primitive. But the telegraph had profound effects on the delivery and presentation of news. When Henry David Thoreau considered the notion that the telegraph would allow Maine and Texas to communicate, he concluded that the two states might have "nothing important" to say to one another. Of course, they did. And to great extent they said it through the newspapers of the time.

Until the coming of the telegraph, editorials had been the staple of American newspapers. Once Maine and Texas began to converse, news became all important. "The telegraphic dispatch is the great point," said Horace Greeley, publisher of the New York Tribune, the most influential newspaper of the mid 19th century. News became what was new, wherever it occurred. No longer did editors—and readers—have to wait days, even weeks, for word of what had happened at a distance. The telegraph allowed newspapers in Springfield, Mass., and Springfield, Ohio, to publish news that happened in Springfield, Ill., on the same day it was published in the Illinois State Register of Abraham Lincoln's day. The content of newspapers was transformed, and so was the way people thought about news. News became what was current.

The way in which news was written began to change as a result of the telegraph. At the time of the laying of the transatlantic cable, James Gordon Bennett, publisher of the New York Herald, predicted that the telegraph would have tremendous impact on news writing. It would "bring us back to that succinct, simple and condensed method of expressing our ideas which prevailed in ancient times. . . . Condensation of words to express thought will prevail." And prevail it did, if for no other reason than it cost money to send words by telegraph. The toll for use of the Atlantic cable was $5 a word.

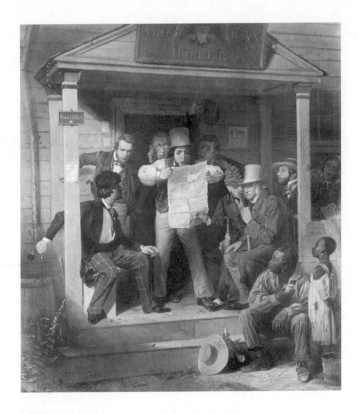

MEXICAN NEWS. The telegraph was used to transmit news from battlefields to newspaper for the first time during the Mexican War, and the new device soon changed journalism in both form and content. The inverted pyramid style of newspaper writing came about as a result and benefitted both writers and readers.
(The Bettmann Archive)

Although linemen began stretching wires across the country almost as soon as the dots and dashes of Morse's first messages were fading, it was the Civil War, and the American public's demand for news from the battlefields, which gave greatest impetus to use of the telegraph and to changes in the structure of the news story. For one thing, as Bennett predicted, expenses dictated that stories be condensed. Reporters had to be less flowery in their language and more direct. And because telegraph lines themselves were sometimes brought down in battles or by sabotage, reporters sending stories from the field could no longer use a narrative style that detailed events in chronological order. Lest the lines be cut while their stories were going out, they learned to tell the most important facts first, followed by less important facts, and then by the least important facts. The resulting form came to be known as the inverted pyramid.

THE INVERTED PYRAMID

STUDY PREVIEW   Today fiber cables and satellites carry the news from reporter to consumer, but the inverted pyramid has remained as a most useful writing device for reporters whose work is printed. First of all, it helps them organize their thoughts quickly against a deadline. Reporters who deal primarily with event-based stories hardly ever use another style. Second, it is a help to copy editors faced with the need to make stories shorter to fit an available news hole. They can cut from the bottom of a well-constructed inverted pyramid story. The form also helps busy readers, who can skim the first few paragraphs of a story and get to the heart of the matter. Most spot news stories follow the inverted structure, with less important details being introduced as the story continues. Depth stories take a wider variety of structures but require no less discipline in keeping the audience's attention and interest. Once readers are hooked, the challenge becomes keeping the story compelling.

Structuring the Story

The facts of the situation or event should dictate the kind of lead you, as the writer, choose and the wording you use, and what is in your lead determines what follows. In effect, you make a promise, a commitment, to the reader in the lead: "This is what I'm going to talk about." In the body of the story, you follow through.

Once you have developed your main point, satisfying immediate reader and listener questions about what happened, you can move to lesser points, and then to even lesser points, until you have nothing more worth including and you are done telling your story.

Let's analyze an Associated Press story constructed in the form of a simple inverted pyramid as it appeared in the News of Boca Raton, Fla. The "what" lead clearly states what the story is about. The remainder of the story develops points made in the first paragraph and adds new, secondary elements in succeeding paragraphs.

TALLAHASSEE, Fla. — A $295 fee on vehicles registered by newcomers to Florida would be cut in half if legislation endorsed by a House committee Wednesday becomes law.

The lead contains the principal fact in the story. The writer promises to tell the reader about the new legislation.

The bill, approved 17-0 by the House Transportation Committee, would also reduce from $100 to $50 the "new-wheels-on-the-road" fee for vehicles registered for the first time.

The second paragraph develops the first by providing specific details: the name of the committee, and the vote count. The paragraph also adds a second element. In the writer's view, apparently, cutting the $100 fee was of secondary importance.

The sponsor, Rep Mario Diaz-Balart, said the legislation is intended to improve compliance with fee schedules that aren't bringing in anticipated dollars anyway. The impact fees, passed last year by the Legislature, were initially projected to bring in $83 million but may raise only $27 million.

The third paragraph further develops elements of the first paragraph—the "who"—and the new point in the second paragraph. It also explains the "why" of the legislation.

The bill would drop the $295 fee to $150. It attempts to improve compliance by requiring proof of auto registration before a newcomer can enroll a child in public schools, apply for a homestead exemption or obtain a driver license.

Expansion of detail from the first paragraph. Also provides the "how" of the paragraph immediately preceding.

The reduction in the new-car fee would be offset by a flat increase of $3 on motor vehicle license taxes and permits.

Further development of the second paragraph.

The bill next goes to the House Finance and Taxation Committee.

A new element is introduced. A succeeding paragraph might quote the bill's sponsor or a legislative leader on the chances of its passage.

One measure of how well a story follows the inverted pyramid form is the cut-off test. If a story can be cut at any paragraph without seeming to leave something out, it passes. Read the story again but without the last paragraph. Repeat the process four more times, each time eliminating another paragraph. Does the story still make sense, even when it is reduced to one paragraph? It is not as complete, but the essential element remains.

Another way to look at the inverted pyramid is in comparison with other forms of presentation. In a chronological presentation the story would begin at the beginning and progress sequentially, presenting the most important element at whatever point it occurred.

CHRONOLOGY

Main
News
Could
Occur
Anywhere

The climatic form is one that readers of mystery stories are used to. The who-done-it is delayed until the very end.

CLIMACTIC FORM

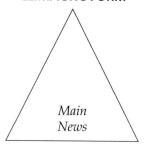

Main
News

The point in writing spot news is to tell what happened, not to create mystery or suspense or to toy with your audience. As a consequence, spot news is most often written in the inverted pyramid form.

INVERTED PYRAMID

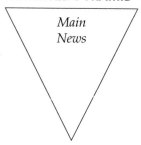

Main
News

The inverted pyramid serves readers and listeners who want the high-lights right away. It lays out the main points at the beginning. For those who want to know more, additional details follow later. When their interest is sated, whether at the third sentence or the 30th, they can move to another page.

Following Through

Most event-based stories capitalize right away on the interest that the lead generates. In this example, a Chicago Sun-Times writer chose to make specific the general points in the lead:

Two employees were stabbed Wednesday night by a scissors-wielding patient who broke out of the psychiatric ward at the Veterans Administration's West Side Medical Center, officials said.

Nurse Rosanna Alexander, 44, was stabbed several times in the face with the scissors, and therapist Eddie Lovitt, 60, suffered superficial facial wounds when he came to her aid and subdued the patient, officials said.

In similar fashion, a publicity writer on a U.S. senator's staff immediately developed the lead on a story of an appointment by telling what the appointee would do:

Sen. John Breaux, D-La., today said Ivory Crockett, a former college sprinter who still shares the world's record in the 100-yard dash, will join his Louisiana office as a staff assistant.

In addition to representing Breaux throughout Central Louisiana, Crockett's duties will include constituent relations and assistance.

If you are wondering why Breaux's name was first in the story, keep in mind that the public relations person's job is to get attention for the boss. Most likely, the story would be edited on a news desk to put Crockett's name first.

When writers do not develop the lead right away but shift too quickly to a second subject, they leave the lead to dangle undeveloped, and that can lose the reader's interest. A dangling lead signals that the story probably is choppy and disorganized and will be tough to get through. Here's an extreme example:

The St. Gertrude College Student Senate voted 10-9 Monday to suspend student body President Charlene Rhodes pending an investigation into charges that her campaign supporters violated spending limits to get her elected last spring.

The Senate also authorized $25 for flowers for the podium at winter commencement.

WRITING A RELEASE. A Pepsico public relations staff member works on a news release. Like writers for newspapers and broadcasting, she knows the importance of following through on the lead immediately. Whether the story contained in a news release is picked up by the editors depends in large part on how well it is written. (Courtesy of The Pepsi-Cola Company)

An unrelated, tertiary Senate decision about flowers is not a good follow-through. It would be in the reader 's best interest to develop the "why" of the suspension:

> In a fiery two-hour session, Rhodes was accused by Sen. Chuck Frye of concealing $500 in printing costs for four-color campaign posters.

A good rule of thumb: If it is worth leading with, it is worth immediate development.

An exception occurs when two closely related developments are important. In the following story, rather than expanding right away on the lead-sentence accusation of the military dictator of Panama, the writer moves to a second development:

Gen. Manuel Antonio Noriega accused the United States on Friday of instigating the failed effort to end his military rule and said Washington waged a campaign of "psychological warfare" against him.	Eric Arturo Delvalle, ousted by the legislature after trying to fire Noriega, refused to accept defeat and told reporters at his home: "I am the president of Panama this morning."

The juxtaposition of the two items in the two lead paragraphs lets readers know that the writer thought both developments were of equal, or nearly equal, importance. In subsequent paragraphs, the writer will give more detail. Noriega's complaint will be fleshed out, then Delvalle's stance.

Writing Depth Stories

In the 1950s, television detective Joe Friday wanted "just the facts, ma'am." This was also the journalistic convention of the time. But in a more complex world, "just the facts" is not enough. For depth stories, which seek not just information but understanding and explanation, traditional spot news techniques will not work. Just as Five W leads are inadequate for depth stories, so is the inverted pyramid. Depth stories have to maintain audience interest, rather than assume dwindling interest and then accommodate it.

As reporters venture beyond the relative comforts of the Five Ws and the inverted pyramid, they learn that writing is an art. There is not one and only one right way to go about the process. After days of interviews, observation and research for a depth story, it is not unnatural for you to be overwhelmed by the massiveness of your material.

What to do? Remember, it is your enterprise that is bringing the story into being. Without you, it would never be told. You are far more central in shaping the depth story than you are in writing spot news. You must look more to yourself than to spot news conventions in deciding what is worth telling.

One technique is to put aside your notes for the moment. Forget all the specifics and details they contain—figures, dates, spelling, quotations. Ask, "What do I know that is worth telling?" Think it through, perhaps for an hour, perhaps a day, and then—still without looking at your notes—begin writing. Don't worry about details for the time being. Just write. If a name is misspelled, you can correct it later. If you can't remember a name or figure, type in "XXX." Don't worry about supporting detail, but focus on the points you want to make. Do this quickly.

Look critically at what you've written and ask if the story flows logically. If it doesn't, rewrite the rough parts, still without concern for spellings and details. Are there points that have to be added? Can parts be dropped without detracting from the point? Rework until you have a structural core for the story.

Then, haul out your notes. Plug in quotations where they support a point you've made. Do the same with examples, illustrations and anecdotes. Fix spelling. Add details that you couldn't remember without your notes. Insert color to make it more interesting or drive points home.

No matter how gripping your first few sentences, you can't expect readers to stay with you if you do not let them know where the story is going, so you have to get to the point, to the "nut" of the story, fairly soon. Usually the best place to state the subject is in the transition from the introductory section. Here is how Washington Post reporter Bradley Graham did it in a story about violence as a way of life in Colombia:

Maria Luisa Mejia, a television reporter, stopped going for walks after her name turned up on a death list a few months ago.

Ernesto Samper, a ruling Liberal Party senator, travels with eight bodyguards but knows he is still vulnerable to anyone who really wants to kill him.

Gloria Triana, an anthropologist, used to feel safe living next to a police station but now worries that she could get caught in the crossfire if leftist guerrillas decide to attack the station.

In ways big and small, Colombia's mounting violence has disrupted the lives of many people in the nation's capital and across the country, forcing them to alter old routines and endure a constant state of fear.

The number of killings per capita in Colombia is more than five times the U.S. rate, according to official statistics. Assassination is the principal cause of death for men aged 14 to 44.

The transition paragraph, beginning "In ways big and small," plays a critical role in the story's development. It is like a link in a chain, tying what has gone before to what comes after. In each of the three paragraphs preceding that focused on individuals, Graham showed disruptions in people's lives. In the paragraphs to follow, he will take up in greater detail the "mounting violence" in Colombia.

Avoiding Tangents

Reporters gather so much interesting information in preparing depth stories that they may be tempted to stray from the main point. Avoid the temptation. You will lose your audience by taking tangents that do not help develop the main point. In his story on violence in Colombia, Bradley Graham would have lost readers had he spent a few paragraphs on the fascinating boyhood of

Simon Bolivar, the role of coffee in the Colombia economy, or the excellent cuisine in Bogota cafes.

Tangential matters, no matter how interesting, should be put aside. They will make good stories another day.

Ending the Story

How do you end the story? By putting down the final fact or quote and typing a period. Some novice reporters believe it is necessary to add what can be called a storybook ending—"and they all lived happily ever after"—as the final paragraph. A writer for a college newspaper closed a story on a new and expensively appointed concierge desk in the student union this way:

Even Knipfing admitted that the fancy office would be a little intimidating at first. "It's going to take time. People have got to learn that that's what it's there for; it's there to be of service. We did it to please the students and to show them that in this area of the university we want to provide the best service we can."

Well, maybe he's right. It might just take time for students to become comfortable with the idea. Then again, it might take a few scratches on the oak veneer until students realize just how helpful Thomas and her fellow concierges can be.

The story ends nicely at the end of the quotation in the penultimate paragraph. But for some reason the reporter added an editorial comment—and one that is not quite clear—as the ending. That wasn't necessary.

Another student reporter closed with an unjustified viewpoint in a feature on a student union piano and the people who play it.

He points out that it would be difficult to steal a piano, but someone did steal the stool last year. "Someone needed a bench for their apartment," Taylor said.

This could be true, but perhaps someone just wanted a piece of school tradition.

A Miami Herald story on a Virgil festival at Florida State University included a report of a talk by Charles Segal of Harvard University. The last two paragraphs read:

Segal's conclusion: Virgil's epic, along with Homer's poems, instill "cosmic consciousness." They present the reader with "a wide horizon of radiant acts and

future glory that make life worth living."

As Virgil said: "*Forsan et haec olim meminisse iuvabit.*" Maybe it will profit us to remember these things in after times.

A quotation is frequently used to end stories, and this reporter tries a clever twist, ending the piece with Virgil's words. But it just doesn't work. The story's real end is the quotation from Segal's talk.

If you can't quite overcome your compulsion to end with a summary paragraph, a comment or a clever twist, go ahead and write it. But having written it, lop it off. Over time, you will find that the paragraph that is left at the end is actually the end. And over time you will be able to wean yourself from writing the superfluous ending.

SUBORDINATE STORIES

STUDY PREVIEW   Editors have found that stories that go on for column after column can discourage readers from even starting to read them. As a result, reporters working on lengthy depth stories often develop some subordinate material into separate stories that are printed alongside the main story. The most common of the subordinate stories are sidebars and point of entry stories.

Sidebars

Sidebars provide elaboration of certain aspects of a main story. In effect, they say to the reader, "By the way, did you know this about x or y or z?" Stories about major tragedies often carry sidebars. When an old building goes up in flames, the main story will cover the fire and the way firefighters battled it. A sidebar might give the building's history or provide some interesting information on the businesses housed in it. A sidebar to the story of a fatal traffic accident at a spot where other fatalities have occurred might provide readers with a history of those accidents.

When two Navy P-3 Orion airplanes from a base near San Francisco collided off the southern California coast early one Saturday morning, editors at the San Francisco Chronicle assigned five staff members to gather details. The team, headed by John Wildermuth and Susan Sward, pulled together the basic facts: who was involved, as much of what happened as the Navy knew, the time of the accident, where the planes collided, the preparations for counseling families of the crew members who were killed and the reaction on the base.

That spot news material filled the page one story under this spot news lead:

Twenty-seven Navy crewmen based at Moffett Naval Air Station in Mountain View are missing and presumed dead after two planes collided yesterday

> during anti-submarine exercises that were being conducted in stormy weather.

Wildermuth and Sward made only passing reference to the airplanes. But because readers have questions about the aircraft involved in accidents, Chronicle editors assigned staff writer Jack Viets to dig up information about the P-3 Orion and its safety record. His sidebar, printed alongside the main story jump on Page 4, described the plane, detailed its weaponry, told how it carried out its missions, and gave some of the history of its development and of its use at the field where the doomed planes were based. It began this way:

> The Navy patrol planes from Moffett Field that collided in a fireball off San Diego early yesterday were long-range submarine killers that evolved from a popular Lockheed commercial airliner.
>
> The sleek, white P-3 Orions, powered by four jet-prop engines in slender nacelles, have been a familiar sight in Bay Area skies since they were first assigned to Moffett Field late in 1963.
>
> Stretching from their tail is a distinctive "stinger," a magnetic detector that is part of its highly sophisticated sub-hunting gear.

To further illustrate, the first story about a roller coaster accident won a place on the front page of the Orange County, Calif., Register. The story by reporters Ricky Young and Donna Davis began this way:

> A distracted attendant who failed to hit the brakes on the Cyclone roller coaster caused an accident that injured eight people at the Orange County Fair, officials said Tuesday.
>
> The pileup occurred at 11:30 p.m. Monday. The accident will be investigated by the California Division of Occupational Safety and Health.

The story then told what happened from the point of view of the victims and of the ride manager, who said the operator "was distracted." Inside, readers found sidebars on the safety record of the company that operated the roller coaster, comments from a woman who sued the same operator after a previous roller coaster accident, and a report on the inspections required of carnival rides. All were important to the reader, but none could easily be incorporated into the main story.

Points of Entry

What is called the "point of entry story" appears alongside the main story, like a sidebar. However, while a sidebar develops a distant subtheme of the main story, as did the sidebar on the P-3 Orions or those printed with the story of the carnival mishap, the point of entry story contains material so closely related to the main story that it could be incorporated into it easily.

Point of entry material is usually something the editors believe will pique reader interest, especially because it often focuses on individuals involved in the story. The idea is to entice readers who otherwise might pass up a lengthy main story by giving them a taste of it in bite-sized form. Rather than looking at a 50-inch story, readers see one 20-inch story and three closely related stories that are each about 10 inches long. After trying the tasty 10-inch morsels, editors reckon, readers will want more and will dig into the main story. The separate story becomes a point at which readers enter the main story.

The Times-Picayune of New Orleans uses point of entry stories skillfully with lengthy and complicated investigative pieces. To cite just one example, in a series by reporters James O'Byrne and Mark Schleifstein on air, land and water pollution in southeastern Louisiana, the newspaper printed one major story of about 35 inches on each of four days. Accompanying each story were at least two, and sometimes three, point of entry stories.

A Page 1 story on threats to drinking water had three points of entry, all of which could have been developed in the main story. The lead of the main story read this way:

> For the past 30 years, 243 million pounds of toxic liquid and sludge have been oozing through the dirt toward the Plaquemine Aquifer, a thin underground layer of loose sand that bears a vast reservoir of pure, fresh drinking water.

The main story jumped to Page 5, and across from it, on Page 6, was a boxed point of entry story headed "The Big Ooze," which developed one aspect of the lead:

> To understand how groundwater gets contaminated, it is helpful to know a little about the geology of south Louisiana.
> In crudest terms, the underground terrain is arranged like a multilayered cake, with each layer separated by frosting.

A detailed explanation followed. Alongside it in the box was a colorful graphic showing how aquifers are contaminated. Another graphic showed what is done to clean an aquifer.

The second point of entry originated in a series of bulleted items in the main story. Each item in the list supported the reporters' assertion that efforts to maintain the purity of underground drinking water aquifers were moving slowly. Among the items was this one:

The companies all express confidence that they will never contaminate the aquifers. But their assumptions are based on unproven experimental recovery and treatment techniques, and often on an insufficient number of samples to prove that the chemicals won't continue to sink, state officials and groundwater experts say.

The reporters could have developed that point within the main story. Instead they chose to develop it in a separate story (sometimes simply called a "separate") that began this way:

Attempts to clean up contamination of groundwater at Louisiana's chemical plants are experimental, and officials admit they don't know if the efforts will succeed.

The third point of entry was related to references throughout the main story to the tension between governmental agencies and chemical companies with groundwater problems. The point of entry zoomed in tightly on the positions held by the two sides.

Frank Burgos of the Chicago Sun-Times also used main story, sidebar and point of entry effectively in a series entitled "The New Immigrants." The last segment in the series reported on a lawsuit against a company that helped immigrants fill out government forms. A point of entry focused on "a self-proclaimed immigration expert" who, some said, bilked clients by promising to get immigrants resident status and ultimately citizenship.

The point of entry was so closely related to the main story that it could have been incorporated into it. The result would have been a story on two suspect immigration businesses rather than just one, and that story would have been so long that readers might have been turned away. As it was, the shorter point of entry might well have drawn readers into a slightly longer main story.

Briefs

Whereas depth stories are so lengthy that elements are sometimes pulled out for separate presentation, "briefs" are condensations of the news. They are often bare bones recitations of the central information about a situation or event, with little, if any, fleshing out. That is true whether they are about local happenings, national and international events, celebrities, sports or entertainment, and regardless of the newspaper or magazine that prints them. Editors have found that the brief is a handy way to present the news to busy readers who want just the nut of what has happened.

Briefs printed in a column on the front page may have a line tacked on that refers readers to an expanded story elsewhere in the newspaper—a "refer," it's called, with the accent on the first syllable. Collected as refers, the briefs serve also as a table of contents.

Briefs may be as short as USA Today's "Gov. Cuomo won't be rushed" or as long as six to eight sentences, chopped into three to four paragraphs. An average length would seem to be about three sentences in one paragraph. This example, from the Minneapolis Star Tribune, illustrates the form:

A ban on cameras in federal courtrooms ended when judges allowed live telecasts of arguments in appeals cases in Boise, Idaho. The move by judges from the San Francisco–based U.S. Circuit Court of Appeals came three days before Monday's scheduled start of telecasts, on a limited basis, of civil cases in courts in several cities. The American Bar Association adopted the ban in 1937.

Other examples abound. The first column in each USA Today section carries a string of very brief briefs and refers. For example, "Newsline" is billed as "A quick read on the news," and "Sportsline" is "A quick read on the top sports news of the day." The Wall Street Journal devotes three of its front page columns to somewhat longer briefs. One focuses on news of business and finance and another on national and international news. The subjects of the third column vary from day to day: labor situations, tax developments, trends in industry and finance, and Washington items. Other newspapers have their own headings and their own categories.

BROADCAST STORIES

STUDY PREVIEW   Broadcast news writers have the same restriction as the writers of briefs: they must develop their stories in the barest minimum number of words. The average newscast story normally contains no more than three or four sentences, and sometimes only one or two sentences. One type of broadcast story is the "reader." Another is the "lead-in" that introduces an "actuality" (an audio or video report from a correspondent, or a sound bite from a source).

Readers

A "reader" is a story written to be read in its entirety by a newscaster. It stands alone, without an audio or video actuality, though on television a related graphic may appear behind the anchor reading it. It is the type of story listeners hear most often on radio and frequently on television. Because "readers" are so short, a lot has to be put into a small package. And it has to be put in a way that will hold the listener's attention and inform at the same time. That's the way it was done by the ABC radio writer who wrote this story:

> Most of us say we turned to TV for most of our information about the Gulf War. A Roper poll finds the majority of people surveyed mentioned only television as their source of news in February. Radio, newspapers, magazines and talking to people—according to Roper—ranked considerably lower as sources of Gulf War news.

Another example, also from ABC radio, nails down the point:

> Investigators in Sterlington, Louisiana, are trying to find out what caused an explosion that wrecked a fertilizer plant. Fires burned for hours killing three people. Five others, unaccounted for. More than 120 people were injured in the International Minerals and Chemicals Company in northern Louisiana.

The listener doesn't get all of the detail that would be in a newspaper or magazine story about either event. But the essentials are there, and as a UPI Broadcast Stylebook once said of good broadcast copy: "'It listens good.' It's active, it has pace, it's clear rather than confusing, and it builds interest." There is no better recipe for the broadcast news writer to follow.

Just as an aside here, notice the line "Five others, unaccounted for" in the explosion story. In broadcast copy, it is permissible occasionally to use an incomplete sentence. Like any other device, however, if incomplete sentences are overused they will draw attention to themselves and away from the content.

Lead-Ins

The lead-in is an introduction to an audio or video actuality (in television the term is "sound on tape," abbreviated on copy as "SOT," though occasionally you may hear it referred to as "sound on film," or "SOF"). As in this example from ABC radio, the lead-in can provide a setting into which an on-the-scene reporter can step:

> Nearly 40 thousand people are known dead in a cyclone that wiped out or flattened wide sections of Bangladesh. One-hundred-forty-five mile an hour winds hit coastal areas Tuesday. There are fears the death toll could hit 100 thousand.

Having read that lead-in, the announcer introduces the reporter:

> A-B-C's Nathan Thomas is in Dacca:

The reporter tells his story:

> (THOMAS) The land around the Bay of Bengal is topsoil that has washed down over the years from the rest of the country. But because there are so many bad storms here there has never been a chance for trees to grow. There is no protection down there at all. But still, even knowing the danger, hundreds of thousands of people moved there because it is the best topsoil in the country and they risked the danger and every so many years this happens and whole villages are just wiped out—disappear.

At this point, the end of the story, the reporter should be identified again for listeners who may wonder who was speaking:

> A-B-C's Nathan Thomas.

The lead-in can also give a context for a newsmaker's statement:

> There may be a lower interest loan in your future. Many of the nation's biggest banks have loosened their belts, responding to yesterday's moves by the Federal Reserve. Banks like Citibank and Chase Manhattan have cut their prime rates to eight and a half percent. Bank rate expert Robert Heady thinks the size of the cut—a half percent—may be just the medicine the recession needs.

Then comes the actuality with Robert Heady. The sentence before the actuality introduces Heady's actual words. The construction of that sentence is particularly good in light of the old saw that "what can go wrong will go wrong." A cartridge tape occasionally is not cued to the sound bite, or a tape machine may not operate properly, or there's some other gremlinesque failure. When that happens, the announcer can go on to the next story without apology, something that could not be done if the introductory line read something like "Here's what bank rate expert Robert Heady has to say about it."

Echoes and Stutter Quotes

Whatever the lead-in, keep in mind that it must make the listener aware of what will follow. And avoid what some call the echo chamber effect:

> . . . and Smith said he is **going to ask for a recount**.
> (SMITH) I'm **going to ask for a recount**. The vote was so close, etc.

Be aware that the echo chamber effect is not limited to broadcasting. Writers for print commit the same fault—though in print it's called a stutter quote—when they paraphrase a statement, then follow the paraphrase with a direct quote, as in this example:

The President said the United States still has a strong national interest in Korea and its determination to maintain **Korea's security remains undiminished**. American troops will remain there as long as they are wanted and needed.	"Our commitment to **Korea's security remains undiminished**. The Korean peninsula remains a vital American interest. Our troops will stay here as long as the Korean people want and need us here," the President said.

Voice-Overs

We have all watched home movies or amateur videos and listened as the movie maker or videographer tells the captive audience something like, "This is Billy on a horse," or "In this shot, Sally is blowing out the candles on her birthday cake," when it is perfectly obvious that Billy is on a horse or Sally is blowing out the candles. The television writer's dilemma is to avoid that sort of redundancy when writing a story that will be read while the viewer looks at videotape, what's called a "voice-over," abbreviated as V/O. The words that tell the story must complement the pictures that illustrate it.

When San Francisco police evicted a group of homeless people from a house they had moved into three weeks earlier, KRON-TV reported the story with a voice-over script. Viewers saw the police gathered in the street and the squatters leaving the building. They heard anchor Catherine Heenan provide explanation:

> Police moved in at 6:20, using a bullhorn to warn a dozen people they had ten minutes to get out. With a minute left, they came from the building. The group "Homes-Not-Jails" had taken over the building as a protest and now accuse Mayor Frank Jordan of betraying them.

The words filled in what the picture did not show and added detail. The phrase "now accuse Mayor Frank Jordan of betraying them" serves as a lead-in to back-to-back statements by the leader of the homeless group and the U.S. attorney.

Writers of photo-captions have to take care that their words under the pictures add to the pictures rather than describe what's in them. If readers can see Ellen Jones and Bill Smith shaking hands, don't tell them the two are shaking hands. Tell them she is congratulating Smith for an achievement or he is welcoming her to an event. Don't be redundant.

CHAPTER WRAP-UP

News writers have a great deal of freedom in presenting their stories. While spot news stories normally are poured into the tried-and-true inverted pyramid, even spot news writers have a degree of latitude in presenting the news. Writers of depth stories are limited only by their imaginations. What is common to both is that the form should be appropriate to the story itself and that the commitment made to the reader in the lead should be responded to in the body. Depth stories are often complemented by subordinate stories, including sidebars, points of entry and briefs. Broadcast stories include readers, lead-ins and voice-overs.

STUDY QUESTIONS

1. Describe the structure of the inverted pyramid. How does it differ from climactic form and chronological presentation?
2. How did the inverted pyramid come into being?
3. Describe the impact of the telegraph on newspaper content.
4. What is the danger in not developing the lead immediately?
5. Describe the process a news writer ought to follow when seemingly overwhelmed by material.
6. Define the terms "sidebar" and "point of entry." How do they differ?
7. Define "brief" and "refer." How do they differ and how are they related?
8. What are "readers" and "lead-ins," and how do they differ?
9. What is the most important thing to keep in mind when writing a video script to be read while pictures are on the screen?

PUTTING YOUR LEARNING TO WORK

> EXERCISE 1   Organization

You are a police reporter for a morning newspaper. When you check with police headquarters one afternoon, you are given the following information by the public relations officer (usually referred to as "a police spokesperson"). You follow up with an interview with Sgt. Mark Thomas, commander of the 2nd District narcotics unit. Use the information to write a 200-word story for tomorrow's edition.

A squad of the narcotics unit from the 2nd District station staged a raid on a house at 1504 Mulberry St. this morning. They arrested four people: Joseph Louis, 23, 1504 Mulberry St.; John Williams, 18, 2666 W. Adams St.; Bert Jacobs, 25, 201 E. Miller Ave.; Martha Hogan, 17, 333 9th St.

All were booked with possession with intent to distribute heroin and cocaine. They also were booked with possession of a firearm while distributing narcotics. Police confiscated one weapon, a .25-caliber semiautomatic pistol. They also confiscated ammunition for an assault rifle.

From Sgt. Thomas: For some time police have been staking out the corner of Pine and Olive streets watching drug deals going down. Last week, a patrolling officer saw what he thought was a drug deal, someone buying heroin, and when he approached two men on the corner, one of them pointed a gun at him and ran. The man was arrested a short time later a few blocks away.

Police had information drugs were being distributed from the Mulberry St. house. They got a search warrant and served it about 11 a.m. They found 432 foil packets of heroin and 224 cellophane packets of crack cocaine. They also seized 132 grams of unpackaged crack cocaine. Heroin packets sell for $25 each. Crack cocaine packets go for $10.

"This isn't one of the biggest hauls we've made. But this was an active and profitable operation. Every time we can put a dealer like this out of business, it sends ripples up through the whole drug organization. It also sends a message to other dealers in the area. We have some of them targeted too, and we'll have more raids like this one in not too long a time."

EXERCISE 2   Organization

Write a story of 300 words for your campus newspaper based on the following facts:

In covering the Office of Student Affairs, you learn that a new smoking policy will go into effect on the first of next month. You question the office's policy coordinator, Paul Dombey, and learn that the policy is the result of a vote last month in the student senate on a resolution to ban smoking everywhere on campus except in the Lower Depths Lounge of the student union, the union bowling alley and in some wings of the dormitories. Previously smoking had also been permitted in the Green Room of the union, in faculty offices and the majority of dorm rooms, but those areas were put off limits for smokers.

Dombey: "The new policy simply continues our efforts to limit the number of smoking areas on campus. The union's Red Room, selected dormitory wings, classroom building lounges and hallways and classrooms were already smoke free."

Dombey: "Before the senate voted, students were polled on their opinions as to which areas on campus should be smoke free. They were given a list of areas on campus and were asked to answer 'yes' or 'no' in regards to where smoking should be permitted or banned."

The faculty and staff were also asked if they supported extending the smoking ban, and they agreed overwhelmingly.

Only about 10 percent of the students expressed an opinion, but the senate used the survey to proceed with the vote on the resolution.

Spot interviews:

Esther Summerson, university comptroller: "I would prefer to be able to smoke in my office, but it's not an inconvenience for me."

Richard Carstone, junior in business administration: "People who smoke stink up the world for the rest of us so I'm in favor of a complete ban on smoking. Everywhere."

Matilda Price, assistant professor, mathematics: "It's reasonable not to allow smoking in classrooms and in public spaces, but I don't know why people who choose to smoke shouldn't be allowed to smoke in their offices. My office is my private space and what I do there is my business."

EXERCISE 3   Endings

Read the following public relations release:

"Flyway," a 15-foot steel sculpture on the grounds of the multi-million-dollar Nickelby Hall, will be unveiled today.

Gov. Barnaby Rudge and Dr. Ada Clare, president of the university, will be the main speakers at the ceremony, which will take place at noon.

The sculpture depicts 18 species of birds that pass over the university campus each spring and fall.

It is the work of Joe Willett of Prairie Village, Kan., and was commissioned for Nickelby Hall under a special program of the state's Center for Art in Public Places. The center funds art works in an amount up to one percent of the cost of new state buildings.

"Flyway" cost $16,000.

The birds on the sculpture include a tundra swan at the base with birds such as the bald eagle, Canada geese, the common night hawk rising above it.

Choose the best final paragraph for the story and justify your choice:

"Flyway" is a truly beautiful piece of work and one that should uplift the hearts of all who pass by.

"I wanted to blend the university and its environment, and to my mind the birds in their natural state also serve as symbols of the intellectual life," Willett said.

Two other pieces are also being considered for placement on the grounds of Nickleby Hall.

"I got a call from the architect last summer, a year ago, asking if I was interested in doing a sculpture," Willett said, "and fortunately I had the time to do it."

This program is one of the most imaginative the state has undertaken in many years, and university officials are grateful to benefit from it.

EXERCISE 4   **Sidebar**

As an assistant in the university's public relations office, you are assigned the job of interviewing Joe Willett for a sidebar about the sculptor that is to go with the release above. Construct a story out of these notes:

Willett was born in Prairie Village, Kan., 1960, went to Prairie grade school and Shawnee-Mission High School. Graduated, art, University of Kansas. Advanced study, Layton School of Art, Milwaukee. Returned and built a studio on grounds of his parents' home.

Sold first sculpture when in high school—bald eagle—to principal. Made specialty of birds.

"We had a birdbath in the back yard of our house—it's still there—and I used to sit for hours and watch the birds drinking from it, and one day I just started sketching them and trying to sculpt them."

Got MSU commission: "I had done a piece showing the birds of the Midwest for a small college in Missouri, and a story about it was in the Chronicle of Higher Education. Then I got a call from the architect last summer, a year ago, asking if I was interested in doing a sculpture, and fortunately I had the time to do it."

Spent three months studying detailed prints and anatomical drawings of native birds, another three months doing models, and six months constructing the piece.

Concept was most important: "I wanted to blend the university and its environment, and to my mind the birds in their natural state also serve as symbols of the intellectual life. At the university, the mind soars and dips and rides the air like birds, you know."

Says it's his favorite work. "But then, I always think the work I've just finished is my favorite."

Now working on bird sculpture for federal prison, Marion, Ill.

"I hope someday I might be considered to rank in sculpture as Audubon does in painting."

> **EXERCISE 5**   **Broadcast Stories**

Rewrite the four stories above for broadcast. Consider that you have the direct quotes on tape to use as audio actualities.

FOR FURTHER LEARNING

Theodore M. Bernstein. "Watch Your Language." Atheneum, 1965. When Bernstein was an assistant managing editor of the New York Times he occasionally distributed a mimeographed sheet called "Winners & Sinners," on which he noted examples of writing, both good and bad, that appeared in the newspaper. This is a compendium of some of that material. The chapter entitled "Storytelling" is especially useful.

Andre Fontaine. "The Art of Writing Nonfiction." Thomas Y. Crowell, 1974. Fontaine, a free-lance writer, discusses how rigorous reporting can be put in effective writing showcases by employing techniques once reserved for fiction.

John Hohenberg. "The Pulitzer Prize Story." Columbia University Press, 1959. Hohenberg has collected examples of stories that have won the Pulitzer Prize through the years. Prize-winning editorials, cartoons, and pictures are included. A second volume, "The Pulitzer Prize Story II," was published in 1980.

Louis L. Snyder and Richard B. Morris, editors. "A Treasury of Great Reporting." Simon and Schuster, 1949. This text belongs on every journalist's bookshelf.

Louis M. Starr. "Reporting the Civil War." Collier Books, 1962. Starr has woven many examples of news writing and reporting into his story of journalistic coverage of the Civil War.

Kendall J. Wills, editor. "The Pulitzer Prizes." Simon and Schuster, 1987. This annual series, beginning in 1987, reprints Pulitzer-Prize-winning news stories.

Incorporating Other People's Words

In this chapter you will learn:

+ Quotations are the words of a subject, so you must put in quotes only the words a source actually used.

+ Quotations differ significantly from paraphrases.

+ Quotations, used correctly, can give life to a story.

+ Sometimes a source's words should be quoted directly, and sometimes they should be paraphrased.

+ Quotes must be attributed to the source, and in a way that does not interfere with the story.

+ Various forms of attribution are punctuated differently.

+ Attribution in broadcast copy differs from attribution for print because of the nature of the media.

+ Special problems arise in quoting someone who uses derogatory racial terms or obscenities.

+ Dialect usually should be avoided.

THE REPORTER AND THE PSYCHOANALYST

Readers of The New Yorker magazine who worked their way through a two-part profile of Jeffrey Masson in December 1983 found a fascinating story of a psychoanalyst who had come to his profession after undergoing analysis himself, had served as director of the Sigmund Freud Archives, and had later become a critic of some of Freud's theories. Little could they have known that the profile, written by Janet Malcolm, would result in a legal argument and an ethical discussion.

Both centered on remarks that Malcolm attributed to Masson. Malcolm quoted Masson as saying he was "an intellectual gigolo" who wanted to turn the Freud Archives into "a place of sex, women, fun" and become known as "the greatest analyst who ever lived." He didn't say those things at all, Masson contended in a $10 million libel suit filed against Malcolm. And, he said, the fact that she put words in his mouth constituted actual malice.

The suit went up to the U.S. Supreme Court, then back to the trial court, Federal District Court in San Francisco. Justice Anthony Kennedy wrote the Court's decision. He said reporters must often alter quotes to get them into print, and the fact that a quote is altered is not proof of actual malice. But he said Masson presented enough evidence to require a jury to decide whether the quotes in question injured his reputation and whether Malcolm showed actual malice. Subsequently, a San Francisco jury decided Malcolm had altered some of what Masson had said and the quotes libeled him.

The ethical questions about doctored or fabricated quotations were put succinctly by Doreen Carvajal in Fine Line, a short-lived newsletter on journalism ethics: "How far can a writer stray from the words? And just how sacred are the sentences between quotation marks?" Publications and individual writers must answer those questions on the basis of their own guiding principles. They have a major stake in the discussion. But as the historian Gertrude Himmelfarb has pointed out, news audiences have a stake in it too, and they have assumed, at least until recently, "that direct quotations are indeed direct, unmediated by any interpreter."

In this chapter, we take a hard line and side with the reader. What's put between quotation marks is not just sacred but sacrosanct. How do you deal with the source who uses bad grammar or swears or who punctuates nearly every utterance with "like, I mean, you know?" As the B-movie interrogators always seem to say in soup-thick accents, "We haf vays!"

BASICS OF QUOTING

STUDY PREVIEW   The words of other people are indispens-
able to the news writer. Whether reporting a company president's speech or a
police officer's investigation, the writer relies on someone else's words to help
tell the story. Those words can support a point, make graphic a description, or
add drama to a story. But as the Malcolm case illustrates, writers must be concerned about the way they use the words.

Quotes and Paraphrases

A quotation, by definition, is the repetition of a source's words. Part of the discussion that swirled out of the Malcolm case revolved around whether quotations must always be the source's *exact* words. Some contend that quotes
should be cleaned up—"er" and "uh" and "ya know" vacuumed out of conversations, "ain't" scrubbed away, and obscenities and profanities flushed
down the journalistic drain.

On the other side of the argument is the Associated Press, whose stylebook
commands staffers: "Never alter quotations even to correct minor grammatical
errors or word usage." The AP does allow the use of ellipses to replace minor slips
of the tongue, "but even that should be done with extreme caution." The AP's Rene
J. Cappon underscored that rule in "The Word: An Associated Press Guide to Good
News Writing" when he wrote: "Like other facts, quotes are not subject to revision." Efforts to revise, Cappon warns, "are high crimes and misdemeanors."

The AP rule recognizes that a quotation is precisely that: a quotation. If a
president of the United States says, as a recent one did, "You see, there's some
fairly good fundamentals getting out there," reporters should not correct the
president's grammar or syntax, if they choose to use the statement. On the
other hand, they can use an indirect quotation, or paraphrase. That is, they can
provide the sense of what the president said in their own words: There are
signs the American economy is basically sound, the president said.

Quotation marks signal readers that they are reading a direct quotation,
the exact words of the source. If the quotation marks are not there, but the
writer has attributed the words to someone, then what is written is an indirect
quotation, a paraphrase. The paraphrase allows the writer to deal easily with
the words of sources who can't get out a sentence without interjecting barracks
language or the stumbling "like, I mean, you know."

What to Quote

Try this exercise sometime. Turn on a tape recorder during a lunchtime conversation or a dormitory bull session, then play it back. Chances are that what

was a perfectly clear conversation will come out on tape like a partially completed jigsaw puzzle. We often speak in broken phrases rather than complete sentences, and listeners fill in a great deal and show their understanding through facial expressions and nods of the head. Even when you play back the tape of an interview, in which a source is concentrating on making clear statements, the result may be something of a jumble—what Malcolm has called "tape-recorderese."

Rather than quote, then, experienced news writers find they can relay a source's thoughts more succinctly, precisely and clearly through paraphrasing. They use direct quotes only sparingly.

When is a direct quote preferable? For one thing, when the source's statement is particularly significant. Normally, if a source says "I'll go to Atlanta next week" or "I'll be going to Walla Walla," the statement is not worth a direct quote and can be paraphrased: Jones said he would go to Atlanta (or Walla Walla). But when, in the 1952 presidential campaign, in the midst of the Korean War, candidate Dwight D. Eisenhower said, "I will go to Korea," the words made such a striking political statement that they were quoted in stories and headlines. Similarly, when Chicago Mayor Richard M. Daley told police, "Shoot to kill," if they saw looters during the riots of 1968, his words were so shocking that Chicagoans needed to see them quoted to believe them.

Quotes can also be used to convey the uniqueness of a personality or the drama of a situation. Jack Wardlaw of the New Orleans Times-Picayune realized no paraphrase could have captured as dramatically as the exact words the exchange between the surviving candidates for the Louisiana governorship when they came face to face the day after the primary election. As Wardlaw told it, Edwin Edwards was being interviewed outside a Louisiana Superdome suite when David Duke happened by.

> "You ran a better second than I thought you would," Edwards told Duke.
>
> "I'm ready for a debate whenever you are," Duke said.
>
> "How about 6 o'clock tonight?" Edwards shot back, as onlookers roared with laughter.

Quotes should also be used if a source has said something especially clever or poignant. Craig Wilson led his Page 1 feature for a USA Today Thanksgiving Day issue with an excerpt from a telephone interview. As you read it, imagine listening to Stella Rentz as she told Wilson about her stuffing and the meal at her daughter's home. Note the few brief quotations he picked from the interview and how he interwove them with paraphrasing for dramatic effect. Note also how paraphrasing gave him license to embellish what Rentz told him.

Stella Rentz of Poughkeepsie, N.Y., is a good mother.

Or at least she thought she was, until last Thanksgiving. She's still not sure where she went wrong.

For decades, she made her famed holiday dressing. Onions, celery, butter and parsley, with juices from the giblets and liver seasoning the bread crumbs.

Her family loved it, and when it appeared every November, all seemed right with the world once again. It would be served down through the generations.

But last Thanksgiving she went to her daughter's home in Manhattan and politely ate the dressing placed before her.

"She prepared a different kind of stuffing. Different from mine," says Rentz. She can't remember what it was.

She does remember one thing, however: "No one liked it." You could hear her smile over the phone.

"It was a pecan cornbread stuffing," confesses her daughter Joan. "Very dry."

So it's back to Poughkeepsie and Rentz's time-honored, don't-mess-with-this-recipe dressing.

Direct quotes can lend authenticity to a story and enhance its credibility. For that reason, John Wildermuth and Susan Sward of the San Francisco Chronicle let an official speculate on the chances of finding survivors from two Navy planes that collided off the California coast. His direct statement underscored the hopelessness of the situation better than the reporters could have by paraphrasing him:

> "I think we have to be realistic here," said Howard, who is spokesman for the air forces of the Pacific Fleet. "It is very cold out there. We're talking about what apparently is a midair collision ... I would say it would be very grim."

Where to Quote

Quotations can be used almost anywhere in a story, as you can see in the stories above, but usually they are used in such a way as to support a general statement in the text.

Quotations are frequently used to end a story, and for an ending a writer may select a quote that summarizes or punctuates the story. Adria Bernardi, for example, writing on an English newspaper in the Womanews section of the Chicago Tribune, ended her story with this summary quote:

MODERN INTERVIEWERS. Print reporters, as well as radio and television news people, now use tape recorders to supplement their handwritten notes in conducting interviews and in getting news conference statements. They want to be sure that they quote exactly what their sources say.   (Mark Cardwell/Reuters/The Bettmann Archive)

Other journalists say that issues important to women are covered in general news and features pages and that a woman's page represents a throwback and a "ghetto," Chunn says. She disagrees.

"My answer is always that if you don't call it a women's page, or if you don't have a page like that, then I think that women's issues aren't covered in the paper properly—because on papers the majority of people at the top and in editing positions are men, and I think you would lose that voice if you had a general features page. You would lose that focus."

Similarly, an annual report story on the Retix company's computer internetworking products ended with a quote:

Founder David Anderson emphasizes AC&C's dedication to customer satisfaction: "To the greatest extent possible, we protect our customers' investments by recommending networking hardware and architectures that provide conformance to industry standards, flexibility, and expandability. Retix Internetworking Products, and especially the new RX 7000, satisfy these critical requirements and provide the foundation for future growth."

Attribution

Much of what the reporter puts in a story can be verified and does not need attribution. Miami Herald police reporter Edna Buchanan made the point graphically in "The Corpse Had a Familiar Face":

> Take a bullet-riddled body lying in plain view in the middle of a shopping center. I saw it and so did 30 people who heard the shots, saw the victim fall, and watched the killer run, smoking gun in hand. I say that we can simply report, "He was shot." We don't have to attribute that information to authorities by writing, "He was shot, police said."

On the other hand, anything in a news story that is not readily verifiable should be tagged to a source through attribution. Here are some guidelines to follow.

Opinion or information that isn't readily verifiable should be attributed:

> A medical waste incinerator is needed and would have to be built somewhere else if it isn't allowed in Tulsa, a state official said Tuesday.

Attribution of opinion applies to lead sentences and the copy that follows. Otherwise, the opinion sounds like the reporter's, and that is editorializing. A reporter stands behind any unattributed information.

Because attributives clutter, use them only when necessary. An exception: Almost all stories should have one attributive to establish authority beyond the reporter's even if all information is readily verifiable.

The attribution usually comes at the end of a sentence, the shirttail of the sentence, because the assertion is the most important element, not the attribution.

> Mayo Clinic scientists have discovered the gene that causes arthritis in mice, an early but significant step toward possible cures for arthritis, multiple sclerosis, lupus and related crippling diseases in people, **a clinic spokesman said Monday**.

Exceptions include accusations:

> **Wilson State College's 1989 valedictorian charged** Tuesday that Academic Vice President Marty George is "opening the floodgates of mediocrity" by changing admissions standards.

Another exception is when the source is significant:

> **Mayor Eric Dorn said** Monday that giving the city manager more budgetary authority was an undemocratic proposal which he won't support.

Occasional mid-sentence attribution can add variety:

> The accident, **Lopez testified**, could have been prevented had mechanics checked the flaps.

Active verb forms are best for attribution, but passive forms can avoid clutter if the source is clearly implied:

> Smithson **was charged** with the May 9 burglary.

However, once a source is established, putting the attribution first becomes a distraction for the reader.

Reverse attribution can be effective if not overdone. One place to use it is where you have a long title separating the attributive from the statement, as in this example:

> "Mann will deliver on time," **Marche,** the director of the shoe company, **said.**

Reversing the attribution makes the sentence less awkward.

> "Mann will deliver on time," **said Marche,** director of the shoe company.

Avoid attributing a statement to more than one person:

> The administration is not ready to compromise on the tax issue, White House **officials** said.

The wording makes it sound as if the White House officials said it at the same time, chanting the statement in unison.

For the sake of clarity, a good rule to follow is "one source per paragraph, one attribution per source." This paragraph illustrates what happens when the rule is broken:

> "The river spilled over the bank and covered the house in the blink of an eye," **Sheriff Jones** said. "What a catastrophe," he said. "It was awful. I just couldn't believe it," **Sarah Hawkins,** a neighbor said. Another neighbor, **Eloise Hart,** said, "I looked away for an instant, and when I looked back everything was gone."

The number of quotations and their attributions, all lumped together, can be confusing for the reader, and can confuse the writer trying to keep them all straight. To avoid confusion give a separate paragraph to each quote.

Double attribution is unnecessary and wordy:

> "The river spilled over the bank and covered the house in the blink of an eye," **Sheriff Jones** said. "What a catastrophe," **he said.**

Keep it simple and spare by dropping "he said."

Attributives

"Said" is a special word to journalists. It pegs a statement to a source unmistakably and unobtrusively. That is, readers are so used to seeing it they know it signals attribution, but it does not stand out and stop them. Their attention remains on what was said, not how it was said. To skilled news writers, it is the best attributive.

There are occasions when the way in which something is said becomes important. "Whispered," "sang," "whimpered," "screeched," "cried"—even "screamed" —are all good words if they are accurate. But they must be used sparingly.

> "Coach, I'd like to play for you," announced his visitor, who stood a quite-sizable 6-11.
> "Yeah, right," Floyd muttered aloud.
> "This has got to be a joke," he thought silently.

While individuals may announce words or mutter them, no one can smile words, laugh them, grin them or frown them. It is nonsensical to use such verbs as attributives with direct quotation. Words can, however, be said with a smile and said laughingly, and someone can speak and frown at the same time.

"According to" has a slight connotation, as if the writer has some doubt. If that is the case, use it—but only in paraphrasing. Because "according to" signals a tinge of doubt about whatever is attributed, it does not make sense to use it with a direct quotation.

Punctuation

Attributives should be set off with commas, whether they are before, after or in the middle of a quoted sentence:

> "After one day, a wet bag of grass smells like silage," he said.

> He said, "They don't really need any more surprises."

> "The democracies established there," she said, "are very fragile and can be easily hurt."

You may use a colon to add emphasis to pre-assertion attributives:

> Johnson said: "Let's win this one for Joey."

A colon is best for a reverse attributive ahead of a quotation:

> Said Perot: "Absolutely not, never ever."

With multi-sentence quotations, the attributive usually is best after the first sentence:

> "Our countries are dangerously slid-
> ing into a political, economic and
> security vacuum," **she said.** "The old,
> imposed political, economic and secu-
> rity ties have collapsed, yet new ones
> are developing slowly and with
> difficulty."

When a multi-sentence quotation is broken into several paragraphs, each paragraph begins with quotation marks, but closing quotation marks appear only at the end of the quotation:

> Byron explained it this way:
> "The man jumped on the bus, pulled a gun on the driver, and demanded to be taken to the Igloo drive-in.

> "It was frightening, especially when the guy pumped three shots through the windshield.
> "The woman next to me fainted."

Fragmentary quotations require no special punctuation:

> Smith said there has been "a pattern
> of indiscriminate shootings in El Paso's
> neighborhoods."

But avoid linking a full sentence to a fragment within the same quotation marks:

> The question, the drag racer said, was
> whether "to go full bore. We didn't
> know whether the 389 hemi could take
> it."

This version is an improvement:

> The question, the drag racer said, was
> whether "to go full bore."
> "We didn't know whether the 389
> hemi could take it," she said.

Or better still:

> The question was whether "to go full bore," the drag racer said. "We didn't know whether the 389 hemi could take it."

Commas and periods normally go inside the quotation marks, as shown above. Colons and semicolons go outside:

> According to Marlowe, these were among the "many mistakes the party made": failing to hold open selections, selecting weak candidates and taking extreme positions on the issues.

Question marks go inside the closing quotation mark only if the quoted material itself constitutes a question:

> "Do you take the position that every misquote gives rise to an inference of actual malice?" Justice O'Connor asked.

If the quoted material is part of a question, the question mark goes outside the closing quotation marks.

> Did she ask whether they would be "wimps forever"?

When quoting someone quoting someone else, use single quotation marks for the interior quotation:

> "He can talk, but it's disconnected," Lawton said. "You'll say to him, 'What did you do last night?' And he'll say, 'My friend has a new pair of shoes.' "

Try to avoid quotations within quotations within quotations. They can confuse readers. If you do use quotations within quotations, be sure to have the proper number and type of quotation marks when you end:

> "The place fell silent," Gordon said, "when the chief quoted Reagan, 'Again let us "do it for the Gipper." ' "

QUOTES ON THE AIR

STUDY PREVIEW   Radio and television listeners have a need for special signals so that they have no doubt about whether a statement is a quote and who said it. To help them out, broadcast writers pay special attention to attribution and verbal quotation marks.

Attribution

Attributive phrases are not the shirttail of a quotation in broadcast writing. Most of the time they must come ahead of the quote so that the listener knows a source is speaking, not just the reporter or anchor. This lead would be fine for print but not for broadcast:

> President Clinton is playing politics with the crime issue, **a Republican senator charged today.**

The problem is that a listener may tune out before getting to the attribution, and without the attribution the statement can sound like an editorial rather than a news story. For broadcast, the lead should be written this way:

> **A Senate Republican says** the President doesn't have the votes to win passage of the bill.

Punctuation

Readers have quotation marks to signal quotes. Radio and television listeners must rely on verbal roadsigns, and there are many variations. The simplest, though often overused, is "quote," "unquote." Here are some other possibilities:

> The president said, **quoting here**, "I'd like to see the cash registers ring at Christmastime."

> The president told reporters he wants to see Americans buying more. **Mr. Clinton's words now**, "It would be very good for the economy."

> Asked whether Americans should be buying more on credit, Mr. Clinton said, **in these words**, "That should be a decision made by individuals."

Additional possibilities:

> Waite urged his former captors to find **what he called** "peaceful, humane and civilized ways" of resolving Middle East problems.

> Sutherland said hostage Terry Anderson is no longer chained to a wall but he is in a room **Sutherland described as** having "very little fresh air and no daylight whatsoever."

SOME PITFALLS IN QUOTING

STUDY PREVIEW   Just as good drivers know to slow down when they encounter hazardous conditions, savvy writers know to beware of certain usages, especially if they have read their newsroom's stylebook. The hairpin curves of journalistic usage normally forbid obscenities and vulgarities, derogatory words referring to race or nationality, sex, and dialect or vernacular terms. Reporters also know never to pass off the exact words of others as their own.

Derogatory Terms

Many persons the world over, especially the uneducated, are contemptuous of, and even hate, peoples of other nationalities and other races, and they express their contempt in a wide range of derogatory terms. Such terms are not used in polite society, and reputable news organizations avoid using them. The general rule is that derogatory terms for nationalities and races should be used only in direct quotes, and then only when essential to the story.

Dialect

Dialect is a peculiarity in pronunciation or syntax, like a twang or drawl of a particular region or the accent of an ethnic group. Novelists make use of dialect when they consider it to be appropriate. Movie and TV script writers use it. Remember "We haf vays!" But writers of non-fiction generally avoid dialect because outside of groups which share a dialect, it is considered substandard, even illiterate, and citing dialect diverts audience attention from what was said to how it was said, which usually is gratuitous.

The rule is simple: Change pronunciation peculiarities into standard English. Following that rule, you would not write, "I'm a'go'in' to town fir uh spell." Instead you would write, "I'm going to town for a spell."

Similarly, you should paraphrase syntax peculiarities. Jones might say, "I called June, and I'm going shopping with," but the good news writer would write it: Jones said he called June and decided to go shopping with her.

In rare situations you may judge that dialect is essential to a story. In such instances try, first, to let the reader know that the speaker spoke in dialect, but without actually reproducing the peculiarities of expression. For example: With his Cockney clip, Dillard snapped back, "I was onto it at once."

If you must cite dialect, spell words phonetically, use apostrophes for missing words and sounds, and be consistent in spelling the same words in the same way each time you use them: "Ain't ya fum Nuh Joysey too?" he asked.

Otherwise, it is best to follow the advice of William Strunk Jr. and E. B. White in "The Elements of Style": "Do not use dialect unless you are a devoted student of the tongue you hope to reproduce."

Vernacular

Be careful with vernacular terms that have not received wide recognition. In Milwaukee, everybody knows what a bubbler is. But a listener in Florida likely would have no idea that it is a water fountain. What is a neutral ground in New Orleans is a median strip in Kansas City. And the Bostonian's frappe is a milkshake in most other places. If a source uses such a term, paraphrase it or give the more common meaning with the regional term.

With foreign words, it is best simply to give the translations of common terms. A reporter writing about land reform in Mexico might wish to cite the revolutionary war cry of Emiliano Zapata, "tierra y libertad," but that would add little to the story. It would be enough to say "land and liberty."

On the other hand, it would be important to use the term "ejido," the specific name for parcels of farmland, since reform has been aimed at eliminating the ejido system. The word can be translated easily: "The land is broken into collective societies called 'ejidos,'" or, "The land is parceled into 'ejidos,' collective farms." When the word is used in a quotation later, the reader will know what it means. It is always helpful to give the pronunciation: "ejidos (pronounced ay-HEE-dohs)."

Offensive Language

In his biography of Red Smith, Ira Berkow reports that the great sports writer tried often to get the phrase "son of a bitch" into the New York Times. Berkow quotes Howard Pincus, then a Times copy editor, who told him Smith made one pass at it in writing an anecdote about a sports editor who had been transferred out of

JOCK TALK. The sportswriter and columnist Red Smith spent his professional life listening to the language of locker rooms. Given the strictures of newspaper style, however, he could not use the saltier expressions he heard—even though alert copy editors caught him trying from time to time. News organizations generally avoid printing language that is obscene, vulgar, or derogatory to a person's race or nationality.   (The Bettmann Archive)

New York to Cleveland, where one night he was driving in a blinding snowstorm. Another car came alongside and the driver shouted, "Excuse me, pal, how do you get out of town?" The sports editor, according to Smith, replied, "You silly son of a bitch, if I knew, do you think I'd be here?"

Pincus told Smith that the term couldn't be used in the Times, and while Smith was mad—"Jesus Christ, when the hell is the Gray Lady going to wake up and learn the way language is today?" he asked—Pincus believed he knew all along it would not get in. So, Berkow wrote, "Though the strength of the story demanded 'son of a bitch,' the story ran with the watered down phrase 'silly ass.'"

Few newspapers would have printed Red Smith's anecdote. The AP stylebook, in fact, cautions writers not to use obscenities, profanities or vulgarities in stories "unless they are part of direct quotations and there is a compelling reason for them." Even then, individual publications—like the New York Times—have their own rules about the use of such language. Some accept Smith's notion that because obscenities or vulgarities are used more commonly in everyday speech, they can be used in print. Others avoid such language by paraphrasing to omit offensive terms.

Some publications censor profanity through various disguises, even though many journalists consider the disguises silly. Disguises include dropping vowels; using just the first letter followed by dashes, asterisks or an underline; inserting ellipses or dingbats (@$%!*&, as in the comic strips); falsifying the word ("silly ass"); or eliminating the word altogether.

Writers should ask themselves whether the profanity is necessary to the story. What do the deleted expletives add to these quotes?

> "We had a lot of injuries this year, and that put us in deep ————," the coach said.

> "These ———— tax assessors have been ———— us over long enough," Jones said, his voice rising.

In both instances, the intimated profanities add nothing of substance, although in the second instance they certainly show that Jones was angry. Both could be rewritten in such a way that the reader misses nothing essential:

> The coach blamed the team's performance on injuries.

> Jones' voice rose and he punctuated his remarks with profanity.

References to specific sexual acts can also be offensive to readers, especially the street names for them, and it doesn't make any difference whether they are spoken on a sidewalk or in a courtroom. It's best to avoid them. Broadcast journalists should be especially concerned about quoting language that might be offensive to the sensibilities of individuals in the audience because their audience can be so varied at any one time, and someone who wishes not to hear offensive language, or a child, has no chance to shut off the set.

Plagiarism

Plagiarism, plain and simple, is passing off the work of others as one's own. A combination of stealing and lying, plagiarism is, like both of those practices, universally condemned. Chances are that your school's catalog or bulletin contains a statement defining plagiarism and spelling out the consequences. An F in a course or even expulsion are common penalties. The penalty in the workplace is termination—and worse. As Albert Hunt, Washington bureau chief of the Wall Street Journal, put it in an editorial: "Purposeful plagiarism is one of the cardinal sins of journalism from which reporters can never recover their credibility."

CHAPTER WRAP-UP

Quoting a source's words is a handy way to show the reader how a source speaks, thereby giving life to the source. A person's choice of words and the way in which they are arranged can give the reader a glimpse of the individual's personality. Quotes can also give a story authenticity and, therefore, credibility. They can be used for dramatic effect. Whatever the purpose of the quotes, readers expect that the words they see between quotation marks (or hear between the broadcaster's spoken clues to quotations) are the words the source actually spoke, in the order in which they were spoken. If reporters cannot quote those words exactly, whether because their sources are inarticulate or ungrammatical or speaking obscenities, the source's statements should be paraphrased. And when a source has said something quotable, the most effective way to attribute it is to use the word "said."

STUDY QUESTIONS

1. Explain why the words between quotation marks should be the exact words spoken by a source?
2. What can quotations add to a story?
3. What is the difference between a quotation and a paraphrase?
4. When is it appropriate to paraphrase?
5. When should attribution be used? When is it unnecessary to use attribution?
6. Why should no more than one source be quoted in a paragraph?
7. Where should attributives be placed in a sentence?
8. What are some appropriate words of attribution? What are some inappropriate words
9. Why should good writers avoid the use of dialect and vernacular?
10. How should obscenities or vulgarities be handled?

PUTTING YOUR LEARNING TO WORK

EXERCISE 1   Using Quotes

Here is a transcript from an interview with Geoffrey Quatrain, a poet and associate professor of English at Middle State University. He has an M.F.A. in poetry that he earned at Petitfours College 15 years ago. Since then he has taught poetry writing at Middle State. Use the material to write a profile of about 500 words. In the story, demonstrate your ability to use both quotation and paraphrase.

Q: I understand English wasn't your original major?

Quatrain: No, it wasn't. First I was an engineering major. I had a cousin in college who was in engineering. But once I got into the college-level calculus and physics and with my poor high-school background and unscientific mind, I found it tough, so I dropped out of engineering and went into business because I didn't know what else to go into.

Q: How did you finally become interested in English?

Quatrain: I tried English as a major, thinking I would be a secondary teacher, but being rebellious at the time, I found the education courses ridiculously juvenile and dropped them when I'd take them. So I knew I couldn't finish this English major either.

Q: So what did you do then?

Quatrain: After three years in college, I became so discontented with my possible career choices I quit college and joined the Army for two years. Once I got out, I went back and finished my business degree.

Q: Why didn't you stick with a career in business?

Quatrain: I guess I've always had an anti-capitalistic and anti-materialistic view. I've always been uncomfortable about going into business, but I think now some of my anti-business feelings were rather immature and silly.

Q: Did you ever get a job in business?

Quatrain: The first job I got when I graduated was writing commercials for a television station. But one day I realized that one could be a college teacher without taking education courses. As soon as I discovered this, I decided that I was going back to finish my English degree. I don't think it ever crossed my mind prior to that time to teach at the college level.

Q: What are some of the things you like about teaching?

Quatrain: My loves in life, as far as subject matter is concerned, happen to be literature and writing, and I consider myself privileged to have the opportunity to meet with young people and talk about the thing I care so much about.

It's exciting when a student comes back a few years later and says, "I really liked that class."

Another thing I like about teaching is that what I'm teaching is important. You get to know yourself and think about your place in the world.

Q: What is your favorite class?

Quatrain: Poetry writing.

Q: Why?

Quatrain: There are a couple of reasons. Poetry is my favorite literary genre, and I prefer teaching poetry to other genres.

Poetry writing enables me to teach reading and writing. It combines both of my interests in the particular genres I like best. I think I learned how to write poetry myself through trial and error, and I can pass things on to my students.

One more thing I like about teaching this course is it doesn't tend to be all English majors. It's a mix of a number of different majors.

Q: When did you begin to express an interest in poetry?

Quatrain: I used to avoid poetry in college because I was afraid of it and found it difficult. Then in my senior year in college I took a poetry course as an elective. I had a teacher, Dexter Green, who really taught me about reading poetry, fiction and drama.

Q: What are some of your favorite subjects to write about?

Quatrain: I've written about a lot of different things. My heritage is one of the areas I like to explore in my poetry.

But I also like to respond to what my life is like now with marriage, parenthood, and what it's like to be approaching one's old age.

Q: What do you mean by "heritage"?

Quatrain: Well, I've written about where I grew up in Wheat, a small farming community in northwestern Nebraska. I've written poems about the people that live around there, the landscape. I've written about a great-grandfather and about grandparents.

Q: How often do you sit down and write?

Quatrain: I admire some of my colleagues here who are more disciplined and regular writers than I am. I tend to write in spurts. What I tend to do is jot down, on little slips of paper that accumulate all over the place, ideas for poems I have or images that strike me.

Q: How many poems have you published?

Quatrain: About 50 poems all together. Thirty were in various magazines and 20 were published in a book.

Q: Do you plan to publish any more?

Quatrain: Oh yeah. Whenever I get around to writing and produce any poems I feel satisfied with, I send them off to a little magazine. I would hope some day I would have enough accumulated that I could send off a full-length manuscript.

Q: Who is your favorite poet?

Quatrain: It's hard to pick. I'd rather say who are my half dozen favorite poets, and even that I find difficult. Ever since I first discovered him, I've always liked Wallace Stevens for his philosophical positions. He's interested in relationships between language and reality and how we know what we know.

William Butler Yeats. The thing I like about him is how he developed and changed as a poet and never stood still. All through his life, he continued to develop and change and respond to historical times as well as respond to what it's like to be alive in the world.

Q: What are some of the things you would like to do in the next few years?

Quatrain: I would like to travel. I'm possibly thinking about applying to teach at Minnesota State University in Akita, Japan.

EXERCISE 2   Quoting in Style

Rewrite the following story to make it conform to the principles of quotation discussed in this chapter:

Between $30,000-$45,000 is collected each semester from student ID fees, stated Director of Auxiliary Services Otis Ormonde.

The fee that students pay each semester to validate student ID cards is put into a budget for ID services, Ormonde told me in an interview.

"That money goes to pay for the computers that run the ID system, pay the salary of the person who maintains the ID system, repairs to the computers, etc.," Campus Dining Director Sally Carrol claimed.

"Campus Dining is responsible for that budget, as they are for budgets of all the Campus Dining area. The only reason they were assigned that responsibility is because of location. It's in the Campus Dining facility, so they monitor the expenses and income of that operation. The money is left in that budget during the course of the year, July through June. All expenses related to that area are taken out of it. At the end of the year, there's money left over to put in a reserve account with other Auxiliary funds. In other words, the Auxiliary operations are merged at the end of the year. All of the monies from all of the Auxiliary departments are merged together. The net difference, some areas will lose money, some areas will make money. If there is a net surplus, that money is put in a reserve account," Ormonde detailed.

The fee to validate student ID cards, like any other fees they pay, goes to the particular service provided, Carrol explained patiently.

The ID service is an auxiliary operation at MSU, Ormonde said, and "auxiliary operations do not get any funding from the state legislature. The sole source of funding is the student services the Auxiliary Services provide—the payment of those services by the students."

"So each year, at the beginning of the new fiscal year, the Auxiliary Services begin with zero money, and as the year goes on, the sales of various products and services, such as housing, food, bookstore supplies or rent the Auxiliary services receive from the bookstore," Ormonde told me. "The ID service fee is how all of the bills that are incurred cost, which includes labor, insurance, interest on the debts and the debts themselves. So all of the areas that are considered by this university as Auxiliary enterprises are supposed to survive from year to year simply on what the university designates as 'the revenues that they generate' and they are supposed to 'maintain the costs within those revenues.' The ID fee is the same thing, isn't it," Ormonde asked?

The Auxiliary Services does not have any money from the state. For any of the services they provide the students they charge the students. They then operate those particular services within the money they get, Ormonde pointed out.

"That's why there is a validation fee each semester, because the cost of the card is a one-time thing. It's $1.50 or $2 to print the card and maintain it," Ormonde claimed.

Stated Ormonde: "But the maintenance of the files, the employment of the people to run the system, to keep up with where students eat their meals, if there are any problems, all of these things require money. And the ID fee goes to help support these activities".

EXERCISE 3   Quoting for Broadcast

Rewrite the story in Exercise 2, Quoting in Style, for broadcast.

FOR FURTHER LEARNING

Gertrude Himmelfarb. "The Right to Misquote." Commentary (April 1991): 31–34. Himmelfarb discusses aspects of the Janet Malcolm-Jeffrey Masson case.

G. Michael Killenberg and Rob Anderson. "What Is a Quote? Practical, Rhetorical, and Ethical Concerns for Journalists." Journal of Mass Media Ethics, 8, No. 1 (1995): 37–54. This is an excellent examination by two journalism professors of the problems of quoting.

Adrienne Lehrer. "Between Quotation Marks." Journalism Quarterly, 66, No. 4 (Winter 1989): 902–6; 941. After determining that many newspaper quotations are inaccurate, the author suggests ways to improve accuracy.

Mitchell Stephens and Eliot Frankel. "All the Obscenity That's Fit to Print." Washington Journalism Review (April 1981): 15–19. Stephens and Frankel discuss the ways in which obscenity and profanity are dealt with by the news media.

CHAPTER 7

Making Your Writing Likeable

In this chapter you will learn:

- ✦ News writing is a highly intellectual and creative undertaking which reflects the writer's personal values.

- ✦ The writer's presence should remain in the shadows of a news story so the subject has the fullest possible attention of the audience.

- ✦ The news writing style should be friendly and conversational.

- ✦ News stories are best when they have an informal tone that does not undermine the authoritativeness of the writer.

- ✦ Upbeat word choices and writing help keep audience interest.

- ✦ News writers should be sensitive to how labels and other identifying words are perceived.

FATHER TEUFEL'S LESSON

Lee Teufel, a journalist turned priest, loved relating lessons from his younger days as a reporter. He took special delight in telling his Gonzaga University students that writing was "putting your brains on paper." It was a scary concept for aspiring journalists who never had thought about writing in quite that way.

Father Teufel's point was that journalists have to muster all the intellectual and creative resources at their command for every story they write. Further, he would tell his wide-eyed students, every story is a test. Hundreds, perhaps thousands, even millions of people in a mass audience will be able to keep score on how well the writer's mind works.

Father Teufel's point was well taken. By its nature, writing news is a creative act. Journalists, like artists and composers, begin with a blank sheet of paper, and the story that results is their intellect on display.

This chapter will help you find ways to put your brains on paper so you look as bright as you really are, and so your writing is likeable, effective, and true to the personal values you bring to your work.

CREATIVITY AND PERSONAL VALUES

STUDY PREVIEW   News writing is a creative activity, but creativity cannot get in the way of the story you're telling. The presence of the writer's technique, as in all writing, should be subtle. Just as journalists don't flaunt their creativity, neither do they flaunt their personal values, even though their values are present in every story.

Creativity in News Work

In spot news, a reporter's creative energy is focused on finding good sources for the latest information. Imaginative and creative writing are good, but the focus is on gathering information.

Deadlines put a premium on quickly telling what happened. Cleverness and poetic touches can slow the process. Worse, stylistic flourishes can obscure the telling of what happened, especially if done in haste.

Even so, writing spot news is a creative more than a formulaic activity. Consider these different treatments for the lead on the same event, each reflecting an emphasis that flowed from each writer's individual application of intellect to the facts at hand:

From the Associated Press:

> ORLANDO, Fla.—Squirming and chewing a gum drop, a 12-year-old boy went to court Thursday seeking a "divorce" from his parents in a case that could help give children more protection against parental abuse.

From the Wall Street Journal:

> A 12-year-old boy went to court Thursday, seeking a "divorce" from his parents.

From the New York Times:

> A 12-year-old boy who wants to choose who will be his parents began a trial that will substantially alter the legal rights of children and broaden the debate over the structure of contemporary American families.

Reporters usually have more time with depth stories than spot stories to concentrate on their writing, but never is there a license to embellish in ways that get in the way of telling the story. News audiences are not trapped. They have choices. With a morning newscast that misses the mark, the listener tunes to another station. With a bad newspaper story, the reader's eyes dart elsewhere on the page.

This chapter suggests many ways to use your intelligence and creativity to improve the creative aspects of both spot and depth stories.

A Window to the Soul

News writing involves putting not just your brains on paper but also your values. Writing is a self-revealing activity, sometimes unwittingly. Consider the advertising copywriter who employs sexist stereotypes in a billboard. Her insensitive word choices say much about her, either as a sexist herself or someone willing to stoop to sexism to make a pitch. In the same sense, every word written by the pioneer environmentalist Rachel Carson bespoke her commitment to saving the earth from human ravages. The sincerity of Billy Graham, Robert Schuler and many religious leaders is obvious in their writing. In the same way, the personal values of news writers are evident in their word choices and emphasis.

While personal values are inherent in every story, careful news writers avoid letting their values get in the way of a story being effective with an audience. In this sentence from a radio story, the newscaster's words smacked of male chauvinism, which diverted the attention of gender-sensitive listeners away from the news to the newscaster's sexism:

> Three Stanford University students—two girls and a man—were abducted from a research station in Africa.

Here is a soft lead by a newscaster who seemed somehow to have missed the sorrow that people feel about the loss of a life, especially a child's:

> Bang! Bang! Lead in the head, now she is dead. A 12-year-old west suburban girl was killed yesterday when her four-year-old brother was playing with a handgun. The gun went off and . . .

When the communist leader of North Vietnam, Ho Chi Minh, died, one radio reporter chose to begin a newscast in a hearty Santa Claus voice:

> Ho! Ho! Ho! Ho Chi Minh is dead.

The United States was at war with North Vietnam at the time, and Ho was widely vilified in this country, but the writer's attempt at cleverness revealed an irreverence about death that was out of tune with American values that flow from a Jewish and Christian tradition.

The same problem occurred when a sniper killed 13 people and injured 34 others from a tower at the University of Texas at Austin before police killed him. In a misdirected attempt at dark humor, one journalist cast the news like a sports score:

> Texas Sniper 13, Police 1.

TELLING THE STORY UNOBTRUSIVELY

STUDY PREVIEW   News audiences are interested in what is happening, not the writer's flair. To keep their presence in the story as minimal as possible, news writers use numerous techniques to let the news have center stage.

Writing in Third Person

Think about your favorite novelists. Whether Margaret Mitchell or Ernest Hemingway or Danielle Steel, you like them because they tell wonderful stories. Their skill as writers is important but only in a supporting role. It is their stories that attract readers by the million. It is the same with news. People read news not because of the writer, whose skill is presumed, but because news is interesting stuff. The challenge in writing news is telling stories in ways to stir maximum audience interest while being true to the subject. News writers, like novelists, are successful when they are invisible, with the story itself holding the attention of the reader or viewer or listener.

Letting the subject shine is difficult. Natural human egoism is to tell stories with the first-person "I," but this tendency works against effective story telling because the teller is getting in the way of the story. The result is a counter-productive diversion of audience attention from the story to the writer. Also, first person can come across as unflattering egocentricity. For these reasons, news almost always is told in third person.

Misguided Variations on First Person

Besides using outright first-person words like "I," "me" and "we," a writer can needlessly intrude into a story in other distracting ways. Knowing the liabilities of first person, some beginning news writers substitute the third-person "one" for "I." The result, however, is stilted. There are alternatives. Compare these sentences:

Egotistic first person:

> **I** came over the pass and saw the village in smouldering ruins from the air attack.

Veiled first person:

> Coming over the pass, **one** sees the village in smouldering ruins from the air attack.

Third person:

> The village was in smouldering ruins from the air attack.

FIRST PERSON. In most news, writers avoid telling the story in first person to help keep the audience's attention focused on the event or issue being reported, but there are exceptions. When science reporter William Lawrence witnessed the explosion of an atomic bomb against the Japanese city of Nagasaki in World War II, his exclusive eyewitness account justified first person. In fact, the poignancy of his story was in his personal reaction to the historic event.   (The Bettmann Archive, Wide World Photos)

Another usually misguided tactic is to use the second-person "you." Like "one," it too is a veiled egotistical "I":

> **You** come over the pass and see the village in smouldering ruins from the air attack.

Sometimes, "you" can be a clumsy attempt to put the audience in the writer's shoes.

Eyewitness Stories

While first person generally should be avoided, it has a place. In 1887 when Nellie Bly went undercover to report on abuses at a New York asylum, the poignancy of her account would have been lost had she told it other than in first person. Without first person, science reporter William Lawrence could not have relayed his awe at seeing the atomic bomb explode over Nagasaki from a B-29 bomber.

But even on those rare occasions when the reporter's presence belongs in the story, try to downplay it. In an interview story, for example, the reporter's presence can be skillfully incorporated without seeming to be either intrusive self-praise or personal back-slapping, or stealing valuable time or space. Consider the writer's blatant first-person intrusions in these examples cited by writing critic Bill Earls:

> Over dinner, the senator said to **me** . . .
>
> When **I** interviewed Bruceton, he said . . .
>
> So-and-so told **me** that . . .

If it's important to note that statements originated in an interview, Earls suggests a subtle approach, like these hardly intrusive yet colorful hints at the reporter's presence:

> Madonna poked her veal with a fork and said . . .
>
> Quayle smiled, recalling his guard duty. . . .
>
> Hussein loosened his tie . . .

Letting the interviewee shine can be done as simply as:

> In an interview, Gore said . . .

Avoiding a Superior Stance

The veiled self becomes its most obnoxious when the Latin "sic" is added to a quotation after a grammatical error. At its worst, "sic" smacks of arrogance:

> Dear Editor:
>   I read your article and it stinked [sic].
> Please cancel my subscription.

In a news story, "sic" in a quotation can come across as a snotty intrusion by the writer. It's like poking somebody in the ribs: "Hey, look, he don't talk English good."

Almost always, it is better to paraphrase the quotation to fix the error. If the exact words uttered are so important that they must be quoted, you may have no choice but to use "sic." Such situations are unusual.

BEING CONVERSATIONAL

STUDY PREVIEW   Just because news is important doesn't mean that news writing should be stuffy. Skillful news writing requires finding ways to be both authoritative and conversational.

Writing "People Talk"

"Well, chums, here's the latest scoop." No reporter would start a story that way. So casual a tone would vaporize the audience's faith in the reporter's authority. The other extreme is formality that borders on pomposity. A challenge in writing news is finding the line between being authoritative, which risks sounding officious, and being conversational, which may undermine credibility. The middle ground, necessary for telling news effectively, is being conversational yet authoritative.

Early radio writers, working in a medium whose delivery was through conversation, led the way to conversational news writing. These broadcasters pioneered an easier writing style. In one of its early broadcast stylebooks, the Associated Press advised: "Aim for 'people talk.' . . . Use the simple phrase, the precise word, the word the listener has no trouble understanding—in other words, 'people talk.' . . . The broadcasters . . . who handle on-the-air news best use a conversational style. That's the best approach to writing copy for them to use, or to edit for their own personalized use—the easy, conversational style. . . . Let Who, What, When, Where and Why come naturally into your story. Let one thought flow into the next."

Taking a cue from broadcasting, newspaper writers are shifting to a friendly style. In fact, the case can be made that a conversational style is even more important in the print media than in broadcasting because the printed word by its nature lacks the humanness of the spoken word. A conversational style helps overcome this inherent disadvantage of news in printed form.

Ron Davis, who spent nearly four years as news director at a Springfield, Mo., radio station, KSMU, before moving to a Springfield newspaper, put it this way: "We always wrote conversationally in radio, and I've tried to bring that to newspapering. In radio and TV, you can hear the inflections of voice. But in newspapers, you've got to bring that to life just with words."

Tom Corwin, of the Jackson, Tenn., Sun, champions writing naturally. Stilted writing, he notes, can originate with sources who become stiff in the formality of an interview: "People think that they have to sound official, but that's boring. People don't respond to that, and that doesn't sound like a real person. Put your notes away and just kind of stand there and talk to him as a person. See if they respond to that."

Contractions

The Wall Street Journal employs contractions to be conversational: "isn't," "hadn't," "they've." It's how people talk. Some publications disdain contractions as substandard, but the Journal has a conscious policy of using them as reader-friendly communication, which has neither detracted from the general respect in which the Journal is held nor hindered its growth. With 1.8 million circulation, the Wall Street Journal is the nation's largest daily.

It is true, however, that contractions can be overdone, and some contractions, like "could've," have a distracting slovenliness. Others, like "we'd," are ambiguous: "we had" or "we would"?

Contractions don't work in broadcast writing. News script writers avoid contractions to encourage announcers to be precise in their enunciation.

The Second-Person "You"

Although the second-person "you" can be misused, as mentioned earlier in this chapter, "you" can add a conversational quality by incorporating the audience into the story. James Hirsch did this skillfully for the lead article in the Wall Street Journal on June 24, 1991:

> Go shopping at Phar-Mor, the nation's largest, brashest and fastest-growing deep-discount chain, and **you** never know what **you** may find.

Second person, however, can be hazardous. Avoid it if it comes across as preachy.

Also, people not in the group indicated by "you" may conclude that the story was written for an "in" group, not them. It's no fun being left out. Imagine how a low-income reader who couldn't possibly afford to buy a house would be alienated by this lead:

> The next time you receive your property tax bill, you will find a surcharge for your automatic dishwasher and your underground lawn sprinkler system.

Understandably, a reader who does dishes by hand and has never had a lawn can conclude that this publication is being written for somebody else. That's no way for a newspaper, or other news medium, to build a following.

WRITING INFORMALLY YET AUTHORITATIVELY

STUDY PREVIEW   News writing that smacks of formality and officialism is a turn-off. Conversational delivery presents news in a friendlier way.

Shortened Names

The formality of referring to people by their payroll signatures, with full first name and middle initial or maybe even the whole middle name, is hardly conversational. While some news organizations insist on formal identifications, a friendlier, informal quality is possible by referring to people as they're known by their friends and associates.

Broadcasters, capitalizing on the conversational nature of their media, led the way out of the traditional stilted formality of, for example, "Thomas F. Stark" for someone whom reporters and everyone else always call "Tom." In most newsrooms, it's "Bill Clinton," "Al Gore," "Spike Lee." Still, some newspapers and magazines stick with a more formal style, and many newsrooms honor the preference of the person for "Barbara" instead of "Barb," for example, even if no one ever uses the longer form in conversation.

Avoiding stiltedness does not extend to making up a shortened form for people known by their full names. Some Richards are known as Dick and others as Rick or Rich, and some have been known only as Richard all their lives. If friends and associates know someone by the full given name, like Richard, William, Christiana and Pammylou, use the full name.

Names should not be shortened for people in the news in a negative way. To protect yourself legally, use the full name including middle initial or middle name so the other "Jack Smith" doesn't feel libeled. This lesson was learned by the Washington Post when it reported that Harry Kennedy had been charged with forgery. It was Harry P.L. Kennedy who was arrested, which prompted Harry F. Kennedy to sue, and a judge ordered the Post to make a substantial payment to the wrongly maligned Harry F. Kennedy.

Shortened Word Forms

If a shortened form is universally recognized, use it: "dorm" for dormitory, "prof" for professor, "disk" for diskette, "math" for mathematics. A campus audience would immediately recognize "polysci" and "phy-ed," terms that might puzzle a general audience. The key in deciding whether to use a shortened form is whether it is in tune with the audience. Ask yourself: "Would my audience find this obscure?" and "Is it conversational without undermining credibility?"

People Words

Words that refer to people rather than institutions make writing friendlier. Whenever appropriate, make it "firefighters" instead of "the fire department."

In stories about government, people words have the additional advantage of reminding the news audience that government is operated by human beings who are approachable and accountable. This is especially important in an era when many governmental units have grown into such bureaucracies that many citizens perceive them as monolithic institutions no longer responsive to the people. Even if the audience is affected only at a subconscious level, journalists can contribute to the proper working of democracy with words that put government into human terms. Compare these lead entries:

> **Institutional reference:** Fines totaling $50,000 were levied Tuesday against members of the Wildwing Club in court.

> **Institutional reference:** The city approved a 10 percent hike in TCI cable television subscription rates Monday.

The following variations illustrate the advantage of human references over institutional references.

> Fines totaling $50,000 were levied Tuesday against members of the Wildwing Club by **Judge Jenn Slovotky.**
>
> **Mayor Tom Langer** signed his approval to a 10-percent hike in TCI cable television subscription rates Monday.

Institutional Parentage

Unless clarity requires that a governmental subdivision be identified by its parent agency, avoid citing the institutional parentage. Almost always it is clearer to use "the Student Senate budget subcommittee" instead of the "Student Senate finance committee's budget subcommittee." Better than the "Family Support Administration of the U.S. Department of Health and Human Services" is the "U.S. Family Support Administration."

BEING UPBEAT YET APPROPRIATE

STUDY PREVIEW   Even with gloomy news, writing should be lively. Negative words like "no" and "not" work against keeping the audience interested. When the news is bright, the writing, of course, should be too. Another way to improve audience interest is to use present-tense story introductions, which creates an aura of immediacy.

Alternatives to Negative Words

People with sound psyches don't revel in gloom and doom, yet news sometimes is awful. When the news is bad, on pestilence, death, poverty, war or other suffering, writers should avoid negative sentence structures and word choices that can bog down already heavy subjects and turn the audience away. When news is upbeat, of course there is no need to choose negative prose structures.

Some negative prose is obvious with words like "no" and "not," which insidiously slow down and discourage the audience from staying with the story. Often these negative words are avoidable:

The jury found Hanks **not guilty.**

The jury found Hanks **innocent.**

The prof demanded a new photo lab because, he said, existing labs had **no** adequate ventilation.

The prof demanded a new photo lab because, he said, existing labs **lacked** adequate ventilation.

This is not to say that news writers should put a positive varnish on bad news, which would be a pollyannaish distortion. The challenge, rather, is to find wording that sidesteps negative words.

Present-Tense Intros

Broadcasters like present and present-perfect tense for their soft leads to give stories immediacy and to help avoid repeating "today" near the start of every item. By avoiding past tense, broadcasters can go with "say" instead of "said." It's a technique that also can add a peppy, conversational tone to a newspaper story too—if the time element isn't essential. Compare the formal and conversational tone of these newspaper leads:

FLAGSTAFF, Ariz.—Two psychiatrists **testified** Thursday that it is safe to release John Leafler from a state institution where he's been a patient since the slaying of his stepfather in 1978.	FLAGSTAFF, Ariz.—Two psychiatrists **say** it's safe to release John Leafler from a state institution where he's been a patient since slaying his stepfather in 1978.

In both broadcast and print news, it usually is best to switch to past tense soon after the lead. Past tense is the form that people normally use to tell about things that have already happened.

EXHIBITING SENSITIVITY

STUDY PREVIEW   The news audience may be offended by some news, but seldom is there a justification for the writing to be offensive. Choosing words that tell the story yet are sensitive to right-minded people's preferences is important.

Race and Ethnicity

The word "Negro" has largely fallen by the wayside since the 1960s because many African Americans found offense in connotations that had developed around the word through history. The news writer's choice of the word "black" or "African American" today demonstrates not only sensitivity but awareness of changing usage.

Because of the fluid situation in society on minority references, reporters must listen carefully to the terminology that knowledgeable, sensitive people are using. Terms vary from community to community and are evolving. For example, "people of color" appears with some frequency as an accepted term for most racial minorities, which is almost full circle from "colored people," a term that fell into wide disrepute 30 years ago.

"Hispanic" is used in many places for people with a Spanish heritage, but some readers are insulted by the word, contending that it misleadingly lumps many dissimilar cultures together. Alternatives include Latino and Chicano or even the more specific Cubano or Mexican American.

Some people take umbrage at "American Indian" and opt for Native American, aboriginal people or native people.

Journalists must know both local usage and the preference of the individuals being written about to make intelligent choices that are accurate and also sensitive to as many of their readers' sensitivities as possible.

For media with national or large regional audiences, reporters can consult with national organizations representing minority groups, most of which have offices in the District of Columbia. Keep in mind, though, that there is dissension within many minority groups about what to call themselves. Sometimes the leadership can do little more than steer you in a direction that will stir the least antagonism.

Sometimes it takes a heavy whack on the side of the head to overcome insensitivity. Incredibly, not until a 1960s' study did sports writers, then almost entirely white, realize they were using first-name familiarity for their second references to black athletes, like "Reggie" for baseball star Reggie Jackson, and last names like "Smith" and "Jones" for white athletes. Embarrassed at their unwitting racism, white sports writers shaped up immediately.

Offense can take many forms. Some terms left over from older times have stereotypical, one-dimensional connotations that are increasingly resented: indian trader, going dutch, jewing down, being scotch.

Diminutive Words

For many minority people, the word "boy" has an onerous connotation of servitude, like "Fetch my shoes, boy." "Girl" has a similar diminutive taint for adult women. Sensitive writers today avoid "boy" and "girl" except for children.

For teen-agers, "youth" won't have anyone taking unintended umbrage. It may be boys' and girls' basketball in junior high school, but by college it is men's and women's basketball.

Gender Sensitivity

The English language's lack of a gender-free personal singular pronoun poses all kinds of problems for sensitive writers. At one time, "he, "him" and "his" were widely used generically:

> Every member of the seven-man, five-woman jury exited through the rear basement door to **his** car and went home, exhausted from the three-month trial.

But the masculine "his" ignores the gender of the five women. That's male-centered sexism, probably unintended but nonetheless sexism.

Although some conservative grammarians may argue that "he," "his" and "him" are generic and genderless, sensitive writers have found alternatives. Sometimes a pronoun can be avoided entirely:

> Every juror exited through the rear basement door and drove home, exhausted from the three-month trial.

Switching a noun from singular to plural can avoid the problem because the follow-up pronoun will become the gender-free "they":

> The jurors exited through the rear basement door, got in **their** cars and drove home, exhausted from the three-month trial.

Beware, however, of using the pronoun "they" and its variations to refer back to a singular antecedent.

> Every juror got in **their** car and drove home.

Gender stereotypes can be offensive. Men, for example, have every reason to be offended when news writers reflexively use the masculine pronoun "he" to describe a criminal before police even have a suspect in mind because the underlying assumption of the "he" is the false stereotype that all criminals are men.

Consider this line from a college newspaper article, which bespeaks either the writer's ignorance of the growing number of men entering nursing careers or, even worse, insensitivity to gender issues:

> When **she** enters her senior year, the nursing student is ready for intensive "clinicals," as they are called, at city hospitals.

Economic Implications

Besides offending readers and damaging a writer's credibility, insensitivity can undermine the economic foundation of a news organization. To be economically viable, these organizations must retain large audiences. Insensitivity can hit the bottom line when it offends women, who are approximately 50 percent of the nation's population; men, another 50 percent; racial minorities, about 20 percent; and homosexuals, perhaps 2 percent. What if these people, offended and angry, quit subscribing or tuning in?

CHAPTER WRAP-UP

Journalistic writing is a cerebral, creative process, but the creativity must be channeled into seeking relevant information and telling the story. News stories are not a vehicle for writers to show off stylistic flourishes. Flair has its place, but it becomes self-indulgent and unacceptable when it intrudes into the story and diverts the audience's attention away from the subject to the teller of the story.

Good news writing has a natural, conversational quality, although never to the point of eroding audience confidence in the message being told. Write with the words that bright, knowledgable people use in discussing a story, being careful to avoid in-group obscurities.

For an audience-oriented writing style, avoid formal titles, payroll signatures for names, and lengthy labels when shorter, more commonly used ones are available. Good news writing is also marked by direct, positive sentences. Too many "no's" and "not's" can bog down a story.

Word choices that upset readers, even a small minority of readers, can be a reflection of a writer's insensitivity. "Black," for example, has none of the offensive baggage that "Negro" has acquired.

STUDY QUESTIONS

1. Aspiring news people are sometimes told that writing is "putting your brains on paper." In addition, writing news is putting your soul on paper. Explain how writing a news story is a highly creative undertaking. How do news stories reveal the writer's values?

2. How can writers keep their presence in the shadows of a news story so the subject has the audience's full attention?

3. Why has news writing become more conversational in recent years? Discuss techniques for making news stories conversational.

4. What are the advantages of an informal tone in writing news? Is it possible to be conversational without sacrificing authoritativeness?

5. What are techniques to keep a news story lively and interesting even if the subject is gloomy?

6. How does a news writer avoid offending readers sensitive to race, gender or class issues?

PUTTING YOUR LEARNING TO WORK

EXERCISE 1   Sidestepping the Egotistical "I"

These excerpted sentences from hypothetical news stories contain first-person "I" words and veiled "I" words in the form of the second-person "you" and the third-person "one." Because good news writing keeps the focus on the subject of the story, not the teller, it generally is better to tell the story in third person. Recast these sentences to avoid first person or veiled first person:

Entering the kitchen, I saw the blood-spattered table and chair.

When you reach the front door, you hear a loud, static-riddled radio.

On any given day, one can find clam rolls, tofu, and double-chocolate cheesecake at the Eclectic Cafe.

EXERCISE 2   Being Comfortable with Contractions

Because people talk in contractions, they can contribute to conversational writing. What possibilities for contractions do you see in the first few sentences of a 1994 Wall Street Journal article by Quentin Hardy?

> Drink your plutonium, it is good for you.
>
> A Japanese nuclear-power lobby is spreading the word that, when used properly, plutonium is not dangerous but downright friendly.

EXERCISE 3   Being Conversational with Names

Take the stuffiness and formality out of the names in these sentences from news stories:

President William Jefferson Clinton renewed his offer Friday to help Russia ease the shock of private ownership.

Thomas F. Stark, president of the university, denied the charge.

Franklin Vincent Zappa, 52, who covered the waterfront of contemporary American music and who didn't shy from controversy, died at his Los Angeles home after a long battle with prostate cancer.

EXERCISE 4   Opting for People Words

These news story sentences contain references to institutions that can be converted to people words. Convert the institutional references to put the sentences in more human terms.

The fire department received the call at 1:12 a.m.

The Bethel air control station sent a coded message to the pilot of the Korean airliner.

The U.S. Justice Department filed the criminal complaint.

EXERCISE 5   Offsetting Negativity

News comes across livelier when writers avoid negative words like "not." Can you find alternatives to negative constructions in these sentences:

Paris Bass was found not guilty and set free.

Childers' ACT college entrance exam scores were not good enough for Yale.

The husband was accused of not providing enough income for groceries.

EXERCISE 6   Avoiding Presumptuous Gender References

Because the English language lacks gender-free singular personal pronouns, many people use awkward "he or she" references. Can you find a way to avoid clumsiness or inappropriateness in the following sentences, without resorting to male pronouns?

Every club member agreed to go to his or her roommates for a donation.

Gladys Sherwood, chairman of the committee, was given Dec. 22 as a deadline.

Congressman Mary Streeter was elected in 1992.

FOR FURTHER LEARNING

Walter Fox. "Writing the News: A Guide for Print Journalists," 2nd ed. Iowa State University Press, 1993. Fox, a veteran journalist and teacher, puts newswriting in its historical context in this compact guide. Excellent examples.

Casey Miller and Kate Swift. "The Handbook of Nonsexist Writing for Writers, Editors and Speakers." Lippincott & Crowell, 1980.

William Strunk and E.B. White. "The Elements of Style," 3rd ed. Macmillan, 1979.

Alice Tallmade. "Covering AIDS: A Handbook for Journalists." Pacific Media Center, 1987.

Writer's Digest. This monthly magazine carries regular articles on improving the effectiveness of writing.

William Zinsser. "On Writing Well." Harper & Row, 1976.

CHAPTER 8

Building Color into News Stories

In this chapter you will learn:

✦ Writing effectiveness can be improved with word illustrations and small details.

✦ Quotations can provide evidence to support a point.

✦ Well-chosen examples can enliven a point and back up a general statement.

✦ Analogies can make a point clear by likening one thing to another.

✦ Anecdotes enhance points through a brief story within the story.

✦ Good observation yields sensory details that bring a story to life.

✦ Visual detail creates word pictures that evoke sensory impressions.

✦ Hearing and smelling words help create scenes that give a deeper sense of what happened.

DAVE HENDRICKSON TELLS ABOUT WAR

Dave Hendrickson of the Milwaukee Journal was among the first reporters into Kuwait after it was reclaimed by Allied forces in the 1991 Persian Gulf War. Personally witnessing the war-ravaged Kuwaiti landscape, Hendrickson was able to write a riveting, colorful account that came close to transporting readers to where he had been to see what he had seen.

KUWAIT CITY, Kuwait—The highway south of here has been chewed up and its pieces spit out.

It is littered with already rusting carcasses of cars, trucks, armored personnel carriers, tanks. They have been tossed about as though a giant arm had swept a destructive arc through the countryside.

Miles south of Kuwait City, black smoke billows from burning oil fields, the orange of the blaze a dull, sickly color. The smoke fills your nose. The smell is of burning tires.

The desolation is complete.

In all honesty, if a dragon were to appear on the horizon, you might be terrified but you wouldn't be surprised.

The reports of constant celebratory gunfire and non-stop victory parades do not ring true once you get away from the Kuwait International Hotel where a swarm of journalists has gathered to watch the people who came to perform for the journalists.

Away from the International, Kuwait City is deserted and eerily quiet.

During a long, dark night at what would normally be a bustling metropolitan intersection, the only two noises are the howl of a cat and the collapse of a storefront awning.

The hotel that stands on that corner also is silent. There is no water, no electricity, just an owner who wanted to offer free rooms as an act of appreciation for the liberation of his country from the Iraqis.

The hotels seem to have taken the worst beating. The Meridien, a building made of amber-smoked glass, was hit by a bomb and burned. The bottom few floors were destroyed and the shards of smoked glass look like shredded carbon paper slapping in the wind.

The techniques that Hendrickson used to make his story so potent are the subject of this chapter. These include sensory appeals and illustrative techniques.

ILLUSTRATING THE POINT

STUDY PREVIEW   News writers can add to their effectiveness by illustrating what they are writing about. Good advice: "Show, don't just tell." Small details are good for this kind of "showing."

Show, Don't Tell

Covering a political meeting at which everyone was affected by the day's mugginess, the writer might tell that it was "a horribly hot humid day which affected everybody." Better, the writer could go beyond telling to show it. Relman Morin, a Pulitzer Prize reporter for the Associated Press, gives this example for showing how miserable it was in the muggy meeting room:

> A farmer fanned his face with a red bandanna, and another, instead of clapping, applauded by snapping his green galluses.

Small details help show, rather than just tell. Showing "gives a picture," says Morin.

Value of Small Details

In an article about a bounty hunter, Ray Hall, a Sunday magazine writer for the Louisville, Ky., Courier-Journal, might have said at one point in his story that the

DESCRIBING DETAILS. A CNN reporter at the scene of the 1994 Los Angeles earthquake. The importance of seeing and describing the details of an event cannot be overestimated.   (© Copyright Cable News Network, Inc. All rights reserved.)

man relaxed. Instead, Hall wrote that the bounty hunter ate a bag of Doritos, leaned back in the captain's chair of a van, put his feet up on the dashboard and fell asleep. "If I tell you that," Hall says, "I don't have to say he was relaxed."

In the same article, Hall showed the calmness of the bounty hunter.

> Under stress, Meredith is calm to the point of eeriness. An hour after a collar, he may be fast asleep. His conscience, he says, is clear. So are his arteries: the last time his blood pressure was checked, it was 118 over 78, figures a teenager would envy.

In her series on elderly people for the Danville, Ill., Commercial-News, Jean Byram could have said simply that a nursing-home patient had many memories. Showing, not telling, Byram instead wrote:

> She had this beautiful quilt on her bed which was made from patches from her life. There was a patch from the dress of her baby daughter who died, a patch from a wedding dress, a patch from an apron that she probably cooked Christmas dinner in.

Detail like this is not pulled from thin air. It comes from constant observation to spot the things that will help the audience to recreate the reporter's experience.

ILLUSTRATIVE QUOTATIONS

STUDY PREVIEW   Quotations can strengthen writing by providing evidence that supports a point. This is another method of going beyond telling to showing.

Quotes as Supporting Evidence

Direct quotations add credibility to the writer's point. Reporter Craig Wilson of USA Today backs up his general statement with a quotation:

> Gay and lesbian groups are outraged at the portrayal of a serial killer in the thriller "The Silence of the Lambs," opening nationwide today.
>
> **"It combines yet another negative stereotypical image of gay people as villains, with extreme violence against women,"** says Richard Jennings of the Gay and Lesbian Alliance Against Defamation.

Wilson goes on to explain that the killer hunts women for their skin.

Follow-Up Technique

Debbie Howlett, of USA Today, writing about U.S. troops in Operation Desert Storm, uses a direct quote to follow up on her point that combat changes people:

> Most had never seen combat. But it would change them.
> **"I killed my first man today,"** said a subdued Maj. Robert Williams of the Army's Tiger Brigade after a tank battle. **"I'm not sure I feel very good about it."**

Note how Mike Kurilovitch used an illustrative follow-up quotation in a Niagara Falls, N.Y., Gazette article on drunken driving:

> The system does little to discourage drinking and driving. It does, however, frustrate police officers, who feel their enforcement efforts are being wasted, and victims, who harbor little hope that the ordeals they suffered can be prevented again.
> **"We tell our recruits not to follow what happens in the courts—within reason—because otherwise they'd give up,"** said Niagara County Sheriff Francis Giles.

CITING EXAMPLES

> STUDY PREVIEW   Well-chosen examples can bring color to a story. Examples also can cement a writer's point by backing up a general statement.

Examples to Enliven

Examples bring writing to life. They illustrate the abstract, clarify the complex, and drive points home. With examples, you can show, not just tell. Reporters on the scene with a keen eye pick up examples.

In reporting the haste with which Philippines dictator Ferdinand Marcos and his wife Imelda fled their palace, Manila bureau chief Mark Fineman of the Los Angeles Times didn't merely say they left in a hurry; he showed it:

> Beside Imelda Marcos' 12-foot-wide bed was a half-eaten banana.

Backing Up a Point

An example can support a main point, as Amy Wilentz of Time magazine did. Backing up her conclusion that speed kills, she wrote:

In April, when Congress permitted all states to raise the speed limit on rural interstates to 65 miles an hour, 38 states chose to do so. The results thus far have been ominous. **The National Highway Traffic Safety Administration reports that in 22 of those states, highway deaths jumped 46 percent between May and July over the same three months in 1986.**

In an interview, reporters often receive advance warning when an example is coming. When a source begins a sentence with "for example" or "for instance," an example is coming, although there isn't always such an obvious signal.

LISTENING FOR ANALOGIES. When sources say something was "like" something else, they are telling you an analogy that might help make a point quickly and clearly in your story. Other key words to listen for are "if," for hypotheticals, and "so-that," which also can make for a colorful, right-on comparison. (John Reis/PHOTOLINK)

ILLUSTRATING BY COMPARING

STUDY PREVIEW   Analogies, likening one thing to another, can help make a concept clear. Hypotheticals, taking a "what if" approach, can also help explain. An example built around a "so-that" sentence structure can work well too.

Analogies

When an interviewee says something is like something else, listen up. When you hear the word "like," you probably are about to hear an analogy, a comparison in which one thing is likened to another. Consider how Lorene Hanley Duquin, writing in Mother's Today magazine, created an analogy to explain compactly how babysitting co-ops work.

> A babysitting club can work **like a savings account.** But instead of money, members deposit the number of hours they spend babysitting and they withdraw hours when another member babysits for them.

Notice how Ray Hall of the Louisville, Ky., Courier-Journal, describing the work of a private investigator, uses a war analogy to illustrate his point:

> But Meredith's physique isn't the greatest ally in his job, which, **like warfare,** involves hours of tedium, punctuated by seconds of quickening terror.

P.J. O'Rourke has fun with analogies. In a historical aside on the Middle East for Rolling Stone magazine, O'Rourke wrote:

> When the Turks backed the wrong horse in World War I, the French and English divvied up the region in a manner both completely self-serving and unbelievably haphazard, **like monkeys at a salad bar.**

Ralph Blumenthal, covering the 1993 terrorist bombing inside the 110-story World Trade Center, wrote:

> Hampering the inquiry was the precariousness of the site at ground zero, which gaped **like a cored apple through the bowels of the complex.**

The word "like" sometimes is unstated but understood, as in this lead sentence by Craig Medred of the Anchorage, Alaska, Daily News on the celebrated Iditarod dog race marathon:

> HAPPY RIVER GORGE, Alaska—
> Coming down into this cleft through the
> Alaska Range, **the Iditarod Trail is an**
> **angry serpent.**

Hypotheticals

When an interviewee says "Imagine this" or "Let's suppose" or "If," a reporter can expect to hear a hypothetical situation that will make a point. Listen carefully. You might want to use the example.

When Daniel Pearl of the Wall Street Journal was interviewing people in Braselton, Ga., population 500, about the $20 million purchase of their town by film star Kim Basinger, he picked up a hypothetical that made for a colorful quotation:

> Terry Kitchens, an auto mechanic: "I
> want to meet her, but I don't know if
> I could handle it. **If I was a racing en-**
> **gine, I'd probably get over-revved and**
> **blow up.**"

Linda Caricaburu of the Great Falls, Mont., Tribune was interviewing a rural woman about the adversities of life in sparsely populated Garfield County, and the conversation turned to the difficulty of being accepted socially even though the woman and her family had been on their ranch 11 years. Explaining the situation, the woman illustrated her point with "if":

> "**If you haven't been here for three**
> **generations, you're still new to the**
> **area.** A lot of people are pretty friendly,
> but others wait and see. We're newcom-
> ers and will be forever."

So-That Constructions

"So-that" sentence constructions can illustrate a point graphically. Consider this passage by Don Marsh of the Charleston, W.Va., Gazette on the miseries of coal mining:

> The top is **so low that** men work on their backs or from a crouch. They can't straighten up to eat a sandwich, drink water or urinate.

Ron Davis of the Springfield, Mo., News-Leader began a story with a so-that construction, setting the stage for the details that unfold in his following paragraphs:

> Deep within the Medical Center for federal prisoners, locked inside a fortress unlike any other in the country, is a man **so deadly that** he cannot be trusted even to touch another human being.
>
> Clayton Anthony Fountain has killed five men, always blaming his victims for making him shoot, stab or strangle them.
>
> For five years, Fountain was kept under nearly constant surveillance in the strictest lockup of the nation's toughest prison in Marion, Ill.
>
> There he claimed four of his victims, including a prison guard.
>
> He couldn't be executed. There was no federal death penalty then.
>
> Stumped over what to do, the government spent $40,000 in 1984 to build a special cell for him in Springfield.
>
> Fountain has been kept there for the last 2,029 days.
>
> But the unrepetent killer says he now can control his inner demons.
>
> He wants out of the double-caged confines built specially for him—confines **so restrictive that** he cannot eat with anything but a white plastic spoon, or walk outside his isolation without having his legs locked with irons, his wrists frozen with two sets of handcuffs. With every movement, a sea of guards surrounds him like an armada.

Sources sometimes will use so-that constructions that make good quotes. In interviewing athletes who aspired to the big leagues but who didn't make it, sports writer Rick Starr talked to a former minor-league baseball player who described the frustrations with a so-that construction, in this case with the "that" implicit. Starr used it in his article in the Tarentum, Pa., Valley News Dispatch:

> "I saw guys beat their heads on lockers and tear up the locker room after pitching a bad outing or an 0-for-4 performance," he said. "The pressure was **so tremendous,** they would lose it."

ANECDOTES

STUDY PREVIEW   Anecdotes are stories within a story that illustrate a particular point. For complex subjects, anecdotes can be excellent leads to entice readers into the story, a technique called "Dow-Jonesing."

Stories Within Stories

Anecdotes are short stories that underscore a point. In describing the deterioration of life in Baghdad during the Persian Gulf War, Tony Horwitz and Geraldine Brooks of the Wall Street Journal used an anecdote to illustrate what was happening. Here is an adaptation from their story:

Three days after the first Allied bombing raid on Baghdad, Jemis Mut, a Sudanese waiter at the city's five-star Babylon Hotel, made his way carefully down to the water.

In the lull between air raids, crowds lined the normally deserted banks, washing dishes, washing clothes, washing each other.

Dipping a pail in the muddy green water, the 27-year-old Mut did what he had promised himself he never would. "I was very thirsty," he said. "I drank it."

Recalling the moment a week later, as freezing rain raps against his canvas tent in a Jordanian refugee camp, Mut shrugs fatalistically. "To save your life, you risk your life," he said.

Anecdotal Leads

Anecdotal leads can personify complex issues to illustrate issues that don't lend themselves to interesting treatments. This technique is called "Dow-Jonesing" because it has been refined into an art form by the Wall Street Journal, which is owned by Dow Jones and Company, Inc.

In a roundup on consumer spending in 1991, the Wall Street Journal took reports from many bureaus but focused on a single person to illustrate the issue:

George Price is a worried man.

"I've completely changed my spending habits. I'm not buying a new car. I've paid off all my bills. I'm starting to stockpile money," the American Airlines flight attendant in Dallas says.

Given his seniority, he isn't concerned about job security, but he is pessimistic because of the Middle East. . . . "I'm trying to be ready."

Most people interviewed by a nationwide survey by this newspaper aren't quite so worried, but Price is hardly the odd man out of the spending game.

A lot of people are cautiously cutting back.

The story continues, moving from George Price as a microcosmic illustration to the macrocosmic issue that he helped bring home to readers who might otherwise skip what would appear to be "just another consumer survey story."

SENSORY APPEALS

STUDY PREVIEW Strong news writing creates word pictures for the audience. One technique is to cite colors, textures, sounds, smells and tastes to evoke sensory impressions. Observational detail also can create ambiance in the nonvisual world of words.

Beyond Skeletal Facts

Spot news, written against a deadline, often is a barren telling of facts, the writer having no time to go beyond a sterile account. Most journalists revel in the adrenalin surges that go with covering a breaking story, but once the deadline is met they almost always regret not having had time to capture the drama better and tell the story more effectively.

News writers who have an opportunity to redo a story, perhaps an expanded, interpretive piece for a Sunday edition, or to write the script for a documentary wrap-up, will cull their memories for details to help the audience experience the event, albeit vicariously, in ways the deadline-driven spot coverage did not allow. These follow-up stories are marked by deliberate attempts to share the writer's sensory response to the situation with the audience, citing color, texture, sound, smell and taste.

Observation and Sensory Appeals

Such colorful writing is a highly cerebral process, bringing the observation of keen eyes, good ears, and other sensory organs into sharp, coordinated play. The result will be rich impressions for the audience.

VISUAL DETAIL

STUDY PREVIEW   Visual detail helps the audience experience what the reporter experienced. Skillfully employed, this technique makes for evocative writing.

Color

In a series on farm life, John Camp of the St. Paul, Minn., Pioneer Press appealed to many of his readers' senses to help them experience the life of modern farmers. Note Camp's color words:

> The **black** fields dominate the countryside, interrupted here and there by woodlots, by pasturage where lambs play in the **fading sunlight,** by **red-brick** or **purple-steel** silos, Grant Wood barns and Sears, Roebuck sheds, and by the farmhouses.

Besides color words, Camp implies additional colors: the dark greens and browns and grays of a woodlot, the bright greens of pasturage, and the reds and browns of barns in Grant Wood's paintings. Although words, strictly speaking, are a nonvisual medium, Camp has created an impression so rich for the reader that it might rival the reader's recollection of a Grant Wood painting.

Texture

Elsewhere in his series on farm life, Camp cites texture, which is picked up by the sense of touch, to transport his readers closer and closer to the heart of his subject. He moves from the surface of a precisely engineered freeway, to the less even state highway, to the bumpy county road, to the gravel road, to the unfinished farm lane:

> Go down to Worthington. Get off Interstate 90, off the state highway, off the blacktopped county road, and finally go down the gravel track and into the farm lane, listening to the power lines sing and the cottonwoods moan in the everlasting wind, watching a red-orange pickup a mile away as it crawls like a ladybug along a parallel road between freshly plowed fields, leaving behind a rising plume of gravel dirt, crawling toward the silos and rooftops that mark the Iowa line.

The length of Camp's second sentence, 79 words, proves that ironclad rules have limited application in artistic endeavors like news writing. It is a wonderful sentence, in part because of its length. In fewer words, Camp would have had difficulty moving the reader from familiar territory to new places. Also, note how he builds the visual impression with more sensory appeals: "red-orange pickup," "freshly plowed fields," and "rising plume of gravel dirt."

Being Cinematic

Ray Hall, whose work at the Louisville, Ky., Courier-Journal is noted for its evocative detail, prides himself on creating what he calls "cinematic scenes." As with his description of the Dorito-crunching bounty hunter a few pages back, Hall sets scenes with color and sound and smells and revealing detail, which add interest to his writing with no loss of respect for his motivation as a journalist.

Revealing detail can include brand names. Johnny Walker Black Label scotch creates a different picture than Thunderbird wine. It makes a difference whether the subject of your story uses Aramis cologne or Old Spice, or has on an Oleg Casini designer scarf or a Kmart apron. With brand names, the millions of dollars lavished on advertising has created an image on whose connotations news writers can piggyback.

In a story on a country-western saloon in Berlin as an example of American pop culture spreading globally, Fortune magazine writer John Huey noted that the patrons, "in snakeskin boots and Texas hats," drink from "whole bottles of Jose Cuervo tequila, smoke hundreds of Marlboros, and howl 'Yee-haw!'" What is less German than Jose Cuervo tequila, and what cigarette has more of a cowboy image than Marlboro?

Huey was selective in choosing relevant detail. Plugging detail into a story unthinkingly doesn't work. In creating a precise impression for the audience, reporters must decide which details support the point at hand.

Tom Corwin, a reporter with the Jackson, Tenn., Sun, says a detail will often stick in his memory, "like the color of the guy's shirt. Then you have to figure out why that was significant." If it isn't a telling detail, including it will only divert the audience's attention onto a pointless tangent.

Misusing Evocative Detail

Some novice news writers are wary about using observational detail. They note that propagandists and other biased writers stack up prejudicing details to manipulate the audience to their point of view. While observational details can be misused, they also can be used to enhance a story's credibility by strengthening the audience's sense of being there. Color does not detract from a skillful writer's detached, neutral tone if the writer is motivated to use it to better communicate a story.

REPORTING WITH SOUND AND SMELL

STUDY PREVIEW Hearing and smelling are sensory activities that good writers use to create scenes that help readers to a deeper sense of what happened.

Hearing the Details

When Pete Wasson of the Richmond, Ind., Palladium-Item covered a warehouse fire, he wanted readers to feel right from the start that they were witnesses. See how his aural and other sensory references help do that:

> Glass rained onto the street and flaming roof timbers **creaked and crashed** to the ground as Richmond firefighters fought a three-alarm fire on the old north side of the city today.

To relay the feeling of battle from aboard the USS Wisconsin during the Persian Gulf War, USA Today's Debbie Howlett combined colors and sounds:

> Each shot began with a **hum.** The ground-hugging missile's engine ignited with a **blinding white flare.** As the Tomahawk screamed away, the **yellowish halo** in its wake turned the **deep blue sea pale.**

In February 1994, when a shell exploded in a Sarajevo marketplace, Tom Post had the job of putting together Newsweek's cover story in a matter of only a few hours. Notice how he employed sound words to recreate the tragedy:

> **Silently** and without warning, a 120-mm mortar shell sailed into the crowd, hitting a table in the middle of the market.
>
> It exploded with **a ferocious blast,** tearing heads and limbs from bodies and scattering arcs of blood for yards around.
>
> Some corpses were so badly dismembered that they couldn't be identified as men or women.
>
> On one table lay the remains of flowers, shopping bags and a prosthetic leg—a surreal still life.
>
> The marketplace shook with the **cacaphony of grief: the shrieks of the injured,** the **sirens of the police cars and ambulances, the sobbing of Bosnian policemen** who grabbed each other for comfort.
>
> And hour after hour came the **scratchy sound of bodies being dragged across broken glass** and loaded onto beds of trucks that sped them off to the city's hospitals.

Smelling the Details

When John Camp went to rural Minnesota for his series on farming, he not only was watching and listening but also smelling, so he could cite aromas and odors of all sorts to give his readers a stronger feel for the place. Rather than say that it was haying time, Camp talks about "scorching sun," "south wind," "the sweet smell of fresh-cut alfalfa mixed with gravel dust thrown up by passing cars and the scent of diesel fuel." In another passage, moving the reader into a farm house, Camp is both implicit and explicit with smells:

The walk to the porch is guarded by **lilacs** and **lilies** of the valley and a patch of **violets**. . . .

The door swings open and Sally-Anne Benson is there, navy sweatshirt, blue jeans, tan work boots.

"Hi," she says. "Come in. David is still in the field, with the oats."

From behind her come the kitchen **smells of fresh bread and noodles and sauce.**

Combining appeals to different senses can be exponentially powerful. In this article, condensed from the Springfield, Mo., News-Leader, Ron Davis combines descriptions of what he saw, heard, smelled, and felt to give readers a potent impression of an inadequate jail:

"Hey! Turn up the damned heat!"

The **voice richochets** down the **concrete and steel halls** and is immediately followed by a series of **violent booms,** as an **inmate pounds on the walls.** Something is wrong with the heating system at the Laclede County Jail. But what's new? The inmates say this happens every night.

It's **38 degrees** outside on this March night, and the men in the upstairs security cellblock are too cold. They always are, no matter how high the guard at the main-level dispatch desk cranks the thermostat. The heat never makes it to the security wing.

Down the hall from security, Cell No. 5 is cold too. John Mallory keeps himself busy by **tapping** every few minutes on **the battered heating duct.**

"Nothing, man," the 24-year-old inmate grumbles, firing up a **Kool.**

Saturday night in the Laclede County Jail, and 25 inmates—half awaiting trial, the others serving sentences up to one year—are trying to stay warm. No one tries to sleep. It's only 10 p.m., and who can slumber with all this racket, anyway?

Built in 1955, the jail looks older than its 35 years. Paint peels from walls. The cells **smell like sweat and socks and smoke.** On one wall, **a pin-up of Jamie Lee Curtis** competes with **graffiti comparing a state trooper to a bowel movement.**

In the basement is the drunk tank, **a cavernous bunker** that **reeks of urine and vomit.** A hole in the floor serves as toilet and trash can.

The tank is empty tonight, but its **stench overpowers the smell of food** from the adjoining pantry.

CHAPTER WRAP-UP

Bringing a story to life keeps the audience interested. Some writers talk about being "cinematic," providing detail and color that create a "word picture." Useful advice: "Show, don't tell." Covering the trial of Sirhan Sirhan, who had assassinated presidential candidate Bobby Kennedy, a reporter could have "told" his audience that the defense attorney was worried as the jury began deliberating. Instead, one reporter "showed" the worry by quoting the defense attorney as saying: "I'll bet you $5 it's death." Later, reviewing the story, Associated Press court reporter Arthur Everett focused on the defense attorney's quote and commented: "How can any writer better tell of a defense lawyer's anxiety, his fear, the hopelessness enveloping him." It was an example of showing, not telling.

Especially effective in giving the audience an eyewitness feel for what happened is to use sensory words. Details like color and texture help create this verisimilitude. So do words about how the situation sounded and smelled and felt. News writing is no place for what fiction critics call "purple prose," which is soaked with irrelevant detail. To be effective, the use of detail in news stories must be highly disciplined and controlled.

STUDY QUESTIONS

1. Explain how the "Show, don't just tell" principle makes for colorful news stories.

2. How can you use quotations to strengthen a point in a news story?

3. Where do examples usually fit best in a news story to back up a point?

4. How are analogies, hypotheticals, and so-that constructions similar and different? How can they make for more colorful stories?

5. Discuss how anecdotes can help make points colorfully.

6. Why are keen observation skills essential to make news stories colorful?

7. Can you give examples of how words describing color and texture make for evocative writing?

8. Can you give examples of sound and smell words that give the audience a deeper sense of what happened?

PUTTING YOUR LEARNING TO WORK

EXERCISE 1   Visual Detail

In this chapter, you read an excerpt from Tom Post's Newsweek cover story on the Sarajevo marketplace massacre to study his use of sound words. Now, reread the excerpt for the visual details that contribute to his word picture:

Silently and without warning, a 120mm mortar shell sailed into the crowd, hitting a table in the middle of the market.

It exploded with a ferocious blast, tearing heads and limbs from bodies and scattering arcs of blood for yards around.

Some corpses were so badly dismembered that they couldn't be identified as men or women.

On one table lay the remains of flowers, shopping bags and a prosthetic leg—a surreal still life.

The marketplace shook with the cacaphony of grief: the shrieks of the injured, the sirens of the police cars and ambulances, the sobbing of Bosnian policemen who grabbed each other for comfort.

And hour after hour came the scratchy sound of bodies being dragged across broken glass and loaded onto beds of trucks that sped them off to the city's hospitals.

Look also for Post's words that evoke color: arcs of blood, remains of flowers, prosthetic leg. Sound and visual words are only two among many elements that make for powerful news writing. Verbs are important too. Go back and look at Post's verbs: sailed, hitting, exploded, tearing.

EXERCISE 2   Noting Colors

This exercise will heighten your sensitivity to color and help enliven your writing with words that have sensory appeal. Visit a darkish place, like a church during late services, a supper club with low lighting, or a smoke-filled biker bar. Take a thesaurus and a pad of paper on which you've drawn five columns. Sit down, close your eyes, and then open them and take note of the largest object that you see.

In Column 1 of the pad, list the object.

In Column 2, write down the basic color of the object. If the object has several colors, focus on the dominant color.

Now, open your thesaurus to the color you assigned to the object and look at words that describe variations of the color. Red, for example, has a wide range: maroon, crimson, scarlet, vermilion, pink, magenta, cherry, carmine. In Column 3, put the more precise color of the object.

In Column 4, use your imagination to create a more-descriptive synonym for your color: more scarlet than Madonna's lipstick, hotrod crimson, funeral-parlor maroon.

In Column 5, add words that give a feel for the texture or tone: a high-gloss cherry; a deep, elegant maroon; a slippery pink finish; a matte vermilion that absorbs the light; a brilliant neon magenta.

Repeat this exercise with a second object, then a third. This is an especially good exercise to do with a small group because you can share ideas with classmates about using color words effectively.

FOR FURTHER LEARNING

Roy Peter Clark, editor, then Don Fry. "Best Newspaper Writing." Poynter Institute. This ongoing series of winning entries from the annual American Society of Newspaper Editors competition, begun in 1979, includes interviews with the reporters about their work.

Andre Fontaine. "The Art of Writing Nonfiction." Thomas Y. Crowell, 1974. Fontaine, a freelance writer, discusses how rigorous reporting can be put in effective writing showcases by employing techniques once reserved for fiction.

Charles A. Grumich. "Reporting/Writing From Front Row Seats." Simon & Schuster, 1962.

Louis L. Morris and Richard B. Snyder. "A Treasury of Great Reporting," 2nd ed. Simon & Schuster, 1962. This classic collection covers 1586 to 1961.

Kendall J. Willis, editor. "The Pulitzer Prizes." Simon & Schuster. This annual series, beginning in 1987, reprints Pulitzer Prize–winning news stories.

CHAPTER 9

Using the Language Effectively

In this chapter you will learn:

+ News writing follows the generally accepted rules of good English with only a few exceptions.

+ Essential to writing news are a grammar book, a dictionary and a news stylebook.

+ News writers depart from mainstream composition rules on a few matters to more quickly communicate with the mass audience.

+ Writing that is effective for communicating with mass audiences is plain, simple and compact.

+ Correct spelling is important for a writer's credibility.

+ Euphemisms, jargon, abstract nouns and certain sentence constructions work against direct, clear news writing.

+ Numbers can enhance the clarity of your news writing, but they can be overused and badly used.

+ Readability formulas give journalists a general sense of how readable their stories are.

THE "ONLY" ISSUE

When wordsmith Dave Burkett taught journalism at Trinity University, he started class by writing this six-word sentence on the blackboard: "She hit him in the eye." Then he would ask students to insert the word "only" in the sentence. The variations elicited laughs, especially when read aloud:

Only she hit him in the eye.

She only hit him in the eye.

She hit only him in the eye.

She hit him only in the eye.

She hit him in only the eye.

She hit him in the only eye.

She hit him in the eye only.

By the time the chuckling subsided, sudents realized that Burkett had made an important point: The English language has a tremendous ability to communicate information precisely—and also, in the wrong hands, to be very misleading.

This chapter, which offers dos and don'ts of effective writing, will help you use the language to make your writing sparkle with clarity.

GOOD ENGLISH IS GOOD ENGLISH

STUDY PREVIEW News writing follows the rules of good writing that students begin learning in elementary school, which means every college student already has a good foundation for writing news.

Your Headstart on Writing News

Everyone in a college journalism course has a good start on mastering the techniques of writing news. The language we speak is the language we write. Many journalists, to test whether their writing is clear, read their stories to themselves out loud before turning them over to editors. A trend in recent years has been toward writing news conversationally. In short: If you can talk it, you are on your way to writing it effectively.

More than you may realize, you already know a lot about writing news from writing courses all the way back to elementary school. The rules of effective writing taught in the obligatory first-year college composition courses also apply.

On some small matters, journalistic writing departs from convention to meet the special needs of the mass audience, which needs information in a hurry, and also to meet limitations of the medium, but the similarities between journalistic and other writing far outweigh the differences.

Other good news for beginning news writers is that osmosis works. Many writers say they imitated the style of their favorite author until they had it mastered, and then took the style to new lengths with their own flair.

The key is reading. Read what you enjoy. If you like Car & Driver magazine's tight editing and irreverence, your writing will show it. Time magazine's sprightly, sometimes flippant style will rub off too.

This isn't to say that it does not take hard work to polish writing, but people who read have a headstart at becoming effective news writers.

Rules of the Road

Good writing works at two levels. In a broad sense, writers need a good feel for what they are writing about. This involves perspective and a sense of how their subject fits into larger issues and into the lives of their audiences. At a narrower level, good writing requires attention to details of expression, including grammar, spelling and punctuation.

Some beginning news writers bristle at the tedium of mastering the mechanics of the language. There is, however, no choice. Otherwise, communication is put at risk.

The reality, absolute and nonnegotiable, is that writing effectively is somewhat like driving a car. The rules of the road, including stop signs, curve markers and center lines, help drivers get where they are going without colliding. In the same way, agreed-upon symbols of language help us understand each other. Writing, to be effective, must be built on the conventions that literate men and women have developed over the centuries. We call these conventions "good English."

For starters, grammar, spelling and punctuation must be correct. This seems impossible to some beginning news writers, but it really isn't. Even the least confident writer can put a sentence together, which is an excellent starting point.

BASIC REFERENCES

STUDY PREVIEW   News writers must keep a grammar book and dictionary in easy reach. Most newsrooms follow a stylebook for uniformity on issues on which grammarians differ and to comport with local custom.

Grammar and Spelling

When you feel wobbly on a spelling, grammar or other usage question, plenty of resources are available to help you get it right, starting with a grammar book and a dictionary.

Even accomplished writers keep a grammar book at their keyboard to check on fine points of, for example, comma usage. The help is there, within reach. All that serious news-writing students have to do is go to an authoritative reference when they aren't sure about a mechanics question.

The process is much like an athlete in training. Continuing attention to the basics results in their mastery, and once mastered they are performed reflexively. Making the right comma decisions, for example, eventually becomes reflexive in all but the most exotic situations.

Dictionaries. Because dictionaries differ on small matters, most newsrooms choose one as their authoritative source. The most used is Webster's Third New International Dictionary, published by G. & C. Merriam Co. of Springfield, Mass., which is the base reference used by the Associated Press.

The AP also leans on the second edition of Webster's New World Dictionary, published by Simon & Schuster, although it doesn't have as many entries.

Grammar books. Like dictionary compilers, grammarians don't agree on all issues. On unsettled issues, like whether to use a comma before "and" in a series, most newsrooms have a house style, which omits that final comma.

In addition to their news organizations stylebook, most news writers have a favorite authority on grammar, generally a worn-out grammar book from high school or college with which they have become comfortable over the years.

Other respected sources include R. Thomas Berner's "Language Skills for Journalists," E.L. Callihan's "Grammar Skills for Journalists" and Lauren Kessler and Duncan McDonald's "When Words Collide."

Stylebooks

To help their writers and editors, almost all news organizations have a stylebook that lays out a preference for issues on which grammarians and dictionaries have not reached consensus. A stylebook specifies a newsroom's preferences for spelling, capitalization and abbreviations.

News people take stylebooks seriously because, with so many hands involved in writing and editing the product, a uniform guide promotes consistent style. A newspaper looks silly with "theater" in one article and "theatre" in another. So does a station with an anchor saying "Missour-ah" and a stand-up reporter saying "Missour-ee." A news release that abbreviates "Co." in the copy but has "Company" spelled out in the letterhead seems careless.

The most influential newspaper stylebook was a joint venture by the Associated Press and United Press in 1950. Since then, these news services have parted on minor points. Even so, both the AP and UPI stylebooks are standard newsroom references. AP and UPI also have broadcast stylebooks, which help writing effectively for the ear.

Stylebook entries can be unusually thorough. Consider this one from the Associated Press stylebook:

> **airport** Capitalize as part of a proper name: *La Guardia Airport, Newark International Airport.*
>
> The first name of an individual and the word *international* may be deleted from a formal airport name while the remainder is capitalized: *John F. Kennedy International Airport, Kennedy International Airport* or *Kennedy Airport.* Use whichever is appropriate in context.
>
> Do not make up names, however. There is no *Boston Airport*, for example. The Boston airport (lowercase airport) would be acceptable if for some reason the proper name, *Logan International Airport*, was not used.

AP and UPI style dominate, but many organizations have their own. The New York Times gives an address as "12 Maple Street" while the Los Angeles Times uses "12 Maple St." In an absolute sense, neither is right nor wrong. Stylebooks are arbitrary rules to minimize style dissonance for the audience.

This arbitrariness is disconcerting to some beginning news-writing students. Why should stories conform to a particular style when the experts themselves are not of one mind? A quick answer: Learning one stylebook helps you develop a sense of the kinds of elements that style governs, so you will know when to look up something in whatever stylebook your newsroom uses.

While dictionaries, grammar books and stylebooks are essential, good writing is an art, not merely a mechanical application of rules. The rules are essential starters, but what distinguishes good writing is how the writer uses a mastery of the rules in the creative process.

JOURNALISTIC ADAPTATIONS

STUDY PREVIEW   News writers are faithful to the conventions of good English except when departing from the rules helps them communicate better with their mass audiences. Among journalistic departures are occasional verb-subject sequences for attributives, one-sentence paragraphs, and bulleted sentences.

Departures from Standard English

Writers who understand and appreciate the rules of the language know when to break the rules to enhance effectiveness. Poets do it with unorthodox indentations, mid-sentence capitalization and other departures from standard English which serve their purposes.

Newspaper headline writers also take liberties with the language, dropping articles like "a" and "the," omitting the conjunction "and," using colons and single quotation marks to indicate attribution, and truncating sentences so mercilessly that not even a period is used to conclude them. Consider these headlines from USA Today during the 1991 Persian Gulf War:

> Troops set; U.S. mulls date
> Poll: Most support U.S. in gulf war
> Bush 'prepared' for ground war

Headline writers adapt the language to convey messages compactly for readers who are hurried and who want information in a no-nonsense format. These adaptations depart from the conventional rules of the language, but they accomplish their mission. They work.

News writers, like poets and headline writers, can enhance their effectiveness by departing selectively from the "standard English" which is emphasized in composition courses. News writing hardly goes as far as poetry and headlines, but a few journalistic deviations from standard usage have proven themselves over time, and some even have influenced the mainstream rules of prose that dominate composition courses. One deviation is "Timespeak."

Timespeak

Fresh out of Yale in 1923, classmates Henry Luce and Briton Hadden took a major gamble. With borrowed money, they founded Time as a new kind of magazine. Part of their gamble was an irreverent, smartalecky tone that included unprecedented liberties with the language. These liberties, which came to be called "Timespeak," set English teachers abuzz, which focused additional attention on the upstart magazine and contributed to its success.

One Time unorthodoxy was transposing the subject and predicate in parenthetical attributives: Instead of "she said," it was "said she." The unorthodoxy caught on, and today it's common to add emphasis to a direct quotation by introducing it with a transposed attributive, adding even more emphasis with a colon:

> Said Anderson: "It was schlock."

While some Timespeak creations have not survived, placing the verb "said" ahead of the noun, a highly unconventional form, came to be recognized as an effective way to smooth sentences in which the source has a lengthy identifier.

Weak:

> "It was schlock," **Anderson,** president
> of the Purdue Glee Club, **said.**

Stronger:

> "It was schlock," **said Anderson,**
> president of the Purdue Glee Club.

Paragraph Length

After years of writing English essays, you, like many college students, are conditioned to long paragraphs organized classically. Now that you are enrolled in journalism, and looking afresh at your local newspaper, you notice many one-sentence paragraphs. Remembering all the lessons pounded in since eighth-grade composition, you might well ask, "How can this be?" Who's right? Who's wrong? As with Timespeak, the issue is not so simple.

Composition teachers are concerned about formal writing that is intended to be read carefully, even studied. When people read essays, they sit down and concentrate, look for nuances, search between the lines, really work to understand. People don't approach news that way. They zip through stories, jump midway to other stories, get up in the middle if the baby's crying, and maybe don't come back.

People read news with the idea of quitting a story the instant their interest flags or they're distracted. The end of a paragraph is a natural exit point, and a story with frequent paragraphing signals visually that the reader has many options to leave the story easily. Lengthy "grafs," in contrast, signal that the reader has to sit down and tackle the story seriously. Newspaper writers, who have learned that their effectiveness with their audience is best served with frequent paragraphing, follow these rules of thumb:

✦ One-sentence lead paragraphs attract more readers.

✦ Readers stick longer with frequently paragraphed stories.

✦ Two sentences should be combined in a single graf only if dividing them would disrupt closely related thoughts.

Most broadcast news writers, on the other hand, don't paragraph at all. Their stories are heard by the audience, never seen. Only the announcer sees the copy. Without the uneven lines created by paragraphing, announcers can gauge at a glance how long a story will take on the air. Eight full lines of type, 60 characters each, take about 30 seconds. Paragraphing makes quick estimates difficult.

Bulleted Lists

Bulleting a sentence is a typographic technique to speed readers through complex, multi-point spot stories.

Gov. Rudy Bloodstone called Tuesday for 30 percent more state money for schools to assure the state's future as a center for high-tech industry.

"It's an investment we must make," Bloodstone told legislators in his State of the State address.

"Unless we keep our schools in peak condition, other states will graduate students who will make a more attractive work force for the kind of industry that represents the future."

The governor said he would request $145 million for education in his budget proposal to the legislature—compared to $110 million now.

The governor also called for:
- Major rural highway improvements, including 81 new bridges.
- State incentives for employers to set up day-care centers.
- Greater tax breaks for apartment dwellers and other renters.
- Doubling state subsidies for family-owned cotton-growing operations.
- Construction of prisons at Rigby and Farrellton.

In proposing more state funding for education, the governor . . . .

Those black dots in front of the governor's proposals are bullets. They allow readers to zip through several of the governor's major points before getting into details on the main item—the proposed education spending hikes.

English comp purists cringe at bulleting a sentence. It's no wonder: The writer takes a single sentence, puts a colon between the verb and the compound complement, paragraphs at mid-sentence, adds a black dot before each complement, replaces three commas with periods, and eliminates the serial conjunction "and." A bulleted sentence breaks a lot of rules. Even so, it works for quick readers. Consider this unwieldy unbulleted sentence:

The governor also called for major rural highway improvements, including 81 new bridges; state incentives for employers to set up day-care centers; greater tax breaks for apartment dwellers and other renters; doubling state subsidies for family-owned cotton-growing operations; and construction of prisons at Rigby and Farrellton.

When bulleting a sentence, remember these points:

✦ **Parallel construction.** Each bulleted item is a conclusion to the same sentence. Keep the grammatical construction the same.

✦ **Economy.** Put as much of the wording as you can ahead of the colon. Starting each bulleted item with "to" would be parallel construction but needless repetition. Put the "to" in the introductory stem of the sentence, just before the colon.

Weak	Better
In other action, school board members voted:	In other action, school board members voted to:
• To expand the Sheridan High School library to include a separate study area.	• Expand the Sheridan High School library to include a separate study area.
• To close the Jefferson School kitchen and truck lunches from Sheridan High School.	• Close the Jefferson School kitchen and truck lunches from Sheridan High School.
• To cut the district's instructional supplies budget by 10 percent next year.	• Cut the district's instructional supplies budget by 10 percent next year.

✦ **Remember the editor.** Ending each bulleted sentence fragment with a period makes it easier for an editor to drop an item if space is tight. For the same reason, it also helps not to use the serial conjunction "and" at the end of the next to last item.

✦ **No double indentations.** About five words fit on a line of type in a narrow newspaper column, about 30 characters total. There is no room for double indenting to show subcategories.

✦ **No numbering.** Bullets take numerous forms depending on a newspaper's style—dots, squares, dashes—but never numbers. Bulleted items are implicit enumerations. Explicit numbering only diverts reader attention away from what's being said to the order in which it's being said. It generally is a pointless diversion.

PLAIN WORDS AND SENTENCES

STUDY PREVIEW   The crisp, direct writing that is effective for communcating with mass audiences has all kinds of enemies. Among them are big words. Why use a polysyllabic if a one-syllable word can do the job? Convoluted sentences are another enemy of news writing. Why bog down the audience in complex sentences? Write plainly, simply, compactly.

Simple Words

Why say "dessicated," a strange word to many people, when you could say "dried-out"? Common words will help your audience comprehend your story at a glance. Highfalutin words won't. An extensive vocabulary gives you flexibility in telling your stories, but there is a danger. Flaunting your vocabulary will irritate your audience and get in the way. You will come across as pretentious, perhaps arrogant.

This does not mean an absolute ban on polysyllabic words, which must be used if anything less lacks precision. When using complex words, though, it is essential that you define them or make their meaning clear from context. When defining a term, don't imply condescenion toward the reader: "Dear dunderhead, just in case you are too dumb to know what this means, here's a definition."

Here Jerry Bishop of the Wall Street Journal has smoothly inserted a definition as an appositive:

> The same analysis found that men with high blood levels of alpha-linolenic acid, **a fatty acid that researchers say comes from red meat,** ran two to three times the risk of prostate cancer as men with low bolod levels of the acid.

Here, also from the Wall Street Journal, the writer has built a definitional phrase with the obscure term as an adjective:

> WASHINGTON, Del.—DuPont Co. said a Florida jury ruled in its favor in a lawsuit brought by two blueberry growers, who alleged that the company's **Benlate DF fungicide product** had harmed their crops.

Context is an especially smooth way to deal with complicated or obscure words. In the 1950s, scholar Wilson Taylor devised a way to measure whether context was working. He would take a passage of writing, blank out every fifth word, and ask people to fill in the missing word. The more missing words that Wilson's respondents could guess correctly, the better context was working. Here are examples from the Christian Science Monitor in which complex words come across clearly from context:

By James Tyson

In Chicago, as in cities throughout the ages, the **vox populi** has sounded a great cry and compelled city leaders to secure that necessity of daily life: salt.

By Howard LaFranchi

PARIS—Picture the world 10,000 years ago, on the threshold of the **neolithic** period: In the valleys of northern Syria, retreating ice has left behind rich soil in which rich grains thrive.

By Peter Grier

WASHINGTON—By agreeing to reopen part of its nuclear program to international inspectors, North Korea may avoid threatened United Nations economic sanctions without giving up what many in Washington now believe already exists: a **nascent** nuclear weapons arsenal.

Direct Sentences

Many editors tell their reporters to think "S-V-O" when they write. That's short for "subject-verb-object." The idea is to write straightforwardly and directly:

S-V-O: Clinton defeated Bush.

O-V-S: Bush was whom Clinton defeated.

V-S-O: Defeated is what Clinton did to Bush.

Sentences departing from the S-V-O construction reverse the most common sequence of the English language. Deviating can add variety to your writing, but at a high price. Non-S-V-O sentences are built backward, usually lack punch, and are wordy. Unless you have a reason for passive construction, make the doer of the action the sentence subject.

O-V-S: The body was retrieved by sheriff's divers.

S-V-O: Sheriff's divers retrieved the body.

Complex sentences can take a heavy toll on the news audience. New York Times editor Theodore Bernstein campaigned long for writers to restrict their sentences to one idea each. Bernstein argued that a sentence making more than one point was trying to do too much. "Generally it speeds reading if there is only one idea to a sentence," Bernstein said.

Active Verbs

Strong, lively writing is dominated by sentences with active verbs, not passive verbs:

Active: Clinton **defeated** Bush.

Passive: Bush **was defeated** by Clinton.

Put the doer of the action, in this case Clinton, who did the defeating, at the front of the sentence.

A tipoff that you may be using a passive verb form is an auxiliary verb like "was" and "has." In self-editing your copy, check sentences for passive constructions, then play with the word order to see if an active construction is possible.

The problem with passive verb forms is especially obvious in scripted stories. On the air, they come across flat. This flatness is less obvious in the written word, but nonetheless detracts from lively storytelling.

Some public relations people working in an institutional environment find it's hard to cut through the passive constructions that are common among their colleagues in other departments. Lionel Fisher, who has written on corporate journalism, once noted: "Bureaucrats, academicians, politicians and corporate executives thrive on the passive voice because it lets people off the hook, skirts blame, points limply at amorphous companies, institutions, agencies, divisions and departments, instead of singling out culpable individuals." The challenge in PR writing is that the editors and news producers who decide whether to use a news release are more attracted to good rather than bland writing. The quality of writing affects whether a news release is picked up. In-house news also must be understandable by everyone in the audience, not just those who thrive on obfuscation at headquarters.

Even so, passive constructions have their place. When the recipient of the action is the most important element in the story, an S-V-O construction would mean burying the news:

> Three Albuquerque women **were killed** Tuesday when their light plane crashed in the Sangre de Cristo Mountains.

If an S-V-O construction means delaying the news until the end of the sentence, a passive construction generally is better. Don't be so slavish to S-V-O construction that you warp the emphasis:

Delayed emphasis:	Immediate emphasis:
The commission approved **a 40 percent rate hike** for Pacific Bell customers.	**A 40 percent rate hike** for Pacific Bell customers was approved by the commission.

Also, passive constructions can help you streamline a sentence by dropping words that identify the doer of the action. In this sentence, the electors are sufficiently implied:

> Sharon Steward, a former Miss Arkansas, **was elected** student body president at Drury College.

Expletive Constructions

A sentence beginning with "there" or "it" is an expletive construction that usually signals looseness:

Expletive construction:	Improved:
There were nine senators at the meeting, one short of a quorum.	Nine senators attended the meeting, one short of a quorum.

SPELLING

STUDY PREVIEW   People sometimes laugh off a misspelled word as "creative spelling," but it is no laughing matter. Bad spelling undermines the credibility of a piece and can slow down readers and tongue-tie announcers. When dictionaries list multiple spellings, news writers look to the AP stylebook.

Virtues of Correct Spelling

Misspelling in the print media undermines reader confidence in you and your story. Worse, readers can misunderstand what you're writing. Misspelling can be just as disastrous in broadcast writing. An announcer zipping through your story at 160 words a minute can be distracted by an errant spelling and stumble on the air.

Common Misspellings

Among words most misspelled in campus newspapers:

a bit: Two words.

a lot: Also two words.

accommodate: Memory aid: This word is long enough to accommodate two "c's" and two "m's."

athlete: Just because many people mispronounce it "athalete" is no excuse to misspell it. Memory aid: Athletes use two legs—two legs, two syllables.

baccalaureate: The only double letters are the "c's."

camaraderie: More syllables than you might think.

disk: With a "k" for computer disks.

dormitory: With an "i." "Dorm" is more conversational and sidesteps the spelling issue.

embarrass: With one "r," it's not only wrong but embarrassing.

guerrilla: Memory aid: "Guerrilla warfare" is a heavy-duty subject. The word for it is sufficiently heavy-duty to handle two "r's" and two "l's." Don't confuse with "gorilla," a type of ape.

harass: One "r."

liaison: Memory aid: If you and I are both "I's," it takes two for a liaison.

lieutenant: Memory aid: "The *lieu*tenant *lie*d."

marshal: One "l," as in homecoming parade *marshal.*

occur, occurred, occurrence: Two "r's" with a third syllable.

professor: One "f," two "s's." "Prof" not only is more conversational, it sidesteps the problem.

separate: Memory aid: There are "e's" and "a's" in "separate" to separate—two "a's" and two "e's." Also, think about "a rat."

sergeant: Not "sar-." Memory aid: Police *serge*ants wear blue *serge* uniforms.

sheriff: One "r," two "f's."

sophomore: Three syllables, not two. Memory aid: Sophomores are bound for their third year—third year, three syllables.

tenure: It may take a prof 10 years to earn tenure, but the spelling is neither "10-year" nor "ten-year."

Stylebook Spellings

The people who edit dictionaries differ on some spellings, which is why news people create stylebooks. Here is how the Associated Press stylebook, the most widely used reference for journalistic writing, resolves some discrepancies:

catalog: When dictionaries differ, AP generally opts for the shorter form, "catalog" rather than "catalogue," for example, which conserves space.

DIRECT TALK. News is often dramatic, as in the 1993 truck-bombing of the World Trade Center in New York. Reporters need to be direct and clear in their writing to convey the drama of what has happened. Loose wording, passive sentences, and expletive constructions drain the story of its inherent drama.
(Mark Cardwell/Reuters/The Bettmann Archive)

citywide: One word. Also "statewide, "nationwide" and "worldwide."

employee: Two "e's."

-ly: Adverbs ending in "ly" never take a hyphen when part of a compound modifier—"a widely known fact."

theater: AP prefers the American form to the European "theatre."

toward: no concluding "s."

vice president: no hyphen.

AVOIDING BOGGED-DOWN WRITING

STUDY PREVIEW   Effective writing avoids nicey-nice words and phrases, which usually are flabby and detract from a straightforward news tone. By definition, jargon doesn't work for a mass audience. Unnecessary abstract nouns also bog down good writing.

Euphemisms

News is written to the point. An enemy of direct expression is the euphemism, a word that veils what's being written about. Real estate people talk about "homes," a word with connotations of love, hearth and happiness. What they're really selling are "houses."

Don't become part of the sales pitch.

Image-conscious institutions tend to subvert perfectly good words. One Midwest college avoids the word "campus" in news releases. "What we have is a 'community,' not just a 'campus,'" said the public relations director in reprimanding a news reporter. The same PR person bristles too at "dormitory," pointing out that "We have 'residence halls.'"

Some euphemisms are meant to cushion against unpleasant realities. "Died" is a simple, direct, clear verb, yet many people opt for "passed away" or "passed on." Some go further: "returned to her maker," "was called by the grim reaper," "crossed to the other shore." Among the worst offenders are morticians, who call themselves "funeral directors" and call their places of business "funeral parlors."

Euphemisms obscure expression. Worse, they erode the detached, neutral tone that your news audience expects.

Jargon

In gathering news, reporters pick up expertise on specialized subjects. They can also pick up the specialized language of their sources. You may have to know "code blue," "stat" and "post-op" if you're covering a hospital story, but those terms are jargon to your mass audience.

For those rare instances in which you must use jargon, either define the term or make its meaning clear from context.

Redundancy

One enemy of compact writing is redundancy. Each of these phrases can be tightened by eliminating unnecessary elements:

at **the corner of** Main and Elm

is **now** the company manager

at 1 p.m. **in the afternoon**

The store made $500 **in profits,** Kilmer reported.

Abstractions

Go for the specific over the general, and the concrete over the abstract.

Lionel Fisher, who has long crusaded for better public relations writing, offers these examples for cutting through the muck of abstractions:

Fuzzy: In the area of formal written communications, the lowest dissemination-level vehicle has the highest credibility quotient.

Direct: Of all the company publications, the newsletter is the most trusted.

Wordy: In an environment characterized by constrained financial resources and intense competition . . .

Direct: In a tight, competitive economy . . .

Fuzzy: Extension to private industry of a public law on rehabilitating the handicapped may become an effective means of expanding the tight U.S. task force.

Direct: A law to help rehabilitate handicapped people may create jobs.

Wordy: . . . in a fraction of the time required previously.

Direct: . . . quicker than before.

NUMBERS

> **STUDY PREVIEW**   Numbers can enhance the clarity of your news writing, but numbers are tricky. If overused, numbers introduce clutter and confusion. Citing percentage of change is a way to streamline comparative numbers. Rounding off numbers can help the audience understand at a glance what the numbers indicate.

Indicators of Significance

Numbers are an indicator of significance, extent and scope. When Ron Scherer of the Christian Science Monitor was writing about sailboat sales, he began with a catchy lead:

> ATLANTIC CITY, N.J.—Masts ahoy! The sailboat industry is finally showing some signs of vitality.

Then Scherer supported the point with numbers:

> After years of trimmed sales, this bat-
> tered segment of the marine-purchase
> business is starting to enjoy smoother
> waters.
> Manufacturers at Sail Expo '94 report
> that sales are running **15 to 20 percent**
> over last year.

This Reuters story uses numbers to indicate the extent of what was happening:

> TORONTO—Police have detained scores of curious Canadians who attempted to bring in copies of U.S. newspapers that printed details of a grisly Ontario murder case that is under a court gag order.
>
> A total of **61 drivers** had been arrested or spoken to and **187 copies** of the Buffalo News had been confiscated, Staff Sgt. Paul White of the Niagara Regional Police said today.

Numbers are valuable tools for implementing the "Show, don't tell" principle.

Numbers in Context

A number by itself doesn't say much. Should someone be impressed to learn that a university budget is $36 million? Most people have no idea what a university budget should be. Is $36 million a lot? Not enough? Generally you have to provide a context for numbers so your audience understands what they mean. Raymond Serafin, writing in the trade journal Advertising Age, might have said the Saturn automobile company had dropped its advertising spending to $50 million, but instead he wrote:

> Saturn is striving to counteract a sales
> slowdown that began after it **halved** its
> ad budget to an estimated $50 million in
> 1993.

An AP writer might merely have said a newspaper had hiked its cover price to $1.75, but instead put the new price in context:

> The Minneapolis Star Tribune has
> raised the newsstand price of its Sunday
> edition **by 25 cents** to $1.75.

Here are ways that numbers can be put in context:

TELLING IT STRAIGHT. Newspeople are not in the business of coddling their audience with euphemisms that cushion the reality of what is happening. After 66 people were killed and 200 wounded when a mortar shell hit a marketplace in Sarajevo in February 1994, reporters used words that captured the horror of it. Anything else would distort the reality of the massacre.   (Corinne Dufka/Reuters/The Bettmann Archive)

✦ Compare a number with a previous number: "Enrollment, at 1,400, is **100 more than** last year."

✦ Compare a number with a number in a different but similar situation: "MSU's student activity fee, at $110 a semester, is **half** the fee at Metcalf College."

✦ Compare a number with an ideal: "The football budget, at $213,000, is **far less than** the $650,000 Coach Rogers requested."

So Numbers Don't Overwhelm

Too many numbers, just like abstractions, can obscure a point. As a rule, keep numbers to the bare minimum. In this hypothetical lead sentence, you can see how overwhelming and confusing numbers can be:

> The record enrolment, 7,521 full-time equivalent students, represents 5,401 full-time and 7,101 part-time students for the 1994–95 academic year, compared to 6,992, representing 5,388 full-time and 6,700 part-time students, for the 1993–94 academic year.

The key number in this sentence seems to be 7,521 full-time equivalent students. Drop all the rest of the numbers, even the years, do some simple math to calculate the percentage of change, and you instead could write:

> The record enrolment, the equivalent of 7,521 full-time students, is running 7.6 percent ahead of last year.

Almost always the significance of two numbers is clearer if you use one as a base number, in this case 7,521 students, and the percentage of change. You don't have to burden your audience with all the other figures.

To calculate percentage of change, find the difference between the two enrollment figures that are being compared. Then divide that difference by the earlier figure. For example, if 42 Moslem students were enrolled in 1985 and 53 in 1995, you would subtract 42 from 53, which gives you 11. Then to find out the percentage of increase you divide 11 by the base number 42. The result: The number of Moslems at the college increased 26 percent over 10 years.

Generally round numbers off. No purpose is served writing that the legislature approved a budget of $2,411,998,002.33. On radio and television, it would be impossibly silly: "Two billion 411-million 998-thousand two dollars and 33 cents." Write "$2.4 billion" for the print media. For broadcast, make it "almost two and one-half billion dollars." You are not an accountant preparing to do an audit, nor is your audience.

Here are tips on using percentages:

✦ "Almost 20 percent" is better than 19.9145 percent.

✦ "Almost double" is better than 98.42 percent increase.

+ "More than triple" is better than a 205.1 percent increase.

+ "Halved" is better than a 49 percent drop.

Here are AP style rules involving numbers:

+ Use "more than," "less than" and "fewer than." The words "over" and "under" are best reserved for spatial relationships.

+ One to nine are spelled out, 10 and up are in figures.

+ Avoid starting sentences with figures, but if you do, spell them out.

+ Spell out dollars in broadcast instead of using the dollar sign: 102–thousand dollars.

+ "Percent" is one word, as is "percentage." Use the symbol "%" only in tables.

READABILITY FORMULAS

STUDY PREVIEW   Readability formulas are valuable diagnostic tools for news writers. The formulas can alert you if you are wandering from basic principles of good writing, such as using short, direct sentences. Formulas can also help you make your writing more interesting.

The Flesch Scale

Many word-processor programs allow you to calculate your average sentence length and to make other mathematical assessments of your writing. These calculations derive from studies in the 1940s and 1950s by Rudolf Flesch, Robert Gunning and others on what makes readable writing.

With the Flesch formula, you choose a 100–word sample and measure the average sentence length and number of syllables. You multiple the number of sentences by 1.015 and the number of syllables by 0.846. You then add those numbers and subtract them from 206.835. The result will fall somewhere on Flesch's scale:

0–15:   Very difficult, suitable for college graduates. Scientific writing falls in this range.

15–50:   Difficult, for college students. Academic writing is in this range.

50–60:   Fairly difficult, for high school students. This includes quality journals like Harper's and Atlantic.

60–70:   Standard, for eighth and ninth graders. This includes Reader's Digest.

70–80: Fairly easy, for seventh graders. This includes slick fiction.

80–90: Easy, for sixth graders. This includes pulp fiction.

90–100: Very easy, for fifth graders. Comics fit this category.

Most newswriters shoot for the 60–70 range or easier. The Associated Press hired Flesch to conduct two studies of its writing, and from those studies the AP recommended its writers keep their average sentence length at 19 to 20 words. Note: That's average sentence length, not maximum.

Measuring Human Interest

Flesch devised a second formula as an indicator of a story's human interest. In a 100-word sample, you add the number of personal names, like "Bill Clinton" and "Mary"; words with gender, like "actress" and "brother"; and group words, like "people" and "folks." Then add the number of sentences that contain an attributive; the number of sentences that are addressed to the reader, like questions, commands, requests; the number of sentences with exclamation marks; and the number of incomplete sentences whose full meaning has to be inferred from context. Now multiply the number of personal sentences by .314 and the number of personal words by 3.635. Add these sums for Flesch's human-interest score. Zero is no human interest, and 100 means the story is full of human interest. Here's Flesch's human interest yardstick:

0–10: dull (scientific writing).

10–20: mildy interesting (trade writing).

20–40: interesting (Reader's Digest).

40–60: highly interesting (New Yorker magazine).

60–100: dramatic (fiction).

Some writing is off the scale, like many insurance policies. Flesch found one policy that rated –12.

Gunning's Fog Index

Robert Gunning had a similar formula, which United Press used to evaluate its daily report. He figured the average sentence length in words; the number of words of three syllables or more (except capitalized words and easy-to-recognize words formed from smaller words, like "butterfly"); and the number of verb forms made into three syllables by adding "-ed" or "-ing." He added those three components, then subtracted the sum from 0.4 for what he called his "fog index." A 10, where Time magazine fits, would be suitable for 10th-graders. A nine would be ninth-graders, an eight for eighth-graders, and so on.

Critics of Readability Formulas

Readability formulas have their detractors. The critics bristle that formulas try to reduce writing to a science, which it is not. The formulas make no attempt to measure content, context or story structure. In fact, gibberish can be cranked through Flesch or Gunning's formulas and score well. Even so, readability formulas are excellent tools for serious writers to assess their work. A monthly check with Gunning's Fog Index, for example, might alert you that you have let your writing become flabby. Alerted to that, you can take corrective measures.

Flesch and Gunning and their detractors agree, however, on the principles of clear writing, and these are principles that readiability formulas reward:

+ Short sentences on average.
+ Simple sentences rather than complex.
+ Familiar words.
+ Only necessary words.
+ Action verbs.
+ Conversational writing.
+ Terms that the audience can picture.
+ Words that tie in with your audience's experience.
+ Variety in sentence length and constructions.

CHAPTER WRAP-UP

News writers should be so comfortable with the rules and conventions of the written language that they can adapt them to their special needs. These adaptations include breaking and bending some conventions to be effective in reaching news audiences.

What distinguishes news audiences from other readers and listeners is that they comprise people who want a quick fix. While these audiences are largely intelligent people, they don't approach news with the undivided attention that they give to essays, poems or interoffice memos. When it comes to news, they are quick readers and hurried listeners, and they are easily distracted.

Breaking the rules and bending the conventions of the written language are justified only when it helps to meet the individuals in these audiences on their terms.

STUDY QUESTIONS

1.   Name three common reference sources for news writers.

2.   News writing follows generally accepted rules of good English, but there are exceptions. Why these exceptions?

3.   What are the occasions for bending the conventions of good English?

4.   Why is news writing dominated by plain words and simple direct sentences?

5.   Why is correct spelling important in news writing for both print and broadcast media?

6.   What are euphemisms, jargon and abstractions, and how do they detract from direct, clear news writing?

7.   How can numbers enhance a news story? What are the hazards of incorporating numbers into stories?

8.   What are the strengths and weaknesses of readability formulas?

PUTTING YOUR LEARNING TO WORK

EXERCISE 1   Redundancies

Redundancies are flab that consume valuable news space or broadcast time without adding to the message. As empty words, they contribute nothing. Worse, they sap vitality from a sentence. Look for the redundancies in these sentences and then trim them down:

Munson was struck at 8 p.m. last night at the corner of Huff and Sarnia.

Early on in the play, Hendricks' character wanders by the new cinema that is under construction to look for his missing cat Felix.

The common mutual distrust was shared by the two women, Grogan testified.

The man's bodily injuries include two broken wrists.

The bookstore offered the backpack free of charge.

Jane Morrison, an alumna of Wichita State, was graduated in 1977.

EXERCISE 2   Sentence Sequence

None of these sentences is in S-V-O sequence. Recast them so they are:

Bush was defeated by Clinton.

Kreuger said he was called 17 times by Murphy that afternoon.

The fire was caused by a frayed wire on a space heater, the inspector said.

The body was retrieved by sheriff's divers.

The mall is used before business hours by retirees for walking exercise.

EXERCISE 3   **Expletive Constructions**

The sentences below contain expletive constructions, which are common in a first draft. Revise these sentences to rid them of the expletive construction:

There were nine senators at the meeting, one short of a quorum.

It was not until 7:10 p.m. that Foxx called the meeting to order.

It is estimated by Exxon officials that 1,700 gallons spilled into the Hudson River.

EXERCISE 4   **Using Numbers**

Identify the most important numbers in these passages, calculate the percentage of change, and then rewrite the sentences to avoid number clutter:

> The record enrollment, 7,521 full-time equivalent students, represents 5,401 full-time and 7,101 part-time students for the 1994–95 academic year, compared to 6,992, representing 5,388 full-time and 6,700 part-time students, for the 1993–94 academic year.
>
> The librarians said they may as well shut down, noting their budget has slipped from $520,000 in 1990 to $286,000 and probably $260,000 next year.

FOR FURTHER LEARNING

Edgar Dale and Jeanne S. Chall. "A Formula for Predicting Readability." Education Research Bulletin, 27 (Feb. 18, 1948), 45–55. Dale and Chall, of Ohio State University, list 3,000 words known to four out of five fourth-graders. The more words outside that list which appear in a sample of writing, the more difficult the writing.

Lionel L. Fisher. "The Craft of Corporate Journalism." Nelson–Hall, 1992. This lively primer covers the whole range of public relations writing, including news releases and in-house publications.

Rudolf Flesch. "The Art of Readable Writing." Harper & Row, 1949.

Christopher W. French, editor. The Associated Press Stylebook and Libel Manual. Associated Press, 1986. This is the most used newspaper stylebook. Many bookstores stock stylebooks from the Los Angeles Times, New York Times, and Washington Post. The leading radio and television stylebook, compiled and edited by James R. Hood and Brad Kalbfeld, is The Associated Press Broadcast News Handbook (Associated Press, 1982).

Robert Gunning. "The Techniques of Clear Writing." McGraw-Hill, 1952.

Lauren Kessler and Duncan McDonald. "When Words Collide: A Journalist's Guide to Grammar and Style," 2nd ed. Wadsworth, 1988. Every writer needs a desktop grammar book, and this is the liveliest treatment available for news people.

Wilson L. Taylor. "Close Procedure: A New Tool for Measuring Readaibility." Journalism Quarterly 30, No. 4 (Autumn 1953), 314–33.

CHAPTER 10

Following Up and Expanding

In this chapter you will learn:

+ Reporters look for new angles to update their audiences on already-reported news.

+ Updating a story requires a skillful blending of new information and tie-backs to earlier stories.

+ Peppering background throughout a story is more effective than whole blocks of background.

+ Follow-up stories require imagination to expand on underdeveloped angles and create new ones.

+ Reporters sometimes write chunks of breaking stories ahead of time, revising them as developments occur.

+ Fresh follow-ups come from localizing, new questions, new sources and new angles.

+ Reporters apply their expertise to write interpretive follow-ups, analytical pieces and commentaries.

AFTER THE CRACK OF THE BAT

Each summer night at 6:05, the boy James Michener picked up the Sports Extra edition of the Philadelphia Inquirer and rushed through his village hawking the paper.

"I remember how avidly the men grabbed for my wares," recalled Michener years later in a book on sports in the United States. In those pre-television days when baseball wasn't even much carried on radio, the fans in Michener's village were eager to find out how their beloved Athletics and Phillies had done that afternoon.

For sports writers, no less so than for fans, the adrenalin surges with a bases-loaded hit. But sports writers know too that fans are interested in stories about their teams even on days when no games are played, and even in the off-season.

Sports writers scour the locker rooms, head offices and player hang-outs for new stories and fresh angles that tell more than a play-by-play story. These are anticipatory, before-the-game stories and follow-up, after-the-game stories that interpret and explain and offer insights and color, and all news reporters, not just sports writers, do them. Public relations people, always eager to land a favorable story in the media, know how to capitalize on reporters' ongoing hunt for fresh material.

Many people don't realize that most news coverage occurs before and after the events that stick in their memory. Political writers, for example, write dozens more stories on pending legislation than on the vote itself. When a disastrous storm occurs, reporters cover what occurred but then follow up with many more stories on the aftermath and recovery.

Sociologist Herbert Gans noted the significance of follow-up stories in a study of Newsweek magazine's coverage of 1967 race riots. A mere 3 percent of the coverage was on the riots, and only 2 percent dealt with injuries and deaths. Thirty-four percent of the coverage focused on restoring order. Gans found that Newsweek gave four times as many words to police and Army attempts to restore order than to describing the disturbance.

Anyone who looks at the Gans study will realize that news people are hardly the gloomy doomsayers of folk wisdom.

In this chapter, you will learn ways to seek follow-up angles and to expand the coverage of events. You will learn also that these follow-up stories offer special opportunities to bring imagination and creativity to your work.

UPDATING THE BREAKING STORY

STUDY PREVIEW   As events unfold in breaking stories, reporters report not only new developments but also enough background so the new information makes sense. This is no easy job. The challenge is to write simultaneously for people who have been following the story as it has unfolded and for people who missed the earlier stories.

Deadline After Deadline

Except for the most routine announcement stories, reporters are constantly updating their stories. When an airliner goes down, reporters scramble to gather as much information as they can to make a deadline. Once the deadline is met, they have yet another deadline—the next edition, the next newscast. And they keep scrambling to stay on top of unfolding developments.

The pressure for follow-up stories can be incessant. Some metropolitan newspapers have multiple editions, each with updated stories. The afternoon Atlanta Journal, for example, goes to press four times. The deadline for the first edition, which is trucked to outlying Georgia, is 7:30 a.m. With a breaking story, Journal reporters have three more deadlines until the final Blue Streak edition that goes to bed in the early afternoon.

In broadcasting, deadlines come even more quickly—hourly at many stations. At an all-news station, a reporter might be on the air live every few minutes with every new development. A reporter for ABC radio, which operates six news networks, each with newscasts at different times, faces several deadlines every hour.

In his history of United Press, Joe Alex Morris tells of a UP reporter talking about his deadline: "Our deadline is now. Someplace around the world at this instant a newspaper is going to press. We've got a deadline every minute." Given the speed of modern communication, the public's hunger for news, the proliferation of media agencies and the competition among them, it's not just news service reporters but all journalists who have a deadline every minute.

Emphasizing New Developments

With a breaking story, the challenge is to focus on what is new for every revision, yet make the story clear to readers or listeners who missed earlier versions. This requires integrating enough information from earlier stories so newcomers can figure out what's happening, without burdening the story with so much background that you turn off people who caught the earlier stories.

STARTING FOLLOW-UP STORIES

STUDY PREVIEW   The lead sentence of many follow-up stories should have a tie-back to previous stories but not so much as to bog down the lead. The challenge is finding the thin line between too much background, which can bore people who already know those details, and too little background, which fails to give a context for the update.

Tie-Backs

Because many people will not have seen or heard the original story, it is important to have a tie-back high in the follow-up, preferably in the lead. This orients newcomers to the core event. It also provides an anchor to the original event for people who have followed the story.

Michele Apostolos of the weekly Quaker Campus at Whittier College based this lead on a new development but included a tie-back:

> A 17-year-old Rosemead youth was released Monday from the hospital and "is home and doing OK" **after jumping out of a second-floor window** of a Whittier College dorm Sunday.

Her point: The youth is OK.
The background: This was after a dorm incident the day before.
Detroit News writer Norman Sinclair kept the focus on the new development but tied back to earlier stories:

> GAYLORD, Mich.—The star witness **in a retrial hearing in the Jerry Tobias murder** case Friday created another twist in her long-standing claim that she witnessed the killing.

His point: This witness testified.
The background: This added a twist to her earlier claim.

Lead Sentence Construction

Confining background to a subordinate role in the lead sentence of a follow-up story keeps the thrust of the lead fresh. One approach is to build the lead sentence around a subject-verb-object that tells the new development, with the background in a subordinate phrase or clause. Robert Imrie of the Associated Press, reporting a court case, started this way:

> WAUSAU, Wis.—A boy who confessed to strangling his 11-year-old sister after she ridiculed him and a friend was sentenced Thursday to juvenile prison until he is 21 and then a year in county jail.

The subject-verb-object core of Imrie's lead sentence is the new development:

boy | *was sentenced* | *to prison*

A bare-bones core needs embellishment to read well. Notice below how elements are added while keeping the subject-verb-object core intact:

> WAUSAU, Wis.—A boy was sentenced Thursday to juvenile prison until he is 21 and then a year in county jail.

The grammatical core remains:

boy | *was sentenced* | *to prison*

From the grammatical core, you build background detail into the sentence until you are confident that the lead will bring every reader, even the ones new to the story, up to speed. Look at the first example again, noting that the background is in the subordinate clause beginning with "who":

> WAUSAU, Wis.—A boy **who confessed to strangling his 11-year-old sister after she ridiculed him and a friend** was sentenced Thursday to juvenile prison until he is 21 and then a year in county jail.

This approach is true to the inverted-pyramid principle that most lead sentences should emphasize the latest development. A less skilled writer who foresakes the inverted pyramind might end up emphasizing the old news with a weak, chronological approach:

> WAUSAU, Wis.—A boy confessed several weeks ago to strangling his sister after she ridiculed him and a friend. On Thursday he was sentenced to juvenile prison until he is 21 and then a year in county jail.

Among the problems with this flawed lead is that readers who had followed the story would see no reason to read on. The lead seems to indicate that the story contains nothing they do not already know.

The challenge in updating stories, then, is to emphasize new angles while incorporating sufficient background so that people who missed preliminary accounts will understand the new developments.

Broadcast Updating

While newspaper reporters can integrate new developments and background into a lead sentence, radio and television reporters have a different challenge. In broadcast writing, sentences have to be short to appeal to the ear, and short sentences can seldom accommodate both old and new information. The solution, usually, is to build background into the flow of the first two or three sentences of broadcast stories while keeping the emphasis on the latest development:

> A family tragedy that kept townspeople abuzz in tiny Rothschild, Wisconsin, for weeks has come to a conclusion. A 14-year-old boy **who admitted strangling his sister to death** is going to juvenile prison. Brian Lee Kirksey received the sentence in a Wausau courtroom this morning.

At stations with frequent newscasts, a major story that has no new developments requires constant reworking so listeners won't become bored hearing the same story word for word. Some news writers revel in constantly finding new elements to emphasize while being ever mindful of the core of the story that needs telling. To them, reworking the same story is both an art form and a challenge to outdo themselves every 20 or 30 minutes or however often newscasts come. Other writers so disdain reworking the same material that they leave broadcasting because of it.

Here are reworked radio stories, each with a different sound:

> A 14-year-old northern Wisconsin boy is headed for prison. A judge in Wausau has sentenced Brian Lee Kirksey of Rothschild to juvenile prison until he is 21 and then to county jail. The Kirksey youth **had admitted strangling his 11-year-old sister to death and then having sex with the body.**

> The Rothschild, Wisconsin, boy **who got mad at his sister and strangled her to death** has been sentenced. Fourteen-year-old Brian Lee Kirksey was told today that he will be in juvenile

> prison until he is 21. Then he will spend a year in county jail. Judge Vincent Howard passed the sentence. The judge said he could extend the sentence if Kirksey ever violates parole. The maximum could be 20 years.

In these rehashes the tie-back is built into the story near the top. The emphasis is on the new development, the sentencing, but the background is not neglected.

WEAVING BACKGROUND THROUGHOUT

STUDY PREVIEW   Writers who dump whole blocks of background into a follow-up story are inviting their audience to stop reading or listening at that point. More effective is peppering background throughout the story in subordinate clauses and phrases.

Background Breaks

In this adaptation of the Wausau sentencing story, note how the four-sentence block of background interrupts the telling of the news and the courtroom drama:

WAUSAU, Wis.—A boy who confessed to strangling his 11-year-old sister after she ridiculed him and a friend was sentenced Thursday to juvenile prison until he is 21 and then a year in county jail.

Brian Lee Kirksey, 14, shook his head no when the judge asked him if he had anything to say before sentencing.

Kirksey earlier confessed to strangling Laura Kirksey Nov. 17 with his right arm at their apartment in Rothschild, a village of 3,500 near Wausau.

In a statement to police, Kirksey said that his sister told him: "Your friend's dumb and stupid and you shouldn't even have friends."

Two months later, Kirksey pleaded no contest to first-degree reckless homicide after he waived his rights as a juvenile and the case was transferred to adult court.

Kirksey, who a prosecutor said was "abused severely" when he was younger and suffered "deep-seated rage," also admitted to having sex with his sister after she died.

In sentencing Kirksey, Judge Vincent Howard followed the recommendations of a plea agreement.

At a prison school, the boy can receive more treatment for his problems than if he was sentenced to prison, lawyers said.

The judge withheld a prison sentence, reserving his options should Kirksey violate his probation, which will continue until he is 35.

"Twenty years is still hanging over his head," said Judge Howard, referring to the maximum sentence for first-degree reckless homicide.

Kirksey, wearing a red Wisconsin Badgers jacket, hugged his mother and grandmother before being placed in handcuffs and led out of the courtroom.

Such a background block interrupts the telling of the news. Better is integrating background unobtrusively throughout the story.

Integrating Background

Avoid getting bogged down in background. Use just enough information from earlier stories for the new story to make sense. Too much background is flab that will not be a good use of your audience's time.

As much as possible, integrate background into sentences that carry forward the momentum of the new story. This means trying to avoid entire sentences that do nothing more than provide background. Background breaks signal the audience that this is a point at which to stop reading the story.

Over-Emphasized Background

Blocks of background do their worst damage when they are high in a story. Here, sentences of background leave the lead dangling undeveloped:

MANHATTAN, Kan.—The general manager of the nation's largest beef cattle operation told 500 cattle-growers Friday that increasing their income will require identifying profit-limiting factors.

Paul Genho manages 30,000 head of cattle and forestry, citrus and wildlife operations at Deseret Ranches of Florida.

He was hired in 1981 as a cattle manager and worked to make the operation more profitable.

Those last two sentences tell nothing about what Genho said, which was the main point of the lead.

See how the background block can be avoided by integrating it into sentences that keep the story moving:

MANHATTAN, Kan.—The general manager of the nation's largest beef cattle operation told 500 cattle-growers Friday that increasing their income will require identifying profit-limiting factors.

Paul Genho, **who guided the giant Deseret Ranches in Florida to increased profitability over the past 12 years,** cautioned against a formula approach to profits.

"The limiting factors are different for each rancher," he said.

In the first example, the grammatical core of the first sentence is news:

manager | *told* | *cattle-growers*

But the core of the next two sentences is background:

Genho | *manages* | *Deseret Ranches*

He | was hired | as manager

In the second example, background is subordinated in the sentences and the grammatical core focuses on what the man said, which was the news:

manager | told | cattle-growers
Genho | cautioned against | formula approach

Background is best peppered through a story, the most important background higher, less important later. And avoid turning over entire sentences to background. Let's revisit the Wausau, Wis., sentencing story to see how this can be done:

> WAUSAU, Wis.—A boy **who confessed to strangling his 11-year-old sister after she ridiculed him and a friend** was sentenced Thursday to juvenile prison until he is 21 and then a year in county jail.
>
> Brian Lee Kirksey, 14, shook his head no when the judge asked him if he had anything to say before sentencing.
>
> Judge Vincent Howard followed the recommendations of a plea agreement in sentencing Kirksey, **who earlier confessed to strangling his sister Laura Nov. 17 at their apartment in a village near Wausau.**
>
> Kirksey, **who admitted to having sex with his sister's body after she died,** hugged his mother and grandmother before being placed in handcuffs and led out of the courtroom.
>
> The judge withheld a prison sentence, reserving his options should Kirksey violate his probation, which will continue until he is 35.

Other background could be similarly woven into sentences, each of whose grammatical core carries forward the telling of the new developments.

Unavoidable Background Breaks

In rare situations when a background block is unavoidable, it should come at a transition point in the story so it has minimal interruption of the story's idea flow.

RETHINKING FOR THE SECOND CYCLE

STUDY PREVIEW   Follow-up stories are an opportunity to apply your imagination to catch up on underdeveloped angles and create new ones. Even when fresh information is unavailable, reworking a story is a challenging, creative enterprise.

Fresh Follow-Ups

Morning newscasts are dominated not by breaking stories but by recaps of events that occurred overnight. Some listeners and viewers, whose habit is to pick up only the morning newscasts, expect a summary of everything from the past 24 hours. These recaps are called "second-cycle stories." In the newspaper business, there are two cycles in places served by morning and afternoon papers, with each cycle updating the previous one.

Just as with updates against a deadline, second-cycle stories must satisfy two kinds of audiences: those who know the story and those who are new to it. To make the story fresh, reporters try to generate a new angle.

The revised status of a situation can make a good second-cycle lead. For some stories of a routine sort, a quick phone call can do it:

First cycle:

> Deer hunters found a boy, believed to be 8 or 9 years old, wandering lost and incoherent in a wooded ravine seven miles east of Chilton late Friday afternoon.

For the second cycle, a writer in a short-staffed newsroom, which could not spring someone free to go to the scene, called the sheriff and the hospital:

> A 9-year-old Mason City boy who disappeared from a playground Friday afternoon and was found two hours later in a wooded area 12 miles away could give no clues Saturday as to how he got there.
>
> The boy, Jonathan Weiss, son of Keith and Marsha Weiss of Mason City, was questioned by police, but Sheriff George Wilson said the boy recalled no details on what happened.
>
> Attendants at the Chilton Hospital, where the boy was examined, said he was mentally traumatized although in good physical health.

More calls and digging sometimes will yield a story more interesting than the original event:

> How 9-year-old Jonathan Weiss got from a northside Mason City playground to a remote wooded area 12 miles away during a couple of hours Friday afternoon is a mystery to his playmates.
>
> But his mother says she knows.
>
> "The flying saucers are back," said Marsha Weiss.

Here are two follow-ups to a mass killing, the first from the Des Moines, Iowa, Register:

> NORWALK, Iowa—Preliminary autopsies show that Jolene Forsyth and five children did not all die of gunshot wounds, authorities say.
>
> At least one was strangled.

From the Dubuque, Iowa, Telegraph Herald:

> NORWALK, Iowa (AP)—After a caravan of three ambulances hauled six bodies from a quiet neighborhood Monday, Police Chief Mike Richardson was trying to piece together an apparent domestic dispute that turned into mass murder.

Here are approaches for second-cycle leads:

- ✦ Ask about cause or motive.
- ✦ Interview witnesses for their reaction or more detail.
- ✦ Look for a future angle.
- ✦ Explore the effects of what happened.
- ✦ Go into greater detail so the audience can understand the event better.
- ✦ Lean on experts for analysis.
- ✦ Draw on your personal experience and expertise as a reporter to give background and discuss implications.
- ✦ Correct erroneous information in the earlier story.

Misinformation sometimes finds its way into stories reported under deadline pressure from a confused situation. "Correctives," as they are called, can be integrated smoothly into a story:

When errors are the fault of a reporter or editor, most news organizations run a separate correction.

Public relations people, as soon as an error in a news release is discovered, rush a revised release to newsrooms by fax, telephone or hand-delivery in an

> An initial report from an off-duty night clerk that 120 people were staying at the motel was "way, way high," according to Sheriff Susanne Gunn.

effort to replace the errant release before it is used. The corrective is plainly labeled and includes an explanation. If a release has already been aired or printed, a corrective is issued with an explanatory note to editors.

Reworking a Story

When deadlines limit the legwork that should go into the second cycle, reporters rework the earlier story. In this "rehashing," as it is sometimes called, reporters look for an angle in the first story and build a new lead around it, being careful not to distort the emphasis:

First cycle:

> Norman Haynes, who admitted killing his wife and his girlfriend during a frenzied alcohol binge in May, was sentenced to life imprisonment Tuesday.

> Judge Frieda Larson issued the sentence, following the unanimous recommendations of a jury, and **ordered Haynes to prison immediately.**

Reworked:

> Convicted murderer Norman Haynes **was transported to the Stillwater, Minn., state prison Tuesday** to begin a life sentence.

A rehash, essentially, is a new presentation of the first story. Rewording is important for people who read or heard the original.

The second cycle is not the only situation in which reworking is done. Many newsrooms have a policy of reworking news releases so their stories are not word for word that of their competition.

Because news releases are written to serve the purpose of whoever is issuing them, a good standard newsroom practice is to look at releases carefully to determine if a worthy lead is buried. The rehash, then, will have a stronger audience-oriented thrust than the release itself.

No News Can Be News

In 1993, when a giant explosion blew a 50-foot crater in an underground garage at the 110-story World Trade Center in New York, the first stories focused on the blast and the deaths and injuries. The next day, second-cycle stories not only concentrated on follow-up developments, like the investigation into the cause, but also background and context.

Still, there were no major new developments, which prompted the New York Times to build a story on what wasn't known:

> In a briefing at police headquarters by Gov. Mario Cuomo of New York and Gov. Jim Florio of New Jersey, the most pressing questions were left unanswered:
>
> Who planted the bomb or bombs, and why?
>
> What was the bomb made of?
>
> Was it a time bomb, or was it set off by remote control?
>
> Did it blow up accidentally?
>
> Had it been placed in that vulnerable area by malicious design, or happenstance?
>
> Who had access to the site?
>
> Where had the bomb been concealed? In a car or van or somewhere else?
>
> Was there any complicity by employees of the Vista or the Port Authority of New York and New Jersey, which own the trade center?

Speculation can make a good second-cycle focus:

> NEW YORK (AP)—Terrorists might have been responsible for a deadly explosion at the World Trade Center, authorities said Saturday.
>
> But exactly who did it, and why, remained objects of pure speculation.

ANTICIPATING DEVELOPMENTS

STUDY PREVIEW   When reporters know that a story is about to break, they can take the information already at hand, write a basic story and add developments to it later. This gives reporters a running start on a story and reduces deadline pressure.

Getting a Running Start

Broadcast reporters go on the air live with breaking news. The process of getting a story into print, however, takes longer, through all the steps of editing, headline writing, layout, typesetting, and rolling the presses. To make deadlines, newspaper reporters try to get a head start on their stories by writing a core story and then grafting new information into that core.

The Associated Press and other news services, with clients on deadline every minute of the day, have refined this piecing together of stories almost to a ritual. Terms devised by the news services and used in many newsrooms to identify stages in building a breaking story include "B lead," "new lead," "insert," "add" and "write through."

B Stories and B Leads

In the days when big-city newspapers had multiple editions, many morning papers put out a first edition the afternoon before for street sales. These "bulldog editions," as they were known, frequently carried background stories on events expected to break later in the day. Rather than write both an anticipatory story for the bulldog and a whole new story later, reporters organized their bulldog stories so they would make sense to afternoon readers and be easily updated for morning readers by adding a few sentences to the top. These were called "B stories" or "B leads," the "B" for bulldog.

The B story approach works well for things like a major political address:

Gov. Stan Rose was expected to call on legislators for a major tax increase in his state of the state address Tuesday evening, following through on the "quality" campaign theme that carried him into office in November.

In the campaign, Rose had vowed to . . .

This B story goes on with information that the reporter expects will survive through the final edition. This could include background on the governor's campaign theme, the size of his victory, his relationship with the legislature, and the size of the current state budget.

For unexpected events, like an airplane crash, there is no opportunity for B stories. The first story is however many paragraphs a reporter can write by deadline. Then, that first story becomes the basis for adds and new leads.

New Leads

As soon as developments warrant, the reporter writes a new top for the story. This "1st lead," as it is called, includes a transition into the earlier B story:

Gov. Stan Rose, following through on his "restore quality" campaign pledge, laid a record $10.2 billion budget before state legislators Tuesday.

"Quality costs," said the governor.

At $10.2 billion, Rose's proposal is almost 20 percent more than current spending, and far exceeds what most Capitol watchers had expected.

In the campaign that led to his election in November, Rose had vowed to . . .

Against a deadline, a reporter may be able to write only a few sentences for a 1st lead. Then, having met that deadline, the reporter goes to work on a "2nd lead" with more detail:

Gov. Stan Rose surprised legislators Tuesday by calling for a record $10.2 billion budget that caught veteran Capitol observers off guard.

The governor, who won election in November after a campaign promising to "restore quality" in state government, had been expected to recommend more spending, but no one was expecting a near 20 percent increase.

In laying out his plan in rough form, the governor said: "Quality costs."

Rose did not detail how he proposes financing the record budget but promised to send "the whole package" in a document to the Legislature next week.

On where he wants more spending, the governor said the detailed budget plan will include:

• A 5 percent across-the-board pay hike for state employees.

• $260 million for bridge and highway improvements.

• Major increases for school districts statewide and for higher education.

In the campaign that led to his election, Rose had vowed to . . .

A "3rd lead," or even later leads, could add more detail or include reaction. Having pre-written the B story, reporters on breaking stories can spend less time at the keyboard and more time gathering information at those crucial times when developments are occurring and deadlines looming.

Inserts

An insert, usually a few sentences at most, adds information into the story, either into the original B story or into a lead that has already been added to the story. With an insert, always tell editors exactly where it should go:

| After 8th graf, 2nd lead xxx higher education.

Democrats interrupted the governor with applause seven times during his address. | But Republicans were less enthusiastic. After the speech Minority Leader Jessica Bloom said: "He's going to spend us into the poor house."

In the campaign, xxx |

Adds

Seldom will it be necessary to add anything to the bottom of a B story, but if so it should be called an "add." What often happens is that the bottom paragraphs of a B story are deleted to create room at the top of the story for the new leads.

Deletes

Developments sometimes necessitate that a portion of a B story or earlier lead be dropped. Make the instructions to desk editors simple: "Delete the 14th and 15th paragraphs, starting: Rose, who xxx," and offer a quick explanation: "Information outdated."

Write Throughs

Usually a well-crafted B story will not need any changes except new leads. Sometimes, though, developments are so unexpected that a whole "write through" is necessary—a completely rewritten story.

Broadcast Advance Packaging

In broadcasting, reporters have their own version of B stories—pre-packaged stories that can be incorporated into later coverage. For example, in a death-watch story, when the death of a prominent person is imminent, a television reporter can prepare a biographical piece in advance for use at the appropriate time.

SEEING POSSIBILITIES

STUDY PREVIEW   Imaginative reporters can devise fresh approaches with interesting and significant insights. This includes localizing stories from far away, asking questions that haven't been asked before, and going for new sources and angles.

Localizing

Reporters who look for local angles can make far-away news more relevant to their local audiences. To localize, look for local effects, interview local experts, and seek local reaction.

FLIGHT INSURANCE

An airliner's lights trace a path around an intense summer thunderstorm, a routine maneuver for pilots on approach to Tucson International Airport.

On average, individual commercial jets are hit by lightning once a year and suffer only slight damage where the current enters and exits. Designed to meet Federal Aviation Administration requirements, the crafts' metal surfaces and framework provide safe paths for the current—even through vulnerable fuel lines and tanks. Airliners use special shielding to protect delicate electronic guidance equipment from the crippling burst of electromagnetic energy emitted by a lightning strike.

Before a new aircraft takes flight, its lightning protection designs are tested on the ground. At Lightning Technologies, Inc., in Pittsfield,

Massachusetts, a 1.5-million-volt simulated strike zaps a scale model of the new Boeing 777 airliner (above). Repeated tests, with the model in different positions, reveal likely places for lightning to initially enter and exit the aircraft.

Planes with nonmetallic surfaces—which conduct electricity poorly and can thus suffer severe damage from a lightning strike—pose a special challenge

for lightning protection. Lightning Technologies president Andy Plumer (below) holds two laboratory test panels made of carbon-reinforced plastic, used in aircraft construction. The sample at right was punctured by a simulated lightning strike. The test panel at left fared much better. Coated with a lightning-conducting copper mesh, it emerged intact, aside from some paint damage.

Lightning

WRITING TO THE PHOTOS. The magazine National Geographic has been a pacesetter in packaging photographs and then telling stories around the photos. As newspapers become more visually attentive, they are picking up this technique, which reverses the traditional newspaper emphasis on photographs accompanying the articles to articles accompanying the photos.   (Courtesy of National Geographic)

Out-of-town story:

> WASHINGTON (AP)—Rep. Tim Penny, the maverick turned power broker who helped save President Clinton's tax bill, stunned colleagues Friday by announcing that he will not seek reelection next year, saying, "My roots call me home."

In the congressman's home district, Bob Berg of the Winona Daily News began a localized sidebar this way:

> U.S. Rep. Tim Penny's retirement announcement surprised leaders of both political parties **in Minnesota's 1st Congressional District** and ignited speculation about who would run for the seat.

Campus Localizing

Many college newspapers are adept at a specialized form of localizing, finding campus angles in local news, as in this story from the Dakota Student at the University of North Dakota:

> UND students going to bars won't see stripping, or even dancing, any time soon.
> The Grand Forks City Council killed an ordinance Monday that would have loosened restrictions on bar entertainment.

BEING ANALYTICAL

STUDY PREVIEW   Reporters apply the expertise that comes from covering an event or issue in interpretive follow-ups and commentaries. These follow-up stories add depth, provide context, explain background and raise questions—all of which may not be possible under daily, hourly or more frequent deadlines.

Writing Think Pieces

Many news organizations deserve criticism for fixating on day-to-day events and not putting it all together. To address this criticism, some reporters write occasional expanded wrap-ups to put the daily events in perspective. These go by many names, including "situationers" and "think pieces." Think pieces often run in Sunday newspapers and weekend broadcast programs, when many people in the audience have extra time to catch up and put recent events in perspective. In newspapers, think pieces sometimes appear in the editorial section, although, because they come from reporters, they are really interpretive stories, not opinion pieces.

A fine line exists between interpretation, in which a reporter tries to explain the significance of what is happening, and editorializing, which is an attempt to win the audience to a particular point of view. It is the difference between being an expert, which a reporter is, and being a partisan, which a reporter is not.

Being Interpretive

In an earlier time when the world was less complex, someone whose interests spanned all human knowledge was called a "Renaissance man." Today, human knowledge has exploded into so many directions that it is hardly possible for a single person to dabble in everything, even over a whole lifetime.

These growing complexities have rendered obsolete the idea that journalists need merely lay down the facts and let readers figure out what they mean. While some people still adhere to the notion that journalists should provide "just the facts, ma'am," in Joe Friday sterility, most people look to journalists to give them a head start on figuring out what the news means.

Since the 1930s, journalism scholar Curtis MacDougall argued for what he called "interpretative journalism." MacDougall's ideas got a boost in 1947 when a blue-ribbon group of scholars, the Hutchins Commssion, issued an influential report on the news media that called for news to be told "in a context that gives it meaning." Otherwise, with the world so complex, more facts just add to information overload and clutter.

With a breaking story, reporters may not be able to offer much interpretation or context as they scramble to get core information against deadline. The second cycle, however, is a platform for context, background and understanding.

Tips for analytical writing:

+ Tell the big picture, pulling together singular events and developments to help the audience understand what they all mean.

+ Identify trends.

+ Look for the implications of what is happening.

+ Apply your expertise as a reporter who is on top of events to speculate on possible outcomes and effects.

+ Avoid speculation about motives. Nobody has a pipeline into a source's mind.

+ Lean heavily on readily verifiable information and cite expert sources, just as in regular news stories.

+ Keep a detached, neutral posture toward the subject.

+ Acknowledge different points of view and interpretations.

+ Avoid the first person "I" or the editorial "we," unless you are sharing your personal experience as a reporter.

+ Don't be categorical. Even the most knowledgeable experts don't have perfect crystal balls.

+ Extrapolation is OK. If a reasonable person would see the facts suggesting a certain conclusion, then it is reasonable to extrapolate. Share your reasoning with your audience.

+ Cite precedence to point out how a similar situation in the past worked out.

+ Attribute. Name the experts whose opinions make sense to you.

CHAPTER WRAP-UP

Working against deadlines, news reporters inevitably miss information and angles that merit coverage. Reporters have their chance to catch up when they write follow-up stories. These follow-ups also are an opportunity to update people on new developments and to bring people who missed the earlier stories up to speed.

Updating a story requires a skillful blending of background into the new article. To make sense to people who missed earlier stories, follow-ups need tie-backs to the previous stories. So stories don't appear to be rehashes of old material, tie-backs must be subordinated to the new information. Massive chunks of background should be avoided because they bog down a story with old information, giving little incentive for people to read on if they have been following the coverage.

When reporters know that a story is about to break, they can take the information already at hand, write a basic story and add developments to it later. This gives reporters a running start on a story and reduces deadline pressure.

Follow-up stories can have an analytical bent. Reporters apply the expertise that comes from covering an event or issue in interpretive follow-ups and commentaries. These follow-up stories add depth, provide context, explain background, and raise questions—all of which may not be possible under daily, hourly or more frequent deadlines.

STUDY QUESTIONS

1. How do news reporters write follow-up stories that simultaneously serve people who missed earlier stories and people who have tracked developments closely?

2. What is the role of tie-backs in follow-up stories?

3. What is the problem with dropping large segments of background in a follow-up story?

4. Why is creativity and imagination especially important in writing follow-up stories?

5. How do reporters get a head start when they know that new developments will break near deadline?

6. How would you localize a major far-away story that is in the news now?

7. What advice would you give a news reporter who is assigned to write an interpretive follow-up or analytical piece?

PUTTING YOUR LEARNING TO WORK

EXERCISE 1 Incorporating Background

One complaint about the news coverage of the ongoing unrest in the Balkans is that most Americans have problems figuring out who is who. There are Bosnians, Croats, Moslems, Serbs and others. Go to the library and look at several weeks of stories on the Balkan situation and notice how writers identify the various parties. What are the best examples? What techniques do they use? Undoubtedly you will find many examples of writers doing a good job on this. Considering that, then why are so many people in the news audience still confused? How could writers do a better job?

EXERCISE 2 Continuing Story

Review the New York Times in your library for January and February 1994 on court stories from Portland, Ore., involving Olympic ice-skater Tonya Harding. Examine how the writers have explained where the case was in the judicial pipeline from day to day. In writing an ongoing story, one challenge is to tie the new event to what went before and what is next. This is particularly important in court stories because often the story's heart is where the case is in the judicial process. Writers find ways to include step-by-step coverage of the procedure in their stories without seeming to be giving a civics lesson.

EXERCISE 3 Commentaries

Write a think piece on a local or campus issue you have been following. The idea in a think piece is not to expound your opinion or to win people over to your position. Rather, your goal is to offer background and context to help your audience understand the issue better. A think piece often is an opportunity to reintroduce an angle that a reporter couldn't fit into breaking stories or that didn't receive the prominence it deserved.

FOR FURTHER LEARNING

Bob Baker. "Newsthinking: The Secret of Great Newswriting." Writer's Digest Books, 1981. Baker recommends a pre-writing process that helps reporters identify new angles that can be especially helpful for updates and sidebars.

R. Thomas Berner. "The Process of Editing." Allyn and Bacon, 1991. This fundamental editing textbook covers important information for reporters on fitting into the collaborative work of producing a newspaper, including pre-writing leads for breaking stories and packaging the news visually.

CHAPTER 11

Fitting into the Organization

In this chapter you will learn:

✦ Newspapers, radio and television stations, magazines, news services and public relations organizations are organized similarly—but differences do exist.

✦ News operations of the media are similar, but technological considerations create differences.

✦ News cycles vary from medium to medium.

✦ The reporter plays somewhat different roles in different news organizations.

✦ The work of public relations departments in companies can be distinguished from that of public relations agencies.

✦ Public relations has four major functions: information gathering, planning, action and evaluation.

✦ In hiring, employers look for people who are skilled and will fit into an organization.

✦ Working with editors and other supervisors is easier if you know what's expected.

✦ Work in media organizations is most often a cooperative venture.

THE NEWS DAY BEGINS

The time is 5 a.m. The clock radio by the bed of a public relations person triggers and the voice of an announcer for a news-talk radio station fills the bedroom. She listens for a minute or two before forcing her feet to the floor. Shuffling to the kitchen, she switches her television set on and punches up the channel that gives her a local news show, then goes to the front door, picks up her newspaper and takes it to the kitchen table.

As she sits down to drink her coffee, she hears the anchor read a lead-in to a videotaped story about an industrial accident the night before at a company that she advises on public relations questions. She listens and watches intently as the on-the-scene reporter describes the accident and questions the plant manager. She had been there during the interview, and she notes once again that the reporter asked intelligent questions and the manager gave answers that reflected well on him and on the company. She's happy to see that the finished report was edited to give a balanced view of the situation.

She flips through the newspaper to find its report of the event and reads the story. The telephone rings. It's a reporter for the radio station she awoke to. He would like to ask a couple of quick questions about the accident. Would she mind if he taped her answers?

At the same time, in the newspaper's city room, an assistant metro editor is planning the day's assignments to reporters. The industrial accident needs a follow-up. He taps a combination of keys on his computer that puts the assignment in a reporter's queue.

The assignment editor at the television station also decides that a follow-up is in order. She assigns a reporter and a photographer to the story. She'll discuss the angle with them when they come in to work. She spins her Rolodex file to the name of the public relations person and jots down the name and number on a note to the reporter.

The news day has begun.

Scenes like that are played out in cities large and small all across the country. The actors are reporters, editors and public relations people from a variety of backgrounds and with a range of personalities and differing amounts of professional experience. In this chapter, you will get a cross-section view of the media businesses, how they operate, and how to fit in.

NEWSPAPERS AND BROADCASTING STATIONS

STUDY PREVIEW   The management structures of individual newspapers and radio and television stations in the United States are organized in much the same way. Their executives perform many of the same functions, but carry different titles.

Management Structure

Almost all media in the United States are part of chains with headquarters far from most of their properties. Gannett, for example, is headquartered in Arlington, Va., and publishes more than 90 daily newspapers in states from Washington to Florida and from the Virgin Islands to Guam. Knight-Ridder's executives, based in Miami, oversee publications as far away as San Jose, Calif., and Walla Walla, Wash. Many media companies also have far-flung broadcasting properties.

A typical chain has a chairperson of the board, a president, one or more vice presidents, a secretary and a treasurer. The officers assign an executive to each property to supervise its operation. For print media, that post carries the title publisher. Broadcasting stations have a general manager. The people in those jobs have authority over all of the operation but, as a rule, give most of their attention to its business aspects.

The Federal Communications Commission requires that radio and television stations provide annual financial reports with expense categories that are based on station functions: administrative, technical, sales and programming. Roughly the same structure is in place in print media organizations as well. Let's look at what falls under those areas.

Administrative. The administrative area includes most of the support functions for the organization, including personnel, payroll, accounting and purchasing. Those are common to almost any business.

Technical. The technical department in a television or radio station is frequently called engineering. Engineers make sure all of the equipment works, that it is properly maintained and that new equipment is purchased. They see to it that the station stays on the air.

For newspapers and magazines that are printed "in house," the technical aspects are handled by the production department, which keeps the printing presses up and running. Even publications that job out their printing have production departments that set schedules and insure that schedules are met. The publications are distributed by the circulation department.

Sales. Sales departments of broadcasting stations market the stations' audiences to advertisers. In other words, sales personnel sell commercial time. More people are employed in sales than in any other department of a broadcasting station. At public stations, the department responsible for income is called development. Development personnel write grant applications, seek underwriters and coordinate other fund-raising efforts.

The equivalent for a publication is the advertising department. On a newspaper, it is charged with selling display and classified advertising. Depending upon the size of the newspaper, the advertising department may have separate units for those two functions, or it may have different sections for sales of local, regional and national advertising, or any other breakdown appropriate to the size and location of the newspaper. Magazines also have advertising departments. One office may handle all advertising, or the magazine may have regional offices for selling advertising.

Programming. The programming department produces all of the non-advertising material that is broadcast on a radio or television station, including news. It schedules news and entertainment programs, commercials, public service announcements and promotional announcements. On a publication, non-advertising material is referred to as editorial matter.

Newsroom Managers

Typically, newspaper and broadcasting station newsrooms have three levels of management:

Top newsroom management. The newspaper editor or radio or television news director normally deals with long-range planning and articulates the vision of the organization. The editor or news director also develops and manages the budget for the newsroom.

Day-to-day newsroom managers. The newspaper's managing editor or a television station's senior producer or assistant news director supervises the day-to-day operations. Because their staffs are relatively small, radio news directors usually also supervise daily operations.

News editors. The news editor is a key position at many newspapers. That person oversees the work of the copy desk, which is responsible for checking verifiable information, polishing copy and writing headlines. The news editor may also lay out the pages of the newspaper. The producer of each news program is the equivalent executive in television.

City editor and assignment editor. The city editor, or metro editor, as the position is called at many larger newspapers, is first among subeditors reporting to the managing editor. The city editor coordinates the reporting staff that covers the city, including governmental units, police and education. At a television station, the assignment editor takes on those responsibilities. The radio news director wears the city editor's hat as well.

Graphics editor. Graphics is a relatively new position at many newspapers, having evolved from the use of computers and colored inks. The graphics editor is in charge of production of the colorful maps and charts that appear each day to help the reader grasp the details of the news. Television stations that employ sophisticated graphics computers have a similar position.

Subeditors. The number of a newspaper's subeditors and their duties depends on the size of the community and the circulation of the newspaper.

The larger the newspaper, generally the more sections or departments it has, and the more editors overseeing them. The size of a television station's news staff depends on market size and the station's commitment to news.

NEWSROOM OPERATIONS

STUDY PREVIEW   The newsrooms of newspapers and radio and television stations operate in much the same way in gathering each day's news. The packaging and distribution, of course, are different.

Differing Roles of News

Changes in federal regulations have allowed radio stations to reduce news programming, and because that is financially attractive, many stations have done so. Most simply subscribe to a news service and have a disc jockey tear the latest newscast from the service's printer and read it on the air, a practice known as "rip and read." If a station does have a news department, it is unlikely to have more than one or two news people. Even in larger cities, or "markets," as broadcasters usually refer to them, few stations report local news, usually only those stations that have adopted a news-talk format, and they seldom employ more than six to 10 persons.

As on radio, most television programming is entertainment programming. News, however, has a special role to play on television, since news is the most prominent local programming a television station does.

News is central to newspapers, of course.

Gathering the Day's News

The news day begins with the arrival of the person who makes the day's assignments. On a newspaper, that is frequently an assistant city editor or assistant metro editor. It's the assignment editor on a television station, and the news director on a radio station.

The first step is to go through the futures file, an expanded combination of an appointment book and "things to do today" notes. For any one day, the futures file might contain public relations releases announcing one or more news conferences to be held that day, public events such as a meeting of the zoning commission, for which an agenda might be inserted in the file, or the ceremonial ribbon-cutting to open a new stretch of highway. In it too might be notes to follow up on earlier events or announcements. If, for example, the city's director of public housing said in September that new smoke detector systems would be installed in all units by May 1, the futures file for that day would have a copy of the story clipped to a note to call the housing director. A newspaper's city editor or a broadcast assignment editor decides which of the items need follow up and assigns reporters to them.

Reporters begin their day by checking their assignments in a mail box or, on fully computerized newspapers, by opening their video display terminals to their "queues," as computerized in-baskets are called. In following through on assignments, reporters may confer with an editor or producer on the importance of the story, the backgrounds of the people involved and the angle that the editor sees.

Newspaper reporters will go to the morgue—the newspaper library, which may be on the computer—and look up earlier stories or related information. Then they'll begin making telephone calls and appointments.

Reporters assigned to beats keep futures files of their own and may handle items in the day's file as they make their rounds.

After talking to the right sources and doing the background work necessary, a reporter may again confer with an editor about the story and how it ought to be structured, then sit down at the computer to write. When the story is finished, a keystroke sends it to the city editor's queue where it is edited and sent to the copy desk for more editing and a headline.

The editing process puts stories into many different hands, and it's not uncommon for an editor on the city desk or the copy desk to rewrite part, or for reporters themselves to be asked to rewrite portions or to gather new information. Along the way, a news editor will determine where in the newspaper the story is to appear and whether it is to have a one- or multi-column headline. When city and copy desks are satisfied that the story is complete, another keystroke sends it to the composing room to be set in type and pasted up on the layout page.

At the television station, as reporters and photographers arrive they are handed their assignments and begin to prepare for them. In some instances they simply jump in a news car and go. In others they may do some background reading, especially in the newspaper. They may also call favorite sources to get a further understanding of the story and may make appointments for interviews.

A reporter and photographer team sent to cover a school board meeting may capture some of the debate on an issue, then travel to a school that might be affected by a board action to get interviews with teachers and students, and some video, and then head back to the station. In the meantime, as breaking news occurs—a fire, perhaps, or a police action—the assignment editor orchestrates the movements of reporters and photographers throughout the city. One reporter and photographer team might be ordered to a fire and another to a news conference, or a photographer alone might be sent out to cover a story for which information can be gathered easily by telephone but for which video footage from the scene is needed.

While a team is returning to the station, the reporter may review notes and even go over the video footage they've shot to see what footage they'll want to use in the story. That will shorten the amount of time they have to spend in the editing booth. The reporter generally writes copy that will fit the edited video. The type of story that results will depend on the needs of the producers. The team may produce what's called a package, a piece of a minute or more that includes the reporter's narration, pictures of the event and on-camera interviews. They may provide only video and a "reader," a story to be read by the anchor, or a reader alone. The stories go to a producer who reviews them before scheduling them into a newscast.

At both newspapers and television stations the news executives gather once a day to discuss the "budget," a term for the local, national and international stories that will be available. Sometimes editors argue over the stories to include and what stories to put on Page 1. Business news most often goes in the business section, but on occasion the business editor persuades the other editors that a story has enough general interest and impact to be put in the main news section. The news meeting gives all of the editors a broad view of what the day's newspaper will contain and the angles of the stories, though of course everything can change if a major story breaks.

At television stations the producers of the various news programs sit down together to allocate among themselves all the stories expected that day. On some days a major story will make all of the shows, though it may be a full package on one or more and a reader on one. Otherwise a brokering process goes on among the producers. One will want a story on a water main break that created a geyser and left a neighborhood without water while another will ask for a feature on a special summer program for high school students. When all the stories are distributed, producers of the individual programs will "stack," or arrange, the stories they have available into a complete news program.

NEWSGATHERING AGENCIES

STUDY PREVIEW   Two organizations in the United States devote themselves to gathering news from whatever corner of the globe it occurs and transmitting it almost instantaneously. The Associated Press provides a news report rapidly and accurately to member newspapers and radio and television stations across the country and around the world. Cable News

Network transmits the news directly to viewers world-wide on a 24-hour basis. Other smaller, cooperative news services exist to gather and disseminate news on a more limited basis. Regardless of size, because of their special functions the agencies are organized differently from other news organizations.

Associated Press

The Associated Press has headquarters in New York and more than 200 bureaus in major U.S. cities, state capitals and in major cities all over the world. The size of the bureau is measured by the number of reporters and editors assigned to it, and that depends on the importance of the city as a news-making center. Each major bureau is headed by a chief of bureau and may have a news editor, a broadcast writer or editor, and reporters attached to it.

Newspapers hold memberships in the Associated Press and direct its policies and control the news product. Radio and television stations are called "associate members," but are, in effect, subscribers. They have little to say in its operation except as customers.

The Associated Press is a cooperative organization. That means that it has access to the news reports of its member newspapers and broadcasting stations. As a result, a bylined story in the Orlando, Fla., Sentinel may be transmitted to AP's New York headquarters and then transmitted to clients nationwide, or to a state or regional control bureau for regional distribution. AP editors may decide that the story is of interest only in Florida and transmit it as part of the state report, or they may distribute it throughout the southeast.

AP news writers sometimes transmit the stories as they were written for member newspapers or broadcasting stations. Sometimes they gather additional information and incorporate that into the stories they transmit. AP reporters may gather the news themselves, either by going to the scene of an event or by making telephone calls.

The AP operates on two 12-hour cycles, beginning at noon and at midnight. At the start of each cycle the main news desk sends out a list of stories that will be transmitted during the cycle. The "budget," as it is called, tells editors what stories are scheduled to break during the cycle, which ongoing stories will be rewritten with fresh leads and how many words each will contain.

Breaking stories are added to the report as they occur. Some have priority over others. Fast-breaking stories that the AP news desk believes editors will want to take special note of are marked "urgent" and take precedence over any non-priority story. A "bulletin" is a major story—a disaster of some sort or a news event that affects many people. It will interrupt a regular story or an urgent in mid-sentence. The "bulletin" designation is given to the first paragraph or two of the story; succeeding parts of the story, called "takes," are marked "urgent."

The highest priority is given to the "flash." The AP stylebook defines a "flash" as the report of "a development of transcendent importance." It is rarely used—for an outbreak of war, the first landing of astronauts on the moon, the assassination of a president. When a flash is sent, it normally is only a few words to alert editors, followed by a "bulletin" lead and "urgent" takes developing the story. The AP stylebook gives as an example the flash that was sent the moment Neil Armstrong set foot on the moon in 1969:

> SPACE CENTER, Houston (AP) —
> Man on the moon.

Radio and television stations receive a report written especially for them. It is prepared by broadcast news editors in New York who rewrite news stories from the international and national reports in broadcast style for transmission to stations across the country. In the bureaus, broadcast news writers rewrite the local report and stories from member newspapers and send them as part of the local or regional report. AP also distributes audio cuts to radio stations, video stories to television stations, and operates what's called AP NewsCenter, a television newsroom, automated and capable of producing a full newscast.

Cable News Network

CNN is an international television and radio newsgathering organization based in Atlanta with 1,800 journalists and technical personnel who work out of nine domestic bureaus and 19 international bureaus. News programming is carried by cable and satellite throughout the United States and to 136 other countries and territories,

Like AP, CNN relies on its own correspondents for newsgathering and on correspondents of affiliate stations. In turn it broadcasts complete programs on CNN, CNN Headline News and CNN International. Two Spanish newscasts are carried daily via Noticiero Telemundo-CNN.

CNN also provides television news and news feature programming to its affiliate stations. Prior to each satellite news feed, it sends producers a printed rundown that includes story scripts, suggested anchor leads and often transcripts of interviews. With all that in hand, local stations can customize the material for their audiences.

A radio arm provides newscasts to 500 affiliate radio stations.

Other Agencies

United Press International was organized for news gathering much like the Associated Press and once competed fiercely with the AP for news. It has declined as a major journalistic force in recent years, however, after going through a series of ownership changes. Cost-cutting has left it with relatively few major bureaus and no staff members in most states. In an effort at reorganization, it has been enlisting newspaper and broadcasting station clients to gather news and share it with each other.

In most media groups, newspapers and broadcasting stations share news they've gathered among themselves. Some groups have set up separate organizations for gathering news and distributing it to members of the group. Services like Gannett News Service and Copley News Service have bureaus in the capitals of states in which they own newspapers and broadcasting stations. Others, like Newhouse News Service and Scripps Howard News Service, are organized to gather news in Washington and transmit it to members. While such services are organized primarily to serve group members, they also sell to non-member newspapers and broadcasting stations.

MAGAZINES

STUDY PREVIEW   An estimated 16,000 magazines of great variety are published in the United States. They are an important medium for both readers and writers. Readers look to them for a range of general information and for quite specific information. The publications usually have small staffs, so editors rely heavily on free-lance writers to provide stories.

Types of Magazines

The magazines that come into our homes and that we pick up from drugstore racks are mass circulation publications, but they focus on special interests within the mass audience. Periodicals are published for golfers, bicyclists, weightlifters, runners, walkers and people who engage in just about any other activity. You can buy magazines to learn how to plan a wedding, decorate your apartment, cook, sew, build furniture and raise a child.

A host of trade publications—newspapers and magazines with smaller circulations and aimed at individuals who work in specific fields—are also published. Print journalists read Editor & Publisher, broadcasters read Broadcasting & Cable, and public relations practitioners read O'Dwyer's PR Services Report. People in other fields have their specialized publications too. Travel agents, auto mechanics, dentists, motel owners, morticians—you name the occupation, there's a magazine for it.

Other magazines go to members of specific organizations. Members of the Society of Professional Journalists are sent Quill. The International Association of Business Communicators publishes Communication World. The Journal of

Broadcasting and Electronic Communication goes to members of the Broadcast Education Association.

Magazine Organization

Like other media enterprises, magazines are most often parts of larger groups. Corporate officers include the president, vice presidents for special areas and a treasurer or controller—sometimes called the "comptroller." Each magazine in the group is normally assigned a publisher who oversees both business and editorial activities of the magazine and who may manage more than one magazine in the group.

The editorial staffs of most magazines are spare. They may consist of only a handful of editors, headed by an editor-in-chief and a managing editor. Copy editors are responsible for reviewing grammar and spelling, and fact checkers are responsible for ensuring that all the facts in editorial content are correct.

Many magazines have an art director who lays out the magazine and is responsible for photos and other art. Most have a production editor who sets deadlines and sees to it that they are met, arranges for copy to be sent to the printer and supervises proofreading.

Most of the content comes from free-lance writers, sometimes called "stringers," who work for themselves and sell their stories to magazines and newspapers. Some free-lancers specialize in topics. Some may write on science, others on sports, others on cemeteries. Some free-lancers cover a broad range of subjects for a variety of publications.

The best free-lancers get to know editors and the audiences of their magazines and become expert at targeting their work to specific publications. Free-lance writers often test ideas on editors with a one-page proposal and follow up with a story if the proposal is OK'd.

Public relations writers frequently operate as free-lancers to place articles about an industry and the role of their organization in that industry, especially in trade magazines. The articles can appear not only under their own bylines but under the bylines of their clients or top executives.

News Magazines

News magazines like Newsweek, Time and U.S. News and World Report have much larger editorial staffs than other types of magazines. They employ reporters rather than rely on free-lancers, and those reporters work out of bureaus in the United States and around the world. Editors oversee various sections of the magazine.

The reporting process on news magazines can be tedious. Reporters in bureaus may be assigned stories or may suggest development of stories occurring in their areas and, when given approval, will pursue them. Drafts go to an editor, who may change them, ask for more information, or simply seek clarification. Other drafts follow, with more editing. Any one story may go through two or three editors and dozens of full or partial rewrites before appearing in the magazine.

PUBLIC RELATIONS

STUDY PREVIEW   Public relations is carried out in a variety of situations. Many PR people work for public relations agencies or in the public relations departments of advertising agencies. Others are employed in the public relations departments of organizations. Others set themselves up as self-employed counselors. Wherever it is based, public relations is a staff function, supporting the work of those who are engaged in an organization's principal business. As an example, doctors and nurses carry out the main work of hospitals, but public relations people help them communicate with the hospital's employees and the general public.

The Public Relations Department

In organizations that place a high value on public relations, the public relations staff is headed by a vice president who is equivalent to other major officers and who has a strong influence on their decisions. In other organizations, public relations may be headed by a mid-level manager who serves an advisory function to the major officers, or in some instances only as a megaphone for policies determined at the executive level.

Public relations personnel are concerned with both internal relations and external relations. Communication functions of internal public relations personnel include publications of various sorts written and edited for employees. Magazines, newsletters, news bulletins and even bulletin board notices—both cork board and electronic—emanate from the public relations department to provide employees with information they want to know and information that management wants them to know. Increasingly public relations personnel are called upon to produce messages in non-traditional forms, including individual videos, video networks and computer networks.

People charged with external relations communicate the organization's messages in order to build and foster good will among its external publics or audiences. Those include customers or clients, stock holders, legislators and officials of governmental agencies, special interest groups and the general public.

The external publics of a university include potential students, high school counselors, parents of students and alumni. Less obvious as external publics are donors, including foundations that make grants, other institutions, the general public and state and federal legislators who determine budgets. On a day-to-day basis, department personnel cover the campus like a beat and prepare stories about the activities of faculty, staff and students to be sent to the media. On a large campus, the PR newsgathering staff may be divided into two or more beats. Often external relations personnel publish a magazine that goes to those publics.

Public relations personnel also encourage community relations by the organization and its employees. They often coordinate the organization's participation in charities such as United Way and the volunteer activities of employees. If the chief executive officer of a company takes on a high-profile position with a local non-profit organization, the company's public relations department may be called upon to prepare brochures and public service announcements for the news media and to conduct other activities.

Special events often come under the public relations department. Graduation exercises are planned and directed by the public relations people on many campuses. The exercises serve a number of publics, including the graduates, their parents and the individuals given honorary degrees in the hopes that they'll give the school money in return.

Crisis management is a major public relations function. It is activated when an Exxon Valdez runs aground, when someone deliberately poisons capsules of Tylenol, when Perrier water smells like Benzene, when a fast-food restaurant serves something that makes a large number of people ill, or when a tornado strikes. Any public crisis, in fact, requires public explanation with a steady flow of information primarily through the news media. The public relations department plays a central role in determining what ought to be said and how it should be said.

When, during the summer of 1993, some people made claims that they found syringes in Diet Pepsi cans, Pepsico, Inc., immediately began an investigation. The public relations department made spokespersons available to discount the claims. It distributed videos of company production lines that showed cans speeding along on conveyers. The videos, widely played on newscasts, helped to persuade consumers that it would be next to impossible for anyone to put a syringe in a can. The company complemented the videos with full-page advertisements in newspapers all across the country headlined "Pepsi is pleased to announce . . . nothing." The ad minced no words in telling consumers that the claims "were a hoax. Plain and simple, not true." The effectiveness of the campaign was enhanced by Pepsico's public relations initiative with news organizations during the crisis, which resulted in countless news items—most of them reflecting positively on the company.

A CRISIS CALLS FOR PUBLIC RELATIONS. When people began reporting falsely that they had found hypodermic needles in cans of Diet Pepsi, the company's public relations people set out to undo the damage. Among their tools was a widely shown videotape of cans speeding along a conveyer, which gave viewers the impression that it would have been next to impossible for anyone to drop a syringe into a can.
(Courtesy of The Pepsi-Cola Company)

The Public Relations Agency

Some organizations turn the work of public relations over to an outside agency. Others maintain their own departments but contract with outside agencies for specialized work. An airline, for example, might call on an agency to devise a communications plan to be used in the event of a plane crash and to implement the plan if a crash occurs. Or a company celebrating a milestone—the 100th anniversary of its founding, for example—might contract with an outside agency to do most of the planning rather than requiring the in-house staff to add that to its day-to-day work.

Most large agencies can provide a full range of public relations activities, including crisis management, media relations, publications, public opinion polling, image building and fund-raising for non-profit organizations, including colleges and universities. A trend toward specialization is evident, however, and one can find agencies that do work almost exclusively in a functional area such as media relations, special events or lobbying, or in an industry or service area like entertainment, sports or health care. Some public relations people have become rich and famous by working exclusively for political candidates.

Public Relations Functions

Public relations personnel undertake four principal tasks, and bits and pieces of each one consume their working day:

◆ They gather information, much as reporters do.

◆ They make plans and develop tactics based on that information.

◆ They carry out the plans.

◆ They evaluate what they did.

The functions are illustrated well by the case of a university in a history-conscious community that wanted to tear down three buildings that were once fine homes to build a new and modern building. The public relations staff spent many days discussing the problem and possible solutions. The staff people were well aware that the university was situated in a wealthy area of the city, and the old houses sat on the area's main thoroughfare. A recent governor of the state had grown up in one of them. The university's neighbors, many of them pillars of the community and politically influential, did not take kindly to change, and the preservationists among them were especially influential and vocal. Many of the neighbors had not forgiven the university for its last building. In the midst of red-brick buildings reminiscent of an English country church, the school had erected a five-story block of now graying concrete with irregularly placed windows that looked like bathtubs seen from the top.

With that information at hand, the public relations staff decided before making any announcement to persuade the neighbors that the homes would not be a major loss and that the new building, even though modern, would be a handsome contribution to the area.

To accomplish the first aim, they employed an architectural historian to report on the historic significance of the houses and an attorney to conduct a title search. The study showed that no one of public distinction except the governor had lived in any of them. And the houses were neither old nor distinctive examples of an era or a style of architecture. In fact, a well-respected member of a neighboring university's architecture faculty had written a monograph some years before in which the three houses were described as being out of keeping with other homes in the area.

University officials directed their architect to design a building that would be in keeping with the university's dominant architectural theme. The result was a plan for a four-story building of red brick, certainly modern, but with features that tied it unmistakably to the other college buildings on the avenue. The architect built a scale model of the portion of the campus, showing the new building in relation to the old ones.

The next step was a series of meetings with neighbors to unveil the plans. Staff members put together a list of the most influential people in the neighborhood and those known to be staunch preservationists. They sent personal invitations to those people, and two members of the staff with excellent handwriting addressed the invitations.

PR staffers arranged for attendees to be welcomed warmly by the president and members of the board of trustees, some of whom were residents of the area themselves. The architect discussed how the new structure would blend into the campus. The historian presented his findings. Questions were answered frankly.

The public relations department commissioned a poll of the neighborhood designed to elicit attitudes about the project. Had their effort worked? Respondents included both people who attended the meeting and those who did not. The results showed that most of the neighbors were either unenthusiastic about the project or neutral, but only a few opposed it. The persuasive effort had been successful, and the university proceeded to conduct a successful fund-raising drive, demolish the old buildings, and put up the new one. And the neighbors remained friendly.

IN THE WORKPLACE

STUDY PREVIEW   The first days on a new job can be confusing and intimidating. Most communication organizations, however, try to make new employees feel at home. And the person who has a sense of how one learns in a new position and what to look for is going to have an easier entry.

The Newsroom

When A. M. Rosenthal was a student at City College of New York, he took on the job of the college's campus correspondent for the New York Times. The first time he entered the Times city room he was so awed that when he sat down at a typewriter he froze. All he could do was sit and stare at the activity around him. "Then," as Gay Talese told the story in his book "The Kingdom and the Power," Rosenthal was "startled by the soft voice of a stranger behind him" who asked his name and what he did.

"Do you need paper to type on?"
"Yes."
"Do you know where we keep the paper around here?"
"No."
"It's over there in that box," the man said, and then he proceeded to walk down the aisle, to grab a batch of paper, and to place it on Rosenthal's desk.
"Do you know how to slug a story?"
"No," Rosenthal said.
The man showed Rosenthal where his name should go, at the upper left-

hand corner, and with a single word to describe the subject of the story.

"Do you know what you do after you finish your story?"

"No," Rosenthal said.

"You give it to that copyboy standing over there."

Rosenthal nodded.

"By the way," the man said, "my name is Mike Berger."

"Thank you, Mr. Berger."

"Mike," the man said.

Mike, or Meyer Berger as his byline read, was then a 15-year veteran of the Times and a star reporter and writer. In 1950 he would win a Pulitzer Prize. Rosenthal himself would have a distinguished reporting career with the newspaper and ultimately rise to the editor's chair.

That situation is not atypical. Many offices have someone like Mike Berger, who is kindly and who unselfconsciously goes an extra step to help a new person adjust. For people entering the business, that person becomes a role model, someone to watch to see what appropriate behavior is, and someone you know you can question without having the question thought stupid or inappropriate.

Learning the Ropes

Young men who went sea in the days of sailing ships had to learn first what all the ropes on a ship were for, which raised a sail and which lowered it, and which, if let fly, would send a sail flapping in the wind and raise a storm of anger in the bo'sun. Today, young men and women who enter the various news fields also have to learn the ropes and how to manipulate them when they must sail into the wind or with the wind.

The sociologist Warren Breed examined the socialization process in the newsroom to determine how new reporters learn what newspaper policy is. What he found serves as a blueprint to how reporters, and other communication professionals, generally learn what's expected and begin to fit in. Breed cited these as among the ways the new person "learns to anticipate what is expected of him so as to win rewards and avoid punishments":

+ Reading the newspaper and the broadcast report. In so doing the new person learns to fashion "his own stories after others he sees in the paper." As Breed described them, "news columns and editorials are a guide to the local norms."

+ Observing how stories are edited, what stories are followed and which aren't, what topics are fair game for investigation and which are "sacred cows."

+ Becoming attuned to the "characteristics, interests and affiliations of their executives."

+ Hearing "what is said and what is not said by executives" when reporter and editor sit down to discuss the shape of a story, the angles and the reliability of the sources.

Breed cited three other means whereby one can learn about the organization's policy:

+ Reading the publication's house organ, if there is one.

+ Watching the publisher or editors meeting community leaders.

+ Listening to the news executives voice opinions.

What Editors Want

Veteran journalist Madelyn Ross, then managing editor of the Pittsburgh Press, gave even more specific advice on how to get along in the newsroom, especially with editors. Speaking at the 1988 Roy W. Howard Public Affairs Reporting Seminar at Indiana University, Ross gave six suggestions, all of which apply not just to fledgling newspaper reporters but also to individuals going into public relations or broadcast journalism.

Know the community. This means knowing where the city hall is, who public officials are, what the demographics of the neighborhoods are.

Ross told of an intern who walked around the Press's newsroom with a green metal file box. In it he kept "index cards with the names, titles and phone numbers of every government official in the entire Allegheny County." Said Ross: "He was ready. He did his homework. He was prepared." And he was later hired by the Press and became its Washington correspondent.

Self-edit. "Do the first edit" on everything you write. Before hitting the send button, go over your copy to correct grammar and spelling, especially spelling of names. That's the reporter's job, not the editor's. "Your editor is not supposed to clean up slop," Ross said.

Read widely. Read everything you can, from the New Republic to Rolling Stone to the New York Times and Mad magazine. That echoes advice the UPI's broadcast stylebook once gave new staffers: "Read, read and read some more. Papers, magazines, books . . . anything that gives reliable background material essential to your profession." The complexities of the world require that reporters know enough to help readers make connections.

Research. "Learn how to research," Ross advises. Among other things, reporters need to know how to get information under the Freedom of Information Act through an FOI request, how to get and read company financial reports and how to distinguish earnings and profits.

Write to the audience. Write any story so that it is comprehensible and relates to the reader or listener. "If you don't do that you're telling a story of numbers, bureaucracy and census figures and it doesn't get to the people you are trying to reach."

Know what not to say. Ross said she wished she had been told never to say to an editor, "I couldn't find out," or "But that's the way they do it on '60 Minutes,'" or "I ran out of gas." Never say, "It was an unimportant mistake," "You ruined my story," or "You ruined my life." Never ask, "Did we already have this in the paper?"

"And never say to an editor, 'When I get old and can't report any more, I want to be an editor.' That ticks them off," Ross said.

What You Can Expect from an Editor

There was a time when editors were known for being intimidating. Older journalists tell stories of legendary editors who would yell across the room voicing obscene displeasure with something a reporter might have done. Charles E. Chapin was city editor of the New York Evening World in the first quarter of the century, before he was sent to prison for killing his wife. He was pictured by a contemporary as having "a cold objective attitude toward his own work. 'I gave no confidences; I invited none. I was myself a machine, and the men I worked with were cogs. The human element never entered into the scheme of getting out the paper.'"

O. K. Bovard of the St. Louis Post-Dispatch was an easygoing and congenial friend to other reporters at the newspaper until the day he was promoted to city editor. He immediately became the icy and domineering "Mr. Bovard," even to those who had been his close companions, including a friend with whom he had been out drinking the night before. A contemporary later described him as a "more intelligent edition of Chapin."

Ben Maidenburg, editor of the Akron, Ohio, Beacon Journal, was out of the same mold in the eyes of a reporter named Robert H. Giles. Maidenburg's "impatience with the seeming stupidities of his staff could boil into action quickly, and we all dreaded the moment when a mistake or misjudgment would capture Ben's attention and ignite his temper," Giles wrote later. Among the lessons Maidenburg tried to teach Giles was, "you've got to learn to be a son of a bitch" to be an editor. But by his behavior, he reinforced in Giles the "basic instinct that there are other ways to run a newsroom"—ways Giles later delineated in his book "Newsroom Management."

Today's editors, news directors and public relations supervisors are much more likely to have read books on management and taken seminars and special courses in management. They have come to deal more judiciously with staff members and give them more respect. The human element is a part of their operating procedures, and they seek to bring about excellent performance by motivating and developing reporters rather than browbeating them.

TEAMWORK IS THE KEY IN TELEVISION. Reporter Mark Mullen of San Francisco's KRON-TV is on screen when he's reporting a story, but photographer Lou D'Aria is just as important in getting the story. The two work as a team. Teamwork is an essential in all news and public relations operations. (Courtesy of Mark Mullen)

Not that you can expect to be coddled. Writing in The New Yorker magazine, Ken Auletta noted, "There is a conflict between deadlines and democracy, news standards and niceness." Editors have newspapers to get out and news producers have newscasts to put on the air. In the pressure of the moment they haven't time to worry about bruising egos and hurting feelings. But you will be treated as "a member of a professional team," as Ross says, if you show your editors that you are a professional, a person with a sense of mission who will "devote whatever it takes to get it done."

On the other hand, if you believe your work is just a job and "come in the morning, take an hour for lunch, leave 8 ½ hours later," your supervisors will try to be good managers for you, but they will treat you differently.

Working with Others

The work in journalism and other mass communication fields is a cooperative venture. Getting any one day's newspaper from news event to doorstep requires the smoothly integrated teamwork of an army of reporters, photographers, artists, editors, advertising staff, production personnel and the circulation department down to the last newspaper carrier. A television news program requires the meshing of the work of reporters, photographers, producers and technical personnel from computer graphics operators to video switchers and broadcast engineers. A public relations campaign will involve writers, promotion specialists, artists and production specialists.

True, the legwork of reporting—interviewing sources, digging in records, observing the world—is a solitary endeavor. So is the writing. But the reporter works with editors to shape a story and, if need be, to rework it. That can create tension, because writing is an activity that involves the ego, and individuals who put words on paper can be deeply wounded by criticism of their work. Writers must leave their egos at the office door, however, if the news process is to flow smoothly.

Editors will find flaws in your work or see unexplored angles or elements that are insufficiently developed, and as reporter you ought to be open to that. On the other hand, editors should recognize, as does the Pittsburgh Press' Madelyn Ross, that the reporter is "an equal partner" in the journalistic enterprise, and when the editor goes too far in taking a reporter's style out of a story, "you have the right to say 'Wait a minute.' You have every right to talk about a process or procedure."

Once upon a time editors blue-pencilled copy without explanation. The modern editor's view, as Ross expressed it at Indiana University, is that "you have the right to ask editors to allow you to pull up your chair next to the VDT while he/she is editing your story because if you don't know what is in their head when they are editing, you will never learn and you will never have an opportunity to argue the point."

On some stories, especially stories that require a good deal of legwork, two or more reporters may team up. Bob Woodward and Carl Bernstein of the Washington Post worked together on a story that grew from a simple office break-in to the vast conspiracy that came to be known as Watergate. A reporter team from the Chicago Sun-Times set up the Mirage bar in cooperation with the Better Government Association to investigate the soliciting of kickbacks by city and county government officials.

Mark Schleifstein and James O'Byrne of the New Orleans Times-Picayune worked together on an ambitious series that detailed the extent of air, water and ground pollution in Louisiana and who was responsible for it. O'Byrne, who had been covering the environmental beat, had the idea and developed an outline. From that, the two reporters fashioned a list of tasks that each was to take on.

On occasion they worked together even though it might have been more economical to work separately. They conducted many interviews at chemical plants as a team, for example, and included their photographer, Andrew Boyd. They found that two could listen intently to an answer while the third took notes. That allowed more time for thought about what was being said and better follow-up questions. And because Boyd was taking part in gathering the information, he had a better sense of what the story was about and what pictures should illustrate it.

Given the importance of photography, graphics and visual presentation in a newspaper, it is important that reporters have a sense of the visual, Schleifstein says. He tries to ask questions that might lead to a photograph: "What goes on in area x?" "What happens during process y?" He may ask the source to demonstrate an activity, then move away while the photographer gets a shot.

It is becoming more common for reporters to work with graphics editors in developing appropriate charts and graphs to go with complex stories. At the New

Orleans Times-Picayune, one of the newspaper's graphic artists was assigned to the Schleifstein-O'Byrne team. The two reporters frequently sat down at the computer with the artist, and the three worked through ideas. In gathering information for today's publications, whether metropolitan newspaper or in-house newsletter, the reporter must give thought to how to display the information graphically. To help the graphic artist turn information into a pictorial display, the reporter must be able to make suggestions in the artist's own terms and know how graphics are put together —what is possible and what isn't.

Not everything runs smoothly in collaborations. The person who is used to working alone may not take to having a partner. The person who has collaborated as a senior partner may not enjoy being the junior partner. Personalities can clash. And in major projects it is sometimes difficult to keep in touch with everything that is going on, though a computerized master list of tasks helped Schleifstein and O'Byrne.

Turf battles also occur. The Times-Picayune's pollution story involved the city editor, who had supervision over the reporters; the copy desk, because a copy editor was assigned to the project; and the graphics editor, who had authority over both photographer and graphic artist. All had to sit down together, and with the metro editor and the newspaper's editor, to work out problems of presentation. If only limited space is available, and the graphics editor and reporter argue over who is to have it, someone has to referee, and someone has to compromise.

The members of the team that worked on the pollution series were able to compromise to the benefit of the series and, thus, the reader. The series was a finalist for a Pulitzer Prize.

Similar tales can be told of ventures in broadcasting newsrooms and public relations offices. The point is that much of the work of communication is cooperative in nature, and you must be ready, willing and able to work as part of a team.

CHAPTER WRAP-UP

News organizations are organized on much the same lines, although each medium has its particular ways of operating. Management styles have evolved from that of the irascible and profane editor to that of the modern supervisor who feels a responsiblity to develop employees in a humane and understanding way. But employees have responsibilities, including that of devotion to their work. They also have to understand that much of communications work involves close cooperation with others.

STUDY QUESTIONS

1. What is the division of labor in a newspaper?

2. How is a newspaper's news operation divided?

3. What jobs do the editor, managing editor and news editor perform?

4. How does a story work itself from assignment desk into the newspaper?

5. What is the division of labor within a radio station?

6. How does the radio station news-gathering operation differ from those of other media organizations?

7. How is a television station organized?

8. How does a television news story go from assignment desk to evening news-cast?

9. What are the jobs of the news executives in television?

10. How are magazines organized?

11. How are the news services organized?

12. What is the difference between the organization of a public relations depart-ment and a public relations agency?

13. What different functions do public relations agencies and departments per-form?

14. What behaviors do editors want to see in staff members?

15. Describe the behaviors that can help and hurt relationships with co-workers.

PUTTING YOUR LEARNING TO WORK

EXERCISE 1   A View of the Work

Write a 500-word profile of a reporter for a news organization or a public relations prac-titioner. Make arrangements to be with the person for at least one day to conduct an interview and observe the person at work. Highlight what is typical about the day's activities.

EXERCISE 2   Teaming Up

Write a 500-word story about the way in which a team operates in a news or public rela-tions organization. Talk to members of the team about the way in which it functions, what has gone smoothly and what has caused snags and the importance of teamwork in their organization. Observe the team members at work on a project separately and together.

EXERCISE 3   Managing the Organization

To determine for yourself what is expected of new employees, and what new employ-ees find on the job, set up interviews with an editor, news director or principal in a pub-lic relations firm, and with a relatively new employee. Among the questions you should ask of the supervisor are these:

✦ What expectations does the supervisor have of new employees?

✦ Are those expectations met?

✦ Where do new employees fall short?

✦ What sort of probationary period is there? How is the probationary period designed?

✦ What does the supervisor want the person to learn during that period?

Questions to ask the new employee:

✦ Are the employer's expectations made clear?

✦ What expectations did you have as a new employee?

✦ Were they fulfilled?

✦ In what ways was the probationary period successful and how did it fall short?

✦ To what extent have you fit into the organization and how did your supervisors help you fit in?

Write a memo of about 400 words to your instructor setting out your findings.

FOR FURTHER LEARNING

Ruth Adler, editor. "The Working Press." Bantam Books, 1970. New York Times reporters tell how they covered major stories. Their teamwork is evident in nearly all the tales.

Ken Auletta. "Annals of Communication: Opening Up the Times." The New Yorker 69, No. 19 (June 28, 1993), 55–70. A capsule look at New York Times publisher Arthur L. Sulzberger Jr. and the sociology of the newspaper.

Warren Breed. "Social Control in the Newsroom." In "Mass Communications," edited by Wilbur H. Schramm, University of Illinois, 1960, 178–94. A classic study of the way publishers' preferences are filtered to the newsroom and the way reporters and editors respond.

Robert H. Giles. "Newsroom Management: A Guide to Theory and Practice." Media Management Books, 1988. This detailed manual, written especially for editors, allows reporters to gain insights into the management thinking of their supervisors.

Sydney W. Head and Christopher H. Sterling. "Broadcasting in America: A Survey of Television, Radio, and New Technologies." 4th ed. Houghton Mifflin, 1982. The text includes descriptions of the structure of broadcasting.

Dennis L. Wilcox, Phillip H. Ault, and Warren K. Agee. "Public Relations: Strategies and Tactics." HarperCollins, 1992. An excellent overview of the field of public relations. The authors detail ways in which public relations personnel must work together.

CHAPTER 12

Getting a Job

In this chapter you will learn:

+ Careful preparation is necessary for getting a job in a media organization.

+ An internship is a way to practice classroom lessons in the workplace, and it can be the pathway to a job.

+ An effective job application letter tells who you are, what you have done and what job you want.

+ An effective resume is a key tool for the job search.

+ In preparing for a job interview you need to give thought to who you are and what your goals are.

+ Networking is an important aspect of the job search.

+ Seeking advice can provide leads to jobs or a job itself.

+ Careers in media organizations normally follow a stairstep progression.

HODA KOTB GETS A JOB

Hoda Kotb was scared.

She had just graduated with a degree in communication from Virginia Polytechnic Institute in Blacksburg, Va. All of her friends had gotten jobs, or so it seemed, but she had not.

One morning she got up early and borrowed her mother's car. She was going to drive to Richmond to get a job at a television station, she told her mother. She had her resume and an audition tape.

At the station, she remembers, the news director sat her down in his office, put her tape in his video playback machine and watched for what she estimates was about 15 seconds.

"You know, you're really green," she remembers him telling her. "But I have a friend at a station in Roanoke who's looking for a reporter."

Hoda called her mother at work to tell her that she would be late getting home and got back in the car for the nearly 200-mile trip.

In Roanoke, the news director watched her tape for about 30 seconds, punched the "eject" button and told her "No. You're not what we are looking for." But he had a friend who was a news director in Memphis, Tenn., who needed a reporter.

"You'll have to get there early," he said. "He's leaving on a trip at 8 in the morning."

Hoda called her mother again. Could her mother find another way to work the next day? She got back in the car for an all-night drive across Tennessee. At one stop she bought a portable iron and some hair curlers.

In Memphis, Hoda touched up the jacket of her suit in a restaurant restroom and sped to the station where the news director was just heading out the door. He took her inside and looked at her tape.

"He was real nice," she says, "but he told me I was not ready for this level." He recommended she see a friend of his in Florida.

"They kept sending me to other places," she says, and she kept going. She would stop in a town, buy a newspaper for a cram course in the names of local political leaders and issues, put on fresh makeup and knock on the door at the local television station.

She drove at night with her curlers on. She kept a cup of ice water on the seat beside her and dipped her hand into it now and then and splashed her face. When she could drive no farther, she pulled into a truck stop and curled up for a couple of hours of sleep. She ironed her suit wherever she could find a restroom large enough.

Before starting out, she had believed that "if I could just meet a news director face-to-face and sell myself I could get a job, but it wasn't working," she says. With so many rejections she was losing confidence.

HODA KOTB. Hoda Kotb's first job search followed a long road, but at the end of it she found a camera and a microphone. She had prepared herself well in college and involved herself in extracurricular activities. She was tenacious in going after her first job, and as her story clearly shows, she was willing to go anywhere.
(Courtesy of WWL-TV of Louisiana)

The low point came at what she describes as "a rinky-dink station in Florida where the guy kept mocking me: 'Do you know where to put the tape in? Now, what button do you push? Very good.'"

Hoda, depressed, headed home.

Then, somewhere—she's not sure where—she took a wrong turn and found herself traveling through Mississippi. Near Greenville she saw a CBS eye looking down on her from a billboard sign promoting WXVT, the local CBS affiliate.

"I knew I'd be rejected, but at least I could get a map so I could find my way home," she says.

But WXVT News Director Stan Sandroni liked what he saw.

"When can you start?" he asked.

The job paid $11,000 a year, less than she had made working in a fast-food restaurant as a student. She would be on call 24 hours a day and have a police scanner at home. She would have to use her own car. She would have to be her own photographer, sometimes setting the camera up on the hood of the car, though on Wednesdays she got the station's tripod.

The conditions were such that "if I had gone there first, I probably would have turned it down." But she had driven hundreds of miles and had been to at least 20 stations during her 10-day odyssey through the Southeast.

She took the job.

Hoda Kotb was a television reporter.

WHAT YOU CAN DO IN SCHOOL

STUDY PREVIEW   Professionals who lecture in journalism and mass communication classes often emphasize the competitive nature of their fields and the difficulty of obtaining jobs, if jobs are to be had at all. At the end, they advise, "Go into some other work." Jobs in journalism and mass communication are available, however. After all, the professionals who lecture to you have them. The trick is how to prepare for one, how to snare one and how to turn the first job into a career.

First Things First

Job hunting isn't always easy, as Hoda Kotb's story illustrates. But it can be made less painful and more fruitful if you start to prepare early in your college career. These are proven tips for success:

College courses. Be serious and enthusiastic about your studies. It's easier to find a job if you show potential employers that you have learned something during your years in school. They may not look at your transcript, but they will probe your mind to see what's in it and how it operates.

Extracurricular participation. Work on student publications or in student broadcasting. Join a student chapter of a professional communication organization. Among those with campus chapters are the Society of Professional Journalists; National Federation of Press Women; National Association of Black Journalists; Public Relations Student Society; Alpha Epsilon Rho, the national broadcasting society; International Association of Business Communicators; and Women in Communications. Your membership will show your interest in the field and your commitment to it. You will also be able to put into practice what you have learned in the classroom, and you will make contacts that will last you a lifetime.

Flexibility. Be willing to go anywhere. Many students want to go back to their home towns after graduation and settle into a job with a public relations firm, the local newspaper or the top-rated television station. Unfortunately it doesn't always work that way. To pursue a media career is to climb a staircase, from small town to large town to big city.

Tenacity. "You have to be tenacious when you're looking for a job," Hoda Kotb tells students she talks to. "It's so important not to stop and throw your hands up." Career counselors will tell you the job search has to be full-time work, six to eight hours a day, five days a week, until you find one.

Doing an Internship

An internship can be an excellent opportunity to test what you have learned in the classroom, to learn more about your field and to show a prospective employer what you can do. A good internship, in fact, is an extension of the classroom, and a good internship supervisor is a teacher in a professional setting. An internship is a job, but in a situation in which the employer understands that you are still a student and are there primarily to learn. An intern will put in a limited number of hours—perhaps 10 hours a week—and at little or no pay. Some companies, in fact, require that you receive class credit for the internship in lieu of pay.

Most internships are for students who are in or have completed at least the junior year. At that point you are more likely to have had the basic courses in your field, and with those behind you, you will be able to learn more from the experience and to make a greater contribution than if you knew nothing about it. Faculty members usually know of available internships, and some departments post internship openings. Usually, it's up to the student to contact an internship supervisor and to take care of whatever paperwork the company and the school require.

PUTTING YOURSELF ON PAPER

STUDY PREVIEW   You need to catch a potential employer's attention with a letter asking for an interview in which you say what you can do. You also need a resume that describes what you have done and a collection of work that shows what you have done.

Writing an Application Letter

Some people use a gimmick of some sort to gain attention. Agents for the writers of a movie script called "The Ticking Man" delivered alarm clocks to Hollywood producers before sending the script out for sale. It was bought for more than $1 million, the highest price ever paid for a script there, though

Eloise Abelard
4444 West Forth-fourth Street
Huntley, Montana 59999

January 1, 1996

Mr. Franklin Benjamin
News Director
KZZZ-TV
Cronkite, Idaho 83599

Dear Mr. Benjamin:

I have been a reporter, anchor and news director of the campus closed-circuit television station during the four years I have studied journalism at South Central Montana University. Last summer, I was an intern in the news department of KWW-TV. I will receive my bachelor's degree in May and I would like to start my career at KZZZ-TV.

My studies included courses in news writing and reporting, broadcast news writing and electronic news gathering, and I earned A's in each of them. I minored in American history. Among the other courses I took were in English and American literature, sociology, geography and Spanish.

My grade point average in journalism courses is 3.35 of a possible 4.0. Overall, I have a 3.08.

Joe Noticias, news director at KWW-TV, monitored my internship. On my evaluation he wrote that I was "one of the best interns" he has had. He said I "was well prepared and enthusiastic."

Now I would like to put my preparation and enthusiasm to work for you as a reporter.

I will be in Cronkite on Wednesday, January 15, and I would like to meet you. I will call your office in a few days to set up an appointment.

Sincerely,

Eloise Abelard

ironically the movie has never been produced. An advertising man in Dallas at one point went after new clients by enclosing a match in his letters of introduction with the note, "We don't put out fires. We start them." A recent graduate of our acquaintance wanted a job with a New York advertising agency known for its creativity. He sent the president a mannequin's foot with a note that read, "Now that I have my foot in the door, please give me an interview." When he called for an interview everyone in the office recognized him as "the guy who sent the foot." He got the job. Years before he became a famous Chicago Cubs announcer, Harry Caray was hired by KMOX in St. Louis after sending a letter marked "personal" to the station manager's home.

It's important to note that while each of those introductions was out of the ordinary, it was appropriate to the audience and to the end the senders wanted to accomplish. The point is that each person seeking a job needs to find a way to get attention, even if not so flamboyantly. Perhaps the best way is to write a lead for your letter that encapsulates an accomplishment and build on it so that the letter itself becomes a mini resume:

> My reporting for The Forum, my university's newspaper, won me first place in the South Central Journalism Conference reporting competition two years in a row. I would like to be able to do the same kind of excellent work for your newspaper.

> I produced the PSA that was a key element of the campaign our Public Relations Student Society developed to bring a new home for battered women to the attention of our community. Now I would like to use my skills for your clients.

As a member of a student organization you will have the chance to meet professionals in your field from time to time. When you do, be sure to introduce yourself. They'll be happy to give you their business cards, if you ask for them. When you are ready to send out resumes, send to them first:

> It was good meeting you after your presentation at Communications Day. Based on what you said about your firm, I'd like to have the opportunity to work there.

However you begin your letter, be sure to tell your reader what skills you have, where you have used them in the past and how they can apply to the job that you want. That means you need to find out in advance, as best you can, what the employer's requirements are. Include in your letter and resume only information that is pertinent to the job you are trying to get. You may be a magician or a part-time silversmith or make all your own clothes, but unless those have something to do with the job, don't mention them.

Make sure that every word on every page is spelled correctly, that your capitalization and punctuation are consistent, that your grammar is flawless and that you have made no typographical errors. For newspaper and news service jobs, follow Associated Press style. And your pages should have no thumb prints, ink smudges or crinkles.

Resume of Eloise Abelard

4444 West Forty-fourth Street
Huntley, Montana 59999
(609) 444-5555

Broadcast News Experience:
September 1990-May 1994: Newsroom, South Central Montana University closed circuit television system.
September 1993-May 1994: News Director
September 1992-May 1993: Senior Producer
September 1991-May 1992: Reporter, photographer, news anchor
September 1990-May 1991: Reporter

Newsroom produces the daily 30-minute news program broadcast each evening at 6 p.m. on the university's closed circuit television system. It is a student-run organization with a faculty adviser. Students gather campus news and relevant city news with ENG equipment and write and edit it. They also include a segment of state, national and international news rewritten from the Associated Press broadcast news wire.

May 1992-Aug. 1993: News department intern KWW-TV, Murrow, Montana.

In this position I had a chance to see how all aspects of the news department function. At various times I sat with the assignment editor and the producers. I also went out on stories with reporters and sat with them as they edited the stories. In my last three weeks, I covered one feature story each week for air.

Education:
B.A., South Central Montana University, May 1994.
Major: Broadcast journalism. Minor: American history.

Major courses: Newswriting and reporting, broadcast news writing, electronic news gathering, advanced reporting, feature writing, news practicum, internship, history of journalism, communication theory, media in society.

Professional Organizations:
Society of Professional Journalists. Secretary, SCMU Chapter, 1992–93.
Women in Communications. Treasurer, SCMU Chapter, 1991–92; President, 1993–94.

References:
Dr. Deana Ecole, Department of Journalism, South Central Montana University, Mott, Montana 59998.
Mr. Joe Noticias, News Director, KWW-TV, Murrow, Montana 59999.
Ms. Julie Voz, Producer, KYYY-TV, Reynolds, Nebraska 68999.

Preparing Your Resume

Prospective employers will want to see a resume, which is a summary of your education, work experience and life. Keep in mind that you are trying to sell yourself with your resume and that the first impression the reader will have is most important. Put first what has best prepared you for the job you are applying for. In most cases, that's education. But rather than listing only your degree and the date you received it or will get it, put down your specialty, the most pertinent courses you took and—if they were B or better—the grades you got in them.

Then mention your internship, if you had one, and your extracurricular work. If you're seeking a job in public relations, cite your service as PR chairperson for your fraternity or sorority, for example. Did you participate on award-winning PRSSA teams in competitive campaigns or with a team that devised a campaign for a non-profit agency? Put that near the top.

For a job in journalism or public relations, you want to lead with the education that has prepared you for the job and the internship or work experience in journalism that you have had. That's going to have more impact on an employer than your most recent part-time job working in a restaurant.

Your resume should have a short list of references, the people who will be able to tell potential employers something about your personality, your social skills and your professional abilities. Give their names, addresses and telephone numbers.

Those you would like to include will expect that you ask for their permission to list them. Most will readily agree and may even suggest persons to whom you might apply. Some, however, may turn you down. They may not think that they know you well enough or they may not have enough confidence in you to give you a good recommendation. In either case, accept their decision gracefully and ask someone else.

It is common practice to send out a resume with an application letter, but experts like Richard Nelson Bolles, author of "What Color Is Your Parachute?" say job applicants may be wasting paper and postage in doing so. Resumes do not win interviews or jobs. Bolles suggests the best use for a resume may be as a memory jogger sent after an interview.

What's better than a resume, Bolles says, is a full-time commitment to the job search, involving yourself in it six to eight hours each day, five days a week, until you find the job; personally knocking on doors of any organization that interests you; and using contacts to get interviews.

Showing Your Work

Prospective employers will want to see work that you've done. That's usually presented in one of three ways:

Clip file. A collection of your published work, called a clip file, is expected if you are seeking a job in print journalism.

Audition tape. In television journalism, employers want to see a videotape of stories you have reported. The first items should be your best examples of the sort of work for which you are applying, since it is unlikely that a news director will watch for more than 20 to 40 seconds. If you are applying for a radio job, you need an audio tape of your work.

Portfolio. For public relations applicants, a collection of news releases, campaign materials like posters or ads, public service announcements or other written or graphic materials will show prospective employers what you can do.

The work you show should be as professionally done as you can possibly do it. It can come from work you did for classes, a campus publication or broadcasting station, a campus organization or an internship. Your materials need not be extensive. Editors know you have not had time to compile a large collection of work. But you need something to show them that you have been interested enough to do the work and let them get a sense of its quality.

GETTING A FOOT IN THE DOOR

STUDY PREVIEW   Getting an interview requires persistence, imagination and sales skill. You need all that to get to people who make hiring decisions and to impress them that you are the best person for the job.

Networking

An old expression has it that when it comes to job hunting, "It's not what you know but who you know." In this increasingly complex field, you need to know the "what." But it certainly helps to know the "who," the people who hire or who can put you in touch with the people who hire. They constitute a network of contacts, and getting to know them is called "networking."

One of the best-known networks today is referred to as "F.O.B.," or Friends of Bill, the wide network of friends and acquaintances of President Bill Clinton. News stories about them have identified some as friends Clinton made as far back as kindergarten. He met others, both faculty and students, at Georgetown University and Yale Law School, and still others during his years as a Rhodes Scholar. His involvement in politics yielded more. When he wanted the job of president, they banded together to help him get it.

Students in journalism and public relations network by getting to know each other in classes and through their work on publications and team projects. They solidify relationships among themselves by joining student chapters of communication organizations. The contacts made in college years can blossom into professional opportunities later in a career.

Faculty members should be part of your network. They can open doors among two groups. They keep in contact with many of the students they have had through the years or know where many of them work, and the old school tie is a strong one. Faculty also usually have a wide acquaintance among professionals to whom they will recommend students in whom they have confidence.

Student organizations frequently meet with professional organizations. Groups like the Society of Professional Journalists, the Public Relations Society of America and the International Association of Business Communicators open their doors to students at local meetings and at regional and national conventions. A handshake and an introduction give you the chance to meet a public relations executive or a news director, learn something of that person's work and make an impression. Dinner-table conversation at a PRSA meeting won't wind up with a job offer over the coffee and dessert, but it provides a contact point for your network.

Professionals who come to campus to speak, whether to give an informal lecture in a class or a major address, can also serve as contacts. If you take the time to introduce yourself afterwards, ask a question or just thank the speaker for coming, you will have made a contact that you can follow up later.

Make use of anyone and everyone. Let your dentist know what kind of a job you are looking for. A principal in a public relations firm may be in the chair later that day. Or the waiter in a coffee shop you frequent may know the local newspaper editor. Perhaps you decide you would like to write news for a television station. Use every resource you can to find someone who works at the station who can introduce you to the person who hires news writers.

The Guidance Interview

One way to extend your network is by asking for guidance from people who are in the field you want to enter. Use your network to get an introduction to a managing editor, for example, or a news director. Make clear that it's not a job you want, but advice. Develop a set of questions about the job market and specific positions that interest you. Let the person know who you are and what you have done, and ask what you might be qualified for.

It's likely you will develop rapport with at least one of the individuals you interview, and the person may well be moved to help you in your job search by suggesting people to talk to and even introducing you to someone who might have a job for you. It is possible too that you will impress the person to such an extent that a job offer will come from the interview. Or you may win consideration for a job with a thank you note stating you were so impressed that you would like the opportunity to work for the company and that you could offer the company particular skills.

The Job Interview

In preparing for the job interview, it's a given that you'll dress in clean, well-pressed clothes; that, on meeting the interviewer, you'll smile, give a firm handshake and try to impress upon the interviewer that you are poised and articulate. Beyond that, you have to give serious thought to who you are and what your aims in life are, because that's what interviewers are most interested in. They want to know what makes you tick, what motivates you and whether you have the mental and emotional qualities required of a good employee.

They also want to know how you will fit into their firm, so they will measure you against the company's own special character. That means you have to know the organization. If you have a date for an interview at a television station, study the program listings in the newspaper to become familiar with what the station puts on the air. Watch all of its newscasts. Set your alarm and get up early to watch the station's morning show.

If you are trying out for a newspaper, read it thoroughly for days before the interview. When you set up an interview with an out-of-town newspaper, ask for some copies to be sent to you ahead of the interview. That should score some points in itself. When the copies arrive, familiarize yourself with the newspaper. As Hoda Kotb did during her job search, try to get a sense of what the local issues are and who the public officials are. For any news job, be up on as much as you can, including international and national events.

You should also be aware that an interview allows you to get information about the organization. You can get a sense of what the boss finds important by asking about key players in the organization and why they are valued. You should ask how the organization functions and how employees advance. Keep in mind that it is just as important for you to know about the company as it is for the company to know about you. And just as a potential employer will decide whether to hire you or someone else, you need to be ready to turn down a job offer if you are uncomfortable with the employer.

Saying Thank You

One step in the job-hunting process is crucial: send a thank you note to the person who interviewed you. It is a simple matter of common courtesy, but one that often is overlooked. A thank you note will bring your image back into the interviewer's mind, and it could well make you stand out from others who have been interviewed and do not send a note.

Attach your resume to the thank you note. That's important. The resume will remind the interviewer who you are and what you have done, and you'll reinforce the impression with your thank you.

Send a thank you to anyone else who helped you, including the interviewer's secretary. Did the secretary's friendliness help calm your nerves? Say so. It's not uncommon for a secretary to remind the boss of "that nice young person you interviewed yesterday." But say something a little different to each person. They may compare their notes, and identical notes can hurt more than help.

The Tryout

Many newsroom supervisors give job candidates a tryout to see what they can do. According to researcher Ron Smith, candidates typically are asked to do basic newsroom tasks: "Do some interviews, write some obituaries, and answer the phones." Editors want to find out how skilled you are, whether the clips you have shown them are mostly your own work or heavily edited. They also want to know whether you can think for yourself, "ask questions, and show creativity." Some want to get a sense of just how you would fit in.

PURSUING YOUR CAREER

STUDY PREVIEW   If you follow the stairstep method of progressing in a media career, your first job will be with a newspaper or station in a small community or with a small public relations department or agency. From there you will move on to successively more important jobs and, possibly, in successively larger communities depending upon your talent and ambition.

Starting Out

In your first jobs you will pay your dues, to use the vernacular of the trade. You will learn the business from the bottom up, taking a hand at everything. You'll get a chance to learn what you like to do and what you don't, what you are good at and what you aren't so good at. A great advantage is that you will be in a situation in which the stakes aren't very high. James Reston went to the Dayton, Ohio, Daily News upon graduation from the University of Illinois journalism program. Reston, who later had a distinguished career as reporter and Washington bureau chief of the New York Times, wrote in "Deadline," his autobiography, of his continued education at the Daily News:

> I learned the importance of deadlines, for one thing. When Bert Teeters, the managing editor, called for copy, I began to pay attention. When he shouted "COPY!" I knew I was in trouble. "We're not getting out a weekly paper," he would say, and when he was really sore, "Reston," he'd yell, "what do you think this is, a quarterly?"
>
> I learned to write headlines, an artful challenge in discipline and compression. We all knew the horror of the careless editor on one of the midwestern dailies who wrote a headline, MAN FALLS OFF BRIDGE, BREAKS BOTH LEGS, and left out the "g" in bridge. In short, I discovered that you learned this business the way you learned how to play baseball, not by meditating about it but by practicing it and by ducking at the right time.

JAMES RESTON. A University of Illinois journalism graduate, James Reston started up the ladder to an editorship of the New York Times with a job at the Dayton, Ohio, Daily News. Learning journalism was like learning baseball, he said. You learn it "by practicing it and by ducking at the right time." (The Bettmann Archive)

Talk to established reporters or editors and they will tell you similar tales about what they did and how much they learned working long hours for low pay on small publications or stations. They had a chance to cover every type of story and sit at every desk. They also had a chance to make mistakes that would not be tolerated at larger newspapers or stations. And when they made mistakes, they learned how to duck.

Moving Up

The stairstep method of progression is well illustrated by television reporter Hoda Kotb. Greenville, Miss., where she started, is the country's 178th largest market. From there she went to Moline, Ill., the 84th market, then to Fort Myers, Fla., the 88th, and then to New Orleans, the 40th largest market—all in less than 10 years.

NBC News anchor Tom Brokaw began as a part-time radio announcer in Yankton, S.D., while he was still in high school and worked his way through the University of South Dakota as a radio reporter. On graduation, he took a job in Omaha, Neb., a relatively small market, only 73rd largest in the United States, moved on to Atlanta, the 10th market, then went to Los Angeles, the second largest. His next stop was NBC, where he had a variety of reporting jobs, including White House correspondent, before being tapped for the evening anchor position.

CO-ANCHORS. Dan Rather and Connie Chung followed different paths to the CBS Evening News anchor desk they once shared. Chung started her career as a part-time copy clerk at WTTG-TV in Washington while a student at the University of Maryland. Rather studied journalism at Sam Houston State College while working part-time at a local radio station.   (Craig Blankenhorn/CBS)

Former CBS anchor Connie Chung worked part-time as a copy clerk at WTTG-TV in Washington while finishing her journalism degree at the University of Maryland. On graduation, Chung took a full time job as the news department's secretary just to be there, and when a news job opened up, she got it. From there she moved to the Washington bureau of CBS News, then to KNXT, now KCBS, in Los Angeles. After seven years as a local anchor in the country's Number 2 market, she was hired by NBC. Six years later she went back to CBS and, within four years, she was made an anchor on the network's evening news program.

CBS Evening News anchor Dan Rather worked part-time for KSAM radio while studying for his journalism degree at Sam Houston State College. After teaching journalism for a year, he joined United Press International as a reporter, then went to the Houston Chronicle and then to a Houston radio station where he moved from news writer to reporter to news director. From there he went to the CBS television affiliate in Houston and then to the network.

Not everyone, of course, wants to move around like that, and some people find a career with just one or two organizations. For example Jane Healy, managing editor of the Orlando, Fla., Sentinel, went there as a reporter in 1973 after a stint as a copy girl in the Washington bureau of the New York Daily News. In the next 20 years, she moved to a position as the Sentinel's regional editor, won promotion to the editorial page, was made associate editor overseeing the editorial page and then was elevated to managing editor.

Of course, a major metropolitan newspaper like the Sentinel or a television network may not be everyone's goal. One person may find a niche as an editor for the Houma, La., Daily Courier, circulation 22,084, and someone else as a reporter for the Las Vegas, N.M., Daily Optic, circulation 5,286. But like a stairway, wherever a career may lead, it generally starts at a bottom step.

CHARLAYNE HUNTER-GAULT. Charlayne Hunter-Gault graduated from the University of Georgia to a career path that went from a magazine to a television station to a newspaper and to the PBS television network, where she is seen nightly on the McNeil-Lehrer News Hour. Here, she interviews former U.S. secretaries of state at a forum in Atlanta.   (AP/Wide World Photos)

Moving to a New Field

Many people start out on a career path in newspaper journalism or broadcast journalism or public relations and never turn from it. Others, for various reasons, move from field to field. R. W. Apple Jr., Washington bureau chief of the New York Times, knew from practically the first day he read the Times as a young man that he wanted to work for it. But after leaving Princeton University short of his degree he went to the Wall Street Journal, a job that was interrupted by Army service in the late 1950s. Apple completed his degree at Columbia University while working for the Journal, then moved to NBC as a news writer on the overnight shift, midnight to 8 a.m. He won promotion to writer-correspondent with NBC television where Times editors saw his work and hired him.

Charlayne Hunter-Gault of the PBS MacNeil-Lehrer News Hour got her foot in the door as a secretary at The New Yorker magazine following her graduation from the University of Georgia's journalism program. She became one of the magazine's staff writers, then moved to a reporting job with a television station in Washington, to the New York Times, and to the MacNeil-Lehrer program. The program's Jim Lehrer edited a camp newspaper during a hitch with the Marines after graduating in journalism from the University of Missouri. On his discharge, he went to the Dallas Morning News, then switched over to the Dallas Times-Herald, where he moved up from reporter to city editor. From there he jumped to the city's public television station, then to WETA in Washington.

It is not uncommon for journalists to move into public relations. Indeed, it is the norm among all but the youngest public relations people to have worked in journalism first. Those who make the switch are looking for a bit more money, perhaps, and more regular hours.

Public relations people return to newspaper or broadcast journalism on occasion. Individuals who go into political public relations may do so for the term of an elected public official, then return to journalism.

Bill Moyers, a Baptist minister and protege of Lyndon Johnson, worked in the Kennedy Administration as a Peace Corps official. When Johnson became president, Moyers went with him to the White House on the news staff. Soon he was press secretary. Moyers left government life and became publisher of Newsday, a commentator on CBS and a well-known producer and host of public affairs specials on the Public Broadcasting System. Now he is doing commentary on NBC.

The lesson is that the individual who is intelligent and takes advantage of educational opportunities is able to take advantage of varied career opportunities as they come along. Be prepared for and open to challenge and change.

CHAPTER WRAP-UP

Opportunities are available for rewarding careers in journalism and public relations, though the job search may be frustrating. Individuals who want to follow a media career should prepare themselves well through education and involvement in co-curricular activities and internships.

Getting the first job can be made easier with an effective application letter and a resume that stress accomplishments that are related to the job the applicant is seeking. Both networking and making advice calls can open doors. But applicants must be well-prepared for the job interview with samples of their work and a knowledge of the company with which they are interviewing and the community in which it is located.

Seekers of communications jobs should be prepared to start out with a low-level job in a small organization and in a small community, understanding that through dedication and hard work one can move to successively more rewarding positions.

STUDY QUESTIONS

1. How can the student prepare for a first job?
2. What is the importance of an internship?
3. What should be stressed in the application letter and the resume?
4. When is the best time to present a resume?
5. What do potential employers look for in an interview?
6. What should the applicant try to learn during an interview?
7. What do editors look for during an applicant's tryout period?
8. What behaviors do editors want to see in staff members?

9. Describe the behaviors that can help and hurt relationships with co-workers.

10. What are traditional career paths in media organizations?

PUTTING YOUR LEARNING TO WORK

EXERCISE 1   The First Job

Interview someone in news or public relations about how the person got his or her first professional job. Write a 350-word story based on the interview.

EXERCISE 2   Company Profile

Develop a list of sources for information about news and public relations organizations. Choose one company you might like to work for and develop a profile of it as you might do prior to a job interview.

EXERCISE 3   Self-Assessment

Prepare a resume and an application letter. On a separate sheet of paper, list gaps in your experience that might weaken your chances for a job. Next, list specific ways in which you can remedy those weaknesses prior to going on the job market.

FOR FURTHER LEARNING

Perry J. Ashley, editor. "American Newspaper Journalists." Dictionary of Literary Biography. Vols. 23, 25, 29, and 43. Gale Publishing Co., 1983–1985. The lives of journalists can be instructive and entertaining, and the sketches in these volumes are worth reading on both counts. Both historical and contemporary figures are represented.

Perry J. Ashley, editor. "American Newspaper Publishers, 1950–1990." Dictionary of Literary Biography. Vol. 127. Gale Publishing Co., 1993. Biographical sketches of publishers and major news-service executives.

Richard Nelson Bolles. "What Color Is Your Parachute?" Ten Speed Press, 1981. This is a classic text on searching for a job.

Robert H. Giles. "Newsroom Management: A Guide to Theory and Practice." Media Management Books, Inc., 1988. Giles discusses management techniques as applied to newsrooms and includes views of other editors on their practices.

James Reston, "Deadline: A Memoir." Random House, 1991.

Sam G. Riley, editor. "American Magazine Journalists." Dictionary of Literary Biography. Vols. 73, 79, and 91. Gale Publishing Co., 1988–1990. Biographical sketches of magazine writers, editors, and publishers.

CHAPTER 13

Writing and Rewriting for Public Relations

In this chapter you will learn:

+ Different circumstances require different types of news releases.

+ News releases for print publication differ from those for broadcasting.

+ Broadcasting stations should be sent releases in broadcast style.

+ Special types of releases include the tip sheet and the request for coverage.

+ Audio releases and video news releases take advantage of the special technology of the broadcast media.

+ Both preparers and users have special ethical concerns about releases.

+ A public service announcement is a release but with a difference.

+ Writing copy for a newsletter is much like writing for a newspaper.

A RAID ON A SWEATSHOP

Some years ago a U.S. Secretary of Labor named Raymond Donovan under-took a campaign to wipe out poor working conditions in the nation's garment factories. To dramatize the campaign, Donovan himself led a raid on a factory in New York, and rather than relying solely on news coverage, his depart-ment's information office issued a news release:

The drunk on the trash-strewn side-walk barely lifted his head as the un-marked van pulled up in front of a loft building in Manhattan's Chinatown.

Crouched inside the van, Secretary of Labor Raymond J. Donovan and a team of his wage and hour compliance officers were about to investigate sweatshop working conditions in the garment facto-ries above. . . . Donovan, the compliance officers and their Chinese-speaking in-terpreter bypassed the broken elevator and raced up the stairs. They fanned out to two separate floors of the building. It was time to go to work.

In the same tone, the release reported that Donovan's raid had turned up a 90-year-old Chinese woman who was earning $1 an hour and "a terrified 10-year-old girl, reportedly a recent arrival from Hong Kong." It ended this way:

Meanwhile, sewing machines whirred on in Chinatown, as the drunk nodded on in the street below. The bent-backed women of the sweatshop had found a new and powerful friend.

The release made news all right, but not entirely the sort of news its writer intended. It was reproduced in a Page 1 story in the Wall Street Journal, where it was characterized as having "the flourish of a pulp novel." Journal reporter Robert S. Greenberger quoted union officials as saying many of Dono-van's assertions were flat-out wrong, including the charge that the elderly woman was paid $1 an hour. "I think the whole thing was a gimmick," Sol Chaikin, president of the International Ladies Garment Workers Union, was quoted as saying. "Whoever wrote that press release should be writing hot, sexy novels."

The news release failed on two counts. The content was suspect, and that alone should have doomed it. Even had the piece been accurate, the writ-ing, with its "flourish," was inappropriate for newspapers and newscasts—and, therefore, for a news release.

As a public relations writer you must write in a style suitable for pub-lication or broadcast, and your work must meet that most basic of all journalistic standards—accuracy. That is true whether you are writing news releases, news ideas, public service announcements or newsletters. You must also be attuned to the organization's policies, so you can articulate those policies clearly and forcefully. The public relations writer, in effect, becomes the organization's voice.

TYPES OF NEWS RELEASES

STUDY PREVIEW   News releases come from everywhere. Politicians in and out of office, private individuals, corporations, churches, citizens groups, trade groups, schools, fraternities, sororities—anyone who has a story to tell to the public issues them. And they serve many different purposes. So many, in fact, that it is nearly impossible to categorize them. At heart, however, they seek to draw attention to the person or group distributing them or to provide information from the distributor's point of view. Most often they are separated into announcement releases, position papers and backgrounders.

Announcement Releases

Announcement releases are written to gain publicity for an individual or an organization. They may be designed to promote an activity—a church bazaar, a fund-raising dinner, a public lecture. Announcement releases are sent out before the event and include essential information: the name of the event, the day and time it is to occur, the place and the individual or organization involved. Announcements also should note whether admission will be charged.

Many television and radio stations carry such announcements in community calendar features. Newspapers may print them as separate stories or list them in an events calendar.

Larger newspapers may have events calendars in different sections of the newspaper, so the person sending out the release should know which section of the paper is most appropriate. A release about a school fashion show sent to the business desk will end up in the trash just as fast as an announcement of a seminar on international trade that goes to the amusement editor.

Organizations also announce managerial-level appointments and promotions with news releases. Sending a photo increases the exposure potential. A personnel announcement might be run as a separate story or in a column on promotions, depending on the space available and how an editor perceives the importance of the company, the position and the person.

Middle State University Theater
#1 Campus Drive

FOR IMMEDIATE RELEASE

Contact:
Thelma Ryan
(504) 555-5555

Moliere's masterpiece "The Misanthrope," directed by guest artist Solomon Gills, opens the 1992–93 Middle State University Theatre season Oct. 2 at 8 p.m. in Nickleby Theater.

Performances run Oct. 2–3 and Oct. 8–10 at 8 p.m. with matinees at 3 p.m. on Sunday, Oct. 4 and 11.

Gills will direct Tony Harrison's adaptation set in the 1960s France of Charles de Gaulle, Givenchy and Chanel, hanging at the precipice of cultural, political and social revolutions.

Harrison's version, commissioned by the National Theatre of Great Britain, retains the couplets yet places the comedy 300 years after its first performance.

Tickets are $6 for general admission and $4 for students, senior citizens and MSU faculty and staff.

School and community groups are welcome at a special discount.

For more information, call MSU's Department of Drama at (555) 555-3826.

Moliere's "The Misanthrope" presents a world filled with superficiality and hypocrisy; a society of slandering gossips and artificial poets where the moral dilemma invades the personal, social, ethical and political realms.

Harrison's adaptation presents a de Gaulle regime that echoes the court of Louis XIV, pointing to a period between 1959 and 1966 when no less than 300 convictions were made under a law which made it a crime to insult the Head of State.

"Story Theatre" by Paul Sills and directed by Joe Gargary opens Nov. 13.

ANNOUNCEMENT RELEASE. This example is adapted from a release that was sent to drama critics, entertainment editors and community calendar editors.

1000 POTOMAC ST., NW, SUITE
204 WASHINGTON, DC 2007

TELEPHONE 202-298-7512
FAX 202-337-7092

FOR RELEASE: CONTACT:
     Immediate   Ruth Domboski
                                   (202) 298-7512

DOMBOSKI NAMED DIRECTOR OF COMMUNICATIONS

Washington, Sept. 1, 1992 -- Ruth Domboski has been named director of communications for The Media Institute.

Domboski will handle the overall communication efforts of the Institute. She also will provide editorial assistance on Institute publications, coordinate special events and the Institute's luncheon series, and will work on the Environmental Reporting Forum, a joint program with the Radio and Television News Directors Foundation.

Domboski previously was marketing coordinator for the broadcast division of the Associated Press. Before AP, she worked for the investment firm of Folger, Nolan, Fleming & Douglas in Washington.

The Media Institute is a nonprofit research foundation specializing in media and communications policy issues. The Institute publishes studies, conducts conferences, and files court briefs and regulatory comments on a host of communications topics. Through its First Amendment programs, the Institute advocates free-speech rights for individuals, media, and corporate speakers.

###

PERSONNEL ANNOUNCEMENT. The Media Institute's communications director, Ruth Domboski, sent out news of her own appointment in this release. She uses this format to report on other Media Institute activities.

Some announcement releases are designed to win coverage of an event as well as to let the public know that something is coming up. Releases may be sent to a television assignment editor and to the station's community service manager, or to both a city editor and a section editor.

As a public relations person, you may also do your own reporting on a publicity event. You gather information as the event unfolds and put it in news story form, then send it out to news organizations. Some studies, however, show that "after the fact" releases are rarely used because news organizations want to control their reports of what happened.

Backgrounders

Backgrounders, as the name implies, provide background information that helps to explain an event or a situation. As such, they provide a context for understanding. If a university finds it necessary to raise tuition rates sharply, the public relations department may put together a set of statistics showing how costs have risen at a faster rate than income. The backgrounder may also describe the school's pressing needs and new programs that have been instituted to benefit students. It could include a discussion of what would happen if the tuition were not increased and what the impact of the increase will be.

Whatever the topic, the backgrounder gives a look at the past, the present and the future. It gives historical context for a situation, describes the situation as it exists and looks to what might come from a course of action. It does so without making a judgment.

Backgrounders are issued to news organizations. They are often made available to the public. They serve as an information base for other publications, including news releases, annual reports and informational brochures. They are also used as the basis for speeches given by organization officials.

Position Papers

While the backgrounder is free of opinion, the position paper is not. It gives the organization's position on an issue or situation. One might describe company efforts to meet governmental safety or environmental regulations or detail the damages caused by an explosion in a manufacturing plant. Another might be issued as a response to an external situation. If a reporter makes an error in a story, a position paper might be prepared to set the record straight.

Citizen watchdog groups accuse corporations of not operating in the public interest, government attorneys bring charges of malfeasance against elected officials, and news organizations raise questions about all sorts of public and private groups. In those and similar instances, the responses come in the form of position papers.

WHITE HOUSE PUBLIC RELATIONS. Dee Dee Myers, President Clinton's first news secretary, served as a spokesperson for the president. In daily briefings, the news secretary explains administration policy, gives reporters the president's views on issues of the day, and funnels reporters' questions to the president. Behind the scenes, the White House news office prepares scores of news releases each day.
(Rick Wilking/The Bettmann Archive)

Tip Sheets

Closely akin to the news release is the tip sheet. It consists of a paragraph or two describing a story that a reporter might wish to cover and that the public relations office can help with. Tip sheets may contain one story idea or several ideas grouped together.

One of the concerns of the Recording Industry Association of America is protecting its members against exploitation by people who counterfeit, or pirate, sound recordings. It investigates counterfeiters and works with law enforcement agencies to have them arrested, and when it is involved in a case it issues a tip sheet it calls a "piracy alert,"

Middle State University
Office of Public Affairs

News Tip Sheet

Jan. 1, 1996
Contact: Basil Lee
(504) 555-5888

Teacher's Strike

Dr. Emmy Pinkard of Middle State University's College of Business Administration is a leading expert on the economics surrounding the impending Metropolis public school teacher's strike. Pinkard has been following the development and ramifications of this local labor issue.

Pinkard, assistant professor of economics, was selected for the prestigious national Sears Roebuck Foundation Award. She earned her Ph.D. from George University and her master's degree from Northern Kansas. Pinkard joined the MSU faculty three years ago.

If you would like to interview Dr. Pinkard on any of these issues, call Basil Lee, assistant director of public affairs, at 555-5888.

###

TIP SHEET. The tip sheet is not meant for publication. It's designed to give editors story ideas and to alert them to help they might get from a public relations department in developing a story.

News

RIAA

Contact: Alexandra Walsh
(202) 775-0101

PIRACY ALERT

WHAT: Simultaneous raids were executed on both sides of the United States/Mexican border as a result of the first joint sound recording piracy investigation by the Recording Industry Association of America and the Mexican office of the International Federation of the Phonographic Industry. The investigation revealed not only the alleged manufacture and sale of counterfeit cassettes on both sides of the border, but the alleged trafficking of raw materials and finished product back and forth across the border.

WHEN: August 6.

WHERE: One residence and two storage facilities in El Paso, Texas, and the Mercado Juarez Flea Market in Juarez, Mexico.

ENFORCEMENT: Agents from the El Paso FBI Office under Special Agent Leo Navarette, officers of the El Paso Police Department supervised by Det. Jerry Palmer, officers of the Federal Judicial Police located in Juarez, with the assistance of representatives of the RIAA and IFPI.

PRODUCT SEIZED: Approximately 100,000 alleged counterfeit cassettes were seized from vendors at the Mercado Juarez Flea Market. In El Paso, an alleged illegal manufacturing facility housed in a residence yielded equipment and materials capable of producing 1.7 million cassettes per year (representing an annual loss to the legitimate recording industry of $17.5 million in displaced sales) as well as 300,000 alleged counterfeit cassette labels. In addition, a total of 6,500 alleged counterfeit cassettes were seized from the El Paso sites and two arrests were made.

POTENTIAL PENALTIES: Jose Manzano and Guadalupe Garcia were arrested and charged with federal copyright violations. If convicted, they face up to five years imprisonment and $250,000 in fines.

AVAILABLE FOR INTERVIEW: Frank Creighton, RIAA coordinator, investigative operations and Gabriel Abaroa, RIAA/IFPI anti-piracy unit, Mexico City.

ADDITIONAL COMMENTS: Photographs are available.

###

8/10/93

RECORDING INDUSTRY ASSOCIATION OF AMERICA, INC.

1020 Nineteenth Street, N.W. ▪ Suite 200 Washington, D.C. 20036 ▪ Phone: (202) 775-0101 ▪ Fax: (202) 775-7253

PIRACY ALERT. The Recording Industry of America issues a piracy alert like this one to provide basic information on investigations into record counterfeiting and to let news people know who to contact for further information.

RIAA public relations person Alexandra Walsh credits the piracy alert with getting more coverage for the raids than traditional after-the-fact releases did. She sends them to reporters who cover the recording industry for publications like Billboard, Variety and Hollywood Reporter. She gets local coverage by targeting newspapers and radio and television stations in the area in which a raid occurs. She sends them to crime reporters who appreciate the bare-bones Five Ws and the H in the "piracy alert" but want to get the details for themselves, "not from a prefabricated release," Walsh says. She also finds the alerts spark the interest of consumer reporters in the broader issue of the impact of sound-recording counterfeiting on the record-buying public. But, Walsh says, "the amount of coverage depends on the follow-up," making personal contact with reporters and having available the information they need.

It's important to note that Walsh does not send out a piracy alert following every raid. She exercises editorial judgment and considers the impact on the audience and the newsworthiness of the event. A raid that nets 500 counterfeit cassettes isn't especially newsworthy, but the one cited in the example in which 100,000 were seized is. She'll also cover a raid that has a novel element, such as the joint effort by U.S. and Mexican authorities, and that will be highlighted in the alert.

Requests for Coverage

Linda Yasnyi, principal of the advertising and public relations firm You Ain't Seen Nothin' Yet Ink. in New Orleans, has developed what she calls a "Request for Coverage." To remind assignment editors of an event she is promoting and feels is newsworthy, or to let them know about the event in case they have not yet seen a release, Yasnyi faxes target media organizations one page on which she has condensed the Who, What, When, Where, Why and How. An assignment editor can drop the "Request for Coverage" in the tickler file and on the day of the event hand the sheet to a photographer or reporter.

PREPARING NEWS RELEASES

STUDY PREVIEW   News releases are heavily used. Any editor will tell you that. Much of the business and financial news in newspapers comes from news releases. News releases, in whole or in part, are the basis for stories elsewhere in the newspaper as well, from Page 1 to the food section to the sports pages. Many more would be used, however, if writers paid more attention to editors' needs.

September 28, 1996

REQUEST FOR COVERAGE—Oct. 2, 1996
Opening Night—Middle State University Theater
Moliere's Comedy The Misanthrope

WHAT: Tony Harrison's adaptation of Moliere's masterpiece is set in the 1960s France of Charles de Gaulle, Givenchy and Chanel, on the edge of cultural, political and social revolutions. It presents a de Gaulle regime pointing to a period between 1959 and 1966 which echoes the court of Louis XIV, when no less than 300 convictions were made under a law which made it a crime to insult the Head of State.

WHEN: 8 p.m. curtain, Friday, Oct. 2
Performances run Oct. 2–3 and Oct. 8–10 at 8 p.m. with matinees at 3 p.m. on Sun., Oct. 4 & 11.

WHERE: Nickelby Theater, MSU Campus
63 South Campus Blvd.

WHO: Middle State University Theatre
Solomon Gills—Guest Director
Adele Craw—MSU Drama department chairperson and scenic designer
Tony Harrison's adaptation of "The Misanthrope," commissioned by the National Theatre of Great Britain.

COST: The tickets are $6 for general admission; $4 for students, senior citizens and MSU faculty and staff. School and community groups are welcome at a special discount.

CONTACT: Adele Crawe — (555) 555-3826, (555) 555-6112
Basil Lee   — (504) 555-5888
Edith Bradin — (504) 555-7229

###

REQUEST FOR COVERAGE. The request is a no-frills statement of the facts. It is designed to let news people know exactly what event is to be covered and when and where it is taking place.

Writing News Releases

Writers of news releases should think of stories in terms of newsworthiness and audience appeal and should understand that perhaps the most important member of the audience is the editor who first reads a release. The results of a study of business editors by Brouillard Communications provides a glimpse of the questions that will be foremost in the mind of an editor unfolding a release.

Does the story have any interest or relevance for the larger audience and, particularly, for the local audience? Editors who answered the Brouillard questionnaire said much of what they received had no relevance or significance and no local connection. And frequently the significant or relevant information was buried.

Is it timely? Too often, releases arrived after an event was over.

Late or timely, however, many of the releases were badly written, the editors complained.

Television newscaster David Brinkley has been widely quoted as saying, "News is what I say it is." News is what editors select, and while they generally agree on the elements of newsworthiness, different editors have different tastes in news just as they have different tastes in automobiles or clothing. Pay attention to the publications and stations for which you are writing so you will know what the editors believe is news. Then you can tailor your releases accordingly and increase the chances of usage.

In assembling the news release, determine which of the Five Ws and the H is most significant and interesting and make it the lead, as news reporters do. Within some organizations there may be pressures to put the spotlight in every release on people at the top of the organizational chart. But news release writers have to assess whether the "who" is the most important and most interesting element, or if an executive "who" is more important than the "who" at the center of the story. And they have to be prepared to argue that a release with a journalistically sound lead is more likely to be used than one that begins as a puff piece for the boss. Editors want to see in the first paragraph why the news being offered to them is important and what it will mean to their audiences.

Quotes may be handled differently in a news release than in a news story. A news reporter wants the actual words uttered by a source. The writer of a news release, however, may make up quotes on behalf of the individuals to whom statements are attributed.

In devising quotes for others, the writer either senses from long experience with them what the sources might say or has consulted with the sources and knows what they are thinking about the matter being written about, at least in general terms. The practice is similar to that of a speech writer ghosting a speech. The quotes must ring true, however, and be approved prior to release. That is, they must sound as if they had been spoken, and sources ought to be given the opportunity to edit the words that have been put in their mouths so that the words, in effect, become their own.

Whereas news reporters are loathe to show their copy to a source, it is not uncommon for news releases to be checked by one or more persons in supervisory positions. Supervisors will want to make sure the facts are right and that any interpretation of the facts is in accord with the organization's policies and beliefs.

Following Style

Following style guidelines is as important for writers of news releases as for reporters. Nearly all newspapers in the United States follow the style outlined in the Associated Press Stylebook and Libel Manual. You will find variations, however. Whereas most newspapers do not use an honorific like "Mr." or "Mrs." in front of someone's name, the New York Times does, and publications vary in their use of "Mrs.," "Miss" or "Ms."

When in doubt, adhere to AP style, especially if preparing a release for wide distribution. If a release is going to only one publication, the style should be tailored to fit. In fact, if you find yourself writing for one publication consistently, you should ask for and use its stylebook.

Precision counts. Be consistent in using a reputable dictionary. AP stylebook readers with spelling, style and usage questions not covered in the text are directed to Webster's New World Dictionary, Third College Edition, or to a backup, Webster's Third New International Dictionary.

For broadcast copy it is a good idea to follow the AP Broadcast News Handbook, a standardized guide to the style used in most radio and television newsrooms. Among its valuable features is a pronunciation guide you can use to lessen the chance announcers will mispronounce the name of a town or company, or worse, a major executive's name.

Formatting for Print

Releases should be prepared in a format that permits easy reading and easy editing. Use standard 8 ½ x 11-inch paper, preferably not letterhead—at least not letterhead with an imposing logo that overwhelms the message. Margins should be 1 to 1 ½ inches all around. Copy should be typed at least double-spaced or, preferably, triple-spaced. The white space allows for editing.

The organization's name, address and telephone number should appear in the top-left corner of the form. Also include the name of a contact person or

news release
Internal Revenue Service

For release: **EMBARGOED UNTIL MARCH 26**   Media contact: Teresa Bailey
(504) 589-2458

<u>IRS ATTACKS UNDERGROUND CASH</u>

NEW ORLEANS—Drug traffickers are using Louisiana businesses to "clean up" money gained through illegal activities, and the Internal Revenue Service is working to put a stop to it.

Twenty-two teams from the IRS will sweep the state during the next two weeks, checking 140 businesses to see if they are complying with the federal law requiring them to report cash payments of more than $10,000. About 60 businesses in the New Orleans/Houma area are expected to be contacted. IRS District Director John Wendorff said.

"This is one way private industry and law enforcement can take the profit out of selling illegal drugs," he said. "If someone hands you $50,000 in cash to pay for a new car or real estate, it should arouse suspicion."

Large cash payments may mean the buyer is trying to evade taxes or to hide profits from illegal activity, a procedure known as "money laundering." For example, an Alabama drug dealer recently pleaded guilty to money laundering charges based on his cash payments of $160,000 for luxury cars, including a Rolls Royce.

Banks and other financial institutions are also required to report cash transactions of more than $10,000. While IRS statistics show that financial institutions are very cooperative in filing the reports, compliance in the business and professional community is poor. In 1990, 114,374 currency transaction reports were filed by Louisiana financial institutions, compared to only 295 Forms 8300 from businesses and professionals reporting large cash transactions.

If the IRS check shows unreported cash transactions involving amounts of more than $10,000, the business may face substantial penalties. In November, Congress increased the penalty to the greater of $25,000 or the amount of cash in the transaction, up to $100,000. Previously, it was 10 percent of the transaction amount. The new legislation defines cash as including "monetary instruments" having a face amount of less than $10,000.

Additionally, if it appears that the violations were willful, the IRS agents may refer the case to the criminal investigation division for a more in-depth investigation. Those convicted of intentionally disregarding the law may face fines of up to $25,000—$100,000 for corporations—and prison sentences of up to five years, in addition to any civil penalties imposed.

Cash transactions under $10,000 may also be suspicious.

"Drug dealers and other criminals are aware of the laws and frequently try to skirt the reporting requirement," Wendorff said. "A drug dealer may go to 10 different banks and purchase 10 cashier's checks of $9,000 each rather than buy one $90,000 check." This, too, is a violation of the money laundering statutes.

For businesses or professionals, a similar type of transaction that should be reported would be if a car dealer received $4,000 on three separate occasions during one year for a $12,000 car. That transaction must be reported to the IRS within 15 days of the time when the amount exceeds $10,000 using a Form 8300. "Report of Cash Payment Over $10,000 Received in Trade or Business."

A suspicious cash transaction or buyer who refuses to provide information needed to complete the Form 8300 should be reported by calling the IRS toll-free at 1-800-800-2877.

RELEASE FORMAT. This release is an example of a proper formatting. Use it as a model in preparing your own releases.

persons, with both office and home telephone numbers and beeper and fax numbers too. The contact person must be accessible, no matter the hour, should a reporter or editor have a question about the release.

Some stories are for broadcast or publication as soon as they arrive at a news office. Those should carry the line "FOR IMMEDIATE RELEASE" ahead of the text.

Sometimes you want stories in the hands of news people but you don't want them broadcast or published immediately. For example, the president of your company is to announce a new product at a shareholders' meeting and you want them to hear it from him, not from a newscaster. Or you have a feature story you want played in the Sunday newspaper. That news can be sent ahead of time with the understanding that it is to be held for release later, or "embargoed."

Whatever your reason, note the embargo at the top of the release, and state the time and date for release. For example: "HOLD FOR RELEASE AT 6 P.M., FEB. 29," or "EMBARGOED UNTIL 6 P.M. FEB. 29." It's always prudent to follow up with a telephone call to insure that the editor will honor the embargo.

Editors prefer shorter stories than longer, so it is always best if you can fit everything on one page. If you must carry a story over to additional pages, finish a paragraph before going on to the next page, and at the bottom of the page center the word "MORE." That lets editors know more is to come. At the end of the story, type "-30-" or "###"— both are standard symbols signifying that there is no more.

Formatting for Broadcast

Too many organizations send the same tailored-for-print release to broadcasters as to newspapers, and when the release is not formatted for print, much less broadcasting, nothing is better designed for a slam dunk into the wastebasket.

Head the sheet as for the print release, and indicate if the story is "FOR IMMEDIATE RELEASE" or "EMBARGOED UNTIL" a certain time. Take the time to write the story for the ear, condensing where you have to. And use broadcast style.

The Internal Revenue Service release might be rewritten for broadcast like this:

> Internal Revenue Service agents in Louisiana are out to stop what's called "money laundering"—buying big ticket items with cash to hide profits from illegal activities or to evade taxes. It's a favorite practice with drug dealers, and now there's a federal law outlawing it. The Internal Revenue Service district director in New

Orleans, John Wendorff, says anyone who tries to put down 10 thousand dollars or more in cash to buy something is supposed to be reported to the I-R-S, but many aren't. So Wendorff's agents are fanning out across the state in the next two weeks to make sure businesses are complying. If they're not, they face heavy fines. Even jail.

Audio News Releases

Many organizations make available stories designed especially for radio that contain audio cuts, so-called "actualities" or "sound bites," in place of written quotes. The releases are prepared on audio tape and mailed to stations, or recorded on answering machines for telephone distribution, and are formatted like, and sound like, radio news stories. In an effort to localize them, to make them appeal to local stations, producers of national audio releases will include interviews with people in the local stations' immediate geographical areas.

One variation provides stations with a script and one or more audio cuts, or the cuts with explanatory material that a staff member at the station could work into a script. More common is a release that contains a lead-in the station's news announcer might read, followed by an organization's announcer providing details, then an actuality and a tag line at the end. Releases should be constructed so that the stations can use the actualities with their own voiced lead-ins or wrap-arounds. It's common practice to include a transcript of the audio portion.

Keep in mind that news actualities ordinarily are only 20 to 30 seconds long, so actualities in audio releases should run no longer. And whereas news reporters must fashion a story out of what a source actually says, the public relations person conducting an interview for an audio news release can coach the source. If the first take is long-winded, the interviewer might suggest ways to condense the statement or to make it more forceful or more colorful.

Video News Releases

A relatively new phenomenon, but one that is becoming successful, is the video news release, or VNR. As the name implies, it is a news story prepared for airing on television. It should be kept between 60 and 90 seconds, the outside length of stories on most newscasts. And it should have the look and the sound of a news story.

Most television news stories tend to be mini-dramas, showing a problem and how that problem has been or will be resolved. The writer-producers of VNRs should mimic that form but show especially how the client's product or service can help with the solution.

Like television news stories, VNRs should be shot on location. A reporter off camera should set the stage, conduct one or more interviews with coher-

VIDEO FASHION. One form of the video news release is the feature designed to help market a product. Fashion designers do public relations by having fashion shows videotaped and the tapes distributed for showing, especially on cable television magazine-format programs. Nicholas Charney has taken the concept a step further by launching Videofashion Monthly, a fashion magazine on videocassette. Important to remember, a well-crafted script must go hand-in-glove with the video.
(Courtesy of VIDEOFASHION, Inc.)

ent transitions, then wrap up the story and give a tag: "This is Joanna Doe reporting."

One difference between a VNR and a news story is that stations show their own reporters doing stand ups, especially at the end, but they prefer that the reporter on a VNR go unseen.

As are audio interviews, interviews for VNRs are little more than 10- to 20-second sound bites, and just as audio interviewers do, interviewers for VNRs

NASA News

National Aeronautics and
Space Administration

George C. Marshall Space Flight Center
Huntsville, Alabama 35812

For Release

Mike Simmons   OCTOBER 1, 1992
Marshall Space Flight Center
Huntsville, Alabama 35812
(205) 544-0034

NASA & VIRTUAL REALITY, A NEW WAY OF LOOKING AT THE WORLD

RELEASE NO. 92 – 157

NOTE TO PRODUCERS

RUNS: 1:43
SUPERS: @ 1:01 - Joe Hale/NASA
OUTCUE: " . . . this is MIKE ARRINGTON reporting."

[SUGGESTED LEAD]

ON ANCHOR: An emerging computer technology now allows
                                users to view and interact with computer-gen-
                                erated images, even to "get inside" things and
                                places that don't exist yet—like the interior of
                                NASA's Space Station Freedom. Scientists
                                and engineers at the Marshall Space Flight
                                Center in Huntsville, Alabama are using this
                                new technology to design the Space Station
                                and to train the astronaut crews who'll live and
                                work there. We have more in this report . . .

VIDEO NEWS RELEASE. The National Aeronautics and Space Administration's Marshall
Space Flight Center in Huntsville, Ala., sent television news departments this script
along with a ¾-inch video tape. All a newscast producer had to do was to find a place
for it in the newscast and hand the suggested lead-in to an anchor.

VIDEO	AUDIO
MARS ROVER, USER MOVING HAND/ARM, ROBOT ARM MOVING	Imagine moving across Mars, and being able to see through the eyes of a robot and pick up and move objects.
FLYING THRU SOLAR SYSTEM	Imagine flying through the solar system to learn the order and movement of the planets.
SPACE STATION	Or imagine entering NASA's Space Station Freedom where you can explore an orbiting laboratory and grab and manipulate objects. You can make all of these "trips" without leaving earth through the use of a new computer technology known as "Virtual Reality."
USER WITH EYEPHONE AND GLOVE NEAR COMPUTER	This Virtual Reality computer system at NASA's Marshall Space Flight Center allows people to interact with computer-generated, three-dimensional, artificial environments. Humans can, if you will, step inside by using special goggles and a glove that enables the computer to sense human body movements and the human to see and manipulate artificial objects inside this virtually real world.
JOE HALE/NASA	["You actually enter the virtual environment. Instead of being on the outside looking in, in Virtual Reality you are actually on the inside, looking out."]
USER WITH EYEPHONES AND DATA GLOVE	When the user looks up or down or right or left, the image shifts to appear in those locations.
JOE HALE/NASA	["Training is an application we think has broad appeal for not only astronauts for mission training but for ground support crews also."]
LOCATIONS	Since its beginning, NASA has relied heavily on simulations. Now, the space agency is exploring the limits of "Virtual Reality."
[SUGGESTED TAG]	In Huntsville, this is _____ reporting.
ON ANCHOR:	NASA is planning to launch the first segments of the real Space Station Freedom in 1996.
[SUPPLEMENTAL VIDEO]	

can suggest that the source edit the statement. The interviewer might also look to the source's appearance. Is the source speaking to the interviewer, as the best interviewees do, or looking up at the ceiling or down at the ground or, even worse, directly into the camera?

An interview that does not sound or look good can easily be shot over. In fact, while a television reporter-photographer team normally must get its story in a hurry, a professional production unit will want to shoot scenes over and over again from different viewpoints.

THE VIEW FROM THE NEWSROOM

STUDY PREVIEW   Occasionally you may see a saying tacked on an editor's wall: "The strongest drive is not love or hate. It is one person's need to change another's copy." Whether a release is well written, just passable, or a horror, if it contains information an editor judges worth putting in a newspaper or a newscast, it could be rewritten or edited. Few are willing to carry a story that the audience has read or heard somewhere else.

Rewriting the News Release

When over-written news releases come into the newsroom they are more likely to be tossed in a waste basket than be rewritten, so rewriting should take place in the public relations department. Public relations writers should make sure their releases are in news style and tightly written. That will improve the appeal to editors. Consider how you could rewrite the Yellowstone Association's release on the next page.

The edited version of the Yellowstone Association release on the following page shows how the fat could be pared. In this case, two-thirds of the words have been cut, and more could go if space were tighter.

Even with editing, the piece is dry and little more than an announcement. To make a more interesting story out of it, a reporter might conduct a telephone interview with the association's director, who was given as the contact person. ("We try to give people the most relaxing and educational vacation they could possibly have.") He could provide the names of instructors who could breathe some life into the course descriptions. ("For us, it is a natural wonder," Jones told the students. "For the Indians, it was home.") People who took the course in the past would also be good sources. ("The next year, George and I wanted to go to Disneyland. The kids persuaded us to go back to Yellowstone.") Assuming a budget were available, the story might be one that an editor would want to cover on the scene and expand into a longer feature, with photos.

The Yellowstone Association for Natural Science, History & Education, Inc.

FOR IMMEDIATE RELEASE
March 11, 1991

CONTACT: Don Nelson, Director
(307) 344-7381 ext. 2384

YELLOWSTONE LEARNING ADVENTURES

For travelers headed toward the northern Rockies and Yellowstone this summer, there is a way to learn more than the typical "drive-through" the Park allows. Located in the northeast corner of Yellowstone in scenic Lamar Valley, the **Yellowstone Institute** is offering 70 classes this year. From its special location excellent instructors lead field explorations that delve into the specifics of nature's most unique classroom and provide a distinctive kind of close-to-nature learning vacation.

For example, consider that courses are offered in: horsepacking and llama packing, streams through the eyes of a trout and flyfishing, grizzly bear biology and folklore, Indian use of Yellowstone and other human history, canoeing and backpacking, numerous wildlife ecology courses, geology courses, and even writing and sketching, and philosophy of nature. Six different classes are specifically designed to offer a diversity of learning experiences for families. Two classes are designed for children.

The classes run from one to six days and are primarily designed for adults from all backgrounds. Over twenty classes can be taken for college credit, but all classes can be taken for fun, interest and the satisfaction of learning about various intricacies of Yellowstone and the surrounding area.

One three-day class makes trips to important geological sites to investigate the area's volcanic past and its layers of fossil forests. A new class, "Environmental Education for Teachers," will feature short field studies that lead to the development of classroom activities for elementary students. "Wilderness Medicine" will consider detailed aspects of prevention and treatment of illnesses and injuries in the backcountry and "Streams Through the Eyes of a Trout" will give you a detailed look at how trout survive in Yellowstone's streams and rivers. Yet another class will involve its students in philosophically exploring their relationship with nature and the wilderness.

Most participants stay in rustic cabins which overlook the expansive Lamar Valley, a haven for bison, elk, antelope and other large and small mammals. Classes are kept small at 10 to 15 people. the total daily cost averages $40 to $45 per day for the classes, and cabins are only $7 per night. A community kitchen is available. Courses that require horses, canoes or other outfitting cost more.

For more information on fees, options for credit, and free 24-page catalog, write: Yellowstone Institute, Box 117, Yellowstone National Park, Wyoming 82190; or call (307) 344-7381, extension 2384. Details about lodging and travel can also be furnished. The Institute is sponsored by the Yellowstone Association, a nonprofit association.

READY FOR REWRITING. This release might be appropriate for a travel section with lots of space to fill, but most editors would say it needs work before it can be published. Editing should begin with the first three sentences, each of which starts with a dependent clause.

Vacationers heading for Yellowstone National Park this summer might want to take a course or two at the Yellowstone Institute.

The Institute will offer 70 classes, including "Environmental Education for Teachers," "Wilderness Medicine" and "Streams Through the Eyes of a Trout." Other courses will teach students horsepacking and llama packing, canoeing and backpacking, wildlife ecology, geology, writing and sketching and philosophy of nature.

Most of the classes are designed for adults, but six are for families and two are for children.

Classes run from one to six days. More than 20 can be taken for college credit.

Tuition averages $30 to $35. Cabins are $7 per night. A community kitchen is available.

For more information, write: Yellowstone Institute, Box 117, Yellowstone National Park, WY 82190 or call: (307) 344-7381, extension 2384.

The Institute is sponsored by the Yellowstone Association, a non-profit association.

Ethical Considerations

Questions about the ethics of presenting releases and other publicity material without labeling them as such have been raised numerous times. At the heart of the questions is the notion that the news and information we receive through the media ought to be filtered through an independent editorial process to eliminate bias.

It is believed that, at the very least, the sources should be clearly labeled so members of the audience can make judgments based on their own knowledge of the sources. Otherwise, the news media become only viaducts for special interests who wish to promote their own causes and put themselves in the best possible light. When that happens, the media break the bond of trust they ought to have with their audience. Their credibility, and by extension the credibility of all media, is tarnished.

That being so, both the public relations person preparing an audio or video release and the news person using it ought to make sure the piece is clearly labeled as a release. They should also identify public relations staff people who are acting as reporters but actually are representatives of the organization that is employing them. For example, if Mike Arrington of NASA does a standup in a video release, he should be identified as a NASA person so there is no misunderstanding who he represents. To do otherwise would imply he is affiliated with the stations, which would be dishonest.

PUBLIC SERVICE ANNOUNCEMENTS

STUDY PREVIEW   In addition to carrying information about public activities of non-profit organizations in community calendar listings, radio and television stations also broadcast public service announcements. The PSA is a cross between a news release and a commercial and contains information about non-profit organizations or their activities that a station considers to have importance. The announcement of a school fair, for example, would probably be carried on the community calendar, while a United Way fund drive would merit a PSA.

The PSA has two advantages over a news release sent to a radio or television station. It will be run as you wrote it, assuming it is written well. And it could be run often, like a commercial, depending on the availability of time.

Writing the PSA

PSAs take a variety of forms. Some consist of live copy alone, a script to be read by a radio announcer, or a television script to be read over a slide with the name of the organization or event and a telephone number. Those are obviously the most inexpensive. For radio, an organization with a budget for PSA production might consider producing a tape with script backed up by music or sound effects. For television, it might look to professionally produced videos.

In some cases radio or television stations will help with production, but given costs, most will produce simple free spots for only a few organizations, usually those that appeal to a broad segment of the audience. They also tend to produce those that their own air personalities agree to tape or those for organizations with which the stations are associated.

The most frequently aired PSAs are those that run only 10 seconds, but stations also accept spots of 20, 30 or 60 seconds. The best thing to do is to check with the stations you want to air your PSAs to learn what their requirements are. Ask also how far in advance of the first air date they need the PSA. Some need up to two weeks to get it into a continuity book or have it taped.

A PSA should be typed double-spaced on a sheet of 8 ½ x 11-inch paper. As with the news release, put the name of the contact person at the top and the person's telephone number or numbers. Be sure to show the inclusive dates the PSA is to be aired. You should include a line under the contact person's name and number that reads, "For use between," with the dates. Neither you nor the station wants a PSA announcing an event that has already occurred. It is also helpful to note that the copy is a public service announcement and how many seconds it runs.

As with other broadcast copy, the writing should be conversational, "talked" into the typewriter or word processor, and with relatively short sentences. Open with a grabber, your most important point, put in such a way as to grab the listener's attention. Make sure everything else in the spot supports that idea. And—the most important point—be sure to tell listeners exactly what you want them to do.

To increase the chances that your event will get coverage, prepare your PSA in different lengths, 10, 20 and 30 seconds. Here's how the variations might read:

Run for the Roof. It's a five-K run at 8:30 Saturday morning to help fix tornado damage to Live Oak School's roof. Register at Four Minute Mile shoe stores. (:10)

Run for the Roof Saturday morning. Runners can get their exercise and help the Live Oak School raise money to fix damage caused by last month's tornado by participating in the five-K Run for the Roof. Run for the Roof— Saturday morning at 8:30. Sign up today at any Four Minute Mile shoe store, get a free T-shirt—and Run for the Roof. (:20)

Run for the Roof Saturday morning. Last month's tornado ripped off a corner of the roof of Live Oak School. Now you can help the Friends of Live Oak raise the money they need to repair the damage by running in the five-K Live Oak Run for the Roof. Run for the Roof begins at 8:30 Saturday morning at the intersection of Washington and Adams. You will get your exercise and a specially-designed Run for the Roof T-shirt. Live Oak will get your registration fee. Sign up today for the Live Oak Run for the Roof at any Four Minute Mile shoe store. (:30)

Stronger messages can also be delivered via the PSA. Consider one written by Julie Burmeister of the Atlanta branch of the Ogilvy & Mather agency for the Centers for Disease Control:

> KRISTA: I bet I know what you think about H-I-V. You think only certain people get it. Like people who mess around a lot . . . or drug users. You think it happens mostly in big cities . . . certainly not in little towns. You think it's no big deal because you don't know anyone who has it. And you think it won't happen to you. Sound familiar? Now think about this. My name is Krista Blake. I'm 19. I'm an honor student. I live in a town with a population of 5,000. I've never touched drugs. And guess what? My old boyfriend has H-I-V, and now so do I. Do you know why? I used to think like you.
> ANNCR: Find out how you can prevent H-I-V. Call 1-800-342-AIDS. A message from the Centers for Disease Control.

The PSA carries the message forcefully by listing common ideas about the HIV virus, then showing them to be misconceptions. It is written in a conversational tone that dramatizes the message and gives it more impact than a simple listing by an announcer. Note that at the end the listener is told what to do.

Adding Video to the PSA

An additional element has to be added when writing for television—visuals. The examples above could easily be transformed for TV. The PSA for the race could be presented by an announcer while the screen showed the name of the race, perhaps superimposed on a slide photograph of the school. Or a spokesperson, someone familiar to the audience, might stand in front of a neutral background and deliver the announcement. Similarly, "Krista," against a plain background, could deliver her message.

Of more interest would be a scene acted out, no matter how uncomplicated. That was the tack the Minneapolis advertising agency Martin/Williams took in producing a 15-second PSA for the American Humane Association. An overhead camera showed a couple in their late 60s in bed but wide awake and staring at the ceiling.

VIDEO	AUDIO
TIRED BEYOND BELIEF, THE COUPLE CONTINUES TO STARE INTO THE CAMERA LIKE TWO ZOMBIES.	SFX: HOWLING OF A CAT
NO RESPITE FOR THE COUPLE	SFX: HOWLING OF A CAT

| SUPER: Get a Good Night's Sleep | SFX: HOWLING CONTINUES UNDER |
| SUPER: Neuter Your Cat
CARD: AMERICAN HUMANE ASSOCIATION
    1-800-227-4645 | |

The Leo Burnett agency branch in Toronto produced a somewhat more detailed, though still relatively simple, 60-second PSA for the Addiction Research Foundation. The scene was a teenage boy's bedroom.

VIDEO	AUDIO
OPEN ON A MAN AND HIS TEENAGE SON. THE BOY IS ABOUT TO GO OUT AND PLAY BALL.	DAD: Hey, son . . .
CU: BOY	SON: Yeah, Dad.
CU: FATHER	DAD: Sit down a minute. You know son, when I was your age, things were different . . . kids were a lot different . . .
MCU: FATHER AND BOY	kids were a lot . . . well we would smoke 'cause we thought we looked cool but I think we looked more like . . . ah . . . more like . . . ah . . .
CU: BOY	SON: Geeks
CU: FATHER	DAD: Ah, I don't know if geek was the word I was looking for, but . . . well, you know we used to think it was pretty cool to go out, have a few drinks, get a little, . . . ah . . .
CU: BOY	SON: Drunk
MCU: FATHER AND BOY	DAD: Yeah, sometimes, ah, we even, ah . . . smoked a little . . .
	SON: Dope?
CU: DAD	DAD: Dope . . . yeah . . . Um . . . I guess . . . what I'm trying to say son, is ah, um, um . . .
CU: BOY	SON: Don't be like you?
CU: FATHER	DAD: Well, I guess . . . you know. Uh.
MCU: FATHER AND BOY	SON: No problem, Dad.

| BOY LEAVES. FATHER THINKS ABOUT THEIR CONVERSATION. | ANNCR (VO): At the Addiction Research Foundation we believe communication is the most important part of prevention. Talk to us. |
| SUPER: Addiction Research Foundation logo. | |

NEWSLETTERS

STUDY PREVIEW   Companies, educational institutions, social service agencies, hospitals and a host of other organizations send out newsletters to their publics, both internal and external. More and more newsletters have appeared with the advent of desktop publishing systems. It is estimated that 100,000 newsletters, both amateur and professional, are being published.

Writing Newsletter Stories

Depending upon the audience and the publication's purpose, the content of a newsletter is news, though of a somewhat limited and directed type. Because the newsletter is so tightly focused, writing one requires a thorough knowledge of the organization and the material. And you must know who your readers are.

A newsletter for the faculty and staff of a university would likely contain items of interest only to those persons. Among the items an issue might present are:

◆ Information about a new benefit.

◆ A change in parking regulations.

◆ How to obtain a special price for a ticket to a campus theater production.

◆ A listing of activities of faculty and staff, including papers published or positions held in community service organizations.

A newsletter published by the same university for its alumni and benefactors might report in some detail on a faculty member's research, the related research activities of several faculty members, a graduate fellowship won by an outstanding student, or the workings of an exchange program with a foreign university. It might also have a series of briefs on alumni activities.

The format of newsletters dictates that the information being reported must be put into a small amount of space. Newsletters of four to eight 8 ½ x 11-

SECOND HARVESTERS FOOD BANK

LOUISIANA'S PREMIER FOOD BANK   WINTER 1995 - VOLUME 10

Second Harvest Sustained Excel

Each year the Greater New Orleans Foundation recognizes non-profit organizations which have demonstrated exemplary performance during the past year in three critical areas: primacy of organizational mission; the partnership between executive staff and governing board; and the organization's capacity to attract, maintain and effectively use sufficient

Community Sup Citywide Grocer

The Citywide Grocery Drive netted over 77,000 pounds of food and over $4300 from personal donations.

Kraft General Foods joined The Times-Picayune and the Greater New Orleans area grocers as 1994 Citywide Grocery Drive sponsors. The Greater New Orleans Broadcasters Association and other members of the print media supported the effort again this year.

POYNTER REPORT

A NEWSLETTER FOR STUDENTS, ALUMNI, AND FRIENDS OF THE POYNTER INSTITUTE ■ FALL 1994

INSIDE

Can TV news be 'family sensitive' and retain viewers?

Tabloid style news put WCCO on top in Minneapolis, but the gains might have had a high price: citizens' sense of community. The station's response was a pioneering effort to chart another path.   Page 6

Let artists go to work on electronic papers

Not much of what passes for "electronic journalism" looks as elegant as this scene from the interactive CD-ROM game "MYST." But the new news products can be much better if we apply sound design principles. A Poynter graphics conference explored this new frontier.   Page 10

Boyd to teach at Harvard; Scanlan joins faculty as writing head   Page 16

Poynter books and tapes now available   Page 17

Poynter gets wired   Page 20

O.J. Simpson and the news media: Both go on trial in Los Angeles

Bob Steele, director of Poynter's ethics programs, couldn't have asked for a more prominent journalism ethics case than the saga of O.J. Simpson. His response: a nationally televised conference to explore the lessons.

BY PAUL STEINLE
UNIVERSITY OF MIAMI

The savage murder of Nicole Simpson and Ron Goldman and the subsequent indictment of O.J. Simpson for the crime has triggered an avalanche of media coverage seen only rarely in the 20th century. Much is being said and written about the news coverage of the murders and the trial, and not much is complimentary.

Simpson stories reportedly boost newsstand sales and court coverage is generating loyal daytime audiences for CNN, Court-TV, and local stations carrying the proceedings. But the murders and the trial coverage have responsible news organizations agonizing over the quality and extent of the coverage they've given the story at the same time they are dishing out each day's report.

Motivated by these concerns, The Poynter Institute,

along with the School of Journalism at the University of Southern California, the Foundation for American Communications, and the Society of Professional Journalists/Los Angeles Chapter, convened a conference titled Journalism & Justice: the Media and the O.J. Simpson Case on the USC campus on Oct. 11.

Harvard Law professor Charles Ogletree opened the conference. His keynote address was followed by a panel

discussion facilitated by Bob Steele, director of ethics programs at Poynter and organizer of the conference.

Ironically, this event itself received wide news coverage. Conducted before an audience of about 125 people at USC, the conference was broadcast via satellite to newsrooms around the country. C-Span carried elements of the discussion in eight different time slots that week.

Highlights of the conference begin on page 2.

A panel of experts discusses media coverage of the O.J. case.

NEWSLETTERS. The ease of producing newsletters on personal computers has led to an explosion in their numbers. The writing, editing, and publishing fall to the public relations person, who must know the organization and the readers.

inch pages, for example, may have a standard story length of only five or six short paragraphs. They normally contain a good many items even briefer—one or two paragraphs of one or two sentences. Newsletters also contain listings, often set off with bullets.

Whatever the designated length, items must be tightly written. They still require the Five Ws and H but in streamlined form, without extensive elaboration or quotation. At the same time, because so much competition exists for the reader's attention, each item must be colorfully, interestingly written.

Appropriate graphics will enhance appearance to increase readership.

CHAPTER WRAP-UP

As a public relations practitioner you must master styles of writing for the various media and be able to write a range of materials for those media. You should be able to craft a news release for a newspaper, for radio or for television. You must be as comfortable writing a public service announcement for radio or television as writing an item for a newsletter. In each instance, you must know what is newsworthy, who your audience is and the publication or station for which you are writing.

STUDY QUESTIONS

1. What is the principal aim of all news releases?
2. What is the difference between announcement releases and detail releases?
3. What is a tip sheet?
4. What is included in a request for coverage?
5. Why is it important for public relations practitioners to know reporters and editors?
6. What should be the writer's major considerations in writing a news release?
7. What is the difference between the way quotes are handled in a news release and in a news story?
8. Why are release dates included on a news release?
9. What is an audio news release?
10. What is a video news release?
11. What ethical question arises over the dissemination and use of news releases, especially audio and video releases?

11. What is a public service announcement?

12. What are the major considerations in writing a newsletter item?

PUTTING YOUR LEARNING TO WORK

EXERCISE 1   Writing Releases

Using the facts below, write:

+ An announcement release for print.

+ An announcement release for broadcast.

+ A tip sheet.

+ A request for coverage.

Middle State University's School of Aeronautics is sponsoring its annual air show, the sixth annual Wings Over MSU, Sept. 25 and 26 at the Middleton airport. Gates open at 9 a.m. both days; show begins at noon.

Admission: $9, adults; $6, children six years and over; 5 years and under, free. Parking is free.

More information: School of Aeronautics, (555) 555-1234.

The event is held every year to raise money for the school's special needs. It has raised more than $200,000 in the past.

Features include:

+ F117A Stealth fighter fly over.

+ U.S. Navy Blue Angels, based in Pensacola, Fla., will perform. Team includes six jets, McDonnell Douglas F/A-18 Hornet aircraft. Fliers demonstrate precision flying, aerobatic maneuvers, solo fly-bys, all showing high-performance capabilities of Navy pilots and aircraft.

+ Le Groupe Parabec, a civilian skydiving team sponsored by city of Quebec, Canada.

+ Sky Is the Limit, skydiving team made up of MSU students.

+ A sailplane demonstration.

On display during the show, many military aircraft including C-5 cargo plane, Apache helicopter, fighter jets.

EXERCISE 2   Rewriting Releases

+ Rewrite the following release to make it more acceptable to an editor.

+ Prepare a release for broadcast based on the information.

According to Squeers County School Board Superintendent Easton Hughes, progress is being made regarding the reconstruction of the new Lake Eden Senior High School.

"The Squeers County School Board and Central Insurance Company have agreed to settle the claim for $4,250,000," Hughes said. "Settlement proceeds were deposited at Squeers State Bank and the First National Bank," he said.

The old high school building was destroyed by the tornado that struck on July 4, 1993. The building was insured by Central Insurance Company.

The School Board, on Jan. 20, 1994, authorized Riply Buckner, architect, to develop construction documents, secure cost estimates and report such findings to the Board as soon as possible.

On Jan. 31, 1994, Buckner, architect, reported that "My engineers are currently working on the project. Hopefully I'll be able to give the Board a month-by-month plan in the near future."

The architect further stated that "More than likely, construction will begin around July 1."

Hughes stated that as additional information is received and approved by the School Board, he would continue to keep the public informed.

"I know that everyone is concerned and anxious and I just want to keep them up to date," Hughes said.

EXERCISE 3   Writing a PSA

Assume you are a public relations writer for Lakeland Hospital. The hospital is sponsoring a series of cooking classes, the latest in a series of health-related programs it offers as part of its public relations effort. Given the information below, write a public service announcement of 30 seconds for area radio stations. Use standard PSA format.

The series is called Healthy Cookin' in Lakeland and is designed to help people prepare nutritious yet healthful meals. It will consist of five classes—four regular classes and the final class, to be taught by Chef Louis Alton, chef and owner of the city's elegant Louis the First restaurant. Dates: Oct. 1, 8, 15, 22 and 29. Time: 11:30 a.m. to 1 p.m. Place: Lakeland Hospital Heart Center in the west wing of the hospital, 1200 Beachfront Ave. The cost is $50 for the series. Individual classes are $10 each for the first four classes and $15 for the last class, to be given by Chef Louis. Make reservations by calling Heart Center Services, 555-2112.

FOR FURTHER LEARNING

Tom Bivins. "Handbook for Public Relations Writing." NTC Business Books, 1991. As the name implies, a handbook covering all aspects of writing for public relations.

Keith Elliot Greenberg. "Radio News Releases Make the Hit Parade." Public Relations Journal 48, No. 7 (July 1992): 6. A report on usage of radio news releases.

Communication World. This monthly periodical, published by the International Association of Business Communicators, provides public relations professionals with a variety of articles on all aspects of their work.

Linda P. Morton and John Warren. "News Elements and Editors' Choices." Public Relations Review 18, No. 1 (Spring 1992): 47-52. A study of how various news elements in releases correlated with their use by editors.

Adam Shell. "VNRs: In the News." Public Relations Journal 48, No. 12 (December 1992): 20-23. Shell discusses the wide use of VNRs and methods being considered to let viewers know when they are seeing a VNR.

Frank Walsh. "Public Relations Writer in a Computer Age." Prentice Hall, 1986. A writing handbook for public relations writers. Of particular interest is Chapter 4, "The Public Relations Writer and News."

David R. Yale. "Publicity Handbook: How to Maximize Publicity for Products, Services and Organizations." NTC Business Books, 1991. A how-to book on preparing materials for print and broadcast and how to place them.

CHAPTER 14

Reporting Accidents, Calamities and Death

In this chapter you will learn:

✦ Some tragedies are newsworthy, but others do not merit coverage.

✦ The reporter must call on specialized sources in covering a tragedy.

✦ Fire departments, hospitals and weather forecasters use terminology the reporter must master and convey accurately to the audience.

✦ In major tragedies, establishing communications is a critical first step.

✦ Obituaries vary with the prominence of the deceased, but all share certain characteristics.

TELLING THE STORY OF TRAGEDY

"When Bad Things Happen to Good People" is the title of Harold Kushner's popular work of get-in-touch-with-yourself psychology. It could just as easily be the heading for this chapter. Much in journalism deals with the bad things that happen to people. Among the most common are automobile accidents that shatter lives, and fires that leave families homeless. Because they are so out of the ordinary, affect people's lives so profoundly, and as a consequence attract our interest, such events consume pages of newsprint and hours of broadcast time each year.

THE BASICS OF COVERAGE

STUDY PREVIEW   All sorts of accidents happen to people. Someone hanging a picture in Miami bangs her thumb with a hammer. A do-it-yourselfer in San Diego receives a severe shock while installing a new electrical outlet. A teen-ager in Minneapolis takes a tumble from his skateboard and breaks an arm. A window washer's rig gives way on a Chicago skyscraper, and the worker dangles from a safety harness until rescued by a firefighter. A school bus driver loses control of the vehicle on an icy road in Iowa, it careens off the roadway, and some children are killed, others are hospitalized with injuries, a few walk away with only scratches. Some of those incidents will be recounted, if at all, only in conversation or in letters. Some will be reported locally. One or two will be deemed worthy of space or time far from the scene. What makes the difference?

News and Non-News

The elements of news are the touchstones reporters, editors and public relations practitioners use to determine whether an event is worthy of coverage. Consider the incidents above. Hitting a thumb instead of a nail is not of much consequence. It happens relatively frequently, it affects only the person with the bad aim and the damage is minor and of short duration. It is hardly anything even to write home about. The same would be true of the shock to the do-it-yourselfer, even the skateboarder's broken arm, though that is the sort of thing that probably would be included in the weekly letter to the grandparents.

Consider, on the other hand, the plight of the window washer swinging 50 stories above Michigan Avenue. Although only one person is involved, such an event is exceptionally unusual. The danger the worker is in makes for breathtaking drama that would draw a crowd of gawkers. As journalism, it is not momentous, but the story is the sort of snapshot of life that makes a newspaper or newscast a bit more interesting, especially if pictures are available. It is primarily of local interest, however, and few if any news organizations in other communities would run the story, although a photo editor might consider printing a dramatic picture. The story of the school bus accident, however, is of widespread interest because tragedies involving children are particularly poignant, and when a number are killed at one time, the story is carried by news organizations across the country.

Prime Sources

In many newsrooms the first job of the day for one reporter is to "make the rounds" of the local police, fire and sheriff's departments by telephone to find out what tragedies may have occurred overnight. A bank of radio monitors tuned to frequencies used by those departments usually is mounted somewhere in the newsroom, and it is at least one person's job to listen to the transmissions throughout the day so that the organization can stay on top of accidents, fires and other tragedies that may occur in the community. When something potentially newsworthy does happen, reporters are sent to the scene or to the telephone to find out from authorities what happened.

Dos and Don'ts of Coverage

The first thing to do, of course, is to introduce yourself to the source as a news reporter and give the name of your organization. Explain that you are asking questions for a story. It is usually unnecessary if you are recording or taking notes, but if you are unsure the source realizes what you are doing, spell it out. Ask straightforward questions and be sure your source understands. Keep questions simple, especially in a confused, breaking situation. You don't want to err because a source misunderstood you.

It is always wise to double check what you have put down, and especially if you doubt what you've heard. Repeat it back to the source so that you get it right. If it is a factual question, verify with at least one other person who has first-hand knowledge or with independent sources.

Make sure that you get names right. Ask how they are spelled. When you hit the keyboard and have to attribute information, you will need the name, and by then the source may be unavailable. If you do not know your source and you think it is appropriate, ask for credentials. Some people make a practice of passing themselves off as officials, and you do not want to quote a faker.

Don't hinder emergency workers. Stay out of the way of firefighters or police officers concentrating on doing their jobs, both for the sake of their efficiency and your own safety. Follow the orders of fire and police officials. Most give reporters a good deal more access to scenes of tragedy than they give the average citizen, but sometimes they deem it necessary to deny access. It is wise to respect their judgment. On the other hand, you ought to challenge what you consider arbitrary exclusion or excessive restrictions on access. When police are antagonistic, it's best not to respond in kind, but it is important that you assert your right to do your job.

In all instances, rescuing victims and calming distraught relatives and friends is more important than your story. If you are against a deadline, tell the best story you can at the moment. There is always a next edition and newscast.

Honor the privacy of the maimed and grieving. Forget the "Front Page" stereotype. Don't think you have to shove a microphone into the face of a victim or a survivor as soon as you spot one and ask "How does it feel?" Always remember that journalists are human beings first, reporters second.

Finally, remember that it is detail that distinguishes an excellent story from a mediocre one, and the ability to gather details that makes reporters stand out from the crowd. Names, ages and addresses are essentials, so are names of hospitals where victims are taken, the conditions of victims, the time an emergency call was first received, the time a fire was put under control, the number of dwellings or other buildings affected, the number of persons left homeless, the dollar amount of damages. Keep an eye open too for physical details that can lend color to your story, and think of how you can describe scenes of devastation in ways that will create sharp images in readers' minds. Avoid cliches, however, such as "the hurricane, packing winds of" or "the scene looked like a battlefield."

Communications

It is essential in covering a fast-breaking disaster story that reporters immediately establish and maintain a communications link with the newsroom. Stories abound of how reporters have used ingenious means to get their stories out from scenes of news events. The legendary Henry Grady learned that all telegraph lines out of Tallahassee, Fla., had been cut the day an investigation team was to release its report on voting irregularities in the state during the 1876 presidential election. He hired a buckboard and driver and drove nearly all night before reaching a small-town telegraph office. He scored a clear beat on the story.

UPI's Merriman Smith held on to the telephone in the press car in President John F. Kennedy's Dallas motorcade after he heard shots fired, even though the AP's Jack Bell in the back seat was beating on him and trying to get the phone so he could file his own story. Arriving at Parkland Hospital, Smith jumped from the car, ran past the president's open convertible and glanced inside to see a bouquet of roses given earlier to Mrs. Kennedy lying in a pool

COVERING THE PRESIDENT. Merriman Smith was White House correspondent for UPI from Franklin D. Roosevelt to Lyndon B. Johnson. Here, he interviews President Kennedy. One key to his Pulitzer Prize-winning coverage of Kennedy's assassination some months later was his ability to arrange communications—an essential in covering any disaster.   (UPI/The Bettmann Archive)

of blood on the back seat. He asked a Secret Service agent Kennedy's condition and heard the reply, "He's dead."

Smith sprinted toward a hospital door. Inside he immediately ran to a receiving station, told the clerk he had an emergency, asked how to get an outside line, called the Dallas bureau and began filing his story, trying to watch the scene around him at the same time. Peter Lisagor of the Chicago Daily News, also knowing he had to secure communications, had a nurse dial his office for him, and her hands were shaking so badly she could hardly find the holes in the dial. When she finally got the number, it was busy.

Telephones were so scarce, Smith reported in a story the next day, that he stayed put "lest I lose contact with the outside world." He left the telephone only to go to the news conference at which Kennedy's death was officially announced.

Smith directed a local UPI reporter to find a pay phone, then persuaded a nurse to lead him to a phone in one of the offices, only to find that the other reporter had reached the office first. After that call, Smith learned he had been tapped to be a pool reporter on Air Force One flying back to Washington. He hurried to the airport. There he noticed a bank of telephones on the side of the runway and got permission to inform his office of the plan. "Then began another telephone nightmare. The Dallas office rang busy. I tried calling Washington. All circuits were busy. Then I called the New York bureau of UPI and told them about the impending installation of the new president aboard the plane."

As he showed that day, Smith's communications savvy was at the heart of his reporting skills. He won a Pulitzer Prize for his coverage of the Kennedy assassination.

Today cars are equipped with two-way radios or cellular telephones reporters can carry with them. But as with any piece of technology, these too can fail. Every reporter can tell a story similar to that of Rob Masson, then of WWL-AM, New Orleans, whose cellular phone gave out as he moved west of the city following the path of Hurricane Andrew. He filed for the rest of the night from outdoor pay phones, battered by high winds and rain. The point is that, in a disaster, your story may be only as good as the communications you have established.

Hospital Condition Reports

The American Hospital Association has published guidelines for condition reports, and many hospitals use them. The conditions apply to victims of accidents or violence or to persons who are ill.

> **Good**: Vital signs are stable and within normal limits. Patient is conscious and comfortable. Indicators are excellent.

> **Fair**: Vital signs are stable and within normal limits. Patient is conscious but may be uncomfortable. Indicators are favorable.

> **Serious**: Vital signs may be unstable and not within normal limits. Patient is acutely ill. Indicators are questionable.

> **Critical**: Vital signs are unstable and not within normal limits. Patient may not be conscious. Indicators are unfavorable.

Public Relations Support

In many instances public emergency agencies and companies will set up media information centers, or a combined center, near the site of a disaster. One person will be designated as spokesperson and provide most information. At times, two or three officials will join together to provide news briefings. In the case of airline crashes or industrial accidents, company spokespersons may provide numbers and names. Larger companies have prepared crisis communications plans that call for setting up public information and media information centers, including emergency newsrooms. One person is designated as the contact person. A team of people drawn from various parts of the organization provide support, including gathering basic information that reporters will want to know.

While both public and private media contacts will give reporters an abundance of information in emergencies, they will provide just factual material, and the facts that officials want them to provide. They normally will not speculate, as reporters often want them to do, on causes or possible effects of an incident. They may provide access to some areas, or may not.

Casualty Lists

Disaster stories always contain the number of people injured and killed. The casualties are the best gauge to the degree of tragedy. In instances involving only a few people, the count is relatively easy to obtain. A hospital spokesperson can tell a reporter how many individuals were admitted as a result of the incident, how many were dead on arrival, how many were injured and the extent of their injuries, whether they were admitted or treated and released.

In major calamities, an airliner crash for example, or a natural disaster, many people may be involved, and the more there are, the more the counting of the dead and injured becomes a problem. Think for a moment of the problem of determining the number of casualties resulting from a tragedy like the 1995 bombing of the Oklahoma City Federal Building. In such instances, of course, news organizations detail many reporters to various hospitals and to sites where corpses may be taken.

Official casualty counts at disaster sites are announced by media contacts. But because emergency officials have many other concerns, they may not be making an accurate count. As a result, many reporters try to get their own counts. A team of reporters from one organization may divide a site into sectors in order to make a count. Or editors may detail reporters to hospitals to count victims being brought in by ambulance. Others may do a count at the city morgue or at a temporary morgue, if they can get in. However the count is obtained, reporters must make every effort to be accurate.

An Ethical Caution

It is the practice of most emergency departments to withhold the names of people killed in accidents or natural disasters until the next of kin can be notified. On occasion, however, names are prematurely released, or news organizations get the names and release them without determining whether relatives have been notified. Imagine the shock to mother or brother or wife to hear over the

OKLAHOMA CITY BLAST. When a terrorist bomb ripped the face off the Murrah Federal Building in Oklahoma City, news reporters and photographers were on the scene as soon as emergency crews. One key to disaster coverage is identifying the people through whom information flows. These sources include fire chiefs and police captains. Do not overlook less authoritative sources, but be sure to have credible corroboration before using the information.   (Reuters/The Bettmann Archive)

radio that a loved one has been tragically killed or to receive a telephone call from someone who has heard the news. Reporters and editors have to ask themselves whether the benefit of prematurely broadcasting or publishing victims' names outweighs the harm.

COVERING CALAMITIES

STUDY PREVIEW   Among the stories that are told in newsrooms is one about the young reporter on assignment whose editor, seeing a story on a news service machine, sends a message asking why the reporter hasn't filed anything. The reporter wires back: "All is confusion. Can send nothing." Certainly much is confusion at the scenes of disasters, but the reporter's challenge is to compile a set of facts, organize them and present them to the audience in a way that makes them intelligible.

Automobile Accidents

The so-called "fender bender" automobile accident is so common an occurrence that it could not win news space even on the slowest of news days. But auto accidents do make the news, depending on the circumstances of the accident and the size of the news organization. The smaller the community, the more likely a routine accident will get at least a line or two of attention. The involvement of a prominent person will also make an event news, as in this AP story that appeared in the Dallas Morning News. The incident took place far away, in Miami, and days before the story became public, but it was deemed newsworthy in Dallas because of the person and his Texas hometown:

A member of the Waco singing group Hi-Five has been hospitalized in Miami after a car accident left him partially paralyzed, according to the group's record company.

New York–based Jive Records said Roderick Clark was in stable condition Wednesday at Jackson Memorial Hospital recovering from surgery.

Hospital spokesmen refused to comment further on the singer's condition, following a request by family members.

But Clark's brother, Rodney, told the Waco Tribune-Herald on Monday that the crash broke the singer's neck.

Three other group members, Marcus Sanders, Tony Thompson and Treston Irby, suffered minor injuries in the multicar collision that occurred last week.

The hip hop R&B group was in Miami to promote its new single, "Playing Hard to Get." The song is the first single to be released from the group's second album, "Keep It Going On."

The fifth member of the group, Russell Neal, did not attend the promotional trip and was in Texas at the time of the accident, according to the company.

"It was a pretty bad accident," said Sanders, who broke his nose in the collision. "It could have been worse. I thank the Lord we're all still alive."

Accidental death is less common, and certainly more tragic, than injury. Automobile fatalities are normally reported, even in big-city newspapers. This story, adapted from the St. Louis Post-Dispatch, includes all of the elements that readers are likely to want to know.

A driver was killed Tuesday afternoon when his car was crushed in an accident on westbound Interstate 70 at Kingshighway.

Fatally injured was Nathaniel Laster, 54, of the 4600 block of Margaretta Avenue.

The accident forced police to close down westbound I-70 and reroute traffic from about 1:25 p.m. to 4:15 p.m.

Police were questioning a 19-year-old man Tuesday evening who may have been responsible for causing the accident, said police Maj. Ronald Henderson.

Henderson gave this account:

A car that police believe the 19-year-old was driving apparently struck Laster's 1984 Nissan in the rear, knocking it from the right lane into the center lane, where it was struck by a tractor-trailer rig.

The tractor-trailer was unable to

immediately stop. It crushed the Nissan along the guard rail for a short distance. The car eventually flipped onto its roof.

Laster was pronounced dead at the scene.

No one else was injured.

Hollace Weiner and Amy Keen of the Fort Worth Star-Telegram produced a Page 1 story on a fatal accident in their area. Note that the questions they asked were much the same as those that resulted in the Post-Dispatch story:

Five people were killed, three of them Arlington residents, and 10 were injured in a fiery crash yesterday when a Richardson church van carrying teenagers to an East Texas youth camp collided with a cement truck.

The van, one of three from Dallas Chinese Bible Church, apparently ran a stop sign at U.S. 69 and Farm Road 564 near Mineola and collided with the truck, said Trooper Brad Tullis of the Texas

Department of Public Safety in Tyler.

The vans were headed to Brookhaven Youth Camp in Hawkins.

The three Arlington residents who died in the crash were identified as Audrey Chiang, 16, and Adelina Lau, 18, who were best friends and classical violinists, and Raymond Ng, whose age was unknown late last night.

Lau planned to study pre-med this fall at the University of Texas at Austin.

Succeeding paragraphs gave the names of the others who were killed, more details about the accident, the truck driver's name and his condition, and reaction of the people in the other vans.

The main sources for both stories were police officers. Normally the state or local police force or sheriff's department will authorize the main investigating officer at a crash scene to speak to reporters or will designate an officer as a spokesperson to answer reporters' questions about disasters, and those individuals are usually easily accessible by telephone. Fire departments delegate responsibility for providing information in similar fashion. Hospitals also have public relations staff members or other people designated to answer questions about conditions of accident victims.

Among the immediate questions to be asked are these:

+ Where and how did the accident occur?
+ What were the weather conditions and did they contribute to the accident?
+ Who was involved?
+ Who was killed?
+ What were their ages?
+ Were they pronounced dead at the scene or at hospitals?
+ Who was injured?
+ What is the condition of each of the injured?

+ To what hospitals were they taken?
+ What did the crash scene look like?
+ Were citations given for traffic violations?
+ Where were they going when the accident happened?
+ Where had they been?

The Star-Telegram reporters also spoke to an aunt of Adelina Lau, who provided personal information about the young woman and her friend, Audrey Chiang. Details of that sort could be used in a follow-up story, a human-interest story after the funeral perhaps, in which the loss is underscored by showing the promise that the young women had.

Fires

In addition to the injuries they cause to humans, fires are measured by damages caused and by alarms, and both should be included in any stories about fires. Damages are put in dollar amounts and are usually given out by fire department officials in consultation with the owners of the property damaged or destroyed.

Fire departments designate the extent of a fire by a system of alarms. Each alarm requires a certain complement of personnel and equipment needed to cope with an escalating fire. For the New Orleans Fire Department, for example, sounding of one alarm will bring two engines, one ladder truck and a district chief. A second alarm calls for an additional three engines, one ladder truck, a salvage unit, a squad and a district chief. A third alarm requires sending two more engines, a hazardous materials unit, a squad, a district chief and a deputy chief. A fourth alarm calls for two more engines. A three-alarm fire, in most instances, is a major fire, and anything over four alarms is a potential disaster.

Fires are treated in much the same way as accidents in most metropolitan media. Unless a death occurs as a result, or unless the fire is a spectacular one—in a large commercial or residential building, for example, or in a skyscraper—it is rarely covered. Even when a fire causes a death, the story may be given only one paragraph or relegated to a column of briefs. However, in community newspapers even a house fire may rate a paragraph or two.

This report, adapted from a column of briefs in the Dallas Morning News, is a good example of the elements that go into a fire story. The questions the reporter asked should be apparent as you read through it.

A 31-year-old man was killed Sunday morning during a two-alarm blaze at his Lake Highlands-area apartment. The victim, whose name was not disclosed because his family had not been notified, was pronounced dead at the scene.

Fire Capt. Don Benda said firefighters were summoned to the Sunflower Apartments, 8401 Skillman St., about 1 a.m. by neighbors.

Firefighters found the man on the floor in his living room. Fire investigators believe that the blaze began in his apartment and was smoking related, Benda said.

The blaze caused $65,000 in damage to three units in the building.

In fire stories, if injuries or fatalities have resulted, those are mentioned first. If no one was hurt but the fire caused considerable damages, the extent of the loss in dollars is put in the lead.

Industrial Accidents

Industrial accidents are frequent occurrences. An engineer on a construction site is killed in a fall from an exposed girder. Half a dozen miners are trapped in a cave-in. A barge veers off course into the pier of a bridge over a river. All are the stuff of news and have to be covered. And all too often they occur on deadline, which puts extra pressure on both reporters and public relations people.

One such accident occurred at an ammonia processing plant in Westlake, La., late one Tuesday evening just after the next day's issue of the weekly Westlake-Moss Bluff News had been put to bed. Word came to editor Cliff Seiber, by then in a neighboring town seven miles away, that an ammonia reactor at the plant had exploded. Staffers in Westlake tuned to police scanners. As they listened, they realized the explosion had been significant and resulted in many injuries.

Seiber returned to Westlake. He headed for a command post that had been established at the city hall by the mayor. There he could talk to sources like the chief of police, the fire chief, ambulance company representatives and company officials, all of whom gave what information they had about the cause, damages, injuries and response to the blast. Staffers sought out eyewitnesses and what Seiber later called a "nose witness." They included a worker repairing a leak that had occurred the day before and a motorcyclist who had found himself driving into the ammonia cloud that covered an interstate highway near the plant. Calls were placed to professors of environmental science at nearby McNeese State University to find out what ammonia is used for and what its dangers are.

The already printed copies of the newspaper were tossed aside, and the front page and two inside pages were remade. Page 1 carried the main story on the explosion and two photographs. A sidebar based on the interviews with the professors was printed on the jump page. On the jump page too was another sidebar. Seiber had seen two Secret Service agents huddling outside the city hall with the police chief. The agents were in the area for a planned visit the following day by presidential candidate Bill Clinton. As Seiber learned when he asked the chief about the meeting, they were concerned about possible danger to Clinton. None, the chief told them.

The main story, which Seiber wrote under tight deadline pressure, began this way:

An explosion at the Arcadian Corp. ammonia processing plant in Westlake resulted in the injury of at least 36 people Tuesday night.

At about 7:30 p.m. police closed nine miles of surrounding roads including Interstate 10 following the explosion and advised area residents to remain indoors with windows and doors closed.

The smell of ammonia was strong at Sampson and McKinley streets at that time.

Westlake Police Chief "Hawk" Herford said chances are debris found on roads were chunks of steel parts from the reactor measuring approximately 24 inches apiece.

The cause of the explosion was unknown as of press time Tuesday night.

The story reported damage to stores in the area and to cars parked at nearby motels. Then came the eyewitness account of the pipe repairman:

"I didn't hear anything, I just felt the explosion," Dominge said. "It threw me."

Dominge said he saw a 600-pound beam fly about 150 yards from the build-

ing. He was hit by another piece of debris.

"A pipe hit me in the hand," he said. "I'm just lucky it didn't hit me in the head."

The story gave as complete a picture as could be given at the time. But the quotes made it more than a mere recitation of dry fact. They helped give it life, and in such a way that readers could empathize with the man, almost to the point of feeling the force of the explosion itself.

The next week, the newspaper's lead story followed up on the explosion:

Arcadian Corp. officials are still assessing damage and possible causes of an explosion that hospitalized seven people, injured more than 100 and added the U.S. Secret Service to local emergency response agencies last week.

Paul Moore, employee relations man-

ager of the plant, just off Interstate 10 adjacent to the Olin facility at Westlake, said the Tuesday night blast occurred when pressure built up in a reactor in which ammonia and carbon dioxide were combined to make fertilizer pellets during normal plant operations.

The newspaper reported that officials from state and federal agencies toured the plant with company officials after the explosion, but they had not determined why the pressure built to explosive force. Cleanup had begun, but repairs would take "several months to complete."

The story contained news gathered from the State Police that members of Clinton's advance security team had volunteered to help police, that an assistant police chief opened his home to a family whose car had been hit by debris and who were unable to find a motel room in the area, and that the blast had been heard 25 miles away. The story also developed eyewitness accounts that had been only touched on in the first story and included the first-person accounts of two ambulance drivers who had helped evacuate the injured.

Besides those mentioned, sources for the story included the company's director of investor relations, the chief of police, an auxiliary police officer, and six other area residents. Readers learned that the plant had been bought from Olin Corp. in 1989 and was "one of seven facilities owned by the company, which was formed in 1989. Arcadian Fertilizer is the largest producer and distributor of nitrogen fertilizers and related products in the company."

Readers got as complete a story of the aftermath of the explosion as they might have expected from a weekly newspaper, although there was one glaring omission: the reporters did not follow up on the conditions of the injured mentioned in the lead. Readers would want to know who they were, whether plant employees or not, what injuries they suffered and their conditions, especially if any were in serious or critical condition.

TELLING THE STORY OF BAD WEATHER

STUDY PREVIEW   Conflict, as you have learned, is a news value. Most often we think of conflict as between individuals, whether they are fighting wars or playing in championship games. But conflict is involved, also, between humans and the natural world, and news is made when humans fight nature or nature flays humans. Earthquakes, tornadoes, hurricanes, tidal waves, heavy snow storms and even violent thunderstorms—all have an impact on human lives, and the greater the impact, the greater the public interest and the greater the news coverage.

Weather Terms

It is important in telling the weather story that a common set of terms be used, and most news organizations use definitions provided by the National Weather Service. Those can be found in the Associated Press Stylebook and Libel Manual. A heavy snow (an accumulation of four inches or more in depth in 12 hours, or six inches or more in 24 hours) is different from a blizzard (wind speeds of 35 mph or more, and considerable falling and/or blowing snow with visibility near zero). And freezing drizzle or freezing rain (the freezing of drizzle or rain on objects as it strikes them) differs from sleet (solid grains of ice formed by the freezing of raindrops or the refreezing of largely melted snowflakes).

Similarly, the National Weather Service distinguishes between a watch (a storm of some sort may pose a threat) and a warning (violent weather conditions exist in an area or are expected to occur). Reporters have to master those terms so that they can use them correctly to tell accurate stories.

Radio and Television Coverage

The job of radio and television reporters covering a breaking story is complicated by their need to get something on the air in a short time after their arrival, if not immediately.

Radio reporters normally work alone. That means a brief personal look at the situation immediately to take in as much as possible in order to be able to describe it clearly and concisely for listeners. Then follows a quick taped interview with the ranking official on the scene covering little more than the who, what, when and sometimes how of the situation. Then it's air time, to report the essentials to listeners and to give them some sort of feel for the scene. Once off the air, and as the story unfolds, the reporter has to keep observing, picking up color, and to talk to other officials.

Television reporters normally work in teams, with an on-air reporter or producer gathering information from on-the-scene sources while a photographer captures video of the situation. Unless they are dealing with an exceptionally important story, they go live only during newscasts. Depending on how close they are to a newscast, they may have a bit more time in which to gather more complete information.

A continuing problem for any reporter in a breaking situation is that confusion frequently leads to misinformation, and misinformation to inaccuracies in reports to the public. Newspaper reporters, even with a backup team in the newsroom and on the copy desk, still make errors. But there is often time to correct the errors before the newspaper hits the subscriber's front walk. Radio and television reporters, reporting, editing and publishing all at the same time, are more prone to reporting conflicting information, even inaccurate information. That being so, they have to be on constant guard to make sure that their information comes from reliable sources and that they double check it before putting it on the air. And that they air corrections promptly.

Reporting Storms for Newspapers

When bad weather is on the way, one of the jobs of the media is to inform audiences about what they might expect and how others are preparing to cope with what is expected. When Hurricane Andrew was heading for the Louisiana coast after devastating a portion of south Florida, reporters Sunny Brown and Seamy Thomas Stokes of the weekly Westlake-Moss Bluff News reported on preparations in its area:

Local businesses began feeling the effects of Hurricane Andrew on Monday.

Some handled services to Cameron Parish residents and others sold supply items to local residents, but a lot of early preparations were made for the possibility of the worst case scenario—a local hurricane.

All public schools in Calcasieu Parish will be closed today, Aug. 26, and McNeese State University has suspended classes because of the threat of Hurricane Andrew.

Assistant Supt. George Clyde said no decision has been made on whether Calcasieu Parish schools will hold class Thursday.

He advised residents to follow radio and television news for status reports.

Brown and Stokes checked with local motels and included information about availability of rooms. They called grocery and variety stores to ask how stocks of food and emergency supplies were holding up. They asked managers of local lumber yards how lumber sales were going, since many people living in the path of a hurricane board up windows. All of that information went into a story that let readers know what they ought to do to prepare for the storm and gave them a sense of shared experience.

One of the hardest hit areas in Louisiana was the community of LaPlace, upriver from New Orleans. Although the hurricane's eye passed farther to the west, high winds, heavy rain and a tornado did such damage that the parish was designated a disaster area by both federal and state governments. One man was killed. The town's weekly newspaper, L'Observateur, devoted much of the issue that followed to reporting the aftermath. The main story was written by reporter Amy Miller:

As National Guardsmen, State Police troopers and St. John the Baptist Parish sheriff's deputies patrolled the tornado-ravaged streets of LaPlace and Reserve Thursday, residents whose lives were uprooted by the winds of Hurricane Andrew began piecing together the tattered remains of their homes, their community and their existence.

Throughout the city, life was returning to normal.

Most traffic lights were back in operation and businesses had reopened their doors.

In putting together her story, Miller spoke to the parish civil defense director, Bertram Madere, and learned how many residents were without electric power and gas service and when they could expect those utilities to be restored. Madere provided information about shelters still open and gave telephone numbers that people could call to volunteer for the clean-up. He also told Miller how residents could apply for federal loans.

For an accompanying story on the destruction caused by the tornado, Miller got Madere's estimate that the hurricane had caused $7.3 million in damages. The figure included the loss of 52 houses and 14 mobile homes that had been destroyed and another 56 homes that had been damaged.

Sixty-six families had been left homeless. Her story continued:

Eight businesses were either destroyed or suffered substantial damage.

The roof was blown off River Parishes Technical Institute, and the Regala Park public recreation building was 75 percent destroyed.

One man, 63-year-old Carlos Cabrera, died when his Belle Pointe South home caved in, trapping him until his body was found early Wednesday.

In a check of the local hospital, Miller learned that it had dealt with 33 patients hurt in the storm, and of those, 27 had been treated and released and six had been admitted. Three of those were later transported to a hospital in a neighboring parish, including a child badly injured when a brick wall in her home collapsed. Miller learned that the child had later been moved to a university hospital and, in speaking to a spokesperson there, that the child was in critical condition following surgery for head injuries.

Other follow-up stories included a feature based on interviews with surviving victims. Written by reporter Keith Darce, it began this way:

Attribute Sylve looked at the remains of her West Fourth Street home for the first time Thursday morning after a tornado spun by Hurricane Andrew ripped through LaPlace and Reserve Tuesday night.

Sylve stared at the small wood-framed home—where she was born in 1928— from the front yard of her cousin's home across the street.

"I haven't gone over there yet," she said. "It's just too hard."

A steady stream of neighbors filed past her, wishing their best and gawking at the rubble in disbelief.

Darce interviewed five others in the areas struck by the tornado. They told what they were doing when the tornado struck, their immediate reactions, and the effect on them. He quoted them liberally.

Darce also provided his readers a view of the scene through his own eyes. "The twisted steel frame of the main production area towered over piles of split lumber and bent sheet metal," he wrote of one building. In a subdivision, "Dark clouds drifted over the area and a light rain fell Wednesday afternoon as dozens of people moved from house to house cutting downed trees, moving furniture and carrying sandwiches to neighbors." At another subdivision, "An American flag flying near the entrance of the neighborhood stood as a testament to the whirlwind fury. The blue field of stars and three stripes were all that remained of the tattered piece of cloth."

Darce's was a graphic recreation of the tornado's impact on the people of the area and on the places in which they lived. His words and those of the people he interviewed provided a special view, even for those who had seen the pictures provided by television.

WRITING OBITUARIES

STUDY PREVIEW   The writer Alexander Woollcott was handed an obituary to write as a young reporter on the New York Times. When he finished, he gave it to the night city editor. Woollcott had led with "the sad news that Mary Van Rensselaer Whoozis had just died of heart failure. When he got that far, the boss gave a low moan and began plucking hairs from his auburn beard. Next he seized his pencil, struck out the word 'failure' and in its place wrote the word 'disease.' Then, turning as if to rend me from limb to limb, he noticed for the first time that I was a newcomer, and straightway took the trouble to give me my first lesson in journalism. 'Not heart failure, Dearie,' he said, 'we all die of that.'

"In 10 seconds he'd taught me more than I'd learned in all my courses in composition in school or college."

Like Woollcott, new reporters often are assigned to write death reports, and they may see it as more of a chore than an opportunity, especially since obituaries are usually printed deep inside the newspaper. But obits are among the most read items in any newspaper and, hence, among the most important. Writing obits also gives new staffers a quick introduction to the realities of the news business. And it gives them the chance to demonstrate their capabilities as writers.

Death Notices

Two types of death notices are the norm on most newspapers. One type, normally placed as paid announcements by morticians, contains only minimal information: name, age, cause of death, survivors and information about funeral services and burial. It is frequently written in a florid style and printed in agate type, like classified ads. For example, on March 19, 1986, the Times-Picayune of New Orleans carried this report:

> Jorge E. Canarte on Tuesday, March 18, 1986 at 2:30 o'clock a.m. Beloved son of George Canarte and Maria Isabel Grimm. Brother of Christian and Humberto Canarte. Age 19 years. A native of New Orleans and a resident of this City. The Relatives and Friends of the Family are invited to attend the Funeral Services from Leitz-Eagan Funeral Home Chapel, 4747 Veterans Blvd. near Clearview. A Mass of Christian Burial from Leitz-Eagan Chapel. Interment in Garden of Memories Cemetery. Friends may call Wednesday after 6 o'clock p.m.

The other type of obituary is a somewhat longer report printed as a regular story. Writers follow news style and avoid the flowery language of the funeral home. They also may include more and different information:

> Jorge E. Canarte, a student at the University of New Orleans, was killed Tuesday when the truck he was in ran off Interstate 10 in Gonzales, La. He was 19.
>
> Canarte was born in New Orleans and lived in Metairie.

In the three sentences that followed, the writer gave the names of Canarte's survivors, the time of the funeral, and the names of the funeral home and cemetery.

The Philadelphia Daily News features obituaries of people who are not well known outside their immediate neighborhoods, but whose lives may be of interest to the broader readership of the newspaper. On the same day that the Canarte obituary appeared in the New Orleans newspaper, readers in Philadelphia found this one on what the Daily News calls the "Deaths" page:

> Edward E. "Ace" Clark, who hauled ice through Port Richmond by horse-drawn wagon and by truck for nearly 40 years, died Saturday.
>
> He was 85 and lived in Port Richmond.

Clark's story, written by Jim Nicholson, ran on for 21 paragraphs and recounted the life of "a man of many friends who had a zest for life." In the final paragraphs Nicholson named Clark's immediate survivors, told when and where funeral and burial would be, and when friends might call.

Obituary Styles for the Rich and Famous

On that same March 19, the New York Times printed a 40-paragraph obituary that began on the front page. It was the announcement of the death—and a recounting of the life—of a man renowned throughout the literary world:

> Bernard Malamud, the novelist and short story writer who won two National Book Awards and the Pulitzer Prize for his chronicles of human struggle, died yesterday at his Manhattan apartment. He was 71.

In the remainder of the obit, the writer, Mervyn Rothstein, provided details of Malamud's personal life and his literary achievements. A sidebar carried excerpts from some of Malamud's works.

Since 1965, in addition to the funeral home death notices and the slightly more expanded obits for people who achieved a degree of fame or notoriety in life, the Times has run lengthier obituaries for individuals deemed to have particularly significant lives. Those can run up to four pages, the length the Times gives to presidents of the United States. And most of those are prepared in advance. The news services also maintain a file of obituaries, kept ready through updating for the moment when a great heart fails.

Alden Whitman, who began the practice of writing such longer obituaries for the Times, has described the nature of the obituary in such a precise way that it bears consideration by anyone who writes obituaries—or reads them. First, an obituary is not a biography. It sketches just the main features of the person's life, not details, and it does not take a point of view, as good biography does. It should be many-sided, however, "telling what the person thought of himself, what his friends thought, and what his critics had to contribute."

"A good obit has all the characteristics of a well-focused snapshot, the fuller the length the better," Whitman wrote in his introduction to "Come to Judgment," a collection of his work. "If the snapshot is clear, the viewer gets a quick fix on the subject, his attainments, his shortcomings and his times."

How to put together a longer, advance obituary? Whitman started in the newspaper's morgue, where files on various individuals are kept. He also made use of the newspaper's reference library and, when necessary, the public library. And he sought out academic experts, such as the critics who contributed to the obituary on Malamud.

Finally, in a method he pioneered, he went to the subjects themselves and interviewed them. By and large, he said, his subjects cooperated. "Only the young are immortal," he wrote, reassuring those who might think the process ghoulish. "Elderly people have reconciled themselves to mortality and are thus often willing to look back over their lives with a mixture of pride, candor, detachment, and even amusement." Indeed, in most instances, the subjects of obituary interviews respond more freely because they realize their words will be printed only after they are gone. The material he obtained in the interviews he integrated with his research material.

Mervyn Rothstein, in writing the Times obituary on Malamud, included a listing of the writer's works, with brief descriptions of the better known ones. And he interwove interview material, as in this paragraph:

Malamud's first novel, "The Natural," an allegory about the rise and fall of a baseball player, was published in 1952. It is different from most of his work in that there are no Jewish characters.

After the book was made into a movie starring Robert Redford in 1984, Malamud said in an interview that he was grateful for the film because it allowed him "to be recognized once more as an American writer" as opposed to a Jewish writer.

But "The Natural" is similar to his later novels and stories in that it lies in the realm of a morality play.

In some portions of the obituary, the interview material stood alone. Malamud had discussed his writing at length, and at one point Rothstein included this telling paragraph:

He did not find writing an easy task. "The idea is to get the pencil moving quickly," he said. "Once you've got some words looking back at you, you can take two or three—or throw them away and look for others. I go over a page. Either it bleeds and shows it's beginning to be human, or the form emits shadows of itself and I'm off. I have a terrifying will that way."

The Malamud obituary not only sketched the man and his work, but the interview did precisely what Whitman believed a good interview should do. It added "an extra dimension to the finished obit—a sense of intimacy." In so doing, it gave the reader something of Malamud's "unique flavor."

Broadcast Obituaries

Broadcasters also report obituaries. Small-town radio stations regularly get reports from local mortuaries and broadcast them. Stations in larger communities report the deaths of only more prominent persons, and then only give a few lines to the report. One outstanding example of a broadcast obituary was carried at the end of the CBS Evening News with Dan Rather on Oct. 10, 1985:

As it must to all men, death came to Orson Welles—that, a paraphrase borrowed from his own film, "Citizen Kane." David Browning has more on Orson Welles.

The opening sentence, linked as it was to the lead of Kane's newsreel obituary in the film, was artfully crafted. Following Browning's report, which included highlights from Welles' films and excerpts from interviews, Rather had the last word, also from Citizen Kane.

Rosebud.
That's the CBS Evening News for this Thursday.

Not all broadcast obituaries lend themselves to such treatment. For the most part, they are simply told:

Former Anytown Mayor John Jones died during the night at the age of 95. Sources at the Overlook Nursing Home, where Jones had lived in recent years, said Jones died in his sleep. Jones served as mayor from 1951 to 1959, and again from 1963 to 1967.

Sources

As you can see, sources for obituaries are varied. Information can be provided by family members, friends, neighbors or business associates. Nicholson's prime source was Clark's son, whom he quoted throughout the piece. Rothstein based Malamud's obituary on his own reading of the author's work, on the comments of critics and on an interview with Malamud himself. In each instance, contact with the sources was made by the reporter.

On occasion someone will call with the report of a death and provide details. It is always advisable to double check the sources. Ernest Hemingway was very much alive the first time he was reported dead. So was Mark Twain, who laughed off the premature obit by saying, "Reports of my death are greatly exaggerated." A 91-year-old former Chicago alderman and his family were not amused when they found his obituary on the front page of the Chicago Tribune one Sunday morning. The newspaper had received the report from a source "with a track record of reliability." Reporters checked with the fire department and got comments from prominent political figures, but they did not call the man's home. It was actually the politician's brother-in-law who had died. The slip-up would have been an embarrassment to the Tribune under any circumstances, but the story appeared on the opening day of the American Newspaper Publishers Association's Chicago convention.

The Detroit Free Press has been burned by phony obituaries twice in recent years. After the first time editors required reporters to check with a mortuary or the police any report of a death provided by a friend or relative. But a new reporter, working part-time, did not follow confirmation procedures when a woman claiming to be the aunt of a prominent physician called to report his death, and the obituary ran. In an explanatory article later, the newspaper told the story of a physician, very much alive, who had been harassed for more than two years by a woman who had developed a romantic obsession for him. It was she, he believed, who had made the call.

What to Include

Whether a mini-biography such as Malamud's, or a single paragraph, each obituary has common elements. Readers immediately learn the "who," "when" and "where" of each death, and to greater or lesser degree something of the "what" of the person's life. As for any story, it is important to capsulize and to develop detail only as space, usually dependent on the person's prominence, allows. Whether the "what" of the death—the cause—is given depends on whether the cause is known. In many instances, it cannot be known without an autopsy. In a survey conducted not long ago by the Society of Professional Journalists, only 16 percent of the editors responding said they always included the cause of death in obituaries, while 61 percent said they publish the cause when they can get the information.

AIDS

The increasing number of deaths as a result of AIDS has raised questions in news offices about whether to attribute the cause of death. In the SPJ poll, only seven of 32 editors said they would give AIDS as the cause of death, if that were known. Ten might cite a death as AIDS-related, though half of those said they would do so only with the family's permission. Certainly if family members provide the information, news organizations may use it, but as the survey showed, policies differ from newspaper to newspaper. Some will tell readers the cause of death, including AIDS. As in these examples, the cause is usually put in the second paragraph, with attribution:

> Corona died of complications from AIDS, said Professor Hugh Edmonds, his companion.

> He tested HIV-positive five years ago and died of pneumonia, said Helen Hoch, his executor and friend.

> He died of AIDS, said Keith Williams, a friend.

Suicide

Suicide can be an even more sensitive issue. Most of the editors surveyed by SPJ said they would not report a death as a suicide unless the person were prominent or the incident took place in a public place and drew attention, and in such instances the deaths would be reported in news stories. Whether in a news story or an obituary, the death of a person who has taken his or her own life ought to be reported straightforwardly, yet with the understanding that suicides can be especially painful for surviving relatives and friends. When individuals are not prominent, the circumstances should be recounted in much the same way as causes of other deaths.

A reporter for the New Orleans Times-Picayune handled the death of a high school football star with concern for the young man's family and friends and yet provided readers with the information they would want to have:

A star tight-end for the Bogalusa Lumberjacks died Sunday from an apparently self-inflicted gunshot wound, authorities said Monday.

Christopher Eugene Robertson, 18, was found dead by his brother John at about 11 a.m. Sunday in his home at 1005 Union Ave., Police Chief Aubrey

McMillan said.

Robertson, 6-foot-3 and 210 pounds, was hit in the left temple by a single shotgun blast, police said.

Jerry Thomas, Washington Parish coroner, said he is awaiting laboratory tests before ruling if the death was an accident or suicide.

Robertson was last seen alive about midnight Saturday at home, McMillan said.

Robertson was regarded as "one of the top tight-end prospects in the state," said his coach, Lewis Murray.

Robertson caught a 23-yard touchdown pass in Bogalusa's 20-0 victory at home Friday night over Woodlawn.

"It's not only a tragic event for his family, but it's also a tragic event for this football team," Murray said.

Robertson, a two-year starter described by Murray as "a good student," resigned from the team after the Bogalusa Jamboree and missed the season opener at Picayune, Miss.

"He just said he was tired of it," Murray said.

But Robertson reconsidered and rejoined the Lumberjacks before their second game of the season, against Varnado.

"He was the type that when you got the ball to him, he was big enough and strong enough that a 6-foot boy would have trouble taking him down," Murray said.

"I'd say he would have been one of the top tight-end prospects in the state. . . . He was on everybody's list."

As the team's best football player in a small community that takes special pride in its football team, Robertson was well known. For that reason, and because the problem of teen-age suicide is alarming, the newspaper covered his funeral. Staff writers Joseph Garcia and Mike Strom began their 26-inch story this way:

The Bogalusa High School Lumberjacks buried their brightest star Thursday afternoon under a warm October sun.

With his teammates serving as honorary pallbearers, Christopher Eugene Robertson, 18, was laid to rest at the city cemetery off Louisiana 21.

His football was at his side in the chrome and metal casket.

As the casket was carried through a line of players clad in black and gold jerseys, junior quarterback Eric Brister banged it and yelled, "Why, Chris?"

"I just don't understand it," Brister said later.

To put together their story, Garcia and Strom described the funeral in the church and quoted portions of the eulogies. They also spoke privately to the school's acting principal, to Robertson's homeroom teacher and to other students and teammates. While the two reporters could not answer the "why" in their story, they did draw a sympathetic portrait of the young man and treated the reaction to the event with sensitivity.

CHAPTER WRAP-UP

Readers want to know about the tragedies that befall other human beings, and news organizations try to satisfy their interest. While stories of accidents and other tragedies must be reported, and reported completely and accurately, they must be told with sympathy and a sensitivity for the victims, their families and their friends. That marks the difference between yellow journalism and responsible, informative journalism.

STUDY QUESTIONS

1. Why would an editor consider one accident news and another not news?
2. What are the sources of news about accidents?
3. What are the condition reports issued by hospitals and how are they defined?
4. What are the two types of death notices.
5. What are the sources of news about death?
6. Why is it so important to be accurate in writing obituaries?
7. What safeguards should you use to avoid reporting a phony obituary?
8. What elements normally go into an obituary?
9. When is the cause of death included in an obituary?
10. When is AIDS listed as the cause of death?
11. How should suicides be reported?

PUTTING YOUR LEARNING TO WORK

EXERCISE 1   An Auto Accident

✦ Read the scenario below. Taking the role of a reporter for the afternoon Centerville Mercury, write a front-page story of 300 words.

✦ Next, take the role of a newswriter for the local radio station and write a broadcast story for mid-day newscasts.

You talk to state police spokesman Cpl. Carl Miller and learn:

A woman has died in a Squeers County car accident: Cary R. Sloan, 19, of Centerville. Two others injured.

Accident occurred 4:05 a.m. along westbound Interstate 10 five miles south of Centerville.

Part of a chain reaction. A car was stalled and parked along the inside shoulder of the highway but blocking a portion of the left lane of traffic. Another car hit it. Both vehicles landed in the middle of the highway, blocking westbound traffic. Two persons, unidentified, were in the car that hit the stalled car.

Robert Bourgeois, 49, of Newman, was driving a double tractor-trailer, an 18-wheeler. He stopped on the interstate behind the wreck to help the victims. The car with Sloan in it hit the truck.

Sloan was pronounced dead at Squeers County Medical Center soon after the accident. She lived at 1410 Louise St.

Driver of the car she was in was Tammy Von New, 29, of Centerville. Also taken to the med center. Another passenger in the car, J. D. Buck, 25, of Centerville.

Investigation continues into the accidents. No citations have been issued.

You talk to Squeers County Medical Center spokesman Dexter Green and learn:

Sloan died at 5 a.m. Von New was treated for a cut to her lip and a puncture wound in her hip and released. Buck is being observed by doctors for possible internal injuries. They expect to release him sometime this weekend.

EXERCISE 2   A Hunting Accident

+ Read the scenario below. Taking the role of a reporter for the morning Middleton Clarion, write a front-page story of 250 words.

+ Next, take the role of a newswriter for the local television station and write a broadcast story for the 10 p.m. newscast.

A reporter, you call the sheriff's office on a Tuesday night to find out what might be new. You talk to Deputy Judy Jones, department spokesperson, and are told that a man who lived in your city was shot in the head and killed by a friend while the two were hunting that day.

You take these notes:

Victim: George Packman, 31, a self-employed fisherman; department isn't giving the name of the other man. Happened about 5:30 p.m.

The two men were hunting from a small boat on Lost Lake, south of Middleton. Hunting partner told deputies he was preparing to fire his rifle, a .22-caliber, at a nutria along the shoreline when Packman stood up. Packman hit the muzzle of his partner's weapon, caused partner to pull the trigger.

The bullet hit Packman in the back of the head. The partner said he brought the boat back to the shore, immediately called 911. Lost Lake Fire Department rescuers took him from the scene to Squeers County Medical Center in Middleton.

Sheriff's deputies think shooting was accidental, but are investigating.

No charges have been filed against the partner.

You call hospital spokesperson Phillip Dean and he tells you:

Packman died there 8:05 p.m. while doctors were operating. Autopsy will be held tomorrow. Body taken to Unger Funeral Home.

From funeral home you learn:

Packman was married, wife Ida; two children, Maurice and Warren, both at home: 1212 W. Monroe. Parents, Mr. and Mrs. Hamilton Packman of Middleton. Furneral services are pending.

E X E R C I S E   3   **The Obituary**

Write two obituaries, one for a newspaper, one for a broadcast, based on the information below:

Daisy Smythe Solomon died yesterday, Squeers County Medical Center, Middleton. b. 1910, Adams, N.Y.; moved to Middleton as a child.

Taught school in Middleton for 42 years. Was retired. Taught science, math and history for many years at Middleton Junior High and Squeers County High. Early in her career, taught at one-room schools; was principal at Haredale and Pirrip schools.

B.A. degree, Middle State University, 1922; also attended state Normal School at Parallel.

Member, Business and Professional Women, Middleton (also, past president); American Association of University Women; number of genealogical societies incl. Daughters of the American Colonists, Colonial Dames of the Seventeenth Century, Daughters of the American Revolution and Daughters of the Confederacy.

Lifelong member of the First Baptist Church in Middleton. Served on building committee.

Survivors: daughter, Mary Solomon Brown; sister, Mildred Smith Walk; a brother, Stanley Smythe; and two grandchildren.

Funeral today, noon, Unger Funeral Home, 1414 S. Tippecanoe St., Middleton. Visitation 10:30 a.m. to noon.

Burial, Pilgrim's Rest Cemetery.

Family suggests donations to First Baptist Church or AAUW, Education Foundation.

FOR FURTHER LEARNING

Ruth Adler, editor. "The Working Press." Bantam Books, 1970. Tom Wicker's story about the way in which he and other New York Times reporters covered the assassination of John F. Kennedy leads this compilation of "how they did it" pieces by Times reporters. "The Story Behind the Jewish Klansman" by McCandlish Phillips is also must reading.

Bill Cantor. "Inside Public Relations." Longman, Inc., 1984. A compilation of articles by outstanding public relations professionals. How public relations people prepare for disasters is discussed in Chapter 3, "Crisis Management," by Michael D. Tabris.

Joe Alex Morris. "Deadline Every Minute: The Story of the United Press." Doubleday, 1957. Morris's history contains many examples of the way in which reporters for the news service covered stories of accidents, tragedies and death.

Alden Whitman. "Come to Judgment." Viking, 1980. A collection of Whitman's obituaries. Whitman pioneered interviewing subjects for material to be used in their obituaries, and in the introduction he discusses his work.

Alden Whitman. "The Obituary Book." Stein & Day, 1971. The first collection of Whitman's obituaries, with an introductory essay on the writing of obituaries.

CHAPTER 15

Reporting Public Speech

In this chapter you will learn:

+ Understanding the structure of a speech will help you construct better speech stories.

+ The reporter must master the mechanics of covering speeches, panels, meetings and news conferences.

+ In using a prepared speech, the reporter must be alert to departures from the text.

+ Speech coverage has an ethical side.

+ To attract reporters to a news conference, public relations writers must craft compelling invitations.

+ Coverage of panel discussions requires listening for each panelist's central points.

+ Meeting coverage should give positions on all sides of issues raised.

+ The public has a right to access to almost all governmental meetings.

THE PRESIDENT GIVES A SPEECH

The newspaper correspondents were frustrated. They had journeyed to Gettysburg with President Lincoln, but his secretary did not have an advance copy of the president's speech for them. The chaplain of the House of Representatives had handed out copies of the prayer he would give, and even Edward Everett, the most noted orator of his day, had made copies of his address available—a blessing for the reporters since he was to speak for two hours and four minutes. But at the time the president got up they still had been given nothing, and they worried about how long he might talk. Some feared they could be facing hours of transcribing.

Lincoln's speech that day, of course, was brief. It was only 10 sentences long. Short as it was, however, some in the press corps managed to mangle it. In fact, had the public relied solely on what reporters could reconstruct from their notes, Lincoln's Gettysburg Address might not be considered a literary masterpiece. Consider just this one line of a jumbled transcription that came from the Philadelphia Inquirer's reporter on the scene: "The world will little know and nothing remember of what we see here, but we cannot forget what these brave men did here." Fortunately for the newspapers of the day, Lincoln's reputation, and posterity, the Associated Press managed to get a manuscript, and its version was faithful to Lincoln's elegant language: "The world will little note nor long remember what we say here, but it can never forget what they did here."

REPORTING SPEECHES

STUDY PREVIEW   In Lincoln's time, it was common for newspapers to publish the full texts of speeches, or what passed for the texts, as the Inquirer demonstrated. As space became a more precious commodity, editors began excerpting from speeches. After all, readers did not need all of the examples and oratorical flourishes in a speech. They were far better served with a summary and occasional sentences and paragraphs that gave the speaker's main points and illustrated the tone. By mid-20th century the New York Times was a rarity in occasionally giving the full text of speeches by major figures. The person on the scene had to be a reporter, not simply a recorder, and that required even more skill than the ability to use shorthand.

How Speeches Are Written

Before concerning ourselves with how to cover a speech, let's examine how speeches are written. That will provide some insight into what the reporter should be aware of while listening to a speech and writing a coherent report of it.

A speaker a reporter has been sent to hear is likely to be someone with a message of some importance and someone skilled at delivering a message. Otherwise the reporter would not be there. In preparing the speech, the person will have given thought, first, to its purpose: whether to inform the audience, to persuade them, to move them to action or simply to entertain them.

Accomplished speakers also consider the makeup of the audience, what their prior understanding of the topic might be, and what their expectations of the speaker are. For example, the different knowledge and interests each has would influence an editor to tailor a speech on responsibilities of the news media in one way for a meeting of the Society of Professional Journalists and quite a different way for the American Management Association.

The occasion will also help shape the form of the speech. A luncheon speech will normally be shorter than a speech given at an evening banquet, and a speech prepared for a panel will be briefer still.

A well-written speech will have an introduction, a body and a conclusion. The reporter has to be able to distinguish each section. The introduction is designed to get the listeners' attention and to tell them what the talk is about. In the body, the speaker will give the meat of the speech, but usually no more than two or three key ideas. An audience can absorb no more than that at one sitting. Frequently a speaker will highlight those or signal when they are coming: "There are three principal reasons why the media are essential in a democratic society. First . . ." Each of the points will be developed with specific instances or examples: "Consider, for example, trying to vote with little information about the candidates." The conclusion should be the speaker's call for some sort of action: "As linchpins within the democratic society, you must . . ." Good speakers remember the old Chinese proverb, "To talk much and arrive nowhere is the same as climbing a tree to catch a fish."

Knowing that, your job as a reporter should be somewhat easier. First, listen for the purpose, and as the speaker moves from the introduction to the body of the talk, be alert for the signals designed to alert you to key points. Listen especially for apt examples or examples that the speaker has worded forcefully or imaginatively. And listen for the action the speaker wants the audience to take.

Backgrounding

Assuming you have time, you ought to learn something in advance about the person who will give the speech and something about the topic. Reference works like Who's Who in America, including the regional volumes, can give some background on the person, as can Current Biography. A national figure and the issue may have been written about in the New York Times, which is indexed. Computer services such as CompuServe, America Online and Prodigy may have information on the person and the topic in a reference forum.

A public or university library may have an index that will lead you to articles the individual has written and which you may want to read before attending the speech. The public relations staff of the organization to which the individual will speak, certainly if it is a large organization, may have compiled some background information on the person and the topic that you may find valuable.

The background knowledge is essential to help you determine what is important in the speech, if anything, and whether what the person has to say is fresh and newsworthy or whether it is stale. That is particularly important in the case of politicians. Many repeat the same theme as they make what they call the rubber chicken circuit, speaking at dinner after dinner. Long before the soup is put on the table, the reporter needs to be aware of what the politician has said before.

Covering the Speech

When you arrive at the banquet room or auditorium where the speech is to be given, locate a seat that will give you a clear view of the speaker and, without contortions, a look at the audience. An aisle seat a few rows back from the front and to the side on which the speaker will sit should give you a line of sight to the podium and to the audience. It will also provide you an easy exit if you have to leave early to meet a deadline or a clear path to the speaker afterwards if you want to clarify a point.

One element that helps to give life to a speech story is a count of the number of people in the audience. In a banquet room, count the chairs at a table and multiply by the number of tables, or ask a headwaiter how many places are being set. In an auditorium, count the seats in a row and the number of rows, and when the seats fill you can get an estimate of the attendance. Glance at the audience from time to time during the speech. Are they enthusiastic or indifferent? Do they respond spontaneously or perfunctorily?

Using a Prepared Text

If you are fortunate, the public relations staff will have gotten a copy of the speech in advance and duplicated it for reporters. That will give you a chance to read it over, find the most important elements and even start organizing the story. Just because a speech is prepared, however, does not mean that the reporter can pick it up and head back to the office to write. Too many tales are told of reporters who did that only to learn after their stories were in print that the speaker had laryngitis and had to cancel at the last minute or was stuck at an airline hub in a snowstorm. Neither can the reporter with a prepared text in hand daydream while the speaker is talking. Speakers sometimes depart from their prepared texts, and the departures can hold the person's most important remarks. The best practice is to follow along with the speaker, making sure to get down all the ad libs. That way you will not miss anything, and your quotes will be accurate.

Coverage Without a Text

If the speech is not available in advance, your task is somewhat more difficult but not insurmountable. You have to be ready to take down those words you think you may use in a story exactly as they are spoken, and to keep up you'll need to do that in shorthand. Over time, many reporters develop a kind of shorthand of their own for note taking. Some buy a book on the technique and learn some of the most frequently used symbols. Others spend a semester in a community-college stenography course.

A cassette tape recorder with a counter is an essential if you are a radio reporter. That's the way you'll collect actualities for your story. Listen carefully and jot down the numbers at which the speaker makes the most important points. Put a check mark next to the quotes you think you can use.

If you are reporting for print, you'll find a recorder a handy backup to your pencil and notebook. Turn on the recorder and take the most complete notes possible, as if the recorder were not operating properly. It may not be. When you hear something you consider particularly important or especially quotable, write down what you have heard and, next to it, put the counter number. That way you can check the tape to make sure you have the quote as it was spoken, and in context.

In writing the story, it's time consuming to play back the whole speech. Write the speech from your notes, and use the tape only to verify quotations.

Interviewing the Speaker

After a speech you may find that you have a question about something the speaker said or a question that came up as you were doing background work. It is an easy enough task to take the person off to the side for a few moments for a private chat. Those "exclusive" interviews can make a routine speech story into solid news or, certainly, different from the stories of the competition.

Writing the Speech Story for Print

On reviewing your notes after the speech or going back over the printed text, you should be thinking about the two or three main points the speaker made and deciding which of those is the most important for the lead. Inexperienced reporters sometimes find a quote that seems especially noteworthy and lead with the quotation, but quotations are support elements. They do not adequately set up the story, as in this front page story from a state university newspaper.

COVERING A SPEAKER. When a prominent person like Gloria Steinem speaks, a reporter is there listening, ready to present the words to a larger audience. The reporter wants to get the words down accurately and give the feeling of the occasion.   (AP/Wide World Photos)

> "What would have happened if a woman had lied to the country and then later said that she did it so that her daughter's wedding wouldn't be ruined?" Gloria Steinem asked a full house at the Fine Arts auditorium Monday.

The lead tells little about the content of Ms. Steinem's speech. The quote is striking but not the main point. Rather, it supports a point Ms. Steinem made. But what was the point? The reader gets a hint of it in the second paragraph, but it is not clearly stated.

> She was using Ross Perot's on again-off again presidential campaign as an example of America's societal double standard as it relates to women.

In the third paragraph the reader gets still another element of support for the point, but note that "the point" does not have a referent, and the introduction to the quote is convoluted:

> To further illustrate the point, Steinem cited an incident that occurred earlier this year involving President George Bush. "Or what if a female representa-

tive had fainted and thrown up all over some Japanese officials?" Her conclu-

sion: "We never would have heard the end of it."

Another effort to state the point fails because it is couched in muddy phrasing:

> According to Steinem, what these examples demonstrate is that bias is often unnoticeable unless a situation is scrutinized using different variables. If reaction to the situation is different because of race or gender, then prejudice is a factor.

To see just how vague that paragraph is, try to rewrite it.

As readers get into the story, they find that the element the reporter chose to highlight was secondary to a broader concern Steinem voiced and one that the reporter barely touched on by mentioning her reference to "race or gender."

Her battle to end prejudice and "caste bias" is what has made Gloria Steinem a household name. Her battle began in force when she co-founded Ms. magazine in 1972, during what she now terms the "first wave" of feminism in which women were struggling to reclaim their identity. She said that the United States has now moved into the second wave of feminism: achieving equality for all people.

That "second wave," in fact, constituted Steinem's major point in the speech and, in terms of news, a fresh point. Four goals she set for the movement made up the action element. Unfortunately, the writer buried them. A more experienced writer might have structured the story this way:

The feminist movement has taken up the cause of racial equality as part of "a second wave" of activity, Gloria Steinem told a packed campus audience Monday.

Steinem, one of the pioneers of the movement and founding editor of Ms. magazine, said women realize they need to join with minorities to fight prejudice and "caste bias."

"Individual differences are what should matter," Ms. Steinem said. "Sex and race are irrelevant."

Steinem, speaking in the 1,000-seat Fine Arts Auditorium, won her greatest applause of the night when she said soci-ety still uses a double standard to judge the actions of women and men.

Steinem said a woman would have been treated much more harshly had she claimed that someone tried to sabotage her daughter's wedding, as did Ross Perot during the presidential campaign, or had she gotten sick at a state dinner, as President Bush did in Japan.

"We never would have heard the end of it," Steinem said.

Steinem outlined goals for the movement toward gender and racial equality:

• "Establishing reproductive freedom as a fundamental human right."

- Work needs to be redefined as something other than work men do.
- Fathers need to share homemaking and parental duties equally.

- The public needs to depoliticize the culture by challenging institutions that protect inequality, especially education and religion.

The second version develops the main point as Steinem herself did, but it does so more economically. Paraphrasing helps condensation while portions of quotations add the speaker's flavor.

Michael Berg, a staff writer for the Tampa Tribune, made a story out of an advance copy of a speech. Notice that Berg capsulized the content of the talk in the first two paragraphs through paraphrasing and added emphasis by using the speaker's own words.

Universities must improve teaching and adjust to tight budgets or risk the fate of General Motors, whose stubborn management has been blamed for billion-dollar losses and plant closings, Florida university system Chancellor Charles Reed said Thursday.

In an advance text of a speech to an educators' group in Boston, Reed proposed revamping tenure to reward teaching as well as research.

He said schools will be held accountable for spending money wisely and satisfying demands of students, alumni and employers.

"Universities are not automatically seen as engines of upward mobility or tools of regional economic development," Reed said. "We have to work at convincing people to see us that way."

A reporter sometimes may take a soft approach to a speech story. That would be inappropriate for a serious presentation, such as Chancellor Reed's. But notice the touch Gail Gibson, then of the Philadelphia Inquirer, used in reporting on a talk at Ursinus College in Collegeville, Pa., by columnist Eppie Lederer, who writes under the name "Ann Landers."

Dear Ann Landers: I know you've been in this business for 37 years. You still look like you're in pretty good shape. How old are you? Also, how did you get started writing an advice column? I would like to try it.
—Curious in Collegeville

Dear Curious: You're right. Ann Landers is in pretty good shape. But if you are serious about starting an advice column, well, she just might urge you to get some counseling.

The advice business, according to its 74-year-old diva, is a far cry from just reading letters and writing replies.

When Eppie Lederer took over the "Dear Ann Landers" advice column in the Chicago Sun-Times in 1955, most of the letters she received were from women. Most had the same complaint: My husband never kisses me.

Today she doles out counseling information as often as old-fashioned advice. And her subjects range from AIDS to teenage sex to random violence.

When she visited Ursinus College in Collegeville Saturday night to talk about her work and offer the audience some advice—even about starting a column—

Landers said her job has made her "positively shockproof. I would believe anything about anyone now."

Her job has not shocked her into looking her age. Landers has smooth skin and blondish-gray hair and looks a lot like the photograph that runs with her column every day. She said she exercises every day, has never smoked a cigarette and has never had a drink.

This divorcee, who acknowledged that she is dating a younger man, knows some people are reading her column for entertainment. And that, she said, is fine.

"I have absolutely no problem with that," she said, "but I don't go out of my way to be funny."

Gibson set the tone for the story by preceding it with a question and answer that might have come from a Landers column. Then she went into her lead. As she reported what she heard, she also wove in background material and what she saw.

A Note on Ethics

When speeches follow a luncheon or dinner for which members of the audience have paid, whether directly or as a donation, the sponsoring organization may want to give you, as a reporter, a complimentary meal—"comp" your meal, as it is sometimes said. The best policy is not to accept. Taking any gift of value given to you only because you are a reporter can create a conflict of interest or the appearance of a conflict of interest. If you are starving, pay for the meal, get a receipt, and give your editor an expense voucher.

Assume you don't want to eat but a waiter offers you a cup of coffee. Can you drink it and remain—or appear to remain—ethical? Certainly. A cup of coffee has little real value.

Occasionally door prizes may be given out at events that feature a speaker. You might be tempted by the chance to win a free vacation in the Bahamas or a shopping spree in a local mall, but it's best not to give in to the temptation. You just might win, and that would be a conflict of interest. Certainly you can imagine the other members of the audience thinking that as you walk to the dais to claim your prize.

REPORTING PANELS

STUDY PREVIEW   Covering a discussion on one theme involving two or more persons—a panel discussion—is somewhat more difficult than reporting a speech. Prepared texts are not available, and discussions can take on the character of verbal ping pong. It may be difficult to keep up with the conversation, write down the main points, get quotes right, properly identify each of the speakers and then write a story that lets your audience know clearly what was said. But it can be done.

Covering the Panel

You need to find a chair near the panelists so that you can hear what they are saying, distinguish among them and hear questions members of the audience ask. Get the names of the participants, if they are not on a written program. If you are unsure how the names are spelled or what the participants' titles are, ask the persons themselves.

It is a good idea to tape the presentation, but the advice given for covering a speech holds true for panels: take notes as if the recorder were not working. In your notes, identify each speaker with an initial, with the person's statement beside it. Place an identifying mark next to statements you consider noteworthy at the moment, and record the number from the tape counter. That will make it easier for you to find the important quotes when you sit down to write.

Writing the Panel Story for Print

The writer's first task, as with any story, is to decide what the lead should be, and the lead should contain something of substance. It could summarize the outcome of the discussion, if that is possible, or it could center on a major point of agreement or a point of disagreement.

As you develop the story, be sure to support the lead, usually by stating and expanding points made by each of the speakers. As with a speech story, you will find it most economical to paraphrase the statements and to use direct quotations that illustrate a point exceptionally well or colorfully.

Mimi Whitefield of the Miami Herald did a good job of relating a written study of Cuba's post-Castro economy and a follow-up discussion of the findings. Notice that she used four paragraphs to develop the lead. She covered the "who," "what," "when," "where" and "why" in the first three and used the fourth to provide a smooth transition from the study to the panel discussing it. She showed points of general agreement by using the attribution "participants said" and followed the general statements with supporting or contrasting quotations. The reader can imagine one panelist making a statement and the others following up with, "I agree with Carlos, but," or "I'll endorse everything the others have already said."

Cuban specialists on Thursday questioned a new study that foresees a "quick and strong recovery" for Cuba's economy after a change in government.

The study, previewed at the 16th Miami Conference on the Caribbean, projects that within five years of a transition, the island's foreign-exchange earnings would rise from $2.7 billion to $9.7 billion.

Ernest Preeg, a former ambassador to Haiti, directed the study for the Washington-based Center for Strategic and International Studies. It will be published in February.

The key to assessing Preeg's figures is how transition will come about in Cuba, said participants in a panel on "Anticipating a Post-Marxist Cuba."

"It's impossible to make an economic calculation about post-Castro Cuba because everything depends on what scenario produces change," said Madrid-based writer Carlos Alberto Montaner, president of the opposition Cuban Liberal Union.

A major hurdle in a smooth economic recovery will be the handling of claims by U.S. citizens whose property was nationalized and by Cuban Americans who may try to recover their former homes and property, panelists said.

"Investment for the Cuban-American community will probably wait for settlement of claims," said Teo Babun, a Miami businessman who has started a fund for future investment in Cuba.

Robert Gelbard, the State Department's deputy assistant secretary of inter-American affairs, agreed that Cuba's future depends on "how change takes place and when."

Although Cuba's economy has declined an estimated 50 percent over the past three years, Gelbard said, "we now see Castro is still firmly in control."

Gelbard said he is "somewhat more pessimistic" about how Cuba's economy would respond to a change in leadership. He cited the problems of settling claims, the island's deteriorating infrastructure and the difficulties of retooling to a market economy after more than 30 years when the government has been "the sole landlord and employer of virtually the whole island."

If there is a violent transition, Montaner said, it could result in a long period of political turmoil that would set back economic recovery and investment.

The best possible scenario—one that Montaner said doesn't appear very likely—is that President Fidel Castro would enter into a negotiated transition resulting in a change of government and free elections.

However, Domingo Moreira, a director of the Cuban American National Foundation, disagreed, saying the fundamental prerequisite for change in Cuba is Castro's ouster: "No meaningful change will occur in Cuba unless Castro goes."

For that to happen, he said, the U.S. trade embargo against Cuba must stay in place because lifting it "gives up the only leverage the U.S. has in bringing about change."

Lisandro Perez, director of the Cuban Research Institute at Florida International University, said the United States should be sending a message to Cuba that "we're not your enemy and we're not interested in turning the clock back 30 years."

"The Cuban government has demonstrated that it can handle isolation very well, but not openness," he said.

Whitefield sought to record a major point made by each of the participants, and she was able to recognize those points because she was aware of the issues. As should be obvious to you, however, she judged Robert Gelbard's remarks to be of the greatest importance.

The so-called political debate is another type of panel. It has little in common with classical debate, but is a panel discussion that allows candidates to present their own views and attack the views of opposition candidates. The reporter's problem in covering a debate is to try to find something new, thus newsworthy, in what the candidates have to say, and to present their views clearly and succinctly and in a balanced fashion. Read this story from a college newspaper and ask yourself how the reporter could have told it to the reader better—more interestingly, more completely and more economically.

Several ideas were presented during a debate between Congressional candidates Democrat Tom Barlow, Republican Steve Hamrick, and Reform Party candidate Marvin Seat held Oct. 8 in the Student Center ballroom.

Hamrick, a Hopkinsville native, said we must make changes in Congress.

"I am for a balanced budget amendment to the Constitution and for term limits," he said. "I am opposed to any legislative body being able to pass a law which exempts them from the same laws they pass for the American people."

Barlow, from Paducah, said this is an historic year in politics.

"We all can feel it," he said. "It has been building for months now. Washington has not faced up to the tough jobs. It's time for Washington and for our Congress to be moving on these tough jobs."

Seat, of Fulton, said he is concerned with term limits for Congress as well as such issues as trade agreements.

"We have got to get rid of career politicians and the only way I know to do it is to have term limits. We have got to get eight-year Congress term limits," he said. "We have got to do something about this Free Trade Agreement. I am for fair trade, but the biggest things we've been exporting are our jobs and our tax dollars."

The candidates also discussed the problems with the country's health care.

"Affordable health care is going to have to be some kind of national approach," Barlow said. "We are going to have, I believe, a state coordination in this national framework. Young families can't afford $3,000 insurance premiums on $10,000 to $15,000 salaries."

Hamrick said that he believes a national health care policy would be wrong.

"I am for an open market when it

comes to our health care," he said. "I am for reformation but I want to start by taking the regulations that the government has put on the backs of people who provide health care off of their backs."

Seat said he does not see the need to have a national health care policy.

"We do not need another branch or department in Washington, D.C. They can't run what they're running now," he said. "We, the working people, do not need any more loads on our backs."

Take another look at the lead. It falls into the "say nothing" category, doesn't it? In addition, the reporter used a sort of scattershot approach just below the lead in presenting what the candidates said. She apparently reported the event chronologically, rather than topically.

Had she been more aware of campaign issues or had spent some time talking to her editor about what was said at the panel she might well have come up with a more substantial and better-focused lead. One of the major issues to emerge in the presidential campaign of 1992 was health care. And in the issue of the newspaper in which her story appeared, the editors devoted the op-ed page to columns that discussed health care plans at the national, state and university levels. What would be more appropriate, then, than to lead with the candidates' views on that issue. Once again, be aware that the general statement is backed up by specific quotations.

Candidates for the First District congressional seat sharply disagreed on the need for a national health insurance policy in a debate in the Student Center ballroom Oct. 8.

Democrat Tom Barlow said "affordable health care" will require a national plan. He said he favors state coordination within a "national framework."

"Young families can't afford $3,000 insurance premiums on $10,000 to $15,000 salaries," the Paducah Democrat said.

Republican Steve Hamrick of Hopkinsville disagreed. He said a reform of health care coverage is necessary, but in an "open market."

"I want to start by taking the regulations that the government has put on the backs of people who provide health care off their backs," Hamrick said.

Marvin Seat of Fulton, candidate of the Reform Party, said he also opposes a national health plan because it would mean more bureaucracy in Washington and a heavier tax burden.

The federal government "can't run what they're running now," Seat said. "We, the working people, do not need any more loads on our backs."

Voters want to know the differing views candidates hold on all of the major issues, and the reporter could have given that information. In the original story, readers learned Hamrick's stand on the balanced budget amendment and should have been given the positions of the other two. The reporter should also have given the views of all three on the issue of term limits and on the North American Free Trade Agreement.

PRESIDENTIAL NEWS CONFERENCE. Reporters are invited guests at a news conference, like this one in the East Room of the White House, but the persons staging it have control. Reporters, however, can provide balance by seeking out contrary views. (Greg Gibson/Wide World Photos)

REPORTING NEWS CONFERENCES

STUDY PREVIEW   News conference formats are relatively simple. The person who called the news conference makes an announcement. The reporters ask questions on the announcement and on anything else that seems to have happened since the previous news conference. The format allows the announcement to be made in a controlled situation and for reporters to have equal access to a source for questions and answers.

Arranging the News Conference

The public relations person who arranges a news conference will send out invitations stating the reason for the event, naming the participants, and giving the day, date, time and place. Invitations should go out well in advance of the event and should be followed up with phone calls a day before.

Middle State University
Office of Public Affairs

<u>EDITORS AND ASSIGNMENT EDITORS</u>

Legislative budget cuts are threatening to do serious damage to the state's institutions of higher learning. Colleges and universities suffered cuts of 30 percent in this year's allocations, and the prospects are that unless something is done, budgets will be cut another 40 percent in the next fiscal year.

Dr. Wilhelm Wilhelm, chancellor of the state university system, will announce the system response at a news conference on Friday, Dec. 15, at 10:30 a.m., on the steps of the university's Alumni Hall.

Photo opportunities:
Crowd of students and faculty in attendance.
Dr. Wilhelm will lead a tour to show physical deterioration of campus buildings.

ANNOUNCING A NEWS CONFERENCE. The invitation to a news conference is, in effect, a request for coverage. Notice that this one is also designed to appeal to photo editors.

On the day of the news conference, reporters are given a media kit that includes a release, fact sheets, feature stories when appropriate and biographical information on key people. Media kits sometimes also include photographs. The more advance preparation, generally, the more coverage that will result, especially from radio and television reporters who usually have too much to do and too little time in which to do it.

Covering the News Conference

The guidelines for covering a news conference are similar to those for covering a speech. The major difference is that the reporters are the audience at the news conference and everything is arranged to suit them, though the situation is tightly controlled by the people who have staged it.

The heart of the news conference is the announcement that is to be made, and the text of that may be in the media kit. The news source will read the announcement and may elaborate on it, then take questions. Sources usually make themselves available afterwards to answer individual questions, either at the scene of the news conference or by telephone.

Because the news conference is controlled by those who arrange it, the news that comes out of it can be one-sided. George Kuempel of the Austin bureau of the Dallas Morning News attended one in the Texas capital that was obviously set up not only to provide news but to serve the interests of the state's Democratic politicians.

Comptroller John Sharp said Wednesday that the state will have at least $529 million in the bank at the end of the current budget year Aug. 31, and he credited Democratic leaders for the unexpected surplus.

"Every single bit of this happened because of some folks in state government and some actions that were taken either by legislative leaders or agencies themselves," he said in a news conference.

"It had absolutely nothing to do with the economy. It was supposed to be going up in June, and it's getting worse in Texas."

Sharp, a Democrat, conceded that the surplus could quickly evaporate if the economy worsens or if state agencies increase their spending during the next fiscal year. The current two-year budget period ends Aug. 31, 1993.

He earlier had predicted that the state would close out the current fiscal year $168 million in the red.

To provide balance, Kuempel made some quick calls after the news conference to get reaction from some Republican officials. In writing the story, having gotten the main point down, he turned to the reaction.

State GOP Chairman Fred Meyer of Dallas said he was pleased with the news of the surplus, but he said that it doesn't say much for Sharp's ability as the state's official revenue estimator.

"We are delighted. We assume, therefore, he will probably want to reduce the corporation income tax so we can bring more jobs to Texas because it is severely

hurting us economically," Meyer said.

State Treasurer Kay Bailey Hutchison, the Republicans' only non-judicial statewide elected officeholder, said the surplus is further evidence that Texas doesn't need to raise taxes.

And she said her office helped make it possible.

"Interest income, the unclaimed property program, and the collection of tobacco taxes—all programs run by the state Treasury—exceeded the comptroller's estimates by $70 million, she said.

Gov. Ann Richards congratulated the agencies and state employees, who she said are responsible for the "good news," but warned that the battle to hold down spending continues.

"The message today is that tougher times lie ahead. Agencies that have already begun the belt-tightening process must be prepared to take in another notch in the next biennium," she said in a prepared statement.

After veering to the GOP reaction, Kuempel turned back to the news conference with a simple transition.

In his news conference Wednesday, Sharp, the state's chief tax collector, said his figures reflect both good and bad news in the Texas economy.

The bad news, he said, is that state unemployment was at 8.2 percent in June—up 2.4 percent from last year; oil- and gas-tax collections were off $50 million; and motor vehicle taxes were $10 million below estimates.

A bit of enterprise on Kuempel's part made this a better story. He was able to provide balance that would have been absent had he confined his reporting to attendance at the news conference.

The Chicago Tribune's Susan Kuczka had a different problem in covering a news conference held by the parents and attorney of a young man accused of murder. She had to select her information from among the responses each gave. She had to report on the arraignment that preceded the news conference. And she had to weave in the background so that readers would have context in which to place the news conference responses.

Tense but composed, the parents of murder suspect Richard Church said Tuesday that they had been devastated by the 1988 killings of a Woodstock couple they had known all their lives.

The three years since the crime, his mother said, have been "the worst years of my life."

"We're sorry about the tragedy," Eugene Church told a press conference after his 22-year-old son pleaded not guilty to two counts of murder in the August 1988 slayings, which shocked the tight-knit McHenry County Community.

"We feel sorry for the other family," said the elder Church, referring to the surviving relatives of Raymond and Ruth Ann Ritter, who were savagely beaten and stabbed in their home during an early-morning attack.

Richard Church's ex-girlfriend, Colleen Ritter, now 20, and her youngest brother, Matthew, 14, were injured in the attack, which occurred shortly after Colleen Ritter broke off a two-year romance with her onetime high school sweetheart.

Church, who had eluded authorities for more than three years before his arrest in Utah last month, also faces two charges of attempted murder and one count of home invasion. He is being held without bond in the McHenry County Jail.

His parents said that they never heard from him while he was on the run, but they have visited him in jail since his arrest. They said they had no idea why he might have committed such crimes.

Prosecutors have indicated they will seek the death penalty if Church is convicted of the only double homicide in the history of Woodstock, a community of 14,353 residents.

The pain felt by Church's parents, who watched their only child enter his plea to the charges during Tuesday's arraignment in the McHenry County Courthouse in Woodstock, was evident as they responded to reporters' questions after the five-minute hearing.

"We've known them [the Ritters] all our lives," Eugene Church told reporters gathered at the Crystal Lake offices of his son's attorney, Harold McKenney. "We're just devastated by it. I don't know any other word I could use.

The two, who were separated at the time of the crime and are now divorced, both still live in the Woodstock area.

Tuesday was the first time they had publicly discussed the killings since their son was apprehended in Utah by a Salt Lake City police officer who recognized the fugitive working at a fast-food restaurant.

Although the crime and Church's escape from authorities had been featured on television programs such as "Ameri-ca's Most Wanted" numerous times, the last confirmed sighting was in Wisconsin, where he fled immediately after the slayings in his mother's pickup truck.

Not knowing her son's whereabouts and then learning of his arrest had taken its toll on Church's mother.

"It has been the worst three years of my life," said a trembling Cherry Kot, who has remarried. "I didn't know where he was. I was not even sure he was alive."

Asked if she was relieved to now know her son's whereabouts, Kot replied: "Yes, and no."

Church's parents said that they still haven't learned where their son spent the last three years, although McKenney said Church has divulged that information in "confidential" conversations with him.

"I think it's an interesting odyssey," McKenney said. But he refused to divulge more details other than to say that Church stayed "in certain areas for lengthy periods."

Church's parents also could not shed any light on why their son, a former high school football player who had attended Northern Illinois University as a freshman, might have killed the Ritters.

"He did everything that any normal, ordinary child would do." Eugene Church said. "He never gave us one ounce of trouble that we were aware of. Other than that, he was a good boy. We don't know what happened any more than you do. We'd like to know, too, but we don't. . . . We're not psychologists."

In analyzing her story, you should have noticed that Kuczka was able to interrelate the background with the rather cut-and-dried material from the arraignment and the drama of the news conference, and that she did so with a sensitivity to the pain suffered by all of the individuals.

REPORTING MEETINGS

STUDY PREVIEW   Public meetings to discuss civic problems are a by-product of democratic society. They are held by union members, parents of school children, church members and special interest groups from neighborhood preservationists to environmentalists. They can be thoughtful discussions or they can deteriorate into raucous shouting and name-calling. No matter the topic or the tone, the problem for the reporter sent to cover such a meeting is what to include.

Backgrounding

The need for you to be aware of the issue that is going to be discussed at a public meeting is apparent. Unless you know what the issues are and how they have developed, you will not be able to give an intelligent account of what occurs. Usually much has taken place before the meeting.

If the organization or area is on your beat, you may know the leaders at the meeting. You may know the issues. If not, find out who the leaders are and call them to see if you can get their points of view. If an opposition group exists, get in touch with the people who can speak for it. If you are dealing with community groups, many of those are public relations savvy, and they may have contacted you. But your responsibility is to know and understand the issue and the various positions on it as best you can before you go to the meeting.

Writing the Meeting Story for Print

At the meeting, you have to listen carefully to the arguments on all sides. You have to try to sort out reasonable positions from visceral complaints, though you need to take note of both. Your long-range aim is to let your audience know why the meeting is being held and what the positions are on various sides.

John Blake of the Atlanta Constitution covered a meeting of homeowners plotting strategy to keep a supermarket chain out of their neighborhood. His story made a complex situation clear to readers throughout the newspaper's circulation area.

As it begins its much-publicized push into metro Atlanta, Publix supermarkets has been poised to battle several local competitors, but Sunday it learned about the resolve of another formidable foe— 2,000 homeowners in Dunwoody.

Members of the Dunwoody Home- owner's Association crowded into Austin Elementary School in DeKalb County, exuding confidence as they plotted their strategy for blocking Publix's store on Chamblee-Dunwoody Road.

"To just force what they want on us, it's not going to work," said J. V. "Nick"

Nicodemus, president of the homeowners association.

The group vowed to bombard Publix officials with faxes, phone calls and letters. By Tuesday, they expect to have 4,000 signatures on a petition demanding rejection of the project when the DeKalb Planning Commission takes up Publix's application for the 10-acre site.

The planning commission will make a recommendation on the project, but the DeKalb County Commission will make the final decision.

County Commissioner Jean Williams, who represents the area in question and attended Sunday's meeting, was surprised at the number of people who showed up. "It was probably the largest turnout I've seen in 10 years," she said.

Mrs. Williams would not say how she planned to vote on the matter. "I'm going to listen to both sides," she said.

If Publix is allowed to build its flagship store at the Chamblee-Dunwoody site, residents said they will boycott it. "Most of us are not going to shop at Publix—anywhere," said Ruth Maise, a Dunwoody resident for 10 years.

At least half of the association's 2,000 residents attended the boisterous meeting. The 65,000-square-foot supermarket—to be built on property currently zoned for an office—will flood the area with traffic and create a commercial domino effect, angry residents warned.

Publix officials have said they would be a good neighbor. In addition to the grocery store, Publix's proposal in Dunwoody includes construction of 34,000 square feet in adjacent retail space and 25,000 square feet in supporting businesses, like fast-food restaurants and gas stations

It is apparent that Blake knew the Publix position and felt an obligation to record it, even though representatives were not at the meeting. Of those people who did attend, he identified the leaders of the organization. He also knew the county commissioner and, obviously, spoke to her after the meeting. He probably had to buttonhole Maise afterwards to ask her name and how to spell it. But notice that while he summarized the audience's position, she was the only member of the audience he identified by name, despite the fact that in a meeting attended by 1,000 people many of them probably spoke. Why?

A protest meeting in Delray Beach, Fla., brought a group of citizens face to face with the City Commission. Anthony Marx, a staff writer for The News of Boca Raton, had the task of tightly summarizing what must have been an angry presentation to the commissioners. Marx supported his lead with specifics, carefully selected quotes that seem to sum up best what the complainants argued.

Embittered friends and family of an unarmed man who was fatally shot by an off-duty Delray Beach police officer told city commissioners Wednesday they want the officer fired and brought to justice to prevent another tragedy.

About 40 people who knew Ricky

Guarine asked commissioners to do whatever was necessary to make sure Sgt. Don West, an eight-year veteran, never carries a gun or badge again in Delray Beach.

Relatives of the slain 34-year-old Boynton Beach mechanic vowed to seek a special prosecutor from outside the county to investigate.

They said a grand jury, which exonerated West this month, ignored key evidence that West had threatened to kill Guarine two weeks before his death in November.

"This entire case was improperly handled," said Carl Ray Smoot, Guarine's brother-in-law. "I challenge the commission here to take action."

"Do we have to wait until West makes a second mistake? We want justice," added George Intagliata, who knew Guarine for eight years.

City Manager David Harden said he is awaiting the results of an ongoing internal affairs investigation by the Delray Beach Police Department.

After he has the report, Harden said he would decide quickly about whether to fire West.

Guarine's friends and relatives, who have collected nearly 500 signatures demanding action, walked away from the meeting unsatisfied with the city's response.

"The old boy network is taking care of the police now," Smoot said.

Most readers can understand the story to this point. But Marx goes on to provide background that gives context for the meeting. That provides information for people who may not have seen the original story. It also jogs the memory of individuals who may have read the story but forgotten the details.

After confronting Guarine in a bank parking lot Nov. 16, West followed him and the two got into a fight near Guarine's home.

With five other police officers present,

West fired the fatal shot.

He later said he thought Guarine was pulling out a weapon. But Guarine was reaching for a set of keys.

COVERAGE FOR RADIO AND TELEVISION

STUDY PREVIEW   Radio and television reporters cover public speech events with much the same mindset as reporters from print outlets. They want their audiences to know what was said and in what context. But the audio and video technology they employ makes special demands on the way they cover those stories and present them on the air.

Setting Up for Radio and Television

If you are covering a speech for radio, it is preferable to use a microphone with your tape recorder. That will allow you to check the tape counter when the speaker has said something you think you might use on the air. It will also allow you to turn the tape over, if necessary. Arrive early enough so that you can secure the microphone to the lectern without making a disturbance. If you do not have a microphone, sit in front of the lectern, if at all possible, and when the speaker gets up to talk, turn on the tape recorder and place it in front of the speaker as unobtrusively as you can.

Television photographers set up their tripods wherever they can get the best shot of the speaker, but without blocking the view of others, and camera lenses allow them close-ups even from the back of a hall. Reporters usually stand next to photographers to cue them when to start and stop videotape. At some point the photographer will take the camera off the tripod and move around the room to take pictures of audience reaction. Just when that will be is easier to decide if the reporter has a prepared text. If not, reporter and photographer need to choose a time when the speaker is not making a major point.

The same applies for radio or television coverage of any public events. The point to remember is that only news conferences are staged primarily for the benefit of the media. At speeches, meetings and panels, the media are on-lookers, not the invited guests, and reporters and photographers have to behave accordingly. Three rules of journalistic etiquette will serve you well: arrive on time, be as unobtrusive as possible in using your equipment, and accede to the directions of the people in charge.

Writing the Story for Radio

If you are reporting for radio, you can write a "reader" or, better still, a story that contains one or more actualities. The ability to transmit the voices of newsmakers has been among the main advantages of radio news since the 1920s. A radio reporter sent to cover Gloria Steinem's speech might well have written a story like this for the next morning's drive-time newscasts:

> Feminist Gloria Steinem told a state university audience tonight that equality for women must be tied to racial equality. Steinem is the editor of Ms. magazine and a pioneering member of the women's movement. She told students and faculty the fight for racial equality is a second wave of the feminist movement.
>
> (INTRO) Individual differences. . . . (:10)
>
> (OUT) . . . race are irrelevant.
>
> But, Steinem said, women are still judged by different standards than men.
>
> (INTRO) What would have. . . . (:25)

(OUT) . . . end of it (laughter/applause).

Ms. magazine editor Gloria Steinem.

The writer of the broadcast story has to be especially careful to set up the actuality, to provide a context for it but without repeating in the script what the source will be heard saying in the actuality—avoiding the echo-chamber effect or its print equivalent, the stutter quote:

Steinem said individual differences should matter.

(INTRO) Individual differences should matter.

Writing the Story for Television

A story for television can take a variety of forms as well. It could be a reader, much like the radio story. With tape, it could be a voice over, showing the speaker but not broadcasting her words. It could be made up of an anchor's introduction and the speaker with sound on tape. Or it could be a package that includes a reporter who tells the story with shots and sound bites of the speaker interspersed with pictures of audience reaction.

	ANCHOR: When our Nancy Newshound came to work today she asked for some advice—what should she cover. We sent her to Ann Landers.
LS LANDERS	*VO*: An Ursinus College auditorium full of her faithful readers heard Ann Landers talk about the job of writing an advice column. Landers—whose real name is Eppie Lederer—said things have changed over the 37 years she's been writing the column.
CU LANDERS	*LANDERS*: Most of the letters I got were from women, and most of them had the same complaint: My husband never kisses me. Today, they want to know about
MCU AUDIENCE	how to avoid AIDS. Teenagers ask whether they ought to have sex.
CU LANDERS	Mothers want to know how to protect children from violence.
MCU AUDIENCE	*VO*: Even with all the seriousness, she gets letters that give her and her readers

	a chuckle. Like the one that asked which way the toilet paper should hang.
CU LANDERS	*LANDERS*: Should it hang with the edge hanging along the wall or on the outer part of the roll? Well, we got 15,000 letters arguing over it.
MCU AUDIENCE	Finally, I got a letter from a health club janitor in Minneapolis who said the debate had people at the club so divided
CU LANDERS	he had to put two paper holders in each stall. That ended that.
CU NEWSHOUND	Landers told this Founders Day crowd that if she could give only one piece of advice to everyone it would be, be kind to one another. A smile and a kind word can go a long way. At Ursinus College, Nancy Newshound, Action News.

The same method of putting together the television story applies to the other public-speech stories discussed in this chapter. Show the main speaker or speakers stating a central point. Include audience reaction. If time allows, include a few seconds of an individual interview. In covering panels or meetings, you can provide variety and show the flavor of the event if you include members of the audience making statements or asking questions.

EMPLOYING THE LAW TO COVER MEETINGS

STUDY PREVIEW   Federal and state sunshine laws provide reporters access to most policy-making meetings of government units. The provisions of the state laws vary, but generally a meeting can be closed only for a specifically stated reason allowed by the law, like strategy discussions for labor negotiations and personnel matters.

Open Meeting Requirements

Implicit in any democracy is that public policy be developed in open sessions where the people can listen in as their elected and appointed leaders discuss public matters. The people also need to be able to monitor their representatives' votes.

Every state has an open meeting law, which specifically declares that legislative units, including state boards and commission, city councils, school boards, and county governing bodies, be open to the public, including journalists. These laws also apply to executive agencies, like the state commissions that regulate telephone and other utility rates. The idea is that public policy ought to be created and executed in the bright sunshine, not in the shadows of secrecy.

Open meeting laws vary. Some insist that almost every session be open. But the state legislatures that create the laws are not always as strict about requiring themselves to meet openly as they are in demanding that city, county and school units and state executive agencies do so. In fact, some states permit legislators to caucus privately to devise party strategy.

Some of these laws proclaim the virtues of openness but lack teeth to enforce openness. In contrast, some states specify heavy fines and even jail terms for public officials who shut the doors.

Here are provisions of strong open meeting laws:

- ✦ Legislative units are required to meet at regular times and places and to announce their agendas ahead of time.
- ✦ Citizens can insist on quick judicial review if a meeting is closed.
- ✦ Closed sessions are allowed for only a few reasons, which are specifically identified, like discussion on sensitive personnel matters, collective bargaining strategy and deciding security arrangements.
- ✦ Any vote in a closed session must be announced immediately afterward.
- ✦ Decisions made at a closed meeting are nullified if the meeting is later declared to have been closed illegally.
- ✦ Penalties are specified for any presiding officer who authorizes a closed meeting illegally.

If the presiding officer at a government meeting proposes to close the session, or entertains a motion to do so, you should object. That is one of the few occasions on which a reporter should intrude into a meeting that is being covered. The formal objection helps establish a record that can be important in legal action against anyone who acts to close a meeting illegally. You need to notify your newsroom supervisors to determine what to do next.

Many reporters carry a wallet-size card with a protest that they can read out loud when a meeting is being closed—a kind of script. The cards normally specify the laws that would be violated if the meeting were closed and quotes from the statutes. Individual newspapers and broadcasting stations may issue the cards. Most state broadcast and press associations also provide them. So do many chapters of the Society of Professional Journalists.

Federal Sunshine Act

At the federal level, the 1976 Government in Sunshine Act requires about 50 federal agencies, boards and commissions to announce the time, place and agenda of meetings a week ahead, whether the meeting is open or closed, and the name and telephone of a person who may be contacted for more information.

Among the agencies to which the Sunshine Act applies are the Federal Communications Commission, Federal Trade Commission, Securities and Exchange Commission and National Labor Relations Board. While most meetings of the federal bodies covered by the Sunshine Act do most of their business in Washington, reporters elsewhere need to know that they have access to the occasional meetings convened outside of the capital.

CHAPTER WRAP-UP

Public speech activities, such as the ones discussed here, take place in every community across the country and are covered every day by radio, television and newspapers. Readers and listeners want to know what was said and how it was said, and the job of reporters is to convey both. They must record the words of the speakers accurately and try to put them in the context of the entire event.

Many private organizations invite reporters to attend meetings at which speeches will be made, and both public and private groups often set up special news conferences at which reporters are the principal guests. On the other hand, some governmental boards and committees on occasion attempt to carry out the public's business in private. Reporters need to know what meetings should be public and how to go about getting access to them.

STUDY QUESTIONS

1. How is a speech constructed?
2. Where can you find background information on a speaker and a topic?
3. What should go into the lead of a speech story, and how should the story be expanded?
4. What should the reporter put in the lead of a panel story, and how should the story be developed?
5. What is the reporter's major problem in covering a political debate?
6. What does the public relations person do to prepare for a news conference?
7. How can a reporter build a balanced story out of a news conference?
8. What must a reporter do to give a coherent report of a public meeting?

9.   What are the special considerations of public speech coverage for radio and television reporters?

10.   Explain what open meeting laws provide?

11.   What does the federal Government in Sunshine Act require?

PUTTING YOUR LEARNING TO WORK

EXERCISE 1   Writing the Speech Story

The following is the edited text of a speech given by President Clinton to students and faculty at Howard University in Washington, D.C., on Martin Luther King Day, Jan. 19, 1994. The text was prepared by the White House press office, which inserted the audience responses.

✦   Use the text to write a story about the speech for broadcast in the evening of that day. Assume that you have the text on tape.

✦   Write a 300-word story based on the text for a newspaper on the following day.

Only three American citizens, one from each century of our history, are honored with a holiday of national scope. Two were presidents, but the other never occupied any office, except the most important in our democracy. He was a citizen. George Washington helped to create our union, Abraham Lincoln gave his life to preserve it, and Martin Luther King redeemed the moral purpose of our United States. (Applause.)

Each in his own way, each in his own time, each of these great Americans defined what it means to be an American, what citizenship requires and what our nation must become. Dr. King, his family, and those who join in his cause set in motion changes that will forever reverberate across America, across the lines of geography, class and race.

For all of you who are very young here today, many of you who were not even born when Martin Luther King died, it may seem to you that the struggle was a very long time ago. But if you look around you, you can see that the history of that struggle is still alive today, still being written and still being made, still waiting to be fully redeemed.

We cannot—we cannot—meet our obligations to the young people in this audience today unless we say to them if you work hard, you get an education and you do what is right, you will have a job and an opportunity and a better life. We cannot do that. And to do that, we have to live in a world where all of us are working together.

Today, I pledge to you continued and aggressive enforcement of the Fair Housing Act. In a few moments I will sign an Executive Order that for the very first time puts the full weight of the federal government behind efforts to guarantee fair housing for everyone. (Applause.) We will tolerate no violations of every American's right for that housing opportunity. (Applause.)

But, my fellow Americans, the absence of discrimination is not the same thing as the presence of opportunity. (Applause.) It is not the same thing as having the security you need to build your lives, your families and your communities. So I say to you, it is our duty to continue the struggle that is not yet finished to fight discrimination. We will and we must. But it is not the same thing as the presence of opportunity.

National service is a part of our effort to create opportunity by building communities from the grass roots up and at the same time to give young people the opportunity to pay some of their costs of college education. And it is a part of the work that the Secretary of Education, who is here, has done to try to revolutionize the whole way we finance college education.

We know right now that 100 percent of the people need not only to graduate from high school, but to have at least two years of education after high school in the global economy. We know it, but we're not organized for it.

And so under the leadership of the Education Secretary and the Labor Secretary, our administration is working to set up a system to move all young people from high school to two years of further training while they're in the workplace, in the service or in school. (Applause.) And we are doing our dead level best—(applause)—and we're doing our dead level best to make sure that the cost of a college education is never a deterrent to seizing it, by reorganizing the whole student loan program. (Applause.)

Last year the Congress adopted our plan to reorganize the college loan program, to lower the interest rates, string out the repayments, require people to pay back as a percentage of the income they are earning when they get out, not just based on how much they borrow when they're in school. (Applause.) No one should ever refuse to go to college because of its cost. (Applause.)

When he spoke here at Howard, Martin Luther King said the following things. Dr. King said, "Human progress never rolls in on wheels of inevitability. It comes through the tireless effort and persistent work of dedicated individuals who are willing to be co-workers with God. And without this hard work, time itself becomes an ally of the primitive forces of stagnation. And so we must help time, and we must realize that the time is always right for one to do right." "Time is neutral," he said. "Time can either be used constructively or destructively." All he asked from each of the rest of us was to put in a tiny little minute.

When I think about it I'm often sad that Martin Luther King had so few precious minutes on this earth. Two days ago he would have celebrated his

65th birthday; and the older I get the younger I realize 65 is. (Laughter.) But, you know, he did a lot with the time he had, and I think we should try to do the same.

Thank you. (Applause.)

EXERCISE 2   Writing the Meeting Story

You have just returned from covering a meeting of the student government association.

✦   Write a story of about 250 words for the campus newspaper based on the following notes.

✦   Write a story for the campus radio station. Consider that you have the quoted material on tape.

One agenda item: funding for student organizations.

Report from William Kennedy, chair, SGA finance committee: 87 student organizations requested $565,200 in funding. Last year SGA allocated $400,000 and only had 56 organizations to fund.

Joanna Roussell, university vice president for administrative affairs: "You have to be aware that you might not have that amount to spend. That money comes from the student activity fee, and that depends on enrollment. It also depends on the overall university budget. We can't divert money from the educational fund into the student government budget."

Question from Louise Cole, fine arts senator: Why can't you give us a definite amount now?

Roussell: "There is a lot of guesswork that goes into this budget process. You never know how many students you are going to have, and what we expect now is a decline. If that happens, the budget will be cut. It's all very iffy. What you need to do is not just give money away with no accountability but to look at how the organizations have spent what you gave them this year. That way you'll have a better idea of how to allocate it for next year."

Tom Greenberg, engineering senator: Doesn't "want to have to raise student activity fees if enrollment goes down." Proposed motion: "That student government freeze funding available to organizations at $415,000, with $400,000 to be allocated to student organizations." Seconded.

Amendment, Rita Lopez, arts and sciences senator: That a committee be established to devise guidelines for allocating the money.

Amendment, Tina Bergeron, communications senator: To strike cap of $400,000 on the funds.

Amendments, passed. Lopez: 16-12. Bergeron: 20-8. Motion, passed. 17-11.

FOR FURTHER LEARNING

"Access to Places: A Guide for Reporters & Photographers Gathering News." The Reporters Committee for Freedom of the Press, 1992. This brief handbook was designed "to give reporters a 'plan of attack' when access to newsworthy events has been unreasonably restricted."

"Cameras and Microphones in Public Meetings: A Broadcaster's Guide to Effective Access in the 50 States & D.C." The Reporters Committee for Freedom of the Press, 1993. A survey of state laws governing the use of electronic news-gathering devices in public meetings.

Doug Newsom and Bob Carrell. "Public Relations Writing: Form & Style." 3rd edition. Wadsworth, 1981. This widely used text has a chapter on writing speeches and scripts.

Dennis L. Wilcox, Phillip H. Ault, and Warren K. Agee. "Public Relations: Strategies and Tactics." 3rd edition. HarperCollins, 1992. Chapter 15, "Spoken Tactics," is useful for seeing how a speech is constructed.

"Sunshine Laws," Quill (October 1992): 27–37. This special section of the publication of the Society of Professional Journalists summarized open meetings and open records legislation in the 50 states.

Preparing for the Interview

In this chapter you will learn:

✦ Making an appointment for an interview requires skill and, sometimes, perseverance.

✦ Some places are more conducive to interviews than others.

✦ Backgrounding yourself on the source and the issue is essential.

✦ Lists of questions developed ahead of time can be helpful.

✦ Reporters use a combination of open-end and closed-end questions depending on circumstances.

✦ Circumstances determine whether to use questions that move from specific to general or from general to specific.

✦ While reporters are usually neutral questioners, they may find it necessary to ask confrontational or loaded questions.

✦ Background information can be used to elicit direct quotes, details and color that will give life to a story.

✦ The skillful interviewer uses a variety of techniques to keep information flowing.

THE JOURNALISTIC INTERVIEW

The journalistic interview took form in the 1830s when the first mass-circulation newspapers sought new ways to generate interesting copy. James Gordon Bennett, editor of the New York Herald, conducted a spot news interview in 1836, and other reporters soon adopted the technique. Among them was Henry Grady of the Atlanta Constitution who interviewed most of the great figures of his time for newspapers North and South. He called the interview "the neatest and handiest thing in journalism." But not all found the form to their liking. As late as 1874 magazine writer Richard Grant White called interviewing "the most perfect contrivance yet to make journalism an offense, a thing of ill savor in all decent nostrils."

In-depth biographical articles emerged in the 1920s as journalists pushed for more and more detail. The New Yorker magazine led the way with increasingly intense examinations not only of individuals but also of great public issues. It was verbal autobiography, typified later by the intense, self-revealing Playboy magazine interview.

Television interviews are frequently superficial, largely because the medium does not allow for hard, sustained questioning. But reporters like Mike Wallace, David Frost, Leslie Stahl and Dick Cavett have made names for themselves because of their ability to gather information one on one.

ARRANGING THE INTERVIEW

STUDY PREVIEW   The first job in arranging an interview is to make contact with the source to set a time and place. But that can sometimes be easier said than done. Public relations people can expedite some interviews. Otherwise, use the telephone to reach the source yourself.

Using the Telephone

Reporters usually set up interviews by telephone, sometimes directly with the interviewee, sometimes through intermediaries. They dial and ask.

It can go easily. Sources who are readily available usually say "yes" right away. When that happens, be prepared to suggest a time and place and even to conduct the interview over the phone right then if the source won't grant an in-person interview.

In arranging an interview, it is generally best to identify what you are interested in asking about, but save your specific questions until the interview. Tell your source, too, how much time you think you will need.

Reporters often have to work through intermediaries. If you want to interview someone with a large organization, you might ask the organization's public relations people to help set it up. Their media relations responsibilities include accommodating journalists, although they occasionally are under orders to run interference. If you do get a run-around from PR people, or from secretaries, receptionists and other intermediaries, you are on your own to get to your source.

Most receptionists and secretaries will inform their boss that you called. If you've treated them well, they may go further and prod the boss into returning your call. Because you will have to ask by name for the person you want to interview, know how to pronounce the name. If you don't, you may not be treated seriously, perhaps not even cordially.

When you call to request an interview, expect to be asked three things: Who are you? Whom do you represent? What are you writing about? All are reasonable questions, but you run unneeded risks with an intermediary if you go on at great length. When asked "Who's calling?" give your name confidently and directly. The intermediary may only want to let the boss know who is on the line. If you go further and say you are from a particular newspaper or broadcast station, you could slow down getting to your source. If you are asked whom you represent, keep it simple: "I'm with KFMJ." Again, detail could increase the chances you will be put off. To say "KFMJ News" could raise a warning flag, and you would certainly trigger alarms if you say, "I'm with KFMJ's investigative reporting team."

What do you say if you are a free-lancer? If you have an assignment, say so. But never lie and say you are with a news organization if you are not on staff. If you are free-lancing on speculation, you have to say that. Even if you hope to peddle your article to Smithsonian magazine, it is misleading to leave an impression that you are with Smithsonian.

Some intermediaries will ask why you are calling. Offering details could slow you down, especially if the intermediary is asking so the boss can be briefed before being put on the line. If you give specifics, you run the risk of your source declining to come to the phone. It is best to be general without sounding secretive. Say you are working on a story. If pressed, explain it is something you really need to talk to the boss about.

Mentioning another source may help get an interview. In effect, you are saying you've been cleared by others. The technique can also help in introducing yourself: "Mr. or Ms. X told me you could probably help me."

Hard-to Reach Sources

Persistence is sometimes the interviewer's most important virtue. Journalist Oriana Fallaci said that to meet many of her subjects "was often an exhausting chore. My request for an appointment was almost always met by cold silence or a refusal . . . and if later they answered yes, I had to wait months for them to grant me an hour or half hour." However long it took to get an interview, when she sat down with the source Fallaci made the most of the opportunity, and her work has won her Rolling Stone's praise as "the greatest political interviewer of modern times."

Free-lancer Larry Miller wanted to interview CBS journalist Diane Sawyer on breaking into television. It took him 27 calls—including several at 3:15 a.m., just after she ordinarily got to work. His 27th call, the successful one, was at 10:30 a.m. "All the effort," he recalls, "turned out to be worth it." He got his story.

You may have to try a variety of means to reach sources for quick telephone questions or to arrange a sit-down interview. Every reporter has heard it hundreds of times: the potential source "is in conference." Often that is true. But the line is also an office tactic for taking names and numbers to help the boss decide whose calls to return first, if at all. Muster a tone that conveys the importance of your call. The result may surprise you: "Oh, she just walked in."

Harry Romanoff, a reporter out of the Front Page days of Chicago journalism, was brilliant at telephone interviews. In fact, a colleague said Romanoff could "play the phone like Heifitz playing the violin." Except that Romanoff played false notes. He impersonated anyone he needed to, from police captains to governors, to get a story by telephone. These days most journalists have qualms about misrepresenting themselves, and rightly so. Not uncommonly, though, reporters frustrated at obstacle-erecting intermediaries sometimes let false inferences go uncorrected. They may only give their names and ask for the person by first name in a tone and manner that indicates they have known the person for years. That can pave the way to a call back, even if by a puzzled source who wonders if you are friends. If you try this, however, be sure you know what first name your source uses. Many people use their middle name or a nickname, and to ask for "Ed" when you are seeking "Edward J." may get a quick turn-off from "John" or his secretary.

Sam Schuth, at radio station KLSE in Rochester, Minn., learned early that telephone companies assign sequential numbers for related offices. If the receptionist is 555-5017, the boss may be 5018. Try it if the source's phone number is unlisted and the receptionist uncooperative. You may reach your source directly. If you don't, try 5019, then 5020.

If you reach your target, the fact that you dialed directly may lead your source to think that somebody who knows the unlisted number gave it to you, and that can give you instant credibility. On the other hand, you may irk a source by interrupting a meeting. And you need to be prepared to explain how you got the number.

Reporters usually try to reach sources at work, but sometimes it is necessary to call someone at home. Some novice reporters may hesitate to do that, not wanting to invade anyone's privacy. But anyone who has a telephone accepts the idea that the phone may ring, and it is the rare public official who will complain at the chance to get his or her name in print or on the air. If a source does feel you are intruding, you will be told. If you call again, then you are trespassing. Is it rude to call at 1 a.m.? Yes, to most people with usual sleeping hours, although urgent situations may leave no choice. It is a good general rule not to call before 9 a.m. or after 9 p.m., except in emergencies.

Early evening is best for reaching most people with answering machines. Arriving home after work, they listen to messages, then turn the machine off for the evening and answer personally. When an answering machine answers, leave your name and number—nothing more. If your message cannot be distinguished from, say, a prospective client, you are more likely to receive a prompt return call than if you announce you are from a news organization. Call back every few hours with politeness, never exasperation, and leave your name and number again.

SETTING UP THE QUESTIONS

STUDY PREVIEW   Most reporters would agree with New York Times columnist Russell Baker that the "toughest thing for a reporter is finding the right questions to ask." How do you find the right questions? By backgrounding yourself on the person and the issue—and by thinking.

First Things First

John Sweeney, writing coach for the Wilmington News-Journal in Delaware, says you decide first what you want to get out of the interview. Do you want a feature story or a profile? A depth story or a couple of quotes for a brief? When you know that, you will be able to shape the interview accordingly.

If it's a profile you are after, you need to background yourself on the person. CBS' Mike Wallace has said the interviewer must know what the subject "has said in the past, and what his point of view on various subjects is and has been. The interviewer must research what others have said on the subject or about the person being interviewed." ABC's Barbara Walters does thorough research on people she is going to interview, enough so that "you really feel you know the person."

How do you do that? "Read the book or report the subject wrote," Sweeney says. "Study the issue. Look at your newspaper; read other newspapers and magazines. If you're talking to a legislator, find out her voting record, who she represents, how long she's been there, and so on. Get the spelling of her name, get her name and occupation before the face-to-face interview." Shelves of reference works are available to help you. Skeletal information on individuals can be gotten from biographical dictionaries like Who's Who. More detailed material is contained in works like Current Biography. Go also to the Reader's Guide to Periodical Literature and to the New York Times Index.

Sterling Green of the Associated Press said he "put in considerably more time in preparation for an interview" than in conducting or writing it. One advantage of doing the background work, obviously, is that the interviewer will know the source and the subject and feel more comfortable with both. Moreover, Green said, "it builds the confidence of the subject when you know his problem and his business."

Making a List

Many reporters prepare a set of questions ahead of time. According to Sweeney, Steve Kurkjian of the Boston Globe puts together three lists. He'll have a short list and a long list and a "hello-goodbye" list, depending on the amount of time he anticipates having with the source. The "hello-goodbye" contains one big question for a subject who's likely to bang down the phone, "the one you need an answer for before he hangs up."

With a list drawn up, the experienced reporter may not even refer to it or may use it only as a memory aid to make sure the important questions all get asked. But it can serve other purposes. The AP's Saul Pett argues that prepared questions help the spontaneity of an interview. "The spontaneous interview is never less spontaneous than when you let the guy just roam anywhere he wants to—and he's just telling you what he wants to." Prepared questions are also helpful with sources who are taciturn. Without them, "you'd just be at a total loss," Pett says. "And if you're going to sit there and grope—well, it ends too soon."

Going Tough or with Fluff

Going into the interview, you also need to decide whether to lead with a hard question or a soft one. Reporters vary in their preference for one or the other, though most will tell you that the kind of interview frequently dictates the kind of question. Fluff is often best for a personality interview. For a spot news or in-depth story, a no-nonsense question lets the source know right away that you mean business.

QUESTION TYPES

STUDY PREVIEW   "Silly, meaningless questions lead to silly, meaningless stories," says Mike Kautsch, dean of journalism and mass communication at the University of Kansas. A major element in conducting an interview is developing a sequence for questions that will generate the kinds of information and truths that will make a worthwhile and interesting story. Such questions are usually one of two types, open-end or closed-end. Each type has its place. For lengthy interviews, a mix of open-end and closed-end questions generally is best.

Closed-End Questions

Closed-end questions focus on "who," "what," "when" and "where," and tend to be binary, like a true-false examination. Unless you have a gregarious source, closed-end questions elicit only bare-bones information without the flavor and color that make interesting stories. Despite their shortcomings, however, closed-end questions have value. For two paragraphs on something being reported for the record, closed-end questions work well. They make for quick, efficient interviewing against a deadline, as in covering routine stories like traffic accidents. For example, a reporter making a telephone check of police agencies close to a midnight deadline might ask a desk sergeant a series of closed-end questions:

+ Any news tonight?
+ Anybody hurt?
+ Where was the accident?
+ What was the name of the driver?
+ How do you spell that?
+ Have an address?
+ Age?
+ Nobody else in the car, right?
+ Much damage?
+ How did the car end up in the ditch?

Except for the last one, those are closed-end, fact-seeking questions which elicit terse, to-the-point answers.

With their frequent deadlines, short stories and headline formats, broadcast reporters tend to write more stories from closed-end questions than newspaper reporters.

Open-End Questions

Open-end questions, those that seek the "why" and "how," generally are more fruitful. They encourage sources to go into detail, recall anecdotal color, spontaneously offer opinions and expand on observations. Open-end questions also allow room for tangents, which is their advantage—although that can be a problem, because tangents can detract from the efficiency of the interview.

Interviewer Hugh Sherwood advises against questions so open-ended that they are vapid. He encourages reporters to begin putting their stories together in their minds while the interview is in progress. Then they can sense when things are on track and when they veer off on the dead-end tangent.

QUESTION SEQUENCES

STUDY PREVIEW   To be more effective in drawing out information, reporters usually arrange their questions in a sequence, rather than taking a scattershot approach. There are five sequences for questioning: narrowing, broadening, quintamensional, direct focus and conversational.

Narrowing and Broadening

Interview questions fall into two primary categories: narrowing and broadening. With the narrowing sequence, reporters begin with broad, general questions and funnel into narrower questions. The broadening sequence is the opposite, moving from narrow, specific questions to broader questions. Both sequences have a role in journalistic interviewing, and the sequences can be mixed.

At a chemical spill, for example, a reporter might open an interview with the county civil defense director by asking, "What happened?" That is a broad, general question that will give the reporter a sense of the situation. Narrower questions for details follow: "How big a crew do you have here? What's your target date for getting the lake cleaned up? Do you know where the spill came from?" Later, the reporter is back with the civil defense director. "I was just over the ridge," she tells the chief, "and the muck in that bay smells like rotten eggs. Does this mean the spill is from the Kovatch sulphur plant?" The reporter, having explored the situation for herself, is back with specific narrow questions.

For spot coverage, the narrowing sequence can be as uncalculated as making a morning telephone check of police agencies:

Reporter: Anything happen overnight? (Broad Question)

Deputy: We had a car go in the river.

Reporter: Anyone hurt? (Narrowing)

Deputy: The driver, a 17-year-old kid from Bluffton, drowned. At least we think he did. The coroner has the body now.

Reporter: Do you have the name? (Further narrowing)

Deputy: Larry Johnes.

Reporter: How do you spell that? (Further narrowing)

Deputy: J-o-h-n-e-s. Regular Larry for the first name. Middle name is Kyle, K-y-l-e.

In enterprise and depth interviewing, funnelling can help establish rapport with new sources. Broad questioning gives them a chance to size you up before you move to detailed questions that may be sensitive. Starting with narrowly focused questions gets right to specifics, and such questions can be effective with no-nonsense sources who value their time.

In enterprise and depth interviewing, you want a scope that narrow questions usually can't provide. You want your source to explain how specifics flow from general principles or to explain motivations in broad terms. This can be done by putting questions in a broadening sequence.

Mixing Sequences

Interviewing can be a hybrid of broadening and narrowing questions. In interviewing Mohammed Reza Pahlevi, then Shah of Iran, Oriana Fallaci began with a question so narrowly focused that it almost required a yes or no answer:

Fallaci: Your Majesty, is it true you've taken another wife?

Shah: A stupid, vile, disgusting libel.

At that point, Fallaci had enough to state in her story that the Shah denied he had taken another wife. But Fallaci was less interested in the shah's answer to her specific question than in how he viewed women. She persisted according to her plan and prodded him into illuminating elaboration, using the broadening sequence:

Fallaci: But, Your Majesty, you are a Muslim. Your religion allows you to take another wife without repudiating Empress Farah Diba.

By broadening her questions, Fallaci learned how the Shah fit specifics of his views on marriage in a general framework. Then she narrowed her questions to push the Shah on his initial claim of fidelity.

Broadening questions are helpful not only in high-powered interviewing. Some sources feel more comfortable with specifics of their specialty. Talking first about details can help sources not used to being interviewed relax before moving to broader issues.

Whether you choose narrowing or broadening, you are making a judgment call based on what you know about your source ahead of time. It is like Russian roulette. What works with one person may not for another. The better you prepare, the better you can "psych out" your source and make the right call.

Quintamensional Sequence

Pollsters devised quintamensional sequencing in the 1940s. It is a five-step method to test how strongly sources feel on an issue. You start by asking if the person knows anything about the subject.

Imagine you are interviewing a candidate for attorney general the morning after a gambling raid in the state capital. Here's how quintamensional sequencing would work:

"Did you hear about the raid in Des Moines last night?"

Has the source given any thought or attention to the issue? Essentially, these are filter questions.

"Would raids of that sort be part of your law enforcement plan for Iowa?"

Does the source have general attitudes on the issue? These are open-end questions through which sources may reveal a general direction of their thinking, sometimes in the process bringing to light things otherwise overlooked in the interview.

"Would you authorize a raid like the one on Smelzer's Saloon last night?"

Does the source have specific attitudes about the issue? These tend to be yes or no questions, what pollster George Gallup calls "the questions which ask the public to stand up and be counted."

"What's wrong with a little roulette or blackjack among friends at a private club?"

Why does the source hold such attitudes? These questions provide opinion from a different angle, asking for rationale.

"Would you move against all gambling even if it cost you re-election four years from now?"

How intensely does the source hold these attitudes?

Asking the questions in sequence is important so you can identify a pointless line of questioning early. If a source knows nothing about an issue, you will learn that with your first question. The quintamensional sequence also precludes embarrassing a source with advanced questions that presume knowledge that the source lacks. Of course, a reporter does not always

THE SKILLED INTERVIEWER. Larry King interviews politicians like former Vice President Dan Quayle, movie and rock stars, and other celebrities on his CNN program, "Larry King Live." His interviewing skills have won him a large audience, and the size of the audience attracts the high-profile guests. Like other good interviewers, King shows an interest in the people he interviews.   (CNN/Reuters/The Bettmann Archive)

have the time to make methodical use of quintamensional sequencing. It takes planning.

Direct-Focus Questioning

In spot coverage, question sequencing usually is spontaneous. The event itself suggests your questions, most of them fact seeking or reaction seeking. The focus is directly on the unfolding situation being covered. In such situations, questions designed to elicit lengthy and reflective answers are unnecessary. Sometimes this is called the tunnel or train sequence—one question leads to another with no grand design. One question just follows the other.

The Conversational Interview

For New Yorker profiles and Playboy interviews, reporters employ the gamut of question sequences. They narrow, they broaden, they filter, they test. Interviews extending over days, sometimes weeks, cannot be reduced to a single question-sequence model.

Depth interviewing may seem a meandering, exploratory, relatively free-form approach. It is not. Open-end questions are designed to invite reflection. Closed-end questions seek detail and documentation. The mix of open-end and closed-end questions moves the interview in productive directions. Methodically, questioning moves from subject to subject, and then back again—to tackle a sensitive issue from another perspective.

To conduct a conversational interview successfully, the reporter must be a skilled conversationalist so the interviewee remains interested in going forward. Dumb questions can cause the interviewee to doubt whether the interview is worth the time. A. J. Liebling wrote of an interview with Gen. John J. Pershing in 1940 in which the journalist was unable to make headway with his questioning. Finally he asked, "When they started to cut down the Army after the Armistice in 1918, General, you were against it, weren't you, because you foresaw this new European crisis?" Pershing looked at him, Liebling wrote, "in an angry disgusted manner and said, 'Who the hell could have foreseen this?' End of interview.

Elaborate preparation is essential for a conversational interview. It is not as much putting questions to someone as it is, true to its name, conversing intelligently. The conversational interview is a two-way exploration.

Confrontational Questions

Truth-seeking sometimes requires journalists to ask questions that sources would rather not be asked. Asking straight out is one approach, but a narrowing sequence or a diversionary approach can work in some situations. Andrew Schneider and Matt Brelis of the Pittsburgh Press spent four months tracking reports of sick, drug-addicted, and alcoholic commercial-airline pilots. They heard tales that federal air surgeon Frank Austin cavalierly allowed grounded, impaired pilots to return to the skies—with passengers. Involved were more than 250 professional pilots and co-pilots grounded by potentially fatal or debilitating conditions. Finally Schneider and Brelis had to confront Austin. Readers needed the whole story. And fairness required that the accusations be put squarely to Austin. Such situations occur on every beat: What does the athletic director say after reports that overzealous boosters have written checks to football players? How does the mayor explain taking a city car across the state line to a topless go-go joint? What did the president know and when did he know it?

Few reporters revel in asking confrontational questions, but some questions, no matter how unpleasant, have to be asked. Usually the issue is not whether to ask but how. When sources expect a confrontational question, ask it straight away. Frank Austin, the federal air surgeon, knew the question that the Pittsburgh Press reporters had in mind when they arranged an appointment to interview him—and he had an answer. Austin explained he had used his professional opinion in evaluating appeals from grounded pilots. In fact, he prided himself in doubling the number of recertifications from 1984 to 1985 and reducing a backlog of applications by 80 percent in his first six months on the job.

Straight-out questions, however, will not always work. Ask most crooks if they are crooks and they will say no. An alternative to straight-out questions is a variation on the narrowing sequence: the box-in question, moving from broad questions to specifics that lead to the confrontational question. Handled poorly, boxing-in smacks of entrapment, but it can be done skillfully. Tough questions can be framed carefully to give a source an opportunity to explain and elaborate. The goal after all is to seek truth, not make a source squirm.

If a source is cagey, journalists sometimes respond in kind. Moving back and forth from sensitive questions to benign questions, a reporter can keep a source off guard until ready to spring the confrontational question. The technique is one of interspersing easily answered and tough questions, open-end and closed-end questions, and friendly and antagonistic questions.

The GOSS Model

Let's be philosophical a moment. All existence is in movement—bills becoming laws, candidates becoming office-holders, the Toronto Blue Jays starting 0-0 and becoming World Series champs. Journalists report these changes.

Borrowing from philosopher Frederick Nietzsche, journalism professor LaRue Gilleland noted that changes do not occur automatically. To become law, ideas must receive legislative approval. To become world champs, the Mets must win games. To win office, candidates must woo voters. There always is an obstacle between a starting point and a goal.

Gilleland took this concept and designed the GOSS model for interviewing. G stands for goal and S for starting point. Between them, O is the obstacle and S is the solution to overcome the obstacle and reach the goal. Questions fall into four categories:

+ *Goal questions:* "What are you trying to accomplish?" "What was the real purpose of your organization back then?"
+ *Obstacle questions:* "What problems did you face?" "What stands in your way now?"
+ *Solution questions:* "How did you handle the problem?" "What plans do you have for resolving the conflict?"
+ *Start questions:* "When did the program begin?" "Whose idea was it?"

The GOSS technique has been criticized as simplistic, but it can help you organize your thoughts for an interview. Flowing from a universal principle, GOSS is so workable and flexible that it can help work up new question lines extemporaneously when an interview hits a dead end.

Exceptions to Value-Free Interviewing

As detached, neutral, dispassionate inquirers, journalists favor value-free questions which do not portray them falsely as partisan. Even so, there are

DAVID FROST. Among television journalists, David Frost has won a reputation for eliciting information in very public interviews. He knew his subject well before he sat down to do a series of television interviews with former President Richard Nixon. (UPI/The Bettmann Archive)

times and places for loaded and leading questions. Loaded questions really aren't questions. They are statements disguised in interrogative form: "Have you stopped embezzling company funds?" Unless the guy is an embezzler, the question is an indictment. To answer yes is to admit embezzling, perhaps once, perhaps habitually. To answer no is saying he still does.

With loaded questions you risk derailing an interview—even being punched in the nose. Then again, no matter how unfair and inciting, loaded questions sometimes will so excite a source that an interview that had been progressing mundanely suddenly breaks open. It worked for Oriana Fallaci. In an interview with Henry Kissinger, Richard Nixon's secretary of state, Fallaci asked an outlandishly flattering loaded question that prompted unexpectedly revealing answers:

Fallaci: Dr. Kissinger, how do you explain the fact that you have become almost more famous and popular than a president? Have you any theories?

Kissinger: Yes, but I will not tell you what they are.

Then, at Fallaci's persistence, he proceeded to do so. Kissinger displayed an unbecoming pomposity that surely he would have avoided had Fallaci asked him whether he saw himself almost as famous and popular as the president, instead of how it was so. Kissinger fell for Fallaci's loaded premise. Loaded questions require a sixth sense on whether they will work. A successful question in one situation might backfire in another.

Leading questions condition sources to answer a certain way, putting words in their mouths. The result can be answers that may not reflect the source accurately. Leading questions can be useful, however, in two situations:

◆ *To expedite an interview.* If a source has rambled at great length, you might ask: "Are you saying, senator, that you lean toward an embargo?" That sums things up, and the interview can move forward.

◆ *To maintain a friendly momentum.* This can be tricky. Interview expert John Brady says the effectiveness of leading questions rests on how perceptive the interviewer is about the rapport of the interview. If the reporter and source are hitting it off splendidly, the source rolling with the questions and having fun in the process, then leading questions can work.

Leading questions also can ruin an interview. Says Brady: "The leading question requires a subject with a sense of spirit and fight—and an interviewer with a sense of timing. When injected into a touch-and-go exchange, it may disrupt rapport. But in secure surroundings, it may spark a surprisingly honest answer. The difference, perhaps, is whether the subject sees his interviewer as closed-minded or simply not persuaded. The success of the leading question—and the success of much of interviewing—is a matter of trust, of rapport."

SEEKING INFORMATION AND COLOR

STUDY PREVIEW   By doing their homework, journalists can make good use of valuable time with their sources to break new ground, rather than asking basic biographical and background questions. The interview is a good opportunity to generate direct quotations and anecdotes.

How to Use Background

An interview is an opportunity to develop fresh material, not rehash what is already in the record. It would be unpardonable, for example, to ask Bill Clinton his views on gays in the military. The journalist's general knowledge has to include the great issues of our time. Just as unpardonable is not checking basic references before an interview. Never is there reason to ask the birth date of a state legislator. It is in the Blue Book. Nor should there ever be reason to ask where a professor went to college. It is in the college catalog.

Information from biographical sources like the state Blue Book and Who's Who in America is a starting point for eliciting fresh information and color. Consider these questions from a hypothetical interview with Chrysler wonder-worker Lee Iacocca:

"When were you born?"

> This is a biographical question that says the reporter has not prepared adequately for the interview. Iacocca's birthday is a readily available bit of information.

"Am I correct that you were born Oct. 15, 1924?"

> This closed-end question indicates that the reporter has done some homework, but it doesn't move the interview anywhere. It is a dead end.

"You grew up in the Depression, a child of the 1930s. How did that shape your values?"

> This question puts biographical detail to work creating an open-end question designed to elicit source comments that might make excellent direct quotes. It also could elicit colorful detail and examples to help bring a story to life.

Asking questions that flow from facts and numbers, you guide sources into rich material. In answering, your sources likely will refer to facts that you want to confirm. Talking about values growing up, a source may refer to brothers and sisters. You then do not have to ask the dead-end question, "How many brothers and sisters did you have?" If family size interests you, it can be pursued in the conversational exchange that open-end questions start. Consider this hypothetical question to Lee Iacocca: "In your book you talk a lot about your father and mother when you describe growing up, but your sister Delma is hardly mentioned. Weren't you close to Delma?"

Except in book-length biographies, journalists seldom organize stories chronologically. A person's life begins at birth, but birth seldom is what makes someone worth writing about. Everybody is born. Although birth rarely makes gripping leads, a chronology helps you sort out facts and organize your thoughts before you hit the keyboard. Human thought processes work sequentially, starting at the beginning and moving forward. Once a source opens up, things usually are told by starting at a beginning point. In the process of telling a story from beginning to end, whether a life story or an account of a project or a crisis, let the source proceed chronologically. Likely there will be colorful material recalled along the way. You can stop the story at promising points to push for detail and background.

Working for Quotations and Anecdotes

Successful interviewers use a variety of techniques to get their sources to talk and, in talking, to provide quotations and anecdotes that will make their stories come alive. The best technique is to listen closely. Ed Bradley of CBS' "60 Minutes" has attributed much of his success to being a good listener. "When you listen well, people tend to talk more," he told E. J. Kahn Jr. of the New Yorker, himself a superb interviewer.

Play it again, Sam. Prodding a source to retell things you already know can yield good quotes. When familiar stories are retold, they often take on new compactness and color. You can be explicit in asking that something be retold: "Your experience in the Bataan Death March has been widely told, and it is central in your book about coping with adversity. Would you mind retelling for my listeners what you learned about the human condition from that experience?"

Paralanguage. Paralanguage can keep a source talking. Barbara Walters takes up a position in an interview designed to create intimacy. As described by Bill Carter of the New York Times Magazine, "She leans toward her subject, her eyes boring in, almost squinting with intensity. But her facial expression is benign, her body language unthreatening. The unspoken message behind her gaze is: 'I understand; I care; I'm here for you.'"

Affirmative nods say you are listening and hearing and interested. Re-enforcing "uh-huh's" can do it. Sometimes an awkward silence can keep a source talking. If your source signals that a question has been sufficiently answered by stopping for your next question, and you just sit there, the source almost invariably will go on. Mike Wallace is a master of that "dead air" technique. "The interviewee may find that the protracted silence is too much for him," Wallace said once, "and—so—frequently the pudding comes tumbling out." Wallace also prods sources to add to statements with a simple "And?" or "But?"

The master television interviewer Jack Paar could also use the "dead air" technique to good advantage. Hugh Downs recalled a Paar interview with film star Mickey Rooney in which Paar "simply sat there and looked at him," and Rooney kept talking.

"It's a hell of a technique," Downs said. "It can also be a very cruel technique."

Leading questions. Although disparaged, leading questions can result in good quotes. Imagine interviewing a state Republican official about the 1992 election when George Bush lost to Bill Clinton. An assertion like, "You must have been terribly disappointed," may spur a quotation that recaptures the chairman's feelings at that distant point.

Seek examples. Your quest for anecdotes can be absolutely explicit. If a source has been general, you might ask: "Do you have an especially poignant example of that?"

You can push a source to detail a specific incident. "In court, you said Margaret was a ruthless, brutal woman on her way up the corporate ladder. What kind of behavior and incidents led you to conclude that?"

Shared experiences. Some sources will open up if they think you have had similar experiences or hold similar views. To get the on-air confession he wanted from an accountant reported to have been involved in a tax avoidance scheme, CBS reporter Mike Wallace told the man, "Look, between you and me . . . you do it, everybody does it." The source replied, "Yeah." Such an approach is likely to work even better in a softer interview. For instance, in interviewing author Bob Greene, who wrote a book on fatherhood, a journalist who is a new father might say that the birth gave him the same feelings that Greene wrote about. But take care not to reverse roles. Listen and let the source do the talking. Otherwise you could defeat the purpose of the interview.

DEAD-ENDING AN INTERVIEW

STUDY PREVIEW   Some questions are confrontational by nature, and those may dry up an interview. Leading questions may have the same effect. The effective reporter prepares questions that will keep the conversation flowing and elicit information.

Questions That Go Too Far

In the quest for truth, journalists ask all kinds of questions, sometimes even causing their sources discomfort. Most journalists agree, however, that there are limits—although agreement is lacking on where to draw the line between questions that must be asked and questions which shouldn't be asked.

The Washington Post ran a story suggesting that unusual staff practices in Maryland Congressman Roy Dyson's office reflected the homosexuality of a senior Dyson aide. Later in a news conference—in front of Dyson's family and friends, with no evidence whatsoever that Dyson was homosexual—a television reporter asked the congressman, "Are you gay?"

Some journalists would defend the question, but not others, like Abe Rosenthal, retired executive editor of the New York Times. Said Rosenthal: "What does the congressman's homosexuality or lack of it have to do with the price of peanuts—because a member of his staff was supposed to be? The idea that you must get the last detail, whatever the price to your own self-respect or the other person's, I just do not agree with it."

When asked in a public forum, some questions have an indicting quality. To ask someone whether he's a traitor plants doubts whatever the person's answer. That can be destructive.

Asking for Insufficient Answers

Questions have to be framed in such a way as to get more than yes or no answers. To illustrate with an admittedly silly situation: A reporter turned a corner and saw a crowd. A man said a woman had jumped off a ninth-story ledge, and pointed to a witness. The reporter approached her.

Reporter: Did you see the woman jump?

Witness: Yes.

Reporter: Had the police talked to her?

Witness: Yes.

Reporter: Did she respond?

Witness: No.

Such an exchange would be pointless. The responses would not be enough for a story. To get information, the reporter would have to ask questions to get at the who, what, when, where, why and how.

"Yeah, well . . ." Interviewing

Failing to listen to a source's responses can slam the door on an interview. Hugh Downs has labeled the reporter who doesn't listen the "Yeah, well . . ." interviewer. The interviewer asks a question and while the source is answering begins thinking of what the next question will be. "If the interviewee says, 'I've been in New York for 155 years' this chap will blandly say, 'Yeah, well where do you go next. . . ?' If you don't listen to the answers it can't be much of an interview."

Not listening to the answers can also put the interviewer in the embarrassing position of asking a question the source has already answered.

The interviewer who listens closely to what the source is saying can home in on responses to get elaboration or clarification or to clear up inconsistencies.

CHAPTER WRAP-UP

Securing an interview is sometimes difficult, so reporters need persistence, especially on the telephone. When a source does allow an interview, the reporter should keep the interview as short as possible and hold to the point. The reporter also should maintain control despite obstacles the source might put up, including inconsistencies and outright lies. In the writing the reporter has to draw color from the interview situation and the words of the source. But the reporter ought to stay out of the written picture and keep the focus on the source.

STUDY QUESTIONS

1. How does a reporter go about getting an interview?

2. What do you do when a potential source is not available to you by telephone?

3. Where is the best place to conduct an interview?

4. What are closed-end questions and what sort of information do they elicit?

5. What are open-end questions and what is their value in an interview?

6. How do narrowing and broadening question sequences differ, and what are the advantages of each?

7. What is the process involved in quintamensional sequencing?

8. What is direct-focus questioning?

9. What goes on in a conversational interview?

10. When are confrontational questions appropriate?

11. How does one use background fact in an interview?

12. How does the interviewer elicit quotations?

PUTTING YOUR LEARNING TO WORK

EXERCISE 1   Arranging an Interview

Set up an interview with a local reporter. After the interview, ask the reporter to critique the session.

EXERCISE 2   Planning an Interview

Assume you have been assigned to interview the top administrator of your school on the person's accomplishments in office to date and goals for the future of the institution. Plan the interview on paper. In the plan, cover the following:

+ The purpose for the interview—the type of story you want to result.

+ Determine where you can get the necessary background.

+ Devise the questions you want to ask, and put the questions in the order you believe will be most effective.

FOR FURTHER LEARNING

Oriana Fallaci. "Interview With History." Houghton Mifflin, 1976. Fallaci's interviews with 14 world political, religious, and military leaders are models of probing questioning and keen observation.

Ken Metzler. "Creative Interviewing." Prentice Hall, 1977. Metzler's is one of the best guides to interviewing on the market.

Hugh C. Sherwood. "The Journalistic Interview." Harper & Row, 1969.

Eugene J. Webb and Jerry R. Salancik. "The Interview, or The Only Wheel in Town." Journalism Monographs, No. 2, November 1966. Austin, Tex., 1966. Webb and Salancik have applied the methods and findings of social science to help journalists gather undistorted information in interviewing.

CHAPTER 17

CONDUCTING THE INTERVIEW

In this chapter you will learn:

+ In-person interviews are better than telephone interviews.

+ Making a good first impression can help the interviewer get the interview off to a good start.

+ Sources are sometimes difficult, but techniques for handling them exist.

+ The report of an interview can be enlivened with examples and quotes.

+ Some sources will want to review your copy before publication, and you will have to decide whether you should allow that.

+ Television and radio interviews require the skill to direct the conversation so it is both interesting and informative.

IN THE INTERVIEW

A. J. Liebling was one of this century's finest reporters. He covered war, boxing matches, political campaigns, and the operations of the press, and he wrote about all with equal facility. He revealed at least part of the reason for his success in a piece on interviewing that he wrote for the New Yorker, and young reporters (and not a few older ones) could learn a great deal from the very few words he put down about the technique of preparing for an interview: "I knew that I would have to document myself on his views, his past, and enough of his technical background and jargon to make him feel that I knew what he was talking about. The preparation is the same whether you are going to interview a diplomat, a jockey or an ichthyologist. From the man's past you learn what questions are likely to stimulate a response. After he gets going, you say just enough to let him know you appreciate what he is saying and to make him want to talk more."

In the same piece Liebling said that one of his best preparations came before an interview with the jockey Eddie Arcaro. Among other things, he learned that jockeys on American tracks kept their left stirrups longer than their right, so he asked Arcaro first, "How many holes longer do you keep your left stirrup than your right?" Arcaro picked up the conversation at that point and galloped with it. Liebling was able to get in only about a dozen words, but after about an hour and a half Arcaro said, "I can see you've been around riders a lot." Liebling's question had given Arcaro confidence in him as an interviewer and that put the jockey at ease. The result was a relaxed and rewarding interview.

CONDUCTING THE INTERVIEW

STUDY PREVIEW   Where you conduct an interview can affect it. Most interviews are best conducted in person, not on the telephone, and at a place where your source is comfortable and there are minimal distractions. Once you sit down with the source, you need to be able to direct the interview. And you need to be able to deal with inconsistencies and outright lies.

Telephone Interviews

The telephone is efficient and expedient for arranging interviews, seeking spot news for brief stories and confirming information. If a source is across the country, and if time and budget are tight, the telephone may be the only means to conduct an interview. Some sources are accessible only by phone. And in newsrooms employing only a few staffers, especially radio newsrooms, it is all but impossible to get out of the office, so the telephone is the only option.

For most depth interviewing, however, the telephone is inferior. The rapport between journalist and interviewee that makes for good interviewing is impossible to develop and nurture without in-person conversation. It is harder to establish trust with new sources. You can't read body language. Eye contact is impossible. Many journalists use the telephone only for simple querying, confirming details, and setting up face-to-face interviews.

Face-to-Face Interviews

A source usually will be more comfortable if the interview is held in the person's own surroundings, either at home, where the person will likely be more relaxed, or in the office, if distractions can be eliminated. Some reporters prefer the office for tough interviews. According to Sterling Green of the Associated Press, at a person's home "you have to be polite. You can't come on very strong. In his office—there is the place where you can talk to him in a business-like way."

If at all possible, you should avoid interviews in distracting situations. Lunch, for example, presents the awkwardness of handling a fork and pen at the same time, interruptions from a solicitous waiter or waitress, and the possibility of getting spinach caught in your front teeth.

The Associated Press' Saul Pett has another rule: "Keep your hands free at all times in interviews." Pett once interviewed President Lyndon Johnson, who began giving evidence for his assertions by shoving classified documents at Pett, then grabbing them back. Pett was a smoker, so he had cigarettes going during much of the interview, with an ashtray on the arm of his chair. He had also accepted a cup of coffee, which he had to balance. He finally spilled the coffee and dumped over the ashtray.

For depth interviewing, you may want to see your source in several environments. Journalists P. J. O'Rourke and Hunter Thompson both work hard to find their sources in places where they are relaxed and unguarded. O'Rourke wants "to tell the readers what these people tell each other at 10 o'clock when they've had 11 drinks." Thompson holds to the "theory that the truth is never told across a desk. Or during the 9 to 5 hours. Even on the telephone. I call people at night."

O'Rourke and Thompson are looking for color, insights and tips as part of a lengthy process for major pieces. They don't take notes in their hob-nobbing approach to truth-seeking. They have years of practice in which they did take notes, however, and until reporters have the practiced ability to rely on memory they should record what they have heard on paper or tape.

Setting Time Limits

Telephone interviews, obviously, should be brief—no more than 10 to 15 minutes. No one likes to sit for a long time with an ear sweating itself onto a receiver. If you anticipate an interview running longer, make an appointment.

How much time should you ask the source to set aside for a face-to-face interview? That depends on the type of story you are working on and the medium for which you are writing. For the daily story, probably no more than half an hour. That should be plenty of time to get the essentials that you need. Even if you are a television reporter, 30 minutes allows for the setting up and breaking down of equipment and a set of pertinent questions.

Reporters for newspapers and broadcasting stations putting together in-depth stories or documentaries will want to set aside longer blocks. An interview with a business person on international trade might take an hour. An interview with a school superintendent for a depth story on problems in the school district might last two or three hours.

Still more time is needed by reporters researching magazine pieces. Conductors of the Playboy interview feature get their subjects to commit as many as 40 hours, lasting over many months. The magazine's interview with Robert Redford took writer Larry DuBois two years, interviewing in bits and pieces.

Establishing a Tone

In meeting a source for the first time, remember that first impressions count. Experts on interpersonal communication say the first few seconds of a meeting, even before an introduction is completed, can be essential in establishing a tone for the interview, especially if the reporter does not know the source. A strong stride, head up, rib cage high, can set your momentum. Except for somber occasions, convey energy and excitement. A friendly smile says "I'm glad to be here." A firm handshake conveys warmth.

Keep notepads and pens tucked in pocket or purse. Pull them out later. Concentrate first on making an impression as a person, not as a reporter. If you cannot avoid carrying something, keep it in your left hand so you can shake hands with your right. Avoid holding anything in front of you. It can look like a shield.

Some reporters establish rapport by commenting on a picture on a person's wall or on a souvenir on the desk. Then they segue into the interview. That is especially helpful if the interview is likely to be a cordial one. If the subject is a difficult one for the source to deal with, many interviewers like to get down to business right away.

Handling Sources

On a news beat, reporters come to know personality quirks that flavor what their regular sources say. Yea-saying or nay-saying tendencies, for example, show themselves after just a few meetings. Beat reporters acquire a vast background against which to assess the accuracy and completeness of new information. With sources seen less frequently, journalists rely on homework to come to know new subjects and new interviewees. Whether the source is an old acquaintance or a stranger, here are a few helpful rules:

- Keep interviews short. You are busy. So are most sources.

- Be detached and neutral. The interview is for your source's views, not yours. Let the source talk.

- Interrupt only for clarification or to keep the interviewee on track.

- Confirm figures and comments that seem carefully worded, even if you are tape recording. Remember that machines can fail, and they often do so at critical moments.

Interview Conditions

Reporters like to identify their sources in their stories. That aids credibility. But reporters also like good stories, and some information is available to them only on condition that they don't use it or if they promise not to tell who their sources are. When a source says "I want this off the record" or "I've got some information for you, but only on condition that you won't use my name," what's a reporter to do?

First, both you and the source need to be aware of the terms. In the 1960s Alfred Friendly, then managing editor of the Washington Post, put labels on interviewing conditions:

- *On the Record.* This is what journalists prefer. Anything said may be quoted directly and attributed by name.

- *Off the Record.* Information offered off the record may be given so that a reporter will better understand a confusing or potentially harmful situation, or it may be intended to head off a damaging error that a source thinks a reporter might make if not informed. The information is not to be disseminated, even in conversation.

Those are the generally accepted definitions. In Washington, where politicians and journalists have a special, well-storied relationship, two other conditions sometimes come into play:

+ *On Background.* What's said may be quoted directly but the source cannot be identified. For example: "A source close to the governor said . . ."

+ *On Deep Background.* The source's information may be used but neither quoted nor attributed. As a result, the story must stand on the reporter's reputation alone when it's printed.

Outside of Washington, sources are likely to understand only "on the record" and "off the record." Even so, both reporter and source should be clear about how these terms are being used. The source should state any condition before giving information, so any interview is on the record until otherwise stated. A source cannot avoid attribution by trying to put something off the record after it has been uttered.

You don't have to accept information on condition. If a source wants to go off the record, you can reply that you are there for a story and that you need the comments on the record. You don't know what you might be missing, but neither can there be any misunderstanding. If a source insists on putting something off the record, you are committed to the condition even if you don't explicitly agree. Silence is tacit agreement. However, you ought to try to negotiate a source out of conditions right away. You can try again to change the person's mind later, but your chances are best at the outset. Sterling Green of the Associated Press said he always began interviews assuming that everything was to be on the record. During a background interview, he might ask if he could use a particularly apt quote and, he said, more often than not the source would give permission.

Fair play is essential. It is sometimes prudent, and necessary for continued good relations, to let a source "take back" a slip of the tongue, especially a source who is inexperienced in dealing with reporters. Peter Arnett, now with CNN, said that in his interviews with military officers during the Vietnam War he assumed they were speaking off the record. "I learned that most military people are just not conscious of being quoted, or they're unconscious of the impact of that quote because they see newspapers so infrequently," he said. Arnett's fair play technique was to tell an officer at the end of an interview that he would like to quote from what he had been told. Usually, he said, the officer would agree.

The Experienced Source

Marquette University journalism professor George Reedy, who had once served as news secretary to President Lyndon Johnson, was often sought out by reporters for his comments on political events. He was brilliant and articulate to begin with, but on a day when he might expect a call, one could hear him perfecting what he was going to say as he made his way down the long hallway to his office. He might stop to talk about the event to the switchboard operator, whose cubbyhole was just inside the entrance. A few steps beyond, he would have a somewhat more refined response for a faculty member. For another professor or a student, perhaps, he would have a more tightly edited version. By the time he reached his own office, his thought on the matter at hand had clarified and he had honed his comment to such an extent that no editor, print or broadcast, could resist it.

Politicians, performers and sports figures have faced the same questions so many times over the years that many have developed almost rote, and predictable, responses. When one says, "I'm glad you asked that question," you can be assured the person is glad because a well-practiced answer is at hand. The trick with such a person is to ask the usual questions, listen to the usual answers, then raise the interview to another level with different, more probing questions. Of course, to ask questions that move the interview beyond the pedestrian requires thorough research to know the questions that everyone else has asked and to know the person and the subject well enough to pose those that have not been asked.

OVERCOMING INTERVIEW PROBLEMS

STUDY PREVIEW   It should be obvious that people do not always communicate clearly with each other, even when they have the best of intentions. What's called "static" often interferes, even in face-to-face conversations. That's true also in the formal interview. No matter how skillful a reporter might be in asking questions and listening to answers, problems in communication can occur. It's up to the reporter to try to surmount them.

Inconsistencies

Going into an interview, journalists carry understandings of reality. The goal is to sharpen, correct and update those understandings. If a source's statements don't square with your understanding, you have to reconcile the problem, either on the spot or through further checking. You need to know if a source is trying to mislead you or is misinformed to begin with.

Discrepancies are not necessarily deceit. People are imprecise, even slovenly with spoken language. In a 30-minute interview, especially if it is relaxed, a source may be inconsistent countless times if words are taken literally, especially if the reporter and source are sitting down together for the first time. New to each other, they may not be on the same wavelength.

Literal inconsistency is a fact of life. As long as you are hearing what is meant as well as what is said, you don't have to square contradicting words. Eugene J. Webb and Jerry R. Salancik put it this way: "Literal interpretation is a shallow criterion of consistency. Accurate interpretation requires that the reporter heed the context as much as he attends the barebones statement."

When a discrepancy confuses you, ask. Ask too if you want a quotation. Words in print and on the air have to be precise. Asking for clarification can be done smoothly: "I'm not sure I followed you on that." The source almost always will recast the point, this time being more attentive to wording.

Some inconsistencies are conceptually consistent. A senator concerned with avoiding major war may favor U.S. intervention abroad when the risk of casualties is low but oppose involvement when the risk is higher. Although inconsistent in particulars, the senator is consistent to a broader principle. The literal inconsistency makes sense: "That was then, this is now." In the 1950s, civil rights leader Martin Luther King was called radical. Although his views remained largely the same, King was considered moderate in the 1960s. How so? On a scale of political positions, the extremes shifted from the mid 1950s to the late 1960s. King was near an extreme in his early work. By the late 1960s, when the militant Black Power movement emerged, King, although still true to his original principles, was no longer extreme.

Not all shifts can be explained ideologically. In political campaigns, some candidates shuck long-held positions overnight—a revealing expediency of the moment. When ideological loyalty extends only to doing what's necessary to win, serious questions can be raised journalistically about a candidate's principles.

Almost every fact can be checked. Corroborating new information, especially if it is dubious, is a standard safeguard against inaccuracy. In their Watergate reporting, Bob Woodward and Carl Bernstein used information only if they could confirm it with a second source. Sometimes more than two sources are needed.

You can corroborate within a single interview by asking the same question twice. Double-asking is less obvious through counter-stacked questions. Asked one way, the question requires a positive response. The second way, it requires a negative response. First question: "So you were 13 when you were converted to Christianity?" Later question: "It was in Jordan, when you were 14, that you became Christian?"

INTERVIEWING ON THE RUN. Reuters reporter Bernd Debusmann interviewed a captain of the Colombian narcotics police in the field near Miraflores. Reporters need to be prepared to conduct interviews in various locations, from plush offices to foxholes. (Bob Strong/Reuters/The Bettmann Archive)

Interview information can be corroborated with other information-seeking methods. If a source says new safety measures will prevent another tragic cave-in, you can visit the quarry to see for yourself. Observation would be your methodology for corroboration. Documents can help too. You might check invoices with safety equipment suppliers about recent quarry orders.

Sources on the Offensive

Sources who are being asked tough questions may try to divert the questioning, and in not so subtle ways. Oriana Fallaci said she found that "it became a game to reach the truth" in some interviews. Intimidation is one tactic sources use, sometimes so blatantly it throws a journalist off guard and gives the source the upper hand. Some sources try to buffalo reporters away from delicate areas.

Reporter: The Harvard tales you mentioned will make good reading, but I also must ask about what happened in History 420. Were you suspended because of plagiarism?

Source: I thought you were on my side, and now you ask a question like that.

Or:

Source: The Gazette wouldn't print that. You should know better than to ask.

Or:

Source: That question is rude. It is an invasion of privacy, and you are out of line asking.

Or:

Source: I've been in public life 36 years and I have talked with hundreds of journalists. None has been so uncouth as to ask that kind of question.

Intimidated, a novice journalist might shrivel, even apologize, and move to safer questions. That's unfortunate. If an important question is not answered or not even asked because the reporter feels intimidated, the audience loses.

How do you deal with challenges to your motive, your civility, and whether you know what you are doing? In preparing for an interview, identify sensitive areas. If you are unsure what is appropriate, talk with your editor or news director. Think through whether the sensitive questions are important for your audience. If you go ahead, develop backup questions so you are ready to follow through if your source attempts to intimidate you away from a subject.

Source: That's not important. Nobody cares about that.

Reporter: I know it's a subject that's difficult to address, senator, but it is a question that has to be asked.

Considering the trust people have in you by virtue of your position and responsibility, I must ask whether you cheated. Let me ask again: What's your explanation for what happened in History 420 in the Spring 1972 semester?

When a Source Lies

Nobody wants to be caught lying, so the more knowledgable you present yourself, the less likely a source will take a chance. As Webb and Salancik explain it: "The source who is considering lying must ask himself two questions: Can this statement really be checked? And, more important, is this reporter likely to check it? Since it is not probable that the reporter will check every statement, the adept reporter might occasionally check a statement and let it be known, subtly: 'You were really right on X. I talked to Y and Z. They didn't learn about it until a week later.' By such a tactic, the reporter demonstrates his thoroughness and competence and discourages deliberate distortion."

Educational psychologists Mark May and Hugh Hartshorne agree. They asked fifth graders to correct their own exams. Far more of the students erased wrong answers that were in pencil than those in ink. Changing an ink mark shows. Erasing a pencil mark doesn't. Except for the reckless, May and Hartshorne concluded, the decision to lie is preceded by calculating the risk of being caught.

Even so, sources occasionally lie, not just unwittingly or from perceptual weaknesses, but out and out lie. If a lie is at the heart of a story, you may have to confront the source. Washington reporter Jack Anderson recommends knowing the answers to tough questions before asking. If a source begins to lie, Anderson interrupts: "Now, wait a minute. Court testimony indicates . . . ," or "I have a document that says . . ." Knowing that Anderson has done his homework, the source quickly gets back on track.

Confrontation, however, has hazards. The reporter becomes an adversary, and that can color the rest of the interview. Also, if your homework hasn't been thorough, you risk the embarrassment of being wrong. In many situations, pushing a source into a corner can be pointless.

Journalist Hugh Sherwood recalls interviewing a surgeon on a malpractice suit. Talking generally, Sherwood asked whether the surgeon had ever been sued. Though Sherwood didn't intend to set the surgeon up, he already knew that a patient had sued a few weeks earlier. But promptly, the surgeon answered no. "It was one of those moments nobody likes," recalled Sherwood. "I knew he had lied. And he knew that I knew. Yet I did nothing. After a moment's hesitation, I passed on to another matter. The lie was not pivotal to the story."

Reflecting on the episode, Sherwood said "There can be no easy rule of thumb about what to do when a man lies. But if there were to be one, I would say that, in most cases, disregarding the lie is probably the wisest course. The reason is that if you call the man's bluff, you will immediately put him on the defensive. The rest of the interview is likely to be defensive, awkward and unproductive. Certainly the man who lies—and who is caught at it—will not want to be interviewed by the same person again."

If you decide the lie is on an important matter, and you are on a tight deadline, you have to follow up on the spot. If possible, however, let the lie ride a few days and then check back. Tell the source that you found a discrepancy in your notes and that you would like some clarification. That is a gentle approach, and you likely will be received graciously. The delayed follow-up helps preserve your source's dignity, and your audience is none the worse. Of course, you need to decide how to deal with the lie in the story, or whether to touch on it at all.

Caustic Interviews

Caustic approaches are as old as interviewing, the product of occasional caustic personalities. The caustic approach became standard in every journalist's repertoire in the adversarial 1970s, although a technique of choice for only a few. The approach can be insulting. At its worst, it has a prosecutorial quality. Sources are presumed guilty unless they can convince their journalistic inquisitors otherwise.

Not every source should be in a hot seat, and most journalists are uncomfortable with the caustic interview. It is, however, a mode for eliciting truths when other approaches don't work, though only a last resort.

When Your Mind Goes Blank

No matter how carefully you may have prepared for an interview, your mind may go blank at some critical point. That has happened to nearly every reporter. You are hearing what your source is saying, but when the source pauses for your next question, you are without words.

When that happens, all you usually need is a second or two to group your thoughts. To gain those few seconds, try repeating the last three or four words uttered by your source but put them in interrogative form.

Source: ... and as a result the building was in terrible shape.

Reporter: In terrible shape?

Source: Yes. The plaster was sagging from the walls, and fixtures had been torn from the pipes.

Almost always, the source will restate the last point, usually in different words. As the answer is being repeated and restated, you have gained valuable time to decide your next question. Your source, meanwhile, probably has given more detail and better stated the point.

Previewing Copy

Some sources want to see copy before it goes to print, but most news organizations do not provide drafts to sources. It is rarely done, and when it has been, publications have sometimes paid dearly. Playboy, for example, once allowed subjects of its interviews the right to approve publication after an interview was written, and some subjects edited their statements. The singer Bob Dylan objected so strenuously when he saw his words in print that the editors told him to redo his answers if he wished. Dylan did, and the magazine ran his rewritten version. Playboy has long since changed its policy and doesn't allow sources to look over the interview before it's published.

Pre-publication review, however, has its champions. Steve Weinberg, a freelance writer who was once executive director of the organization Investigative Reporters and Editors, has argued strongly for it. Weinberg put into four categories the objections journalists have to allowing their copy to be previewed. They worry that sources might "deny direct quotes or other information, thus censoring the story." They are concerned sources could pressure editors to kill the story ahead of publication. They fear sources might threaten a suit if they don't like what they read. Finally, many journalists consider pre-publication review unprofessional.

Weinberg dismisses those objections and argues for allowing sources to review copy. If a source objects to the quotes, the reporter should preview his notes or tape recordings, and if the source is right, the quotes should be changed. On the other hand, if the evidence confirms the quotes, there is no need to alter them. The objection that higher-ups might try to kill a story Weinberg describes as melodramatic and unfounded. If one did try to kill a story, he says, he would show his evidence and, if still pressured, would not work for the editor again. And he would broadcast the editor's cowardice.

As for fear of suits, Weinberg says, courts consistently throw out efforts at pre-publication censorship. He also suggests that someone who threatens a suit before publication might sue after publication, and "many judges and juries would be impressed that the reporter offered an opportunity to check accuracy."

Weinberg dismisses the question of professionalism by saying too many errors occur, as evidenced by the frequent corrections and clarifications newspapers print. The bottom line: Weinberg sees it as a journalist's ethical responsibility to be accurate, and in his view, "accuracy encompasses a great deal, including getting facts straight, quotations verbatim, paraphrases in proper form when eschewing exact quotes, and providing context." He argues that pre-publication review allows journalists to meet those aims while maintaining control over the story.

Even so, a reporter who is skittish about showing a complete story to a source might wish to check quotes and context with the person, especially if the reporter is at all concerned about the wording. That would allow the person to make statements more precise and to clarify, if need be.

Some publications make exceptions to non-review policies for important interviews or when a source will give significant information not otherwise available only if guaranteed the right of review. In such an instance, if the source insists on substantive changes after reviewing it, editors must decide whether to run the story. If it is run, the audience should be alerted that the story is in a form cleared by the source.

INTERVIEWS ON THE AIR

STUDY PREVIEW   The technology of radio and television allows the audience to hear for itself the words of sources, in their own accents and with their own style of speaking. But the technology imposes perhaps an even greater burden on interviewers. They must get microphone and camera, or microphone alone, to the scene of a news event, help the source cope with the strangeness of talking to an interviewer and a machine at the same time and, if a live interview, report, edit and publish the interview in plain view of the audience. In the end, interviewers have the job of making plain talk interesting and pertinent to great audiences.

Spot Interviews

Tune to almost any broadcast news report of a tragedy and you are likely to hear the "feel" question:

"You returned here to find your home destroyed by fire. How do you feel?"
"What did you feel when realized the plane was going to crash?"

The "how do you feel" question is not limited to tragedies, however. It's used whenever reporters are not adequately prepared for an interview. Think back to the CBS coverage of the 1994 Winter Olympics. How often did you hear reporters ask both winners and losers how they felt? The question was even asked by an NBC reporter of a defense attorney following the murder trial of 11 Branch Davidians.

STUDIO INTERVIEWING. Morning news show interviewers in New York City had a chance to talk to the city's new mayor, Rudolph Giuliani, the morning after his election. That did not allow the reporters much time to prepare, but those who asked questions beginning with "what," "when," "where," "how," and "why" got better answers than those who asked "feel" and "thoughts" questions.   (Malcolm Clarke/Wide World Photos)

The "feel" question's first cousin is the "thoughts" question, usually asked by sports reporters:

"What were your thoughts when you watched the ball go into the stands?"

"You grew up playing basketball in hand-me-down sneakers on an asphalt court in a public housing project and today you are the NBA's most valuable player. What are your thoughts?"

The questions are not only trite, they signal the audience that the interviewers are lazy, if not inept. The interviewers have not taken the time to think through more substantive questions. And the answers they get, more often than not, are strained and artificial.

Of far greater interest to the audience, and less certainly intrusive on the sensitivities of the source, would be responses to more specific questions, either open-end or closed-end:

+ "What caused the fire?"
+ "Where were you when it happened?"
+ "What was your greatest loss among your possessions?"
+ "When will you rebuild?"

In an interview with the survivor of a tragedy, ask:

+ "Tell me what was going on in the airplane?"
+ "What did you do?"
+ "What happened when the plane hit the ground?"

Even sports reporters can get more interesting, less predictable responses if they ask more specific questions.

+ "What did the manager say to you when you got back to the dugout?"
+ "How did your teammates respond?"
+ "When you talked to your mother after being named most valuable player, what did you say? What did she say to you?"

Depth Interviews

Depth interviews conducted at the station or in the source's home or office require the same amount and type of preparation as for a print interview. In addition, they demand that the interviewer make an extra effort to see to it that the source feels comfortable. The presence of a microphone, or cameras and microphone, floor crew fussing over mikes, perhaps a make-up person dabbing powder on a sweating forehead—all that can be unnerving for people who might be apprehensive about even a paper and pencil interview.

It is a good idea to try to take their minds off the hubbub by introducing them to members of the crew and answering technical questions they might have. It is sometimes well to explain the general subject, but do not let the source know the specific questions in advance. That can result in a stilted interview.

Dealing with the Scene Stealer

Inexperienced radio or television interviewers can fall into the trap of allowing sources to make speeches. Politicians and spokespersons for various organizations are particularly good at taking command of an interview. Many have taken courses taught by former broadcasters in how to present themselves on the air, take control of an interview and get out the message they wish to present and nothing more. The best way to deal with such individuals is to follow Mike Wallace's advice: "If you want a straight answer you simply have to be dogged. You must go after it and keep after it." And you do that by mastering the question-asking techniques spelled out here.

CHAPTER WRAP-UP

A reporter preparing to conduct an interview should have a purpose in conducting the interview and should develop a set of questions that will lead to fulfillment of that purpose. Preparation for the interview, the sorts of questions developed, depend upon the situation. Gathering spot news usually requires closed-end questions. Depth interviews require a mix of closed-end and open-end questions arranged in a variety of sequences that the reporter believes will best secure the greatest amount of information, the best quotes and the most rounded view of the person. The reporter must not be bound to a set of predetermined questions, but must learn to listen carefully and be flexible in response to the answers. Whether for print or for broadcast, the interview is best when it flows under the direction of the interviewer. Then, to use Mike Wallace's words, "if you do it well there is a moment of truth—a moment in that time period when your eye suddenly fixes on his and you are talking to each other."

STUDY QUESTIONS

1. Give the pros and cons of telephone interviews.
2. What are the categories that sources use to avoid attribution?
3. How does an interviewer deal with a source who takes the offensive?
4. How does an interviewer respond to inconsistencies in a source's responses?
5. How does an interviewer confront a source's lie?
6. How does one gather color for a report of an interview?
7. When is a caustic interview appropriate?
8. How does one respond to a source who wishes to review an interview story?
9. How do broadcast interviews differ from print interviews?
10. Why should interviewers avoid "feel" and "thoughts" questions?

PUTTING YOUR LEARNING TO WORK

EXERCISE 1   Evaluating Interview Types

Conduct a telephone interview with a source, then do a follow-up interview face to face with the person. Prepare a critique for your instructor in which you list your own reactions to each type of interview. What did you find were the advantages and disadvantages of each type?

EXERCISE 2   Interviewing Technique

Conduct an interview with a working journalist or with a journalism teacher. When it is over, ask the person to critique your technique with an eye to what you did well and what you could improve.

FOR FURTHER LEARNING

Michael J. Arlen. "The Interview." The New Yorker, 10 (November 1975), 141.

John Brady. "The Craft of Interviewing." Writer's Digest, 1976. Brady, a well-published writer, provides a readable handbook for interviewers.

LaRue W. Gilleland. "Simple Formula Proves Helpful to Interviewers," Journalism Educator, 26 No. 2 (Summer 1971), 19–20. Gilleland gives a more detailed explanation of his interviewing formula.

David Sanford. "The Lady of the Tapes." Esquire (June 1975), 102. A good profile of interviewer Oriana Fallaci.

Barbara Walters. "How to Talk With Practically Anybody About Practically Anything." Doubleday, 1970. An entertaining account by one of television's best-known interviewers.

CHAPTER 18

GATHERING NEWS WITH DOCUMENTS

In this chapter you will learn:

✦ Documents are an important although underrated source in gathering news.

✦ Directories and other reference documents are an everyday source of information for reporters.

✦ In a well-equipped newsroom reporters have access to crisscross directories, trade directories, maps and other documents.

✦ Many news organizations maintain libraries in which articles, scripts and other material are filed for reporters to consult.

✦ Local governments maintain birth, marriage and death documents that are essential sources for many stories.

✦ Documents can be flawed with omissions and statistical and textual errors, and they can be doctored.

✦ Federal and state laws require units of government to maintain documents and make them available to the public on demand.

A FIRE STORY

You are working alone in the radio station newsroom on a Sunday morning. While on the phone updating stories, you keep one ear on the scanner as it monitors high-frequency channels used by emergency agencies. The scanner locks on a police channel: "Three units to 1340 Woodlawn. Fire units en route."

Maybe it is worth a story, maybe not. You reach for the city directory, find Woodlawn Boulevard, move down the column to the 1300 block, and discover that 1340 is an apartment building. The scanner locks next on a fire department channel. There's a call for more units. It's a major fire.

You want to go to the scene, but your newscast schedule has you tied to the station. You know that the police and fire dispatchers don't know more than you've heard on the scanner. No use calling them yet. What do you do?

You check the city directory again. It lists 32 adults living at 1340 Woodlawn. You check to see what's next door and across the street. There, at 1337 Woodlawn, is Georgina Fulvey. You call. She gives you an eyewitness account, which you tape. You make calls to other neighbors, pick up details from the scanner, and put together a story for your next newscast.

Amid it all, you ring your news director at home. She decides to call in an off-duty reporter and send him to the fire for spot coverage.

Then, you go back to the city directory for more calls to neighbors for more eyewitness accounts. After the fire, you can use the city directory to find more people for reaction. City property records will give you the building owner's name. Fire department or fire marshal's reports will provide a damage estimate and conclusions that investigators drew about the fire's cause.

A key in getting this story was documentary sources: the city directory, property records, investigators' reports. They are among many document sources whose value you will learn in this chapter.

THE IMPORTANCE OF DOCUMENTS

STUDY PREVIEW   Documents like dictionaries and directories are an everyday tool for journalists. On the beat, specialized documents are valuable sources. In investigative projects, documents are the "paper trails" that reporters follow to track down and confirm information not otherwise available.

The News-Gathering Triad

News people gather information three ways: by interviewing, by observing and by using documents. Documents are so routinely used that many reporters don't even think of them as one leg of the news-gathering triad. Routine newsroom uses include consulting directories and reference books to check facts and confirm details.

Beat reporters, however, are highly conscious of the value of reports and other documentary sources. Many beat stories are built entirely around documents, some of them routine, others not.

Documents on the Beat

Farm reporters wait for state agencies to issue crop reports. The annual reports issued by corporations are essential to business reporters. These are periodic reports that are hard to miss.

Police reporters pick up story ideas from incident reports filled out by police. Many of these reports are routine, but some are explosive, like the 1972 burglary report in the District of Columbia that led to the Watergate scandal, which forced the resignation of Richard Nixon as president. Police reports were key evidence in the 1992 and 1993 trials in Los Angeles in which police officers were charged with using excessive force against Rodney King.

To be on top of court news, beat reporters regularly check for suits, complaints, motions and other documents filed by litigants. Trial evidence can include especially revealing documents, including financial statements, police documents, and other records not normally available.

A job of every beat reporter is to know what documents exist, when they come into existence, and how to go after them.

Campus beat reporter Jeremy LaCroix, of the student newspaper Winona Campus Life, knew that police had confiscated gambling records while investigating an embezzlement and that the district attorney was ready to introduce the records as evidence at the embezzler's trial. When the embezzler pleaded guilty, the evidence was no longer needed and the district attorney filed it away—until LaCroix asked for a copy. Under Minnesota law, such evidence becomes a public document. The board, as LaCroix suspected, listed everyone who had placed bets. His story started this way:

Several Winona State University bigwigs and leading townspeople bought spaces on an illegal gambling board that police confiscated in last fall's Warrior Club gambling scandal.

Police recently released the confiscated document at the request of Winona Campus Life.

The names of more than 18 university profs and administrators appear on the illegal 1990 World Series gambling board sponsored by the Warrior Club.

Among prominent campus people listed on the board:
- Jack Kane, university vice president for student affairs.
- Jerry Nauman, former men's basketball coach.
- Gary Grob, baseball coach.
- Jon Kosidowski, former assistant to university vice president Jack Kane.

Expense accounts are documents full of many potential stories for reporters who know where to go. At Northwestern University, Mark Mensheha of the Daily Northwestern had been tipped that dorm leaders splurged on a banquet with student funds. When the leaders filed for reimbursement, which was allowed under university rules, Mensheha was standing by to check the receipts. His story started:

Members of the outgoing Allison Hall government threw a party last month for successors at a posh Italian restaurant—and dormitory residents paid the $668 bill.

The meal at the Como Inn in Chicago, also attended by the residence hall staff, included veal sauteed in white wine and gourmet seafood gumbo.

The final dinner tab—minus the amount students paid for their own alcohol—came to $464.79.

An additional $203.31 was used for four taxi cabs and a van provided by the restaurant to transport the group, bringing the total cost of the evening to $668, according to receipts filed with the Student Organizations Finance Office.

The feast was part of an Allison welcoming tradition that has siphoned hundreds of dollars from dorm funds over the past three years.

While documents are widely used to gather news, their full potential for stories is seldom tapped. Reporters generally are more comfortable honing their interview and observation techniques than developing their abilities with documents.

Until recently, when reporters began using computers to delve into databases, working with documents was time-consuming, labor-intensive and tedious. Spending weeks with musky papers in the courthouse attic was not much fun and might not even generate a story. It was no wonder that reporters opted to go after stories by interviewing and observing instead.

Reporters with a complete repertoire of news-gathering skills are able to use the interview, observation and documents, and to move from one method to the other for a better story. Information from documents can lead to interview questions that otherwise would never be asked. Observation can raise issues that send a reporter into documents for background checks. Without a sense of the potential that documents hold, a reporter is hobbled and may not have the whole story.

Documents in Investigative Stories

Documents are especially important in investigative reporting, which goes after information that people are attempting to hide.

Los Angeles Times reporters went into Federal Election Commission records to pursue a hunch that the giant Disney entertainment company was donating more money to political campaigns than law permitted. Times reporters found that Disney was rounding up money from executives, their spouses and family members and giving it to candidates in a single bundle but reporting the donations to the Federal Election Commission as coming from the individuals.

Most of the individual donations were within legal limits, but the bundled total far exceeded the limits. Disney was circumventing the law, and the Times' document-based stories raised serious questions about whether election laws needed reform. Those questions had additional potency when the Times noted that Disney was benefiting from taxpayer-funded projects, including one that built a superhighway right to the parking lot of a Disney amusement park.

Documents were the key to the Times' Disney revelations. It was a story that the other two news-gathering methods, interviewing and observation, probably never would have uncovered. Disney executives would have had no interest in divulging what they were doing, and Federal Election Commission officials were unaware.

Documents are valuable also for personality profiles. Going through life, we all leave paper trails that a resourceful reporter can follow. Steve Weinberg, executive director of Investigative Reporters & Editors, a journalists' association, wrote in Washington Journalism Review: "When you are born, you leave a paper trail in the form of a birth certificate and hospital records. When you begin school, you leave a paper trail through enrolment records, report cards, yearbook items and the like. When you marry, you leave a paper trail in the form of a wedding license; when you divorce, your court file might include income tax returns, lists of your property and much more. When you buy or sell a house, the transactions are recorded at the county courthouse and the sales price is often determinable. When you die, the probate court file might contain details that you have kept secret your entire life. Every time you write a check or make a charge card purchase, you leave a paper trail. When you register to vote, obtain a driver's license, buy or sell a car or have an accident, you leave a paper trail."

Many significant stories have been built on documents that are not even public information, like income tax returns, life insurance policies and internal corporate memos.

Says Weinberg: "A journalist skillful at following paper trails can get almost any document if the document exists. It is not always easy, but it almost always is possible."

THE END OF THE PAPER TRAIL. Jeff Brazil and Steve Berry of the Orlando Sentinel won the 1993 Pulitzer Prize for document-based reporting that exposed a sheriff's drug squad for unjustly seizing $8 million from motorists stopped on suspicion of having drugs. Whether or not drugs were found, the motorists' cash was assumed to be drug money and confiscated. The sheriff's department spent the money on equipment that it could not buy with its regular budget.

DESKTOP REFERENCES

STUDY PREVIEW   Anyone who gathers and writes news, including news releases, is opening reference books all the time, checking spellings, looking up details, confirming statistics. Besides dictionaries, stylebooks and grammar books, essential desktop references include telephone directories.

Telephone Directories

Directories published by telephone companies have an outstanding record for accuracy. The spelling of names and addresses can be relied on.

Telephone books also are helpful because they cluster certain listings. All government agencies are listed together either in the white pages or a special section of blue pages. The same with schools.

Yellow pages list all businesses by category—like physicians, construction companies and newspapers—which can help reporters identify additional sources in a hurry. Yellow pages have cross-references to related categories, which also can lead you to additional sources.

With back issues of telephone books, you can track address changes. If a company disappears in one edition, that might be the year it moved out of town, was shut down by the law, met some other fate, or changed its name. The month and year of publication is always on the telephone book's cover and usually the spine.

Because most telephone books are published only once a year, some listings inevitably are out of date. Newcomers who miss a press deadline aren't listed for a year. Transients may never be listed.

Not everyone has a telephone. Those who don't are not listed. Some people with phones choose to remain unlisted in the interest of privacy.

In college towns, listings for many students may be out of date because they move so much. But most colleges publish directories listing names, adddresses, and telephone numbers of students, faculty and staff.

Some companies and institutions publish internal directories, which are essential not only for public relations people on the staff but also for reporters on special beats. An education reporter will have the local college phone books dog-eared in no time.

Some institutions update their phone books with great regularity. Many military posts, for example, issue a new edition every three months to try to keep up with frequent personnel transfers.

The Complete Desktop

Reporters use a number of reference books so often, they have desktop copies. Here are several frequently relied on:

Dictionary. The newsroom standard is Webster's New World Dictionary of the American Language, second college edition. This is the abridged version of Webster's Third New International Dictionary on which the AP style is based.

College editions have a section that lists every college and university in the country alphabetically. This is especially valuable in campus newsrooms for checking spelling and hometowns. A sample listing:

Rensselaer Polytechnic Institute, Troy, N.Y.; independent; founded 1824.

Stylebook. For newspapers, the standard is the Associated Press Stylebook and Libel Manual or the substantially similar United Press International Stylebook.

Stylebooks give preferences on abbreviations, capitalization and other usage questions. The AP and UPI stylebooks identify common trademarks that should be used with care, provide useful background, and offer writing tips.

For broadcast, most stations prefer the Associated Press Broadcast News Handbook or the UPI Broadcast Stylebook. Broadcast stylebooks include pronunciation guides.

Many news organizations maintain stylebook addendums on local usage.

Public relations staffs often have in-house stylebooks that augment AP–UPI style on corporate or institutional preferences.

Thesaurus. An edition of Roget's Thesaurus with alphabetical entries is a quick source for synonyms.

Grammar. Many news people are so comfortable with the grammar book that they picked up in high school that they keep it within arm's reach for their whole career. While good English is good English and a dog-eared grammar book from high school is just fine, several solid grammar books intended for mass media writing are available:

+ Thomas Berner's "Language Skills for Journalists."

+ E.L. Callihan's "Grammar for Journalists."

+ Lauren Kessler and Duncan McDonald's "When Words Collide."

Almanac. General almanacs like Information Please, Statistical Abstract of the United States, and World Almanac and Book of Facts collect data on a great range of facts—from presidential returns, to state flowers, to celebrity profiles. Editors of almanacs pride themselves on accuracy.

NEWSROOM REFERENCES

STUDY PREVIEW   News people, in both journalism and public relations, need directories and references books for quick information and data. Crisscross directories like the Polk and Cole city directories are especially important for news. So are government, industry and other directories.

City Directories

Without a city directory the radio reporter in the chapter-opening story probably would have known little more than fragmentary, perhaps misleading information from the scanner. With the directory, the reporter kept listeners current on a breaking story.

R.L. Polk & Co. of Detroit publishes directories for 1,400 cities, and Cole Publications of Lincoln, Neb., for about 100. Most are annual.

Polk and Cole gather information about individuals, organize it alphabetically by name in one section, by address in another section, and by telephone number in another.

The address and telephone sections are called "reverse directories" or "crisscross directories." Each section is printed on a different color paper for quick reference.

In the case of the imaginary Georgina Fulvey, who lived next door to the burning apartment building in the chapter-opening story, the directory listed her alphabetically under Fulvey in the white pages, by her address in the green pages under Woodlawn Boulevard in the 1300 block, and numerically in the blue pages by her telephone number.

In the alphabetical entries, city directories list the adults in every household, their address, telephone number, occupation and usually the employer.

While helpful, city directories don't have the reputation for accuracy of telephone directories. Polk and Cole gather their information from numerous sources, including door-to-door interviews, which are only as accurate as the person who answers the door. If no one answers, a card is left asking residents to send in information. Some do, some don't. At press time, if new data aren't available, the information from a previous edition may be left in—even if out of date.

Despite their deficiencies, city directories are essential—and they outdo telephone directories by including some unlisted numbers. If Polk or Cole run across an unlisted number in the gathering of data, it goes in.

Government Directories

Federal, state and many local governments publish fact-loaded directories.

The Congressional Directory contains biographical information on every member of the U.S. House and Senate, the President and cabinet members, and much of the federal judiciary, along with telephone numbers and the names of their primary staff members. Maps of congressional districts are included.

Every state has a directory of state office-holders with addresses and telephone numbers. Usually called "blue books," these are the state equivalent of the Congressional Directory.

Some blue books contain exhaustive descriptions of government agencies and biographies of elected state officials, judges and agency heads.

Trade Directories

Newsroom reference sources include directories on subjects that reporters write about frequently. In a college town, every newsroom has American Uni-

ALPHA SECTION

Bollinger Wm M & Violet A; retd h1420
Good Hope St ◎ 335-3743
Bollman Julie rptr Metro Entrtnmt
h654 S Spring ◎ 334-5049
Bollwerk Richd L & Angela G; elem dir Bd
of Educ h1537 Parksite Dr........ 334-0753

Messamaker Arth & Florece; retd h600
Lincoln St ◎ 334-1782

METRO ENTERTAINMENT MAGAZINE

**Steve Agan Editor, Monthly Magazine
on What's Hot Including Calendar
of Arts & Entertainment Events,
712 Washington St, Tel 335-1701**

Meuzelaar Isacc & Gwen; assoc pastor
Faith Christian Reformed Ch
h45 Brook Cir ◎ 335-9929

STREET GUIDE

**MAIN ST N — FROM 20 STATE ST
NORTH**
• ZIP CODE 16125
1528 Burris Myrtle L [9]+ ◎ 335-2403
1530 Ellis Oren O [9]+ ◎ 334-3789
Ellis Oren O Jr 334-3789
1532 Finney Sarah S [5] ◎ 334-8887
1534 Jones Robert A & Mary S [6] 335-7095
1535★Cook Marilyn S ◎
1536 BOB'S BAR-B-Q 334-1200
1540 McNiel Jim & Erin L. [2] 334-5260
1541★Sorenson Mchl S & Susan T ◎
335-1723
7 HOUSEHOLDS
1 BUSINESS

◎ = Homeowner
[1] = Years of residence
★ = New resident

TELEPHONE KEY

**DIAL 651 PLUS THE
FOLLOWING
FOUR DIGITS**
1197 Moore Margaret 1925 Good Hope
1198 Stoops Susan 1822 Dunklin
1199 Wirtmiller Ken 333 N Ellis
1200 ROBERT JONES REAL ESTATE
1534 Main St
1201 Raines Glenn 641 S Spring
1202 King Jeff Rt 1
1203 THOM MC AN 181 West Park Mall

BUSINESS DIRECTORY

INSURANCE

**A A A AUTOMOBILE CLUB OF
MISSOURI Richard Dennis Pres,
1903 Broadway St (63701)
Tels 334-3038, 1-800-922-7621
(52 Emps)**
Aetna Life & Casualty (Joe Meuller)
310 Broadway St (6 emps)........ 334-5086
Aetna Life & Casualty (Vince Rueseler)
113 S Broadview St (9 emps).... 334-5086
**ALLSTATE INSURANCE (Mark Warden)
2119 Broadway (63701), Business Tel
334-9993, Res Tel 335-5848 (10 Emps)
AMERICAN FAMILY INSURANCE Ken
Voepel President, Howard Aslinger
Vice-President, Tel 334-3921
2236 W Hunter Blvd (63701),
(21 Emps) (See Our Advertisement
This Classification)**
American Family Insurance Group 22256 W
Kingsway Dr (6 Emps)............. 335-5822
American Insurance Agency (Kevin A Govero)
718 Caruthers Ave (11 Emps)
.... 335-2329

AMERICAN INSURANCE AGENCY

Kevin A. Govero, CLU, ChFC
Mutual Funds, IRAs, Health Insurance,
Annuities, Limited Partnerships, Life Insurance,
Employee Benefits
Mon–Fri 8:00 AM–5:30 PM
718 Caruthers Ave.........................**335-2329**
Or...**335-5335**

CRISS-CROSS REFERENCES. R. L. Polk & Co., which publishes criss-cross directories for many cities, codes sections by color. White pages are alphabetical names, occupation of the resident, whether the resident is a homeowner, address, and telephone. Green pages are a block-by-block street guide, which includes how many years a resident has been at the address. For each block, the green pages tell how many households and businesses are in the block: residential, industrial, office. Blue pages list telephone numbers numerically. Yellow pages include the principal person at each business and the number of employees.   (Courtesy R. L. Polk & Co.)

versities and Colleges, which lists colleges alphabetically by state with narrative information and lots of data: tuition, enrollment, financial aid. It also is in every college public relations office.

In a military town would be references on military issues: chains of command, weapons systems, terminology. In areas where religion is often in the news, newsrooms have church references and directories.

Every field has directories. In newspaper work, for example, the standard is the Editor & Publisher International Year Book, which lists every newspaper in the United States and Canada. It includes key executives and editors, telephone numbers, and addresses. It also lists a variety of journalistic associations.

The Broadcasting/Cablecasting Yearbook is the equivalent to the E&P Yearbook.

Public relations people consult J.R. O'Dwyer's directory.

Other Newsroom Sources

Following are several references found in most newsrooms.

Maps. A world atlas contains maps and alphabetical listings of countries and cities. You can also check the spelling of geographic place names in the Columbia Lippincott Gazetteer. Other newsroom maps include current U.S. highway atlases and city, county and regional maps.

Wall maps have enough room to show secondary roads, trails, railroads, bus lines and power lines, all of which can help in figuring out what is happening where with breaking stories.

Street maps with mass transit routes are essential in urban areas.

Postal directory. Most news organizations use the spelling of the U.S. Postal Service for place names. The National Zip Code and Post Office Directory lists cities alphabetically by state and with zip code.

Histories. Good no-frills, single-volume references are Richard Morris' Encyclopedia of American History and William Langer's Encyclopedia of World History. A collection of state and local histories is a newsroom fixture too.

Encyclopedias. The Britannica has the greatest depth. Quicker references are World Book and the Americana.

Biographical references. Prominent people, past and present, are often in the news. Good references, available in libraries and well-stocked newsrooms, include the following:

+ Biography Index, a quarterly, lists biographical material in books and periodicals.

+ Current Biography is an annual volume with about 350 articles on living persons. Monthly editions are published too.

✦ Dictionary of American Biography covers distinguished Americans who have died.

✦ Webster's Biographical Dictionary offers brief biographies on 40,000 persons worldwide.

✦ Who's Who comes in many editions, each with biographical information on categories of prominent persons in specific fields or geographic areas. Among the editions are Who's Who in Commerce and Industry, Who's Who of American Women, Who's Who in Theater, and Who's Who in the United Nations.

NEWS MORGUES AND LIBRARIES

STUDY PREVIEW   News organizations file stories from previous issues and newscasts for reporters' background. These files, traditionally called "morgues," have expanded at some places into full-fledged in-house libraries. News people who know the potential of the morgue have a head start plumbing documents for all they're worth.

Clips

For many stories, reporters can build on what others have written before by checking "the clips," articles clipped or entered into a computer database from past issues and newscasts. Even modest news organizations have someone assigned to maintain clip files. Articles are filed by subject. Many broadcast stations similarly file every news script, and some index them for quick reference. At newspapers, these files of clips were dubbed "morgues" in the early days because they helped writers gather information for obituaries. The term stuck, although it is giving way to the more dignified "news library."

Some news organizations have full-time librarians who maintain the clip files or database and whose job includes searching for material that reporters need. News libraries can be elaborate, with subscriptions to news indexes, numerous reference sources and computer databanks.

Public relations shops maintain files of articles about their company or organization and related subjects. Some agencies and offices subscribe to a clip or on-line service that monitors hundreds of publications and major newscasts for items of interest and passes them on.

The Associated Press offers one of many electronic clip services, providing public relations and other clients every AP story on a specific industry. The stories are provided directly to clients' desktop computers or printers.

The AP clip service, and others like it, have many uses. At Thomas Jefferson University, media relations director Cindy Hoffman checks the AP medical wire half a dozen times a day: "We're always looking for news pegs for our physicians and scientists. AP Alert/Medical gives us up-to-the-minute information on medical news and helps us be first in pitching related story ideas and our medical experts to the media."

Indexes

Some morgues, with full-time staffs, maintain a full range of bound indexes to other newspapers and magazines.

The New York Times Index, most used of these indexes because of the Times' extensive national and international coverage, is published in annual volumes with biweekly updates. Every Times story is boiled down to a single sentence and indexed by subject.

Every entry tells when the article was published and the page and column, so a reporter can go to microfilms of back issues to find the full article. Here's how it works:

You want to find when Ross Perot first entered the 1992 presidential race. Under "Ross Perot" as a subject, the 1992 Times index has a one-sentence summary on every Times story on Perot in the year. Entries are chronological. It is easy to zip through them to find the date on which Perot announced his candidacy.

Other indexed newspapers include the Wall Street Journal. Since 1972, Bell & Howell has published a monthly index for the Chicago Tribune, Los Angeles Times, New Orleans Times-Picayune and the Washington Post.

Smaller news organizations with limited budgets may not subscribe to a news index, but reporters can always find the New York Times Index at the local library.

The most used index for articles in popular magazines is the Reader's Guide to Periodical Literature.

For books on subjects they're writing about, reporters can go to the Subject Guide to Books in Print. To read up on what a particular author has in print, Books in Print is the best. For quick orientations to books, there are several guides: the Book Review Index, Book Review Digest, and the New York Times Book Review Index.

The Gallup Poll Index provides survey results with analysis generated by the Gallup organization. More general is Public Opinion Quarterly.

The Nexis computer database indexes many newspapers. CD-ROM indexes to current periodicals are also available.

Photo Libraries

Newspaper, magazine and television morgues maintain files of photographs and video tapes that they have published or aired for re-using. In addition, news organizations buy photographs from companies in the business of filing photos on all kinds of subjects.

All Associated Press photographs go to an AP subsidiary, Wide World Photos. If a newspaper needs a photograph of an F–16 jet fighter belonging to the Saudi Arabian Air Force, Wide World can supply it. The files of Wide World and similar services, like Black Star and Time-Life, are so massive with so many photos of a subject that you might be asked if you would like a vertical, horizontal, aerial, head-on, profile, on-ground, refueling or combat shot.

DOCUMENTS FOR GENERAL ASSIGNMENT

STUDY PREVIEW Rookie reporters often are assigned to gather birth, marriage and death information. These "vital statistics," as they're called, can be helpful in major stories too, like personality profiles and investigative projects.

Vital Statistics

Editors like to assign obituaries to rookie reporters. If a name is misspelled, or a birthdate wrong, or a brother is listed as an uncle, the family is sure to call—and the editor knows right away that the rookie has a problem with accuracy and will need special watching during the six-month probationary period for new employees.

In most newsrooms, obituary information comes from mortuaries, which either call it in or drop off a form. Information from mortuaries usually is accurate but not necessarily complete. Families, for example, sometimes will instruct the mortician not to provide certain information, and morticians, who are hired by the family, almost invariably go along. Obituary writers, of course, may double-check the facts provided by mortuaries or go after greater detail, especially if the person was once prominent, which puts the death more into the category of spot news than routine obituary.

Without exception, a paper trail of public documents is maintained by governmental bodies on the major events in our lives—when we arrive in the world, when we marry, when we divorce. These are documents available to anybody who wants to look them up. Learning how to locate these documents, called "vital statistics," can also be invaluable in investigative reporting.

Birth and Adoption

Pat Robertson, a man of the cloth, decided to give up his television ministry and run for president in 1988. Even before the Iowa caucuses and the New Hampshire primary, the Wall Street Journal reported that Pat and Dede Robertson's oldest child had been conceived before they were married. The wedlock issue was presented in neither tawdry nor sensational terms. Deep in a full-page biographical story, part of an in-depth series profiling presidential aspirants, reporter David Schribman mentioned that the birth was 10 weeks after the Robertsons married.

The Journal's revelation was awkward for Robertson, who had usually been vague on the date of his marriage but who had consistently placed it earlier than it had in fact occurred. After the Journal story, there were questions, naturally, of misrepresentation, of hypocrisy, and of moral fiber. How did David Schribman run across the wedlock issue?

+ If you knew that Pat and Dede Robertson were married in Maryland, you could check their marriage license. It's on file in the state capital.

+ If you knew the state in which their oldest child was born, you could check the birth certificate.

+ If you knew neither state, nor the dates of marriage or birth, you could begin fishing in every state capital until you came up with the dates.

Birth certificates list the given name of the newborn; gender; race; parents' names, including the mother's given name; parents' address; the date and hour of the birth; the place of the birth; sometimes additional information like the number of siblings, the parents' occupations, whether the birth was the first for the mother; and medical details. The attending physician signs the certificate.

Birth certificates are filed locally and eventually forwarded to the state's central vital statistics repository, usually at the state capital.

Birth certificates weren't always required. New Mexico has state files back only to 1920, and Arkansas, Louisiana and Tennessee only to 1914. Earlier birth certificates may be available from county or local officials. Some people whose birth was not certified apply for a "delayed birth registration," perhaps to seek a passport, which creates a public record. Because these delayed records are maintained separately in some states, reporters have to ask specifically for them. For U.S. citizens born abroad, births are recorded with the State Department.

Not only are birth records helpful for a reporter working up a major personality profile or preparing for a lengthy interview, they can help track down sources. Said Jack Tobin, a veteran newspaper and magazine reporter and author of four biographies: "Birth records can lead us, as they have led me, to those few people who have left no other paper trail. A person may not drive, vote or own property, but if he was born in the United States, somebody has a record of it."

In investigative work, birth records can reveal a lot. As investigative reporters David Anderson and Peter Benjaminson put it: "Birth certificates come in handy when a reporter is following the nepotism trail and wishes to find out if a certain official has in-laws on the payroll. By obtaining the official's birth certificate, the reporter may find the official's mother's maiden name on it, and then be able to search for public payrollers with the same last name."

In some places, out of concern for individual privacy, record custodians acting on their own have become hesitant about allowing access to birth certificates. Inquirers may be asked their relationship to the subject. If they aren't related, they may be turned down, or some information, like parents' names, may be blacked out. Some record custodians are especially protective about records of illegitimate births. With 14 percent of the births in the United States out of wedlock in recent years, this promises to be a growing, sensitive issue in access to birth certificates.

Generally though, access is routinely available. Present yourself as if you have the right of access, and a clerk who might otherwise be hesitant to open the birth records to you may do so. In rare situations, it may take a call from an editor or news director, or your news organization's attorney, to see birth records, but usually it is more expeditious to avoid a high-level confrontation. A friendly smile and a good relationship with the custodians of the documents work wonders most of the time.

Adoption records are rarely available, even to an adult who was an adopted child. It's only through accident, or a cooperative records clerk, that reporters have access to them.

Marriage and Divorce

In the wedlock question about the Rev. and Mrs. Pat Robertson, the question was whether nine months of gestation had occurred between the date of marriage and the date of the couple's first-born son. The Wall Street Journal's David Schribman found the marriage date in the Robertsons' marriage certificate.

Marriage certificates list the full names of bride and groom, including nicknames, their address, their ages or dates of birth, and the date and place of the marriage. Whoever performed the marriage signs the documents, and so do witnesses of the ceremony—all of which are leads to further sources in preparing a major biographical or investigative piece. Marriage records are available in the county or city where the marriage occurred, although some states maintain central indexes.

Divorce and annulment documents are also filed in the county or city where the court approved the action. The documents include names, addresses, former addresses, ages, date and place of the divorce or annulment. Divorce cases once required the parties to state a reason why the court should dissolve the marriage, which sometimes yielded information that otherwise was hard to find.

Revelations could be significant. As they say, there can be no fury like a woman scorned, or a man either. When Sen. Herman Talmadge, D-Ga., was divorced in 1978 after 37 years of marriage, the record revealed kickbacks, hidden cash, and campaign contributions that ended up being used personally by the senator. Talmadge, a four-term senator on powerful Senate committees, ended up censured by his colleagues and losing his next race for reelection.

Citing assertions in divorce papers seldom involves a risk of libel because they are court documents, but reporters should approach them with skepticism. Many things can be said in the heat of a contested divorce that aren't true, or which are flawed, self-serving, or get-even reconstructions. Juicy documents don't necessarily make for truthful journalism.

Today, most states allow no-fault divorce, which means a request to divorce is routinely granted without either husband or wife being found wrong. Even so, divorce documents may contain important information.

If there is any dispute on property to be divided or a custody question with minor children, for example, the judge will ask for documents to help make a decision. Those documents, which are filed with the divorce court, list things like income, real estate, bank balances and corporate ownership.

Death Certificates

Many newspapers routinely include cause of death in obituaries, which necessitates occasional checking of vital statistics documents. Not always is the mortician who supplies obituary information as an agent for the family completely forthright, especially if the death was odious in some way or if the family is superstitious about discussing details. In most cases, in deference to the family, the issue isn't worth pressing. Sometimes, however, the cause of death is germane—and it's a matter of public record. Reporters need only check the death certificate, which is signed by a physician or coroner who attests to the cause of death.

Rarely is there a question about the accuracy of information on death certificates. When a death certificate is inaccurate, that generally is newsworthy in itself. Consider the case of Carl Erickson, former president of the giant Dayton's department store chain. In 1987, knowing he was dying, Erickson asked that his

AIDS infection not be reported. The Minneapolis Star Tribune, relying on a mortician's data sheet and not checking official documents, reported death due to cancer. Because cancer was the direct cause of death, the obituary was accurate, but the story was misleading because it failed to mention that AIDS was a factor. A gay newspaper accused the Star Tribune of a coverup. Said Tim Campbell, editor of the GLC Voice: "By hiding the fact that a former star president of Dayton Hudson Corp. died of AIDS, we help convince the rich that AIDS won't touch them."

Physicians and coroners who certify the cause of death are usually specific and forthright, but Erickson's physician attributed death to respiratory complications resulting from a malignancy of the lung. Under pressure after the GLC Voice revelations, AIDS specialist Frank Rhame acknowledged that he had bowed to Erickson's wishes not to report his AIDS condition and had listed death as respiratory failure due to malignancy. Because of the gay newspaper's reporting, Rhame then amended the certificate to state that Erickson had AIDS and that the fatal malignancy was a sort seldom seen except among AIDS sufferers.

Some thought the media attention that suddenly was focused on Erickson's death was unbecoming. Rhame, in fact, was incensed: "The prying constitutes an unseemly dance on this good man's grave." The point here, however, is not the issue of reporting controversial causes of death in great detail, but that death certificates contain potentially significant information.

A similar kind of ethics question can be raised about the Wall Street Journal revelations about Pat and Dede Robertson's first-born son. The issue, however, is not whether the inquiry into public documents is ethical. It is. The proper question is why the material is being used. On the question of whether to include such information, journalists disagree among themselves. But journalists cannot even consider the ethics of using information unless they first have the information that comes from vital statistics documents.

Beyond Vital Statistics

While vital statistics documents are important in news work, their value can be multiplied when tied to other documentary sources. In 1988, when Gary Hart was the leading Democratic presidential candidate, reporters were bothered by some murkiness in the Colorado senator's past. Once the family name had been Hartpence. Why now Hart? And just how old was the Democratic presidential hopeful? Hart himself was inconsistent.

Reporters not familiar with documents as sources might merely have asked Hart to reconcile the inconsistencies about his age that appeared in his own campaign literature. But reporter Brooks Jackson of the Wall Street Journal was not content merely to quote someone on a factual question. Jackson set out, through documents, to find out whether Hart was 47, as rumored, or 46, as his campaign literature said. Jackson consulted:

+ Personnel records with the U.S. Justice Department.

+ Denver Bar Association files, which had records on Hart as a lawyer.

+ A book that Hart had written.

+ The Colorado Division of Motor Vehicles, which had Hart's driver's license information.

+ Biographical information, not only that which originated with Hart but also information in the Congressional Directory and Who's Who in America.

+ Navy Reserve forms, because Hart was a reservist.

+ Transcripts from Bethany Nazarene College and Yale Divinity School, from which Hart held degrees.

+ Voter registration cards.

Jackson's conclusion, firm and incontrovertible: Hart was 47.

PROBLEMS WITH DOCUMENTS

STUDY PREVIEW   Despite their value as a source, documents are not infallible. Inevitably, human beings make unintended errors in creating documents. Some documents contain intentional falsifications. Many documents, including statistical databases, have inherent limitations because they raise questions they don't answer.

Accuracy

Computer people use the term "GIGO," short for "garbage in, garbage out." If something erroneous is entered in a program, the results will be flawed. It is the same with documents.

Statistical errors can occur when a clerk entering information misspells a name or gets a number wrong. Some documents contain intentionally false information. A property owner, for example, might underestimate the value of a construction project in an attempt to keep the property undervalued for tax purposes.

Textual errors in old articles pose special problems for reporters using documentary sources, whether they be clips of old articles in a newsroom morgue or statistics in database tables.

In most newsroom morgues, librarians post corrections beside the original stories. If old articles are stored electronically, some librarians erase the error and replace it with the correct information. Some errors, however, are missed. Only those errors that come to the attention of newsroom librarians are corrected. If no one complained about an error, or if an editor decided not to publish a correction, the error will live forever in the documents.

Some errors are regretted but deemed inconsequential by editors who are less concerned about getting it right for posterity than getting their next edition out. Under deadline, a wrong age or middle initial from the day before may seem hardly worth correcting.

To reduce the risk of propagating an error, check the next few issues to see if there was a correction. It's also good to check the letters column. Some publications, including Time and Newsweek, do not correct errors other than to print reader letters pointing out an error. Also, corroborate information with a second source that would not have picked up information from your first source.

One advantage of documents as sources is that, unlike human beings, they don't change their stories over time. Once a document is created, it exists for posterity. There is a possibility, however, that people have doctored documents after they were created. This happens rarely, but it is something that reporters should keep in mind.

Healthy skepticism can protect reporters from being duped by doctored documents or being misled by statistical or textual errors. Just as they do with information from interviews, reporters have to corroborate what they learn from documents. These questions can help:

- ✦ Does this information square with other findings?
- ✦ Does this information seem right in view of my personal experience?
- ✦ Could the person creating this document have had a motive to misrepresent the information? Or been misled? Or have made flawed assumptions?

Interpretation

Many documents tell what happened but not why. A statistical table might record a drastic increase in infant mortality, or a drop in charitable donations, or a decline in property tax revenue, but the numbers do not offer an explanation. It is up to the reporter to analyze the data and frame questions for follow-up interviews with knowledgable sources. With old data, the reporter may have to delve into historic commentaries to make sense of what the numbers say.

Some documents include explanations. News clips from the morgue may be especially good if they go beyond the "who," "what," "when" and "where" to develop the "why" and the "how." But even clips with explanations for what happened may not be all that a reporter needs for a full understanding. For alternate explanations:

✦ Check alternate sources for different explanations.

✦ Check follow-up coverage, especially for unfolding events in which new developments might have led to revised or new explanations.

✦ Check later issues for letters from readers offering contrasting interpretations. Whether you use information, and how you use it, can be shaped by the reception a story received.

Inherent Limitations

Databases don't chuckle. Statistics are dry and lifeless, which means that when reporters take information from databases they frequently seek liveliness and color from other sources to make an interesting story. Interviews can help bring dry facts to life. So can clips that contain anecdotes, examples, stories, quotations and details.

Some statistical information suggests questions for an interview. On historical issues, biographies and commentaries can yield background that puts numbers in perspective and makes the story more interesting.

Documents can be hard to figure out, especially those prepared by experts like lawyers or accountants. Memos among colleagues can have all kinds of in-house jargon and shorthand that makes no sense to an outsider. Even more obscure can be the notes that people write to themselves as reminders.

KNOWING OPEN-RECORD LAWS

STUDY PREVIEW   State and federal laws specifically allow public access to government documents, but there are exceptions. News people must know what is open and how to ask for it, and government public relations people must know how to comply with open-meeting requirements when they receive media requests.

Access Laws

Federal and state laws require government agencies to allow public access to agency records. These laws are designed to assure that the government is accountable to the people. For journalists, open-record laws are important in tracking policy decisions and actions which they cannot cover personally. Most investigative projects lean heavily on documents, which have long lives and, unlike human sources, do not forget or change their stories.

The federal Freedom of Information Act, called FOIA, which is pronounced FOY-yah, went on the books in 1966, specifying how people could request documents. Since 1974, when FOIA was beefed up, federal agencies have been required to list all their documents to help people identify what documents they are seeking and to help the agencies locate them quickly. Despite penalties for noncompliance, some agencies sometimes drag their feet and stretch FOIA's provision to keep sensitive documents off limits. Even so, the law was a landmark legislative commitment to government openness.

All 50 states have laws regarding public access to documents of the state, county and municipal governments, although the requirements vary from state to state. State open-record laws also apply to executive and administrative agencies, school districts and the courts. Most states have severe penalties, including fines and jail, for withholding records. Some states allow whoever brings a successful court action for records to be reimbursed for their attorney fees and related expenses.

Exceptions to Government Openness

Numerous exceptions have been written into federal and state openness legislation. Among the exceptions are:

+ Documents classified to protect national security.
+ Trade secrets and internal corporate information obtained on a confidential basis by the government.
+ Preliminary drafts of agency documents and working papers.
+ Those police files which, if disclosed, might jeopardize an investigation by tipping off guilty people or, worse, falsely incriminate innocent people.
+ Medical and personnel files whose confidentiality is necessary to protect individual privacy.

Most people concur that these are reasonable exceptions to open-records laws. Less accepted, however, is a growing trend in state legislatures to close many documents to protect the privacy of individuals. While well-intended, legislating privacy protection works against the free flow of information in the society and makes the journalist's job more difficult.

Campus Records

Journalists usually have had problems with access to college records. It became worse in 1974 when Congress passed the Family Educational Rights and Privacy Act, known as the Buckley Amendment, which restricted the release of students' "educational records" without their permission. College officials, wrapping themselves in the Buckley Amendment, closed campus records. As they saw the law, they could jeopardize federal funding by opening any records that included student names—not just grades but campus police and judicial records and all kinds of other documents.

Two significant court decisions have weakened the power of college administrators, at least at state schools, to keep the lid on so many records. A brief account of them follows.

Campus crime. To campus journalists, Traci Bauer is a hero who challenged campus secrecy at Southwest Missouri State University and won. In 1989, Bauer, editor of the Standard, a student newspaper, wanted to see a campus security report about a rape involving a student athlete. The university denied access, citing the Buckley Amendment and claiming the report was an "educational record" and therefore off limits. Two years later, federal appeals Judge Robert Clark swept away the university's case, saying that Congress never meant for campus crime reports to be secret. Further, he said, withholding the reports violated the First Amendment, which guarantees freedom of the press, and the Fifth Amendment, which guarantees due process.

To the university's argument about privacy, Judge Clark said: "An individual's enrollment at a state university should not entitle him or her to any greater privacy than members of the general public when the privacy interest relates to criminal investigation and incident reports." Certainly, he said, Congress never intended "to make university students a specially protected class of criminal suspects." Heeding the judge's unequivocal language, the university's regents voted 6-0 against appealing.

Campus discipline. In 1993, the Georgia Supreme Court ruled against the University of Georgia for sealing records on disciplinary proceedings. The student newspaper Red & Black wanted the records for stories on proceedings against two fraternities accused of hazing. Denied the records, the Red & Black sued. University regents responded that the records of the Organization Court, a campus judicial unit, were not open to the public because they were exempted under the Buckley Amendment. The state Supreme Court ruled, however, that the regents were being expansive beyond Congress' intent in applying the Buckley Amendment's term "educational records" to anything except records held by the registrar. In an eloquent rationale for openness, the court said: "Simply put, having delegated official responsibility and authority to the Organization Court, the defendants cannot hide behind meetings at which official action is taken on their behalf, and for which they are responsible, by contending that a group of students, none of whom are members of the Board of Regents, is taking that action. We are mindful that openness in sensitive proceedings sometimes is unpleasant, difficult and occasionally harmful. Nevertheless, the policy of this state is that the public's business must be open, not only to protect against potential abuse but also to maintain the public's confidence in its officials."

The Red & Black victory meant that Georgia's open-records law would govern access to campus judicial documents. Because Georgia law is similar to open-record laws in other states, campus administrators in other states, at least at state institutions, are under new pressure to soften their hardline position on records access.

Private colleges, however, remain an exception. As nongovernment entities, they are free to make their own rules, open-records laws notwithstanding.

CHAPTER WRAP-UP

Documents are such an everyday source of information in news work that many reporters do not even rate them with interviewing and observation as an important vehicle for gathering news. While common reference documents like telephone books may be taken for granted, other documentary sources are reporting tools that require sophisticated knowledge to use to full advantage. These include documents that beat reporters encounter in their specialized areas. Investigative reporters base much of their work on documents.

For all their value, documents can be flawed with omissions and errors. Sometimes people doctor documents. Statistical tables may yield valuable information for a story, but because they lack the color that makes a story interesting, reporters need to supplement their document research with the two other major ways to gather news: interviewing and observation.

Reporters have a great friend in federal and state laws that require government units to make their documents available to the public on demand. These access laws, however, allow some information to be sealed, and reporters must know the provisions of these laws to make good use of them.

STUDY QUESTIONS

1. Documents are only one of three methods that reporters use in gathering news. What are the other two?

2. How can documents lead to news stories that would not otherwise be told?

3. Telephone directories have voids that make them less than complete references for journalists. What are these voids, and how can journalists bridge those gaps?

4. List sources that many news organizations maintain in their libraries for reporters to consult for stories.

5. What are "vital statistics"? Where can they be found? How are vital statistics used in routine stories? In personality profiles? In investigative stories?

6. How can news reporters guard against the problems in relying on documents as sources?

7. While government documents generally are available to the public, reporters occasionally encounter problems obtaining access to them. Why? How can these access problems be addressed?

PUTTING YOUR LEARNING TO WORK

EXERCISE 1   Biographical Sources

What documentary sources would give you quick background on Attorney General Janet Reno? What was the date she assumed office? What is her age? What previous jobs impressed President Clinton to appoint her to head the U.S. Justice Department? Check your library for these sources: the New York Times Index, Nexis, the Congressional Directory.

EXERCISE 2   Geographical Sources

How can you find the postal zip code for St. Maries, Idaho? How can you find the place name for the 54629 zip code? In what county is St. Maries located? What is the county seat of that county? What rivers have their confluence at St. Maries? How is St. Maries pronounced? "Saint MAH-rees" or "Saint Mary's"?

Imagine you are assigned to get to St. Maries as fast as you can for a major, breaking story. Where is the nearest airport with scheduled airline service? How long would it take to travel by rental car from that airport to St. Maries? Could you charter a private airplane and get to St. Maries more quickly? Does St. Maries have an airport? Could today's weather be a problem getting there?

EXERCISE 3   Criss-Cross Directories

Find the name of a faculty member in your local telephone directory. Be sure it is a faculty member who lives in town. Now take that number and go to a criss-cross city directory to find more information about the faculty member. Who lives next door on each side? Across the street? Is a spouse listed? Are occupations listed?

EXERCISE 4   Vital Statistics

What are your vital statistics? Where would someone find your birth certificate on file? If you're married, where is your marriage certificate on file? If you're single, where is the marriage certificate of a relative on file? Where is the death certificate of someone in your family on file?

Check the social section in back issues of your local newspaper for the engagement announcement of someone who has since been married. Go to the county courthouse to look at the marriage certificate. Who performed the ceremony? What date? What are the full names of the parties? What friends and relatives are listed? Any addresses? This is all information that can be useful in identifying sources and tracking them down.

Check back issues of your local newspaper for a death in your community. Then go to the county courthouse to look at the death certificate. What was the cause of death? Who determined the cause of death? What was the full name of the deceased person? Where did the death occur? What other information is on the death certificate?

FOR FURTHER LEARNING

Kathleen Hansen and Jean Ward. "Quantity In, Quantity Out." Washington Journalism Review 7, No. 8 (August 1985): 53-55.

Celeste James. "Database Journalism: Facts and Figures Spark Compelling Stories." Gannetteer (April 1993): 6-7.

John Ullman and Jan Colbert, editors. "The Reporter's Handbook: An Investigative Guide to Documents and Techniques," 2d Edition. St. Martin's, 1991. This is a thorough reference to sources published under the auspices of Investigative Reporters and Editors.

Steve Weinberg. "The Paper Trail: How to Dig Into Documents." Washington Journalism Review, 7, No. 8 (August 1985): 10-11, 58.

CHAPTER 19

REPORTING WITH NEW TECHNOLOGIES

In this chapter you will learn:

+ The computer offers reporters and public relations people a powerful tool for gathering, organizing, analyzing and disseminating information.

+ Computer-assisted reporting can yield a great deal of information in an efficient manner, but it must go hand-in-glove with traditional reporting methods.

+ A wide array of databases, especially those maintained by the government, hold a rich repository of information.

+ Reporters using computers hooked into networks can locate new sources for interviews and conduct interviews on-line.

+ Television stations equipped with computer systems allow more rapid writing and editing of stories. Satellite transmission gives the capability to broadcast instantly from great distances.

+ Public relations people are using new technologies to gather information rapidly from diverse sources and communicate with employees, news outlets, and clients in an efficient and cost-effective way.

+ The network of networks that is the Internet promises to expand even further the database resources available to reporters.

+ Increasing numbers of newspapers are publishing via commercial on-line services. Others are setting up their own services.

+ Some newspapers are allying with cable and broadcast television to widen their audiences.

+ News organizations are looking to technologies such as CD-ROM as possible vehicles for information dissemination.

- Special interest groups on the Internet give communication professionals electronic forums in which to discuss issues and problems with their peers.

- Increased use of the new technologies in communication fields has given rise to new legal and ethical problems.

UNSAFE—AT COMPUTER SPEED

Reporters Paul D'Ambrosio and Rick Linsk of the Asbury Park Press had questions about New Jersey's bridges. What kind of condition were they in? Were they safe? Were they being adequately maintained?

For answers they turned to the National Bridge Inventory, a computer database holding the results of inspections of bridges 20 feet or longer. Information in the inventory allowed them to compile a list of bridges in their state that inspectors deemed structurally unsound.

List in hand, D'Ambrosio and Linsk pushed their chairs back from the computer and went on the road. They went to state and county offices and examined inspection reports. The reports told them what the specific problems were and what inspectors estimated repairs would cost. They talked to engineers and inspectors about what they had found. Then they took a first-hand look at the bridges themselves. Among others, they saw "bridges with fractured foundations, one that had been struck by a train (but remained in use), and one that had state officials so scared they inspected it daily."

With all that information in front of them, D'Ambrosio and Linsk sat down at their word processors and wrote a story in which they were able to show readers in clear, well-documented detail that one of every six bridges in the state needed major repairs and that the cost to taxpayers would be about $4.8 billion.

The starting point for D'Ambrosio and Linsk, that database search, is what is being called computer-assisted reporting, or CAR. It's a powerful new form of information gathering that is being used increasingly by reporters at newspapers and radio and television stations, both large and small. But it is only one development in the electronic revolution that is taking place in journalism and mass communication. Newspapers are delivering information through on-line computer services. Television stations are going on-line, as are radio stations. Public relations people are gathering information for clients and delivering it via computer.

The technology can sometimes make the head swim, but technology is not what the electronic revolution is all about. As has been pointed out by Ralph L. Lowenstein, dean emeritus of the College of Journalism and Communications at the University of Florida, "It's about more news, more exchanges of opinion, more photographs, and more knowledge delivered in a timely fashion. . . . It's about press freedom. It's about multiplying the channels of information and giving everyone who reads the opportunity to chime in."

COMPUTER-ASSISTED REPORTING

STUDY PREVIEW   Computers are excellent tools for storing information and for retrieving and manipulating it. Reporters are finding that computer databases hold great varieties of information that can be retrieved for quick analysis. And computers networked to other computers serve to put reporters in touch with sources they might otherwise not even have known about.

The Tools

Between 1988 and 1994, stories generated through the use of the computer won Pulitzer Prizes. The ability to find and analyze public records has long been a fundamental journalistic skill. But it has been made easier with the coming of the personal computer. Reporters increasingly are using computers to dig out information from governmental databases and analyze it with spreadsheets and sophisticated statistical software. They have gotten other information out of their own newspapers' computerized morgues. They have conducted interviews via the Internet. In short, they have given the computer a place alongside other essential communication tools. But, as Rebecca Ross Albers wrote in the Newspaper Association of America magazine, "Computers don't make journalists' jobs easier or cut back on gruntwork; they do allow reporters to answer questions that couldn't otherwise be answered, find stories that might stay hidden, and add context that helps readers understand information."

It wasn't too many years ago that sports reporters traded in the typewriters they once lugged up to the press boxes of stadiums on Saturday afternoons for laptop computers. They still struggled under the weight of those early "portable" computers, but they found the burden eased when they were able to punch out their stories a little faster. And then, instead of having to dictate what they had just written, they could cradle the handset of the telephone in a coupler and send the story back to the newsroom in record time. Today, the laptop is as likely to belong to a city-side reporter as to a sports reporter. Putting it to use for computer-assisted reporting can be as simple as equipping it with a modem and linking it to the publication's mainframe or powering it with its own word processing, database, spreadsheet and communications software.

For much analysis, reporters are using desktop, or personal, computers. But since many government agencies transfer records from mainframe computers to magnetic tapes, that data must be transferred into a form that can be manipulated on the desktop computer. NineTrack Express, a software package developed by Pulitzer Prize-winning reporter Elliot Jaspin, serves that purpose. Once the data are transferred, they can be saved in spreadsheet or database form for analysis. For databases on CD-ROM (short for computer disk–read only memory), a CD-ROM drive is a necessary add-on.

Databases can be transported easily. In Connecticut, the Waterbury Republican-American's city hall reporter takes a laptop computer with basic databases to cover city meetings. As Christopher J. Feola, the newspaper's news systems editor, explained the process, the reporter can run an immediate check on people making pleadings before the city council or city commissions and boards. Did someone who has just gotten a concession on zoning from the mayor make a campaign contribution? A few keystrokes into a database and the information is on the screen—and can be in the reporter's story before deadline.

Republican-American reporters can also use their portables or desktop personal computers to take a quick look into standardized test scores at area schools, to tap into census data, or to pull up names of employees of area corporations, with their titles. That sort of information gives life to the routine seven-inch or eight-inch story about a budget or a school. And, as Feola says, because readers are most interested in that kind of story, it is crucial that reporters be able to write it before they undertake more ambitious projects. "If you don't understand how to organize a short story," Feola says, "you're sure to wander far afield when trying to put together a longer one."

In television newsrooms, as in the city rooms of newspapers, where battered typewriters once stood are the terminals of sophisticated computer systems. Denver's KUSA-TV is an excellent example. Every reporter and producer in the news department has a computer terminal on the desk, and whatever stories they are working on, they have news and information from four news services at their fingertips. They can access the Internet, on-line services and bulletin boards via modem, then copy text they find and paste it into their own stories.

Each of KUSA's six remote trucks is equipped with a laptop computer, so reporters in the field can write and edit their stories and send them to the station via modem. Terminals are at control room positions of the producer, associate producer, director, technical director and audio engineer. Tape operators in master control use terminals to track which tapes to load for playback. The system also allows for uploading of character generator displays—the written names of sources or other text material viewers see on the television screen. KUSA-TV may be one of the better-equipped television stations in the country. But other stations, especially in larger markets, are not far behind.

Probing Databases

The United States is a nation that loves to describe itself in numbers. Just glance at the box on the bottom left corner of each section of USA Today to see some of

infoPLUS. The Dayton Daily News polled readers to find out the topics they believe are most important to them. Then it began digging into databases to produce a daily "infoPLUS" page centering on one of those topics. The page combines computer-assisted reporting and state-of-the-art graphics. (Courtesy of Dayton Daily News) the varieties of statistics we have compiled about ourselves. We know how many of us exist, our sexes, our average ages, how much schooling we have had, how much money we make, and how much we spend; what kinds of cars we drive and the numbers of tickets we received for moving violations; how many dishwashers we operate; how many pounds of chocolate we ate last year; how many people were victimized—and in what ways—by criminals in any given time period, and how many people are serving time for those crimes; how many miles of roadway we traveled last year; how many pizzas we ate; how many books we read; and, probably, how many statistics we compiled. And that's just an infinitesimal part of the total.

All of those numbers are deep inside more or less available databases, like genies ready to be let loose with promises of content-rich stories that will enlighten the public—and reporters are going after them. At KHOU-TV in Houston, senior producer Hamilton Masters created and maintained a homicide database for Houston based on police reports. "That database has generated a number of stories," Masters said, "as well as given us a way to provide context in a story—how many murders in this area this year? In the last two years? Is a certain block extremely violent? That sort of thing."

The station has traced political contributions from contributors to candidates using computerized reports from PACs, as political action committees are usually called. "We've also seen how the names of PACs change, but the people behind them don't," Masters said. "Sometimes more than one committee has the same address, even the same chair."

Reporters for the Seattle Post-Intelligencer regularly dig into on-line court records of state superior courts and federal courts, according to Paul McElroy, the newspaper's systems editor. "We also dial into the local bankruptcy court, county hall of records and state bar association," McElroy says. "We're starting to use FedWorld and have peeked into Greenpeace's Environet, the Federal Reserve Board in San Francisco, and the FDA's BBS." Reporters at the Asbury Park Press mine FedWorld, other federal and state government bulletin boards, and a real estate database that yields information about every piece of real property in the state.

In Ohio, reporters and editors at the Dayton Daily News use commercial databases and databases of their own making to produce a special themed page each weekday that focuses on issues readers have told the newspaper are important to them. The Metro section page, called "infoPlus," contains interesting statistics on the day's theme, richly illustrated with graphics. Additional material on the topic is available through the Daily News' audiotex system as well as through a fax-on-demand system. Kevin G. Riley, who coordinates the pages, has said that the infoPlus pages enhance the newspaper's computer-assisted reporting effort and make CAR "part of our daily product and culture."

Open almost any newspaper today and you are like to find a story that relies at least in part on a database search. Reporter Carolyn Tuft of the

Belleville News-Democrat was bothered by persistent rumors that police officers routinely stopped cars of African-Americans who drove into that Illinois city from neighboring East St. Louis. She put her computer to the task of analyzing the races of people given tickets. Data in hand, she could report that blacks did receive more tickets than whites. Two reporters for the Albuquerque Journal, Ed Asher and Lynn Bartels, examined drunk-driving statistics and penalties, and found that while their state led the nation in drunk-driving deaths per capita, the average fine for DUI was $17 and the average sentence only 7.5 days.

Even reporters for student newspapers are delving into databases. At the University of Florida, staff members of the Independent Florida Alligator downloaded information from police files to do a series of stories on a man convicted in the slayings of five students.

Kevin Corcoran, Indiana statehouse reporter for the Fort Wayne News-Sentinel, is a strong advocate of computer-assisted reporting. He used CAR methods to examine information in a database on gasoline octane testing by the Indiana Health Department. He sought to determine what effect, if any, the testing program was having on compliance, and which suppliers were selling gas that didn't meet state standards. A major finding, Corcoran said, was that drivers were "twice as likely to buy gas that exceeded the posted octane rating by seven-tenths of a point or more than to buy gas that fell below the posting by seven-tenths or more." He also was able to point to six distributors who were responsible for about 40 percent of the bad samples found.

Corcoran developed another story by using a spreadsheet "to sort through the state's unclaimed property database to find out how many unclaimed checks the state was holding for itself." His probe turned up the information that "about 90 checks made out to state agencies from the past five years' worth of unclaimed property were being held by the attorney general," Corcoran said. "Nobody from that office had bothered to notify the other state agencies about their unclaimed property."

In Oklahoma City, Griff Palmer, database editor of the Daily Oklahoman, used database software to sort through seven million financial transactions of the state's general fund. The search generated dozens of stories, revealing, among other things, instances of companies affiliated with state legislators doing business with the state government. In another search, Palmer compared a list of 600,000 people who had died against a list of Oklahoma's two million registered voters and found numerous instances in which individuals had cast ballots after they had died. He verified the data against county election board records and against the newspaper's own obituaries, then blew the dust off records in the archives to check election-day signatures against those in card files. "That's fundamental reporting legwork," says Palmer. "Try doing it in a week without computers."

In these and similar stories, what makes them journalistically sound is the emphasis on the information the audience gets. Reporting always comes first, ahead of the technology, as the reporters cited here have shown. As The Daily Oklahoman's Griff Palmer says, "Data analysis is not a journalistic be-all and end-all, any more than public records analysis is a journalistic be-all and end-all." The best reporters who are using CAR methods recognize that behind the numbers lie people, and that the numbers mean very little to readers or viewers unless they are humanized. The computer can provide data, but it is still up to the reporter to give the data meaning, put them in context and make them understandable for the audience—in people terms.

Interviewing by Computer

Free-lancer Brandon Judell set out to write an article for a Rodale publication on bread as a diet tool, and he wanted to know what medical experts thought. He hooked up with ProfNet, an Internet network operated by college and university public relations officers and designed to give reporters access to professors. Reporters making requests like Judell's to ProfNet provide a short heading telling what they need, what the story is about and the questions they want answered, their deadlines, and names, telephone numbers, and e-mail addresses. Judell found his sources, then started interviewing via his computer. When an American Eagle jetliner crashed near Raleigh, N.C., News and Observer reporter Mark Stencel signed onto CompuServe's aviation special interest group forum to locate American Eagle pilots to interview for a story.

Reporters like Judell and Stencel are finding that the computer, linked to an on-line service or the Internet, stands alongside the telephone as an interviewing tool. In fact, they find the numbers of sources available to them for interviews expand considerably when they go on-line. Stencel, for example, may browse the messages in a CompuServe forum "to find people who might be quotable." Then he uses the CompuServe membership directory to locate them.

Once a reporter has identified a source, other advantages soon become evident. The reporter doesn't have to play telephone tag with a source because e-mail gets to the person whether home or not, free-lancer Emory Daniels wrote in an Internet discussion. And written questions avoid misunderstandings. Daniels missed the spontaneity and the body language that occurs in face-to-face interviewing, but he did not find that a major disadvantage.

Another reporter, Nate Zelnick, says he has found on-line interviewing "in many ways superior to other forms." Interviewees have more time to think about how they want to respond, and "oftentimes, be quite eloquent in their responses." Still, Zelnick believes sources are "forthcoming in on-line dialogue." Like many other on-line interviewers, Zelnick tries to follow up by telephone or face-to-face. Free-lance writer Lea Bayers Rapp says the follow-up allows reporters to determine if sources "are legitimate and to get more in-depth information." The downside, according to Bayers Rapp, is the cost of using a commercial on-line service, which cuts into her profits.

Story Ideas for Computer-Assisted Reporting

For a workshop on computer-assisted reporting, Carol Napolitano, CAR coordinator at the Munster Times in Indiana, sent out an e-mail plea for stories for which reporters could use the computer to good advantage. She listed 50 of those for the workshop. Here is a selection of them to give you an idea of the kinds of work your computer can do to help you in your reporting.

- Rover? Fido? Fifi? Morris? Peanut? Pickles? What's the favorite name for dogs and cats in your area? Analyze animal licensing records and find out.
- Use a spreadsheet to sort and rank salaries for state, county or local workers. Who gets paid the most? Who gets paid the least? Did a ditch digger for public works make more than the mayor because of overtime? Take a look at job descriptions.
- Does your state or town have an employee doing an unusual job?
- Using annual state school reports in a database, analyze for differences in teachers' education and salaries and benefits among area school districts.
- Use local police statistics by zones to chart crime at malls over the holidays. What kind of crime is it and when and where does it happen?
- Create a database documenting every homicide in your town or region. Include vital statistics on the victims and the suspects and data on the weapons used, the times and places of the killings, whether gangs or drugs were involved, etc. Then do a piece on murder trends.
- Use U.S. Census income data to map out a story pinpointing the richest and poorest neighborhoods in town and determine per capita how much each is getting in city services.
- Track the demographics and geographic locations of people appointed to local boards by the mayor or governing body. Are they diverse? Do they truly represent the town in regard to gender, ethnicity, race and income?

COMPUTER-ASSISTED PUBLIC RELATIONS

STUDY PREVIEW   Like newspaper reporters, public relations professionals are using the computer as tool for digging information out of electronic databases speedily, without leaving the office. They also find that the computer and related electronic tools allow them to distribute information more efficiently.

- Use federal Equal Employment Opportunity Commission records (available on CD-ROM and based on the 1990 Census) to gather numbers of minorities in various professions in your county or state. Put it into a spreadsheet and compare data between professions and minority groups and their proportions to total population.
- Analyze the campaign finance data for local politicians to see who is influencing these decision-makers and why.
- Test students' geographic knowledge. With the cooperation of school districts, give students in your area a blank map of the United States and have them name the states. Then input the test results, students' grades, gender, etc., into a database and analyze. What state do kids know best? What state is least known? What are some of the weird answers you got?
- Get disciplinary data from your school districts—numbers of suspensions, detentions, expulsions, etc. Make sure the data include each student's age, grade, gender and race, as well as why they were disciplined. Look for inconsistent applications of discipline. Do males get expelled more frequently than females for the same offenses? Are minority students more harshly treated?
- Look at state traffic accident data for bicycle accidents to show when and where fatalities are most frequent, and whether bicycle riders were impaired by alcohol or drugs. Compare the results of accidents when bikers are not wearing helmets.
- Use state traffic accident data for your area to review drunk driving accidents on New Year's. Is it the most dangerous time to be on the road despite extra enforcement and publicity campaigns?
- Study state traffic accident data for crashes involving emergency vehicles—police cars, fire trucks, ambulances, etc. Are there trends in speed, companies or towns, or geographic locations?

Database Research

The uses of databases in public relations are many. Charles Pizzo, principal of the New Orleans firm PR PR, Inc., says it is important for him to "know a reporter's profile" before providing access to one of his clients. When an unknown reporter calls asking for an interview, Pizzo dips into the newspaper database in Nexis and searches for stories the reporter might have written and reads a sampling. Depending on the tone or the tenor of the articles, any biases he perceives, Pizzo recommends that his client either see the reporter immediately or take extra time to prepare for the interview.

Pizzo also probes databases when he has a story about a client but isn't sure how to shape it to interest editors. He looks at related stories to see how they have been played. That gives him "a broad picture of where the media industry's interest is" on the topic, and he find that enables him to put his information in the context of a trend.

The computer has also given rise to on-line clipping services. Such services once hired people to clip items physically from newspapers and magazines so that public relations firms could show clients where stories had been placed, the kinds of stories competitors had placed, and stories about their industries. A computer does that now. The AP, for example, offers a service called AP Alert, which gathers some 10,000 stories into a database each day and puts them into nine industry categories. Public relations clients get the stories at the same time newspaper members do. That allows the PR people to react to the news and to be prepared when reporters call. Similar databases exist for electronic clipping of radio, television and cable news.

Public relations people like Charles Pizzo can use these services to gather information printed or broadcast about their clients or material of interest to them. When Pizzo arrives at his office each morning, he can call up stories that have been clipped for him and within 15 or 20 minutes know everything that's been said about a client, the competition, and industry issues. Pizzo also subscribes to a service that transmits news releases so he can read releases sent out by unions his clients deal with. If he spots a potential problem, he can fax the copy to his client. Then they confer by telephone and prepare a response. "Then," says Pizzo, "when a television reporter calls later in the day, the company is ready."

Don't get the impression that the computer is a tool public relations people use to stymie or get a leg up on reporters. Rather, Pizzo says, a public relations person who is comfortable with the new technology is better able to respond to reporters' needs. He tells of a weekend when he got a call at home from a television reporter who needed some information about an industry and was having difficulty locating sources. Pizzo dialed his office computer, downloaded a file to his home computer, then sent it to the reporter via an on-line service. The reporter got his story, and Pizzo's client got a mention he might not otherwise have received.

Electronic Newsletters

Increasing numbers of companies are putting employee newsletters on-line because of the speed with which they can reach employees and get feedback. Internal public relations staffs are writing and editing them. United Parcel Service's Martin Welles, the company's internal communication supervisor in Louisiana, publishes Hub and Spoke on the company's computer network for more than 200 employees in the state and for his counterparts elsewhere in the country. He gathers information about recent events involving UPS and its competitors, then condenses it into two-sentence and three-sentence briefs that fill about two pages of a word-processing program or six e-mail pages. The newsletter goes out at one minute past midnight every Tuesday. Welles estimates 80 percent of the people it's sent to read it within 24 hours, and many respond with comments, compliments, or corrections almost immediately after. Following Welles' lead, UPS communication supervisors in Florida and Tennessee have set up similar systems in their states.

The Organization Communication Department of the Insurance Corporation of British Columbia in Canada publishes two electronic newsletters: Newswatch, which is all business, and Intercom, which focuses on personal items. Each comes out once a week for the company's 4,000 employees. The editors chose to write the newsletter in radio style, rather than newspaper style, as a way of seeking to communicate with just one person rather than a mass audience. Stories carry a telephone number for feedback.

AT&T Today sends a daily on-line newswire to more than 120,000 of that company's employees around the world. It includes information about the company generated by the media relations department, material carried in the media, stories about developments in telecommunication and related industries, and responses from readers.

Similarly, in-house bulletin boards are inexpensive and easy to set up, and they can reap public relations benefits. They allow employees, the general public, and reporters to get information about the company quickly via computer.

Desktop Publishing

Hard-copy newsletters from organizations large and small have multiplied since the development of desktop publishing software. Once stories are written, they can be typeset and laid out electronically with relative ease, then sent to a printer as camera-ready pages from a laser printer, on disk, or by telephone via modem.

Desktop publishing has also led to such ventures as Extra Extra, a daily newsletter published by Sandra Driggin for broadcasting- and cable-industry trade shows and conventions. Driggin, Editor Kathy Haley and Managing Editor Sharon Donovan, each living in different cities, have to confer frequently to plan their coverage of a convention. They found it useful to prepare some copy in advance, but since all have different computers with different operating systems, they had a problem with compatibility—one person's disk was not compatible with another's hardware. Mailing hard copy back and forth was cumbersome, slow, and expensive, so finally they all subscribed to an on-line service. Now they upload and download without a hitch.

At the convention site, Driggin hires a small staff of free-lancers who report on convention activities as they would those of a small city. They cover workshops and speeches, conduct interviews, and pare exhibitors' news releases, then return to a networked bank of Macintosh computers set up in a booth on the convention floor to write their stories, occasionally with curious conventioneers looking over their shoulders. When their copy is edited, Art Director Charles Bork lays out the newsletter's pages on a laptop computer and sends

THURSDAY, JANUARY 26, 1995 · NATPE · LAS VEGAS

EXTRA EXTRA DAILY

Interactive Challenge: Make TV Viewers Happy-Users

That new technologies are changing the tv business is no surprise. Still, the financial community and key players in the industry have been, at best, cautious in their approach to the info highway.

This year, NATPE focused on the interactive arena in three separate panels. And at a glance, it's clear that, while everyone knows something is happening out there, they're not sure how to make a profit from it.

The two different views of future communications met head-on at Tuesday morning's session, "The New Media Revolution." Moderator Josh Harris, president of Jupiter, a New York interactive production company, pushed home the point that the "PC is where the action is." Yet the one key element missing in the medium, he said, is the entertainment aspect.

Cliff Friedman of Bear Stearns then offered the Wall Street perspective. In a visual presentation, ironically

CONTINUED ON PAGE 15

Distribs Spar On Program Alliances

No waiting—call now. Syndicators are standing by. At yesterday's general session a bakers dozen of independent syndicators feistily faced off on the effects of alliances and the new weblets.

The pros and cons of station/syndicator alliances, which Worldvision's John Ryan termed a "double-edged sword," dominated much of the discussion. While Turner's Russ Barry believed that an alliance "gets better programming to the public," Multimedia's Bob Turner argued that alliances "clog up the pipeline for a season."

Noting that alliances have been around since tv began, Group W's Derk Zimmerman praised one key beneficial byproduct—the ability to develop a program for a specific time period—that extends beyond guaranteed clearances. But Rysher's Keith Samples questioned the potential benefits of management cooperation, arguing that "blind commitments, based on a business relation-

CONTINUED ON PAGE 5

Exhibit Posts Record Draw

It's the most crowded NATPE I've ever seen," said David Goodman, senior vp for domestic distribution at Saban Entertainment, who echoed the sentiments of many execs doing business in the Sands Expo Center this week. Goodman attributed the throngs to much bigger international participation.

Last year, NATPE set an attendance record with 11,650 registering for the Miami show. Of that, more than 1,500 came from countries other than the U.S. By Wednesday, that record was shattered with 15,622 registrants, of which 2,476 were international. This represents a 34 percent increase in attendance from last year.

EXTRA EXTRA. This newsletter covers activities at broadcasting and cable conventions and trade shows. It is written, edited and laid out in the booth area of the shows, sent to the printer via disk or fax modem, and delivered to convention-goers the next morning. An on-line version was published simultaneously on America Online during the 1995 convention of the National Association of Television Program Executives.

the finished product to a local printer. By the next morning, the 8½ × 11–inch, slick-papered publication is in the hands of exhibitors and others attending the convention. Depending on the size of the convention and the number of ads Driggin can sell, Extra Extra can run anywhere from a dozen to 50 pages.

Driggin moved into electronic publication when she took Extra Extra onto America Online during the 1995 convention of the National Association of Television Programming Executives in Las Vegas. Warner Bros., a major television and cable syndicator, produces a program called "Extra," and at the suggestion of Warner executives Driggin had staffers summarize the stories in each issue of Extra Extra during the five-day convention and upload them to AOL. She and her editors also devised a questionnaire to get the reactions of AOL users to television content, then published the results during the convention.

Fax

Facsimile, or "fax," is another technology embraced by public relations professionals. Fax was invented in 1842, and used by the Milwaukeee Journal and the New York Times to transmit newspapers in the 1930s. Not until the 1980s, however, was the technology developed to the point at which it could be used reliably and economically.

Both print and graphics can be arranged on an 8½ by 11–inch page for easy transmission. Or faxes can be sent directly from a computer on a writer's desk. A system called broadcast fax allows one document, such as a news release, to be sent to hundreds of radio and television stations at the same moment. Names and telephone numbers of the addressees can be stored in computer files and called up instantly, as can letterheads and photos. Those features have made the fax an ideal tool for distributing news releases.

Fax technology has also given rise to fax newsletters—tightly written publications, many of which are laid out in traditional newsletter format. Among these is CableFAX, a daily bulletin published by the Phillips/Maxwell Group of Potomac, Md., that contains information about developments in cable and related industries such as advertising. Political writer and commentator John Maginnis publishes a four-page newsletter, the Louisiana Political Fax Weekly, putting into it a variety of political and governmental policy information of interest to politicians, bureaucrats and businessmen. He writes it on his computer on Thursday afternoon, puts it into a two-column format using desktop publishing, then delivers it that night via fax modem from his computer to subscribers' computers or to their fax machines. The value of Maginnis' information to his 500 subscribers is not just its content but its immediacy. Using broadcast fax, he's able to "keep about one step ahead of the rumor curve," one of his subscribers told him.

An enhancement of broadcast fax is Blast Fax, developed by the news distribution service News USA. News releases for print are reformatted into scripts in broadcast style and sent to newsrooms across the country.

Fax On Demand provides information via fax to individuals who dial an 800 number to request it. An organization called Wall Street By Fax sends out financial information such as stock and mutual fund prices, recommendations of brokerage analysts, and company performance figures. All that is particularly useful to public relations people who want to measure the effect of a news release on the stock or bond market or on the people who trade on them.

Interactive Press Kits

Another new twist in the media relations area of public relations is the publishing of electronic brochures about products and services on floppy disks. More ambitious is the interactive press kit, or IPK, being used by record producers, especially Warner Bros., to help market musical groups and their albums. The IPK was born in 1993 when promoters of Billy Idol's "Cyberpunk" sent out a floppy disk with images and text along with more traditional materials. Not only can the diskettes carry printed information, including favorable comments from critics, but also song samples, original photographs and artwork.

Companies are also making IPKs available through their sites on commercial on-line services or the Internet. The result is what Tom Maurstad of the Dallas Morning News has called a "public kit." That's "a press kit to which the public has direct access without having to go through the filter of some actual press person or to pay collector's prices to vendors advertising in Goldmine magazine," Maurstad says. "This press-to-public transition serves as a testimonial to the much-hyped payoff of the computer-on-line phenomenon—wall-leveling access."

Electronic Tools as Means, Not Ends

Electronic tools enable public relations people to do their essential work more efficiently, effectively and economically. Among the benefits, as PR PR's Charles Pizzo notes, they speed his work, give him more accurate data to work with, and allow him to make better decisions and recommendations on the basis of information rather than instinct. Or, as free-lancer Betsy Wiesendanger wrote in Public Relations Journal, "The advantage . . . of technological advances is not that they replace people. Rather, they free practitioners to focus on the more complex components of a communications program: synthesis, evaluation and strategy."

COMPUTERIZED INFORMATION SOURCES

STUDY PREVIEW   Reporters have more information at their fingertips through computers than ever before. They have access to databases holding dictionaries and encyclopedias. They can even search the files of their own news organizations via computer.

The New Life in Morgues

A typical newspaper morgue once held a shelf of biographical dictionaries and gazetteers, files of photos marked with grease pencil, and yellowing columns of stories tucked away in kraft paper envelopes. At larger newspapers, librarians—often reporters or editors in a final pre-retirement job—were on staff to help locate the right envelope or check a reference book for a busy reporter. As newspapers have become computerized, they have not done away entirely with printed material. But they have entered their historical material into databases and updated it with today's news. They subscribe to on-line services that provide access to databases holding bibliographies and abstracts, full texts of articles and speeches, government publications, public records, personal information, and photographs and other images.

Today, newspaper morgues are usually called "news research departments," and librarians tend to be professionals as skilled in computer research techniques as in journalism. At its most elaborate, the news research department can be as extensive as the library the Gannett company maintains to service USA Today, USA Weekend, Sky Radio, Gannett News Service, the USA Today Information Center, and Gannett's corporate offices. Its 22 librarians also provide research services for reporters and editors at other Gannett newspapers and television stations. The USA Today-Gannett library is not typical of newspaper libraries, but a glance at its contents shows what reporters can expect to find at most newspapers today, though to lesser degree. It includes 5,200 books, articles from more than 100 newspapers and 200 magazines, a database of sources, and access to the most important on-line databases.

At another level is the Rochester Times-Union in New York. Four people make up the full-time staff of the library, which also serves a sibling publication, the Rochester Democrat and Chronicle. They oversee up-to-date reference books, periodicals, and on-line sources like DataTimes, Nexis and Dialog, and the newspapers' own Digital Collections electronic library, an archive that holds text, photos and graphics.

Smaller newspapers may have fewer resources and, perhaps, access to only one or two on-line services. The news research departments of larger newspapers generally fall somewhere between the Gannett library and that of the Rochester newspapers. But even a library with only one service contains vast amounts of information. And today's newspaper librarian is a reporter's willing, eager and well-equipped partner in the search for information.

Bibliographies and Abstracts

The information sources you would look for on the shelves of your college or university library to write a term paper are the same kinds of sources reporters and public relations professionals dig into in computer databases. The starting point for much research is a bibliography or an abstract. Bibliographies contain references to books and articles on particular subjects, listed in a bare-bones fashion with author, title, and where the article or book can be found. Abstracts offer that information plus summaries of the articles. Your school's library may have terminals where you can feed in one or more key words and get back a list of titles of related articles, a bibliography. If a title interests you, you can get a summary, an abstract, with just a keystroke or two.

Full-Text Databases

Having compiled a list of likely sources for a story, people conducting research can go to "full-text" databases for complete texts of articles or major speeches. Or they can go to one of those databases first with a few key words and get every article that holds those words.

Many of the most important reference books and directories are now available in database form, either on line or on CD-ROM. Every word in a computer database is indexed, so pulling out information can be accomplished much more easily than trying to ferret it out of a book's index.

Government Publications

The U.S. Government is the largest publisher in the country. Its presses turn out tremendous amounts of information every day, from presidential proclamations to the transcripts of congressional hearings to instructional booklets on canning fruits and vegetables. Much of that information is now available online. Government documents can be gotten from the Internet, from bulletin boards set up by government agencies, and through commercial databases.

Public Records

Closely related are databases holding public records of state and local governments. As you can imagine, the numbers of such databases are almost overwhelming. But among the most useful are records on motor vehicle registrations and driver's licenses, traffic violations, real estate transfers, and incorporations.

Personal Information

You and your classmates are probably listed in one or more databases yourself. Commercial vendors compile electronic databases from telephone books, city directories, credit reports, change of address forms filed at the post office, and the warranty cards you fill out when you buy a CD player or the cards you send in when subscribing to magazines. All are sources for information on people you might be writing about. But three words of caution: check it out. If you think only about the number of times you or your fellow students might have moved during a year, you have an idea of the problem of keeping personal databases current and, therefore, accurate.

Images

Databases holding images are also available. For graphic artists and desktop publishers, a treasury of clip art, drawings and photographs is at their fingertips, and repositories of images are growing every day.

Garbage In, Garbage Out

Unfortunately, what computer users long ago termed GIGO, for "garbage in, garbage out," exists in computerized journalism. Mistakes printed in the newspaper are fed into the computerized morgue, and corrections, no matter how timely, may not catch up with them in subsequent searches. The result is that misspellings of names, errors of fact, and misinterpretations can be perpetuated.

In doing research for their story on New Jersey's bridges, D'Ambrosio and Linsk found that some incorrect information had been entered into the National Bridge Inventory and some was out of date or incomplete. Sometimes when that happens, mistakes are magnified and take on a life of their own, especially when they are perpetuated in a large database like Nexis. Writing in American Journalism Review, Christopher J. Feola cited the case of former Gov. Richard Lamm of Colorado, who was quoted in the Denver Post as saying that the elderly "have a duty to die and get out of the way." The story was picked to be entered into Nexis. Unfortunately for Lamm and for subsequent Nexis users, Feola reports, the Post did not immediately provide adequate context for the statement, though it did print a correction the next day. Nevertheless, the quote continues to dog Lamm more than a decade later. Feola quotes Lamm as saying, "The corrections move by bicycle while the stories move at the speed of light."

To avoid garbage out, reporters are encouraged to school themselves on how databases are organized, know what they are looking for, and work with a skilled librarian. The librarian can help determine whether it's necessary to go on-line for information. If the decision is to go on-line, the librarian will know which database is most likely to hold the material and what the costs of a search are likely to be. The librarian knows when databases are updated so that the reporter doesn't go poking around in the same material time and again.

The librarian can also help verify the authenticity and accuracy of information retrieved in a search. That's important because reporters need to be as skeptical of a database as of any other source. Says the Raleigh News and Observer's Mark Stencel, "The key is to get multiple clips and look for discrepancies. Was a quote in an AP account a little different from a quote in the New York Times account? Double-check everything, as you would with any clip, and so on."

COMMERCIAL ON-LINE SERVICES

STUDY PREVIEW   A variety of commercial on-line computer database services is available to reporters. Some hold specialized databases, while others provide subscribers with databases and supplementary material. Some also provide access to the riches of the Internet.

Nexis

Among the best-known specialized database services is Nexis, a kind of computerized morgue that provides full-text access to many publications. Reporters and editors value it as a rich, though expensive, resource for research, along with its sibling service Lexis, a business and legal database. Nexis computers hold nearly four million pages of data and can yield hundreds of specific references in just seconds. "Few newspapers can function without it," says the News and Observer's Mark Stencel. "There is no greater on-line library on earth."

Bill McCloskey, director of media relations for BellSouth Corp., used Nexis when he was a reporter with AP. McCloskey calls it "better than a good morgue, especially if you have a librarian or someone else who can construct search strings to get you what you need and not what you don't need." Editor Gary Deckelnick of the Asbury Park Press says simply that use of Nexis and Lexis gives Press staffers "access to everything we need."

Dialog

Similar in scope to Nexis is Dialog, whose hundreds of files hold full texts of some magazines, newspapers, and scientific and technical journals; statistical and demographic information; and Who's Who and Standard & Poors business directories. DataTimes includes material from newspapers, wire services, the Dow Jones News Service, and directories published by Standard & Poors and Dun & Bradstreet.

Burrelle's Broadcast Database

Burrelle's Broadcast Database contains transcripts of news and public affairs programs of the major television networks, including talk shows like "Nightline." Baseline holds information about the world of entertainment, such as biographies of celebrities and movie rankings.

CompuServe

Among the on-line services with a broad content, CompuServe seems to lead the pack, with America Online, Delphi and Prodigy following close behind. All have a range of attractions beyond databases. Subscribers can read magazines and newspapers, news service reports, and scripts of broadcasting programs. They may be able to correspond with the journalists who staff those publications or, by enrolling in special interest groups, they can discuss topics ranging from professional issues to vacation travel. They can make airline reservations, buy and sell stocks and track their portfolios, and play games, if they wish. Each of these services offers much the same content, though in slightly different formats. Trying to compare them is like comparing Chevrolets, Fords and Plymouths—which is best comes down to a matter of personal preference.

Many journalists and public relations professionals like CompuServe for its research services and its wide variety of professional forums, or special interest groups, including groups for public relations professionals, broadcasters and journalists. In those forums, members post messages and responses on a wide range of topics, from technical aspects of their work to their ethical responsibilities.

On one occasion a professor, suspicious that a student's final project in a writing course had been plagiarized, sent out a general message to members of the journalism interest group asking if anyone recognized the topic and the way it was handled. A free-lancer wrote back that she not only recognized the story, she had written it.

America Online

Journalists describe America Online as a versatile service with a graphic approach that facilitates maneuvering around in it. AOL offers easy access to the Internet, including the World Wide Web. And because it has discussion areas devoted to special interest groups from aging to the environment, reporters can reach sources for almost any story they are working on. For detailed information, subscribers have access to databases such as Consumer Reports and Compton's Encyclopedia, and to image databases. They can also call up contents of a large number of publications. Among them are the Chicago Tribune, the San Jose Mercury News, the New York Times, and Time magazine. It's possible to make contact with reporters and editors for those publications and others, from The New Republic to Washington Week in Review to C-SPAN, and to see how readers and viewers react to what they read and see.

TIMESLINK. The Los Angeles Times went on line with TimesLink in the fall of 1994. It's available on Prodigy. From this screen for state and local news, subscribers can choose a great many options, from reading the top story of the day to checking the smog index. (Courtesy of the Los Angeles Times)

Delphi

Delphi has an excellent "on-ramp" to Internet databases. It also offers a gateway to Internet mail. Among its databases are Grolier's Encyclopedia, Kussmaul Encyclopedia, and Hollywood Hotline. It offers access to the St. Louis Post-Dispatch's PostLink and the Orange County Register's Register Online.

Prodigy

Prodigy provides the Atlanta Journal-Constitution, the Los Angeles Times, the Palm Beach Post of West Palm Beach, Florida, and newspapers in Richmond, Tampa and Winston-Salem. Its databases include the Academic American Encyclopedia, Consumer Reports, Events Online, and Magill's Survey of Cinema. Two main features are bright color graphics and a cache of advertisements.

THE RESOURCES OF CYBERSPACE

STUDY PREVIEW   Cyberspace is what William Gibson has called "a new universe, a parallel universe created and sustained by the world's computers and communications lines," and the Internet is its central artery. An evolving computer super network, a network of computer networks, the Internet enables people working at the keyboards of their computers to contact other people and to dig into computerized libraries and databases.

The Internet for Journalists

All that's needed for getting onto the Internet is a modem linked to a computer and Internet access through a commercial on-line system, a free-net system, or college or university system. Internet users can send and receive e-mail or gather electronically with people with similar interests to share what they know about a subject and seek what others know. Most important for reporters and public relations professionals, they can travel the Internet to plumb the riches of new information sources and to communicate with others anywhere around the globe at near-lightning speeds.

The Internet proved a boon to reporters at KHOU-TV when they were putting together a series of stories on automobile emission testing under the 1990 Clean Air Act. When testing began in Texas in 1995, it created a major protest, and the Texas Legislature tried to scrap the program. That would have put the state afoul of the Clean Air Act and might have led to the loss of federal funds.

Using Internet connections, senior producer Hamilton Masters was able to quickly "check the status of Texas bills through the legislature's server and check on bills in the new congress that might have an effect." He found that pending congressional action to amend the act might make the whole issue moot, a fact he was able to include in the story.

"That's one story on one day," Masters said. "We were able to broaden the scope of our story and put it into context. That makes any story better."

And while on that story Masters also located a bill introduced by a local congressman "to do away with the Employee Trip Reduction mandate in the Clean Air Act—an opportunity for a different story."

Masters has been able to cut his newsroom's Lexis/Nexis bill in half by using free Internet resources whenever possible, and he has found information on the net he could not find in Nexis. For example, he needed information on a Houston-area community from a copy of American Demographics magazine for a story he was producing for the station's Sunday morning program. Because the magazine is on-line, Masters was able to find it quickly and retrieve what he needed, and at minimum cost.

On-line News Groups in Communications Fields

Various discussion groups on the electronic highway have special interest to journalists and public relations people. Among them are these. Their Internet addresses are in parentheses:

- COPYEDITING-L allows copy editors discuss the fine points of their work. (listserv@cornell.edu)
- EDUPAGE keeps journalists current with current information on media issues. (listproc@ivory.educom.edu)
- FOI-L is discussion group for freedom of information issues. (listserv@suvm.syr.edu)
- IRE-L is maintained by the professional organization Investigative Reporters and Editors for discussion of investigative reporting. (listserv@mizzou1.missouri.edu)
- NEWSLIB is a group set up for news librarians, but journalists also dial in to learn about Internet resources. (listserv@gibbs.oit.unc.edu)
- NICAR-L is the online news group of the National Institute for Computer Assisted Reporting and is filled with discussion of CAR. (listserv@mizzou1.missouri.edu)
- NPPA-L is operated by the National Press Photographers Association runs for discussion of visual communications topics. (listserv@cmuvm.csv.cmich.edu) Another forum for visual communications is VISCOM. (listserv@templvm.bitnet)

Other journalists tell similar stories of traveling the Internet to locate material they might not otherwise been able to find, and material they might not otherwise have known existed.

Electronic Mail

While it has much to offer, most observers agree that the Internet is functioning primarily as a gigantic electronic post office for the transmission of e-mail. Persons signed on to a free or commercial account have e-mail addresses. They can receive mail at those addresses or send mail to others with e-mail addresses. So common is e-mail now that many people include their e-mail addresses on their business cards and on their stationery (used for "snail mail").

Listservs

Many travelers into cyberspace subscribe to special interest groups called listservs. A member who posts a message sends it to everyone else who has subscribed to the listserv by e-mail address. That person will receive all of the mes-

- ONLINE-NEWS focuses on newspaper technology (online-news-request@marketplace.com).
- PRFORUM deals with issues in public relations (listserv@indycms.iupui.edu).
- RADIO-2000 takes up ways in which the computer can be used in radio production (listserv@radio-online.com).
- RTVJ-L, sponsored by the Radio-TV News Directors Association, allows quick communication among the organization's members and encourages discussion of broadcast news issues (listproc@listserv.umt.edu).
- SPJ-L is operated by the Society of Professional Journalists to keep SPJ members up on the organization's activities and to provide a forum for discussing current isssues in journalism (listserv@psuvm.psu.edu).
- WRITER-L, moderated by freelance writer Jon Franklin, is the site of discussions about various types of journalistic writing (jonfrank@darkwing.uoregon.edu).

These and other special interest groups for journalists and persons in related communications fields are listed in "The Journalism List" compiled by John Makulowich. It can be obtained from CARR-L, a discussion group centering on the use of the data-gathering by computer. You can subscribe to CARR-L files by sending an e-mail request to listserv@ulkyvm.louisville.edu. For "The Journalism List," ask for get journ lists f=mail.

To subscribe to any of the forums, address a message to the subscription address but leave the subject line blank. Ask for the subscription in the body. For example, to join SPJ-L, in the message area type Subscribe SPJ-L Jane Doe, substituting your name for "Jane Doe," of course.

sages sent by other subscribers. A listserv provides those who enter an opportunity to discuss current issues, ask advice on professional problems, and seek information from one another.

Whatever lists you subscribe to, you will be signed on almost immediately and sent a welcome message that will contain information you'll find handy as a member, including ways to sign off temporarily or completely.

Usenet

Usenet, a world-wide conferencing system that links universities, government agencies, commercial organizations, and individual users, contains news groups that operate very much like topical bulletin boards. Individuals post messages and others go to the news group to read them. More news groups are popping up all the time, so it is impossible to say exactly how many are out there. A very rough estimate would be somewhere between 7,500 and 10,000. Reporters surfing through Usenet's news groups can find story ideas aplenty, and experts and amateurs to comment on just about any subject they might be writing about.

Telnet

The Internet allows people working at their desks at home or in an office to turn their computers into terminals for host computers at distant locations. That's done by telnetting, the process of connecting to a host computer by typing in the host's address. Once connected, a person can search databases on the host and download files.

Gopher

Gopher, which takes its name from the mascot for the University of Minnesota, where it originated, is a particularly useful application that allows easy interface among computers so that people can conduct searches of computer files at distant sites. It's menu-driven. One of its most attractive features for journalists is that allows them to enter libraries across the country and browse through their electronic card catalogues. Gopher won't pull a book off the shelf, but it will tell users how to get what they want electronically.

World Wide Web

The World Wide Web, sometimes called the Web or www, is similar to Gopher, but it based on hypertext, so all of the information is linked. An item on one hypertext page can point to another hypertext page, and the user can quickly move from item to item to find out more about a subject or about related subjects.

Wide Area Information Servers

Wide Area Information Servers, or WAIS, offers ways (as the acronym is pronounced) for searching Internet databases to find locations of specific information and, then, the information itself. In his book "The Whole Internet," computer expert Ed Krol describes WAIS databases as "private libraries devoted to a particular topic." A WAIS search on a topic will turn up the appropriate private library, then take you through the library to the books and articles that deal with the topic.

File Transfer Protocol

Files held in other computers can be downloaded to your own computer through a special file transfer protocol, or FTP. FTP permits downloading of text files, pictures and audio from remote computers and on a range of subjects. Using FTP, for example, you can get background on the space program from NASA, statistics on disease control from the World Health Organization, and climatological information from the University of Minnesota.

MEDIA MARRIAGES

STUDY PREVIEW   Newspapers across the country are embracing the electronic revolution. Some are going on-line as part of established services. Some are setting up their own on-line editions. Media conglomerates—companies that include newspapers, radio and television stations, and cable networks—are expanding and, in some cases, finding ways to unite their media agencies to the advantage of the consumer.

Print and the Computer

The most apparent connection between print and the computer has come as newspapers have gone on-line. The Chicago Tribune has a part ownership in America Online, and the Tribune's news, features and classified advertising can be accessed through the service. AOL subscribers can get not only the contents of the day's newspaper, they can also ask for additional information on some stories. They can discuss the contents of the Tribune with each other and with the newspaper's columnists and editors on special electronic message boards. They can get a wealth of other material—schedules of plays, movies and sporting events, for example. The San Jose Mercury News offers a similar range of up-to-the-minute content as part of Mercury Center on America Online. It has also developed a news library in which readers can search for information printed in the past. Other publications allied with America Online include the New York Times, Time, Atlantic Monthly, The New Republic, and Commerce Business Daily. The AP and ABC also offer up-to-the-minute news.

Newspapers that have allied with CompuServe include the Detroit Free Press, the Washington Post, the Gannett Westchester Suburban newspapers in White Plains, New York, and that group's Florida Today. The AP, United Press International, Reuters, and Dow Jones News Service are also available. The Los Angeles Times-Newsday New York, the Atlanta Journal-Constitution, and newspapers in West Palm Beach, Tampa and Winston-Salem have developed electronic editions for Prodigy.

Other publications have developed their own, independent on-line services that individuals can dial into via modem, usually for a monthly fee. The Albuquerque Tribune set up its Electronic Trib as early as 1990 to provide local news and material from the Scripps Howard News Service, most of which does not appear in the newspaper. Among other things, subscribers have been able to get names of people on the payroll of the public school system and names of people convicted of drunken driving, county extension service information, and guides to movies, concerts and libraries. The Electronic Trib also offers a wire package to other newspapers.

A newspaper strike in San Francisco in 1994 spawned two competing on-line newspapers. One was published by the strikers. The other was published by the struck newspapers, the Examiner and the Chronicle. For the newspapers, the strike accelerated a move to going on line.

A more recent entry is the Seattle Times Extra, billed as "a natural extension of the newspaper" by John A. Williams, executive vice president of the newspaper. The Times Extra has content beyond the stories that appear in the newspaper, from local news to business, sports and features. Readers can search classified ads, access a guide to movies, and read restaurant, wine and movie reviews. File libraries provide readers with information about transportation facilities, school districts, and government and community events. The service also includes on-line discussion groups and local and Internet e-mail.

When the Minneapolis Star Tribune began planning an electronic edition, the expectation was that immediacy would become more important as a news value. So reporters were asked "to file brief 'early version' stories on breaking news events," according to Steve Yelvington, editor of the Star Tribune Online. However, that did not bring about a major change in the way reporters operated, since much news for the Star Tribune, as for other newspapers, is not breaking news but self-generated stories. For the most part, reporters write for the newspaper, and the text of their print stories is made available for the electronic version. The service also makes available as-written copy from the Associated Press and other news services to which the newspaper subscribes.

Updating is rare, also, on the Los Angeles Times' TimesLink. Editors put up top stories at 8 p.m., then update them about 11:30 p.m., the newspaper's normal replate time. Updating is largely confined to major local stories, TimesLink editor Dan Jenkins reported. "Our emphasis will be on the type of analytical stories that The Times does so well," Jenkins said.

The Raleigh News and Observer looked into the future for technology and users when it began its NandO service. Like many other services, NandO offers the daily newspaper, classified ads, e-mail, games, a set of reference materials, a bulletin board, forums for discussion, and access to the Internet. What's unusual is that the service is focusing on third-graders. While adults can subscribe to the service, the newspaper is putting its efforts into appealing to the children and their teachers. "A decade from now their interests and enthusiasm will be driving the Info X-way, so we'd better understand what they want from a newspaper publishing company," says Bruce Siceloff, the newspaper's on-line editor.

All told, more than 25 local newspapers offer their own dial-up services. More than 30 others are available through on-line services. On-line versions of more than 30 U.S. newspapers can be accessed via the Internet, as can nearly 20 newspapers from more than a dozen other countries. At least 50 college and university journalism and mass communication programs publish on-line newspapers, from New York's Columbia University Spectator to the Daily Forty-Niner at California State University-Northridge, and from the University of Minnesota Daily to the University of Texas-Austin Daily Texan. Those are the figures as this text is being written. While you are reading the book, Internet users will undoubtedly be turning the electronic pages of even more newspapers, both foreign and domestic.

On-line newspaper services obviously differ from their hard-copy parents, as the comments from those involved show. But they are not replacements. In a publicity release for TimesLink, editor Dan Fisher said he sees the two as complementary. The newspaper has great advantages: "the way we like to read it, its portability, the serendipity of thumbing through it and finding things we didn't know we wanted to read until we saw them," Fisher said. But the on-line version might reach young people who "may not have the same reading habits that we have, and they're already getting information from a variety of different sources."

Newspaper people involved in setting up on-line services say they need to approach the new medium in a different way. TimesLink's Jenkins found, after 25 years as a newspaperman, that he had "to think more interactively and more visually. You have to think how you can best tell a story on a screen. You have to think about engaging people in different ways—you really have to engage them emotionally."

Print and CD-ROM

Another development on the horizon for media companies is information packed into the read-only memory of a compact disk, CD-ROM. This format is useful for computer-assisted reporting. Databases, especially government databases, can be found on CD-ROM, and more CD databases will be available in the future. Private concerns are offering telephone books, directories and business databases on CD-ROM.

CD-ROM is also being used as a news medium. Full text reports of the Associated Press, United Press International, Canadian Press and Kyodo News are being published by a Nashville company, CD-RE, Inc., on CD-ROM, primarily as a resource for libraries. A full six months of the Associated Press report, about 100,000 stories, can be put on one CD. Each word on each disk is indexed so that users have quick access to the information they are looking for.

Newsweek, owned by the Washington Post Company, is publishing stories from the magazine and the newspaper on compact discs. When the Chicago Tribune Company bought Compton's Multimedia Publishing Group, which publishes an interactive CD-ROM encyclopedia, some company executives began to think about how the newspaper also might present material on CD-ROM.

Broadcasting and CD-ROM

Broadcast newsrooms are adopting disk technology, though only to a limited extent. One use is storage. Hours of programming can be compressed and stored on a CD in much less space than would be required for the same amount of material on videotape. But developers are looking ultimately to CD-ROM technology that will integrate news production functions, from image capture to editing and playback. What broadcasters are looking for in CD-ROM technology, as in any technology, is how it will make their work more efficient so that they can better inform the public.

Print and Video

In the 1960s, the parent company of the Chicago Sun-Times and the now defunct Chicago Daily News owned a television station, WFLD, that provided viewers with news delivered by reporters from the Daily News newsroom. Reporters went to a desk in the corner and reported on the stories they had been covering. That linkage of newspaper and television came to an end after only a few years, but the idea did not die. A quarter of a century later, on Jan. 1, 1993, the Chicago Tribune began a 24-hour cable news operation, ChicagoLand Television News. CLTV provides 24-hour programming of news, features, sports and public affairs—doing locally what CNN does nationally, but with a crucial tie between the newspaper and the cable channel.

The main CLTV studio is in suburban Oak Brook, where one newsroom houses the newspaper's 25-member DuPage County news staff and CLTV's 50 employees. The two staffs work independently but cooperatively. They share news tips and they share information they have gathered.

CLTV also has a mini-studio in the fourth-floor newsroom in Tribune Tower on Michigan Avenue, staffed by two producers. The producers use the newspaper's reporters as sources for cable news. They help the reporters to prepare for question-and-answer sessions on television and to ready stories that the reporters themselves will broadcast. When CLTV producers get tips, they share them with newspaper staffers. A camera may look over the shoulder of a newspaper reporter during an interview with a news source and the tape later edited for presentation on CLTV. When the Tribune began publication of a new food section, CLTV developed a weekly television program based on it. Far from being competitors, Tribune and CLTV staffers are "people who act and work in concert," according to Mike Adams, CLTV's director of news and programming.

A similar operation was envisioned by the Boston Globe, which joined with New England Cable News to produce broadcasts by Globe staff members. Other communication organizations are undertaking projects that are somewhat less ambitious but nevertheless illustrate the intimate relationship that can exist among various media. Knight-Ridder's KR Video produces a nightly one-hour newscast that gives the audience a look at the next day's Philadelphia Inquirer. The New York Times features its reporters talking about each day's news on "New York Close-Up," broadcast each night on cable. The Charlotte Observer joined with WSOC-TV to poll voters on the issues they were concerned about. The newspaper produced in-depth stories on the findings throughout an election campaign, while the station used them for background.

These are only halting steps on the road to a multimedia future. But already communication companies are looking farther ahead. By the year 2000, for example, the New York Times plans to spend $1 billion or more each year buying up TV stations and cable networks and developing its own electronic products. And hardly a day goes by without news of some similar, if less costly, ventures.

It has been the practice at some television stations with sibling radio stations to have television reporters carry audiotape recorders while covering stories to capture audio for use in radio newscasts. In the late 1960s, United Press International gave its reporters audiotape recorders so they could prepare stories for the service's news wires and for its audio service. CLTV's Adams sees a day not too distant when technology will allow newspaper reporters to cover stories using small cameras that record images on disk that can be fed back to the newsroom on telephone lines and the stories being distributed in print and video forms and also via a computer service.

Audiotex

Audiotex is a sophisticated form of the telephone-answering machine which allows readers to get more information from the newspaper than it can publish. At the same time, newspapers can use audiotex to get feedback from readers on the stories they publish or get information from readers for stories. Callers dialing into the Kansas City Star's StarTouch can catch up on the latest news, obtain stock market quotes, get the latest ski conditions and pick up homework assignments from school. They may express their opinions on the news, and they are encouraged to leave news tips or story ideas. The Seattle Times Info-Line makes 1,200 categories of information available to callers. When the Spokane Spokesman-Review redesigned its pages, it invited readers to react via its audiotex Cityline. More than 400 people called to express their opinions.

During the commemoration of the 50th anniversary of D-Day, the Fort Wayne News-Sentinel put sound bites of 15 historic recordings on its CityLine system. Included were President Roosevelt's broadcast to the nation announcing the invasion and an eyewitness account of the shooting down of a German plane. The St. Paul Pioneer-Press put recordings from the Apollo 11 moon landing on its service. That newspaper also has a feature on its pages entitled Bulletin Board that imitates an on-line chat line but gets its content from calls and faxes from readers who share their insights and little stories of daily life in both prose and verse. Some 500 calls and faxes come in every day, and the best are used in the column. Raleigh News and Observer reporters do audio versions of their stories for distribution on its audiotex system.

Other News-Delivery Links

By its very nature, broadcasting is technology-intensive, but in recent years, the microphones, transmitters and antennas of the early days of radio have given

COMPUTERIZED CONVENTION. Working under the main camera platform at the Republican National Convention at Houston's Astrodome, Associated Press staff members use a computer to operate a digital electronic camera above them. New technologies make journalistic work more efficient so that those who use them can better inform the public.   (Marcy Nighswander/Wide World Photos)

way to television's portable cameras and satellite dishes. The best example of a news operation that has fully embraced new technologies is probably CNN. It gathers stories from cooperating local stations in the United States and from its 20 foreign bureaus via satellite—stories that have been shot on portable gear and edited electronically—and can rebroadcast them immediately. It isn't just for art's sake that a satellite is prominent in CNN's graphics.

But satellite delivery is not limited to broadcasting. USA Today is faxed via satellite from its headquarters in Washington to 31 printing plants throughout the United States, four-color graphics and all. The technology allows distribution of the newspaper throughout the country bright and early every morning.

Motorola is developing a service called NewsStream that delivers headlines from USA Today to pagers and portable computers. The company's NewsCard can download the same amount of news a reader can get from an average newspaper. The company is developing a device that will allow fans to get the scores of their favorite National Basketball Association teams, quarter by quarter, on a small, hand-held receiver. Plans called for the device to be good for three seasons, after which a fan would have to buy a new one.

The list of new tools for information gathering and delivery is a long one: cellular telephones, chip television cameras, electronic still cameras, radio and television delivery via the Internet, and convergences of various media. Indeed, even a visionary like Barry Diller has called our day "the apex of confusion in this technological evolution." But he encourages people to "plunge in, get confused, get frustrated . . . get curious about it, find a new track to develop, an application in your own work."

Preparing for the Future

What skills are you going to need to adapt to the new world of cyberspace and multimedia? The same skills needed in the old world of typewriters and blue pencils. CLTV's Mike Adams gives this advice: "Learn to report. Learn to ask questions. Learn to be perceptive. Learn to use the telephone. Learn to write. Learn to edit." Only after you have mastered those skills will you be ready to disseminate news and information in multimedia form.

SOME LEGAL AND ETHICAL QUESTIONS

STUDY PREVIEW   New legal and ethical questions have arisen with coming of electronic communication. The most apparent legal issue for journalists seems to swirl around copyright. But the potential for libel exists in cyberspace, just as it does in more conventional communication. Ethical questions center under the heading of respect for privacy.

Quoting Public Postings

Sources interviewed through direct contact—face-to-face, by telephone or by e-mail—expect that whatever they say might be quoted. The same is true of individuals who make statements at public meetings. But what of individuals who post comments on electronic bulletin boards, news groups, or the public areas of on-line services? Is everything they say fair game for reporters? Some on-line areas have stated rules that allow quoting without permission. Others forbid it. And out on the Internet, it's an ethical free-for-all. An extra knot in the tangle comes about because persons communicating via an electronic network don't always use their real names. That means a reporter can't always know whether a source is legitimate.

Another question centers on the use of material in postings that are addressed to someone else, even though the postings are made in public forums. Many journalists would agree that those can be quoted, with attribution, just as they would quote statements made at a public meeting. On the other hand, it is not fair practice to use names without attempting to notify the individuals.

The case of John Schwartz, a science writer for the Washington Post, illustrates the situation. One day he read in a public area a letter sent by a Yale professor to friends reporting that he had opened a letter bomb. Schwartz saw a good story in the letter and tried to contact the professor, without success. He used the letter anyway. Despite the fact that up to 20,000 people could have seen it, some readers took Schwartz to task for printing the letter without permission. Schwartz himself rightly justified his use of the material by the fact that it had been so public. The professor agreed.

Generally, the rule is the same no matter how news is gathered: verify your source and ask for a comment or for permission to quote what the person posted.

Opening Another Person's Mail

While an electronic mailbox may be more accessible than one nailed to the front door, it is no less an invasion of privacy to look into it. Writers as well as readers were outraged when they learned that a small group of reporters had read letters posted in Tonya Harding's electronic mailbox during the 1993 Winter Olympics. Some have tried to rationalize the episode by saying her password, her birthdate, was common knowledge and that hundreds of reporters had a peek at her mail. But the "everybody does it" attempt at justification doesn't wash, on-line or off. Certainly, it may not stand up in court, since the Electronic Communications Privacy Act of 1986 holds that electronic mail is as private as conventional telephone calls.

Copyright Infringement

When material is copyrighted, no one may reprint anything but brief excepts without permission except the holder of the copyright. For that reason, newspapers include in their databases only material produced by staff members and free-lance material for which they hold the copyright. News service stories do not appear in database versions of newspapers. Similarly, database vendors such as Nexis filter out wire service stories from newspaper files. In cyberspace, however, copying and redistribution of material, copyrighted or otherwise, is widespread. One Internet site once offered the lists of the Billboard Top 10 records and the Nielsen Top 10. Both were shut down because they were infringing copyright. Knight-Ridder-Tribune Information Services pulled columns by Dave Barry and Mike Royko from ClariNet, an electronic newspaper distributed on the Internet. Newspapers pay syndication fees for the columns. But the service found that on-line users were simply saving the columns with one set of keystrokes and forwarding them with another. That's a form of stealing, a practice that is both illegal and unethical.

Libel

Libel suits potentially are as much a threat in cyberspace as they are in traditional news work, though the courts are feeling their way in this area. In the first major case, a suit against CompuServe, a federal judge equated the on-line service with a library or bookstore and therefore ruled that it is not liable for users' defamatory statements. But that raised a further question about the liability of services that do police content.

The case of Brock Meeks, who publishes an Internet "newswire," Cyberwire Dispatch, might hold a clue to the way courts view the First Amendment rights of Internet users. Meeks criticized Suarez Corporation Industries in his electronic publication, and Suarez, rather than responding in the same arena, fired back with a libel suit. Whereas reporters for publications or broadcasting organizations normally have the company behind them when they are sued for libel, Meeks was alone in the courtroom. Fortunately, he was able to reach a settlement with Suarez that did not bankrupt him, but his legal bills topped $25,000. That's a chilling prospect for anyone. So the precautions any journalist would normally take to avoid libeling someone also apply in cyberspace.

CHAPTER WRAP-UP

Computers are essential tools for reporters for newspapers and broadcasting stations and for people working in public relations. They serve a variety of needs: gathering information, processing it, analyzing it and presenting it. They offer excellent opportunities for people working in journalism and public relations to provide the public with greater amounts of news and information, so that we can all live our lives better. At the same time, they will spawn legal and ethical problems that must be dealt with.

STUDY QUESTIONS

1. List some of the stories that have resulted from computer-assisted reporting. What types of stories lend themselves best to CAR?
2. What other reporting tools go hand-in-hand with CAR?
3. How are public relations professionals making use of the computer as a communication tool?
4. How do electronic newsletters differ from hard-copy newsletters?
5. What are the advantages of on-line and fax publication to publishers and readers?

6. What are the categories of sources available in computerized databases?

7. Explain why care must be taken in relying on material in computerized databases?

8. In general, what do on-line services provide that would be of value to journalists and public relations professionals?

9. What is the Internet? What does it offer journalists and public relations professionals?

10. Describe ways in which the lines between traditional media are blurring?

11. How do on-line newspapers differ from their hard-copy parents?

12. What sorts of print and television links are being forged?

13. Explain the major ethical concerns arising from on-line communication?

14. Why should libel be a concern of people who communicate on line?

PUTTING YOUR LEARNING TO WORK

EXERCISE 1   Computer-Assisted Research

Jenny Jones is editor of the university newspaper. She opens a discussion area on her university's e-mail network one day and notices a flurry of messages discussing grading policies in different departments. Writers argue that some named departments are more lenient in grading that others. Some name professors who, they say, grade more strictly or more easily. She decides a story may lie within the argument and assigns you and another reporter to work as a team to develop it.

✦ What university databases would you tap to provide the data?

✦ How would you organize it for analysis, and what type of software would you use?

✦ Would you contact those who wrote comments in the public discussion area or not? Why?

EXERCISE 2   Gathering Data

Using records available in a police database, do a story on crimes committed by students. What percentage of crimes in the off-campus community are committed by students? What kinds of crimes do they commit? How many students have been arrested and convicted? What campus disciplinary measures from do those convicted of crimes face?

EXERCISE 3   CAR Story Development

Develop a list of at least five other stories suitable for the campus newspaper that could be developed for greater reader understanding with the use of the computer.

EXERCISE 4   **Data Development**

You are head of a student team developing a strategic public relations plan for a local home for runaway teenagers. In what ways could your team use the computer in developing data to support the plan?

FOR FURTHER LEARNING

Christopher J. Feola. "The Nexis Nightmare." American Journalism Review, 16, No. 6 (July/August, 1994), pp. 38–42. In this article, Feola points out problems that can enter into Nexis and other databases and how those problems can go unresolved.

Martha FitzSimon and Edward C. Pease, editors. "The Virtual Newsroom: New Technologies Create a Newsroom Without Walls." "The Homestretch: New Politics, New Media, New Voters?" Freedom Forum Media Studies Center, 1992. This chapter is drawn from a survey on how reporters used computer-based technologies in covering the 1992 presidential campaign.

Ed Krol. "The Whole Internet User's Guide and Catalog." O'Reilly and Associates, 1992. This is a comprehensive guide to the ins and outs of the Internet, written for "those who want to use the network, but who don't want to become a professional networker in order to use it." The publication is also available on WWW (http://near-net.gnn.com/wic/newrescat.toc.html).

Tom Koch. "Journalism for the 21st Century: Online Information, Electronic Databases and the News." Praeger, 1991. As the title implies, this book details the array of new sources available to journalists and how they can make use of it.

Tracy LaQuey with Jeanne C. Ryer. "The Internet Companion: A Beginner's Guide to Global Networking." Addison-Wesley, 1993. While much less detailed than Krol's book, this is nevertheless a good primer for readers with little experience on the Internet.

Tim Miller. "Information, Please, and Fast—Reporting's Revolution: Data Bases." Washington Journalism Review, 5, No. 7 (September 1983): 51–53.

Philip Meyer. "New Precision Journalism." Indiana University Press, 1991. Meyer's book builds on his earlier "Precision Journalism" to take into account recent developments in tools and techniques of computer-assisted reporting.

Nora Paul. "Computer Assisted Research." The Poynter Institute, 1994. This booklet is written especially for journalists and is a worthwhile handbook for using this new research tool.

CHAPTER 20

USING YOUR POWERS OF OBSERVATION

In this chapter you will learn:

+ Eyewitness reporting has advantages over interviewing and reliance on documents as a news-gathering tool.

+ Observation is an information-gathering tool for both spot and depth stories.

+ Observation skills are essential for participatory and immersion journalism.

+ Reporters using participatory and immersion journalism choose their roles and vantages.

+ Observation reporting requires special note-taking attention to detail to make the story come alive.

+ Using all the senses helps reporters gather information for strong observation stories.

+ Documenting their experience is particularly difficult for reporters in participatory and immersion projects.

+ Observation is underutilized as a news-gathering tool.

AN AWOL SOLDIER

The Army was plagued by desertions in the 1890s—2,842 from a force of 22,000 in one year alone. Jefferson Barracks in St. Louis listed 300 AWOL soldiers. Why? That was a good journalistic question, and Frank Woodward, a St. Louis Post-Dispatch reporter, decided to find out.

Woodward enlisted in 1889, was assigned to Jefferson Barracks, and when he had his answers, he deserted to write his story.

Under the cover of a five-year enlistment, Woodward found recruits brutally mistreated, even tortured. A soldier who upset a sergeant could be sent to the guardhouse, where a favorite torture was to handcuff men behind their backs and then hang them up by their wrists. Sergeants were stealing food for the black market, leaving only scraps for recruits. Beatings were given for no reason. Extortion was rampant.

After deserting, Woodward did nothing to elude the Army. Knowing the number of deserters, Woodward probably didn't expect the Army to spend special energy tracking him down. But he was soon shackled and then court-martialed to Leavenworth. Even from prison, he kept writing.

Finally, President Benjamin Harrison ordered an investigation. Heads rolled. Several Jefferson Barracks sergeants lost rank. Rations were restored to Civil War levels. Living conditions were improved. Harassment eased.

At that point, the Army, embarrassed, was glad to be rid of Woodward. Seventy-six days after he had enlisted, he was discharged by special order. Within a year, he was pardoned.

As with many advanced journalistic projects in which reporters involve themselves in what they are reporting to get at information not otherwise available, Woodward had taken chances. He might have disappeared forever at the hands of abusive supervisors while undergoing training at Jefferson Barracks, especially if he had been found out. He might have been left full term in Leavenworth had his stories not raised the attention they did.

Frank Woodward's experience points out the tremendous opportunities for important stories by using observation as a news-gathering tool. It also points out some of the hazards. Beyond that, it raises a moral question that still divides journalists today: When, if ever, is it ethical for journalists to misrepresent themselves to get a story?

THE IMPORTANCE OF BEING THERE

STUDY PREVIEW   Although not always possible or practical, eyewitness reporting has advantages. It bypasses secondhand sources, who may not be trained observers. It also reduces reliance on records, which can be flawed and usually are late for breaking stories. Observation yields detail not otherwise possible.

Eyewitness Reporting

The world wanted to know what was going on aboard TWA Flight 847. Extremists had hijacked the plane outside Athens, flown back and forth from Beirut to Algiers, released some passengers, kept others, and killed an American passenger, then threw out his body in a brutal display of insensitivity.

Five days later, as the plane stood on the sweltering tarmac at Beirut, 40 people were still aboard. ABC reporter Charles Glass managed the first interview with the pilot, copilot and navigator, shouting questions up to the cockpit as hijackers held guns to them.

FIRST WITH THE STORY. The greatest story in the world doesn't do any good unless the reporter can get it back to the newsroom. ABC's Charles Glass, in Beirut in 1985, managed to interview the pilot of a hijacked airliner through the cockpit window, while hijackers held a gun to the pilot's head. It was an important exclusive, but competing networks, not wanting to be skunked, managed to delay the transmission of the interview from Beirut back to ABC headquarters in New York.   (ABC News/Wide World Photos)

It was a scoop. So envious were CBS and NBC that they denied ABC access to a satellite to transmit Glass report to New York unless they could air it too. That might have seemed petty of CBS and NBC, but that's how important "being there" is. Eyewitness reporting has credibility that is almost impossible to match because it's firsthand, not secondhand or thirdhand.

Being on scene, journalists:

◆ See for themselves, rather than rely on untrained sources who happened to be witnesses but whose observation skills are rough.

◆ Report quickly, rather than wait for documentary sources.

◆ Corral involved persons before they depart the scene.

◆ Head off coverups by anyone who might later put a distorted cast on what happened.

◆ Pick up detail to help readers and listeners see, hear, touch, smell and even taste what happened.

Seeking Revealing Detail

Listening and looking for revealing detail can help the reporter write a story that brings the audience closer to the news, almost as if they were participants.

CBS radio reporter Edward R. Murrow brought the battlefields of World War II Europe into American living rooms with his vivid descriptions. His picture of an air drop over Holland is a classic:

> There they go. Do you hear them shout? I can see their chutes going down now. Everyone clear. They're dropping just beside a little windmill near a church, hanging there very graceful. They seem to be completely relaxed like nothing so much as khaki dolls hanging beneath a green lamp shade.

Arthur Everett, long the Associated Press' pre-eminent trial reporter, suggests going beyond testimony for the tension and drama of the courtroom. Recalling the trial of Bobby Kennedy's assassin and the jury's imminent verdict, Everett said: "When the jury had decided Sirhan Sirhan's fate, chief defense attorney Grant Cooper, his voice quavering, tears in his eyes, told a reporter: 'I'll bet you five bucks it's death.' How can any writer better tell of a defense lawyer's anxiety, his fear, the hopelessness enveloping him."

The verdict was death.

Writing for the Senses

For centuries, novelists have used sensual detail to sweep readers into their stories. In news too, reporting that appeals to the audience's senses of sight, sound, smell, taste and touch can bring an event to life.

Pulitzer-winner Relman Morin gives this advice: "A news story should take the reader to the scene of the action so that he can see and feel and even smell what happened. You do this by piling up pertinent details, a facial expression, a tone of voice, a gesture. Generally it is possible to use color terms, a 'bright-red dress,' 'a blue-and-gold autumn morning,' words that help to evoke a visual image in the reader's mind."

Edward R. Murrow had a knack of painting word pictures for his radio audience. He had an eye for color and detail that made bare facts take life in the mind's eye of his listeners. During an air raid on London, for example, he described the scene around him:

> Here comes one of those big red buses around the corner. Double-deckers they are. Just a few lights on the top deck. In this blackness it looks very much like a ship that's passing in the night and you just see the port holes.

A few moments later he told listeners:

> Many searchlights come into action. You see them reach straight up into the sky and occasionally they catch a cloud and seem to splash on the bottom of it.

Take in what people wear. Did the woman wear a dark business suit? A flowing summery plum chemise? Note the surroundings. What color were the walls? What did the place feel like—crisp, damp, muggy, heavy? Where were the windows? Fans going? Triple storm panes? Oak wainscoting? Knotty-pine paneling?

By being there, reporters are able to transport their audience to the scene as they witnessed it.

Enhancing Detail

Besides adding richness to a story, observational detail enhances credibility. If a reporter is so observant as to get minute detail, then the reporter must have the big picture right too. Or at least such is the impression created in the audience's mind.

A Time magazine story on a retiring physics professor started off:

The short, 5-foot-4, white-haired professor perched on a small stool, his feet
hooked in the lower rung, his hands
extracting scrawled lecture notes from a
manila envelope.

Isidor Isaac Rabi (rhymes with Bobby)
gazed solidly up at his 30 selected students at Columbia University's tiered,
286-seat Pupin physics lecture hall.

The story is vivid and also credible. Readers know that only 30 students
were gathered in the huge lecture hall that could seat 286.

The irony of colorful detail is that it can enhance credibility even if inaccurate, as media commentator Otto Friedrich noted in stories about a spy
exchange in Newsweek which said a car was yellow, and in Time, which said it
was black.

From Newsweek:

One foggy morning in Berlin, a **yellow**
Mercedes from the Soviet zone drew up
at the tollgate at the Heerstrasse crossing
point.

From Time:

Shortly after 5 o'clock in the morning
a heavily shrouded **black** Mercedes
bearing license tags issued by the Allied
Control Commission in Germany rolled
quietly into the no-man's land between
the Western and Russian sectors of
Berlin.

Color and detail like "foggy morning," "yellow Mercedes," "heavily
shrouded black Mercedes" and "rolled quietly" helps the reader experience the
situation vicariously even if, ironically, some facts are wrong.

Details, of course, can clutter a story if they are chosen with no purpose and
incorporated clumsily.

Also on the down side, evocative news writing can delay telling the story.
An on-scene reporter doing live reports, for example, is more concerned with
conveying the latest developments than a newspaper or magazine reporter
who seeks to provide a distinctive account for people who already have heard
the live reports. The more in tune reporters are with their audience, the better
they can judge which details to include to tell the story better and to enhance
credibility—and which to leave out.

Choice of Vantage

Observation lets the reporter choose the vantage from which to watch events unfold. In contrast, reporters who interview to find out what happened are limited to the view that their sources had. A general who was at a rear headquarters, for example, may make for a good interview, but the general's vision, at headquarters, is itself limiting. The reporter on the scene has the option to go into the foxholes.

Every vantage has limitations, but when reporters use observation to gather information it is they who are choosing. And they can move among vantages. Covering a battle, for example, reporters can consider the view from the foxhole and from the ridge. They might hit the command post and the MASH unit too.

APPLICATIONS OF OBSERVATION

STUDY PREVIEW   Observation skills are important for spot news and depth news. A reporter attempting a personality profile without using observation as an information-gathering tool likely will have a flat story that misses detail that can bring dimension and color to the person being reported.

Part of a Reporter's Repertoire

In a breaking story, reporters put their observation skills to work reflexively, whether it is a play-by-play account of a football game, a political convention, or a disaster.

At the Lakehurst, N.J., aerodrome in 1937, Herbert Morrison of radio station WSL gave one of the most memorable on-scene reports in history, at least for the first few seconds.

Matter of factly, Morrison described the giant dirigible Hindenburg easing into port: "It is practically standing still now." Then, suddenly shouting, Morrison captured the sudden horror of what he was witnessing: "It bursts into flames! It's falling on the mooring mast! It's one of the worst catastrophes in the world!" Morrison then dissolved into incoherent sobbing.

A more experienced reporter might have been able to continue telling the story, but for the short period that Morrison was in control he was capturing the horror of what he was witnessing.

For spot news, social commentator Walter Lippmann recommended that reporters consider themselves a "fly on the wall." Unnoticed and not influenc-

BEING THERE. Reporters captured the horrible drama of the German dirigible Hindenburg going down in flames because they were there with pencils, cameras and microphones. "Being there" is essential. So are refined observation skills that help the audience experience what you as a reporter experience. These skills include using descriptive words that appeal to the audience's senses: color sound, scent, feel, shape, motion.   (The Bettmann Archive)

ing the event being reported, the journalist looks for details to tell what is happening to give an audience the feel of the event.

Observation for Depth Stories

Besides their potential for spot news, observation skills are important for depth stories. At the Beirut airport, ABC's Charles Glass was on a spot story. Two years later, Glass himself was seized by Beirut terrorists. Months later he escaped. Whenever Glass now writes of his experiences as a hostage, it is a depth, not spot story, but observation nonetheless is the basis of the story.

Covering the civil war in the former Yugoslavia in 1993, Blaine Harden of the Washington Post used observation to relate the horror. From a story datelined Sarajevo, Bosnia, consider these passages:

The old town's main market, normally splendid this time of year with fresh fruit and vegetables, today sold dried chicken, matches and paper napkins.

One enterprising man sold green onions from the trunk of his car and attracted a 50-deep line of customers.

A six-pack of tonic water sold for $30.

. . .

Isolated cars screech around the city, driving herky-jerky at high speed to elude snipers.

They run a slalom unique to Sarajevo, weaving around downed tram lines, potholes from artillery shells, smashed-up cars, burned-out buses, chunks of concrete, and an occasional corpse.

Many of these speeding cars carry four heavily armed fighters, some Serbs, some Muslims. A few carry journalists.

. . .

Down in the basement workshop of the Muslim High School, in a stuffy, odiferous room without windows, there are 12 children, two sick old women and 18 young adults scrunched together on dirty mattresses.

There is one flicking lantern.

The children cough and have diarrhea.

In personality profiles, observation can be as important as the quoted dialogue in revealing the person. In a Rolling Stone article on country singer Garth Brooks, it took Anthony Decurtis only a few sentences to establish the flavor of the man:

Garth Brooks is a regular at the Pancake Pantry on 21st Avenue in Nashville.

When he arrives for breakfast, the proprietor greets him at the door with a handshake, the waitress embraces him—"Ohhh, how are you, darlin'?"

She takes an order from his guest but doesn't require one from Garth.

With a twinkle in her eye, she says, "I know what he wants."

And when Garth orders a second round of hot chocolate to accompany his meal, she suggests a pitcher.

A pretty young woman, Tracie, comes over to ask for autographs for herself and her friend Kim, who writhes in shyness in a nearby table.

"I guess I'm the one with all the nerve," Tracie says, smiling.

After she leaves, an acquaintance at a table behind Garth leans over and asks about Garth's wife, Sandy, and their new daughter, Taylor Mayne Pearl, born last July.

Bruce Ingersoll of the Wall Street Journal used observation to help personify a story on President Clinton's plan to eliminate the U.S. Board of Tea Tasters with this introduction:

NEW YORK—Robert Dick takes tea every day at work.

He sniffs the aroma of a fresh-brewed cup, sips a spoonful into his mouth and swishes it about thoughtfully.

Then he spits.

A pale brown spurt of tea spatters into a big spittoon on wheels.

Dick has been doing this—sip, swish, spit—for 46 years, from as many as 300 cups of tea a day.

He seldom, if ever, overshoots the spittoon.

The 78-year-old Dick is the government's No. 1 tea taster, a Food and Drug Administration employee devoted to upholding a regulatory anachronism, the Tea Importation Act of 1897.

OBSERVATION FOR ADVANCED REPORTING

STUDY PREVIEW   Observation is essential in two advanced news-gathering forms: participatory and immersion journalism. In both advanced approaches, reporters are involved as participants in what they report. In immersion projects, reporters go under cover because being up front would interfere with getting the story.

Participatory Journalism

Participatory journalism, in contrast to Lippmann's fly-on-the-wall approach, involves the reporter in the event being covered. It's an approach that can yield truths not otherwise obtainable. For a San Francisco newspaper series, Hunter Thompson joined the Hell's Angels motorcycle gang to learn about the biker lifestyle from the inside out. There was no other way to get at the subject.

In participatory journalism, the reporter becomes part of the scene being reported. There are no disguises or undercover ploys, but the journalist tries not to affect what's being observed.

While participatory journalism is a step beyond most contemporary reporting, it is hardly a new approach. Here are some memorable participatory stories this century:

+ John Reed rode with revolutionary Pancho Villa across the Mexican deserts for Metropolitan magazine and the New York World on the eve of World War I.

+ Paul Gallico went into the boxing ring with a great heavyweight fighter to sharpen his perception about his subject for a New York Daily News series.

+ George Plimpton joined the Detroit Lions to experience football life from the inside for his book "Paper Lion."

Plimpton explains how participatory journalism can yield insights not otherwise possible: "It is one thing to go out on the field and catch a curve ball; you learn about skills. But probably more interesting is to join a team and learn, for example, what baseball players are like and what they talk about on the bus." When a writer like Plimpton participates that way, he can present a picture of such color and depth that the reader can have the same experience vicariously.

Immersion Journalism

Immersion journalism takes observation to its ultimate with reporters concealing their journalistic purpose. The goal is to minimize the effect of the reporter's presence on what is being observed. This is in contrast to participant observation, in which reporters let their journalistic purposes be known even though they do not flaunt them.

Here are examples of immersion journalism:

◆ Joining the Marines to check on reports of abuses in basic training, akin to what Frank Woodward did at Jefferson Barracks in Missouri in 1889.

◆ Posing as a druggie to figure out the campus drug scene.

◆ Seeking a job from a placement service to get evidence on whether racial, gender or age discrimination is practiced.

In immersion journalism, the reporter is under cover. Covertness bothers critics, who say it may be an unethical misrepresentation if the story can be gotten in some other way. And even then, many argue that it is a form of lying and should not be practiced. Those who defend immersion journalism note that it is the only way to uncover some significant stories.

Significant Immersion Projects

Immersion projects usually are long-term endeavors that require intense planning. An often-cited example was Nellie Bly's 1887 exposure of abuses at an insane asylum in New York. She faked her way into being admitted to the asylum to do a story that was not otherwise possible.

Nellie Bly at Blackwell Island. Nellie Bly, 20, a reporter at Joseph Pulitzer's New York World, masqueraded as a lonely, unattached woman and moved into a slum apartment. Then she feigned losing her sanity, and authorities committed her to the Blackwell Island asylum.

Once inside she acted normally. Even so, she was regarded as belonging by everybody there. Indeed, she concluded that many inmates were sane but that Blackwell Island was a convenient place for unwanting families to park them. She also found horrifying conditions—poor sanitation, bad food, nurses who tormented patients, doctors who didn't care.

Her stories were afforded lavish play—1½ pages in the World two Sundays in a row. And they got results. A grand-jury investigation followed, and there were improvements.

John Griffin and "Black Like Me." Among the 20th century's most haunting books is "Black Like Me," in which a white man, John Griffin, related how he was treated in the Deep South on a six-week odyssey in black guise.

With a prescription drug, ultraviolet rays and a stain, Griffin turned his skin pigment dark. He shaved his head and the light hair on his wrists.

Griffin's experiences, in 1959, opened the eyes of white people to a racist reality they had not understood and became a compelling, emotional banner of the powerful American civil rights movement of the 1960s.

Gloria Steinem as a Playboy Bunny. Odd as it seems, feminist leader Gloria Steinem, later editor of Ms. magazine, once was a bunny in a Hugh Hefner Playboy Club. She signed on for bunny training under a false name to do a story for high-brow Show magazine. Immersing herself in her subject, Steinem came up with insights about bunny life that hardly coincided with the portrayals in Hefner's Playboy magazine.

Steinem had responded to an advertisement that proclaimed: "Yes, it's true! Attractive young girls can now earn $200-$300 a week at the fabulous New York Playboy Club." She found bunny earnings far short of the promise, working conditions far from fabulous, and clientele hardly the suave, moneyed and handsome young men portrayed in the club's promotion. Her article penetrated the carefully manipulated image of Playboy Clubs and their bunnies.

PREPARING FOR OBSERVATION

STUDY PREVIEW   Advice for observing: Keep your eyes open—and your ears and all your senses. Develop your observation skills so they are reflexive. When covering a story, be unobtrusive so that your presence does not affect events. Carefully choose the vantage or role from which you will observe the world of your story.

Observation for Spot and Depth Stories

You cannot prepare for a breaking story you suddenly happen upon, but if you have developed observation skills, you will reflexively know what to do. Follow what's happening. Look for causes and effects. Note the outcome. Take down detail that will explain what happened.

For depth stories, know why you're observing before you begin. Keeping your eyes open isn't enough. You can't soak in everything. There's too much. Instead, settle on a purpose for your observation, a tentative story line. Then you can focus attention on details that support it, not squander energy trying to absorb too much. Don't, however, glom onto a story line too tightly. Be prepared to chuck one story line if a better one presents itself, then shift to observing detail that will bring your new story line to life.

When planning observation, consider how to be unobtrusive so your presence does not impinge on the event you're reporting. Be a fly on the wall, present but as unnoticed as possible.

Choosing a Vantage

The quality of an observation story can be determined by the reporter's vantage. For some personality profiles, reporters do not let their subjects know that they are observing them in public places and at public events. For some subjects, it may be better to be up front and even tag along with them through their daily routine. Multiple vantages, like observing unannounced at one point and also being up front at other points, can produce a richer array of material for a story.

It is the reporter, generally, who chooses vantages, although circumstances can be a factor. Actor Marlon Brando, for example, spurns most requests for interviews, and reporters end up observing Brando from afar. In World War II, Ernie Pyle told moving stories from the trenches. He was there, reporting things that would have been untold had he sought less uncomfortable, less hazardous vantages. In some wars, reporters have less choice of vantages. Military escorts with their M–16s and AK–47s can be persuasive in keeping reporters from some places where observation could yield good detail.

Resisting Herd Journalism

Most strong observation stories come from reporters who have chosen vantages that competing reporters have overlooked or rejected. Observing what every other reporter is seeing tends to result in what media critics call "herd journalism," in which reporters end up being more attentive to what each other is reporting than to looking for fresh perspectives.

Photographers for Life magazine had the knack of finding vantages from which to take pictures that other photographers missed. Richard Pollard, a former Life picture editor, said that other photographers would "all line up in a little semicircle and shoot what's going on. Shoot right at it. Life photographers went around behind the guy."

One Life photographer, Edward Clark, was on assignment in Warm Springs, Ga., following the death of President Franklin Roosevelt. When the casket bearing Roosevelt's body was being moved by Army caisson to the train station, some 50 to 75 photographers on the scene began shooting. Clark, however, heard the music of an accordian and turned to see Navy petty officer Graham Jackson playing the instrument with tears running down his cheeks. Clark said he thought to himself: "My God. What a picture." And he began shooting. His vantage made his picture a classic news photo.

The herd mentality that works against fresh perspective was documented by Timothy Crouse in his book, "The Boys on the Bus." Crouse tells how reporters covering presidential campaigns come up with remarkably similar stories. The reporters, all on the press bus, talk with each other, share their thinking, even compare notes.

Herd journalism, unfortunately, operates at many levels. Media commentator George Foy once noted that every war has its hotel: "Vietnam had the Caravelle, in Saigon; Rhodesia, the Ambassador, in Salisbury; Lebanon, the Commodore, in Beirut. These are places where the spies, the mercenaries, the arms traders and the journalists can sit in dark corners, listening for bombs, watching the fires burn, plying their trade as they sip drinks served by dark-skinned waiters."

At these hotels, stories abound, many of them good stories. But mingling among the shadowy characters who come and go from a hotel in a war-torn area is not true observation reporting and it misses vantages that could enable reporters to bring the whole story home to their listeners and readers.

When reporters chase each other instead of fresh vantages, the audience suffers. Less independence in gathering news means less is told.

Should journalists never compare notes? Except in extreme competitive situations, reporters commonly lean on each other to verify details. Cross-checking, however, is far short of interviewing one another at the Caravelle or on the press bus.

Choosing a Role

Just as in theater, where not all actors can play all parts, not all reporters can do all immersion projects. Physical factors, like race, generally cannot be disguised. A black reporter, for example, would have problems fitting in with a Ku Klux Klan coven. A Briton with a Cockney accent could not pass as a U.S. urban street-gang member.

Fitting in is essential. Media scholars Peter Johansen and David Grey put it this way: "For the reporter, acceptance is crucial. All groups have private and public behavior; if the reporter remains outside the group, only the public activity will be seen. Thus, the reporter must decide whether, in the amount of time the editor has allowed, the group's confidence can be won."

A practical reason for finding a role that facilitates quick acceptance is the fact that minute for minute, column inch for column inch, immersion projects are an expensive way to fill a news hole. For economy's sake, reporters must do everything that they can to hasten their acceptance into the phenomenon they want to observe. Ready acceptance saves time and dollars. For a story on cattle rustling, for example, become familiar with the jargon before you start mixing with ranch people.

Some reporters have a head start for some roles. Gloria Steinem fit in right away as a Playboy bunny. She was an ex-dancer and beauty queen. A magna cum laude graduate of Smith College, she had the wits about her to play the part. Important too in her fitting in was that bunnies tended to be a transient group.

It would be much harder for a reporter on an immersion project to fit quickly into a group with its own history of complex interrelationships and group experiences over a lengthy period—such as a Ku Klux Klan coven or people in a mental ward.

In choosing a role, reporters have to anticipate problems. Johansen and Grey point out, for example, that a journalist who misreads street-gang horse-play as violence and overreacts will give himself away. Think how you would prepare yourself to get inside an urban street gang.

Also, be prepared to throttle the extent of your immersion. As much as possible, choose a role that allows you to be at the periphery of what you are observing so your effect on what you are reporting is minimal. In using observation as a research tool, social scientist Robert Bogdon advises: "Learn to control some normal participant feelings."

At the same time, immersion reporters should recognize that a situation may unfold that necessitates abandoning their role. Imagine being the only person who can break up a knife fight between two street-gang members. Interfering may undermine your observation, but the alternative—watching two human beings kill each other—is morally unacceptable. San Francisco newspaper reporter Hunter Thompson faced this kind of problem while hanging out with the Hell's Angels motorcycle gang for a series: "At a party many months after I first met the Angels, when they were taking my presence for granted, I came on a scene that still hovers, in my mind, somewhere between a friendly sex orgy and an all-out gang rape."

Immersion reporting can put personal values on the line. Before a project, consider how far you are willing to go for a story. For Kate Coleman, it became a question whether to go all the way. In planning an article for Ramparts magazine on the lives of whorehouse prostitutes, she decided to go with participant observation, but in the middle of the project, approached by a john, suddenly she had second thoughts: "I looked up and saw paunch, shiny suit and horned-rimmed glasses on a doughy face. Omigod, he's asking me to go into the bedroom with him—with him! I stuttered my refusal with the madame's assisting explanation that I was not working. 'But didn't I just see her come out of the bedroom with that guy?' the bespectacled john asked, slightly outraged."

Coleman was adamant, which points up an inherent limitation in participant journalism: No matter how hard a reporter tries to get into a subject by being part of it, the reporter can always go home. As Coleman recalled, one of her hookers chided her: "But you see, that's the point; your research is unreal." Real hookers don't have the choice to refuse.

Cover to Avoid Detection

In immersion projects, reporters need confidence that their cover will work. Gloria Steinem was on edge during her whole period as a Playboy bunny for fear she would be uncovered before she had seen and experienced enough for her article.

Steinem's problem was a flimsy cover. She had used an alias and fake references when she applied. Then she put off submitting a required birth certificate. Being caught was an ever-present worry: "I knew someone was going to come in and say, 'Gloria!'"

Then, as she worked the coat-check room, it happened. From her article:

A man asked for his coat. I turned around and found myself face to face with two people whom I knew well, a television executive and his wife.

I looked down as I took his ticket and kept my back turned while the boy found the coat, but I had to face him again to deliver it. My television friend looked directly at me, gave me a 50-cent piece and walked away.

I breathed again. Neither he nor his wife had recognized me.

Steinem might better have chosen a Playboy Club in another city, not New York where she was known, in the interest of being able to concentrate more on observation.

DOCUMENTING THE EXPERIENCE

STUDY PREVIEW   Observation is an essential technique when the reporter's experience is more important than the event itself. In first-person stories, observation is key. The details that come from observation convey the significance of the experience.

Noting the Details

When Greta Tilley of the Greensboro, N.C., News & Record was invited to a budget briefing at the White House for non-Washington reporters, she knew there would be no hard news. President Reagan's budget was already widely reported. Not much was left to say. So she decided to share with her readers her experience at a White House luncheon, which was part of the program.

The result was an extraordinary piece of observation journalism. In the following abbreviated version, notice the details that Tilley recorded in her mind and in her notes to help readers experience what she had experienced. Also note how she juggled her notepad and dessert spoon.

WASHINGTON—The president doesn't dye his hair.

It is not blue black or sunrise red or shoe polish brown or any other color that the people who describe presidents talk about it being, and it doesn't flounce about in flamboyant pompadour waves like you see in the cartoons.

Ronald Reagan's hair is a subdued black at its darkest, and his cut is on the short side.

There are too many gray hairs to count during a one-hour lunch in the White House—too many to count even if there wasn't anything better to do.

Mention this to the president and he thanks you the way he might if you had surprised him with a prize Arabian stallion to ride in the hills above Santa Barbara.

"All these references to dyeing my hair go all the way back to when I was governor," he says. "I not only never dyed my hair. I never even wore makeup in any of my pictures. Cary Grant never wore makeup either. If your beard doesn't show, you don't need it. I don't need TV makeup."

The president puts the proof on the table. He bends down, lowers his head, and volunteers to have it examined.

"You know what dyed hair looks like," he says, holding still as a Marine at morning muster. "Now, take a good look at the roots and tell me what you think."

An impulsive move to touch the president's hair freezes a few inches above his head. The instructions from the press assistant were not to grab the president's hand, not to solicit an autograph for Aunt Hilda, and not to beg for a private audience. Surely his hair would be off-limits too. Mothers don't enjoy watching their daughters being dragged off hand-cuffed to the Secret Service on the 6 o'clock news.

By the time it would take to get back in, lunch would be over.

Eating consomme Celestine next to the president of the United States in the State Dining Room isn't the same as gulping clam chowder and a frankfurter delight with the girls at the Irving Park Delicatessen.

The noodles are hard to capture gracefully and harder to swallow. A lipstick mark on the water glass stands out like the Scarlet Letter. No one else leaves a grape tottering on the edge of the sterling silver server platter after taking a helping of wild rice amandine.

Maybe White House dining is what makes the president's cheeks rosy without makeup. He says it is getting fit early in life and sticking with it later.

"Nothing is better for the inside of man," he says, "than the outside of a horse."

You want to know how he's going to ride the range since the doctor ordered no more sun after two skin cancers on the nose, but these kinds of questions are considered trivial by the five other reporters at the table.

They have come so they can tell everyone back home that they have eaten mango mousse with raspberry sauce with the president, and that the only person whose dessert kept sliding away from the spoon was the woman on his left who asked inconsequential questions and took notes on everything from the centerpiece to the chandelier.

The president is wearing aids in both ears and a brown suit with dominant lapels and large stripes. In between the big stripes are smaller stripes in rust and navy blue. Nancy has been quoted as saying she would like to weed out his closet. This suit may be one reason why.

His tie is solid burgundy, his shirt white, his Italian loafers cordovan-colored. He must have had them awhile because the leather beneath the presidential shine is cracked enough to look comfortable.

The caricature image disappears two or three minutes after the president starts talking. Ronald Reagan is comfortable being Ronald Reagan. He is real.

Yes, he saw his son Ron in his underwear on "Saturday Night Live."

"We were amazed at his good sense of comedy."

No, he doesn't know who came up with the idea of rolling this year's budget out on a litter and calling it dead on arrival, but he liked it.

"We need more humor in government."

The president says "gov'ment" the way he does on TV. The voice that has been imitated by every impersonator in the business is hoarse but not as strained as it sounds sometimes in news conferences and speeches. It's soothing, almost hypnotic.

His dark blue eyes are his best physical asset. They listen to you talk and respond quickly. The whites are clear except for a spot around the left pupil, perhaps a broken blood vessel.

President Reagan's teeth are white and a little bit uneven on the bottom row.

His smile doesn't have the look of being manufactured in an assembly line for political parts, then used too much.

The waiter brings out a towering cream-colored castle of mango mousse crowned with a blossoming white flower. Around the castle is raspberry sauce circled with slices of kiwi fruit.

Cutting into the mousse is tricky. It shimmies. The kiwi looks good but forboding with memories of the tottering grape from the wild rice amandine. What the heck, it's dessert.

Note-Taking Beyond Quotations

Like most reporters, Greta Tilley took down quotations, numbers and spellings, but her notes also recorded details to help her recapture the mood of the occasion and a bit of presidential charm. These details distinguish fine observation pieces from ho-hum stories.

If you were to read Tilley's whole story, you would get an even stronger idea of the detail that an observation reporter needs to record—for example, the following are the kinds of detail that she crafted into the story:

chandelier huge, ornate and gold, fills center of room, glass enclosed bulbs, too many tiers to count without pointing

draperies yellow gold brocade, high big windows with lots of space between panels, magnolia outside, snow falling, looks like in movies

centerpiece—flowers look real, are real—tulips, red and what look like pinkish red lilies.

cigarettes, filter tips up, and nuts and gold wrapped mints in little silver containers, salem, winston, barclay, rich lights

tablecloth, color of the green Crayon you never used in box, and matching napkins folded in pyramid in middle of a plate—different wildflowers, 10, along inside edge and gold around border.

flowered carpet kind of goes with plate colors, soft greens and beiges and yellows and blues and grays

chairs covered with little twirled gold bars along back and covered whitish cushion; president should have a bigger chair

Those observations helped Tilley reconstruct her experience with details that vicariously put readers in the State Dining Room.

NOTE-TAKING TECHNIQUES FOR OBSERVATION

STUDY PREVIEW   Observation-based reporting requires special note-taking skills because observation stories contain so many details. Notes need enough detail so the reporter can reconstruct what happened when the actual writing begins. Yet note-taking should not be so detailed that it slows your observation.

Employing Your Senses

How does a reporter catch the detail necessary for good observation stories?

Good observation skills include listening for good quotations and jotting down numbers and proper names, just as in everyday reporting. But observation also requires more than listening. Every sense must be employed—the eyes for visual detail, the nose for scents, and the complex interrelationship of senses that enables reporters to talk about a group's anxiety, a courtroom's stuffiness, a summer day's mugginess.

Photographic Eye and Ear

By practice, reporters can develop the photographic eye and ear that are ideal for observation reporting. Truman Capote, known for powerful and detailed nonfiction writing, drilled himself for unusually high recall. Here's how Capote explained it: "Long before I started 'In Cold Blood,' I taught myself to be my own tape recorder. It wasn't as hard as it might sound. What I'd do was have a friend talk or read for a set length of time, tape what he was saying, and meanwhile listen to him as intently as I could. Then I'd go write down what he said as I remembered it, and later compare what I had with the tape. Finally, when I got to be about 97 percent accurate, I was ready to take on this book."

Capote's photographic eye and ear helped reconstruct scenes and experiences. It helped, too, that he sat down immediately after interviewing to make notes that would help him when he hit the keyboard.

Keeping Notes Sparse

So you don't become wrapped up in note taking, which will divert your energy from observing, keep notes sparse. Include no more than you need to jog your memory when you sit down right afterward to flesh them out.

Even for quotation, take down only key words. Plug in prepositions and the articles like "the" and "a" later. If you flesh out your notes right after your observation, your reconstruction of quotations and recollection of details will be incredibly accurate.

Being Self-Conscious

Journalism scholars Peter Johansen and David Grey give this advice: "Reporters should record their own behavior and conversation. In rereading these notes, they can understand their findings better and learn in what ways they have affected them."

Predetermining Your Focus

While observing, you need a sense of the direction that your stories will take. This will enable you to focus your observation. Otherwise, you will diffuse your focus and absorb trivial irrelevancies amid the relevant.

To narrow your focus, make a tentative decision ahead of time on the type of story you want to do. Molly Moore of the Washington Post, who covered a Marine unit in the 1991 Persian Gulf War, had to shift gears regularly for a broad range of observation articles. For some stories on women in the war, she looked for details to illustrate the difficulty that women in the U.S. forces had adapting to the Saudi culture, in which women are veiled head to toe, sit in the back of the bus, and never enter or leave public buildings by the front door. For other stories, she looked for how female and male troops interacted. She also wrote about how women and men coped with being separated for weeks and months from their families.

If Moore had started her day simply wide-eyed, without being any more focused than to "cover the war," she would have ended up the day with gargantuan quantities of material but hardly a poignant story.

This is not to say that reporters should cling inflexibly to a story idea when an event and their experience suggest a shift is in order. The key is finding a balance between focus, which allows you to concentrate, and flexibility, which allows you to see other possibilities.

In Molly Moore's Persian Gulf coverage, she was prepared to abandon a tentative story line when something better suggested itself, like:

+ The scariness she encountered on a convoy through a mine field in the dark, the night all the blacker because of sky-shielding smoke from enemy-set oil well fires.

+ The frustration she saw among military commanders when battle planners left their units out of the action.

+ The anxiety she found among troops who had no idea what was happening in Washington, at the generals' headquarters, or over the next dune.

Each of Moore's stories, based on observation techniques, required a strikingly different focus.

Avoiding Prestructuring

Every reporter has sat down at a keyboard and realized that there was a question that wasn't asked or a detail that wasn't noted. This becomes less a problem with experience because you learn to prestructure your story, anticipating during interviewing and observation the kinds of things that you will want to know when you later write the story.

Prestructuring, however, can go too far if you try to organize the story at note-taking stage. Regard notes as memos to yourself or journal entries—not early story drafts. As Johansen and Grey advise: "Notes are not written in the familiar inverted pyramid form. Rather, they should be chronological, completing a full account of one incident before proceeding to an equally full description of the next. Aids to this reconstruction might include diagrams of the physical layout of a meeting area, seating plans, agendas of topics in lengthy conversations, brief notes scribbled unobtrusively during the sessions, and so on."

SPECIAL PROBLEMS IN NOTE-TAKING

STUDY PREVIEW   Taking notes can be a special problem when a journalist is participating in what's being covered. The problem is especially severe in immersion projects, when taking notes makes the journalist's presence noticeable and can affect what is being observed.

Note-Taking as a Participant

Reporters who participate in what they are covering do so to get an insider's view, which means keeping a low profile. Because note-taking would draw attention to their journalistic purposes, observation reporters are reluctant to pull out a pad and pencil.

Use private moments to jot down what you observe, and keep those notes to yourself. Among reporters, stories are legion about ducking periodically into a restroom to take notes and then returning to whatever is being observed, only to have others ask, after the repeated trips to the bathroom, whether the reporter is feeling OK. In undercover projects, one too many of those trips can raise suspicions that undo the reporter's cover.

In immersion projects, when reporters are under cover, note-taking could blow the cover. Gloria Steinem would have given herself away jotting notes in the Playboy bunny locker room. Pulling out a tablet was impossible for Nellie Bly when she was posing as a patient in an insane asylum.

But there are occasional exceptions. Andy Knott of the Chicago Tribune had no problem scribbling notes when he posed as an emergency medical technician for several weeks. Ambulance attendants are always taking notes as they go about their work, and his note-taking fit right in.

Necessity of Documentation

A record of observations is important in immersion projects because the journalist usually is the only witness. Without a record, the journalist's credibility is vulnerable in a challenge.

Nellie Bly learned this the hard way after unearthing the terrible abuses at the Blackwell Island asylum in New York. Her stories sparked a grand-jury investigation, but when the jurors were taken to Blackwell Island they went in a clean, new boat—not the scow with tobacco-chewing matrons that had carried the "insane" Nellie Bly a few weeks earlier. Some mistreated patients whom Bly had cited in her stories were not to be found. At least one had been shunted to a remote part of the island when the grand jurors visited.

There had been a major attempt at coverup, and Nellie Bly stood to be made a liar. Finally someone spoke up, and the jurors learned the truth.

A lesson from Bly's experience is to plan for corroboration of whatever is discovered—documents, witnesses, recordings. Today, audio and visual documentation sometimes is possible.

A Question of Misrepresentation

A great ethics debate has raged for years about hidden recorders and surreptitious reporting. Journalists who engage in immersion projects defend their undercover role as a last resort to get at truths that otherwise could not be found. Don Hewitt, veteran producer of the CBS news magazine "60 Minutes," sees misrepresentation as "a small crime."

"It's the small crime versus the greater good," he told the Washington Post. "If you can catch someone violating 'thou shalt not steal' by your violating 'thou shalt not lie,' that's a pretty good trade-off."

Used effectively, immersion can penetrate the public posture of an individual or group to see the private face—a face that interviewing, for example, cannot touch nearly as effectively.

DIFFICULTIES OF OBSERVATION

STUDY PREVIEW   Despite advantages, observation is not the most widely used way that reporters gather news. A problem is that a reporter's presence has some impact on what's being observed, in effect distorting it. Observation is also difficult, labor intensive and costly. It can be dangerous.

Heisenberg Indeterminacy

Scientists know the phenomena they test are affected by the test. Perhaps only imperceptibly, a reaction in a test tube is different from a reaction outside the test tube. The concept that observation affects what's being observed is known as the Heisenberg Principle of Indeterminacy. It's a problem in journalistic observation too.

In the urban race riots of the late 1960s, rioting intensified when reporters arrived—especially broadcasters with conspicuous electronic equipment. Rioters played to the camera. Even at something as routine as a city council meeting, as soon as even one council member realizes a reporter is present, the meeting is affected.

Like Walter Lippmann's fly on the wall, the reporter should see all but not be seen. Before television, fly-on-the-wall reporting meant press tags were absent and note-taking was inconspicuous. Even then it was an ideal. Council members know the reporters who cover the council. Rioters note non-rioters in their midst.

To reduce the Heisenberg effect, reporters using observation should keep their presence low key: no logo blazers or gaudy vans, and camera strobes only as a last resort. Also important: Recognize that you affect what you see, perhaps only minutely, and adjust your confidence in your observations accordingly.

Becoming Trapped

Depending on the story, observation reporting carries personal risks.

Nellie Bly, whose cover at the Blackwell Island asylum was shaky, became worried after 10 days that her editor, Joseph Pulitzer, had run into legal difficulties in arranging her release. Might she, like real patients, be there forever? On the 11th day, however, a newspaper attorney arrived and took her back to the city room to write.

As you read at the beginning of this chapter, Frank Woodward of the St. Louis Post-Dispatch might have disappeared forever, just as some regular Army recruits did, if Army sergeants had discovered what he was really up to.

Physical Danger

In planning "Black Like Me," John Griffin was warned over and over. Said his publisher: "You'll get yourself killed fooling around down there. . . . You'll be making yourself the target of the most ignorant rabble in the country." The dermatologist who helped Griffin turn his skin black warned him too.

Risk can be unexpected, as Hunter Thompson learned after assuming that he had won the confidence of the Hell's Angels: "On Labor Day I pushed my luck too far and got badly stomped by four or five Angels who seemed to feel I was taking advantage of them."

There also are dangers in being perceived as part of the group you've infiltrated. Thompson and reporter colleague Don Mohr found themselves inheriting the same enemies as the Hell's Angels at Bass Lake near Yosemite National Park. Tension was high between Angels, who had chosen the area for a weekend outing, and locals who had banded together in understandable hysteria, almost as vigilantes, to protect their town from biker ravages. "Despite the press credentials, Mohr and I had been firmly identified with the outlaws. We were city boys, intruders, and under these circumstances, the only neutrals were tourists, who were easily identifiable."

Thompson and Mohr weren't sure whom to consider the good guys—the Bass Lake locals or the Hell's Angels.

Going Native

People who knew John Reed in college remembered him as a playboy and prankster, hardly an ideologue. A few years later when Reed rode across Mexico with Pancho Villa, his stories were sympathetic to the peasant guerrillas. Later in reporting the 1917 Russian Revolution, Reed was so involved in his subject that he became a Bolshevik propagandist. Immersion journalism, experts tell us, poses a danger of becoming too involved in your subject. Says sociologist Arthur Vidich: "If the participant observer seeks genuine experiences, unqualifiedly immersing and committing himself in the group he is studying, it may become impossible for him to objectify his own experiences. In committing his loyalties he develops vested interests which will inevitably enter into his observations. Anthropolgists who have 'gone native' are a case in point."

By its nature, "going native" means that reporters cannot detach themselves from their subjects. But they need to be forthright with their audience that their perspective may be colored by their experience. Being forthright can be done smoothly, as Hunter Thompson did in explaining the blur that developed between his purpose in reporting on the Hell's Angels and almost becoming one of them: "In the beginning I kept them out of my own world, but after several months my friends grew accustomed to finding Hell's Angels in my apartment at any hour of day or night. By the middle of summer, I had become so involved in the outlaw scene that I was no longer sure whether I was doing research on the Hell's Angels or being slowly absorbed by them."

With a skillful reporter whose motive is truth-seeking, participatory journalism will be recognized by the news audience as a necessary methodology—despite its departure from the orthodoxy of detached, neutral observation. But be sure to spell out your participatory or immersion role. Not acknowledging the departure leaves you suspect for the bias that flows unavoidably from your intimacy with your subject.

How much can a journalist be involved? Critics of John Reed say he went too far when he became a Bolshevik propagandist. Sociologist Arthur Vidich suggests trying to keep involvement short of "genuine partisan action."

CHAPTER WRAP-UP

Eyewitness reporting puts reporters at the scene, bypassing secondhand sources and reducing reliance on records. The advantages include having trained observers doing the reporting, seeing things in a detail otherwise not possible.

Although observation is used less than interviewing as a news-gathering tool, reporters all need solid observation skills to call on when unexpected events occur, like an airplane crash. Observation skills also are essential in many depth projects, including personality profiles and first-person stories. Observation is at the heart of participatory and immersion journalism, two advanced news-gathering forms.

Detailed formulas for observation are impossible because different reporters are effective at it in different ways. General advice is to keep your eyes open—and your ears and all your senses. Observation can yield detail that excites the senses of your audience, coming close to putting them in the situation that you as a reporter experienced. Observation also yields detail which enhances credibility.

Observation-based reporting requires special note-taking skills because observation stories contain so many details. Taking notes can be a special problem when a journalist is participating in what's being covered. The problem is especially severe in immersion projects, when taking notes makes the journalist's presence noticeable and can affect what is being observed.

Despite advantages, observation is not the most widely used way that reporters gather news. It is costly because it takes so much time. Also, it can be dangerous. There also are questions of ethics when reporters go under cover, in effect misrepresenting themselves. Journalists themselves are split on undercover reporting. Those who defend it, including people at news operations like CBS's "60 Minutes," note that some important stories are almost impossible, if not impossible, to unearth any other way.

STUDY QUESTIONS

1. What are the advantages of observation over interviewing as a news-gathering tool?

2. What role can observation play in spot news stories? In depth news stories?

3. Why is observation essential in advanced reporting that involves reporter participation and reporter immersion?

4. Discuss how reporters choose roles and vantages in advanced reporting that involves observation.

5. Why is observation an especially useful reporting tool when a journalist's experiences are more intersting or important than the event itself?

6. How do journalists document their experiences while using observation as a reporting tool?

7. What are the special problems confronting journalists in taking notes during participatory or immersion journalism projects?

8. Why is observation not used more in news work than it is?

9. Why is it important for a reporter to identify a story line early in the observation process, long before hitting the keyboard?

10. Why do reporters try to appeal to their audience's senses by citing color, sounds, shapes, mood, smells?

11. Discuss how a reporter finds the balance between enhancing detail and irrelevant cluttering detail.

12. How does herd journalism work against strong observation stories?

13. Can you distinguish participatory journalism from simpler journalistic observation?

14. Immersion journalism involves the reporter in a covert role. What are the practical implications of this?

15. Why are budgetary concerns usually a hindrance to immersion journalism projects?

16. Finding ways to fit in quickly and being readily accepted is important in immersion journalism. Why?

17. What is the risk of journalists "going native" in sophisticated observation projects?

18. Why should reporters be aware of the Heisenberg Principle of Indeterminacy in participant observation projects?

19. How can journalists establish documentation for their observations when note-taking is difficult if not impossible?

PUTTING YOUR LEARNING TO WORK

EXERCISE 1   A Basketball Game

Many people think that covering a basketball game entails merely sitting in the press box and chronicling what happens on the court. But a good account requires a reporter to seek numerous vantages. You want the overview from the press box to see the game itself, but the press box has limitations. What other vantage points would you seek to offer your audience a complete report?

EXERCISE 2   Marine Boot Camp

Consider how you would prepare yourself to do a story on Marine boot camp as an immersion project in which you are under cover. How would you record the experience if you were a newspaper reporter? A radio reporter? A television reporter? Is there an alternative to signing up for a full two-year hitch to do such a story? Is there a justification for not revealing your journalistic intentions? Are there journalistic methods short of immersion to tell the story?

FOR FURTHER LEARNING

Fred Barnes. "Shiite Spin Control," New Republic (July 15 and 22, 1985).

Robert Bogdon. "Participant Observation in Organizational Settings." Syracuse University Press, 1972.

Kate Coleman. "Carnal Knowledge: A Portrait of Four Hookers," Ramparts (December 1971).

Timothy Crouse. "The Boys on the Bus." Random House, 1973.

George Foy. "In Peshawar, Everybody Comes to Green's," Rolling Stone (Feb. 11, 1988).

Otto Friedrich. "There are 00 Trees in Russia," Harper's (October 1964).

John Howard Griffin. "Black Like Me." Houghton Mifflin, 1961.

Charles A. Grumich, editor. "Reporting-Writing from Front Row Seats." Simon and Schuster, 1971.

Jane Howard. "A Six-Year Literary Vigil," Life (Jan. 7, 1966).

Howard Kurtz. "Hidden Network Cameras: A Troubling Trend?" Washington Post (Nov. 30, 1992). Kurtz discusses a spate of lawsuits filed by people who were subjects of hidden cameras. Charges include fraud, misrepresentation, invasion of privacy, and eavesdropping.

Maxwell McCombs, Donald Lewis Shaw and David Grey. "Handbook of Reporting Methods." Houghton Mifflin, 1976.

A. Kent MacDougall. "The Press: A Critical Look from the Inside." Dow Jones, 1972.

Molly Moore. "A Woman at War: Storming Kuwait With the U.S. Marines." New York: Scribner's, 1993. Moore, a Washington Post reporter, details her ongoing scramble for new vantages from which to tell what was happening on the ground in the Persian Gulf War, so her editors could piece together the whole story day after day.

Mignon Rittenhouse. "The Amazing Nellie Bly." E.P. Dutton, 1956.

Robert A. Rosenstone. "Romantic Revolutionary: A Biography of John Reed." Knopf, 1975.

Louis L. Snyder and Richard B. Morris. "A Treasury of Great Reporting." Simon and Schuster, 1962.

Gloria Steinem, "A Bunny's Tale," Show (May and June 1983).

Hunter S. Thompson. "The Hell's Angels: A Strange and Terrible Saga." Ballantine Books, 1967.

Barbara Tienharra. "Sports Interviewing: Plimpton Style," Quill (November 1980).

Arthur J. Vidich. "Participant Observation and the Collection and Interpretation of Data," American Journal of Sociology 60, No. 4 (January 1955): 354-360.

Thomas Weyr. "Reaching for Paradise: The Playboy Vision of America." Times Books, 1978.

Harry Wilenski. "The Story of the St. Louis Post-Dispatch." Pulitzer Publishing Co., 1981.

CHAPTER 21

COVERING A NEWS BEAT

LEARNING GOALS

In this chapter you will learn:

✦ Beats are an efficient way for news organizations to organize their coverage.

✦ New reporters should check previous beat coverage, contact likely sources, review relevant documents, and learn the rhythms of the beat.

✦ A reporter new to a beat must gain the confidence of sources.

✦ Beat reporters exploit the advantages of being at the scene and avoid the temptation of shortcuts.

✦ Public relations work requires its own beat reporting.

✦ Reporters know the hazards of beat reporting so they can avoid them.

NORTH DAKOTA SHOOTOUT

Jim Corcoran had the evening off from his beat as the federal building reporter for the Fargo, N.D., Forum. He had just uncorked a beer and was about to enjoy the concluding episode of the miniseries "Winds of War" on television when the phone rang. It was the newsroom. "It seems a federal drug bust went bad out in Medina," an editor said. "A federal marshal has been shot. Can you get on it?"

Corcoran, an experienced federal building reporter, knew something was garbled. Normally it was the U.S. Drug Enforcement Agency, not the Marshals Service, that conducted drug raids. Marshals transported prisoners and provided courtroom security. Before heading to Medina, 120 miles away, Corcoran called one of his regular contacts on the federal beat, someone who normally would be home on a Sunday night. He wasn't. Corcoran then called another source, who wasn't home either. Now he knew for sure that something had gone terribly wrong at Medina. This was not just another drug raid.

Forearmed with knowledge from his beat experience, Corcoran headed for Medina with information and hunches that other reporters didn't have. Yes, he learned when he arrived, there had been a shootout. Two U.S. marshals were dead and three other law enforcement officers were wounded. Wounded too was the 22-year-old son of Gordon Kahl, a right-wing religious zealot who was the object of the ambush. Kahl got away.

Jim Corcoran's familiarity with his federal building beat in Fargo equipped him to stay on top of developments in the months ahead with a series of exclusive stories. Corcoran's coverage gave readers insight into the secretive Posse Comitatus, whose political agenda favored converting the United States into a Christian theocracy. That, as Posse Comitatus people saw it, was the intent of the nation's founders. Theirs was a growing subculture involving thousands of people nationwide, but it was not much understood until the nation's attention became riveted on Medina, the follow-up trial of Kahl's companions, and another shootout in Arkansas, where federal agents incinerated a house in which Kahl was holed up.

Four years later, Corcoran recapped it all in a book, "Bitter Harvest," which, again, was possible only because he was, first of all, a good beat reporter. His federal sources trusted him personally and respected his work as a journalist. He had access to people and information that someone less known in the halls of the federal building would have a hard time tapping.

This chapter tells how reporters learn and then work a beat. These are reporters who specialize in a specific area, which gives them an edge as news gatherers and a depth as news writers.

SOMETHING WASN'T RIGHT. Jim Corcoran, who covered courts for the Fargo, N.D., Forum, knew from experience that something big was happening. To check out information that just didn't seem right, Corcoran drove to a small North Dakota town where federal agents were in a bloody shootout with right-wing extremists. His beat reporting background and persistence gave him an edge in an evolving story with important insights into an antigovernment, white supremacist movement.

COVERING NEWS WITH BEATS

STUDY PREVIEW   Beats are an efficient way for news organizations to catch major stories. The traditional beats, like police, are built around places rich in story potential. Today, many beats are built around subjects and issues.

Being Entrusted with a Beat

Ask any editor. There are never enough reporters for all the issues and events that merit coverage. To do the best they can with limited resources, editors entrust experienced reporters with specific story-rich areas to cover on a continuing basis, like the police or schools or the environment. These are called beats.

On a beat, a reporter is the newsroom's primary source of stories from that assigned area. Beat reporters are expected to know what is worth covering on their beats and to generate story ideas on their own. Unlike general assignment reporters, beat reporters are not given a list of things to cover. They are much more on their own, and being assigned a beat is usually a promotion.

Beat reporting goes back to James Gordon Bennett, a pioneering editor who put together the first organized system for news reporting at the New York Herald in the 1830s. He assigned reporters to cover the police, the courts and other sources of news regularly. Bennett's thorough beat system assured him that the Herald would not miss big events.

Economics of a Beat System

Beats make economic sense. Most editors will tell you that if they had to eliminate all beats but one, they would keep a reporter on the police regularly. A tremendous amount of information passes through police stations—crime, accidents, disasters. A newsroom that doesn't have at least one reporter with ongoing access to police sources stands to miss a lot of basic stories. In most communities, the police beat generates more stories than any other, which means police reporters are the most prolific. They write more stories per newsroom salary dollar than any other reporter.

To some people, there is a dark side to the economies of beat systems. Media critic Ben Bagdikian says beats can lead to a distortion in the overall impression that the news audience receives from the media. Referring to police beats, Bagdiakian makes his point this way: "Among all catgeories of news, crime is one of the cheapest, easiest to gather and safest to publish. It is gathered by the police, made available in a central place, and unless handled with gross incompetence is libel-free even though it deals with intimate and damaging events in personal lives. I have been a police reporter and an editor, so I speak as past sinner and confessor: if news organizations had to track down the commission of each crime, gather details with their own paid reporters, and verify the events sufficiently to avoid lawsuits, I can guarantee that the incidence of reported crime in the American news media would plummet."

The number of stories produed on a beat ranges tremendously. A news organization that emphasizes short, event-based coverage, like traffic accident stories drawn from police records, expects far more stories a day than an organization whose emphasis is depth policy questions. There also are slow days and heavy days. A middle range is reflected in the work of Kay Quinlan, who wrote 15 stories in a one-week period that was part of Stephen Hess' massive 1981 study of Washington correspondents. Quinlan's stories, for the Omaha, Neb., World-Herald, ranged from 40 words on a federal grant to the Nebraska

Arts Council to an 890-word compilation on congressional voting. The stories totaled 5,085 words and averaged 339 words.

After a police beat, most editors rank the courts as the second most important beat for hometown coverage. A lot of human drama unfolds in the courts. Also, because court procedures are complex, a newsroom needs someone who covers the courts often enough to understand what is happening and who has regular sources to help sort through the complexities.

The police, courts and city hall sometimes are called the "Big Three" beats for hometown newspapers, radio and television. No newsroom can ignore these areas, and even the smallest news operation will have one or two reporters on them, although maybe not full time.

Beyond the Big Three beats, different newsrooms set up beats differently. In an agricultural area, there might be a reporter who specializes on farm news. For a city with several colleges, there could be a higher education beat. The New York Daily News, whose reputation was built on crime coverage, once had a half dozen reporters on police, backed up by photographers in 11 cars equipped with scanners to monitor police communications. Smaller news operations may barely be able to ensure that somebody drops by the police station for a daily check of records and to stay in touch with sources.

Beat structures are easily adapted to the kind of coverage editors want and the communities being covered. At the University of Pennsylvania's Daily Pennsylvanian, the staff excluding sports and special sections typically ranges from 75 to 120 reporters. Most reporters are on general assignments, but 15 are assigned these respective beats:

✦ Administration.

✦ Administrative and education issues.

✦ Arts and sciences and nursing programs.

✦ Business and education colleges.

✦ Campus neighborhood.

✦ City and state issues.

✦ Crime.

✦ Financial affairs, including the university budget and facilities.

✦ Graduate student life.

✦ Graduate schools.

✦ Labor, including faculty, staff and unions.

✦ Minority affairs.

✦ Performing arts.

✦ Student government.

✦ Student life.

Other campus newspapers might focus more on student life, others less so. Some pay much less attention to finance and budget issues.

Categories of Beats

"Get me rewrite!" That classic movie line typified much about beat reporting in an earlier era. A beat reporter on top of a breaking story was phoning the newspaper and demanding that the call be put through to someone who would take dictation. In earlier days many beat reporters worked from remote sites, like police headquarters, and telephoned information to a rewrite person who put the information into story form, often against a deadline. Today, a newspaper beat reporter more likely will have a keyboard tied directly to the newsroom, and radio and television reporters often are set up to go live to their audiences.

While the tools and methods of beat reporting have changed, the concept has roots going back more than 150 years.

Place beats. James Gordon Bennett, who devised beats in the 1830s, first sent reporters out from the newsroom on regular rounds, but he realized eventually, in those days before mass transportation, computer modem and satellite dish communication, that it was more efficient to station reporters outside the newsroom, where the news was. These early beats came to be defined by the place where reporters did most of their work. Except for forays to crime scenes, police reporters spent their time at police headquarters. Court reporters were at the courthouse, and city hall reporters mostly there.

In 1909, when New York built a new police headquarters, the architects asked the newspapers what kind of pressroom they wanted designed into the structure. The newspapers decided instead to rent space across the street, in part to retain their autonomy, but since then it has become routine for major government buildings to be designed with facilities specifically for the news media, with the media in many cases renting the space they need to avoid charges of being in the hire of the organization being covered.

Facilities can be as minimal as a shared desk and telephone in a converted broom closet, to elaborate facilities with individual computer work stations for competing reporters, a separate interview room and even a small television studio.

Writing about the beat systems used by the Washington press corps, which parallel many hometown beat systems, scholar Stephen Hess observed: "This geographic division of labor—the assignment of reporters to buildings—has advantages. It minimizes jurisdictional disputes between reporters. It is easy to administer. It divides the work into manageable proportions. Geographic beats provide some assurance that the bases will be covered."

Subject beats. As newspapers developed special sections later in the 1800s, other kinds of beats developed, like sports and business. Because these reporters covered subjects that were geographically dispersed, their home base was the newsroom but the legwork for stories took them on regular rounds.

Today, these beats cover an ever-growing range of subjects: agriculture, politics, labor, education, entertainment, the arts, science. Large news organizations also have reporters whose beats are subsubjects. Some sports reporters, for example, deal almost exclusively with a single sport or team.

Part of the move toward subject beats is that the world is increasingly complex and interconnected. This is no less true in covering the federal government than other subjects, as noted by Stephen Hess, who made these observations in his major report on news coverage in the nation's capital:

"Government is a web—everything relates to everything else. Energy policy, for example, is not the exclusive province of the Department of Energy nor urban policy that of the Department of Housing and Urban Development. Therefore, news organziations are increasingly defining beats by substance— what government involves itself in, not the location of its building (diplomacy rather than the State Department, economics rather than the Tresury)."

Hess noted too that subject beats lessen the ability of public officials to set reporters' agendas. When reporters are less dependent on the same sources at a single agency, they have a broader base of information and are less apt to be manpulated.

Issue beats. As the news media have expanded their coverage from events to issues, new issue-based beats have been created. Many urban newsrooms have a minorities beat. The Detroit News in 1991 assigned Deb Price to cover gay issues. Some news organizations have created a beat to cover environmental issues.

Experimental beats. News staffs have grown larger through the 20th century, and many newsrooms have the resources to experiment with new beats. Eager to hook younger readers, many newspapers have set up beats to explore young lifestyles. There also are senior citizen specialists. In Chicago, newspapers from time to time have tried an O'Hare beat to find stories, mostly quick interviews with celebrities changing flights at the busy airport. In southern California, one newspaper, the editors reasoning that news is where the people are, set up a shopping mall beat.

Reporters from different beats sometimes team up for special projects. On CNN business news programs, for example, entertainment reporters and financial reporters often contribute to stories on business aspects of Hollywood movie projects. The overlap between environmental and health beats also can make for significant collaborative stories.

LEARNING A BEAT

STUDY PREVIEW   New reporters should check previous beat coverage, contact likely sources, review relevant documents, and learn the rhythms of the beat.

In-House Orientation

News organizations take different tacks to coverage. The New York Times prides itself as a newspaper of record with great detail on government activity. Many publications and most broadcasters pass up lesser events to focus on big stories. Some hometown newsrooms are especially attentive to traffic accidents. Some revel in unearthing scandal. Others limit themselves to the routine.

A beat reporter needs to know what the editors expect. An essential part of orientation to a beat is asking:

- What strengths of previous coverage do the editors want to retain?
- What do the editors see as weaknesses in previous coverage?
- Would the editors like any new directions in coverage?

A new beat reporter may be lucky to learn some of the ropes from whoever worked the beat before, but often a reporter starts on a new beat all alone. That's not always a disadvantage. Sometimes a predecessor has done a poor job, and it's better for the new beat reporter to be as distant as possible from the predecessor.

Documents for Orientation

Most news organizations maintain in-house libraries with articles clipped, indexed and filed—increasingly in computer databases—on everything that reporters cover. Broadcasters, in addition to newspaper clips, keep their own scripts and video records. These documents are essential orientations to what has been happening on the beat and how it was covered.

A reporter can pick up not only an overview of the beat but also details that can be essential in getting off to a good start.

Upcoming events. A small-town editor once told a rookie: "I don't care when you come to work or when you go home, but you better never miss a story on your beat." The point was that the newspaper depended on the reporter to be on top of the beat 24 hours a day—from the first day.

Recent coverage, which can be checked in the newsroom files of clipped articles, may have references to upcoming events that the new beat reporter should put in a future book. Also, articles from a year earlier will indicate cyclical events or issues that merit coverage during the period that the new reporter is getting started on the beat.

Ongoing issues. A good way for a reporter to learn the issues on a beat is to begin files on issues with information from clips. Reporters organize their notes in many different ways. One useful way is to think about how notes would be helpful in another five years to write a book. In fact, many beat reporters do write books from their experiences.

Names of sources. Clipped articles from old issues will help identify sources on the beat, with the correct spellings of names and titles.

Basis of authority. For beats with elected officials, check the files for election returns to gain an idea of the strength of your sources' base of support. When is the next election? Who were the opponents? What were the issues?

For appointed officials, check on who did the appointing? How was the selection made? Because the power to hire is also the power to fire, a reporter can pick up a good sense of operating relationships among people on a beat by knowing how people got their jobs.

Definitive Documents

Most beats have seminal documents with which new reporters must become acquainted. The state constitution lays out the rules by which counties, cities and other political subdivisions were created. Cities have charters. Police have regulations manuals. Corporations have articles of incorporation that state their purpose, with annual updates that list owners and officers. Election officials have manuals with state rules on conducting elections.

Among a new beat reporter's tasks is to identify the documents that are base marks for how people go about their business on the beat. Some of these documents, like the state constitution and city charter, are in the public library. Corporate documents are a phone call or computer search away with the secretary of state at the state capital.

Beat sources are impressed when a new reporter asks to borrow a copy of a basic document.

At personnel offices, ask for job descriptions of key officials on the beat. To understand how positions are structured, look at the descriptions to identify:

+ What each person is responsible for doing.

+ To whom each person reports.

+ Who is on the staff.

+ Salary, a key indicator of a person's responsibility in a bureaucratic structure.

It is essential for reporters covering public institutions to know the federal and state laws requiring open meetings and open access to records. These include the federal Government in Sunshine and Freedom of Information laws. Other open meeting and records laws vary from state to state. The Society of Professional Journalists' magazine, Quill, carries an annual summary of the state laws, but it is better to have a copy of the actual statutes for your state. Most state media associations can provide a copy. Also, a clerk at the county law library can help.

Forearmed with knowledge of the law, a reporter can protest if someone wants to close a meeting illegally or block access to a public document.

Competitive Coverage

Most beats are covered by several news organizations, which means that a newcomer will be in competition with somebody more experienced. Learn from the competition. Watch their coverage, their sources, their patterns, and let those things shape your approach so you aren't skunked regularly, and so, knowing the competition's patterns, you can score an occasional scoop yourself.

Be sure to introduce yourself to other reporters on the beat. Although they are competitors, reporters often do each other favors out of professional courtesy.

Meeting Regular Sources

A reporter needs to know everyone on the beat, from the custodians to the chief honchos, although this isn't possible from the first day. On a new beat, reporters should introduce themselves first to the most newsworthy people. On the police beat, for example, this would be the police chief and the chief's key lieutenants. For the first few weeks, much of the job will be to expand the number of contacts until, finally, the reporter knows everyone on a first-name basis.

Some reporters go to extraordinary lengths to be in touch with sources. Henry Brandon tells about arriving in Washington as a correspondent for the Sunday Times of London. He chose to live on the outskirts of Georgetown "to establish 'connections' with the mighty, and the best way to do that was to live near them." Brandon also took advantage of his bachelorhood to be available as the "spare man" at dinner parties, which made him a vital commodity on the Washington social circuit. Brandon's connections made him one of the most successful reporters in Washington for four decades, not only on breaking news but also depth coverage. In his memoirs, published in 1988, Brandon wrote: "Access to the men at the top, whether presidents or secretaries of state, defense or the treasury, matters when it comes to predicting the likely outcome of a crucial decision or when editors request a character sketch. For to be able to analyze the man it is necessary to take into considerstion not only his record but also one's own sense of him. And that needs 'eyeball to eyeball' encounters, impressions of the man's behavior at private occasions outside his office. Editors too like to know that their correspondent has access to the top so that they themselves can expect to meet anybody they want on a visit."

Not all beat reporters are willing to create an entire lifestyle built around their job, but a competitor as focused as Brandon will be hard to beat. Being close to the pulse of decision makers and the people around them and privy to the issues on their unofficial agendas can make for important stories. This is especially important for beats where key people are not available every day.

A reporter on the city hall beat may not see the mayor every day, but the daily rounds will include a stop at the mayor's office to check with assistants and others on what is happening. Subordinates, in fact, can be important sources on breaking stories. So can people at the lower levels. A whispered tip from someone on the city hall grapevine can prompt a beat reporter to ask questions that otherwise might never have been asked.

Making the rounds, office to office, source to source, in person, is important. Good beat reporters are at home in the offices they visit and fall into easy conversation with everybody and anybody in the snack room.

The ultimate in reporter-source relations on a beat is when sources reflexively include a reporter on breaking events. For years the Jacksonville, Fla., fire marshal invited a Times-Union photographer to come along on investigations. The newspaper had extraordinary photos, even inside private property which authorities had cordoned off. Such close reporter-source relations can become too cozy and the journalist's autonomy can be jeopardized, but there are ways to cultivate good source relations without surrendering control over what is reported.

FIRST DAYS ON THE BEAT

STUDY PREVIEW   New beat reporters must establish their competence and gain the confidence of sources. There may not be many stories in the first few days, but this is an important period for building relationships and mapping out the beat's long-term potential.

Media Relations Services

Many institutions covered on a beat employ media relations people. Their titles include terms like "community relations," "public information," "institutional relations," "public relations, "public affairs." A major corporation may have a public relations office with a dozen people assigned to media relations. A small organization may have one person assigned to media relations along with other duties.

Whatever the number of people in an organization's media relations unit, these are sources worth contacting right away. Their job is to represent the institution to the public, which includes offering a variety of support to news reporters:

+ *News releases.* These pre-written news stories are official statements of the institution. Some organizations issue releases on routine events, like personnel promotions. Others do news releases only for significant changes in institutional policy.

✦ *Knowledgable sources.* Good media relations people know their institution well, and they also have a sense of what interests news reporters and what their needs are. They are good sources of information. A good media relations person who is stumped by a reporter's question will get the information or steer the reporter to someone who has it.

✦ *Arranging interviews.* Some executives grant interviews only if they are arranged through the institution's media relations staff. In most situations this is advantageous all around. The executives are briefed by the media relations staff ahead of the interview, which gives them a chance to gather their thoughts for a better interview. Also, media relations people usually are eager to help reporters prepare for these interviews.

✦ *Accommodations.* Many institutions provide facilities, sometimes called "press rooms." If reporters have problems with the facilities, like unsuitable electrical wiring for new equipment, it is the media relations staff that should be contacted.

While media relations people are excellent reporter contacts, their perspective doesn't always coincide with the reporter's. They are on their employer's payroll to facilitate a favorable impression to the public through the news media. When reporters are after stories that seem negative, media relations people usually are less helpful and may even try steering reporters to other subjects. The stronger and franker a reporter's relationship with media relations people from the beginning days on a beat, the better the relationship will weather the unflattering stories that inevitably come along from time to time.

Making Introductions

From preliminary research, including discussions with media relations people, reporters learn who the major sources are on their new beat. The introductions, usually at each source's office or workplace, almost always include these elements:

✦ *Greeting.* "My name is Sarah Lory, and I am KQQE's new reporter covering the police." She extends her hand for a friendly shake. "I am here to introduce myself."

✦ *Statement of purpose.* "I'm not after a story today, but as I said, I wanted to meet you and let you know who I am." This is not only clarifies your purpose but puts the source at ease. Many sources are uneasy with a new reporter who charges into a heavy-duty interview on their first meeting.

✦ *Personal touchpoint.* "I see from the pictures on the wall that you like the outdoors." Use office cues or information from your preparation to demonstrate an interest in the source as a person. This may include family, hobbies, outside interests, career goals. Especially good at establishing a camaraderie are interests that you have in common.

✦ *Homework.* "I have been reading that you are in the middle of a major project to increase services." This lets the source know that you have done your homework. Because your purpose at this point is not a story, there is no need to pull out a pad and pencil and recorder.

✦ *Credibility.* "In school I had a professor who talked a lot about her experience doing this kind of work." Your goal is to establish as strong a credential for covering the beat as you can. Alternatives: "I wrote about this field for my college newspaper," or "When I was at the Press-Gazette over in St. Peter, I covered this beat too." Don't belabor your background, for your purpose is only a brief, favorable introduction, not an egocentric recitation of your resume.

✦ *Continuing relationship.* Let sources know that you see yourself on the beat for the long haul. The fact is that editors usually expect reporters to be on the beat for at least a year or so, and some of the best veteran reporters have made a career of a single beat. A source knowing that you will be around for a while is more likely to invest time in establishing a good relationship.

✦ *Future arrangement.* "Do you have time in the next few days to sit down for half an hour or so to talk about the things you're doing and would like done?"

Introductions typically take two or three minutes, perhaps longer if the source has time for more conversation.

For access to many sources, reporters work through secretaries or assistants. It is important in the first foray into the beat to make the same kind of introduction to them as to the sources themselves. Secretaries, receptionists and assistants frequently act as gatekeepers on who sees the boss. Also, they can be excellent tipsters for stories.

Building Source Confidence

A reporter's self-introduction to people on a new beat can be a solid foundation for future relationships, but there are additional things you can do to build source confidence in your work.

Past coverage. Ask your new sources what they see as strengths and weaknesses in past coverage. Not only does this give sources a chance to express their opinions, which most people love to do, but it also establishes your openness about the form that your coverage will take. In talking about past coverage, sources will reveal their attitudes about journalism, which can be helpful in your future tactics for gathering information.

Most sources will be flattered by your interest in their opinion of past coverage, and will be less inclined to view you as an adversary.

Informed querying. While interviewing is a process for gathering information, you can use it also to let sources know that you have done your research. This is important in early interviews, when you especially need to establish your credibility.

Question: "Tell me about the last election."

Informed Question: "You had a big margin in the last election. Tell me about that."

First stories. Sources will be watching the new beat reporter's stories carefully. A misspelled name, a wrong title, or a clumsy reference can undermine whatever preliminary credibility was established in the introduction process and early interviewing. Get it right, make it clear.

Knowing the importance of their first stories to their future success on a beat, many reporters start with easy stories. These include informational pieces that sources have suggested were overlooked in the past. The first week on the beat is hardly the point for blockbuster scandal stories.

BEING THERE

STUDY PREVIEW   The regular personal contact that beat reporters have with sources gives them an inside track on significant stories and an ability to go in-depth. At the same time, beat reporters cannot perform miracles like being two places at once. Imaginative alternatives to in-person reporting are needed when the pace becomes hectic.

The Value of Regular Checks

Photojournalists have a saying among themselves about getting great news shots: "F8 and be there." The point: Pull out all stops to be at the scene. Otherwise, no picture. While it is possible for reporters to catch up after the fact or to gather information by telephone, there is no substitute for being there.

Most beat reporters begin their day by catching a newscast, reading the newspaper, checking the mail and placing some telephone calls to remote sites to see if anything unexpected is occurring in the hinterlands. Then, on beats defined by place, like city hall, the reporter begins the essential ritual of making the rounds.

The process of generating stories is hardly scientific research with highly structured questions that yield neat, clean, precise answers. Many story ideas come from chatting at the water cooler with people on the beat, tapping into office grapevines with clerks and secretaries, and exchanging gossip picked up along the beat. These things can be done best in person.

The telephone has its place, but a limited one, in beat reporting. It is efficient for confirming an occasional detail, checking remote places for tips, and arranging interviews, but it isn't an acceptable substitute for making the rounds. "F8 and be there."

Being Everywhere

Almost every beat has periods when more is happening than the assigned reporter can handle. Sometimes editors will add reinforcements to help, but often the beat reporter has to find ways to be several places at once, like at three simultaneous meetings. That, of course, is impossible. How does a reporter do the impossible?

Recording. If a meeting is being broadcast, pre-set a video recorder to tape it. This has great efficiency in that you can listen to the tape while doing other work, pausing just for the highlights.

Interviewing. Talk with principals at the meeting after it is over. This has some hazards in that your sources may not have your audience-oriented perspective, which means it is best to check with several people who were at the meeting, especially if there were controversial divisive items on the agenda.

Colleagues. If a fellow reporter owes you a favor, ask that it be returned. While this is hardly an ideal way to go about covering an event, skeletal details from a colleague, coupled with a quick check with a few principals at the meeting, can yield an acceptable story on a busy day.

Dividing time. When a meeting moves into a slow phase of the agenda, reporters often leave and come back later. Court reporters are adept at this, knowing in advance from attorneys which witnesses are likely to be the most important. This way, reporters covering several cases being heard simultaneously can divide their time from courtroom to courtroom, and in one sense be several places at once.

PUBLIC RELATIONS AND BEAT REPORTING

STUDY PREVIEW   Public relations people do their own form of beat reporting for their own news outlets and reports, and to respond intelligently and quickly to news-media queries. For favorable long-term media relations, the best policy is giving all reporters an equal shot at stories.

In-House Public Relations Beats

To do their media relations work, public relations people are beat reporters themselves. They make the rounds to tap many of the same sources that reporters do, and they need to think in the ways that reporters do so they can anticipate their questions and respond knowledgeably and quickly, and also to keep their institution's officials abreast of issues that reporters are pursuing.

In fact, public relations people literally are beat reporters when their job includes producing reports, in-house newsletters and other documents designed to keep employees and other groups informed on what is happening. These documents contain the whole range of journalistic content, from bulletin board announcements to depth reports, personality profiles, and analytical pieces.

Issuing News Releases

A basic component of media relations is making announcements on behalf of the institution, usually in the form of news releases. The timing of releases can be critical.

The goal is to get the word out quickly, but a premature announcement can be disastrous. When an Idaho resort manager announced a multimillion dollar, long-term expansion plan without clearance from his parent corporation, all kinds of loose ends began unraveling at corporate headquarters. His higher-ups had not coordinated all aspects of the plan, and the announcement had embarrassing ramifications with other corporate enterprises. The man ended up fired.

If reporters sniff a major story before the institution is ready to make an announcement, public relations people have to move quickly. First they need to buy time, perhaps just a few minutes, by telling reporters they will check on their queries and be back to them as soon as possible. Then those responsible for the policy or issue in question must be informed that reporters are working up a story. The usual public relations advice is to release as much information as is solid. If a project is still at a preliminary stage, that should be stated in just those terms.

In a free and open society, the people need to know what public officials are discussing and planning even at preliminary stages. Otherwise, public participation in policy making is stymied. Access laws recognize exceptions, like security planning, but the wisest course for public officials is to hold back nothing when the media are onto something.

The legitimacy of journalistic inquiries into public issues forms a mindset for reporters on beats in the private sector. While private organizations can be as tight-lipped as they wish, it generally is misguided not to respond forthrightly to news media queries. This common wisdom is especially true if the organization depends on public acceptance, which can be damaged if the organization comes across in the news media as secretive and closed.

In human relations, it is only natural that some people get on better with some than others, but in media relations it is important to treat all reporters equally. This includes issuing news releases simultaneously to everybody. A slighted reporter is an unhappy reporter, which is something that media relations is designed to avoid.

Although the standard practice is to issue releases quickly, some announcements are tied to events, like a company official testifying at a legislative hearing. In such situations, releases often are issued in advance with an embargo. A release distributed on Tuesday might be marked: "For use only after the testimony, scheduled at 10:45 a.m., Wednesday."

Reporters, appreciative of getting information ahead of deadlines, routinely honor embargos, although there is always a risk that someone will break an embargo inadvertantly. When the timing of an announcement is sensitive, advance releases are not a good idea.

Special Projects

An exception to the public relations rule of providing information to all reporters at the same time involves enterprise stories. When reporters are working up a story on their own, like a personality profile or an investigative article, public relations people produce the requested information for the reporter exclusively. Of course, if a second reporter asks for the same information, it is also provided. Only when it seems there is general interest is there a blanket release.

HAZARDS OF BEAT REPORTING

STUDY PREVIEW   Beat reporters need to know the hazards of beat reporting so they can avoid them. Veterans on a beat run a special risk of their stories becoming inside reports for insider readers, rather than the mass audience, because of their daily association with the same people. Also, becoming too comfortable on a beat can lead to complacency that works against lively, imaginative coverage.

Too Close to Sources

Although getting to know sources well is essential on a beat, reporters run a risk of getting to know a beat and its people so well that they see things too

DOCUMENTS ON THE BEAT. When U.S.Supreme Court Justice Harry Blackmun retired, he met with reporters to recount his "fantastic, intimate experience" on the court. It was a rare session. Justices seldom conduct news conferences or grant interviews, which mean Supreme Court reporters rely mostly on documents as sources. Reporters spend most of their time reading up on pending cases so they can write stories quickly when the justices release their written opinions.   (Marcy Nighswander/Wide World Photos)

much from their perspective. The sharp edge that marks the detached, neutral reporter, someone on the outside looking in, softens and the reporter begins writing as an insider.

Editors generally are quick to recognize when reporters have become too close to sources and will rotate reporters to fresh beats. This not only solves the problem but improves reporting in general by broadening the knowledge and experience base of each reporter. Also, it gives reporters who are intent on an editing job a broader range of experience that will be valuable on the desk.

When bad news is brewing on a beat, editors sometimes add another reporter rather than ask the regular reporter to take the heat and lose the close relationship with sources that has been built up carefully over the years.

Too Comfortable with the Routine

Most beats have a pattern that dictates seasonal stories. On a farm beat, there are the crop report pieces during the growing season, the farm policy stories during the legislative session, and the machinery stories in the fall. The religion beat has seasons too, most of them built around holidays and holy periods. Once a reporter has experienced a couple of cycles of seasonal stories, it is possible merely to freshen up old story concepts.

Beat reporting, however, should be more. Although easy, doing the routine becomes boring, which shows in stories and insidiously leads reporters to a disenchantment with their beat and themselves. Worse, the reader is not as well served. While cyclical stories cannot be ignored, like Easter and Hanukah on the religion beat, beat reporters must keep themselves sharp with truly fresh approaches and by recasting the routine in terms of new and emerging issues.

Occasionally an anthropologist will go off to study peoples in some remote place and then never come back. In anthropology, this is known as "going native." All researchers dealing with human subjects, whether anthropologists or news reporters, run the risk of becoming so involved in their subject that they lose their detached, neutral perspective, or even become "one of them."

No matter how close beat reporters are to their sources, they need to reinforce from time to time that their first obligation is to serve their audience. Reporters have different ways to do this. On some beats, reporters lay out all sides in their stories every day, quoting the mayor on behalf of a pet project but also the mayor's detractors. This is a little more difficult on the police and other beats, where suspects, on the advice of their attorneys, are less forthcoming with their side until their day in court.

Here are ways that reporters can remind regular beat sources that the journalist's No. 1 responsibility is to the audience:

+ Ask regular beat sources to respond to information you have from interviewing their adversaries. This can be done gently yet firmly: "This is a difficult question for me to ask, but as a reporter I have to put it to you." The goal is to alert friendly regular sources that you are not their publicist.

+ Ask for the names of people who might be interviewed for other points of view. This too can be done pleasantly: "You've laid out your position strongly and clearly. Where do you expect the opposing position to develop?" Or, "Can you suggest whom I should talk to for the other position?" This too reminds sources that your obligation as a reporter is thorough news gathering and complete reporting.

+ Avoid off-the-job socializing. This reduces the chances that sources will create unreasonable expectations and lean on you as a friend, asking you to shape your stories to their purposes, or even asking that certain stories not be told. Some reporters, however, are able to both work the social circuit and retain the separateness that journalists must have. Henry Brandon of the London Times, who was mentioned earlier, was a master at being a charming dinner guest and also letting it be clear that he was first a journalist. For reporters who find this difficult, it is better to take the easier route of keeping source relationships businesslike and turning down dinner invitations. Some newsroom policies make this decision for the reporter, forbidding socializing that could create an impression of favoritism in coverage.

Myopia

A hazard in beat reporting is getting to know the beat so well that it becomes difficult to put what is happening in a larger perspective.

This myopia is a special problem for foreign correspondents, who can lose touch with their home audience by being away too long. Recognizing this problem, the New York Times and other news organizations with foreign staffs have a policy of rotating foreign correspondents home for a few months every so many years.

Jargon

In learning a beat, reporters have to learn the language of the people being covered. Everyone involved with the courts knows what an "omnibus hearing" is, and terms like "habeas corpus" and "in camera." A court reporter has to know these terms to communicate with the people on the beat. But these words are lost on a mass audience. Some newcomers to a reporting beat, proud that they have learned the jargon of their specialized areas of coverage, like to pepper their stories with these terms. That is a mistake. The job of a beat reporter is to translate what is happening on the court beat into words that ordinary people, not just lawyers, judges and court clerks, will understand.

College students learn this in reporting for their campus media. Words like "tenure" and "associate professor" may trip off the tongues of faculty sources, but they will be lost on a general audience and must be recast in common language.

In beats involving reformists, specialized lingo can take on a slant that can contaminate the neutral tone to which reporters aspire in their stories. John Ledo of U.S. News & World Report made the point this way: "Many reporters tend to absorb the language of their sources and consider it normal. But the sources are often activists bending language to push private agendas. Cover the disability-rights movement long enough, and you too may find yourself tapping out 'mentally and physically challenged.' "

Reporters have to understand the self-serving language common among people on the beat, like "mentally and physically challenged," but stories have to tell it straight: "disabled," "crippled," "mentally handicapped."

Nowhere are self-serving warps of the language commoner than on college campuses and in the military.

When new students arrive on the nation's campuses every fall, they are sat down for orientation. Anxious to learn the ropes, the students listen eager-eared to the people who run the dorms and related activities. These administrators have devised a special language intended to disguise certain truths about dorm life, including a top-down chain of command that assures discipline. Dorm supervisors, for example, are usually called "residence assistants," which has a nice ring, giving the impression that R.A.s are friends and helpers, which is partly true, but more important, R.A.s are an essential part of the university's dormitory governance and disciplinary structure whose primary function is to maintain order among a lot of 18-year-olds who could get out of hand.

To create an ambiance about dormitory living, college administrators tell students that they will be living in "residence halls" and bristle if anybody uses the word "dorm." Cafeterias are transformed into "dining facilities." Campus infirmaries are "health service centers." All this campus lingo is designed to create warm and cozy impressions among students—and make the job easier for those in charge of maintaining order in the dorms.

Sad to say, inflated language extends to many other parts of college life. Consider:

✦ "Learning resource center," for the library.

✦ "Human resources office," for personnel office.

✦ "Development," for fund-raising.

CHAPTER WRAP-UP

News reporters who specialize not only ask better questions and write more knowledgably but are able to produce more stories. James Gordon Bennett, a New York editor, learned this when he established the first news beats in the 1830s, with reporters making regular rounds of places that generated a lot of action.

Police reporters are generally the most prolific, but other fruitful beats for hometown news media are the courts and city hall. These are all "place beats," with reporters spending most of their time at a single geographic location.

Since Bennett's time, news people have designed beats around subjects, like sports and business, and also around issues, like the environment and race relations, because some important issues go undeveloped if reporters focus merely on institutions like police departments and courts and government agencies.

Developing sources is the heart of covering a beat. On some beats there are media relations people whose job includes providing information to reporters and arranging interviews. Thorough coverage, however, requires reporters to tap a great range of sources. This includes being on grapevines, picking up tips while making daily rounds, and being known enough so anonymous sources know whom to contact.

Beat reporting has hazards. Being close to sources is essential, but it can cloud journalistic judgment. Being comfortable with a specialized subject can lead to overly detailed, jargon-loaded stories that don't communicate to a mass audience. Being immersed in a subject can get in the way of placing issues in broader contexts. These are hazards that good beat reporters guard against every day.

STUDY QUESTIONS

1. Why do editors set up beats?

2. How would you begin acquainting yourself with a beat? Which people are worth consulting before even setting foot on the beat? What documents?

3. What is the primary goal of a new beat reporter in meeting sources?

4. When is the telephone an acceptable substitute for "being there" to cover beat stories?

5. Why do public relations people need to know how news beats works?

6. What hazards do reporters face in covering a beat? How can they avoid these hazards?

PUTTING YOUR LEARNING TO WORK

EXERCISE 1   Designing a News Beat

Read three weeks of your daily newspaper's back issues for coverage of your campus. Note who the reporters use as sources. Do not overlook news releases as sources. Then create a list of beat sources you would contact on a regular basis if you were covering the beat. Include each source's official title. Use a campus directory to find each source's office address and telephone number. Use a telephone book and criss-cross directory to find each source's home address and telephone number.

EXERCISE 2   **Creating Story Ideas**

Create a list of possible follow-up stories to your daily newspaper's campus coverage. These could include status reports on matters that are in process, like a construction project, planning next year's budget, fall enrollment expectations. List the names and titles of sources you would contact for each story.

EXERCISE 3   **Building a Beat System**

Imagine you are the news editor for your campus newspaper. You have five reporters to assign to beats to cover campus news. What are the five beats you would create? Now, image you have 10 reporters. Name 10 beats. Imagining you had 15 reporters, do the same. Also for 20.

EXERCISE 4   **Media Relations and Reporters**

Ask your campus public relations person for copies of the 30 latest news releases that were issued to local news media. Read these, and then ask the person in charge of your campus media relations whether there were any media requests regarding those releases, like requests for more information or clarifications. Ask also if any of those releases were in response to media inquiries about a subject. Write a brief report on what you discover about the relationship of reporters on the campus beat for local media and the campus public relations people.

EXERCISE 5   **Public Relations Reporting**

Imagine you are responsible for stories in a monthly employee newsletter for your campus. Whom would you contact regularly on the campus beat for stories?

FOR FURTHER LEARNING

Edna Buchanan. "The Corpse Had a Familiar Face." Random House, 1987. Buchanan, a Pulitzer Prize police reporter, tells a lot about beat reporting in recounting 16 years with the Miami Herald. Buchanan is especially good at source relations.

Jim Corcoran. "Bitter Harvest: Gordon Kahl and the Posse Comitatus: Murder in the Heartland." Viking, 1989. Corcoran bases this book on the knowledge, experience, and sources he developed covering the federal court for the Fargo, N.D., Forum. Corcoran is an especially good observer, which enables him to offer descriptions that help readers experience events.

Stephen Hess. "The Washington Reporters." Brookings Institution, 1981. Hess, a Brookings scholar, used a survey and interviews to answer a wide range of questions about how more than 1,200 Washington reporters go about their work. The study is revealing not just about Washington beat reporting but also about beat reporting everywhere.

Ted Prager. "Police Reporter." Duell, Slon and Pearce, 1957. Prager recounts a career as a police beat reporter for the New York Daily News. Prager's anecdote-rich story is laden with lessons for aspiring beat reporters, especially those interested in crime and courts.

CHAPTER 22

KNOWING THE LEGAL IMPLICATIONS

LEARNING GOALS

In this chapter you will learn:

✦ The U.S. Constitution specifies that the government have a hands-off policy toward the news media, but even that has exceptions.

✦ News stories can lead to libel suits against whoever wrote, printed, aired or otherwise disseminated information that damaged someone.

✦ The courts recognize that individuals have a right to privacy, which affects how reporters pursue some stories.

✦ Copyright law limits the amount of other people's work that news reporters can use without permission.

✦ Some states recognize that reporters sometimes have to keep the names of sources confidential, but this right of confidentiality is tricky and not recognized everywhere.

✦ The Federal Communications Commission regulates radio and television stations but tries to steer clear of influencing broadcast news.

✦ News releases, newsletters and other work produced by public relations people have their special legal hazards.

In other chapters you will learn these additional elements of news law:

✦ Federal and state laws require most government meetings be open to news reporters and the public.

✦ With a few exceptions, documents held by federal, state and local units of government are available to any citizen, including news reporters, to review and discuss and write about.

- The U.S. Supreme Court has ruled that the responsibility for fair trials rests not with the news media but with judges, who can control news coverage of court cases in limited ways.

- Because certain stories and reports pass muster under news law does not mean that there are not ethics implications for conscientious journalists to consider.

ANITA BREWER AND ELVIS

Back when Elvis Presley was alive, the Memphis, Tenn., Commercial Appeal had a lively subject in reporting that singer Anita Brewer was divorced and having a reunion with him. The two had once been close, and in fact Anita Brewer had capitalized on their relationship back then to advance her own budding career.

It turned out that the Commercial Appeal's story had problems. First, there had been no reunion. Second, the story erred in reporting that Anita Brewer and her husband were divorced. Still married and claiming they had been defamed by sloppy reporting, the Brewers sued the newspaper for libel.

A "libel" is a defaming statement, and there was no question that the Commercial Appeal had defamed Anita Brewer. When a news organization is threatened with a libel suit, it sends shivers from newsrooms all the way up to executive suites. To defame someone wrongly is unfortunate enough by itself. Making it worse for news people is that juries have become increasingly inclined to make big financial awards. One award in 1992 topped $50 million.

Considering the inevitability of occasional human error, the quantity of words that pass through a newsroom in a given day, and the amount of news that people would rather not be printed or aired about themselves, it is a wonder that there aren't more libel suits. Journalists, however, have a lot of protection through the First Amendment, which guarantees freedom of expression, if they know how to minimize their vulnerability in telling news. This chapter will tell you ways to tell news safely.

In the Memphis case, a federal appeals court ruled against the Brewers even though the Commercial Appeal had made defamatory errors of fact. The court noted that Anita Brewer had once courted media attention and thereby had chosen to become a public figure. Her public figure status, said the court, gave her special access to the media to set the record straight. The distinction between a public person and ordinary person is significant in news law. An ordinary citizen falsely reported to be divorced and to have reunited with an old lover would have a strong libel suit.

FIRST AMENDMENT AND NEWS LAW

STUDY PREVIEW   The First Amendment guarantees free expression, but the courts allow a wide range of exceptions. These include post-publication suits against the media by people who feel that news stories have defamed them or invaded their privacy.

The First Amendment

The news media are specifically mentioned in the First Amendment to the U.S. Constitution. The amendment, ratified in 1791, says: "Congress shall make no law . . . abridging freedom of speech, or of the press."

The courts have interpreted the amendment broadly. Because the nation's founders in the late 1700s could never have anticipated radio and television, the word "press" has come to include all news media. Because expression is impossible without information, the courts have decided that the First Amendment guarantees the freedom not just to tell news but to gather news. The amendment also has been interpreted to be a guarantee of diverse forms of free expression, including some that are not even verbal—like wearing black arm-bands as a symbolic protest.

Although the wording of the First Amendment is absolute—Congress "shall make no law"—most reasonable people agree that limits are needed. Over the first 200 years of the republic's history, the courts have sorted out conflicts between the media's right to free expression and the rights of individuals who have been wrongly harmed. These court decisions, and also laws originating in Congress and state legislatures, have created a field in jurisprudence known as news law.

News Law

The most visible First Amendment issues occur when the government attempts pre-publication censorship. The U.S. Supreme Court has overruled such censorship consistently, and this is not an everyday problem for journalists. But even on the issue of government censorship, the Supreme Court has said that it could conceive of circumstances, such as national security, in which censorship would be permissible. So even on a basic issue like government censorship, the First Amendment does not give journalists an unrestricted license.

The news law that most affects journalists involves collisions between the media's rights of expression and the rights of individuals who feel damaged by stories that have defamed them wrongly or invaded their privacy. News law also involves copyright protection for the works of creative people. The First

Amendment does not give journalists or anyone else a blanket right to use other people's work without their permission.

While news law places some restrictions on journalists, it also works in their favor. Copyright, for example, protects journalists' work against someone pirating their work. Also, some states have laws which in many situations bar the courts from compelling journalists to divulge their confidential sources.

AVOIDING ACTIONABLE LIBEL

STUDY PREVIEW   People who write, print, air or otherwise disseminate news stories are vulnerable in libel suits if the stories damage someone. Not only can individuals sue but so can small groups and corporations.

Libel as a Risk

News can irk people, especially those who are negatively portrayed. Someone who is defamed may feel hurt enough or mad enough to go to a lawyer and file a libel suit. The stakes are high for a news organization, which, if it loses a libel suit, can be ordered to compensate an injured person both for the damages that can be demonstrated and for punitive damages. Increasingly in recent years, juries have awarded "megaverdicts," as the newspaper trade journal Editor & Publisher calls them. Consider the punitive damages in these early 1990s cases:

+ $41 million to a former district attorney, whom a Dallas television station had reported as dismissing certain drunken-driving charges.

+ $31.5 million to a prosecutor, whom a Philadelphia newspaper had linked to the quashing of a murder investigation 19 years earlier.

+ $12 million to a physician, whose professional competence had been questioned in a Los Angeles newspaper.

Libel suits are not limited to big-city media. The Alton, Ill., Telegraph lost a $9.2 million judgment in a complex 1982 case that, before the amount was reduced on appeal, threatened to put the newspaper out of business.

Nor are libel suits limited to news. A news release from a public relations shop can trigger a libel action. So can an advertisement, a newsletter headline, a caption, a television streamer, or a teaser line to entice listeners to stay tuned for a newscast.

One way to reduce the risk of being sued for libel is to write only happy news, but that won't work. The world is not wholly a rosy place. Robbers hold up banks. Police arrest criminals. Judges sentence crooks. People kill people. Stores gouge customers. Special interests bribe public officials. These things

RULE OF 25. Colonel Harland Sanders didn't much like the extra crispy recipe that was introduced by the new owners of the company he founded. He called it "a damn fried doughball stuck on some chicken." The Louisville, Ky., Courier-Journal picked up the Colonel's colorful quotation, as well as his description of the chain's gravy as a combination of "wallpaper paste" and "sludge." When one Kentucky Fried Chicken outlet sued the Courier-Journal for libel, the Kentucky Supreme Court ruled that the Colonel did not have a particular outlet in mind and that the statement could not be inferred to damage any particular one. In most libel cases, the defamation must be directed at a group of fewer than 25 persons, or in this case chicken stores, to be actionable.

have to be reported. The challenge for news reporters is to tell the negative stories in ways that contribute to a truthful portrayal of the day's issues and events but do not result in losing a libel suit.

Timidity is not a satisfactory approach for reducing the risk of libel losses. Rather, reporters must know the law sufficiently well to distinguish between high-risk, low-risk and risk-free approaches to negative subjects.

Checklist for Actionable Libel

The courts allow a wide variety of defamations. Milwaukee serial murderer Jeffrey Dahmer, to cite an extreme example, was the subject of intensely negative news coverage when he was arrested, yet he would have no grounds for suing. Bill Clinton isn't pleased with many of the news stories about him, but he could hardly sue. Someone accused of shoplifting may find his name in the newspaper, but the newspaper, if the story has been done right, probably has no risk of being sued.

Working through these questions before filing a story can help a news person sort out what is safe and what is not:

+ Is there a defamation?
+ Is someone libeled?
+ Is the libel against a public performance?
+ Is the libel against a public person?
+ Did the libel originate in a privileged forum?
+ Is the libel provably true?

Presence of a Defamation

If you are uneasy about something that you want to include in a story, ask this fundamental question: Is there a defamation?

If the information you are working with includes something nasty, pejorative, humiliating, contemptuous, disgraceful, ridiculing, hateful or otherwise negative, it is, by definition, a defamation. If there is a defamation, you will need to ask more questions from the above checklist.

It is possible, though, that you are uneasy for reasons that have nothing to do with libel. For example, a story on a controversial issue may be a hot item sure to stir strong emotions, but controversy is not necessarily defamation. If there is no defamation, the story will run no risk of losing a libel suit.

Most libel suits stem from accusations or implications of criminal conduct; sexual impropriety; immoral, disgraceful or unusual behavior; professional incompetence; misconduct in a trade or business; carrying a disease; poverty; or financial irresponsibility.

Libel and Identification

A defamation included in a broad stroke is suit-proof. To say an embezzler is on a giant coporation's payroll may not be flattering to either the company or its employees, but the group that the statement defames is so large that no single employee could make a reasonable claim to having been damaged.

To be actionable, a libel must be against an identifiable individual, or the libeled group must be sufficiently small that a member of the group can be presumed to be damaged. It would be risky to write that the 10-person accounting unit in Montpelier, Vt., includes an embezzler.

In cases of group libel, many courts use 25 people as a cutoff point. This Rule of 25 originated in a 1952 case against a book that said "most of the sales staff" at the Nieman-Marcus menswear department in Dallas were "fairies."

No clerks were named, but the judge felt that the group was sufficiently small for individual clerks to go ahead with their suit. Some individuals in a group of 382 clerks also sued, but the judge dismissed their suit because, in his view, the group was too large for individuals to be defamed.

The Rule of 25 is not absolute. The Oklahoma Supreme Court allowed a member of the 1956 University of Oklahoma football team to sue a magazine for an article that implied the Sooners had used stimulative drugs. No names were used. Sixty players were on the squad. The question in such cases is whether a "blanket slur" reaches all members of a group.

Of course, if an individual is identified by name, the defamation carries a risk. There is even a risk if an individual is not named but pinpointed by context. The Kentucky Post reported that one boy had died after a "savage beating." The story did not name the assailant, but the judge allowed him to sue because people who saw the fight were certain to recognize who it was.

Because the law treats corporations as individuals, corporations can recover for libel. Could a giant corporation recover for the previously mentioned hypothetical story that said an embezzler was on its payroll? Probably not. It is almost inconceivable, considering the size of a major corporation and also human frailty, that the company does not have at least one embezzler among its thousands of employees.

Public Performance

Defamations are safe if they are commentary on a public performance. In an often-cited 1901 case, a song and dance group, the Cherry Sisters, were offended by an Iowa writer's newspaper account of their performance:

> Their long skinny arms, equipped with talons at the extremities, swung mechanically, and anon waved frantically at the suffering audience. The mouths of their rancid features opened like caverns, and sounds like the wailing of damned souls issued therefrom.

In a classic ruling, the Iowa Supreme Court ruled that anyone "who goes upon the stage to exhibit himself to the public" may be freely criticized. While the Cherry Sisters case involved reviewing, the doctrine means that news people have great latitude in quoting comments about public performances, whose range includes plays, books, movies, television shows, radio talk shows, newspaper and magazine articles, and newspapers and magazines themselves.

This doctrine of fair comment and criticism, however, does not mean open season on performers. Comedian Carol Burnett, as an example, won a case against the National Enquirer for reporting that she was tipsy and obnoxious at a restaurant. Whatever her celebrity, the Enquirer was hard-pressed to demonstrate that the restaurant incident related to her public performances. It also did not help the Enquirer that Burnett is a teetotaler and that the Enquirer had fabricated the incident.

Public Person

In a landmark 1964 case, in which the Montgomery, Ala., police commissioner sued the New York Times, the U.S. Supreme Court ruled that public officials can sue over a defamation only in rare situations. By and large, the Sullivan decision has made it virtually impossible for public officials to recover for libel.

As a practical matter, however, a news writer trying to determine whether a defamation is safe to include in a story needs to know who is a public official and who is not. The court articulated this broad definition in 1966: "Those among the hierarchy of government who have, or appear to the public to have, substantial responsibility for or control over the conduct of public affairs."

Over the years, various courts have included these people as public officials:

✦ Elected officials.
✦ Secretaries to public officials.
✦ Public school teachers, principals and coaches.
✦ State university administrators and professors.
✦ Police officers.
✦ County medical examiners.
✦ Court clerks.
✦ City and county attorneys.
✦ Public defenders.
✦ IRS and federal drug agents.

Because different courts have drawn the line on who is a public official at different points, news writers should consult with their supervisors, and perhaps a lawyer, on how to make a story safe. The basic principle, though, was articulated by Justice William Brennan when he said that Americans have "a profound national commitment to the principle that debate on public issues should be uninhibited, robust and wide open, and that it may well include vehement, caustic and sometimes unpleasantly sharp attacks on government and public officials."

Besides "public officials," the court has made it extremely difficult for a "public figure" to pursue a libel suit. A definition of "public figure" is even more slippery, but it generally includes people who thrust themselves into the public limelight. People who take public positions on public issues, for example, have chosen to expose themselves to criticism.

PRIVILEGED FORUM. In the interest of robust debate in the creation of public policy, legislators may say anything, no matter how reckless, defamatory or false it is, in legislative hearings. There is no danger of a libel suit. Reporters are also immune from libel action for reporting anything that is said in these sessions. This is how Sen. Joseph McCarthy, R-Wis., right, and the news media escaped libel suits during the Communist witch-hunting in the early 1950s. Like legislative chambers, courtrooms also are privileged forums.   (UPI/The Bettmann Archive)

Even so, news people cannot run roughshod over a public person with defamations. In New York Times versus Sullivan and later cases, the courts have allowed suits if the media are malicious or reckless. These occur when reporters use information that they know is falsely defaming or that they should have recognized as vexatious and failed to check out.

Legislative Sessions

News stories on anything said or done in a legislative chamber are off-limits in terms of libel law, as long as the stories are reasonably true to what happened and what was said. Even outrageously defamatory statements during debate are safe. Neither the utterer nor the reporter can be sued. This applies to Congress, state legislatures, county boards, city councils, school boards and other elected bodies. Committee meetings of elected bodies also are what is called "privileged forums."

The latitudes allowed legislators, and also allowed for news stories on legislative sessions, can be abused. A notorious abuser was Sen. Joseph McCarthy, R-Wis., who used Senate hearings to make reckless, damning charges in the early 1950s. Because McCarthy spoke from a privileged forum, neither he nor reporters who included his charges in their stories could be sued by those who were hurt.

The rationale for giving special privilege to legislators is that they should be absolutely uninhibited in debating public policy issues. If they were constantly second-guessing themselves for fear of a libel suit, the quality of the debate and also the resulting public policy would suffer. Or so goes the reasoning.

The challenge for newspeople in covering legislative sessions with defamatory content, then, is not a legal one but an ethical one. Just because a story would be suit-proof does not mean it should be written. That is a question for the reporters and their supervisors to work through on a basis of conscience and responsibility.

Court Sessions

Like legislative sessions, court sessions are privileged forums. Reporters can be confident that defamations in their stories, like saying that one witness pointed to someone as a murderer, cannot lead to a successful libel suit, so long as the stories are reasonably accurate.

The U.S. justice system is an adversarial one in which two parties each make their best case, including all kinds of defamatory assertions, with judge and jury deciding the truth. The system is also an open one, so citizens or their media surrogates can sit in on trials and most hearings as watchdogs to prevent government abuses of individual liberties.

By extension of this reasoning, documents filed with the court also are privileged. In most states, this means that anything in a criminal complaint or a civil suit may be used in a news story with no fear of losing a libel suit. There are fine distinctions on this immunity in some states, which means that news reporters have to consult with their newsroom supervisors on the particulars of their state's case law. But in general, once officials charge someone with a crime, stories may include the name without risk of a libel action—even if the charge is dropped or the accused person later is exonerated. Such is one price we all pay for an open court system.

Truth as a Defense

If the doctrine of fair comment does not protect defaming information, or if the information did not originate in a privileged forum, news people must be able to prove the truthfulness of the information in their stories. The ultimate

LIBELING A CORPORATION. For a variety of reasons, many corporations avoid suing for libel damages, but this hardly means that journalists have any special license to play loose in covering corporations. In 1993 giant General Motors sued NBC after the television network rigged a truck to explode for a report on the safety of GM trucks. Exposed for engineering the explosion and facing a libel action probably for millions of dollars, NBC apologized for the story within a few hours of the suit being filed. In response, GM withdrew its suit.   (A/P/Wide World)

defense for using a defamation in a story is that it is true. The sexual auteur Madonna might be defamed in the minds of many people if she were called an "exhibitionist" in a news story, but it would be impossible, considering her 1992 book and movies and other performances, for her to deny that she is an exhibitionist. The defamation is true.

In court, the issue is whether the truthfulness can be proven. Consider this hypothetical situation: "After too many martinis, a priest tells a reporter friend that June Smith, a clerk, has embezzled $10,000 from her employer, a local store, and has covered the crime so well that nobody will ever figure it out. The priest says he knows this from hearing Smith's confessions, which he records to help parishioners with later counseling. The priest plays the recording for the reporter and states that he is telling the reporter all this on condition that he not be identified as the source."

Would a story alleging that Smith embezzled the money be safe?

♦ There is a defamation in the embezzlement assertion.

♦ The defamation is against an identifiable person, June Smith.

♦ June Smith is not a public figure.

♦ The libel did not originate in the privileged forum of a legislative or judicial session.

If Smith sued, the reporter would have to prove the truth of the charge. This would be impossible unless the priest agreed to testify and play the tape of Smith's confession. If the priest declined to come forward, or denied that he taped the confession, or admitted to taping the confession but could not or would not produce the tape, the reporter would be vulnerable. The lesson here: Even though a reporter may be confident that a story is true, the issue in court can end up being provable truth.

Attribution and Libel

In some cases, news people can get off the hook in a libel suit if the defamation was accurately quoted or paraphrased with attribution. Whoever was defamed then can go after only the utterer of the defamation.

Attribution, however, is not blanket protection against being sued. It is not always good enough for a reporter to demonstrate, even with a tape recording, that a source has been accurately quoted or paraphrased. The issue can be whether the defamation itself is true.

To be safe, an attributed defamation must have originated with a source in whom a court will agree that the reporter should have had nearly absolute confidence. Also, the reporter may have to demonstrate to the court's satisfaction that there was no reason to doubt the defamation.

Why should a reporter bear the weight of not only quoting a source accurately but also making sure the source was right? The reasoning is that a news organization can do the greater damage. A source, of course, should bear responsibility for wrongful damage caused by a defamation, but the news people compound the damage multifold by passing it on to great numbers of people, perhaps millions.

The safest route is not to use attributed defamations, but timidity can deprive the news audience of information it needs. The challenge for reporters is to be confident that they can explain to a judge and jury that:

♦ The source had a good record of reliability.

♦ The source seemed to be neither maliciously motivated nor sloppy with the facts.

♦ The reporter diligently tried to corroborate the truthfulness of the defamation.

♦ The reporter found no contradictory information from other sources while seeking corroboration.

If defamations are pure opinion, however, there is no problem. The Barre, Vt., Times Argus once called a political candidate "a horse's ass, a jerk, an idiot and paranoid." The candidate sued, but the newspaper won the case. Not only was the target of the defamation a public person, but words like "horse's ass" and "jerk" are hardly provable. They are mere opinion. Words like "idiot" and "paranoid" may have clinical definitions but not in ordinary usage. Words that do not lend themselves to proof are opinion, and quoting a source's opinion is safe. The U.S. Supreme Court has been specific that "imaginative expression" and "rhetorical hyperbole" are allowable.

There is a danger, though, if an opinion seems based on facts. An Ohio sports writer lost a libel case for implying that a high school coach had lied. The writer tried to defend the implication as opinion, but the U.S. Supreme Court was interested in whether the writer had evidence to support his opinion. The writer did not.

Anonymous sources may be good for tips, but using them as a source for a defaming statement is dangerous. Without betraying the confidentiality pledged to an anonymous source, a reporter will be hard pressed to demonstrate to a court's satisfaction that the source was someone who the reporter thought could be trusted.

Deadlines and Libel

Reporters who make defaming mistakes in covering important, breaking news have been excused by some courts. These courts recognize both the importance of quick coverage and the difficulties of making sense of what's happening in an unfolding situation. This "hot news" defense, however, has found less sympathy in other courts. Even so, it can be said that newspaper, radio and television reporters with tight deadlines stand less risk of losing a libel action than do magazine writers who have weeks to work up a story.

The courts sometimes are tolerant of technical glitches that defame someone, like a photo ending up with the wrong story, but not always. Nevertheless, a technical foul-up may mitigate the damage award to whoever was libeled.

RESPECTING PRIVACY RIGHTS

STUDY PREVIEW   The courts have come to recognize an individual's right to privacy, which affects how reporters pursue some stories.

Privacy Versus Free Inquiry

The idea that the news media should pursue information to keep people informed precedes the founding of the republic. The First Amendment to the

U.S. Constitution embodied this principle in 1791. More recently, the idea that individuals have a right to privacy has evolved, and gradually it has been recognized in law. At times, the right of free inquiry that is inherent in the First Amendment is in conflict with the right to privacy.

The issue for news people is knowing when their constitutional right to ask questions and pursue truth is encroaching on an individual's right to privacy. In part, this is a matter of decency and common sense, but in recent years some principles of privacy have been codified into law. Privacy law and court cases also recognize that individuals have some rights to control publicity about themselves.

A Right to Privacy

Dorothy Barber had an unusual disorder, probably of the pancreas, that caused her to lose weight. The more she ate, the more she lost. Tipped to the woman's plight, a Kansas City, Mo., photographer went to a hospital where she was being treated. Despite the woman's objections, the photographer took pictures that ended up in the paper and later were distributed nationwide.

Dorothy Barber sued Time magazine, which ran one of the photos with a brief, flashy story that called her a "starving glutton." She won the case, arguing that a patient should have a reasonable expectation of privacy in a hospital. That point, that there is a right to be let alone, has been underscored in numerous cases since Barber versus Time in 1942.

In some situations, the public interest in a subject outweighs an individual's right to privacy, but these are matters of judgment, which are decided ultimately in court. It is best to seek legal counsel in sorting through how to deal with a particular story. Whatever public interest existed in Dorothy Barber's pancreatic disorder could have been met, for example, in a story that neither identified her nor carried a photo.

If a person consents to surrender his or her privacy, then there can be no cause for a privacy case. Without permission, though, there can be problems, as public relations people for Garfinkel's department store in Washington, D.C., discovered in 1985. A plastic surgeon had used before and after photographs of a patient as part of a Garfinkel's promotion. Garfinkel's got off the hook when it pointed out that the plastic surgeon had assured the store's public relations director that the patient had consented.

Where can a reporter seek information and photographs without risking a privacy suit? Generally, a person in a public place, like on a street or in a park or public building, is fair game, although harassment is not allowed. A photographer who jumps out from behind bushes to get a surprised expression on a celebrity's face, for example, has gone too far. A reporter who hounds someone is vulnerable. The issue of public interest, though, can justify hounding. It is the courts that decide, usually more on the particular situation than on a cohesive body of law.

Private places are protected. At home a person can expect privacy, and also in a hospital, as Dorothy Barber's case demonstrated. In one case, involving a CBS television crew that charged into a restaurant with cameras rolling, the court found that people should have refuge from the media at a restaurant, despite its quasi-public nature.

What about private places viewable from outside? A Seattle television photographer, denied access to a pharmacy for a story on a druggist being investigated for Medicaid fraud, photographed the druggist at work through a window from the street. The court found this permissible, following the general rule that anything visible from a public place is not protected by privacy rights. The druggist could control access to his property but had no reasonable expectation of shielding himself from anyone, including a photographer, from the street.

The pivotal question is whether there is a reasonable expectation of privacy. A backyard sunbather, for example, could have a strong case against a photographer who climbed a seldom-scaled cliff to shoot a picture down into the backyard.

Reporters who use telephoto lenses or hidden electronic recording devices generally will have a hard time in a privacy case. Life magazine lost a case brought by a "healer" who used clay, minerals, herbs and gadgetry. Two reporters used a hidden camera and microphones for their story. The court, in this case, considered the healer's assumption of privacy in his home-office greater than whatever public interest existed.

Key questions in privacy include:

✦ Does the subject have a reasonable expectation of privacy?

✦ Does the story involve private facts whose disclosure would be highly offensive to a reasonable person?

✦ Is the story of legitimate concern to the public?

Controlling Publicity

Celebrities have a high degree of control over publicity about themeslves, but this is more a property right than a privacy issue. The idea is that a celebrity's persona is a commercial asset that belongs to the celebrity. An entrepreneur, for example, cannot market posters of a movie star or rock performer without permission.

In news, however, celebrities have no such control, even though almost all newspapers, magazines and broadcast networks and stations are in business to make money. It is "commercial exploitation" of their likeness that individuals are protected against, and news coverage has been excluded from that description.

Public relations people walk a fine line that has not been worked out by the courts. Is their purpose news? Or is it commercial? In corporate public relations, the safest course is to limit the content of news releases, including accompanying photographs, to things for which the subjects have granted permission.

GIVING CREDIT

STUDY PREVIEW   Copyright law allows news reporters to pick up limited amounts of other people's work without permission. The idea is to facilitate the exchange of information while not diminishing the rights of the orginator of the material. This is called "fair use." Outright thievery, however, is inexcusable as unfair competition.

Copyright Rules

To encourage creative people to be productive, the nation's founders provided an economic incentive. It was called copyright. Any creative work, including books, news stories and photographs, is considered the intellectual property of its creator, who holds a copyright on the work. Like the owners of other property, the owner of a copyrighted work can do just about anything with it—sell it, loan it, rent it, or keep it for posterity.

By and large, this means that news people cannot pick up other people's work and incorporate it into their own. Exceptions are based on the concepts of fair use, public interest, and public domain.

Under the Fair Use Doctrine news people, editors of house organs and others may use small excerpts from a copyrighted work without permission. So that the financial interests of copyright owners are not diminished, there are limits on how much may be taken.

Copyright lawyers give different answers, but conservative advice generally is that as many as 400 words may be quoted from a book, 150 words from a magazine, and less from a newspaper. Among television and movie people, agreements usually allow two minutes from a full-length feature without permission.

A second issue is whether the quantity of copyrighted material in a new work is too much. A 200-word magazine story that excerpts 150 words from another magazine has borrowed too much. The courts have never developed firm guides, which means it is judge and jury who determine how much is too much case by case.

The greater the public interest, the more sympathetic the courts will be to longer unauthorized excerpts. In 1963, Life magazine bought Abraham Zapruder's film of the assassination of President John Kennedy. When the author of a book used charcoal renditions of stills from the Zapruder film, Life sued but lost. The court found the public interest outweighed Life's property interest.

For most creative work, copyrights today are for the creator's lifetime plus 50 years. After that, the work enters the public domain and anybody can use any or all of it. Mark Twain is fair game. So is Shakespeare.

Most news people do not own the work they produce. Under the Work for Hire Doctrine, an employee's work belongs to the employer. The copyright on works for hire, as well as anonymous and pseudonymous works, is protected for 100 years after their creation and 75 years after publication. Then they too enter the public domain.

Using someone else's work under the Fair Use Doctrine is not a license to plagiarize. Out of a sense of decency, one should always give credit.

Obtaining Permission

A work is copyrighted the moment that it is created in tangible form. Formerly a work had to be registered with the Library of Congress to be protected, but no more. Most people who are serious about protecting their property rights do register the material, however, and mark it prominently, using one of the styles shown in the following examples:

✦ © 1975, NBC News.

✦ Copyright 1982, by Seymour Hirsch.

✦ Copr. 1975, by Hill and Knowlton.

For permission, you have to contact the copyright holder. This may take time because the copyright line includes neither address nor telephone number. Also, people move, copyrights are sold, and people die and pass their property interest in a work to their heirs.

Once a copyright holder is located, there may be negotiations over a price for the material, limits on the context in which it will be used, how many times it may be used or how long it may be. All of this discourages news people, especially in breaking situations, from going beyond the limited excerpting allowed under the Fair Use Doctrine. The editor of an employee magazine or other public relations publication would, of course, have more time to seek permission.

Piracy of News

Everybody has heard some radio station somewhere that buys its news on a street corner for 50 cents a copy. You can sometimes even hear the announcer turning the pages. Some low-budget newspapers assign their sports reporters to monitor play-by-play radio coverage of athletic events and then slap their byline and dateline on the next morning's story.

Pirating another news organization's coverage is an unfair trade practice that the courts have been absolutely clear about. In 1918 the U.S. Supreme Court ruled against International News Service, which had been taking AP stories, rewriting them, sometimes heavily, sometimes modestly, and dispatching them to INS subscribers. Justice Mahlon Pitney, who had no tolerance for the transparency of the piracy, found that INS was "endeavoring to reap where it has not sown" and "appropriating to itself the harvest of those who have sown."

There is no prohibition, however, against monitoring competing news organizations for tips. A news event cannot be copyrighted. The first reporter at a plane crash cannot claim any exclusive privilege in covering the event. All that can be protected is the reporter's account. As Justice Mahlon Pitney explained it in 1918, the framers of the Constitution did not intend "to confer upon one who might happen to be first to report an historic event the exclusive right for any period to spread the knowledge of it."

What, then, constitutes piracy in highly competitive news reporting? Reporters are safe legally to monitor competing journalists for tips and story ideas, and then go out and independently gather their own information. It is piracy when a reporter picks up someone else's story whether word for word or by paraphrasing, even if the original source is credited. Cases on this issue will almost always turn on whether the follow-up stories were the result of what Justice Pitney called "independent investigation."

Despite the U.S. Supreme Court's clear decision in the AP versus INS, it seems that there are news people who have not heard of the opinion. In a 1963 case, a Pottstown, Pa., radio station, WPAZ, was reading the Potts-town Mercury over the air. The Pennsylvania Supreme Court declared the practice unfair competition, noting that WPAZ was free-loading on the Mercury in creating newscasts to attract the same advertisers that the news-paper was seeking. It was, in Justice Pitney's 1918 metaphor, reaping where someone else had sown.

Deadline Pressure

Does deadline pressure ever excuse a copyright violation? In libel cases, the courts often are lenient about bad journalistic decisions made under deadline, but this leniency has not extended to copyright or unfair competition questions.

When actor Charlie Chaplin died in 1977, CBS quickly assembled a documentary that included a compilation of Chaplin film clips that had been part of a tribute shown at the Academy Awards five years earlier. The company that owned the Chaplin films had authorized the Academy Awards sponsors to use the clips for the 1972 awards ceremony but for no other purpose. When the clips showed up in the CBS documentary, the owner sued—and collected $717,000 damages.

SHIELDING SOURCES

STUDY PREVIEW   Some states recognize that reporters sometimes have to keep the names of some sources confidential, but the right of confidentiality is tricky and not recognized everywhere.

Protecting Confidentiality

Some news organizations, including USA Today, have policies against confidential sources. Their thinking is that the news audience needs to know the source to assess information intelligently. These policies also prevent a lot of headaches, especially if a confidential source is privy to information that someone needs in a court case.

The problem of confidentiality came home to Paul Pappas, a reporter for television station WTEV in Providence, R.I., in 1970. Members of the radical Black Panthers in nearby New Bedford, Mass., invited Pappas to spend a tense night in their barricaded headquarters. They were expecting a police raid, and they wanted an outsider as a witness from the inside. Pappas, a white journalist, was perfect, and he agreed, accepting the condition that he not divulge information that could jeopardize Black Panther members.

Two months later, Pappas was called before a grand jury to tell what he knew. He testified about what he had seen before being invited inside but declined to say anything about what he saw or heard after giving his word to the Black Panthers. The grand jury was not happy, nor was a judge who ordered Pappas to tell all that the grand jurors wanted to know. Pappas appealed.

About the same time, similar cases had come up in Kentucky, involving Paul Branzburg of the Louisville Courier–Journal, and in California, involving Earl Caldwell of the New York Times. The reporters all noted that the First Amendment implicitly protects news gathering and that they and other journalists would lose important sources if they divulged their identities. These sources, they said, were essential for important stories that otherwise would never be told.

The journalists also argued that compelling them to testify would turn them into police agents, contrary to the basic principle that journalists are separate from government. Also, and not unimportantly, they noted the ethical obligation they had to keep their word to their confidential sources.

The U.S. Supreme Court heard the Pappas, Branzburg and Caldwell cases together, and the decision was not good for journalists who want to protect their sources. The court said that journalists have the same obligation as other citizens to help authorities in criminal investigations. Society's interest in law enforcement outweighs society's interest in whatever understandings and insights might come from stories drawn from confidential sources.

State Shield Laws

After the Pappas-Branzburg-Caldwell decision, state legislatures began adopting laws that recognize the confidentiality of journalists' sources to one degree or another. Twenty-eight states now have these "shield laws": Alabama, Alaska, Arizona, Arkansas, California, Colorado, Delaware, Georgia, Illinois, Indiana, Kentucky, Louisiana, Maryland, Michigan, Minnesota, Montana,

Nebraska, Nevada, New Jersey, New Mexico, New York, North Dakota, Ohio, Oklahoma, Oregon, Pennsylvania, Rhode Island, Tennessee.

Because these laws offer broader citizen rights than the U.S. Constitution, they are subject to judicial review only at the state level, which means they are not subject to the U.S. Supreme Court decision in the Pappas, Branzburg and Caldwell cases.

While shield laws vary from state to state, they generally recognize journalists' notes as off-limits to police and other investigators. Because it is in these notes that authorities would look for names, these laws are fairly good shields to protect confidential journalistic sources.

There are significant exceptions, however. In some states, grand juries investigating wrongdoing may compel a reporter to surrender notes and testify. Also, some shield laws have an exemption if one side or the other in a court case is absolutely stymied in its case without information possessed by a reporter, regardless of any pledge of confidentiality.

A reporter or any other citizen who refuses a court order can be jailed for contempt of court. Because most reporters take their pledges of confidentiality seriously, a reporter occasionally spends time behind bars.

Contempt sentences are open-ended, which means a person can sit in jail until agreeing to go along with a judge and testify fully. Conceivably, a contempt sentence could last a lifetime, but most end up being a few days at most. The record is 46 days, virtually in solitary confinement, by William Farr, a Los Angeles Herald Examiner reporter who had information that a court wanted in the trial of mass murderer Charles Manson. New York Times reporter Myron Farber spent 40 days in jail for ignoring a subpoena for information in a New Jersey murder trial, and the Times was fined more than $250,000.

Newsroom Searches

In their quest for information, police have been known to raid newsrooms for reporters' notes. This happened at the Stanford University Daily, a student newspaper, in 1971. Police, armed with a search warrant, barged unannounced into the newsroom and rummaged through drawers and wastebaskets for unpublished photographs of people at a campus demonstration. The Daily went to court, asserting that the police had no reason to suspect anyone in the newsroom of wrongdoing. The U.S. Supreme Court, deciding the case in 1978, said newsrooms are not off-limits if a judge thinks they should be searched. That, however, was not the last word on newsroom searches.

Two years later Congress passed the Privacy Protection Act, which in general bars newsroom searches. An exception is if someone in the newsroom is suspected of a crime or if time is of the essence to prevent someone from being hurt. A search warrant may be issued if there is reason to suspect that a reporter may be about to destroy information that a judge believes is relevant to a criminal investigation.

Instead of seeking search warrants, investigators now are more inclined to go to a judge for a subpoena instructing a reporter or editor to produce documents or information by a certain deadline. This allows time for a news organization to formulate a response, either to comply or to challenge the right of the court to whatever information is being sought. The subpoena is more orderly than the mayhem of a police raid.

Voluntary Disclosure

In a 1991 case, the U.S. Supreme Court found that a reporter's pledge of confidentiality to a source is binding, barring a subpoena. In other words, neither a reporter nor newsroom supervisors may voluntarily break a confidentiality agreement with a source.

The case stemmed from a Minnesota political activist's leak of campaign dirt against an opposition candidate to several news organizations. The leak came in the waning hours of the campaign, and some news organizations skipped the story entirely. The editors of the Minneapolis Star Tribune and the St. Paul Pioneer Press felt, however, that the leak was an 11th-hour smear and that voters should know the source was someone in the opposition campaign. Disregarding that the source had insisted on confidentiality, the editors of both newspapers, acting independently, published the allegation and named Dan Cohen as the source.

Cohen lost his public relations job, which he blamed on the newspapers' breach of confidentiality, and he sued. Such a suit, said the Supreme Court, is permissible, and turned the case back to the Minnesota courts, which awarded $200,000 to Cohen.

BROADCAST NEWS REGULATION

STUDY PREVIEW   In regulating broadcasting, the federal government has carved out special latitudes for news. For the most part, Federal Communications Commission regulations do not apply to "bona fide" news programs.

Exemptions for Bona Fide News

The Federal Communications Commission licenses radio and television stations and has the power to revoke and not renew licenses. Because stations cannot operate without an FCC license, broadcasters are responsive to commission rules. Some of these rules affect broadcast newsrooms, although the FCC, in deference to the First Amendment, generally treads lightly on news issues. Even so, broadcast journalists work in a federally regulated environment, which affects some things that they do.

By and large, the Federal Communications Commission does not involve itself in what it terms "bona fide" newscasts, news interview programs, news documentaries, and on-scene news coverage. What does the commission mean by "bona fide"? Over the years the commission has had to tinker with the definition, but today a news program is considered bona fide if:

+ Broadcasters control the format and content, as opposed to advertisers, political partisans or political candidates.
+ Content is based on reasonable, good-faith journalistic judgment.
+ There is no evidence of favoritism, like covering one political candidate but neglecting opponents.
+ The program is regularly scheduled.

The commission has had to struggle with defining "news" because it has firm rules on political advertising, political programs, and political forums, which are news in a broad sense. Here are examples of bona fide news:

+ Regular newscasts, like ABC Radio's daily Paul Harvey program; hourly headlines; noon news roundups.
+ Weekly public affairs programs, like CBS' "Issues and Answers."
+ "Later With Bob Costas," on NBC, which the FCC has held is a bona fide news interview program.
+ The Sally Jessy Raphael syndicated program, which the FCC also has held to be a bona fide news interview program.

Broadcast journalists sometimes get involved in sponsoring political forums and candidate debates, and these are not necessarily "bona fide" news in the FCC's view. If a program is not bona fide news or if there is any doubt, the best advice is to consult your station's lawyer. There are serious implications if a program falls outside the bona fide area.

Although stations are required to give candidates for federal office "reasonable access" to their airwaves, a candidate cannot insist on being on a bona fide news program.

What is "reasonable" access? In 1991, the FCC upheld the decision of two New Hampshire television stations not to grant presidential hopeful Michael Steven Levinson three-hour blocks of prime time. There were 19 candidates in the New Hampshire primary at the time, and the stations argued that not only would Levinson's request disrupt programming but a floodgate of requests from the other candidates would leave programming in disarray. The stations instead offered Levinson five prime-time minutes.

According to the Equal Opportunities Rule, if a station gives one political candidate airtime outside of a bona fide news program, it must accept requests for airtime from other candidates for the office. Unlike the Reasonable Access Rule, this rule applies to candidates for all, not just federal, offices.

Under the Equal Opportunities Rule, the FCC ruled in 1976 that any station replaying old Ronald Reagan movies would have to give other presidential candidates air time.

In 1984, the commission said that William Branch, a Sacramento, Calif., television reporter could not continue on the air if he ran for the town council in a nearby community, unless other candidates were given air time. Branch averaged about three minutes a day on the air, which meant the station would have had to allow his opponents 33 hours of air exposure during the campaign. Branch's choice: withdraw from the race or take a leave of absence.

Under the Zapple Rule, if a station sells or gives time to supporters of a candidate during a political campaign, the station must do the same for supporters of the opponent. Bona fide news programs are an exception.

Personal attacks are another area where the "bona fide" distinction comes into play. A station must contact any individual or small group that is subjected to an on-air character attack outside a bona fide news program and offer a chance to respond on the air. The requirement involves providing tapes, transcripts and summaries of what was said.

Slanting the News

The Federal Communications Commission sidesteps many First Amendment issues by not extending its regulatory authority into newsrooms. The commission's tolerance, however, does not include intentional slanting. In 1975 the FCC refused to renew the licenses of stations owned by Don Burden after learning that he was using them on behalf of political friends. At KISN in Vancouver, Wash., Burden had instructed the news staff to run only favorable stories on one U.S. Senate candidate and negative stories on the other. At WIFE in Indianapolis, he ordered "frequent, favorable mention" of a U.S. senator on the air.

In the Burden case, the FCC declared it would not put up with "attempts to use broadcast facilities to subvert the political process." The commission called for honest news judgment, specifically decrying Burden for putting his private interests ahead of his responsibilities as a license holder to inform the public.

While the FCC will act against deliberate, gross distortions in news, it has turned away complaints that allege misquotation and bad editing. Those are competence issues that do not affect "the substance of the news." When it comes to news, the FCC says it neither wants to be nor can be "the national arbiter of truth."

Staged News

The Federal Communications Commission has avoided the ethics debate about broadcasters who illustrate news stories with actors and props, but the commission takes a dim view of illegal activity in staging events. When television station WBBM in Chicago asked college students to come to a marijuana party so it could get video for a story, the FCC was not amused. The "party" was portrayed to viewers as real, but it would never have occurred had the station not arranged it for the sole purpose of photographing it.

Some broadcasters, it seems, were not listening when the FCC reprimanded WBBM for the staged pot party in 1969. Staged news has continued to be an issue, although the FCC in recent years seems to prefer leaving corrective and punitive action to the courts and station management.

To boost ratings in 1990, Denver television station KCNC promoted a four-part series on illegal dog fights as an investigative journalism breakthrough. The series itself turned out to be the scandal. Unable to find any real dog fights, reporter Wendy Bergin and photojournalists Scott Wright and Jim Stair staged a gruesome dog fight that was the series' cornerstone. All three ended up indicted for dogfighting for "monetary gain or entertainment," a Colorado felony punishable by four years in prison.

In 1992 reporters for KCCO in Alexandria, Minn., wanted video to accompany a report on underage drinking, so they bought beer and invited some high-school kids over for a party. A good time was had by all, until later when it occurred to somebody that it was against the law to provide alcohol to minors. Some staff people left the station permanently.

For its story on the safety of General Motors pickup trucks with fuel tanks positioned outside the truck frame, NBC crashed a car into a GM truck. The explosion made wonderful video. Four months later, General Motors sued for libel, charging that NBC crews had strapped rockets to the truck's tank to make sure there was a fiery explosion. The issue was not that viewers were deceived by the videotaped crash, which was identified on air as a demonstration, but that the demonstration was dishonest. In one of broadcast journalism's most humiliating moments, NBC apologized profusely, and General Motors, hopeful that the publicity that its suit attracted would offset the damage of the NBC report, dropped the suit.

On-Air Indecency

The Federal Communications Commission has run hot and cold through its history on on-air indecency. The commission once fined a broadcaster for running an interview with a rock musician who uttered vulgarities. In another case a station was fined for allowing and encouraging sexual innuendos during listener call-in programs. Whether these situations would today be considered bona fide news is unclear.

In 1989 the FCC dismissed a complaint that the words "fuck" and "fucking" appeared 10 times in a segment on National Public Radio's "All Things Considered." The vulgarities were in a tape-recorded conversation that had been admitted as evidence in a mobster trial. The commission voted 4-1 that the context of the vulgarities was part of legitimate news coverage and therefore permissible.

The commission is less tolerant outside of newscasts. Comedian George Carlin's "seven dirty words," made infamous in a 1978 U.S. Supreme Court case, still are forbidden at hours when children might be listening. In 1992 the FCC issued a $600,000 fine for indecency against syndicated radio shock-jock Howard Stern.

NEWS LAW AND PUBLIC RELATIONS

STUDY PREVIEW   Public relations work has its own legal hazards. A corporate news release that makes claims about a company product, or about a competitor's product, must be constructed carefully. And house organs are hardly the safe havens that some people imagine.

News Releases

When Texas Gulf Sulphur found a spectacularly rich copper deposit in eastern Ontario, the company issued a news release that rumors of a major discovery were speculative and "without factual basis." To say the least, the TGS release was misleading. Although chemical tests on the ore had not been completed, company executives knew what they had found.

After the release was issued, but before it was announced 12 days later that 10 million tons of ore had been found, many investors unloaded their TGS stock and company executives bought it up. The Securities and Exchange Commission took the company to court for deliberately influencing investors with misleading information. The vehicle to do it was a news release.

Several lessons can be derived from the Texas Gulf Sulphur case and other cases involving news releases.

Many First Amendment protections for news do not apply to news releases from corporations and other organizations that are subject to government regulation. TGS was a publicly traded company, and the Securities and Exchange Commission has firm rules about stock manipulation.

News media stories can speculate wildly about ore strikes and all kinds of corporate activity, but news releases, as a corporate-controlled medium, have no such liberty—even if issued in response to a news-media query. Mum is the word for prudent public relations people in many situations.

Public relations people must know the government regulations involving their organization's activities, whether they are those of the Securities and Exchange Commission, the Federal Trade Commission, the U.S. Forest Service or any of dozens of federal and state agencies. That is why the Public Relations Society of America emphasizes government regulations in its accreditation exams.

Public relations people have a professional obligation to advise their supervisors, including corporate executives, if they suspect that information they are told to release is wrong or misleading in some way. This is not only a professional and ethics question but also a legal one. A public relations person can be named as a co-conspirator in a legal action.

News releases are not immune from libel suits. Routine personnel announcements, like an executive shakeup, have led to suits from departed people. A news release issued by a public relations firm for the Schlitz brewing company resulted in a $3.5 million libel claim by three former Schlitz executives.

News-Media Inquiries

A general principle of media relations is openness with reporters, but being helpful has some limits. Besides government regulations, there are privacy issues. For example, public relations people often can dip into personnel and other files, but only some information about employees is safe to release:

✦ The employee's title and job description.

✦ When the employee was hired and terminated.

Employees have prevailed in privacy actions when information is released about their address, marital status, family, memberships, and job performance. Some organizations ask employees to sign a standard biography form with consent that it be available for release. To be released, file photos should also have a consent signature from the employee.

Public relations people sometimes can accommodate a reporter and also protect the privacy of an employee by explaining the privacy issue to the reporter and then relaying the reporter's request for information to the employee. It then is up to the employee to initiate direct contact with the reporter and decide what to divulge.

House Organs

A lesson that some organizations learn the hard way is that they do not own their employees. Employees have rights. This point has come up in numerous lawsuits against organizations for items in house organs about employees.

Squibs about birthdays, marriages, anniversaries and vacations in a personals column are especially hazardous, especially if jazzed up with misplaced commentary:

Jill Smart, of accounting, and Joey Frank, a local lawyer, were married last month. What's it like the second time around, Jill?	Rich Zelmer turned his tan blue when he came back to Michigan from his Hawaiian vacation. It was 10 below when he landed.
Joe Gumphrey has lost 40 pounds after joining the SoLongFatso weight-loss program. Way to go, Joe!	

The news media might argue newsworthiness and public interest with personal tidbits about prominent people, but this won't work for a house organ.

No matter how prominent people are in their workplace, their privacy interests will be compelling in court. Advice:

+ Limit coverage strictly to work-related matters.
+ Ask employees to sign a blanket release for coverage of work-related matters.
+ Submit copy to the individuals being mentioned and ask for their permission. Have them initial the copy.
+ Use items in a personals column only if submitted by the individual involved.

CHAPTER WRAP-UP

The First Amendment guarantees free expression, which includes the right of the news media to gather and disseminate news. But there are limits. These include the right of someone who is defamed in a news story to seek damages. To avoid problems in this area of law, called libel, journalists must know how to write deftly to tell the news at minimal risk.

Limits exist on the right to inquiry if it infringes on privacy. The courts recognize that an individual has a right to privacy. In general, anywhere that a person has a reasonable expectation of being let alone is a hazardous place for newspeople to venture. People who have chosen to be in the limelight are not as protected as other people, but this does not mean that they don't have any right to privacy.

Copyright law guarantees that whoever creates "intellectual property," including books and articles, can restrict other people from reproducing their work. This means that journalists who want to quote a passage from someone else or to reproduce a photograph or drawing must seek permission and perhaps pay a royalty fee.

To facilitate the exchange of ideas, however, copyright law allows brief amounts to be reproduced without permission, like a sentence or two from a newspaper article, a snippet from a feature-length movie or a paragraph from a book. It is plagiarism, however, to do so without acknowledging the source.

Some states protect inquiry by prohibiting their courts from compelling journalists to divulge their confidential sources. These "shield laws," which allow journalists to shield their sources, greatly facilitate news gathering because some sources, like mob insiders, will not talk if they know they will be identified.

Shield laws, however, are not a blanket protection. Many of them require journalists to break their confidentiality if police cannot obtain necessary information any other way. There are other exceptions too. Journalists who insist on protecting sources can go to jail.

Broadcasters work in a government-regulated environment because their stations are licensed by the Federal Communications Commission. Throughout its history, however, the FCC has tried to avoid regulating newsroom policies. In general, broadcast journalists are as free as their print-media colleagues as long as they make reasonable, good-faith journalistic judgments on what to report and how to report it.

Broadcast journalists can get into complicated FCC rules, though, with sponsored political forums and candidate debates, which are not necessarily "bona fide" news in the FCC's view.

Also, the Federal Communications Commission is firm against intentional slanting of the news, or reporting that violates the law to stage events.

The courts recognize a difference between news and what public relations people produce. This is especially clear in organizations subject to government regulation. A news release generated on its behalf by a corporation or other organization does not have the same constitutional protection as a news media story on the same subject, even if the release and the story say the same thing. In short, the First Amendment is superseded by the regulations. Also, there is less First Amendment protection when a message is in a self-serving vehicle like a news release or a house organ.

There also is a greater risk of privacy suits for coverage in internal media, like corporate house organs, because the latitudes given the news media for news worthiness and public interest are either lacking or not as strong.

STUDY QUESTIONS

1. If the First Amendment guarantees free expression, then how can a news organization be sued for what it prints and airs?

2. How can journalists reduce the risk of being sued for libel over stories that hurt someone?

3. Can a story lead to a successful libel suit if the story contains no defamation?

4. Can people sue successfully for libel if they have not been named?

5. How far can journalists go with negative comments about a performer?

6. How has New York Times versus Sullivan affected libel law?

7. Why are reporters safe in quoting defamatory statements from legislative and judicial sessions?

8. Does an attributed, accurate quotation of a defamatory statement immunize a news writer from a libel suit?

9. Do the courts ever excuse a defamation because of deadline pressure?

10. How aggressively can reporters pursue a story without violating an individual's right to privacy?

11. When must reporters seek permission to quote someone else's work?

12. Why is it hazardous to a reporter to accept information on a confidential basis?

13. How much does the Federal Communications Commission regulate radio and television news?

14. Why doesn't the First Amendment apply to news releases and house organs in the same way it does to the news media?

PUTTING YOUR LEARNING TO WORK

EXERCISE 1   Names in Crime News

You have been monitoring police channels and hear the First State Bank downtown is being robbed. You arrive about the same time as police, amid much confusion.

James F. Cochran, a pharmacist next door, said he was depositing checks when the robber, whom he described as a woman with a blond wig, pulled a gun on the teller at the next window. "She turned to me, and said to 'stay still, like nothing's happening.' She put a bunch of bills in her purse and turned around and walked out."

Cochran said she was wearing a white and beige pantsuit, lots of jewelry, stood 5-foot-8 or so, well groomed, trim. He believes he was the only person besides his teller and the teller being robbed who realized a robbery was under way. This, he says, was just before 4 o'clock.

Cochran owns James' Medicine Chest, 515 Main Street. He had already made his deposit, $617.82, and had the deposit slip in his hand when he realized the robbery was going on. The robber, he said, had a deep voice. She walked briskly out of the bank and headed left, west, probably around the corner of Main and Sixth Street.

You see Janeen Griech, president of the bank, but she declines to discuss details. She does say, however, the robbery was recorded by video cameras on the walls at 3:58 p.m. and that the police took the tape. The only money taken was in a cash drawer at the teller's window. Griech wouldn't say how much. She refers you to the police.

Forrest Gordon, police captain, doesn't know how much was taken yet. He says the teller and others in the bank are being interviewed. He said the FBI will take over the investigation, which is routine for banks whose depsoits are insured by a federal agency. "I would tell you how much was taken when I find out, but I can't. The FBI has a policy against that."

Outside the bank you find Heidi Mason, a teller, sobbing in the corner of an alley. She had been waiting on James Cochran when the robbery occurred. Mason says the robber was Kerry Davis, who had worked at the bank as a security guard until a week earlier. She recognized his voice. The pantsuit, wig and makeup were a disguise, she says. Mason says Davis was fired, but she didn't know details. She says she dated him once a couple of months ago, but didn't know him very well. He lives in Hopeville, a northside neighborhood, on Oak Street she believes. Between sobs, Mason says she will go back inside the bank as soon as she regains her composure and talk to the police. She says Jonathan Rekord was the teller who was robbed.

You ask Griech, the bank president, to see a criss-cross directory. You find:

Davis, Kerry T. 1642 Oak St. Security Guard, First State Bank. 667–1301.

You call. No answer.

You ask Griech about Davis. She seems surprised but says Davis was let go after being caught napping in the employee lunch room. That was last week. Gordon, the police captain, interrupts your conversation and tells you to go outside. He points to officers putting a yellow ribbon around the bank's front door. "You're off limits in here," he says as he ushers you out. You ask what kind of gun the robber had. "Small handgun, Saturday night special of some sort."

A bystander outside the yellow-ribbon perimeter turns out to be Jonathan Rekord's roommate, Lance Smyth. He's peeved because police also ushered him outside when they took Jonathan into a back room to be debriefed. Smyth says Jonathan told him he turned over about $3,500 in $100 bills to the robber. He said Jonathan was "pretty shaken up."

It is now 4:30 p.m. and you have one-half hour to write a one-minute story for your radio station's 5 p.m. newscast. Your tape recorder has failed so it will be entirely script, no voicers. A news law question you will have to deal with: Do you mention that former bank security guard Kerry Davis was identified by teller Heidi Mason as the robber?

EXERCISE 2   Employee Newsletter

As the new public relations director at Community Memorial Hospital, you are expected to revamp the employee newsletter. One popular feature is "ComMem People." Here are some items from the last issue:

Maxine Rhodes, anesthesiology, has tied the knot with Greg Fogarty, March 14. They are living at 1421 Knotty Road, #14.

Kyle Krueger, bookkeeping, and her family vacationed a week at Hedonism II, a resort in Jamaica. Nice tan line, Kyle.

John Gordon, custodial services, and his wife Hanna are the proud parents of a girl Myrtle Rae, who was born March 18. She was 7 pounds, 14 ounces.

Mike Farr, food services, was promoted to assistant food handler. Congratulations, Mike.

Would you have cause to worry about legal implications if you continue "ComMem People" in its current form?

FOR FURTHER LEARNING

Ellen Alderman and Caroline Kennedy. "In Our Defense: The Bill of Rights in Action." Morrow, 1991. Alderman and Kennedy have an excellent chapter on the First Amendment with special attention to a 1987 Ku Klux Klan attempt to force its way onto the Kansas City, Mo., cable system's public access channel.

Bill F. Chamberlin. "State Media Law Sourcebook." Brechner Center for Freedom of Information, 1983. This pocket-size guide has information on the states' media laws.

Christopher W. French, editor. The Associated Press Stylebook and Libel Manual. Associated Press, 1986. This stylebook, used by all AP reporters and editors, contains a good, brief addendum on avoiding actionable libel.

Fred W. Friendly. "The Good Guys, the Bad Guys and the First Amendment." Random House, 1975. Friendly, known mostly for his CBS documentaries, focuses on the Red Lion case in this examination of the Federal Communications Commission's Fairness Doctrine. Although the doctrine is largely abandoned, this book remains a valuable orientation to FCC regulation of broadcasting.

Fred W. Friendly. "Minnesota Rag." Random House, 1981. Friendly has created the definitive work on Near vs. Minnesota, a significant free-expression case.

Donald M. Gillmor and Jerome A. Barron. "Mass Communication Law: Cases and Comment," 4th edition. West Publishing, 1985. This respected casebook is one of the standards on mass-media law.

John J. Watkins. "The Mass Media and the Law." Prentice Hall, 1990. Watkins, a law professor, has written a comprehensive textbook used in many media law courses.

CHAPTER 23

RECOGNIZING SOME REALITIES ABOUT NEWS

In this chapter you will learn:

✦ Individual reporters are pivotal in determining what is reported and how, but news is a team effort involving editors and other gatekeepers.

✦ The amount of time and space that the media have available is a factor in determining what is reported.

✦ When several major stories occur about the same time, lesser stories are squeezed out.

✦ News reporters miss potential stories because they cannot anticipate everything that is newsworthy.

✦ Media owners sometimes order coverage that is self-serving or that panders to advertisers.

✦ Some advertisers exert subtle and explicit pressure on the news media to shape coverage.

✦ Competitive and sociological factors steer journalists into similar kinds of coverage.

SKEPTICISM ABOUT NEWS

Everyone has heard it said: "You can't believe a thing you read in the papers." While an exaggerated statement, it nonetheless captures the doubts that many people have about the news. Are such doubts warranted?

In this book you have learned how news and public relations people can go about their work as honest truth seekers and truth tellers, and you would be correct in concluding that almost all of them are well-motivated and competent people. Like all human beings, they make mistakes and sometimes fall short of their goals, but the vast majority of their stories merit our trust.

Why, then, are media consumers so skeptical?

The fact is that many forces beyond the journalists' control influence news. Some of them are unpredictable and beyond human control, like a storm cutting off reporters from information. Other influences are sinister, like advertiser pressure to kill a story.

In this chapter, you will learn about many factors which, generally for the worse, shape the news.

REPORTERS AND THEIR JUDGMENT

STUDY PREVIEW   News reporters have a lot of freedom deciding what to report and how to report it. At the same time, many influences affect what ends up being told. One of these realities is that news is a team project, with many people involved in what finally ends up in print and on the air.

Autonomy on the Job

News work attracts many young people because the work is interesting and a high level of autonomy goes with the job. A reporter hired fresh out of college by a small daily newspaper and assigned to city hall deals with interesting, prominent people who decide important issues, and the reporter has a great deal of independence in deciding what to report and how to report it.

Such trust is unheard of in most fields, which dole out responsibility to newcomers in small bits over a lengthy period. Of course, rookie journalists are monitored by their newsroom supervisors, and editors give them some specific assignments and review their stories, but it is that city hall reporter, to cite one example, who is the news organization's expert on city government.

The importance of judgment in deciding what's news bespeaks the need for journalists to be bright, sensitive, well-educated, highly motivated people.

Gatekeeping

Media messages, whether news or art or entertainment, are subject to changes at many points in the communication chain. At these points, which can be likened to gates, are people whose job is to delete, trim, embellish and otherwise try to improve messages. These are gatekeepers.

Just as reporters exercise judgment in deciding what to report and how to report it, so do gatekeepers. In the mass media hardly any message, except live reporting, reaches the audience in its original form. Along the path from its creator to the eventual audience, a message is subject to all kinds of deletions, additions, and changes of emphasis. With large news organizations, this process may involve dozens of editors and other persons.

Some examples:

✦ A reporter decides to emphasize one aspect of an event and neglects others, based on her perception of audience interests.

✦ A public relations writer chooses which points to include in a news release, in the interest of putting a helpful spin on the story.

✦ A television producer decides where to point the camera for images that will tell a story with greater poignancy.

✦ A news-service editor in London trims a story from Africa to 600 words for European and 400 words for North American clients, based on his perception of client interest.

✦ A network newscast producer trims a newscast from seven to six stories, to create a few extra seconds for the lead story.

Gatekeepers sometimes are called "censors," a criticism fueled by the fact that most gatekeepers do their work behind the scenes. To call gatekeepers censors is unfair, and the critics forget that gatekeeping is a necessary and unavoidable selection process because there is never enough space or time to tell everything.

Gatekeeping can be a creative force. Trimming a news story can add potency. A news producer can enhance a reporter's field report with file footage. An editor can call a public relations person for additional detail to illuminate a point in a reporter's story. A news-magazine editor can consolidate related stories and add context that makes an important interpretive point.

THE LIMITS OF RESOURCES

STUDY PREVIEW   The time and space available on a given day, as well as the flow and significance of events, affect what is reported and how well it is reported. Other influences include whether reporters were in the right place at the right time, and whether photographs, sound bites and other supporting material are available.

News Hole

A variable affecting what ends up being reported as news is called the "news hole."

In newspapers, the news hole is the space left after the advertising department has placed all its ads in the paper. The volume of advertising determines the number of total pages, and generally the more pages the more room for news. Newspaper editors can squeeze fewer stories into a thin Monday issue than a fat Wednesday issue.

In broadcasting, the news hole tends to be consistent. A 30-minute television newscast may have room for only 23 minutes of news, but the format doesn't vary. If the advertising department doesn't sell all seven minutes available for advertising, then public-service announcements, promotional messages and program notes—not news—pick up the slack. Even so, the news hole can vary in broadcasting. A 10-minute newscast can accommodate more stories than a five-minute newscast, and, as with newspapers, it is the judgment of journalists that determines which events make it.

News Flow

Another variable affecting coverage is the news flow, which varies from day to day. A story that might be played prominently on a slow news day can be passed over entirely in the competition for space on a heavy news day.

Consider this single day in 1989:

+ Death claimed Iran's Ayatollah Khomeini, a central figure in U.S. foreign policy.

+ Chinese young people and the government were in a showdown in Tiananmen Square.

+ The Polish people were voting to reject their one-party Communist political system.

+ A revolt was under way in the Soviet republic of Uzbekistan.

That was a heavy news day, and the flow of major world-rattling events pre-empted stories that otherwise would have been news.

Theodore Roosevelt, when he was president, claimed to have "discovered Mondays." His discovery was the realization that not much news occurred in the United States on Sundays, with businesses shut down and most people taking it easy. This meant that newspaper editors were especially eager for stories to fill their Monday editions and would give the president's Sunday announcements more play.

Later presidents have been masters of news flow in other ways, delaying announcements on news that reflects negatively on them or could cause them problems until the day of a major plane crash or natural calamity. That way, their "bad news" would stand a better chance of being lost, or at least not as noticed, among the other stories of a heavy news day.

Public relations people know "Mondays." When they have the luxury of choosing when to schedule news releases, news conferences and other activities, they look for slack news periods to get more attention. When the timing of bad news can be manipulated, there are advantages in waiting for a heavy news day.

Staffing Stories

Ask any news editor or producer and they will bemoan not having more reporters and other resources to tell more stories. There are never enough people to do the job that might be done. Consider:

+ A newsworthy event in Nigeria will receive short shrift if the network Africa correspondent is occupied with a natural disaster in next-door Cameroon.

+ A radio station's city government coverage will slip when the city hall reporter is on vacation, or if the station can't afford a regular reporter at city hall.

+ When Iraq invaded Kuwait by surprise in August 1990, almost all the U.S. and European reporters assigned to the Persian Gulf were on vacation or elsewhere on assignment.

For the Kuwait invasion, fortunately for the Washington Post, reporter Caryle Murphy happened to be in the country when the Iraqi attack occurred. Like everyone else, Murphy hadn't expected the invasion, but she was making a periodic trip from the Post's Cairo bureau for a firsthand look at Kuwaiti affairs. By happenstance, Murphy was in the right place at the right time to have what she called "a front-row seat for witnessing a small nation being crushed."

The Post had lucked out with a reporter on the scene while competing news organizations were scrambling to fly people into the region. Such are the vagaries of staffing.

Embellishments

The availability of photographs and video is a factor in what ends up being news. Television news producers, for example, are more attracted to stories that lend themselves to visuals. Radio people revel in stories when sound is available. A barnyard interview with a farm organization leader, with cows snorting and belching in the background, is more likely to make the air than the same leader saying virtually the same thing in the sterile confines of a legislative committee chamber.

Sometimes television is criticized for choosing stories based on titilating video, like fires, and underplaying or ignoring more significant stories that are not photogenic. The pressure, however, is to tell stories interestingly. And video helps do that in television, just as embellishing sound does in radio.

At times, it is the supporting material that makes the story. In Boston several years ago, when an apartment building caught fire, a woman and child sought refuge on a balcony. Then the balcony collapsed. The woman died on impact, but the child somehow survived. The tragedy was all the more dramatic because it occurred just as fire fighters were about to rescue the woman and child. Most local journalists would report such an event, but in this case the coverage was far more extensive than would normally be the case because Stanley Forman of the Boston Herald-American photographed the woman and child plunging to the ground.

On its own merits as a news story, the Boston fire tragedy probably would not have been reported beyond Boston, but with Forman's series of dramatic photographs, clicked in quick succession, the story was reported in visual media—newspapers, magazines and television—around the world.

In short, the availability of embellishing visuals or sound influences what is told and how widely.

NONJOURNALISTIC AGENDAS

STUDY PREVIEW   At most news organizations, the owners seldom involve themselves in what journalists report. When owners decide to be involved, however, they override the autonomy normally accorded reporters in doing their work. Other nonjournalistic factors shaping news include advertiser pressure and direct pressure on reporters.

WHEN THE PHOTO IS THE STORY. The death of a Boston woman and the injury of a child became news worldwide because photographer Stanley Forman of the Boston Herald-American was there. His photos propelled the dramatic tragedy into prominent display in newspapers, magazines and television newscasts far beyond Boston. Without the photos there would have been much less interest in the story. The availability of visuals and audio affects what is reported as news.   (© Copyright Stanley Forman)

Chains of Command

While reporters have significant roles in deciding what makes news, news organizations are corporate structures with the people in charge having the final word on matters big and small. Media owners can pre-empt any and all newsroom decisions, although this does not happen often in most organizations.

It can be galling to journalists when executive decisions on coverage are self-serving, especially when they run counter to basic journalistic values like truth seeking and truth telling.

According to a 1990 complaint to the Federal Communications Commission, the Coeur d'Alene, Idaho, Press had a long record of lavishing coverage on the newspaper's radio station but ignoring the other station in town. In one story, in which the Press could hardly avoid acknowledging the other station's participation in a community activity, the station was referred to only as "an obscure local radio station." The complaint to the FCC accused the Press of being anticompetitive.

Journalists are also appalled when executives of their news organizations pander to advertisers. The Denver Post once offered a shopping center 1,820 column inches of free publicity—equivalent roughly to 72,000 words, a small book—as a bonus if the center bought 30 pages of advertising. The puffery cut into space that might have been used for substantive news.

Some media agencies lean over backwards not to alienate advertisers, as when NBC invited Coca-Cola, a major advertiser, to preview a television documentary that reported the company benefited from exploited migrant agricultural workers. NBC then acceded to Coca-Cola requests to drop certain scenes.

To avoid rankling advertisers, the Las Cruces, N.M., Sun-News once had a policy against naming local businesses which were in the news in some unsavory way. When police raided a local hotel room, the Sun-News offered not even a hint about which hotel was the site of the raid.

Rarely do media owners acknowledge that they manipulate news coverage to their own economic interests, which means that it is difficult to document the frequency of these abuses. Most owners are sensitive to their journalistic responsibilities and assiduously avoid calling the shots on news coverage, but those who do are generally within their court-recognized First Amendment rights, and the journalists who work for them have few choices: Either persuade wayward owners they are wrong, or comply with directives, or quit and go work for a respectable journalistic organization.

Advertiser Pressure

Advertiser pressure can be overt. The managing editor of the Laramie, Wyo., Boomerang complied with a request from the newspaper's advertising man-

PUBLIC INTEREST IN O.J. SIMPSON. For better or worse, most news coverage is audience-driven. Critics said coverage of the 1995 O.J. Simpson murder trial was excessive, but the audience had an insatiable curiosity in every development and revelation. Television ratings confirmed this interest, as did magazine and newspaper sales. The National Enquirer kept the case on the cover for 27 consecutive weeks. An economic reality of the news business is that advertisers buy time and space in media that attract audiences of potential customers—the more, the better. It is advertising that funds most of a news organization's expenses.   (Fred Prouser/Reuters/The Bettmann Archive)

ager not to carry a state agency's news release warning people that Bon Vivant vichyssoise, possibly tainted with fatal botulism bacteria, had been found on the shelves at a Laramie grocery. The ad manager was fearful of losing the store's advertising. In fact, the store did yank its advertising from a Laramie radio station when it aired the story, and the station's news director reported that he was warned to back off the story and later fired.

Probably few advertisers try to coerce the news media, but the extent of advertiser clout is impossible to measure. When it happens, it's usually done quietly.

Without any official explanation or public fuss, Ralph's grocery chain cancelled a $250,000 advertising contract with the Los Angeles Herald Examiner after a story on supermarket overcharging and shortweighting. Did the story trigger the cancellation? News people may never know. But knowing that losing major advertisers can put their employer out of business can have a chilling effect on reporters.

Advertiser pressure can be subtle. Many airlines insist that their ads be deleted from newscasts with stories about airline crashes. From an airline's perspective, this may seem a reasonable policy, but it also is a policy that encourages stations, especially financially marginal stations, to omit stories that would contribute to listeners and viewers having a better sense about air safety.

To their credit, most news organizations place allegiance to their audiences ahead of pleasing advertisers. Consider the letter that Terry Berger, president of an advertising agency, wrote to Conde Nast Traveler after an article mentioned air pollution in Rio de Janeiro:

"As the advertising agency for Varig Brazilian Airlines, an advertiser in Conde Nast Traveler, I cannot for the life of me understand the logic of your telling your readers about the pollution problem in Rio de Janeiro. Somehow it seems a very self-destructive tack for a publication whose editorial ambience is supposed to encourage, not discourage, world travel. Is your editorial policy then to see how quickly you can alienate present and potential advertisers and at the same time convince your readers to stick closer to home? I really think that if you continue with this kind of editorial information, you are doing both your readers and your advertisers a disservice. For this kind of information, people read the New York Times. I therefore find it necessary to remove Conde Nast Traveler from Varig's media schedule."

Unintimidated, the magazine's editor, Harold Evans, did not recant. Not only did Evans print the letter but he followed with this comment:

Mrs. Berger is, of course, entitled to use her judgment about where she advertises Brazil's national airline.

I write not about that narrow commercial issue, but about her assertion that it is a disservice to readers and advertisers for us to print true but unattractive facts when they are relevant.

This goes to the heart of the editorial policy of this magazine. . . .

We rejoice in the enrichments of travel, but our aim is to give readers the fullest information, frankly and fairly, so they can make their own judgments.

Direct Pressure

Reporters sometimes feel external pressure directly. At the court house, valuable sources turn cold after a story appears that they don't like. A tearful husband begs not to use the name of his wife in a story that points to her as a bank embezzler. A bottle of Chivas Regal arrives at Christmas from a sports publicist who says she appreciates excellent coverage over the past year.

Most journalists will tell you that their commitment to truth overrides external assaults on their autonomy. Even so, those external pressures exist.

COMPETITIVE PRESSURE

STUDY PREVIEW   Journalists are always looking for exclusive stories that are theirs alone, but they also are always looking to each other for ideas and playing catch up. This results in a sameness in coverage even among competing media.

COMPETITIVE PRESSURES. The news media constantly monitor each other to be sure not to miss a major story. Often the result is similar coverage. An example of this is the detailed focus on developments in the 1994 dirty-play charges against figure-skating champion Tonya Harding. As Harding left a 10-hour meeting with FBI officials and the prosecutor in Portland, Ore., she was swarmed with photographers and reporters anxious not to miss a new angle on the unfolding story of an attack on rival skater Nancy Kerrigan.   (AP/Steve Slocum/Wide World)

Scooping and Being Scooped

One trigger of adrenaline for journalists is landing a scoop. Journalism is a competitive business, and the drive to outdo other news organizations keeps news publications and newscasts fresh with new material.

Competition has an unglamorous side. Journalists constantly monitor each other to identify events that they missed and need to catch up on to be competitive. This catch-up aspect of the news business contributes to similarities in coverage, which scholar Leon Sigal calls "the consensible nature of news."

Playing catch-up can result in a snowballing effect with some stories being overcovered. As more reporters pile onto a story, they are joined by more and more. In the race to get on top of the same story, other stories go uncovered.

Newsthink

Journalists pride themselves as an independent lot, but the folk notion of the heroic reporter undetered on a long, lonely quest for truth, so popular among news people themselves, is largely fiction. Most journalists share many conventions about how to do their work. For example, they have a common enthusiasm for the six elements that add news value to an event: timeliness, proximity, prominence, currency, drama and consequence.

The term "newsthink" has been coined to explain why so much news coverage is duplicative. Young journalists emerge from strikingly similar college backgrounds. On the job they adapt like other human beings to the social environment of their news organizations. People at the National Enquirer are sensitive to the news values of their supervisors and colleagues, and the same is true at the New York Times and CNN. This gives a lot of news a homogeneous quality.

CHAPTER WRAP-UP

News reporters exercise a lot of judgment in deciding what to report, but many variables beyond a reporter's control also shape what ends up in print or on the air.

On a heavy news day, some stories are squeezed out by the press of other stories. With magazines and newspapers, some issues have room for more stories than others. No newscast is long enough to tell everything that might be told.

While journalists have a lot of autonomy in deciding what to cover, external influences including advertisers and people who own the mass media, for better and worse, also play a role.

Media owners can intrude into news decisions and influence coverage, although this is hardly an everyday occurrence. When owners involve themselves, it generally is for self-serving purposes to placate advertisers.

STUDY QUESTIONS

1. Are reporters the only decision makers on what is reported and how it is reported?

2. What is the "news hole"? How does it affect what is reported?

3. What did President Theodore Roosevelt mean when he said he "discovered Mondays"?

4. What is a heavy news day? How does it affect what is reported?

5. Discuss the effect that the corporate chain of command can have on news coverage.

6. How do advertisers influence news coverage?

7. What factors contribute to a sameness in news coverage?

PUTTING YOUR LEARNING TO WORK

EXERCISE 1   Turning Down a Gratuity

Imagine that you are a sports reporter who has received a holiday gift with a card signed by the coach of a Big 10 football team you cover. The team's sports information director sent the gift, a $200 stadium warm-up blanket with the team logo, to all the reporters who cover the team. The coach's note says the blanket is a token of his appreciation for your coverage. Your news organization has a strict policy against receiving gifts from sources, not because your coverage would be affected but because of perceptions. Draft a cover letter for returning the blanket.

EXERCISE 2   Sacred Cows

Interview a news reporter who has worked in another community about sacred cows that supervisors there cautioned should be given special treatment. Write a report about what you learn.

FOR FURTHER LEARNING

Michael Schudson. "Discovering the News: A Social History of American Newspapers." Basic Books, 1978. Schudson, a scholar, traces the development of journalists and their self-perceptions through U.S. history, with continuing attention to the evolving concepts of news.

Leon V. Sigal. "Reporters and Officials: The Organization and Politics of Newsmaking." D.C. Heath, 1973. Sigal, a political scientist, examines the roots of imitative coverage, which he calls "the consensible nature of news." This phenomenon is well documented in Timothy Crouse's "The Boys on the Bus" (Random House, 1973).

Doug Underwood. "When MBAs Rule the Newsroom," Columbia Journalism Review 26, No. 5 (March-April 1988): 23–30. Underwood, a journalism professor, worries that traditional newsroom values and instincts are being lost as news organizations seek efficiencies by applying management practices developed in other industries.

CHAPTER 24

BEING RIGHT JOURNALISTICALLY AND MORALLY

LEARNING GOALS

In this chapter you will learn:

✦ The ethical principles of Aristotle, Kant and Mill and the Judeo-Christian ethic are useful bases for ethical journalistic performance.

✦ Persons in communications fields should apply ethical principles to their work.

✦ Systematic methods exist for arriving at ethical decisions.

✦ Various professional organizations have codes of ethics that set forth ideal behaviors for professionals.

✦ Competence in communications work is an ethical virtue.

✦ Telling the truth is an essential element in journalism.

✦ The ethics of using deception as a journalistic tool is often debated.

✦ Plagiarism is an unacceptable act.

✦ Privacy of sources and subjects is an ethical concern to journalists.

✦ Maintaining confidentiality of sources is an ethical issue.

✦ An ethical problem is involved in accepting gifts from sources.

✦ Journalists who profit from information they gather are on shaky ethical ground.

✦ A host of ethical problems can arise in relationships between journalists and politicians.

ONE CITY EDITOR'S BAPTISM

William Burleigh was the new city editor of the Evansville, Ind., Courier. The Courier was what Burleigh later characterized as a tough newspaper that prided itself on printing the news—all the news—regardless of the consequences, and that included printing names, addresses and offenses of individuals involved in municipal court cases, the innocent and the guilty. No exceptions. That's the way Burleigh had learned it from his predecessor and that's the way he kept it when he was given the editor's chair. Then one day he got a telephone call asking him not to print two cases. If those records were printed, the caller told Burleigh, two young girls could be revealed as incest victims. The cases were innocent enough in themselves, but a tie-in to a previous news story would make the girls' identities known to careful readers.

Although new to the job, Burleigh had heard his share of pleas for keeping various records out of the paper, but he recognized that this one was different. "It was time for the young city editor to start asking himself some ethical questions," he wrote years later. "Did he really want to be the agent for branding these girls for life? If there was even a remote chance of causing such harm, no rule, however venerated, seemed worth that. Even if it did make him less of a macho city editor." He took out his scissors and sheared the two cases from that day's list of court records before dropping it in the overnight basket.

Calling the episode "one city editor's baptism," Burleigh, now president of Scripps Howard, said he "learned in the process that the job of editing yielded to few hard-and-fast rules and that a little dose of compassion wouldn't get him drummed out of the corps after all."

In making his decision, Burleigh weighed his newspaper's print-all-the-news policy against the principles that individuals have a right to privacy and should be respected as ends, not means, and that one should avoid harm to another person. He decided that the harm that could come to the two young girls outweighed the benefit to the reading public.

Was Burleigh's situation rare? Not at all. There is hardly a reporter, news director or public relations person who does not have to make tough ethical decisions, and frequently under the pressure of a deadline.

Public Relations Society of America
Code of Professional Standards for the Practice of Public Relations
Declaration of Principles

Members of the Public Relations Society of America base their professional principles on the fundamental value and dignity of the individual, holding that the free exercise of human rights, especially freedom of speech, freedom of assembly, and freedom of the press is essential to the practice of public relations.

In serving the interests of clients and employers, we dedicate ourselves to the goals of better communication, understanding, and cooperation among the diverse individuals, groups, and institutions of society, and of equal opportunity of employment in the public relations professional.

We pledge:

To conduct ourselves professionally, with truth, accuracy, fairness, and responsibility to the public;

To improve our individual competence and advance the knowledge and proficiency of the profession through continuing research and education;

And to adhere to the articles of the Code of Professional Standards for the Practice of Public Relations as adopted by the governing Assembly of the Society.

These articles have been adopted by the Public Relations Society of America to promote and maintain high standards of public service and ethical conduct among its members.

1. A member shall conduct his or her professional life in accord with the public interests.

2. A member shall exemplify high standards of honesty and integrity while carrying out dual obligations to a client or employer and to the democratic process.

3. A member shall deal fairly with the public, with past or present clients or employers, and with fellow practitioners, giving due respect to the ideal of free inquiry and to the opinions of others.

4. A member shall adhere to the highest standards of accuracy and truth, avoiding extravagant claims or unfair comparisons and giving credit for ideas and words borrowed from others.

APPROACHES TO COMMUNICATIONS ETHICS

STUDY PREVIEW   Philosophers through the ages have given much thought to what constitutes ethical behavior and the principles that should govern our relations with one another. News and public relations organizations have developed ethical standards for their members based on shared values and have written them down in the form of codes of ethical behavior. The problem for people engaged in communications work is how to apply those principles and values to the situations they face day in and day out.

5. A member shall not knowingly disseminate false or misleading information and shall act promptly to correct erroneous communications for which he or she is responsible.

6. A member shall not engage in any practice which has the purpose of corrupting the integrity of channels of communications or the processes of government.

7. A member shall be prepared to identify publicly the name of the client or employer on whose behalf any public communication is made.

8. A member shall not use any individual or organization professing to serve or represent an announced cause, or professing to be independent or unbiased, but actually serving another or undisclosed interest.

9. A member shall not guarantee the achievement of specified results beyond the member's direct control.

10. A member shall not represent conflicting or competing interests without the express consent of those concerned, given after a full disclosure of the facts.

11. A member shall not place himself or herself in a position where the member's personal interest is or may be in conflict with an obligation to an employer or client, or others, without full disclosure of such interests to all involved.

12. A member shall not accept fees, commissions, gifts or any other consideration from anyone except clients or employers for whom services are performed without their express consent, given after full disclosure of the facts.

13. A member shall scrupulously safeguard the confidences and privacy rights of present, former, and prospective clients or employers.

14. A member shall not intentionally damage the professional reputation or practice of another practitioner.

15. If a member has evidence that another member has been guilty of unethical, illegal, or unfair practices, including those in violation of this Code, the member is obligated to present the information promptly to the proper authorities of the Society for action in accordance with the procedure set forth in Article XII of the Bylaws.

16. A member called as a witness in a proceeding for enforcement of this Code is obligated to appear, unless excused for sufficient reason by the judicial panel.

17. A member shall, as soon as possible, sever relations with any organization or individual if such relationship requires conduct contrary to the articles of this Code.

Codes of Ethics

Codes of ethics specify the minimal dos and don'ts of the professions that have adopted them. As such, they serve as broad guides to correct behavior. A careful reading of the codes will show that the organizations share many values. The Public Relations Society of America sets as goals "truth, accuracy, fairness, and responsibility to the public." The Society of Professional Journalists holds that journalists ought to "perform with intelligence, objectivity, accuracy and fairness." The ultimate aim is the service of truth. The Radio-Television News Directors Association holds that broadcasters report "accurately, honestly and impartially." All three stress respect for others as a basic tenet. All condemn conflicts of interest.

The PRSA code carries enforcement teeth. It obligates members to identify other members believed to be "guilty of unethical, illegal or unfair practices," and it provides that members must appear before any judicial panel investigating breaches. Unlike the so-called ethics codes adopted by many governmental units, the RTNDA and SPJ codes are unenforceable. In fact, members of the Society of Professional Journalists long debated a clause requiring them to condemn breaches of the code. In the end, they eliminated it on the grounds that it infringed the autonomy of individual journalists.

Four Ethical Theories

Four sets of ethical principles developed by philosophers stand out as bases for correct behavior.

✦ *Golden mean.* Aristotle, who lived in Greece in the fourth century B.C., formulated the Golden Mean. The Golden Mean requires that when there are extreme positions in a situation, one seeks a middle ground. One might say journalists are caught between the extremes of publishing or broadcasting everything they know about an issue, situation or event and publishing or broadcasting nothing. Obviously, they choose the Golden Mean and develop stories that are appropriate to the medium, the outlet, the editor and the audience. Public relations professionals may see themselves in something of the same dilemma, to tell everything or nothing. The proper thing to do is to tell what is appropriate in the situation.

✦ *Categorical imperative.* Immanuel Kant, an 18th-century German philosopher, formulated the Categorical Imperative, the theory that people should behave only as they wish everyone else to behave. One is duty bound to do what is right in every instance, unconditionally (or, categorically). One must always tell the truth, for example, and without exception. To follow the Kantian ethic, then, the use of deception to obtain a story is forbidden.

✦ *Utilitarianism.* Perhaps easier to live with is Utilitarianism, developed by Jeremy Bentham, an Englishman who lived in the 18th and 19th centuries, and refined by John Stuart Mill. Utilitarianism would have us judge what is right by asking what will give the greatest good to the greatest number of people. To determine what is ethical behavior in any situation, we must balance right and wrong and act in a way that results in more good than evil.

✦ *Golden rule.* The Judeo-Christian ethic, or the so-called Golden Rule, calls on people to "do unto others as you would have them do unto you." The flaw in the Golden Rule for journalists is that, taking it liter-

---

**Radio-Television News Directors Association
Code of Broadcast News Ethics**

The responsibility of radio and television journalists is to gather and report information of importance and interest to the public accurately, honestly and impartially.

The members of the Radio-Television News Directors Association accept these standards and will:

1. Strive to present the source or nature of broadcast news material in a way that is balanced, accurate and fair.

A. They will evaluate information solely on its merits as news, rejecting sensationalism or misleading emphasis in any form.

B. They will guard against using audio or video material in a way that deceives the audience.

C. They will not mislead the public by presenting as spontaneous news any material which is staged or rehearsed.

D. They will identify people by race, creed, nationality or prior status only when it is relevant.

E. They will clearly label opinion and commentary.

F. They will promptly acknowledge and correct errors.

2. Strive to conduct themselves in a manner that protects them from conflicts of interest, real or perceived. They will decline gifts or favors which would influence or appear to influence their judgments.

3. Respect the dignity, privacy and well-being of people with whom they deal.

4. Recognize the need to protect confidential sources. They will promise confidentiality only with the intention of keeping that promise.

5. Respect everyone's right to a fair trial.

6. Broadcast the private transmissions of other broadcasters only with permission.

7. Actively encourage observance of this Code by all journalists, whether members of the Radio-Television News Directors Association or not.

---

ally, they might print nothing about individuals that would be considered negative. It would be foolish, of course, and contrary to good journalistic practice to say "I would not want my name printed in the paper if I were arrested for driving under the influence of alcohol, therefore I will not report that the mayor was picked up for drunken driving." Journalists should read the Golden Rule, however, as requiring that they treat other people fairly.

THE COMMUNICATOR'S LOYALTIES

STUDY PREVIEW   Ethics deals with what we ought to do in situations involving other people—what we owe to others and how we meet our responsibilities to them. That sense of duty, or loyalty, implies faithfulness in the discharge of our obligations. The "others" to whom communications professionals owe loyalty include the public to whom news and information are directed, our sources and the subjects we write about, our employers and our colleagues.

Loyalties to the Public

"Dateline NBC," a television news magazine program, developed a story on the safety of GM trucks with side-mounted gasoline tanks. The producers attached tiny rockets to the underside of a truck to make sure there was a spark when it was hit by a car. The staged event was successful. The car hit the truck and flames filled the screen. The event also exploded into a highly publicized lawsuit filed against NBC by GM, a subsequent on-camera apology by the network and the departures from the network of high-ranking producers and the president of NBC News, Michael Gartner.

NBC averted legal action, but the company still faced questions about its ethical behavior, and many of those questions were rooted in the responsibilities journalists have. The producers brought the competence of the network, their colleagues and television news producers everywhere into question. They mistreated their subject, General Motors. And they misled their viewers. To put it another way, had the producers given more consideration to the responsibilities they owed the public, they might have performed in a more competent and, thus, more ethical way.

The impact of NBC's ethical lapse was perhaps best characterized by an editorial writer for the New York Times: "A lie by any reputable newsgathering institution—the fabricated event, the made-up quote, the fictitious source—is intolerable. It not only discredits the offender but debases communication by eroding public trust."

The prime responsibility journalists and public relations practitioners have is to the public since the aim of their work is the enlightenment of the public. As the Times pointed out, NBC's offense was, at core, an offense against its audience. Individuals use the information they receive from journalists in making decisions, from whether to take an umbrella with them in the morning to which way to vote on a tax proposition. If they are given faulty information, they have no basis for sound decisions. So journalists have an overwhelming responsibility to their audiences to provide accurate and unbiased information.

Loyalties to Subjects and Sources

Anyone reporting on the activities of someone else has a responsibility to represent the subject's position as accurately and completely as possible, and that is true even—and especially—when the report is negative. To do otherwise is to misrepresent the subject, to show the subject as something that it is not, as NBC did. In dealing with subjects, it is well to follow Immanuel Kant's principle that individuals should be treated as ends, not as means. That is, they are not to be used. To misrepresent a subject to get a story that will gain public attention is to use the subject, and that is true whether the subject is an individual or a corporation.

Journalists also have to present the views of their sources accurately. That means providing context, when context makes a source's meaning clear. Twisting the words of a source or taking a source's words out of context gives an inaccurate portrayal of the words of a source. That misrepresentation can be harmful to the person, even if it is not libelous.

In most instances journalists owe it to their sources to identify themselves as journalists so that the sources are aware they are speaking for the record. On occasion journalists may believe they need to mask their identities, but the rationale should be clearly and logically worked out.

Loyalties to Employers and Colleagues

Communicators have a responsibility to their employers to do the work they were hired to do as competently and as honestly as humanly possible, whether those duties are spelled out in a written contract or a job description or are arrived at by tacit agreement. Journalists or public relations professionals who act in an unethical fashion bring their employers' ethics into question as well. To return to the example of the report on GM trucks, individuals working for NBC produced it, but it was the company itself which bore the responsibility in headlines and in the public mind.

At the lowest rung in the corporate structure, a relationship of trust must exist between reporters and their supervisors, whether in a newsroom or a public relations office. Trust is eroded when reporters show little concern for accuracy or thoroughness or for performing the normal duties expected of them. In turn, of course, reporters expect their supervisors to respect them and their work and to support them when they run into obstacles.

Similarly, communicators have a responsibility to other communicators to perform their work in such a way that all are esteemed by the public. As we all know, people have a tendency to stereotype, to assign the behavior or characteristics of a few individuals to a whole class, and especially in a negative way. Some common stereotypes are that blondes and athletes are dumb, teen-agers are irresponsible, professors are absent-minded, Republicans benefit the rich, and Democrats tax and spend. When journalists behave unethically, all journalists are subject to the blanket indictment of being untrustworthy. Some of the critiques of the NBC story leaped from criticism of that one network to calling into question "television news" as whole.

Society of Professional Journalists
Code of Ethics

The Society of Professional Journalists believes the duty of journalists is to serve the truth.

We believe the agencies of mass communication are carriers of public discussion and information, acting on their Constitutional mandate and freedom to learn and report the facts.

We believe in public enlightenment as the forerunner of justice, and in our Constitutional role to seek the truth as part of the public's right to know the truth.

We believe these responsibilities carry obligations that require journalists to perform with intelligence, objectivity, accuracy, and fairness.

To these ends, we declare acceptance of the standards of practice here set forth:

I. Responsibility

The public's right to know of events of public importance and interest is the overriding mission of the mass media. The purpose of distributing news and enlightened opinion is to serve the general welfare. Journalists who use their professional status as representatives of the public for selfish or other unworthy motives violate a high trust.

II. Freedom of the Press

Freedom of the press is to be guarded as an inalienable right of the people in a free society. It carries with it the freedom and the responsibility to discuss, question, and challenge actions and utterances of our government and of our public and private institutions. Journalists uphold the right to speak unpopular opinions and the privilege to agree with the majority.

III. Ethics

Journalists must be free of obligation to any interest other than the public's right to know the truth.

1. Gifts, favors, free travel, special treatment or privileges can compromise the integrity of journalists and their employers. Nothing of value should be accepted.

2. Secondary employment, political involvement, holding public office, and service in community organizations should be avoided if it compromises the integrity of journalists and their employers should conduct their personal lives in a manner that protects them from conflict of interest, real or apparent. Their responsibilities to the public are paramount. That is the nature of their profession.

3. So-called news communications from private sources should not be published or broadcast without substantiation of their claims to news value.

4. Journalists will seek news that serves the public interest, despite the obstacles. They will make constant efforts to assure that the public's business is conducted in public and that public records are open to public inspection.

5. Journalists acknowledge the newsman's ethic of protecting confidential sources of information.

6. Plagiarism is dishonest and unacceptable.

IV. Accuracy and Objectivity

Good faith with the public is the foundation of all worthy journalism.

1. Truth is our ultimate goal.

2. Objectivity in reporting the news is another goal that serves as the mark of an experienced professional. It is a standard of performance toward which we strive. We honor those who achieve it.

3. There is no excuse for inaccuracies or lack of thoroughness.

4. Newspaper headlines should be fully warranted by the contents of the articles they accompany. Photographs and telecasts should give an accurate picture of an event and not highlight an event out of context.

5. Sound practice makes clear distinction between news reports and expressions of opinion. News reports should be free of opinion or bias and represent all sides of an issue.

6. Partisanship in editorial comment that knowingly departs from the truth violates the spirit of American journalism.

7. Journalists recognize their responsibility for offering informed analysis, comment, and editorial opinion on public events and issues. They accept the obligation to present such material by individuals whose competence, experience and judgment qualify them for it.

8. Special articles or presentations devoted to advocacy or the writer's own conclusions and interpretations should be labeled as such.

V. Fair Play

Journalists at all times will show respect for the dignity, privacy, rights and well-being of people encountered in the course of gathering and presenting news.

1. The news media should not communicate unofficial charges affecting reputation or moral character without giving the accused a chance to reply.

2. The news media must guard against invading a person's right to privacy.

3. The media should not pander to morbid curiosity about details of vice and crime.

4. It is the duty of news media to make prompt and complete correction of their errors.

5. Journalists should be accountable to the public for their reports and the public should be encouraged to voice its grievances against the media. Open dialogue with our readers, viewers, and listeners should be fostered.

VI. Pledge

Adherence to this code is intended to preserve and strengthen the bond of mutual trust and respect between American journalists and the American people.

The Society shall—by programs of education and other means—encourage individual journalists to adhere to these tenets, and shall encourage journalistic publications and broadcasters to recognize their responsibility to frame codes of ethics in concert with their employees to serve as guidelines in furthering these goals.

THE COMMUNICATOR'S VALUES

STUDY PREVIEW   Every profession has certain values that its members prize. The values comprise what members of the profession consider the essential things they should do and the things they should not do. For people in communication fields, as in others, competence is a value—to do the work as best one possibly can. Communicators also regard telling the truth as an essential. They value the privacy of other people. They believe sources need to be protected. They also believe that they should avoid conflicts of interest, including the acceptance of gifts offered in connection with their work.

Striving for Competence

This book has been devoted to helping you develop those skills that will help you become a competent communicator, whether in journalism or public relations. What may not be apparent is that competence itself is an ethical value. That is, to do one's work skillfully, in accord with standard journalistic or public relations practice, is to do it ethically. Unfortunately, as Stephen Klaidman and Tom L. Beauchamp make clear in "The Virtuous Journalist," the expectation that communicators be competent is "among the more frequently violated norms of journalistic practice."

The producers of the "Dateline NBC" segment on the dangers of GM trucks had aired an unbalanced story by putting heaviest emphasis on the dangers posed by the trucks' gasoline tanks and on the victims, and by giving responses by GM attorneys short shrift. They loaded the story still more by tampering with an on-camera test in using small rockets to try to spark an explosion, and they did not disclose to viewers that the rockets were being used. Although some questions about the tactic were raised during the editing process by the reporter, they were dismissed by the producers. Even when executives found out that the test had been rigged, they were unwilling to admit that to the audience until pressed by the GM lawsuit. All of those were failures of journalistic competence—and of ethical performance.

Being Fair

Fairness is another basic journalistic value growing out of the Kantian principle that persons should be treated as ends rather than means. We equate fairness with being balanced in our approach to stories, open to facts and impartial and unbiased in our treatment of individuals and institutions. Fairness, in fact, is woven through the fabric of ethical behavior discussed in this chapter, for fairness implies a sensitivity to the dignity of other human beings.

More specifically, journalists are called upon to deal fairly with those who have been dealt with unfairly in the past because of race, sex, religion, sexual orientation, physical capabilities or status. That means taking women and women's issues seriously. It means treating the handicapped as functioning individuals and not as objects of pity. It means treating people accused of crimes as innocent until proved guilty.

Being fair as a journalist, however, does not mean being an apologist. Juan Williams, a reporter for the Washington Post, a black, pointed out in a column that his fellow blacks frequently wanted him to portray members of that race in a positive light. At the same time, he receives mail from whites who see him as propagandizing on behalf of blacks. But, says Williams, "to write in response to their white racism—or to the demands of black conformity—is to do far more harm than good."

Neither would be fair. Rather, Williams is convinced that "the truth, and not lies, excuses or apologies, will give power to the poor, the disadvantaged, to people without education or a public voice."

TELLING THE TRUTH

STUDY PREVIEW   All of the events in the making of the NBC story added up to a lie, yet truth-telling is central to journalism—as it is to any human relationship. Truth is a universal value. The code of ethics of nearly every professional communication organization addresses it. We rely on truthful communications to make decisions at every level of our lives and our audiences rely on us, as journalists and as public relations practitioners, to tell them the truth so that they can make reasonable decisions. When we lie, we undermine the autonomy of others. They are unable to act as they should on false information. And when we lie we are treating individuals or institutions not as ends, as they ought to be treated, but as means.

Faking Stories

Journalists can lie in many ways. In 1981 Janet Cooke, then a 26-year-old reporter for the Washington Post, won a Pulitzer Prize for feature writing. It was given to her for "Jimmy's World," her heart-rending story about an 8-year-old heroin addict. Two days later, Cooke's world was in a shambles. The newspaper had given back her Pulitzer, and her credibility as a journalist was destroyed.

As Post ombudsman Bill Green explained to readers, the story was fabricated—"piped" as a faked story is sometimes called. In fact, as it turned out, Cooke had gotten to the Post by claiming a bachelor's degree from Vassar, a master's from the University of Toledo and a year of study at the Sorbonne, none of which was true.

The original lie triggered ethical failures at every stage in the making of the story. Cooke broke the trust editors must have in a reporter. She persuaded them that the story was true, although they were too easily persuaded, some critics said later. In the process, she put the Post's credibility in harm's way. She cast doubts on the veracity of reporters generally. And she lied to readers who expected to be told the truth. A virtuous journalist would always tell the truth.

Other Journalistic Lies

The Janet Cooke story may be an extreme example of journalistic lying. Certainly it has been highly publicized. But many other less prominent lies occur nearly every day.

- ✦ Reporters who make up or embellish quotes are guilty of lying. So are reporters who create situations that did not occur or, for some dramatic effect, embellish situations that did occur.

- ✦ At one major Midwestern radio station, it was regular practice for reporters going out to cover an annual parade to call in their first "on the scene report" to the newsroom from the news director's office before leaving the building. That was lying.

- ✦ Photographers who tamper with scenes of news events before shooting them lie, and there is an ongoing debate among photographers as to whether computer editing of photos is a form of lying.

Reporters and editors who are tempted to lie need to ask themselves whether the lie is justified. What end does the lie serve?

Plagiarism

Plagiarism is another form of lying. Simply defined, plagiarism consists of taking the work of others and putting one's own name on it, thereby passing it off as one's own. The turn of the century Chicago sportswriter Hugh E. Keough cranked out a column of brief paragraphs of humorous comment on the sports events and personalities of his day for his "In the Wake of the News" column in the Chicago Tribune. His work was so cleverly done that other sports columnists often reprinted it as their own. That was plagiarism.

Keough exposed the thieves who stole from him with stinging humor. The editor of the Washington Herald, Keough wrote, "grabs the entire column, substituting nothing but a box head, which is not original, and his monicker de plume, which he did not invent." A sportswriter for the St. Louis Chronicle, he complained, "takes it blood raw and attaches his monicker to it."

Modern editors take a less benign view of plagiarism. Usually, those found guilty are disciplined and even summarily fired, as the pages of trade publications attest. Certainly, the publicity they get can be devastating. Among the incidents that have occurred in just the past few years:

✦ A hard-working team of student reporters at the State News of Michigan State University ferreted out detailed information on candidates for the university's presidency and published a four-page special section. Days later, according to the trade journal Editor & Publisher, they saw their work printed in the Lansing, Mich., State Journal, not only nearly word for word, but typo for typo. State Journal editor Zack Binkley apologized publicly in a signed column in his own newspaper and said the plagiarism resulted from "honest mistakes."

✦ Gregory Freeman, a columnist for the St. Louis Post-Dispatch, apologized in print for having taken three sentences from a column by Boston Globe columnist Derrick Z. Jackson. Post-Dispatch editor William Woo suspended Freeman's column indefinitely, the New York Times reported.

✦ Fort Worth, Texas, Star-Telegram columnist Katie Sherrod was fired after she wrote a column that was similar to a story that had appeared in the Washington Post.

✦ At the same newspaper six months later, political writer James Walker wrote a story in which he used quotes from a television story and another newspaper. He resigned.

✦ Editorial writer Bill Youngblood, also at the Star-Telegram, drew a week's suspension when he wrote an editorial that included an unattributed passage from an opinion piece syndicated by the New York Times. The syndicated article ran on the Star-Telegram's op-ed page on the same day. Youngblood drew a lesser penalty because he had included the attribution when he first wrote the story, but cut it to make the editorial fit the space he had.

The Star-Telegram has a clear policy on plagiarism, and it bears repeating here: "Passing off another's words or ideas as one's own is unacceptable at the Star-Telegram. Staff members should not copy the work of others unless credit is given. Using the words or the illustrations of others is plagiarism. Because journalists often cover the same events, similarity in subject matter, and even in story ideas, is inevitable. The reporting, the treatment, the language must be original—or they must be attributed. Violation of this standard may be cause for termination."

A Star-Telegram committee revised the newspaper's policy on attribution following the incidents. Staffers are now expected to follow this rule: "Attribution for quotes used and information contained in copy should be full, complete and honest. Generally, including unattributed material in copy is permitted only when it is unquestionably factual and essentially undisputed."

In handling news service copy, credit must be given for any of the service's material, and editors have to take special care "to attribute any material that might be exclusive to the news service. For example, if the AP quotes a presidential aide as saying something to an AP reporter after a news conference, then that material should be attributed to the AP."

In putting together roundups, Star-Telegram editors must provide attribution to the news services used "so that there will be no confusion about who reported what." In the eyes of the Star-Telegram's editors, "If there is a question on where attribution is appropriate, we should err on the side of giving full credit where credit is due."

And, the Star-Telegram adds: "The electronic media are no different. We should give broadcast full credit where credit is due."

Writing in Washington Journalism Review on the problem of plagiarism, Roy Peter Clark of the Modern Media Institute found nine instances in one 10-year period, and those were only the most glaring cases.

Clark described various forms of plagiarism. Among them was the practice of "robbing the morgue," or using material verbatim from earlier stories on a subject. In the age of computerization, it's all the easier to copy material from one story and paste it into another. But it's important to rewrite or to make clear that the material came from another source.

"Abusing the wires" consists of putting one's own name above a story filed by one of the news services. Editors should make clear what's come in over the wires and what is locally produced.

Reporters who take material from any other source without attributing it also are guilty of plagiarism. Such sources include other newspapers, magazines, books or research articles. And that goes for reporters, writers of releases and broadcast writers.

Similarly, it is plagiarism to print or broadcast news releases verbatim, without rewriting, elaborating or attributing, Clark wrote.

Clark told his readers that if he were a city editor, he would sit his staff down and impress on them that plagiarism is a crime, and for these reasons:

- Plagiarism is "a form of deception."

- Plagiarism is "a crime against the nature of language" insofar as one's own creativity is at the heart of language.

- Plagiarism is "a substitute for reporting." Not only are reporters who plagiarize not doing their own work, for which they are being paid, but they are opening themselves up to perpetuating inaccuracy.

- Plagiarism is also "a substitute for thinking." Reporters who plagiarize are letting someone else do their thinking for them.

- Plagiarism "poisons the relationship" between writer and audience. Clark wrote that reporters who pass off the work of others as their own fail their basic responsibility to their audience, and the trust that is essential in the writer-audience relationship is destroyed. Communicators need to develop the habit—the virtue—of doing their own work and identifying those others on whom they lean.

Deception

Journalists lie when they deceive others to get a story. In his "Deadlines and Monkeyshines," longtime newspaperman John McPhaul of the Chicago Herald-Examiner told of once being among a group of reporters waiting outside the home of a police officer killed in the line of duty. They wanted a picture of him, but the family was secluded.

At last the door opened. "Where's the 'Examiner' man?" the officer's widow asked. McPhaul stepped forward. He had a telephone call, she said. "The captain wants to talk to you."

The voice on the other end of the line was not a police captain, however, but that of Harry Romanoff, then night assistant city editor of the Herald-Examiner. Romanoff told McPhaul that, pretending to be a police captain, he had persuaded the widow that the Examiner was the police department's best friend and talked her into letting the newspaper have a photo of her husband. McPhaul left the house with a silver-framed photograph of the police officer in his uniform.

Changing technology has allowed ever more advanced forms of deception. The miniature camera and microphone of the spy and the private detective have been adopted by television. Television's magazine-format news programs, especially, often use hidden cameras in doing investigative stories. Producers for CBS's "60 Minutes" used hidden cameras to document sales of Romanian babies to Americans who want to adopt. A producer for the ABC program "PrimeTime Live" took a job with a North Carolina supermarket chain to show conditions in one store's meat department. Among other things, she captured a department manager ordering that some old pork chops be put back in the display case because with edges trimmed "they look just as good as fresh." "PrimeTime Live" also took its miniaturized hidden cameras into a day-care center in New Orleans to show the squalid conditions under which children were kept.

Print reporters also practice deception and go under cover. Jonathan Franklin, a free-lance reporter, had some evidence that military officials provided the public with inaccurate casualty figures during the U.S. invasion of Panama in 1989, and he wanted to find out if officers were telling the truth about casualties sustained in the 1991 war against Iraq. When he was unsuccessful in getting anyone to talk to him, he decided to pass himself off as a mortician to get into a military mortuary.

That allowed him to document the fact that combat deaths were being underreported and that the military was deliberately disguising as many fatalities as possible as "training accidents." Franklin's reasoning was that the public needed to know what was really happening so they "could have made informed judgements about a war they financed and supported. That's the way it's supposed to work in a democracy."

Not all agree that journalists should practice deception. In one celebrated case, reporters for the Chicago Sun-Times bought a bar on the city's north side, The Mirage, and posed as bartenders to document shakedowns by city building inspectors. A 1979 Pulitzer Prize jury recommended an award be given to the reporters and editors responsible for the story. The members of the final Pulitzer Prize selection board disagreed. They apparently believed the deceptive means that were used did not justify the end brought about by exposure of corrupt practices.

Another Pulitzer board of similar mind refused to accept a jury's recommendation that a prize go to Merle Linda Wolin of the Los Angeles Herald Examiner, who posed as a Brazilian immigrant to expose working conditions in Southern California sweatshops.

As in making any ethical decision, the news person who contemplates using deception to get a story needs to ask whether the story can be gotten in any other way. If it cannot, then the question has to focus on whether the good to be derived from using deception outweighs any undesirable result. The executive producer of "PrimeTime Live," Richard Kaplan, told a writer for the Washington Post, "If you misrepresent yourself, it better be for a damn important story." Yet even some at the Sun-Times have second thoughts about the propriety of reporters misrepresenting themselves to get the Mirage story. Sun-Times editor Dennis Britton was quoted in the Post as saying, "I don't think we should pretend to be things we're not."

Truth-Telling in Public Relations

Public relations professionals may be held to a less strict standard of truth-telling. It is rather clearly recognized that they are engaged in what Edward Bernays, a public relations pioneer, called the "engineering of consent." Their job is to persuade, and to do so they have to emphasize some elements, play down others, and ignore some altogether. But public relations professionals should be accurate even if they must provide less than the whole truth. And there may well be circumstances in which they must provide the whole truth. As an example, an emission from a chemical plant may threaten the health of a community. To reveal that information may be damaging to the company, but to deny it, or even to shade the truth by withholding it, could endanger large numbers of people.

RESPECTING PRIVACY

STUDY PREVIEW   Individuals have a "right to be let alone," two Boston lawyers, Samuel Warren and Louis Brandeis, argued more than a century ago, a time when many journalists sensationalized the news and often displayed little respect for the privacy of individuals. Quite frequently, however, the right to privacy, as we refer to that right to be let alone, clashes with the public's right to know—or with what reporters and editors believe the public has a right to know—and that results in ethical dilemmas.

Sexual Matters

Most news organizations print the names of individuals accused of crimes, believing their names are of public interest and that the public has a need to know who its criminals are. Usually, too, they will name the victims of crimes. Because sex is such a private matter, however, many news organizations withhold the names of victims of sex crimes and even the names of those who file complaints.

Often the names of perpetrators of sex crimes are also withheld when printing or broadcasting them could reveal victims' names. Editors who withhold names have believed that the harm that could come to victims, whether psychological or physical, would outweigh any good that would result from making the names of the accused public. On the other hand, some editors are coming to believe that the accusers, as well as the accused, ought to be named. They see a certain unfairness in not identifying complainants when the accused are identified. Some believe identification of complainants may help to eliminate the stigma attached to rape.

Many of those concerns came to the fore when William Kennedy Smith was accused of raping a woman in Palm Beach, Fla. Because of his family connection, the case was widely publicized and his name was printed in newspapers across the country. The name of the woman who accused him was not revealed, however—at least until it ran in a British tabloid. Subsequently it was published in the United States in the Globe, a supermarket tabloid, then reported by NBC News, and then by the New York Times in a story that detailed her family background, her driving record, her drinking habits, and the fact that she was the mother of an illegitimate child.

Unfortunately the reasons given by both NBC and the New York Times muddied the discussion of whether the names of accusers ought to be made public. Michael Gartner, the president of NBC News, said the network believed "the more we tell our viewers, the better informed they will be in making up their own minds about the issues involved." He added, "We do not mean to be judgmental or take sides; we are merely reporting what we have learned." Critics took issue with Gartner's statement, arguing that news organizations always know much more than they make public.

The New York Times said "NBC's nationwide broadcast took the matter of her privacy out of their hands," a statement that Deni Elliott, director of the Ethics Institute at Dartmouth College, called a "school yard justification." Her plea for "a reason based on fairness" went unanswered.

News organizations are still grappling with the question of how and when a person's homosexuality should be revealed. Some gay and lesbian publications, most notably Outweek, believe homosexuals, especially those who are prominent, should be identified as such, or "outed," to use the term that has come into vogue. The key to publication would seem to be whether a person's sexual orientation is germane to a story, just as a person's religion or marital status is mentioned only if pertinent.

Normally, anything related to a person's own sexual conduct is considered private, at least for private individuals. Some journalists believe public figures, especially politicians, give up a measure of privacy. When Gary Hart was a candidate for the Democratic presidential nomination in 1987, rumors surfaced among the reporters covering him that he had engaged in extramarital affairs. He challenged them to follow him. Reporters for the Miami Herald staked out his Washington home and later reported that a young woman had spent much of the night there. The revelation led to questions about Hart's fitness for the presidency and ultimately led to his dropping out of the race.

ACCUSER AS VICTIM. Intense media attention focused on William Kennedy Smith when he was accused of rape by a Florida woman. Especially because of Smith's acquittal, the case sparked discussions about the fairness of naming only accusers in rape cases.
(Robert York/Reuters/The Bettmann Archive)

Four years later, candidate Bill Clinton maintained that matters related to sexual activity were private and had no bearing on a person's fitness for office. Still, he was dogged by rumors of marital infidelity and public charges by a woman who said she had been Clinton's mistress.

Those instances and others have raised questions about whether the media do not go too far in exploiting privacy even among public figures. The touchstone for determining what to print about a politician's private life would seem to be the effect private activity has on the discharge of one's public responsibilities.

Illness

Illness is also a private matter, and that is especially true in cases of AIDS. In a Florida case, a judge removed from her courtroom a defendant in a misdemeanor case who, she was told, had AIDS. The Fort Myers News-Press printed the story but left out the young man's name, even though his name was a matter of public record. Executive Editor Keith Moyer said the editors "decided that the public would gain nothing by knowing the defendant's name, but that he would suffer from public scorn if it were divulged that he was an AIDS patient."

In another case, Doug Smith, a sports reporter for USA Today, got a tip that former tennis star Arthur Ashe had AIDS. Ashe deflected Smith's questions and also questions asked later by the newspaper's managing editor for sports, Gene Policinski. Policinski told Ashe the newspaper would continue to pursue the story but would not go with it unless it had confirmation from someone with first-hand medical information. Policinski told Ashe he would contact him if the newspaper neared publication and he told Smith to keep working on the story.

USA Today did not print the story, but the next day Ashe himself called a news conference and announced that he had contracted the AIDS virus through a blood transfusion during heart surgery. He also told the assembled reporters that the attempt to report the story was an invasion of his privacy. A cross-section of editors interviewed later by Christine Spolar, a reporter for the Washington Post, defended USA Today's decision, mainly because Ashe was a public figure. Media observers she talked to, however, including lawyer Floyd Abrams, long a leading defender of the media's First Amendment rights, questioned the decision on ethical grounds. Spolar quoted Abrams as saying "the harm it inflicted or has the potential to inflict is so great and the information it provides to the public so insubstantial that the story should not have been pursued and should not have been published."

The statements made by Moyer and Abrams would seem to hold the answer to a range of privacy questions. The social value of revelation of a private matter, not the satisfaction of mere morbid interest, should determine whether something potentially damaging to an individual should be published.

To put it another way, the good that would be done must outweigh the harm to the individual.

ARTHUR ASHE. Tennis star Arthur Ashe announced he had AIDS after USA Today began asking questions. Ashe said there was another side to the story, as well: the invasion of his privacy by news organizations.   (Jeff Christensen/Reuters/The Bettmann Archive)

PROTECTING SOURCES

STUDY PREVIEW   Most news organizations want sources named. But sometimes the only way to get a person to tell a story is to promise anonymity. In such instances, a promise is considered binding, and on occasion reporters have gone to jail rather than reveal the name of a source, even when ordered by a judge or grand jury.

Four Landmark Cases

In a series of celebrated cases in the late 1960s and 1970s, Paul Pappas of WTEV-TV in Providence, R.I., Paul Branzburg of the Louisville Courier-Journal, and Earl Caldwell of the New York Times served terms behind bars for refusing to name individuals to whom they had promised confidentiality. They argued—fruitlessly—their legal right under the First Amendment to withhold the sources' names. Beyond that, they said, they had an ethical responsibility to maintain confidentiality.

In another instance a court held that news organizations have not only a legal obligation but an ethical responsibility to their sources to keep a promise of confidentiality. In that case reporters for the Minneapolis Star Tribune and the St. Paul Pioneer Press guaranteed confidentiality to Dan Cohen, a political public relations professional, in writing a story on dirty campaign tricks. Editors believed his name was essential, however, and put it into the story.

Cohen sued and the case went to the U.S. Supreme Court, which sent it back to the state court. In its decision the Minnesota Supreme Court pointed out that the newspapers had maintained "the importance of honoring promises of confidentiality," and there was no "compelling need" to break the promise made by the reporters.

Lyle Denniston, who covers the U.S. Supreme Court for the Baltimore Sun, discussed the case in the Washington Journalism Review. He called the revelation of the name "an ethical outrage." He concluded that the press could learn from such cases "that it might improve its chances with the law if it were truer to its own code of ethics."

CONFLICTS OF INTEREST

STUDY PREVIEW   Given their roles in society, journalists are in a position to give publicity or withhold it, to show individuals and organizations positively or negatively. But because they have an overwhelming responsibility to the public and because the public places such trust in them, journalists must avoid conflicts between their journalistic responsibilities and their private interests. Conflicts can arise when sources offer gifts, as they sometimes do. Conflicts also occur when journalists involve themselves in politics. Even one's personal relationships can lead to conflicts.

Freebies

As long ago as 1887 Lucius W. Nieman of the Milwaukee Journal urged his fellow members of the Wisconsin Publishers Association to give up what was then called "the pass system," the taking of passes from theaters, festivals of various sorts and especially from the railroads. A railroad pass might "seem a small consideration, and it is; but still how great is its influence. It makes many of us overlook the interests of the public when they conflict with those of the corporations." Nieman minced no words in telling the publishers why the railroads provided passes: "Because it pays to give them to you."

It was a long time before journalists in Wisconsin and elsewhere, even those who worked for Nieman's Journal, paid much attention to him. In the meantime "passes" became what we call today "freebies," and they were handed out and accepted without a second thought. Reporters were given free tickets to movies and plays, invitations to press parties with overflowing tables of food and drink, and door prizes at some of those parties of jewelry and trips. For specialized reporters, the treasure chest was even richer:

+ Travel writers enjoyed transportation, accommodations at hotels and resorts and wining and dining, all on the house.

+ Sports reporters had free tickets to sporting events for themselves, family and friends, gifts that ranged from team jackets to golf bags and clubs, and Christmas deliveries of candy, boxes of steaks and bottles of liquor.

+ Entertainment writers were treated to trips to Hollywood and to locations of film shoots, all expenses paid.

+ City-side reporters vied with one other to cover banquet speeches where they could dine in unaccustomed style.

Seldom did reporters turn any gift down. And, unfortunately, it was not uncommon for reporters and editors to ask for favors.

But times and ethical sensitivities have changed. Journalists have come to believe that they should not put themselves in positions in which their responsibility to one individual or group might conflict with their broader journalistic responsibilities. In the 1970s, led by the Milwaukee Journal, newspapers across the country adopted codes of ethics that almost universally specified that reporters and editors were to accept nothing of value. The Society of Professional Journalists adopted a similar rule, as did the Associated Press Managing Editors. Now it's common practice when gifts come into the newsroom to return them, when appropriate, or to give them to charitable organizations, with a note to the individuals who sent the gifts. That is a Golden Mean solution that does not offend the givers.

In turn, public relations people, who once staged press parties and junkets and had bestowed gifts, began changing their way of operating. In keeping with their own code of ethics, they are not to "engage in any practice which has the purpose of corrupting the integrity of channels of communications or the processes of government." PR practitioners now focus attention less on entertainment and more directly on providing information.

Still, Walt Disney World threw a media party in Orlando, Fla., in 1986 to celebrate its 15th anniversary, and more than 10,000 people showed up, most of them journalists. It was what columnist Mike Royko called a "multimillion dollar freeload" for the media. "Who ever thought that Mickey Mouse would act like a Chicago alderman?" Royko asked. Many news people, especially those working for small publications, defended accepting the trip. They said the bash was a legitimate news story and they couldn't have afforded to cover it any other way.

New York Times reporter Dudley Clendinen quoted one editor who straightforwardly described the trip as "a form of bribery." Clendinen also pointed out the irony that it was at a meeting at Walt Disney World that the APME had adopted its code of ethics.

Even if a reporter cannot be "bought" for a bottle of scotch or a weekend at a resort hotel, as all would contend, accepting the gifts can give the appearance of impropriety, and that can undermine the person's journalistic credibility. So not only must journalists be as pure as Caesar's wife, they must also give the appearance of purity.

Public relations practitioners have to be aware of conflict of interest situations in two respects. On the one hand, they want to avoid any attempt to corrupt news reporters and editors, and nearly all have gotten away from providing freebies. On the other, they want to avoid any conflicts themselves. For example, no honest public relations person would represent competing entities.

Involvement in Politics

Possibilities exist for other conflicts of interest for news people, especially in politics. Columnists George Will and Patrick Buchanan, who were both covering the 1980 presidential campaign, helped to prepare candidate Ronald Reagan for a debate with incumbent President Jimmy Carter. Less well-known journalists have acted as unofficial advisers to candidates at many levels of government, and many have even lent their talents in writing speeches for candidates.

Are not reporters who act on behalf of candidates failing their responsibilities to those to whom they owe prime allegiance—their employers and their audiences? And are they not also failing their ethical responsibilities to their colleagues, whose effectiveness as journalists might be diminished if audiences saw them, also, as biased toward one candidate or party?

The implied answers to questions such as those led the Fort Worth Star-Telegram to adopt this straightforward rule: "Because of the inherent conflict of interest, it is expected that no member of the News/Editorial staff will (a) seek election to public office; (b) accept appointment to a public board, commission or panel that makes or carries out policy or that advises elected or appointed officials; or (c) work for a politician or a political organization, either as a volunteer or for pay."

What about the activities of spouses and so-called "significant others"? The husband of the publisher of the Natomas, Calif., Journal became a candidate for the Sacramento City Council, and her newspaper gave him unqualified support. That drew complaints from many readers who believed the newspaper had a responsibility to them to be objective in its coverage.

In another situation, when the husband of an editor for a newspaper in the DFW Suburban Newspapers group ran for city council, some staff members called for her resignation as editor. Instead she chose to act on the Golden Mean principle. She wrote a column saying her husband was running on his own, that she would take no stand, and that the race would be treated like any other. Her husband lost and was bitter that she had not supported him.

Conflict of interest questions have been raised as to whether the spouses of journalists should work for candidates or do nothing more than put a sign in the front yard. Former New York Times editor A. M. Rosenthal has said journalists "have to give up any kind of political activity beyond voting; that's the price we pay for being newspaper people." Purists would argue that spouses must pay the same price, and that poses considerable ethical soul-searching in an age when husbands and wives often pursue independent—and conflicting—careers.

Family Ties

Whether in politics or not, reporters and their sources, and reporters and their subjects, occasionally have fallen in love. Sometimes they have married. Clearly such relationships can create a conflict of interest. The New Yorker, for example, ran a story in its "Talk of the Town" section that defended the former East German leader Erich Honecker. The author, Irene Dische, had written for the magazine before, and with no problems. But editors learned only after the Honecker story was published that her husband was Honecker's attorney.

Jim Amoss, editor of the New Orleans Times-Picayune, was more up front. When his wife, an architect, became involved with planning for the renovation of that city's Municipal Auditorium as the site of a temporary casino, Amoss faced the appearance of a conflict of interest head on. In a column on the newspaper's op-ed page, Amoss said he was able to keep his distance from any stories involving the major shipping firm of which his father has been chairman. But, he wrote, he could not do that with any aspect of casino gambling, which had become part of the social, commercial and political fabric of our community." Were he to shun the subject, he would be "truly crippled" as an editor. Hence, he said, "disclosure, however meddlesome, seems the only reasonable path."

Amoss raised key questions to which persons working in the media should give hard thought at a time when couples are pursuing independent professional careers: "Should the demands of one spouse's profession limit the other's right to pursue a career? How much should each spouse's work life be tailored to fit the other's? When careers do conflict, who should yield?"

The Lure of Money

The world of money also can create conflicts. R. Foster Winans, a Wall Street Journal reporter, once wrote the newspaper's "Heard on the Street" column, which is made up of items of information about companies that could result in the rise or fall of the companies' stock. Winans began leaking items before publication to a stockbroker and timing their release so that the broker could garner large profits. The broker paid Winans $30,000. What Winans did was illegal, and he was convicted of violating securities laws. Beyond that, it was unethical insofar as he unfairly manipulated the information he gathered as a journalist to his own financial advantage and the advantage of his friends.

Potentially unethical was the activity of Steve Castner, a reporter for the Milwaukee Journal assigned to cover the financial difficulties of a major bank holding company. When the story came to light, the Wisconsin Securities Commissioner suspended trading in the company's stock. The reporter bought at auction sharply discounted shares of the bank's holding company expecting that he would sell them for a profit when trading resumed. Journal editor Richard H. Leonard said later that Castner believed he could continue to cover the story objectively while holding a significant amount of the company's stock, and he was not concerned about the public's perception. Leonard saw a clear conflict of interest, however, and ordered the reporter to sell the stock. When Castner refused, Leonard fired him.

Public relations practitioners can also face ethical conflicts in financial matters. In 1985, Detroit public relations practitioner Anthony M. Franco had as a client a company that was preparing to acquire another firm with a stock offering of $50 per share. Franco was to write a news release announcing the acquisition. The Securities and Exchange Commission later charged that before the news was made public, Franco had his broker buy 3,000 shares of the client company at $41 a share. While the incident was under investigation by the SEC, Franco became national president of the Public Relations Society of America. When a public announcement was made that Franco had signed a consent decree with the SEC, he resigned the presidency and, later, his membership.

Other Personal Gain

Even mundane personal matters have led to conflicts of interest. Reporters have sought to have traffic tickets fixed for themselves or family members, for example, or have sought jobs for their children with sources. A columnist for the New Orleans Times-Picayune lost his job after it was reported that he enjoyed a free parking spot at the city's airport. A good policy to follow is one enunciated by the Fort Worth Star-Telegram: "Staff members should never use their positions with the Star-Telegram for personal advantage. Company letterheads should not be used for purely personal activities outside company business. Nor should staffers use positions with the newspaper to obtain preferential treatment in personal matters associated with their roles as parents from business, industry or governmental organizations."

COMING TO ETHICAL DECISIONS

S T U D Y   P R E V I E W   How do we make ethical decisions? Largely through a process of reasoning that allows us to apply our values and principles to the dilemmas we face in the work-a-day world. Communication professionals who in good faith follow a carefully thought-out process when confronted with an ethical dilemma may arrive at different conclusions, depending on the relative importance they give to different values and principles. But the important thing is that they follow the process.

A Six-Step Process

The following questions, if answered carefully and conscientiously, should lead to a reasonable, ethical decision in almost any ethical dilemma. As with any exercise, the more practiced one becomes at following the process, the easier it becomes.

- ✦ *What happened?* What are the facts of the situation? Spell them out as clearly and as specifically as you can.

- ✦ *What communication values apply?* Look to the codes that have been adopted by the professional organizations of your field. What in the codes applies?

- ✦ *What are the ethical principles?* Are you dealing with a question of fairness, of telling the truth, of harming someone? Make sure the ethical point on which the question turns is clear to you.

- ✦ *To whom are responsibilities owed?* As you will see below, communicators owe responsibility to the public, their subjects, their sources, their employers and their colleagues. In this instance, who is involved and who will be affected by the decision you make?

- ✦ *What ethical theories apply?* What would be your decision if you followed the Categorical Imperative? Utilitarianism? The Golden Mean? The Golden Rule? With which outcome are you most comfortable?

- ✦ *What are the alternatives?* What would be the consequences of carrying out, or not carrying out, each alternative? Which is the best alternative in the situation?

To see how the process works, assume you are the news editor for your campus newspaper at a university of some 30,000 students. Acting on a tip one evening early in March, you attend a meeting of about 40 sixth-floor residents of Alumni Memorial Hall, a dorm for first-year female students. They are disgruntled because Missy Rosewater, a popular resident assistant on that floor, has been fired by the director of the Office of Campus Residence.

Missy is a graduating senior and in her second year as an R.A. The previous year she was selected from among the dormitory's 20 resident assistants for the annual Outstanding Resident Assistant award. She has a B-plus average in her courses, is vice president of her sorority and an active member of a campus service organization. She is paying for her education herself, and the free room and small stipend she has received as an R.A. have allowed her to complete her final two years.

Both Missy and the dorm director, Hunter "Stoney" Wall, are at the meeting. Missy, who is not married, tells the group that she is five months pregnant, a fact most seemed to know already, and that Stoney told her she was being fired because she was not a good role model for the residents and because her pregnancy had already begun to interfere with her duties.

Stoney confirms that those were the reasons. He reads a section of his office's policy requiring that resident assistants be "of excellent moral character," and he contends that her pregnancy calls her morality into question. He adds that Missy has needed more than normal medical attention and because she has been attended by her family doctor in her home town, about 150 miles away, she had frequently been away from campus and would likely be absent even more often as the school year wore on. Under those circumstances, Stoney tells the residents, he felt it was important to replace her.

The meeting ends with the students signing a petition to the vice president for student life, Stoney's supervisor, asking that Missy be reinstated.

As you head back to the newsroom, you start to think about how the story will go together, and you begin to wonder whether to identify Missy. You review the facts once more. The core of the story is Missy's firing for the reasons cited and the efforts of the residents to win her reinstatement. You have no doubt that the story ought to be told. You also know that names make news, and the names of individuals, especially in controversial stories, ought to be printed. You have a concern that the newspaper might be criticized and come under suspicion of playing favorites for withholding one name when its policy has been to print all names except those of victims of sex crimes. She did reveal to the people at the meeting that she is pregnant, so those involved in the story already know her name.

Would the details of the story identify her to your readers? On a campus of 30,000, chances are that only a small number of people would be able to figure out who she is or would know her even if her name were used. On the other hand, the Society of Professional Journalists Code of Ethics admonishes journalists to "show respect for the dignity, privacy, rights and well-being of people encountered in the course of gathering and presenting news." Even if few people knew her, would not publication of her name attack her dignity and intrude on her privacy and, as a result, disturb her well-being?

You are dealing with a question of harm to an individual. But you have a responsibility not just to Missy but to your reading public. You ask yourself if the public would benefit more by knowing her name than she would be harmed by its publication. You also ask if, in withholding publication, the harm to the public would outweigh the benefit to Missy.

What theory best applies? Considering the Categorical Imperative, where does your duty lie? Do you always print the name, regardless of consequence? Obviously not, though Missy is not the victim of a sex crime. Nevertheless, her pregnancy is a most private matter. Do you concern yourself with the consequences, and if so, what action, printing the name or not printing it, will serve the greatest good? What would you want for yourself in a similar situation? With which outcome are you most comfortable?

Which alternative to choose? If you decide to print Missy's name, you will have exposed a very personal, private matter. Many people who did not know that she is pregnant will know it. If you do not print it, you may avoid harm to her. At the same time, you may open the newspaper to criticism. You may also set a precedent that you might not wish to follow in the future. Which is the better alternative in the situation?

CHAPTER WRAP-UP

If you do your professional work in a competent way, respecting the values of the profession, you will perform ethically. And having a concern for acting ethically should help you perform competently. To act ethically, you should keep in mind where your loyalties lie. That is, know those to whom you have responsibilities. They include the public, which relies on accurate, unbiased communication in the conduct of its daily activities; subjects and sources; and clients, employers and colleagues. To behave ethically is to treat all of them as they deserve to be treated. You need also to hold the shared values of communicators. Those are detailed in the codes of ethics of professional organizations. Among the more important are telling the truth, respecting the privacy of others, protecting one's sources and avoiding conflicts of interest.

Understanding ethics only from an analysis of ethical acts, as most of us tend to do, is somewhat unsatisfactory. Classical ethics always included an analysis of the source of ethics—a person's character. Thus, at various points we have tried to spell out the virtues that a journalist must have.

Principles are important, but there is no substitute for a virtuous character. The former cannot always be applied. The latter can and must be.

STUDY QUESTIONS

1. Name at least three shared values of news and public relations people as enunciated in the codes of ethics of their professional organizations.

2. What is Kant's Categorical Imperative?

3. What is Utilitarianism?

4. What is the Golden Mean?

5. How does the Golden Rule apply to mass communication?

6. What ethical responsibilities do communicators have to their audiences?

7. What ethical responsibilities do communicators have to their sources?

8. What ethical responsibilities do communicators have to their subjects?

9. What ethical responsibilities do communicators have to their clients?

10. What ethical responsibilities do communicators have to their employers?

11. What ethical responsibilities do communicators have to their colleagues?

12. How does competence relate to ethical performance?

13. Why is it important for communicators to tell the truth?

14. When is lying justifiable?

15. When is the invasion of a public person's privacy justifiable?

16. Under what circumstances can one ethically reveal the name of a source who has been promised confidentiality?

17. What is the danger for a journalist in accepting something of value from a subject?

18. Is a public relations person justified in offering gifts to a news person?

PUTTING YOUR LEARNING TO WORK

EXERCISE 1   How Professionals Act

Interview a professional journalist or public relations practitioner about the ethical performance of professionals. What are the major ethical problems in the field today? How are professionals responding? What major ethical challenges has your source faced? How did the person resolve them?

EXERCISE 2   When Personal and Professional Clash

George Lopez is the night editor for his college's daily newspaper. One night before deadline, in a routine call to the city police department, he learns that six students, all over 18, have been arrested and will be charged with one count of burglary each. The six were arrested as they burglarized a local electronics store that police were staking out following a rash of burglaries of similar outlets. More charges may follow because police believe the students have been involved in all of those burglaries.

The officer reads the names of the suspects, and George recognizes all as friends or acquaintances. Three are his fraternity brothers and one of those is his roommate and best friend.

It is the practice of the newspaper to run city crime stories if they involve students, faculty or staff of the university and to give the names of any suspects 18 or over, and as night George has responsibility for getting the story into the newspaper. If the suspects were just names to him, he would not hesitate to get the story into the newspaper—but this case is different. What would you do in George's situation? Why? Be sure to outline clearly your line of reasoning.

FOR FURTHER LEARNING

Clifford G. Christians, Kim B. Rotzoll, and Mark Fackler. "Media Ethics: Cases and Moral Reasoning," 3d edition. Longman, 1991. The authors present a method for making ethical decisions and show how the method applies in specific instances. The book is used as a text in many media ethics courses.

Keith S. Collins, editor. "Responsibility and Freedom in the Press: Are They in Conflict?" The Report of the Citizen's Choice National Commission on Free and Responsible Media. Citizen's Choice, Inc., 1985. Testimony of individuals who appeared at a series of hearings on media responsibilities held by the commission.

Louis A. Day. "Ethics in Media Communications." Wadsworth, 1991. Another textbook for media ethics courses. Day shows the reader how principles apply to solving ethical dilemmas.

Deni Elliott, editor. "Responsible Journalism." Sage Publications, 1986. Nine essays on ethical performance of the media.

H. Eugene Goodwin. "Groping for Ethics in Journalism." Iowa State University Press, 1983. A discussion of the practice of journalism and how ethical principles should apply.

John L. Hulteng. "The Messenger's Motives: Ethical Problems of the News Media," 2nd edition. Prentice-Hall, 1985. How the media have dealt with ethical problems—and how those problems should have been handled.

Journal of Mass Media Ethics. A quarterly publication devoted to the discussion of issues of media morality.

Stephen Klaidman and Tom L. Beauchamp. "The Virtuous Journalist." Oxford University Press, 1987. A text on journalism ethics that ought to be read and re-read by everyone in the media. Among their contributions is the authors' discussion of competence as a virtue.

Edmund B. Lambeth. "Committed Journalism: An Ethic for the Profession." Indiana University Press, 1986. A carefully considered framework for the practice of ethical journalism.

Frank McCulloch, editor. "Drawing the Line: How 31 Editors Solved Their Toughest Ethical Dilemmas." American Society of Newspaper Editors Foundation, 1984. Brief statements by editor members of the ASNE.

Robert Schmuhl, editor. "The Responsibilities of Journalism." University of Notre Dame Press, 1984. Proceedings of a conference on journalistic ethics held at Notre Dame. Presenters were both journalists and non-journalists. The book includes a case study and analyses by three ethicists and an editor.

Zay N. Smith and Pamela Zekman. "The Mirage." Random House, 1979. The story of the Chicago Sun-Times reporters who became bar proprietors to investigate bribery on the part of city inspectors. The two consider the ethics of their effort.

STORY FORMATS

Uniform copy preparation is essential in news because of the great quantity of material processed by many hands for a single issue of a newspaper or magazine, for a news service report, or for a single newscast. Standard formatting is programmed into computers on which most reporters write their stories. In newsrooms using typewriters, however, or when stories must be printed out in "hard copy," reporters need to format their stories manually. On the next few pages, you will see some common formats. Although there are variations among newsrooms, these forms are representative of those generally specified when copy is prepared in paper form.

PRINT FORMAT

The first example is used for magazine and newspaper articles.

Gemstone Homicide

Karen Maraca

Feb. 15

This is a model for setting up a newspaper or magazine story on a page.

The slug, in the upper left corner, is an identifying line for the story.

In this example, the slug is Gemstone Homicide.

A slug helps headline writers, editors and other story handlers keep track of the story as it moves through the editing, composition and layout process.

A story about an airplane crash might be slugged "plane" or "crash" or something similar.

Avoid slugs which could be applied to several stories, such as "city" on a city council story.

Next is the reporter's name, in this example "Karen Maraca."

Then comes the date: Feb. 15.

MORE

Gemstone Homicide/Maraca/Add 1

The story begins one-third of the way down the first page.

This gives an editor room to write instructions to typesetters and other copy handlers on how to treat the story.

In the case of student stories for class, this room at the top provides room for your instructor's comments, questions and suggestions.

Start the second page with the slug, followed with an "Add 1" to indicate it is the first added page.

"Add 2" indicates a second added page.

Some publications use "Page 2" for the second page, "Page 3" for the third, etc., although this is not the usual convention.

The reporter's name should also go on every added page.

Use a 66-character line, indenting five spaces for paragraphs.

Copy should be double spaced. This allows room for editing notations and corrections.

Copy should be on 8-1/2 by 11-inch paper.

Type on only one side of a sheet.

Never break a paragraph in going from page to the next. Finish a paragraph on the page where you begin it.

Always indicate with the word "MORE" that at least one more page follows.

MORE

Gemstone Homicide/Add 2/Maraca

Because it is ambiguous for typesetters, don't end a line with a hyphenated word or a broken hyphenated word series.

Letter-perfect typing isn't required. Editors regard retyping as a waste of time if an error can be corrected by standard copy-editing marks.

Don't correct an error by typing over or erasing.

Strike-overs are ambiguous, and erasing is time-consuming.

Instead, type through the error with a string of "xxxxxxx's" and go on from there.

If you don't spot an error until after a line has been typed, pencil in the correction and cross out the mistake.

This should not be taken as an excuse for sloppy work. Clean copy always enhances the likelihood of clean typesetting.

Above all, make sure your corrections are intelligible to your editor and the typesetter.

Don't confuse the format for print stories with the different formats for radio and television.

When you come to the end, quit. The symbol "-30-" tells the editor there is no more

-30-

RADIO FORMAT

Many radio stations insist that news be typed on half sheets because they don't rattle so much at a microphone as the announcer flips the pages.

Type only one story on a page. This allows a news producer or announcer to change the sequence of stories quickly.

Type on only one side of a sheet..

Type on a 66-character line, the same as for print stories. Fifteen 66-character lines will take about one minute of air time, which means a producer or announcer may calculate quickly how long an item will take on the air by counting the lines.

Double space so an editor may pencil in changes.

Some stations use all caps, but downstyle is better. The AP rules for capitalization work well for broadcast copy.

Never split a word between lines.

Avoid having the same word start successive lines. That can throw an announcer.

Slug each story. The slug should identify the subject of the story in one or two words.

The slug goes in parentheses to alert the announcer that it's for reference and not to be aired.

Sign off the story with your name, the time and date you wrote the story, and the time and date the story should be killed because it will be outdated or stale.

Put the sign-off in parentheses because it's for reference only and not to be aired.

Don't use the copy-editing symbols used for print stories.

Instead use a copy pencil to mark out completely any words that are to be deleted or corrected. Then type or print the correct word or words above the material that has been crossed out.

Retype any copy that will difficult for an announcer to follow.

Be sure to distinguish between the formats for print and for radio and television stories. They are different, each adapted to the copy processes unique to each medium.

See the following example.

(MINE OPENING)

This is the format for setting up a radio story on a page. Place parentheses around words that are only for an announcer's reference, such as the slug. The story is one long paragraph—no indents except at the start. Write the story as a single paragraph. This will help an announcer determine how many seconds a story will take on the air. On average, 15 full lines take one minute. Seek "soft leads." Avoid abbreviations. Be conversational and you will be on the road to listenable broadcast copy. Perhaps most important, listen for errors when somebody else reads your copy. If the announcer gets tongue-tied, there probably was a better way you could have arranged the words.

(MUHAMMAD ABBAS 210P FEB 18; KILL AFTER 7p FEB 18)

RADIO FORMAT WITH ACTUALITY

When a story includes a taped segment, called an "actuality," the radio format needs adjusting. See the following example.

(WILSON MEETING)

    An actuality is a tape-recorded quotation. It lets your audience hear a news source's voice. It spices up a newscast by introducing a voice other than the announcer's. In writing a radio story that contains an actuality, use the basic format as for a radio story without an actuality — but introduce the actuality with a lead-in such as "Wilson Mayor Joan Jett said the tax is important." Then write the first three words of her comment with the time of the sound bite in parentheses. Below that, give the last three words as the out cue.

    IN: This is necessary (:25)

    OUT: a solid proposal.

Use an exit line such as "That was Mayor Joan Jett."

    (ELISA MENDEZ 940P APR 5; KILL AFTER 12M APR 5)

TELEVISION FORMAT

The writing style for radio and television is the same: soft leads, titles ahead of names, short sentences.

How the story is set up on paper, though, is different.

While radio stories deal only with audio, television scripts show second by second how the writer intends the audio and video to be integrated.

See a model television news script on the following pages.

Among frequently used cues in television news scripts:

BG: Background sound on videotape that is run at lower volume under announcer's voice. Same as WS and NATSOT.

CU: Close-up shot.

DROP SUPER: Drop superimposed wording.

IN: In-cue or intro. Includes first few words from SOT.

LIVE: Announcer on camera live.

LS: Long shot.

MCU: Medium close-up.

MS: Medium shot.

NATSOT: Natural sound on tape. Run at lower volume under announcer's voice. Same as BG and WS.

OUT: Out-cue or out-tro. Includes last few words from SOT.

REMOTE SPLIT: Split into side-by-side panels, such as one for announcer and one for reporter.

SIL: Silent videotape.

SLO-MO: Roll videotape at slow motion.

SOT: Sound on videotape.

SUPER: Superimpose wording from character generator.

VO: Voice over. Tell how long it runs: VO :12 would be 12 seconds.

WS: Wild sound, for sound on videotape run at lower volume under announcer's voice.

(POETRY AWARD — AMY STONE — NOV 23)

LIVE ANNOUNCER ON CAMERA 1	Television copy is double-spaced. Notes on the video part of the story are on the left half of the page. Audio is on the right. The audio half is on 30-character lines. Each line of script takes about two seconds of air time for announcers who deliver at a typical 150 words a minute.
SOT	IN: "A bank teller...." RUN: :19 Indicate a sound-on-tape section with the in-cue and out-cue on the audio half of your sheet. Include the length, in this case 19 seconds. OUT: ... . Phyllis Cable reporting."
LIVE ANNOUNCER ON CAMERA 2	Use standard 8½ by 11-inch paper. Type only on the top three-quarters of the page so the announcer's eyes don't drop too far below the camera if there is no TelePrompTer. (MORE)

(FIRST ADD, GEMSTONE HOMICIDE)

                        Use (MORE) to indicate there is
                        another page. Slug the second page
                        as (FIRST ADD), the third as
                        (SECOND ADD). At the end. write
                        END). Some don'ts: Never break
                        sentences between pages. Never use
                        the back of a sheet of paper. Never
                        put more than two stories to a page.
                        (END)

PRESS RELEASE FORMAT

Trolley
Preservation
Association

140 W. 20TH STREET   •   MESA, ALABAMA 34440

Contact: Darnel Kraal
(414) 773-7600
After 7 p.m.: (414) 776-7552

For release at Noon, March 14
and thereafter

TROLLEY CLUB BUYS VINTAGE CAR

News releases follow the basic format used for newspaper stories.

This includes starting one-third down the first page and double spacing.

Usually the same release is sent both to newspapers and broadcast stations

If your organization has letterhead stationery, use it. Otherwise type the name and address single space at the top.

Include the day and night telephone number of your organization's contact person in case an editor or producer needs more information or clarification. Include the contact person's name.

MORE

Trolley purchase/Add 1

Some editors appreciate headlines on news releases.

A headline gives them a quick sense of what the story is about.

Sometimes a suggested headline will give an editor an appreciated headstart on writing the headline that will appear in publication.

In writing a suggested headline, follow newspaper headline-writing rules:

> A headline is a truncated present-tense sentence.

> The articles "a," "an" and "the" are not used.

> Avoid a label like "TROLLEY CAR PURCHASE." A news headline must have a verb.

Prominently on the first page, state when the release may be used. Include the time, day and date.

By providing a release in advance, you help editors and producers plan how they will use it.

Standard newsroom practice is to honor embargoes on routine announcements.

On a major story, however, an embargo probably would not be honored.

MORE

Trolley purchase / Add 2

    If, for example, the president of the trolley club has fired the club director and plans to seek criminal prosecution for embezzlement, a news release doesn't make sense.

    Get on the phone with the media, tell what's happened, and prepare to answer questions and to arrange interviews for reporters with the club president.

    Organization that issue a lot of news releases include filing and reference information at the end.

    This information usually is the sequential number of the release and the date it was sent.

-30-

Release No. 43

March 12

CORRECTION SYMBOLS

These are symbols you can use in stories to correct typographical errors and make minor changes.

PRINT MEDIA

Insert comma	Insert period
Insert a letter	Insert word
Insert apostrophe: don't	Insert quotation marks
Insert a hyphen =	Insert a dash ⊢⊣
Indent for a new paragraph	Delete this word
Delete several the an words	Transpose letters
Transpose words	Delete letter
capitalize a letter	Lowercase a Letter
Spell out Feb.	Abbreviate February
Spell out the number 12	Use numeral for twelve
Forget this correction	Joynes is right spelling
More story fellows more	End of story — 30 —
Separate words	Bring words to gether

RADIO AND TELEVISION

In broadcast, you don't have to learn any editing symbols. Just pencil in changes so they are obvious at a glance to an announcer speeding through copy at 150 words a minute.

copy at
She sped through the coppy att 150 words a minute.

STYLE GUIDE

The Associated Press and United Press International stylebooks, which were developed jointly 25 years ago and remain largely the same today, are the most widely used style references in the news business. The tips on these pages are consistent with AP and UPI style. For questions not addressed here, see the AP or UPI stylebook.

ABBREVIATIONS

AP and UPI style is balanced between compactness and clarity. Print news uses more abbreviations than most other kinds of writing. Abbreviations should help writers be concise and save space but never at the cost of confusing the audience.

Abbreviations are especially troublesome on the air and generally should be avoided. The only abbreviations acceptable in broadcast news are those that are easily recognized, and they should be spelled to help announcers through them: C-B-S, F-B-I, N-C-two-A, N-double-A-C-P.

The following words are never abbreviated: assistant, associate, attorney, building, department, district, fort, government, lieutenant governor, president, professor, secretary, superintendent, treasurer.

academic degrees. Spell them out: Jones, who holds a doctorate in medieval literature, will speak. An exception is in lists in which the degree is relevant: Scott Jones, Ph.D.; Mary Love, M.A.; and Rob Dug, B.A.

acronyms. A rule of thumb is to use periods in acronyms if these spell a real word: M.A.S.H., c.o.d. Because there are exceptions, consult the AP or UPI style book. Among the exceptions: CARE (Cooperative for American Relief Everywhere), NOW (National Organization of Women).

addresses. See *streets.*

courtesy titles. The courtesy titles "Mr.," "Mrs." and "Miss" aren't used much any more, and many publications have departed from AP and UPI style, which are traditional on the issue. Here is the AP and UPI style:

Never use courtesy titles for first reference or when a person's first and last name appear together.

"Mr." is used only in "Mr. and Mrs."

"Mrs." is only for second references to a married woman unless the woman prefers "Ms." or her last name with no courtesy title.

"Miss" is used for second references to a single woman unless the woman prefers "Ms." or her last name by itself.

If a woman prefers "Ms.," include her marital status only if it is relevant to the story.

In direct quotations, of course, writers must stick with the words as they were uttered.

companies. In company names, use abbreviations: Bros., Co., Corp., Inc., Ltd. Hence Shaman Inc., Warner Bros., Jackson Corp.

A comma is not used before "Inc."

government agencies. Most government abbreviations are confusing clutter for readers and listeners. Among the exceptions: CIA, FBI.

junior. Abbreviate "junior" and senior" after a name: James Squires Jr. There is no comma before "Jr." or "Sr."

nations. U.S. and U.N. are all right only as adjectives. As nouns, spell out: United States, United Nations. Spell out all other countries in all uses.

saint. Abbreviate in formal names and cities: St. Christopher, St. Louis, St. Teresa. An exception: Sault Ste. Marie, Mich.

speed. Miles per hour may be abbreviated: mph.

states. Some states are never abbreviated: Alaska, Idaho, Iowa, Hawaii, Maine, Ohio, Texas, Utah. Other states are abbreviated only when used with a city or county: Jacksonville, Fla.; Whitman County, Wash.

State abbreviations: Ala., Ariz., Ark., Calif., Colo., Conn., D.C., Del., Fla., Ga., Ill., Ind., Kan., Ky., La., Mass., Md., Minn., Miss., Mo., Mont., N.C., N.D., Neb., Nev., N.H., N.J., N.M., N.Y., Okla., Ore., Pa., R.I., S.C., S.D., Tenn., Va., Vt., Wash., Wis., W.Va., Wyo.

The two-letter capitalized state abbreviations were designed by the post office for electronic scanning and not human reading. Never use them in news.

streets. Abbreviate these words in numbered addresses: Ave., Blvd., St. Spell out others, including Circle, Drive, Road, Square. Examples: 42 Ralston Ave., 1102 Green Circle, 411 Jackson Drive. But: on Ralston Avenue.

Use abbreviations for compass points in numbered addresses: 320 Raring St. N.W., 2929 W. Wesley. Otherwise, spell out the compass points: on Raring Street Northwest, on West Wesley.

titles. These titles, when used as an adjective before a name, are abbreviated: Dr., Gov., Lt. Gov., Rep., Sen. Example: Gov. Arne Carlson.

These military titles are abbreviated when used as adjectives before names: Adm., Brig. Gen., Capt., Col., Cmdr., Cpl., Pfc., Pvt., 1st Lt., Lance Cpl., Gen., Lt.Col., Lt. Gen., Maj., Maj. Gen., 2nd Lt., Sgt., Sgt. Maj., Staff Sgt., Spec 4, Spec 5, 3rd Lt. Exception: Petty Officer 1st Class.

Titles after names are never abbreviated: Paul Welder, a U.S. senator; Barbara Glace, an Army sergeant.

weapons. Abbreviate bullet and gun sizes: 9mm pistol.

Acceptable on First Reference

Many abbreviations are in-group references that don't work well when communicating with a mass audience. That's why news people are cautious about peppering stories with abbreviations. The abbreviations listed here are widely enough recognized so that they can be used in first references without the full name. Even with these abbreviations, try to make it clear what they stand for from context.

ABC. American Broadcasting Company. For broadcast: A-B-C.

AFL-CIO. American Federation of Labor and Congress of Industrial Organizations. For broadcast: A-F-L C-I-O.

CBS. Columbia Broadcasting System. For broadcast: C-B-S.

CIA. Central Intelligence Agency. For broadcast: C-I-A.

c.o.d. Cash on delivery. For broadcast: c-o-d.

DDT. Dichlorodiphenyltrichloroethane. Thank goodness for abbreviations. For broadcast: D-D-T.

EDT, EST. Eastern Daylight Time, Eastern Standard Time when part of a time: 9:15 a.m. EST (no commas). Same with Central, Mountain and Pacific zones. For broadcast, do not abbreviate the time zones: Central time.

FBI. Federal Bureau of Investigation. For broadcast: F-B-I.

IQ. Intelligence quotient. For broadcast: I-Q.

NBC. National Broadcasting Company. For broadcast: N-B-C.

ROTC. Reserve Officers' Training Corps. For broadcast: R-O-T-C.

TNT. Trinitrotoluene. For broadcast: T-N-T.

TV. Television, but only as an adjective or in a construction like "cable TV." For broadcast: T-V.

UFO. Unidentified flying object. Plural: UFOs. For broadcast: U-F-O.

UHF. Ultra high frequency. For broadcast: U-H-F.

U.N. United Nations, but only when used as an adjective. For broadcast: U.N.

U.S. United States, but only when used as an adjective. For broadcast: U.S.

VHF. Very high frequency. For broadcast: V-H-F.

VIP. Very important person. Plural: VIPs. For broadcast: V-I-P.

YMCA. Young Men's Christian Association. For broadcast: Y-M-C-A.

YWCA. Young Women's Christian Association. For broadcast: Y-W-C-A.

Acceptable on Second Reference

ACLU. American Civil Liberties Union. For broadcast: A-C-L-U.

AIDS. Acquired immune deficiency syndrome. For broadcast: AIDS.

AMA. American Medical Association. For broadcast: A-M-A.

AP. Associated Press. For broadcast: A-P.

AT&T. American Telephone & Telegraph Company. For broadcast: A-T-and-T.

AWOL. Absent without leave. For broadcast: A-W-O-L or A-WOL, depending on how you want it said.

CB. Citizens band radio. For broadcast: C-B.

ESP. Extrasensory perception. For broadcast: E-S-P.

GM. General Motors Corp. For broadcast: G-M.

GOP. Republican Party. For broadcast: G-O-P.

government agencies. EPA, FAA, FCC, FDA, FDIC, FHA, FTC, GSA, ICC, IRS, NASA. For broadcast, most take hyphens, like E-P-A. Exceptions are agencies whose abbreviations are pronounced like a word: NASA.

NAACP. National Association for the Advancement of Colored People. Because the name of this organization is so long, the abbreviation is OK to avoid cluttered leads, so long as the whole name is introduced in the story. For broadcast: N-double-A-C-P.

OAS. Organization of American States. For broadcast: O-A-S.

POW. Prisoner of war. For broadcast: P-O-W

TB. Tuberculosis. For broadcast: T-B.

VD. Venereal disease. For broadcast: V-D.

VISTA. Volunteers in Service to America. For broadcast: VISTA.

VOA. Voice of America. For broadcast: V-O-A.

CAPITALIZATION

Most publications follow a downstyle. This means they opt for lowercase whenever possible. Downstyle makes sense because capital letters are fatter than lowercase letters; downstyle creates more room for articles. Also, studies have found that people find it easier to read a downstyle. This is important in writing radio and television news scripts. Here are newsroom terms to help you with capitalization:

- ✦ Capitalize. Use upper case for the first letter: Albany, Idaho, Jones.
- ✦ All caps. Use upper case for the entire word: FBI, NAFTA, USC.
- ✦ Upper case. Capital letters: A, B, C.
- ✦ Lower case. Small letters: a, b, c.
- ✦ Upper and lower case: Anderson.
- ✦ Upstyle. A generally archaic style favoring capital letters that is not used in news. The rule of thumb in upstyle is, when in doubt capitalize.
- ✦ Downstyle. The rule of thumb, when in doubt, lowercase it.

awards. Capitalize proper names of awards and medals: Elsie Gruber Blue Ribbon Citation, Heisman Trophy, Medal of Honor, Purple Heart, Notre Dame Distinguished Alumni Award.

Lowercase common awards: the alumni awards, first place, a blue ribbon.

brand names. Capitalize trade names: Chevrolet automobiles, Chevrolets, Macintosh computers, Macintoshes, Wrangler jeans, Wranglers.

Capitalize registered trademarks: Band-Aid, Clorox, Coke, Dacron, Frisbee, Jell-O, Realtor, Xerox. Unless the brand is relevant, use a generic word: bandage, sedan, bleach, cola, ultimate disc, gelatin, real estate agent, photocopier.

buildings. Capitalize formal names for buildings: the White House, Sears Tower.

Lowercase general titles: the biology building, the Radio Shack store.

clubs. Capitalize clubs and their members: American Legion, Kiwanis Club, Phi Beta Kappa, Legionnaire, Rotarian.

committees. Capitalize formal names of committees: the Joint Legislative Council on Ethics Reform, the House Subcommittee on Banking. Lowercase shortened forms: the Smith committee, the higher-ed task force.

creative works. Capitalize the first, last, and all principal words in books, films, lectures, musical compositions, paintings, plays, poems, songs, speeches, television programs, and all works of art. Examples: "The Dead Zone," "Boogie Woogie Bugle Boy of Company B."

Capitalize prepositions and conjunctions of four letters or more. Example: "Gone With the Wind."

Also, it's the U.S. Constitution but the word "constitutional" is lower case.

direct quotation. Capitalize the first word of a full sentence that is quoted directly: *Gertrude Stein wrote, "A rose is a rose is a rose."*

Lowercase the first word of a sentence fragment that is quoted. *In Daley's message to police, he used the words "shoot to kill."*

Put another way: If a comma separates the quotation from an attributive, capitalize the first word of the quotation. Otherwise, don't.

flag. Capitalize nicknames for the U.S. flag, including Old Glory, Stars and Stripes.

formal titles. Capitalize formal titles when used as adjectives before a name: President Bill Clinton, Mayor George Latimer, Dean Bonnie Buzza

Lowercase titles used as nouns: the mayor, George Latimer.

Lowercase occupational titles: actress Jody Foster, astronaut Neil Armstrong, secretary Martha Jones, first baseman Harry Jogs, singer Sinead O'Connor.

If there is no name, lowercase the title: federal, first lady, government, priest, president, senator, state.

geographic names. Capitalize widely recognized geographic regions: the Badlands (of the Dakotas), East End, Idaho Panhandle, the Loop (downtown Chicago), Midwest, Northern California, South, Up North (a regionalism for Northern Wisconsin), Upper Michigan, Upstate New York, the West, West Side (of Manhattan, for example).

Lowercase general directions: *Gregg headed north across the river.*

government. Capitalize federal, state and local governmental units in the United States: U.S. Congress, Nebraska Legislature, Ohio Court of Appeals, Dade County, Omaha City Council.

Capitalize second references to these government units: the Congress, the Supreme Court, County Board.

Lowercase references to foreign government units: the senate, the state.

historic periods. Capitalize historic periods, including Gay '90s, Prohibition Era, Roaring '20s.

holidays. Capitalize holy days and holidays, including Christmas, Easter, Hanukkah, New Year's, Thanksgiving.

military. The names of U.S. military branches are capitalized: the U.S. Marine Corps, the U.S. Marines, the Marines, Air Force, Army, Navy.

nationalities. Capitalize nationalities: Irish. Italian.

personifications. Capitalize Easter Bunny, Tooth Fairy.

plurals. Lowercase nouns with multiple proper-noun modifiers: at First and Oak streets, the Mississippi, Missouri and Ohio rivers.

political parties. Capitalize political parties and their members: the Democrats, Democratic, the Communist Party, the Libertarian Party, the Republican Party, Socialists.

Lowercase references to political philosophy: The communist thinker-philosopher Karl Marx never belonged to a political party. Scandinavians have a socialist tradition.

proper nouns. Bill Clinton, Kansas City, Logan International Airport. Without a name, the adjective is lower case: the president, the city, the airport.

Capitalize shortened forms of proper nouns for one-of-a-kind events: the Derby (Kentucky Derby), the Series (World Series).

Lowercase derivatives from proper nouns if the meaning is no longer dependent on the proper noun: french fries, martini cocktail, pasteurize, venetian blinds.

races. Capitalize races: Asians, Caucasians, Indians. Lowercase black and white.

religions. Capitalize religions in all grammatical forms: Buddhism, Buddhist, Catholic, Catholicism, Christian, Christianity, Jewish, Moslem.

Capitalize references to deity: Allah, the Almighty, the Father, God, Jehovah. Lowercase pronouns referring to deity: he, him, thee, thou.

Capitalize holy books: Bible, Holy Scripture, Koran, New Testament. The word "biblical," however, is lower case.

Capitalize religious titles: the Pope, the Rev. Jerry Falwell.

rooms. Capitalize specific rooms: the Blue Room, Room 1101, the Oval Office, Suite 14.

seasons. Lowercase autumn, fall, spring, summer, winter.

times. Lowercase a.m. and p.m.: at 9 a.m., at 7 p.m., at 6:12 a.m.

wars and battles. Capitalize: World War I, the Battle of Little Bighorn.

NUMBERS

Because space is at a premium in print media, news style uses figures more than many forms of writing. The figure 13 takes less space than thirteen. The general rule is spell out one to nine and use figures for 10 and above. For exceptions, see the AP or UPI stylebook.

One exception is when a number begins a sentence. Spell them out: *Eleven counselors were indicted.* Because large numbers are cumbersome spelled out, try to redraft sentences to avoid them at the start:

AWKWARD: *Two-hundred ninety-three Malaysian crew members made it to shore.*

BETTER: *A total of 293 Malaysian crew members made it to shore.*

Don't get carried away, though. The goal is to be compact:

FLABBY: *A total of six seniors tested the parachutes.*

TIGHT: *Six seniors tested the parachutes.*

When you must spell out large numbers, use hyphens only to connect words ending in "y" with another word: forty-three, two hundred seventy-one, three million seventy-six thousand five hundred seventy-one dollars. No commas.

In broadcast, write numbers in whatever way you think will help announcers say them correctly. Generally spell out one to nine, use figures from 10 to 999, and write out larger numbers as you want them spoken: *12-hundred, 119-thousand dollars, one-point-14 pounds.*

In broadcast, round off numbers as much as you can. The ear has a hard time processing long numbers and decimals. For $1,914.20, make it: *more than 19-hundred dollars.*

addresses. Addresses always are in figures: 1600 Pennsylvania Ave., 45 Shore Drive, 10 Downing St.

Numbered street names follow the main rule: First through Ninth and then 10th, 11th, 12th, etc.

In broadcast: *16-hundred Pennsylvania Avenue, 29-29 West Wellesley.*

ages. Ages are in figures: *Dedmon Hanson, 3, earned $14. The 9-year-old horse died.*

An exception is at the beginning of a sentence: *Fourteen-year-old Georgia Hood walked out safely.*

casual uses. When a number is used casually and not meant as a measure, spell it out: *Thanks a million. It seemed a hundred miles.*

centuries. Follow the usual rule: the first through the ninth centuries and 10th thereafter: the 20th century.

dimensions. Use figures: 2-by-4 board, 6-inch ruler, 5 inches long.

Words in dimensions are spelled out: feet, grams, inches, meters, ounces, pounds, yards. Millimeter is an exception: 70mm film; a 105mm antiaircraft gun.

fractions. Below 1, spell out: three-fifths, five-sixteenths. Above 1, use figures: 3¼. Decimals are often better: 3.25.

In broadcast: *three and one-quarter, 17-point-four.*

legislative districts. Always in figures unless at the beginning of a sentence: 4th Congressional District, 167th House District, 6th Ward.

millions. two million, 14 billion, $212 trillion.

In broadcast, avoid dollar signs and spell out the word *dollars.* Also, never write "a million," which can be heard as "eight million." Make it: *one million.*

No. Use figures in numbered rankings: The No. 2 draft pick; Fire Engine No. 4, Page 1.

ordinals. Ordinals follow the usual rule: First through ninth, then 10th, 101st, 223rd, etc.

Exceptions include legislative districts and other political divisions and military units: 2nd Congressional District, 3rd Army, 2nd Brigade, 7th Fleet.

proper names. Follow the organization's preference: 20th Century-Fox, Twentieth Century Investors, Big Ten, Super Bowl XXVIII.

Roman numerals. Use Roman numerals for wars: World War I. For broadcast, spell it out as you want it said: World War One, the First World War.

Use Roman numerals to show sequence for animals and people: Native Dancer II, King Henry VIII, Pope John Paul II. For broadcast, spell it out as you want it said: Native Dancer Two, King Henry the Eighth, Pope John Paul the Second.

serial numbers: Use figures: The Nissan 300ZX serial number was JN1RZ24H8PX538295.

scores. Scores are in figures: The Yankees won 5-4. The score was Packers 21, Vikings 14.

In broadcast: *The Yankees won 5 to 4. The 5-to-3 victory was the Tigers' first of the year.*

series. In a series, follow the rule of spelling out one to nine and using figures thereafter: *Her sophomore grades included 11 As, 13 Bs and two Cs.*

space craft: Apollo 11, Gemini 2.

temperatures. Temperatures are in figures, except zero: 72 degrees, 9 degrees below zero, zero degrees.

If you must begin a sentence with a temperature, spell it out, but try to avoid this.

time. Times are in figures: 2 p.m., 3:14 a.m., 7:10 in the morning, 10 o'clock.

votes. Use figures: *The City Council approved Springfest 3-2. The House voted 103-99 for reform. In a 5-4 split, the Supreme Court rejected the Jones argument.*

With a large number of votes, use "to" instead of a dash to make it easier to read: *The convention favored Haggerty 1,211 to 1,198.*

weights and measures. Use figures for weights and measures: an 8-pound, 7-ounce baby, she stood 6-foot-2, it measured 7 inches around.

years. Years are never abbreviated, even at the beginning of a sentence: 2001 begins the 21st century. Because it looks awkward, try to avoid beginning a sentence with a year.

PUNCTUATION

Because grammarians don't agree on every dot, newspeople put their punctuation preferences in stylebooks. These preferences generally favor clean, modern, minimalist punctuation forms. A hundred years ago, writers peppered their work with semicolons. In contrast, semicolons generally are avoided in news today except for clarity in lists. Similarly, the old-fashioned comma before "and" in a series is also out.

Not being grammar books, stylebooks have skeletal punctuation sections. Their purpose is only to clarify issues on which grammarians are divided. This section, all consistent with Associated Press style, focuses on matters that confound many college students.

Colons

colons for emphasis. Example: *To succeed in real estate, an agent needs to remember three things: location, location and location.*

colons and lists. Colons are effective for introducing lists at the end of a sentence.

colons and quotations. Colons can add punch to a quotation: *Frank was firm: "I will not give up."*

Commas

commas and names. Use commas to separate names and titles only if the title is used as a noun: *A sophomore, Cherry Harm, fell off the chair.* Here, "sophomore" is used as a noun.

If the title is used as an adjective, don't use a comma: *Sophomore Julie Jacob earned an A.* Here, "sophomore" is an adjective describing Jacob.

commas in a series. Avoid commas before the conjunctions "and," "but," "for," "nor," "or," "so" and "yet" in a series: *A tall, dark and handsome stranger.*

An exception is when a component in the series has an internal conjunction, like "ham and eggs" in this sentence: *George ordered juice, toast, and ham and eggs.* Otherwise, it would be unclear whether "toast and ham" or "ham and eggs" go together.

A serial comma is needed when the elements in a series are lengthy: *Crane's goals included strengthening the five-year-old honors program, creating a residential college, and raising entrance requirements for transfer students.*

comma connectors. Use a comma before a conjunction when the conjunction connects two mini-sentences: *Animals rights advocates say bow-hunting of deer is cruel, and they've turned to the state for help in proving their case.* Ask yourself if there is a mini-sentence, what grammarians call an "independent clause," on either side of the conjunction. In this sentence, we have "advocates-say" before "and" and "they-have turned" after "and." So a comma is needed.

comma splices. Do not splice mini-sentences together with a comma if there is no conjunction. Wrong: *The Pacific Coast states were socked in with fog from San Diego to Seattle, the Midwest was clear.* Comma splices are a common punctuation error, but no more forgivable than others.

One solution is two sentences: *The Pacific Coast states were socked in with fog from San Diego to Seattle. The Midwest was clear.*

Another solution is a conjunction: *The Pacific Coast states were socked in with fog from San Diego to Seattle, but the Midwest was clear.*

A grammatically correct although not recommended solution is a semicolon: *The Pacific Coast states were socked in with fog from San Diego to Seattle; the Midwest was clear.* See the semicolon entry.

comma "but." A comma is needed before "but" only if "but" connects minisentences. "But" doesn't take a comma is other uses: *Martinez visited Yale but not Dartmouth.*

commas and attribution. Commas set off an attributive from a quotation: *She said, "The sky is blue." "The sky is blue," she said. "The sky," she said, "is blue."*

Commas do not set off a partial quotations: *She accused Jones of "lowly deceit" in the campaign.*

Commas do not set off attributions and paraphrases: *She said the sky was blue.* An exception is post-sentence or mid-sentence attribution: *The sky is blue, she said. The sky, she said, is blue.*

Dashes

dashes and hyphens. Dashes and hyphens are often confused. Hyphens join words, like compound modifiers: *a 4-year-old girl.* Dashes are separators, not joiners. Use two hyphens to indicate a dash on keyboards without a dash key.

dashes for change. A dash can indicate an abrupt change: *Harvey plans on college—if he ever gets out of high school.*

dashes for series. Dashes can set off a series inside a phrase: *She listed the prof's qualities—punctual, rigorous, unyielding—on the evaluation form.*

Ellipses

ellipses. Avoid ellipses as much as possible. They have multiple uses, which can leave readers guessing what they mean. Also, they are a sophisticated punctuation form that many people forget about after grammar school. On the keyboard, an ellipsis is indicated by spaced-out periods. An ellipsis at the end of sentence takes four spaced-out dots, the last one for a period: . . . .

ellipses in broadcast. For broadcast, commas are often replaced by ellipses to show brief pauses, depending on the style of the news organization. When in doubt, use commas.

ellipses in quotations. An ellipsis indicates words have been deleted in condensing a direct quotation: *Marshall, tears in his eyes, began his speech. "This is* *most difficult decision of my life. The fact is . . . my health won't let me continue as your president."* Generally, a paraphrase is more effective than a quotation that needs boiling down. Paraphrasing sidesteps the need for an ellipsis.

ellipses and pauses. An ellipsis can indicate a pause, but this is a problem, especially in a direct quote. The reader doesn't know whether the ellipsis indicates a deletion or a pause. To avoid this kind of ambiguity, say there was a pause: *"I cannot," she started and then a long pause. "I cannot do it."*

Exclamation Marks

For mildly exclamatory statements, a comma is sufficient. Use exclamation marks sparingly.

Hyphens

hyphens as connectors. Hyphens connect elements in compound modifiers: *A 17-year-old horse caused the fire.*

Adverbs ending in -ly never take a hyphen: *The bulldozer struck the badly parked car.*

Use two hyphens to indicate a dash if your keyboard doesn't have a dash key.

Parentheses

parentheses for insertions. Parentheses should be used sparingly. Too often they are used to insert background into a sentence. Not only do parenthetical insertions clutter a sentence but they are also a sign of clumsy story organization. Alternatives include placing background ahead of where it is needed for improving context.

parentheses and political affiliation. Most news stylebooks specify commas: *Rostenkowski, D-Ill., proclaimed he was innocent.*

parentheses and proper names. AP style calls for parentheses for clarifying insertions within a proper noun: *the Rochester (Minn.) Post-Bulletin.* A cleaner treatment is to consider "Rochester" as an adjective describing a fragment of the proper name: *the Rochester, Minn., Post Bulletin.* Context can avoid the problem: *In Rochester, Minn., the Post-Bulletin. . . .*

Periods

Periods are the least troublesome punctuation form.

Never use double periods, even when an abbreviation ends a sentence: Wrong: *She lived in Selma, Ala..* Right: *She lived in Selma, Ala.*

Quotation Marks

In U.S. usage, periods and commas go inside the closing quote mark: *The council's view is that Pleasantville show "never be annexed," the mayor said.*

In some constructions, the colon, exclamation mark, question mark and semicolon go outside the quotation mark: *Have you read "El Cid"?* It depends on whether the punctuation mark applies to the quoted part of the sentence inside the quote marks or to the whole sentence.

Semicolons

Rightly or wrongly, semicolons scare readers. They assume that the reading is going to get complicated, so they jump to another story. Good advice is to use semicolons sparingly, which isn't difficult because there are alternatives for many situations that could take a semicolon.

semicolons in a series. Use semicolons for clarity in a series in which commas themselves would make for confusion: *Harvey's survivors include two sons, John and Jake; two grandsons, Ken Post and Jason Hale; two nephews, Larry Panty and Brad Forest; and two great-grandsons, Nick Hank and Parker Jar.* Without semicolons, readers could be confused about whether grandsons are nephews.

Keep lists using semicolons at the end of sentences to avoid this kind of awkwardness: *Mary Hudson, 32, of Alma; Heady Swans, 30, of Citroen; and Salvia Gruyere, 31, of Bruiser; represented Buffalo County.*

Better: *Representing Buffalo County were Mary Hudson, 32, of Alma; Heady Swans, 30, of Citroen; and Salvia Gruyere, 31, of Bruiser.* This structure allows readers who aren't interested in the names and detail to skip to the next paragraph and speed their way through the story.

semicolons and complex sentences. Semicolons are correct but not advisable in connecting mini-sentences: *Rodriguez spent his winter vacation at Silver Mountain; Lucas went to Cozumel.* Because semicolons discourage readers, seek an alternative: *Rodriguez spent his winter vacation at Silver Mountain. Lucas went to Cozumel.* Or: *Rodriguez spent his winter vacation at Silver Mountain, and Lucas went to Cozumel.*

INDEX

605